D0065455

CLINTON CONFIDENTIAL

CLINTON CONFIDENTIAL

The Climb to Power

*The Unauthorized Biography of
Bill and Hillary Clinton*

GEORGE CARPOZI, JR.

Emery Dalton Books
Del Mar, California
1995

Emery Dalton Books
1110 Camino Del Mar, Suite C, Del Mar, CA 92014

Library of Congress Catalog Card Number:
94-61245

ISBN 0-9640479-0-X

Printed in the United States of America

98 97 96 95   10 9 8 7 6 5 4 3 2 1

To my son, George Carpozi III, who was a constant inspiration and driving force throughout this project that was two and a half years in the making.

CONTENTS

PROLOGUE

———

A DUAL BIOGRAPHY OF AMERICA'S FIRST CO-PRESIDENTS

This is the unauthorized biography of William Jefferson Blythe IV, a.k.a. Bill Clinton, and Hillary Diane Rodham, a.k.a. Hillary Rodham Clinton.

They are the first couple to occupy the White House in what is now widely viewed and accepted to be a *co-presidency*.

Before the 1992 presidential campaign, they were relative unknowns to America's vast populace.

Bill had been a longtime public servant of Arkansas, first as attorney general, then, after a dozen years, its longest-serving governor.

Hillary had been a lawyer in Little Rock with considerable clout in her home state, but little influence beyond.

The United States was formally introduced to Clinton as the man he was supposed to be—and what he wanted to be—in late 1991 when he announced that he was a candidate for the nation's highest office.

At the outset, Hillary went along for the ride, as the saying goes about traditional presidential candidates' wives.

While the primary focus of this book is on Bill Clinton, Hillary must share in every aspect of the story from start to finish because, by her actions, she has proven she is not the traditional first lady.

Hillary Rodham Clinton is a different spouse from any woman who preceded her as first lady in the 205 years of the presidency. Thus she must be allowed to bask in the spotlight with her husband at every milepost.

Yet, of necessity, since he is the man America elected, the emphasis falls heaviest on Bill Clinton.

We find that no sooner did he launch his campaign than the glib charmer from Arkansas became an instant media darling. His rapport with print and electronic journalists was galvanic as he appeared to be the *mainspring to turn the generational cycle* that Arthur Schlesinger, Jr., spoke about.

After 20 years and more of conservative retrenchment, the nation seemed ready to welcome a new era of active government, public purpose, and middle-of-the-road idealism. And Bill Clinton was ready to accept the challenge of leading the nation in the undertaking.

Clinton was born of a generation touched and inspired by John F. Kennedy. While a high schooler, this teenager with roots in the tiny hamlet of Hope felt himself anointed by the 35th president's handshake at an Oval Office meeting.

When he took to the stump as an adult, many saw him as JFK reincarnate. He was at once deemed to be a brilliant campaigner—a consummate, totally obsessed, round-the-clock politician with a quick grin, a computer-like mind, a joyous addiction to press the flesh, and an inevitable gush of warm words for everyone.

Displaying an almost evangelical faith in the ability of government to improve people's lives and trumpeting his "new covenant" rhetoric, Clinton sent reporters into paroxysms of ecstasy with his views on re-igniting the nation's economic conscience, his conservative values such as responsibility and self-help combined with liberal ones like tolerance and generosity, and his condemnation of the *us vs them* politics of division.

Though they were gratified by the candidate's views, the news gatherers, not uncharacteristically, at once turned on him. They began plying Clinton with questions about his widely whispered sex life.

Accusations of his womanizing exploded on a national scale in *Star* magazine and streaked instantly to the big-city tabloids and TV, then even to the highly respected broadsheets. Accounts screamed about several of Clinton's purported girlfriends, but especially about a 12-year romance with blonde lounge singer Gennifer Flowers.

As the frenzy intensified, it seemed that the media had suddenly developed "buyer's remorse."

Clinton was devastated as the lead in the polls he had brought to New Hampshire for the nation's first primary dwindled precipitately.

Then the *Wall Street Journal* dropped a blockbuster by revealing details of how Clinton tried to evade the draft in his late teens and early twenties; stories about his anti-Vietnam War activities and secret trip to the Soviet Union followed.

Clinton was almost convinced that the campaign, his career, and his dreams of becoming president were over.

Every detail of the problems that affected Clinton's run for the presidency are covered completely in this book.

The results of the New Hampshire primary surprised Clinton when he finished a respectable second behind former Senator Paul Tsongas in a five-candidate field.

But then it seemed to be the end for Clinton as he wound up a humiliating fourth in Maine's caucuses.

The Arkansas governor refused to quit. Instead, he vowed to fight with greater intensity and vigor. He put his campaign into overdrive after deciding he could do better.

And he did.

He won the Georgia primary and saluted southerners as being more forgiving than others. They had seen his sins yet still believed in his promise of economic redemption.

Calling himself the "comeback kid," Clinton went on a roll, capturing state after state and building up a formidable lead over his Democratic Party rivals.

The book takes the reader through every primary to experience what Bill, Hillary, and his campaign team endured, living with them on their historic adventure through one of the most hard-fought, uphill presidential races ever held.

President George Bush's camp is not ignored.

Nor is Ross Perot's, the Independent *now-you-see-him, now-you-don't* "spoiler" who made the election a three-horse race.

A blow-by-blow report leading up to election day takes the reader beyond the polls to show how, after he fell behind in voter popularity, Bush makes a mini-comeback in the last days of the campaign—only to find his resurgence stop dead.

November 3, 1992, dawns with Clinton exhausted and near collapse after a whirlwind, 29-hour, 4,106-mile tour across the country that wound up a year of campaigning.

With tears in his eyes and his voice a near-whisper, Clinton sits with his family in the governor's mansion in Little Rock and waits to see what will happen.

"Keep it short," President Bush tells his aides about preparing his concession speech in the early evening, even before the ballots had been tabulated in the West.

By nightfall, Little Rock is a jumping city as residents celebrate the first time their rural state has sent a son to the White House.

Bill Clinton has effected a seismic change in American politics by giving birth to a new presidency.

The overriding effort in this book has been to penetrate the myths the Clintons created for themselves. To tear away the protective veils they have drawn around their many questionable activities.

The author has made every effort to produce a volume that is both scholarly and refreshingly frank.

And, above all else, to determine whether Bill Clinton, in following his idol JFK's footsteps, has allowed his apocalyptic life to tread that same path that Nigel Hamilton in his recent best-seller *JFK: Reckless Youth* sought to unravel:

"Did he really possess a political conscience, or was he the playboy figurehead of a new generation of liberals?"

- 1 -

BORN IN HOPE

Death Before Birth

William Jefferson Blythe Clinton IV was born in Hope, Arkansas, on August 19, 1946. As it largely is now, Hope then was a rural, backwater community populated by fewer than 10,000, just 30 miles northeast of the Texas state line. There the Lone Star State's more populous city of Texarkana faces its twin community of the same name in the Land of Opportunity that is Arkansas.

Bill Clinton's father, William Jefferson Blythe III, died in an automobile accident before Bill was born, on May 18, 1946. Blythe, who earlier in his life sold automotive equipment in Texas, had changed his occupation to heavy farm machinery salesman. This entailed considerable travel and extended periods away from home. He had served three years in the Army in World War II, and after he returned, he briefly took up residence in Hope, where his fourth wife, the former Virginia Cassidy, lived.

Blythe was married three times before and fathered children in two of those conjugal ventures. All three ended in divorce, but he never told Virginia about any of them. Bill Clinton's mother had to learn about the previous wives from newspaper accounts after her son was elected president. Blythe, described by his previous wives as an uncaring and cheating husband, simply dumped them and their children before marrying the woman who would bear America's 42nd president.

A chance encounter brought Blythe into Virginia Cassidy's life.

Before she met Bill Blythe, the ebony-haired and attractive Virginia Cassidy had cut a wide swath across town with her laughing blue-gray eyes, husky voice, and easy-going personality. Although ebullient and fun-loving, she was strong-willed and determined to make something of herself. She was very much from the ancestral mold that cast her parents, descendants of Irish farmers and Cherokee Indians.

Virginia was born in 1923 in Bodcaw, Arkansas, a village 13 miles from Hope, where her father, Eldridge Cassidy, moved the family in 1924. Hope was a lively community during the Roaring Twenties, and Cassidy enjoyed a modest income as a watchman at a sawmill. The job held out until the advent of the Great Depression in 1929; then the sawmill was shuttered. Cassidy was forced to eke out a much smaller income delivering ice. But he was a frugal man. He saved what he could of his meager income and eventually bought a small grocery store in a largely black neighborhood.

Virginia Cassidy received her formal education in Hope schools. After she graduated from high school in 1941, she headed to Louisiana to follow a calling that was to be her life's work. She became a student nurse at a hospital in Shreveport.

At that hospital in 1942, at the age of 19, she met her future husband.

Virginia, thrice widowed, and married from 1982 until her death in early 1994 to her fourth husband, Richard W. Kelley, a retired food broker, had a gleam in her eye when she recalled her "first true love."

"I was working late one night at the hospital when this tall, ruggedly handsome man staggered in with a young woman alongside him who was writhing in pain," she remembered.

The woman, whose name is lost to history, was Bill Blythe's date, but Virginia Cassidy assumed she was his wife. Her ailment was acute appendicitis that required immediate surgery.

"It was truly love at first sight," Virginia confessed years later. "And I was so ashamed because at first I thought that they were married."

She learned the truth when she addressed Bill Blythe by the woman's last name "just to make sure that I was correct in assuming they were married."

To her surprise—and utter delight—his response was:

"Excuse me. That isn't my name."

Before she could catch her breath, "He asked me out."

The "other woman" recovered from the operation and was discharged from the hospital. But she never saw Bill Blythe again. For Virginia Cassidy now was his steady date.

The romance carried over two exciting months before it was brought to an abrupt halt by Blythe's call to serve his country just after the bombing of Pearl Harbor. It was early 1942, and just as he slipped into his Army khakis, Blythe exchanged marital vows in a civil ceremony with Virginia. Days later, he left for basic training and Virginia remained behind to finish her courses in nursing school.

If Virginia knew of Bill Blythe's former marriages, she never let on to her children or to others. The fact was that Virginia and William Blythe's marriage certificate didn't list his *priors*.

Bill Clinton is said to have become aware that he had a second, older half brother when he returned to Little Rock in early June 1992, after sewing up the 2,145 delegates needed for the Democratic Party's presidential nomination. Until then, Clinton—and his mother—believed that Roger Clinton, born during Virginia's second marriage, to an auto mechanic, was the only sibling he had.

The Arkansas governor was in a state of near exhaustion at the close of the 105-day primary race that began in the snows of New Hampshire on February 13, 1992, and wound down on June 2 with his six-state sweep that included delegate-rich California.

His voice raspy and unable to speak above a whisper, his mind groggy and bones weary from the nonstop politicking for six straight months, the last thing Clinton wanted was to be handed the letter taken out of an envelope by Dee Dee Myers, his press secretary and campaign director. The envelope was postmarked Paradise, California.

It might better have come from *hell*, so far as Clinton was concerned once he began reading.

"Dear Bill...This is to let you know that we both have the same father, William J. Blythe III...He had married my mom in 1934."

"Ohhhh shit!" the sandy voice roared before reading any further. "Who the hell needs this crap at a time like this?"

The writer was Henry Leon Ritzenthaler, a 55-year-old high school dropout who operated a janitorial service until a heart condition forced him into early retirement.

Ritzenthaler, born in Texas in 1938, was married and had two grown children. He wrote that their father, William Jefferson Blythe III, had married his mother, Adele Cofelt, when she was 17. They were divorced a year later in 1935, but they maintained an on-again, off-again relationship for some years.

Ritzenthaler said he had no idea Clinton was his half brother until June of '92.

He learned that only after Clinton was wrapping up the required delegates for his nomination, "and a member of our family told my mother that my biological father was Clinton's father, as well." He explained further:

"What I did then was write to the governor's office in Arkansas and enclose a copy of my birth certificate. But I never got a response. You'd think the least he could do is phone me or drop a letter saying, 'Hey, I know you're alive.' But that didn't happen for a year [after Ritzenthaler went public with the revelation and the author interviewed him on June 21, 1993]."

Clinton finally was shamed into phoning Ritzenthaler to exchange pleasantries. The president closed the conversation by saying he'd drop by and visit his half brother at some unspecified time. As this book went to press many months later, Clinton had yet to visit Paradise, although he skirted the territory in his travels many times.

Ritzenthaler, who took his stepfather's name after his mother remarried, just as Clinton had done during his mother's second marriage to Roger Clinton, resembles the president in two of his most pronounced facial characteristics: blue eyes and bags under the eyes; and he's also "very emotional, as Bill Clinton is," Ritzenthaler says of himself.

According to Ritzenthaler's mother, Adele Cofelt, after Blythe divorced her he married a second time, to her sister Faye. That marriage also ended in divorce a short time later.

When Mrs. Cofelt became aware of her former husband's relationship to the presidential candidate in mid-1992, she believed that Blythe had followed his marriage to her sister by taking Virginia Cassidy as his third wife.

Not so!

It came as another shock to Clinton—and his mother—to learn in the summer of '93 that Blythe's name appears on yet a third marriage certificate before he married wife No. 4, Virginia Cassidy.

She was Wanetta Ellen Alexander Blythe, now a 70-year-old retired bookkeeper from Arizona, who became Blythe's third wife in a civil ceremony performed May 3,

1941, in a judge's chambers in Missouri's Kansas City Courthouse. Blythe was 25, Wanetta, 17—and she was in her ninth month of a pregnancy that bore Clinton's half sister, Sharon, nine days later.

Their child, according to Wanetta Blythe, now living in Tucson, "was conceived in the Netherlands Hotel." That was where her romance with Blythe climaxed—after a brief initial encounter in a Missouri tavern in a community called Nevada.

"I was just standing there when a handsome young man walked over and asked me if I wanted to dance," reminisced Wanetta.

"I said no, but then 'Alexander's Ragtime Band' came on [the juke box]. He said, "You're going to dance with me." And I did.

"We danced and talked, then we exchanged addresses. I must have told him I was moving to Kansas City, because later that year he came through Kansas City to look me up.

"I fell head over heels for him.

"He'd stay for a few weeks at a time at the Netherlands Hotel. We dated whenever he came into town.

"We'd go dancing or go out to eat and hit all the hotels, restaurants, and dance halls downtown.

"He was wonderful—gorgeous, fun, and happy-go-lucky. I loved him and he loved me."

After daughter Sharon's birth, the family moved from Kansas City and took an apartment in Monroe, Louisiana.

"But within six months I found out Bill was cheating on me—and I decided to go home to Kansas City with Sharon.

"Bill sent me a letter in 1942, telling me he'd fallen in love with a nurse down in Louisiana. He said he wanted a divorce."

Court records disclose that the couple ended their marriage in April 1944. The decree, coming through at that time—two years after he took 20-year-old Virginia Cassidy to be his wife—clearly establishes that Virginia's marriage to Bill Blythe was bigamous.

The fourth Mrs. Blythe became future-President Bill Clinton's mother in 1946 after her husband returned from his three-year World War II army hitch.

But Bill Blythe never saw his son. Nor was he to keep up child support of $42 a month for daughter Sharon Blythe, as the divorce court ordered when it granted him belated emancipation from his third marriage.

Bill Blythe died in the auto accident on May 18, 1946.

Not until three years later, in 1949, did the third Mrs. Blythe learn the awful truth.

"I phoned the firm that employed Bill—the J. H. Pereue Equipment Company in Memphis—to determine why he'd never been in touch with his daughter [or kept up her support payments].

"The man who took my call asked who I was. I said, 'I'm his ex-wife.' The man then asked, 'Which one?'

"I didn't know what he meant. Then he told me Bill had been killed in an auto accident years before. I was stunned."

Sharon Blythe grew up, as her half-brother Bill had, without knowing her father.

Sharon, who is going on 53 and is in the 36th year of her marriage to Robert Pettijohn, is the mother of three grown sons and lives in Tucson. She has made it emphatically clear she has no desire for a "reunion" with President Clinton, although her mother says "it would be great if Sharon and Bill could get together."

"I have no plans to contact him," Sharon stated. "I don't want anything from him."

But her mother has gone so far as to propose a family reunion:

"It would be terrific if the president, my daughter, and his half-brother Henry Ritzenthaler could all get together."

After she married Bill Blythe, in 1942, Virginia endured 36 months of loneliness before he returned to her side. The reunion occurred in 1945 after Blythe finished his three years of military service. By then, Virginia was back home in Hope with her parents. Bill joined her there in November.

Blythe served most of his tour in khaki with an army motor pool company as a mechanic. He saw service in Italy after the Anzio landing in 1943 and was stationed near Caserta, about 100 miles north of the invasion site. He spent the rest of the war there, repairing and rehabilitating jeeps and trucks.

Bill Clinton claims he had no awareness of the duty his father pulled as a soldier until 1993. That followed the stories about his father's bigamous past, which revealed that Clinton actually had a half sister and two half brothers—besides Roger, whom the reader will soon meet.

"Until the stories came out, Bill Clinton knew virtually nothing about his father's war record," a senior White House aide stated. "His curiosity about his father prompted inquiries. A military historian then forwarded information to the president about Blythe's war activities."

However, it is difficult to believe Clinton had no inkling of his father's experiences in the war, for in his mother's autobiography, published in May 1994, she clearly relates the role her husband had in the war and speaks of the letters he wrote from Italy. Clinton read the manuscript before it went to the publisher.

Perhaps inadvertently, Clinton himself let on that he knew something about his father's wartime service. That happened when he honored American heroes who fought for freedom in Italy during the opening rounds of the June 6, 1994, 50th anniversary of D-Day.

"A cousin told me that a young relative wrote my father about the beautiful Italian countryside and asked that he send a single tree leaf home for her to take to school," Clinton said during a ceremony at the cemetery where nearly 8,000 U.S. soldiers are buried.

But Bill Blythe couldn't send the leaf.

"My father had only sad news to send back. There were no leaves—every one had been stripped by the fury of the battle."

The *fury of the battle* was over by the time Bill Blythe began his tinkering under the hoods of jeeps and trucks, and was one of the *lucky ones* who returned home in one piece.

Now that he was out of uniform, Bill was eager to pursue a new calling. He had no desire to return to his old job as an auto parts salesman. He left Virginia in late January and drove to Chicago to apply for an opening in heavy farm machinery sales. He landed it and was assigned a lucrative territory in the Midwest.

On May 18, he headed back for Hope to move his wife to Chicago. Virginia was in her fifth month of pregnancy.

Blythe never made it beyond Missouri. Some 150 miles south of St. Louis, in the small village of Sikeston, barely 60 miles from the Arkansas state line and the last 140 miles to Hope in the southeastern part of the state, Bill Blythe lost control behind the wheel of his car on rain-slicked Highway 61.

"He was going around a curve and had a blowout," Virginia recounted, her eyes growing misty. "You know, we didn't have radial tires then. And it was after a big flood, and all the ditches on each side of the highway were overflowed."

She emphasized that "the only mark he had on him was a little bruise on his head."

Bill Clinton took up the narrative that concluded the sad tale.

"My dad would have lived if it hadn't been for a freak happening," he was to say years later after visiting the spot where his father died. "He was thrown out of the car and landed, unconscious, in a ditch filled with water. He actually drowned."

A Mother's Burden

Virginia Blythe gave birth on a Monday to a healthy 8-pound, 4-ounce son, whom she named William Jefferson Blythe IV. Even before he toddled, little "Billy," as he was called by his mother, was placed in her parents' care. She was determined more than ever, now that she was widowed, to make something of herself.

"I knew I'd have to be the breadwinner in the family," Virginia was to say. "My parents didn't have any money to speak of and certainly held no prospects of making any in the years after World War II when the economy in Hope had hit rock bottom."

Before his mother went back to nursing school in New Orleans for advanced training and certification as a registered nurse with a specialty in anesthesiology, Billy was left to spend the next four years with his middle-aged grandparents, Eldridge and Mary Cassidy.

From time to time, when the going got tough and Billy proved to be a burden to the Cassidys, he was sent to his elderly great-grandparents in the rural area of Bodcaw, north of Hope, which was his mother's birthplace. There it was life as one might find in a John Steinbeck novel. Clinton referred to the *Grapes of Wrath* existence of those early years in his speech to the electorate as a five-time governor of Arkansas in late 1991, when he announced that he had had a change of heart about finishing out his fifth term and would seek the Presidency of the United States.

"For four years I lived with my grandparents," Clinton said. "They didn't have much money. Nobody did in Arkansas at the end of World War II. I spent a lot of time in the country with my great-grandparents, who by any standard were very poor. But we really didn't know we were poor because we cared for each other. We didn't make excuses. We believed in the American dream and were the backers of family and hard work."

What Clinton was telling his listeners was to believe he was a child of poverty. Yet his espousal of principles, such as the immutable "American dream," seems far-fetched. What four-year-old is mature enough to hold such a philosophy?

The consummate politician, Clinton knew how to trek the potholed pathways of an office-seeker's campaign, to press all the right buttons to strike resonant chords on constituents' heartstrings.

The story of how his grandfather, a heavy drinker but not an alcoholic in the true sense, got on his feet for a brief spell, is another classic Clinton chronicle with memory colored by the need to tell a story that makes his political point.

"My grandfather was the kindest person I ever knew," Clinton has said. "Yet my grandfather's personality trait was a fault because it was to prove ruinous to him in business."

Clinton was recalling a time when he himself was only two: That's when Grandpa Cassidy opened a small grocery and fruit stand in a neighborhood of Hope whose residents were preponderantly African Americans.

"The people around there were so poor, and he sold so much on credit that he finally went out of business," Clinton would say. "Not because anybody tried to bilk him out of anything but because they just didn't have any money. Of course, this was before food stamps or anything like that."

Hillary Rodham's Beginnings

Barely two months after Bill Blythe passed his first birthday, a celebration was held in a one-bedroom apartment on Chicago's Northside for the birth of Hugh and Dorothy Rodham's first child, a daughter named Hillary Diane. Her mother chose that first name, she said, "because it sounded exotic and unusual." Dorothy also reflected that the baby weighed "more than eight pounds when I brought her home in my arms...she was very mature, you could say." That was three days after Hillary was delivered at Edgewater Hospital on October 26, 1947.

The Rodhams installed Hillary in a white crib in their bedroom where she was to live for the next three years.

The two births were not dissimilar, and in both instances the birth happened after the men came home from the war.

Hugh Rodham and Dorothy Howell met in Chicago in 1937, five years before William Blythe and Virginia Cassidy's encounter in the Shreveport hospital emergency room.

A large, gruff, macho man, Rodham reflected the toughness of the territory of his birth, the northeastern Pennsylvania anthracite coal mining city of Scranton. He was the son of an Englishman who emigrated to America at age four from Northumberland shortly after the turn of the century. He settled in Scranton where he married and found steady employment at the Scranton Lace Company.

Hugh was born in 1914 and, like his two brothers, worked alongside his father at the lace factory. A hard-headed, independent, rugged individual, Rodham eventually became disenchanted lifting heavy crates all day long and quit. He felt that as a graduate of Penn State University he deserved better, although this was 1936 and the country was still in the throes of the Great Depression. He headed for New York to seek his fortune.

Failing to make a score there, Rodham tried his luck in Chicago. Like his future son-in-law's father, William Blythe, he found a new career. He landed a job with the Columbia Lace Company. The year was still 1936. But there'd be no warehouse chores for Rodham at this firm: he was employed as a curtain salesman.

One day a year later his work brought Hugh to the home office. As he entered, his eye caught a pretty young woman seated behind the secretary's desk. She had just come into the job. Hugh Rodham introduced himself to Dorothy Howell and a date for dinner and a movie followed.

In no time at all, Dorothy knew all about Hugh's background and he about most— but not all—of hers.

A Californian who grew up in Alhambra, next door to Pasadena, Dorothy Howell didn't speak in glowing terms about her childhood and preferred to be silent about it. However, she didn't hesitate to tell her beau that her father was Welsh and that her mother, Della Murray, descended from Scottish, French—and Indian—stock (not too dissimilar to Bill Clinton's mother's ancestral roots).

She made it clear that she held no fond recollections of childhood. To escape further unhappiness, she had left for Chicago at the age of 17 to make her life better than it had been at home.

Unlike the two-month breakneck pace Bill Blythe and Virginia Cassidy trekked to their marriage in 1942, Hugh Rodham and Dorothy Howell extended their courtship for over five years before taking the plunge in that same year.

And, just as Bill Blythe went from the conjugal bed to the barracks cot, so had Hugh Rodham. Only his arm of the service was the navy and an assignment that was a sailor's dream. Because his major at Penn State was physical education, Rodham was assigned as an instructor in the rugged naval basic training program conducted by the 1920s' retired undefeated world heavyweight champion Gene Tunney.

Rodham was discharged after V-J Day. He returned to Chicago where he and Dorothy resumed their life together. She was still behind the desk at Scranton Lace, and the salesman's job for the returning G.I. was his for the asking. But Rodham decided not to return to his old job. He had a better idea. He'd go into business manufacturing draperies.

Meanwhile, the Rodhams' occupancy of a small one-bedroom apartment was adequate for a couple without children. And they could still make do with those living quarters after Hillary was born. However, three years later, after Hillary's brother Hugh came along, they had outgrown that single-bedroom flat. They beat a path to the suburbs, as most city folk across the land were doing in the post-war boom years. They settled in the upper middle-class bedroom community of Park Ridge, 35 miles north of Chicago.

The brick house with the flagstone facade and the white wooden front porch, perched in quiet dignity at the corner of Wisner and Elm Streets, was to be the Rodham family home for the next 37 years.

Unlike Hope, where the residents "didn't have much money...at the end of World

War II," as Clinton put it, Park Ridge was a booming community of young families, most well-to-do, all growing up at the same time.

"There must have been 40 or 50 children within a four-block radius of our house and within four years of Hillary's age," Mrs. Rodham explained. "There were more boys than girls, lots of playing and competition. She held her own at cops and robbers, hide and seek, chase and run—all the games that children don't play anymore."

Her daughter was "a good-natured, nice little baby. She liked to have books read to her and she liked figuring out problems by herself. She was never shy and wasn't afraid of people or dogs or anything. When she was old enough to play outdoors by herself, she could beat up on the neighbors' children, but only if she had to. When she did, she'd go out, arms flailing, eyes closed—and whap! She'd get the better of them."

After Bill Clinton won the presidential election, the *Washington Post* assigned Martha Sherrill to do an in-depth, thoroughly researched background on the first lady elect. The result was a three-part series that ran through inauguration day. The reporter interviewed scores of childhood pals, school chums, her family, and associates and produced one of the most intimate and well-rounded portraits of Hillary Clinton ever published.

Among those interviewed by Ms. Sherrill was Hillary's "baby" brother Tony Rodham who was born in 1954 when his sister was seven.

"Sure, my sister is tough as nails," said Tony, then 38 years old and a private investigator in Miami, whom the writer described as "a Rodham with a certain familial pride." He was picking up on his mother's assessment of Hillary's willingness to take on a foe, toe-to-toe, not out of a sense of defensiveness but just as a penchant to take someone on.

"She's a lot of those things that people had said she was," Tony conceded, alluding to the appellatives coined by detractors and critics during the years she was Arkansas's first lady: "Hillary The Hun," "The Iron Lady Of Little Rock," and "The Lady Macbeth of Little Rock," to name just a few.

"But that's just one face [of Hillary]," said her other brother, Hugh Rodham, a 42-year-old public defender, based also in Miami. "That's her business face," he went on. "Like your game face when you play football."

Her brothers also remembered her in her early, formative years, when Hillary was just beginning to get straight-"A" grades at Eugene Field Elementary School.

Not a Nice Stepfather

About the time Hillary was entering kindergarten at Eugene Field, Billy Blythe had just completed the first grade in Hope's tiny, rural public school system.

This was the summer of 1952, and Bill's mother had graduated from nursing school. She received accreditation as a registered nurse with a license that qualified her to assist in the administration of anesthesia, given always under the supervision and direction of a medical doctor, usually a surgeon. She found work at once in one of Arkansas's most thriving communities, Hot Springs.

About the time of Bill's sixth birthday, his mother came to the Cassidys' home in

Hope. She was accompanied by a strapping, well-structured, pleasant-faced man whom she introduced as her new husband. The widow Blythe had remarried to Roger Clinton, a former master auto mechanic who recently had become partner with his wealthy and influential brother, Raymond, in a Hot Springs Buick dealership.

Roger Clinton had been married before and was divorced when he met Virginia. The newlyweds came to stay for awhile in Hope so Virginia could get reacquainted with her son and Billy might get to know his stepfather.

The stay wasn't a pleasant one. Billy discovered—as did his grandparents and the neighbors—that Roger Clinton was a heavy drinker who, more often than not, metamorphosed into a violent drunk. Virginia had already learned this in the short time they had been married. She'd been subjected to her husband's frequent abuses, including physical pummelings.

In September of 1952, the Clintons packed their belongings and took 6-year-old Billy Blythe on the longest journey of his life—a 65-mile ride in a spanking-new 1953 Buick Century sedan. Their destination was Hot Springs, the city in central Arkansas at the eastern gateway to the scenic Ouachita Mountains.

Hot Springs had a population of 30,000, three times larger than Hope. A thriving community, it benefited handsomely from the nearby tourist resort of Hot Springs National Park, where Eastern blue bloods made pilgrimages to reconstitute their tired bodies in the spa's therapeutic baths.

On the ride to Hot Springs, Billy Blythe sat in the back seat, mesmerized by the prospect of living in a big city, wondering what new friends he'd make and hoping, as he was to say years later, that his life at home would be less traumatic than it had been in Hope after his stepfather entered his life.

Home in Hot Springs

Roger Clinton installed his family in a comfortable three-bedroom house in a pleasant, upper-middle-class neighborhood, a far cry from the environment in Hope.

Fortified by her new domestic well-being, Virginia Clinton became obsessed with the desire to better her son's lot, as she had her own by marriage to a businessman of means.

In Hope, young Bill's education was gained in an elementary school system almost too small to be cataloged. Yet the natural transition to the first grade in Hot Springs' considerably larger—and more academically proficient—public school system was ignored by Billy's mother.

She wanted "nothing but the best" for her first-born. So it was off to St. John's, the private Roman Catholic elementary school in Little Rock.

"I was terribly impressed with Billy's enthusiasm and willingness to learn after he entered St. John's," Billy's mother recounted. "He began to read newspapers in the first grade back in Hope, thanks to the efforts of his grandparents to make him well-learned. I'll be forever indebted to my mother and father for instilling in Billy the desire and love for education and learning."

"My grandparents," Clinton recalled, "taught me to read before I went to school. They taught me the fundamentals. And they also tutored me in simple arithmetic before I was introduced to it in the first grade."

In Hot Springs, young Billy found few of the domestic benefits his grandparents had provided. His father was away selling Buicks; his mother was constantly on call at Quachita Hospital.

Yet Billy wasn't neglected. His mother treated Bill almost, as some folks suggested, as an *icon*. That impression was given by Virginia's vast display of photographs of Billy, adorning almost an entire wall of the house.

Her near-veneration of her son provoked friendly jokes by guests of the frequent parties the Clintons tossed—or by friends like Carolyn Staley, who had fond recollections:

"We used to joke that there ought to be candles around the pictures," laughed Carolyn. She was a Baptist minister's daughter of Bill's age who was a next-door neighbor in Hot Springs.

For Billy, the idea of sitting before the TV set in the den and watching Annette Funicello's "Mickey Mouse Club" or a puppet show like "Howdy Doody" was unthinkable. He was a serious-minded youngster who preferred serious programs such as the political conventions during the summer of 1956.

The fifth-grader's eye was attracted by the addictive game of politics. This was the year that delegates anointed Illinois Governor Adlai A. Stevenson and Tennessee's U.S. Senator Estes Kefauver to challenge President Dwight D. Eisenhower and Vice President Richard M. Nixon in their bid for reelection.

"I was hooked on politics then and there," Clinton admitted. "It got to me in a way on television that no amount of reading in the newspapers about candidates running for office and politics in general could impact me."

His interest in politics grew over the next four years and approached euphoric heights in 1960 when Massachusetts Senator John F. Kennedy and Texas Senator Lyndon B. Johnson faced the challenge of the GOP's Vice President Nixon and U.S. Ambassador to the United Nations Henry Cabot Lodge.

"I was gung ho for politics by then," Clinton professed. "My teacher in ninth-grade civics class was Mary Marty, and she had the class debating the merits of the two candidates for the White House.

"Mrs. Marty and I were the only ones in the class who were for the JFK-LBJ ticket. Being that Hot Springs is the seat of government for Garland County and is heavily Republican, my teacher and I were like outcasts in an environment that had everyone else rooting for Nixon and Lodge. But when that Wednesday morning rolled around after the Tuesday of November eighth, Mrs. Marty and I were the jubilant ones in the classroom."

The 14-year-old's eyelids understandably drooped that day in Central Junior High School, because he had gone sleepless watching the returns until dawn.

"I sat at the TV set all night, hoping and praying for Kennedy's victory. What a rewarding moment it was for me when Nixon made his concession speech."

Growing up with Hillary

At no time in Hillary Rodham's background did she ever experience family traumas such as her future husband encountered in Hot Springs, living with an abusive, boozing father. While his mother provided Billy much warmth and loving care, the same wasn't true of her bourbon-guzzling husband. Virginia could no more change Roger's loutish and disruptive behavior than her small son could put Roger Clinton down when he raged.

Hillary's father was a blusterer and a curmudgeon at times, but that was a put-on character. While he growled disapprovingly almost without letup at his family, he would defend and praise them to the heights—when their ears were turned away.

Early in her schooling, Hillary learned not to expect praise from her father when she brought home a report card replete with "A's."

"You must go to a pretty easy school," he'd chide her in a grumpy voice.

Hugh Rodham was a born family person, as was his wife. Unlike Dorothy, however, he was also a born organizer, full of energy, and a tireless socializer. Hillary liked that quality in her father.

One spring, after Hillary was old enough to hold a baseball bat in her hand, Hugh took her to Hinckley Park, where he pitched curveballs to his daughter.

"He threw so many at me that I couldn't help but swat the leather off the ball after a while."

"Maybe that's why she's such an accepting person," Mrs. Rodham observed about Hillary. "She had to put up with *him*."

Rodham was a whirlwind businessman, virtually a one-man show. Almost single-handedly, he molded his drapery-manufacturing business into a prosperous enterprise. With only one full-time employee, Rodham bought fabric, printed the designs on it, cut the bolts, sewed the cloth to the customers' specifications, then went out and installed the curtains with only one helper lending a hand.

As the business grew and the orders got bigger—hotels, airlines, and corporations became his clients—he recruited his two sons to help.

"Dad never paid us," Tony Rodham said, laughingly corroborating the consensus of those who agree Hugh was tightfisted. "What he gave us was an extra potato at dinner."

Rodham wasn't one for affectations. He didn't belong to the nearby Park Ridge Country Club; he didn't want it to seem his nose was up in the air. The boys and Hillary didn't mind, even though it meant they couldn't swim in the club's pool. Hillary found the public facility just as satisfying.

While Bill Clinton was down in Hot Springs cutting his teeth on politics and learning to play a saxophone, sixth-grader Hillary Rodham began piano lessons.

When Bill Clinton was 18, in 1964, and rooting for LBJ's election to a full term in office, 17-year-old Hillary Rodham and the rest of her family sat glued before their own TV set in Park Ridge, shaking their heads in dismay as the returns were tabulated, signaling a landslide over the Goldwater/Miller ticket.

What sort of mother was Dorothy Rodham?

The *Washington Post*'s Martha Sherrill painted this word portrait: "Unpretentious, wise, funny." The reporter captured Dorothy's essence with her reaction to the honors that Hillary received at graduation from Maine East High School.

"I remember…being slightly embarrassed by the honor medley," Hillary's mother confessed, after her daughter walked off the stage with a heap of laurels and her diploma, finishing 15th in a class of 1,000.

Bill Blythe knew by the time he graduated from high school that he wanted to be a politician. Hillary Rodham took longer to decide.

One day she thought about becoming an astronaut. But the next day she wondered what it'd be like being a doctor. "Whatever goal lingered in her mind, her focus was far away, years away, another place," concluded Ms. Sherrill after interviewing several childhood chums, including Jeannie Snodgrass Almo, who runs a day-care center in Washington, D.C.

"She had absolutely no vanity," Ms. Almo revealed. "She was totally unconcerned about how she appeared to people—and she was loved for that."

When her mother suggested she wear makeup, Hillary said no way.

"I think she thought that was superficial and silly," Mrs. Rodham concluded. "She didn't have time for it."

Hillary's a Barry Goldwater Gal

Not unlike Bill Blythe, Hillary Rodham was a political animal. She was vice president of her junior class in high school. When she lost her bid to be president of her senior class, Hillary turned to Barry Goldwater's campaign. She wore a sash that proclaimed "Goldwater Girl" and, as a representative of the student council, she proposed holding a mock political convention in the school gym, replete with posters, podiums, and nominating speeches.

In the spring of her senior year, Hillary—(until then she always lacked much attention from the opposite sex)—ventured forth as a free spirit to snag a guy or two. She and seven girlfriends rented a station wagon, and with a chaperone headed for Pompano Beach in Florida during Easter break. Their inspiration was the movie *Where The Boys Are*. The girls viewed the flick at the Pickwick Theater in downtown Park Ridge, then repaired to Ted & Pearl's Happy House for Cokes to bat the idea about.

"We thought we'd meet boys from all over the world," laughed Betsy Ebeling, one of the girls who made the trip. "But the first walk we took on the beach, we ran into three guys from Maine East and hung out with them the whole time."

By now, Hillary had completed the selection process for college. She aimed for one or another of the nation's foremost women's colleges.

"She was set on going to an all-girls school," her mother remembered. "At first it was a toss-up among Radcliffe, Smith, and Wellesley. But when Hillary saw photos of the rural Wellesley campus—its lake in the middle, the quaint Victorian classrooms, the tiny surrounding town—she decided.

Bill's High School Days

By 1961, when Bill Clinton was at Hot Springs High School, his passion for politics was fanned hotter by his English teacher John Wilson.

"Mr. Wilson and I debated the political issues of the time with great frequency," Clinton reminisced. "He made me want to pursue politics in the worst way."

Bill "Clinton," as he was popularly referred to by then, although still officially carried as Blythe on school records, began to think of the future when he was still a sophomore.

Partway into that semester, he dropped in on guidance counselor Edith Irons. He had a problem.

"What college do you recommend I attend to pursue my desire to study international affairs?" he asked.

"Above all other schools," responded a surprised Miss Irons, "I would tell you to go to Georgetown University in Washington, D.C. It stands out over most others."

The question—coming from a sophomore—impressed the guidance counselor.

"It was refreshing to hear this young man say he wanted to pursue courses in international studies," said Miss Irons. She was amazed also by the handsome student's versatility and participation in myriad activities, both in school and away.

Noting his membership in the school band, Miss Irons offered further reflections:

"He'd be on the football field marching with the band at six in the morning, playing his saxophone. Then by eight o'clock, with rehearsal ended, he'd show up in class. It was go, go, go for Billy all day long. I could never understand how he did it."

Late night TV audiences who tuned in on Johnny Carson's "The Tonight Show" and "The Arsenio Hall Show" thirty years later during the 1992 presidential primaries heard a mellifluous tenor sax jazz recital played by candidate Clinton.

Clinton's solo performance over the airwaves was an extension of his penchant for public performance with the saxophone from his high school days. He was a member of a jumping jazz trio that played during after-school hours in small nightclubs and honky-tonks in Hot Springs and its environs.

An untruth that circulated during the campaign was that Clinton had once given thought to following a musical career.

Nothing was further from the truth. The same can be said about reports that he had intentions of pursuing other interests. Billy was merely spreading his wings over a multitude of extra-curricular activities because he liked doing them. None ever appealed to him as much as politics.

His proximity to Hot Springs National Park enabled Clinton to become a rugged outdoorsman in every sense of the word. He found the hiking trails and bridle paths inviting places to keep fit. He took up two recreations he carried into later years: jogging and horseback riding. The nearby lakes, with their more than 1,200 miles of shoreline, afforded ample opportunity to swim, participate in water sports, and fish, virtually year-round, thanks to Arkansas's mild climate.

Virginia's "Vices"

The Hot Springs National Park also attracted Virginia Clinton, who found the 31-day horse racing meet at Oak Park much to her liking. Her indoctrination in thoroughbred racing turned into a lifelong love—an admirer of the ponies, indeed of all horseflesh, and also made her an incurable bettor.

During the winter thoroughbred racing season in Hot Springs, Mrs. Kelley, as she was known in the last years of her life, frequently held court in her box on the Carousel Terrace of the Oaklawn Jockey Club. She also frequented it during the summer when the track carries broadcasts from other parks and keeps the pari-mutuel windows busy.

Her passion for betting the ponies—her bible was the *Racing Form*—extended to her home. A sampler on a wall reflected that passion: "A race track is a place where windows clean people." One treasure she cherished is a ring with a gold horseshoe circling a horse's head, inlaid with pavé diamonds, a gift from son Bill.

"Funny thing," she mused in an interview with the *Arkansas Democrat-Gazette*'s Noel Oman. "What does Bill know about gambling? These tiny little diamonds? I got the magnifying glass and I counted them and there was thirteen. And I said, 'Oh, my goodness!' So I took it to the jeweler and said, 'Would you please put a little diamond in this horse's eye?' so I wouldn't have thirteen."

Other than at the track, Virginia cavorted with second husband Roger in one or another of Hot Springs' many casinos and nightclubs. One of their favorites was the infamous Vapors, centerpiece in a rakehell of furtive ventures offering illegal gambling and other nighttime pleasures. This nightlife was a magnet for the rich northerners who sought relief from their days soaking in the spas. They couldn't wait for dark to escape to high times.

This was the world of Virginia and Roger Clinton while their son Billy slept in his bedroom, alone and unattended, growing up, seldom able to locate his parents at any given moment. He hardly ever knew when they'd return home, and was never certain of what might happen behind the closed door after they staggered into their bedroom.

The summer of 1963 found Billy Clinton, as he was now best known, attending the American Legion-sponsored Arkansas Boys' State and participating in the mock election for governor. At Camp Robinson, near Little Rock, the state capital, Billy was reunited with his chum from Hope, Thomas F. (Mack) McLarty, who 30 years later would be named White House chief of staff.

McLarty was elected governor of Boys' State over Bill Clinton. But Bill was selected as Arkansas's delegate to Boys' Nation and went off for his rewards in Washington, D.C.

That trip was perhaps the most significant shaping experience in his life. He met President John F. Kennedy—and right then and there decided there could be no course other than a future in politics.

"It was the most engrossing and most memorable experience I ever had," Bill Clinton would say of his face-to-face encounter with Kennedy and with another political idol, veteran U.S. Senator J. William Fulbright.

"I not only shook hands with the President but had my picture taken with him. Then before the thrill of that meeting could wear off I was sitting in the Senate dining room and having lunch with Senator Fulbright. It was just overwhelming, all that happened to me that summer of nineteen sixty-three."

The picture of Billy Blythe with Kennedy was taken on the White House lawn, and the kid from Hot Springs couldn't wait to get home with it.

"I'd never seen him get so excited about something," recounted his mother. "When he came back from Washington holding this picture of himself with Jack Kennedy, and the expression on his face...I knew right then that politics was the answer for him."

Clinton himself was eager to share his experiences with Boys' State and Boys' Nation: "Those were the greatest highlights of my life as a teenager. No one could ask for a more significant or more memorable happening for a young man of high school age."

His meeting with Fulbright, who headed the powerful Senate Foreign Relations Committee, would not be his last. But there'd be no further meetings with Kennedy. In just three months, on November 22, Kennedy was assassinated in Dallas.

Bill Wasn't into Varsity Sports

Bill's high school days were marked by other experiences that usually revolved around the political scene. Although he participated in virtually every extra-curricular activity Hot Springs High offered, Clinton shied away from the one that was his unspoken yearning: organized sports.

He was tall and rugged. He was capable of playing many sports. And he did, but only in loosely organized games with friends. Although he excelled in school yard basketball and touch football, he did not participate in *organized* sports.

Mack McLarty recalled many years after their reunion at the Boys' State get-together: "Bill loved to play sports. He was especially fond of basketball. But I must say he wasn't as coordinated as he would like to remember."

McLarty didn't say why Bill didn't go out for varsity sports. That side of the story was related by next-door neighbor Carolyn Staley, who remains one of Bill's dearest friends.

"His mother put her foot down on high school athletics because she had seen so many sports injury cases at the hospital [where she was a nurse]," said Miss Staley, who became chummy with Clinton after she defeated him in his first-ever political contest, during their senior year.

Bill and Carolyn were candidates for class secretary.

"We were asked to wait outside the auditorium while the students cast their ballots for officers," Miss Staley recalled. "Bill stood alongside me and said that if I should beat him in the election he'd never speak to me again."

Carolyn did win. Bill did speak to her again. And as long as they lived next door to each other, Bill and Carolyn did many things together. One was competing against each other in solving the crossword puzzle in the *Arkansas Gazette*. At a later time, Carolyn visited Bill at college. On one such excursion she accompanied him, after Martin Luther King, Jr.'s assassination, on an outing to a church in a riot-torn area of Washington, D.C., where Bill delivered much-needed food.

Carolyn Staley remained a vibrant part of Bill Clinton's life. He made her a member of his state cabinet, and she headed the Commission on Adult Literacy.

Bill left high school with many fond memories. He was particularly indebted to ninth-grade civics teacher Mary Marty for stirring his interest in political debates, to guidance counselor Edith Irons for putting him on a heading to Georgetown University and the study of international affairs—but most of all to school band director Virgil Spurling, who held Bill in the highest esteem, not only as a talented member of his musical group but also as a highly principled, well-rounded, and well-behaved young man.

"Billy came equipped with all sorts of techniques when he joined the band with his sax," Spurling recalled. "He was a soloist. He could play jazz. He read every piece of music I put in front of him. Even the orchestral kind."

The bandleader also was of utmost importance to Bill.

"He was a real good man, real religious, spent a lot of time with his kids, cared a lot about them," was Clinton's affectionate assessment.

As Gary Wills noted in *Time*, "He was everything Clinton's stepfather was not, and once Clinton startled Spurling by saying he really did not have a daddy of his own."

Before graduation, Bill put into writing how he felt about the bandleader who taught him his deep appreciation of music. In his sophomore year, Bill entered this passage in the teacher's yearbook: "In the years to come, I shall try with all I have to be deserving of your friendship."

In his junior year: "Some things can't be written down...I truly hope I don't let you down next year."

Then in 1964, his senior year: "I honestly tried to do a good job for you."

A Superachiever

Bill did a good job at Hot Springs High. He was dutiful to a fault and always a superachiever, a constant plodder at community service. Not only did he play in the band, but he also helped Spurling organize musical festivals all over the state.

He was a devoted Boy Scout and took part in scouting jamborees and other such activities. His willingness to volunteer was so extensive that his principal put her foot down. She felt adults were exploiting Bill. Even the local heart fund wanted to make him an officer.

"Bill simply just doesn't seem able to say no to these requests," the principal told his mother.

Clinton was an especially well-rounded young man and very well behaved. In fact, Bill's behavior was so prim and proper that it infuriated at least one classmate, who put him down for being too good.

"Don't you ever do anything wrong?" demanded Carolyn Wilson. "You're a teenager, you're supposed to do things wrong."

During the presidential campaign, she was interviewed by reporters looking for "dirt" on Bill from his high school days. But Carolyn Wilson emphasized that there simply wasn't any.

"You won't find anything bad about him," she insisted.

About the only remotely eccentric thing young Clinton did was to "cruise around Hot Springs in his stepfather's car—a 1949 Henry J. convertible—and do impersonations of Elvis Presley," said another childhood friend, Patty Criner. "He did especially well singing 'Love Me Tender,'" she recalled.

When Clinton left high school, his achievements included a term as president of his junior class and of the Beta Club. He was also a member of the National Honor Society and DeMolay, which offers leadership training (when he was serving his fourth term as governor of Arkansas, in 1988, he was inducted into the society's International Hall of Fame).

One of his last high school honors was to become a semi-finalist in the National Merit Scholarship competition.

That was followed by graduation in June 1964, finishing fourth in a class of 300-plus students.

Next stop: Georgetown University in Washington, D.C.

But first there's a detour to take in Hot Springs for a closer look at the young man's oft-harrowing domestic existence.

2

CHILDHOOD TORMENT

A Spooky Deal

"I remember the police coming and taking him away. That was a pretty spooky deal."

Bill Clinton was describing a marital quarrel he watched through terrified eyes between his mother, Virginia, and stepfather Roger Clinton when he was six years old.

His stepfather was "drunker than a hoot owl" and "very obviously he was out of his bird." For during the violent exchange, Roger Clinton whipped out a bulky .45-cal. revolver and fired it.

"The whole neighborhood knew what happened after the police took my stepfather away," Clinton went on. "We were lucky that nothing like that happened again. When we moved to Hot Springs, there never was another *public* incident."

Clinton did not speak about the *private* domestic bloody brouhahas his violent stepfather had with his wife. Nor of the many ways young Bill tried to intercede and make his parents stop brawling, shake hands, kiss, and make up.

"I was forty years old by the time I was sixteen," Clinton admitted in 1992—only after the press broke the story about the turbulent 15 years he lived in his stepfather's house.

"I think my desire to accommodate is probably due in part to the sense that I had from my childhood, that I was the person who had to hold things together in my home, to keep peace. And on balance, those skills are very good...I mean, basically we're living in a world where cooperation is better than conflict."

His need to smooth things over, his anxiety to please, were at times the acts of a desperate teenager caught up in a home under siege.

This family secret was an unmentionable subject for the dozen or so years Bill Clinton held public office in Arkansas. But the ledger couldn't remain closed when he ran for the presidency. No longer was he dealing with reporters from the *Arkansas Democrat-Gazette*. He was in the big leagues now, with the *Los Angeles Times*, the *Washington Post* and *Washington Times*, weekly periodicals like *Time* and *New York*, and the three television networks covering his campaign. All were asking probing questions.

His mother, who married first a Blythe, then a Clinton, followed by a Dwire, and was a three-time widow before taking a Kelley as her fourth husband, all at once found herself in the national spotlight.

Could Clinton have entered the presidential primaries believing he would escape press probing of his childhood, upbringing, and home environment forever?

His mother's reluctance to discuss her harrowing marital experiences was penetrated finally when she described her reaction to her husband's gun play in an interview with the *New York Times'* Todd S. Purdom, who called her responses "variations on the Scarlett O'Hara sentiment."

"I'm the world's greatest person to dismiss unpleasant things out of my mind," reporter Purdom quotes the mother. "You know, I get, like, 'How did you feel when your husband shot at you?' and she responds in a rich controlled chuckle with, 'Well, how does anybody feel when they get shot at?'"

Almost the instant he declared his candidacy, Clinton was deluged by questions about his private life. Going back into his childhood was a painful process that, until then, he had always avoided in public.

He fenced with reporters and fudged answers about his personal life. He was slick. He couldn't be pinned down. Reporters on the campaign trail soon slapped him with the label his political enemies in Arkansas had pinned on Clinton: "Slick Willie."

His evasiveness ended when *New York* magazine's Joe Klein finally broke down the candidate with probing questions about his stepfather that could no longer be sidestepped.

The newsman had come well prepared. He also had interviewed Bill's mother, who let enough out of the bag to warrant this line of questions:

"Was your stepfather an alcoholic?"

"Was he prone to violence?"

"Did he beat up on your mother?"

The questions rattled Clinton and he withdrew into a shell of silence. Then he begged the reporter not to focus on his childhood experiences—because he couldn't remember anything about them. Klein wouldn't back away.

"Your mother remembers...she told me a good deal...but I'd like to hear it from your own lips, Governor."

Klein wasn't giving Clinton a snow job. Mrs. Kelley had indeed lifted the lid on heretofore closely guarded family confidences.

"Roger," began Mrs. Kelley, "was thirteen years older than me. He adored Bill. But he was an alcoholic. A lot of times Bill had to see...unacceptable behavior."

Living with a Bullet Hole

At times, Mrs. Kelley told the writer, her husband was a violent drunk. Klein picked up on that note in his interview with Clinton, who finally relented to talk about the early years—and to recognize the bullet hole incident.

"I remember once when I was four or five and he was screaming at my mother,"

Klein quoted Clinton, "and he actually fired a gun in the house. There was a bullet hole in the wall. It could have ricocheted, hit my mother, hit me. I ran out of the room. I had to live with that bullet hole, look at it every day."

Clinton had more to say about his stepfather's alcoholic stupors and his disposition to batter Bill's mother in his rages. But those words were not spoken to a reporter. *Time* magazine's Gary Wills found them in the records of the Garland County Chancery Court in Hot Springs.

"I was present on March 27, 1959, and it was I who called my mother's attorney, who in turn had to get the police to come to the house to arrest the defendant."

Bill made that statement to his stepfather's attorney at a deposition hearing held sometime in 1961. He was 15 at the time. The proceeding was precipitated by Mrs. Clinton's decision to take no more abuse from her husband and to divorce him.

Bill's formidable testimony helped influence the court in its decision to issue an interlocutory decree of divorce.

"He Was Abusing My Mother"

The most telling blow was this:

"The last occasion in which I went to my mother's aid, when he was abusing my mother, he threatened to mash my face if I took her part."

But take her part he did, not long after his stepfather threatened *him*. By then, Bill had decided to stand up to him. He was still only 14 but had grown to be an eyelash or so taller than his boozed-up parent who "was so consumed with self-destructive impulses," as Clinton put it to Joe Klein.

"One of the most difficult things for me was...putting an end to the violence." He did so by breaking down the door of his parents' bedroom when they were having it out.

"I told him I was bigger than him now, and there would never be any more of this while I was there."

He was true to his word. From that time on, Bill kept an eye out for the first sign of trouble between his parents, ready to leap in and put the old man down. He also kept his antenna up for any problem that might arise at home during his absence.

"If he was out on a date and knew his stepfather had been drinking," his mother explained, "Billy would always call in a couple of times to see that I was all right."

While he had claimed not to recall many of the confrontations he had with his stepfather, Clinton had a vivid memory of the break-in episode.

"That was a dramatic thing," he offered. "It made me know I could do it if I had to. But it made me more conflict-averse. It's a really painful thing, you know, to threaten to beat up your stepfather."

It was an act of desperation, for all other efforts had failed to put the old man in line. Billy had tried many times to reason with him. Even on the night he broke down the door of the bedroom and faced his mother's boozy assailant, his stepson tried to pacify Clinton by inviting:

"Daddy, if you're not able to stand up, I'll help you. But I have something to say."

It was only after he was rebuffed that Billy laid the law down and told him "there will never be any more of this while I'm here."

Bill Can't Recall

When journalists like Wills and Klein wanted to dig deeper about his stepfather, Clinton usually withdrew into his "I can't remember what happened" stance. He even insisted he didn't remember giving a deposition in the divorce proceedings.

"I honestly have no recollection of that," he would say. Later, when other newsmen hounded him for more details, he protested:

"One of the frustrating things about this whole deal, this nationwide attempt to make me look slick—to which I may have contributed—is that people expect me to remember all of, or to share things I thought I was never supposed to share. I mean, it's a strange sort of deal."

His mother put it another way. "Bill and I have always been able to do that. I know you people are amazed at this, but we would always put away anything unpleasant."

Wills embroidered on that statement in his article:

"In fact, his mother does not remember her own deposition given in the same divorce proceedings. The name of her lawyer is a stranger's name now. She doesn't even remember the timing or circumstances of her remarriage to Roger Clinton—a remarkable suppression of the past. In fact, when a cousin suggested she didn't pursue the divorce to its conclusion, she could not deny that with certainty—and neither could her son. Only the court records restore the sequence. Her divorce did become final in May 1962."

But the couple didn't adhere to the ruling. Three months after the decree was granted, Virginia remarried Roger. What brought about the reconciliation has not been spelled out by anyone in the family. But it may be safe to assume that a shared desire to provide a united family for Roger Clinton, Jr., was a major factor.

Bill's half brother, born in 1956, was just past his fifth birthday when his parents divorced. Roger Jr. remained with his mother during the three months of the separation. Shortly after their reconciliation, his school days began.

But before the youngster had gone off to his first day as a kindergartner, his half brother, Bill, committed himself to what he later described as "an expression of family solidarity."

He appeared before a judge in the Garland County Chancery Court and had his name changed legally to William Jefferson Clinton. His mother later offered an explanation.

"Little Roger was entering school and Bill didn't want people confused by them having different names."

Some think it curious that Bill Blythe took his stepfather's name, a man he abhorred during his ungovernable rages. Ironically, he went through the name-change just when he was urging his mother not to reunite with Clinton.

"I didn't think he would straighten up, even though I loved him," he asserted.

All of which illustrates what it's like growing up in the home of a problem drinker: the arguments, the fights, the promises to reform, the reconciliations, all intended to restore harmony in the household and turn a cheerful face to the outside world.

The reunion and remarriage didn't bring about an appreciable rehabilitation in his stepfather. Billy Clinton continued to be torn by the man he loved and hated.

In retrospect, Clinton made this observation:

"Like most families of alcoholics, you do things by not confronting problems early, you wind up by making things worse. I think that the house in which my brother and I grew up, because there was violence and trouble, and because my mother just put the best face on it she could, things did not work out as well as they should have. Especially since in later years a lot of the stuff was dealt with by silence."

Two Brothers, Two Different Paths

Children from damaged homes can take diametrically different pathways as can be seen by charting the courses Bill and Roger Jr. followed after leaving home.

Bill went on to Georgetown University, to Oxford as a Rhodes scholar, to Yale University Law School, to the governor's office in Arkansas, to a candidacy and election to the presidency.

Roger Clinton, Jr., finished his schooling, became a musician, was busted for peddling cocaine, served a year in prison, and then straightened out and settled into a career as a studio musician in Los Angeles.

"My brother and I," said Bill Clinton in an interview during the campaign, "were sort of two prototypical kids of an alcoholic family."

Did that mean they had only two options: Become a president or a coke dealer?

The question was put to Clinton early in the primary campaign by Joe Klein.

"Well, a lot of the literature suggests that's exactly what happens to children of alcoholics," Clinton rationalized.

"Sometimes they do both in different ways...I understand addictive behavior. You know, a compulsive politician is probably not far from that."

Isn't that, indeed, what William Jefferson Clinton has been since high school—a compulsive politician?

Let's now pick up Bill Clinton's trail following high school—and the pathway taken by Chicago teenager Hillary Diane Rodham.

3

GEORGETOWN YEARS

President of His Class

"Hello, I'm Bill Clinton. Will you help me run for president of the class?"

Those were the first words out of Bill's mouth. He was off and running as a politician even before he had settled in his dormitory room on the Georgetown campus.

They were said to Thomas Caplan, a fellow freshman, but from a far different background. Caplan came from a wealthy eastern family. He was a close friend of Massachusetts' *first family*, the Kennedys, with similar social prominence and considerable wealth.

Caplan wasn't yet aware that the handsome freshman with the friendly, winning smile was to be his roommate.

"Yes, I'll vote for you," replied Caplan without further urging. The affable stranger had arrived hours earlier at Washington's outskirts in the 1960 white Buick Special two-door sedan his stepfather had "lent" him in his senior year in high school.

Bill was campaigning for an honorary elective office at the imposing Roman Catholic university, nestled on the "Heights" overlooking the convergence of the murky waters of the Potomac River and Rock Creek, a heading less than two miles from the White House.

To prepare for his election to the highest office in the land and to feel no embarrassment in becoming commander in chief of the armed forces, Bill made all the right moves a young patriotic American could make.

Shortly after reaching his 18th birthday on August 19, 1964, he went to the selective service board in Little Rock and registered for the military draft.

Upon arriving on the Hoya campus later that month, he enrolled in the Reserve Officers Training Corps and dutifully registered for a two-point course in military science, a prerequisite for the ROTC program taught in the classroom once a week.

(This fact about Clinton's college years has never before been brought out. During his years as governor, when he withstood charges of draft dodging, and the further firestorm that blazed during the presidential primaries against five Democratic rivals and the campaign against President George Bush, no one ever noted that he had served in the ROTC. Moreover, Clinton never mentioned that he devoted *two years* to the Georgetown University military cadet corps. Had he done so, Clinton would have exposed his Achilles' heel and opened himself to charges far more serious than merely avoiding the draft: that he knowingly and purposefully committed crimes [fraud, perjury, and filing false instrument] against the federal government to evade military service. A detailed explanation is forthcoming.)

Bill's in the ROTC

As a new member of the ROTC, Bill was issued a green army uniform, combat boots, and an M-16 rifle that he was told must be disassembled, cleaned, and oiled once a week. His only other obligation to the ROTC was taking part in the Tuesday morning drills on the football practice field.

"Bill was an outstanding trainee," said his student company commander, Philip Plascencia, a junior at the time and today a New York banker. "He attended every drill and fulfilled the requisite classroom studies in military science. When I graduated as a senior, Bill was finishing his sophomore year. I don't know what his experience with the ROTC was after that."

Quite revealing, as this author's investigation brings out.

The four-year ROTC program is divided into two parts: a basic course of training given in the freshman and sophomore years, followed by an advanced course in the junior and senior years. Students in the advanced course are obliged to serve two years on active duty following graduation. The commitment to put in those two years is irrevocable. Even if a student signing up for advanced training has a change of heart at anytime upon commencement of the advanced phase, there is no escape from the obligatory two-year tour of active duty that, under the law, could be ordered to begin immediately.

To say Bill Clinton had the fairest cause to be concerned that he might be called to fight and bleed for all of those who preferred not to, is to underestimate the man's intentions. For he who would be president and command the armed forces chose not to carry his membership in the military to unnecessary excess.

On that late summer day of 1964, the newly arrived freshman from Arkansas was campaigning for office. Thomas Caplan had been the first trophy the comet Bill Clinton rounded up for his orbit across the sprawling Hoya campus.

Clinton's first days in the classroom were a mix of serious concentration on the lessons taught by his professors and serious politicking among the students.

With his characteristic fixed grin and handsome good looks highlighted by close-cropped black hair and smiling blue eyes, Bill Clinton had little trouble selling himself.

Especially easy to convince were campus coeds. Fellow freshman Stefanie Weldon, a Maryland native, caved in to his charms before she knew a thing about him.

"I don't know what you're running for..." she leveled with Clinton. "...but," Miss Weldon sighed surrenderingly, "I want to vote for you!"

Though given with the same ease as Stefanie Weldon's, Tom Caplan's vote was made with some apprehension.

"I didn't believe I could trust him," Caplan was to say later. But in time, Caplan's view of Clinton took a 180-degree turn. At Easter break, Bill brought his roommate home to Hot Springs and introduced him to his mother. By then, Caplan was nothing but complimentary in speaking of his roommate:

"Mrs. Clinton, I'll just put it to you as plainly as I know how. There isn't anyone anywhere in this world as good as your son—nobody."

After a brief pause, he continued, "But until I saw how genuine he is...I couldn't trust him."

Clinton was delighted to bring Caplan home to Hot Springs: "Tom's been to Europe, but he's never been to Arkansas."

Virginia Clinton found her house guest a bit stiff, if not stodgy. She was aware of Tom's very proper social rearing, so she made an effort to bring him down to earth. She managed to do that before he and her son drove back to Georgetown.

"I had him reaching for the butter in the middle of the table just like everyone else," Mrs. Clinton boasted delightedly. She was also pleased that she had prevailed upon her husband to be on his best behavior during Tom Caplan's visit.

His Stepfather Is Dying

Roger Clinton laid off the sauce and didn't utter a single harsh word to his wife during the four days Caplan was their house guest. But by now he was no longer the two-fisted drinker and abusive husband he once was. He had been ailing for some time and, after considerable hesitation, reluctantly went to the family doctor and learned he had cancer.

The condition was advanced, and the diagnosis was terminal. When he returned home, he didn't level with his wife. He was too proud to admit he had a fatal illness—or that he was sick at all. Only when the disease began sapping his energy and vitality, and causing increasing discomfort and pain, did Roger finally allow himself this admission:

"Virginia, I'm gonna die."

Still, Roger Clinton's courage and determination to live enabled him to battle the disease for three more years before he finally lost the fight.

Bill Clinton's days at Georgetown were the happiest he had known. With his stepfather mellowed by illness, home no longer erupted with violence. Now he could tackle his studies with a clear head, brimming with confidence.

"I was not only in love with the experience [of attending the university], I was consumed by it," Clinton admitted. "But most of all I got a job in Washington that came at the most opportune time—when I was a nobody from nowhere and as desperate as all *git out*."

This clerical position came his way after he completed his freshman year in the spring of 1965 and returned home with considerable uncertainty about the future. His mother had paid Bill's first-year tuition and provided him with "pin money" for food and other necessities.

But with his father's illness, the drain on the family budget became prohibitive. It didn't seem that Bill would be returning to Georgetown in the fall. But then...

"I received a call at home from Lee Williams who said he had a job for me and asked me to come to Washington to begin work," Clinton explained.

Williams was U.S. Senator J. William Fulbright's administrative aide. The fact that Clinton met the Democratic legislator from his home state during his senior year and lunched with him had little to do with the offer. Clinton had been recommended for the job by Arkansas Supreme Court Chief Justice Jack Holt in appreciation for Bill's efforts as a Democratic Party volunteer working in behalf of the jurist's uncle in the state's 1962 gubernatorial campaign.

"I got the job despite the fact that I was a nobody, that my family had no money and no political influence...simply nothing else at all," said Clinton, recalling the exchange with Fulbright's right hand man:

Williams: We'd like you to come back to Washington and work with the Senate Foreign Relations Committee.

Clinton: What kind of work?

Williams: Clerical...filing...typing...things like that.

Clinton: What's it pay?

Williams: You can have a part-time job for three thousand five hundred a year or a full-time job for five thousand.

Clinton: How about two part-time jobs?

Williams: You're just the guy I'm looking for. Be here Monday.

Clinton packed his bags and drove his Buick back to Washington. He had $50 in his pocket advanced by his mother to tide him over until his first paycheck. The dormitory room he occupied at Georgetown in his freshman year served as his lodging for that summer.

In the fall, Clinton would return to Georgetown and resume sophomore year studies.

Hillary Goes to Wellesley

"Aside from a few trips away with girlfriends, Hillary Rodham hadn't really been away from home," said her mother Dorothy Rodham as she recalled the day she and husband, Hugh, drove their daughter from Park Ridge to the Wellesley College campus in Massachusetts to start her studies as a freshman in mid-September of 1965.

"I loved having my kids around, and when she went to Wellesley, well, it was really, really hard to leave her. After we dropped her off, I just crawled in the back seat and cried for eight hundred miles."

Hillary Diane was at last at the college of her choice. Once settled into her dormitory and attending classes to fulfill the requirements of her political science major, she began a transformation from the compulsive do-gooder high school teen. The Girl Scout badges, the Daughters of the American Revolution service awards, all that rooting for the Grand Old Party and its conservative flag bearers and the quiet, unruffled *It's a Wonderful Life* setting of Park Ridge soon become a faded memory.

Something more powerful was lurking in her future.

No more races for meaningless class offices or organizing folksy neighborhood activities like the "Olympics" she once staged on her family's front lawn. She became a new Hillary Diane Rodham at Wellesley—a political science major with a sharp focus on what she wanted beyond graduation from that tony four-year, all-women's college: to attend law school and then become the best jurisprudent she could be.

However, Hillary didn't give up her penchant to organize now that she was a college student. She merely set her sights higher, as when she won a seat in the student senate and focused on important issues, matters that meant a lot to a 1960s' collegian bent on being an activist.

"I was worried about her," admits her mother, who noted Hillary's activities from afar with a somewhat critical eye. "But Hillary adjusted to Wellesley without a problem. She joined clubs and was active immediately."

Hillary wasted little time rubbing the Wellesley status quo the wrong way. She irked the college's hierarchy by calling for a ban on mandatory classes and campaigned for admissions of more minority students. She also protested curfews and called for an end to the prohibition of bringing men into dormitories.

Because she was paying more attention to her appearance, she was metamorphosing into a far more attractive young woman than she was in high school. She had caught the eyes of the boys at such Boston area schools as Harvard and Massachusetts Institute of Technology. Dating was high on her agenda now—but not a priority. Thus no serious romance resulted.

Martha Sherrill, in her perceptive *Washington Post* analysis, wrote that Hillary was becoming "something more powerful [than a "compulsive do-gooding" teenager]...the further away she got from Park Ridge, every year, every new experience, every new bit of information, the picture inside her head became sharper—about what piece of the world she'd help fix."

One college roommate, Jan Piercy, read the compulsiveness inherent in Hillary and offered this seemingly proper portrait of a peripatetic go-getter:

"Hillary was smart enough to realize that, eventually, she had to make a choice. Lots of people became paralyzed trying to decide where to focus their energy. At Wellesley, certainly, she hadn't found that focus yet—she was involved in everything."

Before she finished her freshman year and returned from summer recess to Park Ridge, Hillary Rodham had begun to zero in on what piece of the world she wanted to help fix. No longer a laid-back activist, she became a fighter of the first rank, exceeding the "blood and guts" pugilist her mother described, who'd "beat up the neighbors' kids...arms swinging, eyes closed."

Now she was rebellious, but purposely so and yet almost always in full command of her rationale.

"I wouldn't say she was angry," observed Jan Piercy. "Intense anger is sometimes the result of frustration—from not being effective. And Hillary has always been effective...She has a vitality that arises from her convictions. She loves talking about ideas. She loves asking questions. Ask her about herself, and I think you'll find she shuts down. Oh, she may answer your question, but I don't think you'll see much energy behind it."

Despite numerous extra-curricular diversions, Hillary fulfilled the demanding requirements of her classroom agendas.

"[Hillary was] intense and very serious...the lowest grade I gave her was an 'A,'" said Patsy Sampson, her professor in a child psychology course at Wellesley. "The rest [of the grades] were 'A-pluses.'"

No one noticed more than her friend Betsy Johnson Ebeling how Hillary had begun to change when she returned home from her freshman year. She had not yet bloomed into full-blown rebellion, as she would in time, when she'd disagree totally with her parents' politics, stand four-square against the Vietnam War, and become resolutely opposed to virtually every cause her mother and father espoused. The change that first year was not perceptible to her family.

She spent the summer socializing with her parents and brothers, going to the Pickwick Theater on Saturday nights with the girls or an occasional beau, and spending the rest of the time with Betsy Ebeling at the public swimming pool getting a deep tan—and discussing her new-found interests on the Wellesley campus.

Inside Information

Bill Clinton's summer of 1966 was not as restful. It was spent, again, as an intern with Senator Fulbright's Foreign Relations Committee.

Working there gave young Clinton access to information about foreign affairs that virtually no college student, let alone any other citizen of the country, could command.

Long before the public knew that Communist guerrillas in South Vietnam were escalating the recently engaged war, or about North Vietnamese attacks on U.S. naval vessels, the information was in the Fulbright Committee files.

When President Lyndon B. Johnson ordered retaliatory attacks on the enemy's military installations, the press and public certainly were told—but not before it was first made known to the Senate body monitoring America's foreign relations undertakings.

Those privy to official dispatches on the progress of the war before they reached the public had a firm advantage over those who did not have such access. When the president announced, despite the rumblings from Vietnam, that he had appointed a commission to study the feasibility of supplanting the Universal Military Training and Service Act with an all-voluntary system, it was very advantageous for a young man of draft age to know it beforehand.

When summer ended and he returned to Georgetown for his junior year, Bill Clinton was not only engorged with information about the future course of selective service procedures and the progress of the war in Vietnam, but he also had the added advantage of knowing what Opal Ellis was up to.

Opal Ellis was the secretary for Draft Board 26 in Hot Springs. Bill Clinton made a pit stop at Mrs. Ellis's stand while on a brief visit home before resuming his studies.

"He was always coming in here to check on where he stood in the draft," revealed Mrs. Ellis who was approaching her 85th birthday as this was written. "He kept wanting to know, 'What's my standing...How high up am I in the draft now?'"

"We knew he was in the ROTC at Georgetown and couldn't be drafted. For the life of me, I could never figure out why he was so anxious to know where he stood."

In time it would become apparent to Mrs. Ellis why Clinton repeatedly checked his status in the draft. But his motive hadn't become obvious yet.

Bill Clinton had retained his draft-free situation to the close of his sophomore year by adhering to his ROTC commitment until the spring break. As already cited, Clinton returned to his job with the Fulbright Committee in that summer of '66.

Much happened in his second year with the Senate body to tell Bill Clinton that he didn't want to suffer beside the combat soldiers his country was sending to Vietnam.

It appears he decided he could do much better on the home front and bide his time until he could offer himself to take on the responsibility for the country's final healing, as president of the United States, however far off that goal may have seemed to him then.

So when Clinton returned for his junior year at Georgetown, his dormitory locker was no longer encumbered with the green army uniform, the combat boots, and rifle issued to him as a freshman. Nor did he register for further study in military science. Bill opted not to go for advanced ROTC training, which automatically would commit him to serve a two-year minimum of active duty in the army upon graduation, or termination of studies at any time sooner.

He saw no need to serve in the ROTC any longer because he left Hot Springs reassured by Mrs. Ellis that his number on the draft board's roster was high enough to give him at least a year, if not more, of freedom from any call to arms.

Clinton would later admit that, as fervently as he opposed and despised racism in America before Vietnam, it was nothing compared to his passion against, and loathing of, the war. His experience with the Fulbright Committee, he would fess up, gave him little opportunity to work against the war. But now, free from military commitment, Bill Clinton had no compunction about speaking out, writing, marching, demonstrating, and inviting arrest for his obdurate stand against the war.

Anti-War Rallies

When students from Georgetown staged a demonstration in Washington against the practice by universities of reporting students' academic standings to draft boards to determine whether or not educational deferments were warranted, Clinton joined the protesters.

He also joined 55,000 demonstrators on October 21, 1967, in a huge anti-war rally at the Lincoln Memorial organized by the National Mobilization Committee to End the War in Vietnam.

Clinton accompanied marchers who left the rally across the Potomac to the Virginia side to another rally and vigil at the Pentagon. That protest got out of hand. A total of 179 persons, including author Norman Mailer, were arrested after clashing with army troops and U.S. marshals.

Another of Clinton's passions was his opposition to the selective service system, which "I never believed in." He joined demonstrators who staged draft card burnings. As the 1968 presidential election approached, he lent his support to the "Dump Johnson" organizations and beat the drums for New York Senator Robert F. Kennedy's candidacy after the beleaguered president decided not to seek reelection.

In the classroom, he wrote a paper that advanced his views about the draft system. He defined it as "illegitimate" and maintained "no government really rooted in limited parliamentary democracy should have the power to make its citizens fight and kill and die in a war they may oppose, a war which even possibly may be wrong, a war which, in any case, does not involve immediately the peace and freedom of the nation."

Those words are appropriated from a letter Bill Clinton wrote from England after he illegally evaded the draft and skewered the ROTC with what has been shown to be chicanery and deception. The letter, to a University of Arkansas corps commandant, will be presented in its entirety in chapter 4, which details when Clinton attends Oxford University in England and maximizes his efforts to avoid military service under any circumstances.

Before being chosen for a Rhodes Scholarship, Bill Clinton first graduated with the class of '68.

A few weeks before graduation, Clinton was caught up in the tumult following the April 4, 1968, assassination of the Rev. Martin Luther King, Jr., in Memphis, Tennessee. The crisis became a mandate for action for the effervescent, always-ready-to-volunteer "Arkie," as he was known.

His Hot Springs next-door neighbor and longtime-chum Carolyn Staley had flown to Washington to visit Bill just when widespread disorder broke out in Washington.

"I remember flying in and seeing the city on fire," Miss Staley related.

The two of them pitched in to assist Red Cross volunteers ministering to the beleaguered victims, burned out of their homes and left without food, medicine, and other necessities.

"Bill and I went in his Buick to a relief center where they put a red cross on the car, then loaded it with food, medicine, and blankets that we took to an area that was in flames. It was very dangerous. We raced through red lights and all. But Bill just had to be there."

"Before we left the shelter, we were advised to pull hats and scarves over our faces because we were white. We got out and walked throughout the city and saw the burning, the looting, and were very much brought into face-to-face significance with what was going on."

After passing out the emergency supplies, Carolyn and Bill turned a corner on foot and encountered a group of black men walking toward them. They quickly hightailed it back to Clinton's car.

"Although our hearts beat with the cause," Miss Staley acknowledged, "nobody could know that by the color of our skin."

Later, she remembered Clinton "wandering around in a daze, muttering excerpts from King's 'I have a dream' speech under his breath—to himself. I don't even think he was aware I was listening. He'd memorized it in high school."

Clinton had also volunteered for another cause some weeks before. A classmate, Neil Grimaldi, asked him to help feed and house homeless alcoholics.

"Bill went to the shelters and impressed me with the way he poured out sympathy for those poor souls," reports Grimaldi. "He even played his saxophone to break the ice with them."

Hillary at the Chicago Riots

The assassination of Martin Luther King was felt in Massachusetts with the same poignancy that prompted college students of every color and political persuasion all over the land to join the masses in mourning.

Hillary Rodham was winding down her junior year studies at Wellesley when word reached the campus that a huge rally and protest parade was to be held in Boston in King's honor. Hillary went to the demonstration, put on a black arm band, and marched with the thousands.

That summer, Hillary and Betsy Johnson Ebeling took the Chicago and Northwestern Railroad commuter train on the rapid 10-minute ride from Park Ridge and made their way to the Chicago Civic Center, where the Democratic National Convention had opened. They didn't have tickets to admit them to the auditorium; nonetheless, their curiosity about the goings-on outside the hall was boundless. They were attracted there by the pre-convention pronouncements that there'd be a multitude of demonstrations by anti-Vietnam War groups and by several radical organizations.

Hillary and Betsy weren't disappointed. Although they didn't witness the first day's excitement when members of the Youth International Party (YIPPIES) announced their candidate for president, a pig, they saw the violence that erupted after Vice President Hubert H. Humphrey won the presidential nomination on April 28.

By then, Chicago was being swept by an epidemic of protests by peace groups. The city's 11,900-member police force and some 13,000 National Guardsmen and federal troops ejected them. When it was over, more than 1,000 demonstrators had been treated for tear gas inhalation and other injuries, and 101 had been hospitalized; 192 policemen were injured, 49 hospitalized, and 63 newsmen were attacked by police. The scenes that Hillary Rodham and Betsy Ebeling took in were terrifying.

"We saw kids our age getting their heads beaten in," Ms. Ebeling related. "Hillary and I just looked at each other. We had had a wonderful childhood in Park Ridge, but we obviously hadn't gotten the whole story."

Hillary Rodham returned to Wellesley at the end of the summer recess. She tackled her senior-year studies and graduated in the spring of 1969.

Her experiences remain as memories that never fade. She'll drift into new locales as the years pass. She'll go on to Yale University to study law; she'll take another year's curriculum in child development; she'll spend two years in Washington for more of life's experiences; she'll then follow the man who'll become her husband and future president of the United States to Arkansas and beyond.

Through it all, Hillary Rodham Clinton, as she calls herself today, will be found always returning to Park Ridge for high school reunions and other special events. She will visit old friends, and she will stay, always, at Betsy Johnson Ebeling's house, the one friend who has remained closest and dearest to the woman who became America's first lady in 1993, and whom Martha Sherrill described in her *Washington Post* chronicle as one who:

"...never got in trouble. Never got detention. Her grades were often perfect...was a chronic teacher's pet...[who] rejected offers to have her ears pierced with a needle and potato, according to her best friends, didn't smoke in the bathroom, didn't make out with boys in 'The Pit' at Maine South's library, didn't even wear black turtle-necks."

All of the above can be added to Betsy Johnson Ebeling's response when asked whether she and Hillary ever cut class:

"Ohhhh no. The only time I remember us doing that was Senior Ditch day, kind of an organized event. And we thought we were being very daring."

Daring?

A powerful description for a very mild venture that cannot hold a candle to the audacious outing Hillary Rodham will take immediately after her graduation from Wellesley in 1969. But first, we must return to another, earlier graduation.

The Death of a Stepfather

In January of 1968, Bill Clinton received the news he expected—his stepfather was nearing death.

As Roger Clinton entered the last months of his illness, Bill left standing orders with his mother:

"You be sure and call me home before it's too late."

When he went home for Christmas in December 1967, Bill knew his stepfather didn't have long. His mother recalls the last time Bill saw Roger Clinton alive.

"I'll never forget how wonderful Bill was to him before he died. Roger had such pride by now. He had always been vain. And as much as he drank, well, he was still one of the cleanest persons you'd ever want to see. He was well-dressed, he had good grooming habits.

"But when he entered the last stages of his illness, he wasn't able to function well. He wasn't able to go to the bathroom, for example. So Bill would pick him up bodily and carry him to the john so that he could maintain his dignity."

Roger Clinton was barely past his 62nd birthday when he died in 1968. Bill was only 21.

He marked his 22nd birthday on August 19, 1968. He had graduated the previous spring from Georgetown University with a bachelor of arts degree and was prepared for a significant milepost: a Rhodes Scholarship and study at Oxford University in England.

The fellowships were established in 1902 in memory of Cecil Rhodes, the British-born South African financier, statesman, and one of the great empire builders of the late nineteenth century. It was because of Rhodes' efforts that the territories of Rhodesia and Nyasaland came under British dominion.

In his will, Rhodes founded scholarships to Oxford that provided approximately $1,000 per year for students "of good literary attainments, a taste for outdoor sports and qualities of leadership from every self-governing British colony, the United States and Germany, so that they might appreciate the advantage of imperial unity and the union of English-speaking peoples."

While the scholarship is considered a high honor, many find that the award—or the method by which it is bestowed—leaves much to be desired. Leading critic is Michael Kinsley, senior editor of *The New Republic* and co-anchor with Pat Buchanan on TV's "Crossfire."

Although a dyed-in-the-wool liberal, Kinsley took a hefty swipe at how Rhodes Scholarships are awarded:

"When people talk about a 'Horatio Alger success story,' they usually have in mind someone who lifted himself up by his own bootstraps. But that is not what Horatio Alger's stories were like at all. The typical Alger hero succeeds by impressing a successful older man or men with his sterling qualities. 'Mentoring' we call this sort of thing nowadays."

Kinsley went on to recite how candidates are chosen for the scholarships:

"The way...is to solicit eight recommendations, compose a personal essay and then submit to a series of intense interviews by a selection committee made up of local dignitaries, mostly former Rhodes scholars, in your state and region. The whole procedure is an institutionalized Horatio Alger story, an orgy of mentoring."

Whether or not Rhodes Scholarships are all they're cracked up to be won't be resolved here. What does matter is the momentous influence that educational trophy played in prolonging one student's ability to further his education on the cuff at one of the world's finest universities, while at the same time dodging military service.

4

A RHODES SCHOLAR
THE FIRST YEAR

Time Magazine to the Rescue

Bill Clinton breezed through the friendly phalanx of home-grown Rhodes Scholarship interviewers. His last hurdle had to be crossed in New Orleans—a final interview by a committee of Oxford scholars.

Before catching his flight, Clinton bought a copy of *Time* magazine at the airport.

"That was the luckiest thing that I could have done," Clinton was to exult.

For when he went before his examiners, he was asked questions about the first heart transplant operation.

"I gave them all the correct answers," Clinton enthused.

He was able to do that because the big story in *Time* that week was the story of the heart transplant!

At home in Hot Springs, Virginia Clinton sat by the phone awaiting a ring from her son.

"For the first time in my nursing career," she was to say, "I turned down a call to go to the hospital and assist in an emergency operation. I had never refused to do an anesthetic before. But I begged off."

The phone finally rang at 5 p.m. after a tense day of waiting.

"Mom, Mom," Bill Clinton fairly shouted. "That London Fog raincoat you gave me for good luck...Well, let me ask you, how do you think I'll look in English tweed?"

The liner United States steamed out of New York Harbor and reached England's port of Southampton six days later, some 20 hours behind schedule after encountering heavy seas. The Atlantic crossing didn't discomfort Clinton, but fellow Rhodes scholars suffered seasickness. One who spent most of the voyage in his cabin, in bed, was Robert B. Reich.

Reich, now one of Bill Clinton's closest confidantes, recalled the trans-Atlantic passage that helped forge a lifelong friendship: "Bill knocked on my door twice a day to see how I was doing and bring me refreshments. I remember being struck at the time at what a kind man he was. He had just met me."

After completing his Oxford studies and obtaining his law degree, Reich was to stand far taller in his later years than his lilliputian height of 4 feet 10 inches. He became a Harvard University professor who counseled Clinton on ways to run Arkansas.

Then during the presidential campaign, he was a key advisor. After the election, Reich was appointed secretary of labor.

Clinton's tenure at Oxford was not as placid or as productive as he had hoped it would be. Most of his American counterparts in the Rhodes program were, like Clinton, subject to military service. Those who had enlisted in the ROTC or obtained deferments as enlistees in other branches of the military were on safe ground. They were assured they would not be called to active duty until they completed their studies at Oxford.

However, those who hadn't taken the trouble, or didn't have the inclination to protect their flanks from a call-up, went through their studies on tenterhooks, never knowing from one moment to the next when they might be summoned back to the United States—to train for duty in the bloody Vietnam "conflict."

Clinton had no such immediate worry. He had avoided a draft call-up by having Senator J. William Fulbright and others get him deferments so he could go to Oxford. It took the better part of the summer of '68 to fashion a loophole that enabled him to sail to England for first-year studies as a Rhodes scholar at Oxford.

The gambit began shortly before Clinton graduated from Georgetown University. After having allowed him a student deferment up to and until he finished college studies, his Hot Springs draft board finally reclassified him 1-A (ready for induction). The date was March 20, 1968.

After he received his sheepskin in May, Bill hurried back to Hot Springs and dropped by his draft board to obtain another deferment that would enable him to go to Oxford.

"We told him he could not have the deferment," said Opal Ellis, the draft board's executive secretary who had had repeated encounters with Clinton during his last two years at Georgetown.

Can't Keep Him out of the Draft

"This time there was nothing we could do for him," Mrs. Ellis went on. "Deferments for post-graduate study had been rescinded by Washington. We told him to expect his notice to report for active duty in the very near future. He asked how soon that would be. He was told it would be a matter of weeks."

When he left the draft board, Clinton carried with him instructions to be ready for his pre-induction physical. The record reflects he didn't take the exam. A multitude of strings were pulled from high places to give him a succession of delays that amounted to nearly 11 months over other draftees, who were allowed but a week to 10 days to answer their summonses to active duty.

The delays were initiated by Bill Clinton's step-uncle Raymond Clinton, the Hot Springs Buick dealer and brother of Bill's late stepfather, Roger Clinton.

Raymond Clinton's first act was to submit an application in Bill's behalf with the Naval Reserve. Although no openings existed, the uncle obtained a commitment for his nephew. That bought time while his uncle engaged influential friends to pressure the draft board to delay his nephew's induction and allow him to attend Oxford.

Robert Corrado is another member of the Hot Springs draft board interviewed for this book. He corroborated what other sources told the author—or his researchers—about the manipulations Bill Clinton's uncle engaged in.

"Bill Clinton's treatment was unusual. The only explanation for the long delay would be some form of preferential treatment. But I wasn't privy to the details," said Corrado.

Raymond Clinton's longtime friend and personal attorney at the time, now a retired Arkansas Circuit Court judge, gave further testimony that showed "the draft board was handled successfully."

That witness is James Britt, who admitted he "assisted in the lobbying efforts" to delay Clinton's induction. The judge recounted "details of a calculated campaign to get what Billy wanted."

"We started working as soon as [Raymond Clinton] got word Billy was going to be drafted after graduating from Georgetown," Britt told *Los Angeles Times* reporter Bill Rempel.

Britt discounted the possibility that Clinton was unaware of his uncle's lobbying efforts. "Of course, Bill knew about it," he attested.

A Republican who lost a bid to be his party's candidate in Arkansas's 1960 gubernatorial race, Britt recalled that Bill Clinton's uncle Raymond had "one goal in my judgment—to delay, delay, delay," so his nephew could attend Oxford.

The law, as Mrs. Opal Ellis already pointed out, made no allowances for deferments to graduate students—except for those attending medical school.

According to Britt, Raymond Clinton also personally lobbied Will (Bill) Armstrong, head of Hot Springs Draft Board No. 26 and Lieutenant Commander Trice Ellice, Jr., commanding officer of the local Naval Reserve unit.

Raymond Clinton, Britt, Armstrong, and Ellice were founding members of the Hot Springs chapter of the U.S. Navy League, a national service organization.

Britt added that the pursuit of the Navy reserve billet was designed to "stall the draft process."

Trice Ellice confirmed that he persuaded officials of the Eighth Naval District in New Orleans to create a billet, or enlistment slot, when none existed, especially for Bill Clinton.

After all the trouble Ellice went to, Bill Clinton turned down the opportunity to join the Naval Reserve.

"I began to wonder why he hadn't shown up for his pre-induction physical," said Commander Ellice, who today is still involved in the Navy League. "So I phoned his uncle and asked, 'What's become of that boy you asked me to get into the Naval Reserve?'

"I'll never forget the response he gave me: 'Don't worry about it...He won't be joining. It's all been taken care of.'"

Before the billet for the Rhodes scholar came through, Uncle Raymond had worked a fix with the draft board that effectively stalled his nephew's call-up for more than 10 months. That obviated Bill Clinton's need to join the Naval Reserve and gave him the immunity from the military he needed to attend Oxford.

His uncle wasn't the only one pulling strings to keep Clinton out of the draft. Senator Fulbright personally phoned the draft board and whispered into member Robert Corrado's ear:

"We'd appreciate it very much here in Washington if you gave every consideration to keep Bill Clinton from being drafted."

"I was terribly annoyed by that additional pressure that was being put on the draft board," Corrado said during the presidential campaign of 1992. "We had been inundated by requests for special treatment from every side."

The Hot Springs draft board postponed Clinton's call to arms into mid-1969, giving him at least the first year of Rhodes scholar study.

The *Los Angeles Times* put it this way:

"Bill Clinton was the only man of his prime draft age classified 1-A by the board in 1968 whose pre-induction physical examination was put off for 10½ months—more than twice as long as anyone else and more than five times longer than most area men of comparable eligibility."

Opal Ellis offered the last word:

"As old as Bill Clinton was, he would have been at the top of the list of draftees. However, we were proud to have a Hot Springs boy with a Rhodes Scholarship. So the board was very lenient with him. We gave him more than he was entitled to."

Bill's English Girlfriend Talks

"Being there was incredible," Bill Clinton told *Arkansas Gazette* reporter Charles Allen. "I got to travel a lot. I got to spend a lot of personal time—learn things, go see things. I read about three hundred books both years I was there."

Clinton had no part-time job at Oxford as he had at Georgetown University. Consequently, he admitted, he didn't have extra money to spend on dates and frills. Yet, incongruously—and curiously—this Rhodes scholar, as few others in his class at Oxford, found the means to travel widely around Europe between studies.

How he managed that feat has not been explained. Clinton himself has never publicly discussed any of his activities off the Oxford University campus, other than conceding that he "got to travel a lot."

Clinton didn't do his heavy-duty traveling until his second year at Oxford. His first year was spent quite close to the campus. There were frequent outings to London with a classmate who became one of his closest friends, Strobe Talbott, a senior correspondent for *Time* magazine in later years—then appointed ambassador-at-large in the Clinton Administration.

Talbott offers that "Bill Clinton's personality hasn't changed greatly since his days in England...he is extremely competitive, and that is what I attribute to his success—his ability to compete with great intensity and not turn people off...he doesn't come across as being mean or vicious and hungry, thus he doesn't frighten or antagonize people."

Further insight on what Bill Clinton was like in England is offered by Tamara

Kennerly, who dated him that first year.

Clinton knew the pretty, dark-haired, 21-year-old English rose by her maiden name, Tamara Eckles-Williams. They met in April 1969.

"I was with my sister and her boyfriend in his student lodging," Tamara recalled fondly.

The boyfriend was a classmate of Bill's.

"Aren't you going to introduce us?" Clinton brashly asked the beau. He did. After that, Bill and Tamara became romantically involved. "He asked me out for a drink," she remembered.

Tamara surfaced in London just days before election day of 1992. She was found by *London Daily Mail* reporter David Gardner, who wrote that after Tamara's introduction to this Yank at Oxford, "an idyllic summer of romance followed as the two shared the heady atmosphere of the university city in the late sixties."

From the first meeting on the stairway, Tamara could see a headstrong young man who was very direct. "I can believe what I have read about him meeting his wife after he kept staring straight at her (in the Yale Law School Library) until she introduced herself."

Clinton had been going with a young American girl in Oxford, Aimee Gautier, before taking up full time with Tamara, whom he called Mara.

Tamara described how the romance blossomed: "I would come to Oxford from London every weekend and he came to see me a couple of times at my flat.

"His favorite pub was The Turf, a short walk from his rooms, where we would all go. We would all get into my Mini and go out to The Trout on the river outside Oxford.

"He came from Hot Springs, Arkansas, and Oxford really blew his mind. He loved the feeling of the place, he loved the people and everything about it.

"*He never had much money and we wouldn't go out to expensive places to eat or anything.*

"He was very easygoing and a very caring person. He was not at all a womanizer. While I was with him he certainly never went with anyone else. He didn't smoke any cannabis while I was there.

"He was very cuddly. I do remember that. We used to have a lot of fun. He didn't appear to work too hard. He certainly wasn't stuck in his books while I was around.

"He thought he wasn't coming back, so there wasn't much point really."

Tamara said she believed Clinton when he told her he would have to fight in Vietnam someday—though he didn't want to.

"We always knew he would be going to Vietnam.

"*He didn't want to go back* [to the United States].

"Two of his friends had got out of it as conscientious objectors."

(In a letter he wrote to Colonel Eugene Holmes [reproduced later], Clinton wrote about those classmates: "Two of my friends are conscientious objectors. I wrote a letter of recommendation for one of them to his Mississippi draft board, a letter which I am more proud of than anything else I wrote at Oxford last year.")

Clinton, said Tamara, told her that much as he opposed the Vietnam War, he couldn't be a conscientious objector "because he didn't think it was right."

"He thought you should fight for your country, but he didn't believe in what was going on in Vietnam. That was his dilemma.

"It was not the thought of fighting that troubled him—it was going to Vietnam."

The relationship lasted into the late spring when Clinton returned to Arkansas for the summer break, as Tamara recalled:

"When he left, it was a very troubled farewell. We both thought he was going to Vietnam. I thought he was going to be killed."

Desperately Fighting Induction

Clinton had reason enough by now to fear a doomsday. For on May 13 he received word from home that his draft induction notice had arrived. His mother had opened the envelope and phoned him at Oxford. The date of his induction was July 28.

That event was recorded by Little Rock attorney Cliff Jackson, who attended Oxford with Clinton as the only other Rhodes scholar from Arkansas. Jackson saved copies of old letters he had written from England to two history instructors in the states.

A former Republican and an unsuccessful candidate in a race as an independent for political office in Arkansas, Jackson went public with the letters during the 1992 presidential race "so voters in the remaining Democratic primaries could know the truth in advance of Clinton's nomination [that occurred at the July Democratic National Convention in New York's Madison Square Garden].

"Bill Clinton was not trying to avoid being drafted," Jackson declared in his first letter to his teachers in the latter part of May 1969.

"*He had already been drafted and was trying to void, as well as avoid, his imminent induction as an army private* [emphasis is the author's]." Jackson signed a sworn affidavit about the accuracy of his letters for the *Washington Times*, which broke the story on page one of its April 7, 1992, edition.

Jackson sent the letters, almost identical in text, to Professor Leslie Campbell, now associate dean of history at Auburn University in Alabama, and Ron Hathaway, most recently a high school principal in New Braunfels, Texas.

Campbell found Jackson's letter in his correspondence file after *Washington Times* reporter Ralph Frammolino got in touch with him. Campbell faxed a copy of the letter to the newspaper and it showed an Oxford postmark and a date of May 9, 1969. The letter confirmed the news about Clinton's induction notice.

Ron Hathaway said he remembered receiving letters from Jackson but was unable to recall Clinton's name. He had not saved the letters.

About a week after Jackson posted that correspondence to his mentors, the semester at Oxford ended.

Bill Clinton decided against crossing the Atlantic on an ocean liner again and booked a flight with British Airways. He was in a great hurry to beat the draft. His last night in Oxford was recalled by Tamara Eckles-Williams.

"Bill had tried to prevent his uncertain fate from blighting our last days together," she related. "He stayed with me the night before he went."

The next day: "Three or four of his friends went to the airport to see him off," Tamara said. She had gone along.

"I just couldn't stop howling. He was very upset. His last words were that he would write the moment he got home. In fact, he wrote his first letter either on the plane or in the departure lounge. Unfortunately, I have lost that one."

Indeed, he was upset. The news that he had just two months left before he was to report for induction didn't sit well with him. He felt the greatest urgency to buy more time to allow him to return to Oxford.

After a brief reunion with his mother and half-brother Roger, Clinton made it his first order of business to make a pit stop at his Draft Board 26. Opal Ellis described the visit:

"He stormed in here and told me we couldn't draft him. He said he was too well educated to serve as a draftee...he was trying to get into everything rather than have me send him [an official letter of induction]," Mrs. Ellis recalled. He was talking about the navy. He was trying to get into the Army Reserves...he was trying to get into anything so he wouldn't be inducted.

"*He just thought he was too good to go* [author's emphasis]," she went on. "I said, 'I'm sorry, but that's all I could do about it.'"

A Republican who was in her civil service position with the selective service system for 20 years, Mrs. Ellis was shaken by Clinton's gruffness and adamant stance. She tried to reason with him.

"When I told him there was nothing more we could do for him at the draft board, that we had extended him more privileges than were given to all the other young men, he scowled and threatened me. He said he was *going to fix my wagon*. He left in a huff, shouting over his shoulder that he was going to pull 'every string I know how to keep out of this lousy draft.'"

When Mrs. Ellis was interviewed by the *Wall Street Journal*'s Jeffrey H. Birnbaum for a story published in its February 6, 1992, edition, she said essentially the same thing. Her account sent the *Journal*'s staff reporter to candidate Clinton, who protested that he had no recollection of a confrontation with Mrs. Ellis.

"He strongly denies using strong-arm tactics to avoid the draft," Birnbaum wrote. "Anyone who says he did, he says, 'has, at best, a faulty memory.'"

Birnbaum added, "In any case, Mr. Clinton says he decided to, in his words, 'look around' for another option. He opposed the war, but if he had to serve he preferred to be an officer rather than a draftee, so he sought an officer's training program to join."

Further insight into the maneuvers Clinton employed to avoid induction is recorded in a handwritten letter Cliff Jackson sent to a friend. Now back in Arkansas during summer recess, as was Clinton, Jackson went to work as a research director in Republican State Headquarters in Little Rock.

Jackson stated clearly in his letter to the friend that "Bill is desperately trying to stay out of the draft."

He also noted: "Bill has gotten very cozy with me after I began working at the GOP. He came up to Little Rock to see what kind of GOP strings I could pull for him."

In 1969, the sitting governor was a Republican, Winthrop Rockefeller. The significance of that will surface shortly.

In his letter, Jackson described how he was besieged by Clinton with pleas to help him stay out of uniform.

> In comparison to others, I or we, don't have any real problems. Bill Clinton visited with me most of yesterday and night. *He is feverishly trying to find a way to avoid entering the Army as a drafted private* [author's emphasis again].
>
> At this moment, though he is still pursuing several leads, all avenues seem closed to him. The Army Reserve and National Guard units are seemingly full completely, and there is a law prohibiting a draftee from enlisting in one of these anyway.
>
> The director of the state selective service is willing to ignore this law, but there are simply no vacancies. I have had several of my friends in influential positions trying to pull strings on Bill's behalf, but we don't have any results yet.
>
> I have also arranged for Bill to be admitted to the U of A law school at Fayetteville, where there is a ROTC unit which is affiliated with the law school. But Bill is too late to enter this year's unit and would have to wait until next April. Possibly, Colonel [Army Col. Eugene] Holmes, the commander will grant Bill a special ROTC 'deferment,' which would commit him to the program next April, but the draft board would have to approve such an arrangement.
>
> They already refused to permit him to teach, join the Peace Corps or VISTA, etc. So Bill has only until July 28 to find some alternative military service. I feel so sorry for him in this predicament—it could have easily been me.

Obviously, Cliff Jackson and the Republicans didn't have the muscle to sit on Colonel Holmes the way others were to do to keep Clinton out of active military duty—despite the fact that there were no openings in the ROTC for the rest of 1969.

With his induction set for July 28, Bill Clinton had few options left.

When he reported to his draft board on the 28th, he received his pre-induction physical, passed it—despite eye and ear shortcomings that kept him out of the air force and navy officers' training programs he tried to join—and was told to report for active duty with the army on August 18.

The situation now was desperate. His time, as the saying goes, was *down to the short strokes*.

Hillary's Speech Embarrasses Dad

"A great miscalculation!"

Those are the words that tumbled from Hugh Rodham's lips as he jested about having consented to let his only daughter attend Wellesley.

She had left home, an innocent. She was a Republican. A Goldwater girl who campaigned for the presidential candidate's election with a sash on her blouse. She was calm. Balanced. A bit shy. Unquestionably modest. A ceaseless public do-gooder.

A far cry from the cascade of negatives that spewed from the mouth of Pat Buchanan at the 1992 Republican National Convention in the Houston Astrodome when he blasted Hillary as a "lawyer spouse." Other detractors frowned upon her 12-year reign as Arkansas's first lady by bashing her as "The Lady Macbeth of Little Rock," "Hillary the Hun," "Yippie Wife From Hell," and with other epithets that don't come close to the picture offered by a friend of 20 years, Sarah Ehrman of Washington:

"What people don't seem to realize is that Hillary's so conventional, so traditional, so Midwestern, so middle-class. Her taste in art is middle-class. Her taste in music is middle-class. Her clothes…she's very simple, brilliant, a nice person, and a product of her upbringing."

A product of her upbringing?

Hillary hardly was that on the May day she received her sheepskin at Wellesley's 1969 graduation exercises.

The day began for Hugh Rodham at roughly 3 a.m. when he awakened, showered, breakfasted, then left in his Cadillac for the Bay State. He drove the 800 miles from Park Ridge to Wellesley alone because Dorothy Rodham had to mind the store and tend their sons Tony, 13-years-old, and Hugh Jr., 17.

Hugh Rodham would suffer the fallout of his daughter's commencement alone. For the moment, his chest swelled with pride, as he would grudgingly admit later, before he took his seat at the ceremony and stared straight out at the podium. He caught sight of his daughter, her thick-lensed "Coke-bottle" eyeglasses straddling the bridge of her nose, her graduation robe fluttering in a gentle breeze as she took swift, measured steps across the stage to the dais. Rodham had been alerted that Hillary would be the next commencement speaker, following U.S. Senator Edward Brooke of Massachusetts.

As he said later, Rodham "wanted to lie on the ground and crawl away." He was nonplussed by Hillary's opening remarks that delicately, but firmly and relentlessly chewed out the Republican lawmaker for "being out of touch" with the times. Hillary spoke extemporaneously, yet it was clear she must have rehearsed her unprecedented address, an address described as "passionate, eloquent, wise, and full of uncompromising language."

Adapting such philosophy class passages as "authentic reality" and "unauthentic reality," and without referring to notes, Hillary trumpeted her message:

"There's a very strange conservative strain that goes through a lot of New Left college protests that I find very intriguing, because it harkens back to a lot of the old virtues, to the fulfillment of original ideas.

"And it's also a very unique American experience. It's such a great adventure. If the experiment in human living doesn't work in this country, in this age, it's not going to work anywhere."

Life magazine was so impressed by the commencement address given for the first time by a Wellesley student that it ran a story about it and dressed up the feature with a photo of Hillary.

There was no photographer about after the graduation rites when Hillary pulled a Katharine Hepburn just a half-century after the legendary actress, then an undergraduate at fashionable Bryn Mawr College in Pennsylvania, almost wrecked the dignity and decorum of the school.

Miss Hepburn made a public spectacle one sunny spring day when she bathed in the library fountain, then rolled herself dry on the grass.

Miss Hepburn left college with a conviction that she would become an outstanding actress.

Hillary Diane Rodham emulated Miss Hepburn's antics by swimming in Lake Waban in the center of the Wellesley campus, where swimming is prohibited. She stripped to her bathing suit, leaving her clothes neatly piled on the ground with her thick-lensed eyeglasses atop them. Hillary then plunged into the lake.

When she finished her swim and clambered onto dry land, she couldn't find her clothes or glasses. A campus guard had snatched them up.

Twenty-three years later, in the heat of the 1992 presidential primaries, Hillary Rodham Clinton returned to Wellesley's campus and delivered another commencement address. The truth about her clandestine aquatic feat came out.

"Blind as a bat," she chuckled after relating how she went for the swim, "I had to feel my way back to my room at David [dormitory]."

With her clothes and other possessions packed in her father's Cadillac and heading back to Park Ridge, Hillary Rodham promised herself she would become a great lawyer.

The "Fix" Made Bill Draft-Free

After so many efforts to keep Bill Clinton out of uniform, who was left to apply the necessary muscle for another reprieve?

Had any thought been given to Senator J. William Fulbright?

Certainly Fulbright—or even someone on the staff of his powerful Senate Foreign Relations Committee—could push buttons again in behalf of Bill Clinton. After all, he had interned for them during his undergraduate days.

Fulbright had already pressured the draft board to help Clinton.

Also noted was the earlier good deed of Lee Williams, the aide on Fulbright's committee who phoned Clinton and offered him the summer clerical job.

Williams is introduced anew as the author of a memo written on United States Senate stationery. The memo, obtained from congressional files through the Freedom of Information Act, is reproduced here in its entirety:

Law School Grad program
Army - ROTC
501-575-4251
Bill Clinton - 623-5076
Sgt. Graves—

Comb Post - 6 weeks, Fort Benning, Ga.
Summer (1970)
Must have first year ROTC def.
Holmes to call me Wed. 16th

Except for the three-line notation referring to Sgt. Graves and the unclear meaning about Fort Benning, the memo provides unmistakable evidence that some powerhouse was pulling strings for Bill Clinton. Clearly a source with the majesty and might of a U.S. Senator.

With the memo out in the open, there's no need to speculate further how Clinton commanded the influence that soon made his fondest dreams come true.

Bill Clinton Was a Republican!

All speculation should promptly end now with the appearance of retired Lieutenant Colonel Clinton D. Jones, administrator of the ROTC program at the University of Arkansas and second in command under the also-retired Colonel Eugene J. Holmes, the commandant.

Jones was located by *Washington Times* reporter Ralph Frammolino, who was assisted in his investigation by reporters Richard E. Meyer, David Lauter, and Doug Jehl. Jones told how Bill Clinton made his way into the ROTC when there were no openings:

"I received calls from Senator Fulbright's office, *from the governor's office*, and from state selective service headquarters. I told all of those who spoke with me to have Clinton come and see me. They didn't have any influence on my judgment because when I met Clinton I found a seemingly sincere young man."

Heavy stress is laid on "the governor's office" to point out that Winthrop Rockefeller evidently was sold a bill of goods on Clinton—that he was a Republican. That's not exactly an off-the-wall assumption, for, according to several classmates at Georgetown, Clinton had been cozy during his undergraduate days with the Young Republican movement.

"Many of his closest friends and associates on the campus were hooked on the Grand Old Party," said one graduate of the 1967 class who served in the ROTC with Clinton and is now a seminarian in Boston. This source gave the author information about Clinton's ROTC activities and other doings on condition that his name be shielded.

"Bill espoused Republican causes as an undergraduate," the seminarian offered. "I believe he did so because he was so dead-set against the Vietnam War, which was being waged in those years by Democratic administrations."

On Wednesday, August 6, 1969, Bill Clinton drove to the University of Arkansas campus in Fayetteville. He walked into the ROTC offices for an interview with Lieutenant Colonel Jones.

But before seeing Jones, Clinton quietly dropped into the office of the commanding officer, Colonel Eugene J. Holmes. Jones was not aware of this pre-arranged encounter. What Bill Clinton and Colonel Holmes discussed will be reported in chapter 5.

What is paramount is that when Bill Clinton left for home after a three-hour sojourn at the school, he was assured he had no further worries about the draft. The very next day, a phone call from Colonel Jones to Hot Springs selective service offices switched Bill's standing in the draft from 1-A to 1-D. That change, according to the deal he struck with the ROTC brass, meant he agreed to enroll for the 1970 fall semester at the University of Arkansas Law School and simultaneously to begin training with the school's ROTC unit.

A Letter for Tamara

Eight days later, Clinton wrote to Tamara Eckles-Williams in Oxford. In that letter, dated August 14, 1969, Clinton told her how, 11 days before he was due to be drafted, he joined a *scheme* (the ROTC) that allowed him to attend law school for three years, then go into the army for two.

"Hopefully," Clinton wrote, "there will be no Vietnam then." He closed the note saying he'd write again.

Later that month, Cliff Jackson penned a follow-up letter to his friend. Now he was told that Clinton's worries were over, that he had been admitted into the ROTC.

But, Clinton was still not pleased with his status. According to that August 27 letter, he was trying to find yet another way to stay out of military service. He was looking now to nullify his contract to participate in the law school's ROTC!

"Bill Clinton is trying to wiggle his way out of the 'disreputable' Arkansas law school," wrote Jackson. "His latest scheme: Because his ROTC training won't start until next year, he is going to ask the ROTC commander to give him special permission to go one more year at Oxford.

"Presumptuous? I don't know. Perhaps I would do the same thing if I were in his shoes."

(That permission to return to England and resume his Rhodes scholar's studies was granted by the aforementioned Colonel Holmes, whose name will soon surface again.)

Attorney Cliff Jackson took special note of that development when he ended his letter with this:

"P.S. Bill has succeeded in wriggling his way back to Oxford!"

5

A RHODES SCHOLAR
THE SECOND YEAR

Bill Surprises Tamara

Tamara Eckles-Williams brushed a tear away as she read the poignant letter from Bill Clinton bearing the Hot Springs postmark.

"Time at home has been boring but beautifully hot, and I do have a pretty good tan," Clinton wrote. "Have been playing my saxophone with a local band, building a house and meeting with some of the town's younger kids for diversion and pleasure."

In the letter, Bill Clinton leaves no doubt he was a smoothy with women—as far back as his college days.

"I just this minute thought of you and I at the University Ball and how lovely it was," he rhapsodized romantically. "Don't know why it just popped into my head."

Clinton wrote about his enrollment in the ROTC and his relief at not facing the draft.

"The idea of not being in the Army now and going to Arkansas Law School is almost more than I can handle—almost having a hard time adjusting," he continued. "You know how much I brood and worry too much."

Not many days later, Tamara answered a knock on the door of her London flat. It was September 20, 1969. Tamara remembers it was a Saturday because "I was home from work."

Asking "Who is there?" Tamara says the response stunned her.

"It's Bill...Bill Clinton...Don't you remember me? Aren't you going to let me in so I can hug you?"

Tamara flung open the door and rushed into Bill Clinton's arms.

"I was astonished to see him," she recalled. "He turned up out of the blue. He said he had been sent to finish his degree." Clinton harbored hopes of rekindling his affair with Tamara, but that was not to be. Back to earth now, she quickly brought him up-to-date.

"Bill," she said as tactfully as she could, "you've been away for three months...I must tell you that my old boyfriend came back in hot pursuit of me...and I'm afraid that I must be loyal to him."

Tamara also told Clinton, "I've been accepted by British Airways as an air hostess, so I've been flying around."

Clinton didn't fuss. He accepted the circumstances.

"He is very astute," Tamara told her interviewer. "I didn't need to spell it out. He knew things were not the same."

As Clinton turned to leave, Tamara's curiosity prompted her to call him back. She wanted to hear how he managed to return after saying in his letter that he was to study law at the University of Arkansas.

Tamara said Clinton told her "he decided to continue his studies at Oxford." Obviously he hadn't given her straight goods. "By going back to Oxford, he was effectively putting himself back in the draft," Tamara went on rather naively, a conclusion that parroted the line Clinton laid on her.

Then Tamara made this observation about Clinton's escape from the draft for the time being:

"I know he had no money so he couldn't have pulled any strings."

Clearly, he didn't tell her about all of the people he recruited to peddle their influence to keep him out of uniform.

Soon after, Tamara married the boyfriend, then divorced him. She married a second time to Stanley Kennerly, who today at 54 has been wed to the 47-year-old Tamara more than a dozen years. They have a 12-year-old daughter and live in the lap of luxury in Chelsea, where Clinton and Tamara spent much time together. Clinton's fondness for the metropolitan borough in the southwestern part of London, on the River Thames, is reflected in the choice of Chelsea as the name for his daughter.

Tamara, who is both a successful businesswoman and natural therapist, wanted to "set the record straight" for people in the United States who have the "wrong impression" about Bill Clinton and the draft.

"He wasn't trying to shirk his duty to his country," Tamara emphasized. "What has been said in America [about his efforts to avoid the draft] is vastly different to the truth."

Yet Tamara contradicts herself when she uses Clinton's letter of August 14, 1969, as evidence of the close relationship she claimed with him. For that correspondence offers Clinton's own words that "...11 days before [he] was to be drafted, he 'joined a scheme [the ROTC]' that saved him from active military duty."

In that statement Clinton appears to repudiate his own insistent claims of "I never received a draft notice," uttered during the 1992 presidential race. For, if he hadn't received the selective service board's call-up, how could he write that he was due to report for active army duty in *11 days*? How could he know his status without being notified in the mail, the only way he could actually learn that his number was up?

David Gardner wound up his story in the *London Daily Mail* with some last words about Tamara.

"She keeps a special place in her heart for Clinton and she believes he'll make a wonderful president."

The last word comes from Tamara herself.

"You have several boyfriends in your life who mean the most, and he is one that I would remember. I would never have forgotten him."

Hillary Goes to Yale Law

"Your fish look black," Hillary Rodham complained to the operator of the fish cannery on a late 1969 July day following her graduation from Wellesley. She had decided to explore Alaska and paid for her way around the newest state by tackling odd jobs.

When the stunned cannery boss heard Hillary tell him, "...and those fish look weird. Maybe they aren't fit to be eaten," he fired her.

Hillary returned to Park Ridge in early September. She had mere days left to pack and ship out to New Haven to begin law studies at Yale University. She had toyed at length with going to Harvard Law. However, she reconsidered when she realized, as Martha Sherrill reported in the *Washington Post*, that "Harvard's [classes had] 1,500 [students], all eating and sleeping and thinking deep thoughts within 100 yards of one another."

Hillary decided to study at Yale, which, compared with Harvard, was a "small aquarium of big fish." That there were only 500 students to a law class on the Eli campus appealed to her.

Before she left for Connecticut, Hillary went to her ophthalmologist in a desperate effort to emancipate herself from the ordeal of wearing "those annoying thick-lensed 'Coke bottle' eyeglasses."

"Look, doc," she complained, "I've had these damned glasses since I was sixteen. I'm going on twenty-two and I think it's time I started to wear contact lenses. Can't you do something about it?"

The answer was no. In 1969, only hard contact lenses were in use and Hillary's eyes couldn't tolerate them. Years later, after soft contact lenses were developed, she'd get rid of her eyeglasses.

So, with the annoying glasses in place, her straight, brownish hair hanging attractively loose to her shoulders, still disdaining makeup, Hillary Rodham headed for the Yale campus and first-year studies at the university's law school.

She was at once inspired by the high degree of public service orientation Yale offered. Many of its professors struck her as models for the path she hungered to pursue. Some had been members of the Kennedy Administration. One of them was the former head of the National Advisory Commission on Selective Service: Burke G. Marshall, the Assistant Attorney General who headed the Civil Rights Division in the Justice Department.

Marshall and his commission had promulgated the random-selection system for the military draft—the plan that President Nixon put into force three years later, which gave Hillary's future husband a permanent immunity from the draft.

Hillary Diane Rodham eloquently expressed her feelings about attending Yale Law School when she was invited to speak during the 1992 presidential campaign at an alumni weekend:

"There was a great amount of ferment and confusion about what was and wasn't the proper role of law school education," Hillary began. "We would have great arguments about whether we were selling out because we were getting a law degree, whether in fact we should be doing something else, not often defined clearly but certainly passionately argued. That we should somehow be 'out there,' wherever 'there' was, trying to help solve the problems that took up so much of our time in argument and discussion.

"Those were difficult and turbulent times, trying to reconcile the reasoned, ordered world we were studying with what we saw around us."

Hillary Rodham nested under the protective wing of Burke Marshall, one of the Kennedy family's closest confidantes. Marshall was the first person Senator Edward M. Kennedy called after he drove Mary Jo Kopechne to her death off the Chappaquiddick Bridge in 1969.

In the August 1992 edition of *The American Spectator*, Daniel Wattenberg noted that "At Yale, Hillary slipped into an intellectual milieu marked by way-out and sometimes vicious left-wing polemics and activism."

The writer reported that Hillary led campus protests "against everything from the Vietnam War to the absence of a Tampax dispenser in the women's law school john."

Hillary joined the staff of the *Yale Review of Law and Social Action* and was quickly seated on its board of editors. The publication was described as "an alternative legal journal devoted to the development of new forms of journalism which combine scholarship of the highest standard with reflections and recommendations based on experience and practice."

The first edition was plastered with a photo on its cover of a National Guardsman decked out in riot-ready garb and paraphernalia. One of Hillary's first contributions to the journal provided "detailed sympathetic critique" of a rambling article that proposed the following:

"Now a new frontier must be found to foster further experimentation, an environment relatively unpolluted by conventional patterns of social and political organizations. Experimentation with drugs, sex, individual lifestyles or radical rhetoric and action within the larger society is an insufficient alternative. Total experimentation is necessary. New ideas and values must be taken out of heads and transformed into reality."

The main problem with Hillary's piece was that it was "...long on rhetoric, short on action," according to a source at the school's publication.

In another issue, a double-length edition largely devoted to the Black Panther murder trial then being held in New Haven, several drawings depict policemen as pigs. In one, rifle-bearing, hairy-snouted pigs with nasal drip are marching in formation oinking and thinking to themselves, "niggers, niggers, niggers, niggers."

Yet another drawing shows a decapitated pig squealing in agony. The caption reads, "Seize the Time!"

If indeed Hillary Rodham approved of her colleagues' art work, "then she appears to have foreshadowed by about 20 years such contemporary traffickers in cop-killing imagery as rappers NWA and Ice-T," concludes Daniel Wattenberg in *The American Spectator*.

The *Yale Review of Law and Social Action* soon went the way of the dinosaurs.

The Black Panther situation took up much of Hillary's attention. She mediated meetings of angry students who had demonstrated and been tear-gassed by riot troops patrolling the streets of New Haven and the courthouse. Here Black Panther leaders Bobby Seale and Erica Huggins were on trial for the abduction and murder of one of their dissident followers.

Hillary became a skilled negotiator in bringing together the students and faculty at odds over the constructive role the law school should play in their lives. Many students felt, as Hillary did, that the faculty was "out of touch" with their generation. She was designated to be the campus "bridge" between the students and law school Dean Louis Pollak's administration.

It wasn't all work and no play for Hillary at Yale Law School, no more than it had been at Wellesley. Her social life much of the time was occupied by one beau, Jeff Shields, who today is a lawyer in Chicago. Hillary began dating Shields in her freshman year when he was attending Harvard. Shields recalls the relationship as more platonic than romantic.

"We spent lots of time with friends sitting around coffee tables in somebody's suite, having a beer or a Coke and talking in an animated way about politics and government and societal issues," Shields is quoted by Judith Warner in her Signet biography *Hillary Clinton: The Inside Story*. "There were lots of animated discussions on civil rights, civil liberties issues, and international issues, particularly in the Southeast Asia context."

From the day he met her, Shields was struck by Hillary's "real interest in government from the point of view of someone who wanted to be involved and have an impact, but didn't know exactly how. She didn't have fixed ambitions in terms of knowing that she wanted to be elected to some office, and she certainly didn't give any indication that she was looking to attach herself to a politician—and I'm sure probably would have been offended by that concept if someone had raised it at that time."

It wasn't all talk about politics and causes between Hillary and Jeff. They often strolled around Lake Waban in the middle of the Wellesley campus. They went to dances, parties at Winthrop House in Wellesley and his dorm at Harvard. Hillary was a good dancer. They danced to the tunes of Motown and the Beatles, and listened to platters cut by the Supremes, Hillary's favorite singing group.

Shields also attended Yale Law School, but by the time he encountered Hillary on the Eli campus their alliance had run its course.

"The primary basis of our relationship was cerebral," Shields professed. "It was a close dating relationship and we had a lot of fun, but it was primarily intellectual. It was one of those situations where both parties become less romantically interested in each other on a parallel track but remain friends."

Hillary was ready for a new relationship, one that would come close to meeting the prediction voiced in a letter of recommendation to the university's admissions office by one of her favorite mentors at Wellesley, Professor Alan Schechter:

"Hillary Rodham is by far the most outstanding young woman I have taught in the seven years I have been on the Wellesley College faculty. I have high hopes for Hillary and for her future. She has the intellectual ability, personality, and character to make a remarkable contribution to American society."

Schechter left no doubt why Hillary set her sights on the legal profession:

"She was going to law school not for the purpose of making money or becoming a corporate lawyer, but for the purpose of using the skills and the opportunities in the legal field to influence the course of society."

Organizing Peace Rallies

"He had plenty of other girlfriends to keep his social life in high gear," said Cliff Jackson about Bill Clinton after he was rebuffed by Tamara Eckles-Williams.

"Bill had other pursuits to follow that weren't what one would term social in the convivial sense," Jackson said cryptically in one of several interviews with the author. "Girls were a passion with him, yes, yet he seemed to be much more deeply committed and involved in societal situations that can't even remotely be equated with affairs of the heart."

Jackson declined to discuss that aspect of Clinton's activities further. "I've said enough," he protested. "Try others and they'll tell you more."

Other classmates interviewed by the author suggested two points in Tamara Kennerly's remarks be checked out:

1. *"He never had much money..."*

2. "We always knew he would be going to Vietnam. *He didn't want to go back* [to the United States]."

This prompted inquiries by this biographer that resulted in some curious findings.

During the presidential campaign, when accounts about Clinton's draft status and unceasing efforts to avoid military service were raised by President Bush, reports surfaced in various quarters that suggested Clinton had sought asylum in several foreign countries as a means to avoid the draft.

Clinton, the stories went, was prepared to renounce his American birthright—just so he could legally avoid serving in the military.

Tales circulated about "feelers" the 24-year-old Rhodes scholar allegedly put out about applying for citizenship in Great Britain, Sweden, Norway, Denmark—even the Soviet Union.

The rumors about Clinton leaning toward a Scandinavian country sprang from accounts by the Rev. Richard McSorley, a Jesuit priest who directed the Center for Peace Studies at Georgetown University.

McSorley knew Clinton from his undergraduate days. He was familiar with his militant anti-war activities on the Georgetown campus and in the Washington area during 1967 and 1968.

Clinton himself leaves no doubt that little time passed after arriving in England before he beat the drums against his country's participation in the Vietnam War.

"After I left Arkansas last summer, I went to Washington to work in the national headquarters of the [Vietnam] Moratorium, then in England to organize the Americans here for demonstrations October 15 [1969] and November 16 [1969]," Clinton fessed up.

The admission came in a December 3, 1969, letter to Colonel Eugene Holmes in which the Oxford Scholar reneged on his commitment to his benefactor in the States to attend the University of Arkansas Law School and participate in its ROTC program.

Clinton has never discussed his anti-war activities in Great Britain. But Father McSorley mentions them in his book of memoirs, *Peace Eyes*, published in 1978. He gives Bill Clinton considerable exposure when he writes about his visit to England and his experience on November 16, 1969—the first of the two anti-Vietnam War demonstrations Clinton organized in England.

On that day, Father McSorley attended an interdenominational service in St. Mark's American Church near Grosvenor Square, about 150 feet from the U.S. Embassy. He states that the activities in London supporting the Moratorium's efforts were initiated by Group 68 (Americans in Britain), backed by British peace organizations—and closely monitored by the Soviet Union through its KGB secret police/espionage organization.

During the 1992 presidential race, his campaign spokeswoman, Betsey Wright, denied Bill Clinton was a member of Group 68 and stated "Clinton never organized *an entire* anti-war demonstration *to my knowledge*...He merely *helped* organize a London religious service in opposition to the war in 1969. He wasn't the only organizer or the leader of it."

Father McSorley vividly recalls his encounter with Clinton in London on that November 16 when he attended the church service with 500 others:

"As I was waiting for the ceremony to begin, Bill Clinton of Georgetown, then studying as a Rhodes scholar at Oxford, came up and welcomed me. *He was one of the organizers*, and asked me to open the service with a prayer."

McSorley, who went to the pulpit and offered a supplication, described the service that followed:

"After my prayer we had hymns, peace songs led by two women with guitars, and the reading of poetry by a native white South American woman. The poems were very moving, especially one about napalm causing a horrible figure of a person who could not sit because his skin was just about gone and he had a crust spackled with pus. Another poem was about a human brain in a museum which had survived the nuclear destruction of the world. It told how everyone had disappeared and the world had all been fused together. Mixed with the reading were more peace songs."

Father McSorley said he was glad to see a Georgetown student *leading* in the religious services for peace.

"After the services," continues the prelate, "Bill introduced me to some of his friends. With them, we paraded over to the American Embassy carrying white crosses made of wood about one foot high. Then we left the crosses [in front of the Embassy] as an indication of our desire to end the agony of Vietnam."

Bill Visits Defectors' Country

Bill Clinton is mentioned in one additional passage of the book, bearing on a trip Father McSorley took to Norway later in 1969.

Inexplicably, who should be on the same train to Oslo with McSorley?

That same Bill Clinton, the Rhodes scholar said to have inquired about getting citizenship in one of five countries, of which one was Norway.

Why was Clinton going to Scandinavia?

Certainly he wasn't traveling there for the same reasons as the Jesuit priest. Clinton didn't even know McSorley was on that train.

He didn't encounter the prelate until he got off the train and ran into him at the station.

McSorley told Clinton he was on his way to visit the Institute for Peace at Oslo University. Clinton opted to go along. While touring the institute, "We met three conscientious objectors working there," McSorley relates. "They objected to Norway's role in NATO. This was a new reason that we had not heard of before."

The conscientious objectors were but three of several hundred Americans who sought asylum in Norway, Sweden, and other northern European countries to escape military service during the Vietnam War.

Afterward, Clinton and McSorley toured the rest of the university and visited other points of interest.

"At the end of the day as Bill was preparing to leave, he commented, 'This is a great way to see a country!'"

If indeed Clinton had gone to Norway to investigate it as a possible haven from the draft, as has been suggested, was there something he saw in this refuge for his fellow American draft dodgers that didn't sit well with him?

Or had the presence of the Georgetown prelate frightened him—instilled the fear that McSorley might blow the whistle on him should Bill Clinton join his "brothers in arms" in the only combative pose they knew: *fighting against the Vietnam War?*

In conclusion, McSorley offered this about the Norway trip:

"You see as much as a tourist, you have an important subject to talk about with the people you meet, and you learn something of the process of working toward peace."

Shortly after McSorley's report about Clinton's London prayer vigil activities came out during the presidential campaign, Congressman Robert K. O. "Bob" Dornan, the feisty California Republican, took Clinton to task for not "telling all there is to tell about your sordid activities" in the British capital.

"Bill Clinton spent his time in London not only organizing demonstrations for prayer vigils," charged Dornan, "but he organized demonstrations where they shouted, 'Ho-Ho-Ho Chi Minh, Viet Cong is gonna win.'"

One of the most intriguing curiosities about the two years Clinton spent at Oxford is the vast amount of travel he was able to put in. For instance, his journey to the Soviet Union in the dead of a 1969-1970's winter—a two-week jaunt with a four-day detour to Czechoslovakia.

That trip was not made until after Christmas 1969. Before then, Clinton had cleared the slate of his obligation to serve in the University of Arkansas ROTC, and he even struck the mother lode in the draft after President Nixon pressed for a lottery to determine which young men would be conscripted into the military and which, by luck of birthday, would be left free.

Choosing draftees by lottery was a method Clinton was acquainted with. During his summer internship with the Foreign Relations Committee, he had seen reports from the White House about the creation by President Johnson of the National Advisory Commission on Selective Service.

The commission strongly recommended a random-selection system, and President Johnson endorsed a lottery in a message to Congress in 1967. But Congress passed a law that year that prohibited the president from establishing a random system without prior congressional approval.

Thus the established draft continued. Men were susceptible to the draft up to the age of 26, with the oldest men called first. In theory, every man without a deferment or an exemption was likely to be drafted. Frequently such eligibles were not called until they approached their 26th birthdays, a time when their careers could be—and were—seriously interrupted. The period of uncertainty carried for seven years.

In May 1969 President Nixon reiterated Johnson's proposal and called upon Congress to amend the Selective Service Act and legalize the lottery system. Congress finally approved that legislation in mid-November, and the first draft lottery was scheduled at selective service headquarters in Washington, D.C., for December 1. There were to be two drawings—the first for each day (or birth date) in the year (366 days, to take leap-year births into account) and the second for each letter in the alphabet for all eligible draft-age men. The order in which dates were drawn was to determine the order by which men between ages 19 to 26 would be drafted in 1970. The second drawing was to determine the order of induction of those having the same birth date, with the initial letter of the individual's last name providing the key.

The drawings were held on schedule at selective service headquarters at 1724 F Street in Washington. A cylindrical glass bowl—like a water cooler—was placed on a table at the front of the room. The bowl contained 366 capsules. In each capsule was a piece of sticky paper bearing a date.

At precisely 8 p.m. on December 1, the futures of young men across the country were decided as, one by one, the dates of their births were drawn in the first draft lottery in a generation. The first capsule was pulled from the bowl by Representative Alexander Pirnie of Utica, N.Y. When the capsule was opened, the date read September 14.

Representatives of the Selective Service System's Youth Advisory Committees drew the remaining 365 dates, and each date was posted on a board. By 9:30 p.m., the drawing was completed.

The lottery affected every man in the country between the ages of 19 and 26 who had not served in the military. Each of those men was given a number.

Across the land, wherever a radio or TV set could be tuned in, young men and their families huddled before them to find out how they fared.

At precisely 9:18 p.m., a selective service aide put his hand in the bowl and pulled out a blue capsule that, when opened, bore the date of August 19.

At that moment, the hands on the clock in Bill Clinton's room at Oxford read 3:18 a.m. This was Tuesday, December 2, 1969, when Clinton let out what some fellow Rhodes scholars from the United States uniformly agreed sounded like a "hoot and a holler."

Clinton had good reason to feel elated at the news he heard on his shortwave radio. His birth date was August 19, and his lottery number was 319. The announcer's words brought Clinton "close to tears from his joy."

"Men whose birthdays are among the last third of those drawn—roughly those men with numbers from the mid-two hundreds through three hundred and sixty-six are almost certain to be free from the draft."

Having drawn number 319, Bill Clinton was now, finally and at long last, free—totally and irrevocably free—from the draft!

Just to be certain his ears were not deceiving him, Clinton phoned Hot Springs and spoke with an unidentified friend who, according to some of his fellow Rhodes scholars, confirmed what he had heard.

Clinton began writing a lengthy letter that he did not finish until the next day. He dated it December 3, 1969, and mailed it to Colonel Eugene J. Holmes, Director of the Reserve Officers Training Corps, University of Arkansas, Fayetteville, Arkansas.

Bill Confesses: No Intention of Joining ROTC

Here is the entire text of the letter Clinton sent to the army officer who rescued him from the draft so he could have another year of study at Oxford:

> I am sorry to be so long in writing. I know I promised to let you hear from me at least once a month, and from now on you will, but I've had to have some time to think about the first letter. Almost daily since my return to England I have thought about writing, about what I want to and ought to say.
>
> First, I want to thank you, not just for saving me from the draft, but for being so kind and decent to me last summer, when I was as low as I have ever been. One thing which made the bond we struck in good faith somewhat palatable to me was my high regard for you personally. In retrospect, it seems that the admiration might not have been mutual had you known a little more about me, about my political beliefs and activities. At least you might have thought I was more fit for the draft than for R.O.T.C.
>
> Let me try to explain. *As you know* [author's heavy emphasis to indicate Holmes *was aware of it*], I worked for two years in a very minor position with the Senate Foreign Relations Committee. I did it for the experience and the salary but not for the opportunity, however small, of working every day against a war I oppose and despised with a depth of feeling I had observed solely for racism in America before Vietnam. I did not take the matter lightly but studied it carefully, and there was a time when not many people had more information about Vietnam at hand than I did.
>
> [How could he not have, snooping through the files of the Senate Foreign Relations Committee to help keep him abreast of ways to beat the draft?]
>
> I have written and spoken and marched against the war. One of the na-

tional organizers of the Vietnam Moratorium is a close friend of mine. After I left Arkansas last summer, I went to Washington to work in the national headquarters of the Moratorium, then to England *to organize the Americans here for demonstrations October 15 and November 16* [author's emphasis and to be weighted beside the aforementioned denial by Clinton aid, Betsey Wright].

Interlocked with the war is the draft issue, which I did not begin to consider separately until early 1968. For a law seminar at Georgetown I wrote a paper on the legal arguments for and against allowing, within the Selective Service System, the classification of selective conscientious objection, for opposed to participation in a particular war, not simply to 'participation in war in any form.'

From my work I came to believe that the draft system itself is illegitimate. No government really rooted in limited, parliamentary democracy should have the power to make its citizens fight and kill and die in a war they may oppose, a war which even possibly may be wrong, a war which, in any case, docs not involve immediately the peace and freedom of the nation.

The draft was justified in World War II because the life of the people collectively was at stake. Individuals had to fight, if the nation was to survive, for the lives of their countrymen and their way of life. Vietnam is no such case. Nor was Korea an example, where, in my opinion, certain military action was justified but the draft was not, for the reasons stated above.

Because of my opposition to the draft and the war, I am in great sympathy with those who are not willing to fight, kill, and maybe die for their country (i.e., the particular policy of a particular government) right or wrong. Two of my friends at Oxford are conscientious objectors. I wrote a letter of recommendation for one of them to his Mississippi draft board, a letter which I am more proud of than anything else I wrote at Oxford last year. One of my roommates is a draft resister who is possibly under indictment and may never be able to go home again. He is one of the bravest, best men I know. His country needs men like him more than they know. That he is considered a criminal is an obscenity.

The decision not to be a resister and the related subsequent decisions were the most difficult of my life. I decided to accept the draft in spite of my beliefs for one reason: to maintain my political viability within the system. For years I have worked to prepare myself for a political life characterized by both practical political ability and concern for rapid social progress. It is a life I still feel compelled to try to lead. I do not think our system of government is by definition corrupt, however dangerous and inadequate it has been in recent years. (The society may be corrupt, but that is not the same thing, and if that is true we are all finished anyway.)

When the draft came, despite political convictions, I was having a hard time facing the prospect of fighting a war I had been fighting against, and that is why I contacted you. R.O.T.C. was the one way left in which I could possibly, but not positively, avoid both Vietnam and resistance. Going on with my education, even coming back to England, played no part in my decision to join R.O.T.C. I am back here, and would have been at Arkansas Law School because there is nothing else I can do. In fact, I would like to have been able to take a year out perhaps to teach in a small college or work on some community action project and in the process to decide whether to attend law school or graduate school and how to begin putting what I have learned to use.

But the particulars of my personal life are not nearly as important to me as the principles involved. After I signed the R.O.T.C. letter of intent I began to wonder whether the compromise I had made with myself was not more objectionable than the draft would have been, because I had no interest in the R.O.T.C. program in itself and all I seemed to have done was to protect myself from physical harm. Also, I began to think I had deceived you, not by lies—there were none—but by failing to tell you all the things I'm writing now. I doubt that I had the mental coherence to articulate them then.

At that time, after we had made our agreement and you had sent my 1-D deferment to my draft board, the anguish and loss of my self-regard and self-confidence really set in. I hardly slept for weeks and kept going by eating compulsively and reading until exhaustion brought sleep. Finally, on September 12 I stayed up all night writing a letter to the chairman of my draft board saying basically what is in the preceding paragraph, thanking him for trying to help in a case where he really couldn't, and stating that I couldn't do the R.O.T.C. after all and would he please draft me as soon as possible.

I never mailed the letter, but I did carry it on me every day until I got on the plane to return to England. I didn't mail the letter because I didn't see, in the end, how my going in the army and maybe going to Vietnam would achieve anything except a feeling that I had punished myself and gotten what I deserved. So I came back to England to try to make something of this second year of my Rhodes scholarship.

And that is where I am now, writing to you because you have been good to me and have a right to know what I think and feel. I am writing too in the hope that my telling this one story will help you to understand more clearly how so many fine people have come to find themselves still loving their country but loathing the military, to which you and other good men have devoted years, lifetimes, of the best service you could give. To many of us, it is no longer clear what is service and what is disservice, or if it is clear, the conclusion is likely to be illegal.

Forgive the length of this letter. There was much to say. There is still a lot to be said, but it can wait. Please say hello to Col. Jones for me.

Merry Christmas.

Sincerely,

Bill Clinton.

Writing about Clinton's avoidance of the draft, which became a central issue during the New Hampshire primary, reporter David Rosenbaum of the *New York Times* noted that Clinton "...appears to have done what many other young men did at the time, especially those with college degrees who opposed the war in Vietnam. He took advantage of every possible <u>legal</u> opportunity to avoid, or at least delay, being drafted [author's highlight under *legal* is to show that the press had not investigated the many <u>illegal</u> methods Clinton adapted to escape the draft, nor had any journalist cited the numerous penalties he faced for being a slacker as a later chapter will detail]."

When Bill Clinton wrote to Colonel Eugene Holmes, he not only reneged on his commitment to serve in the ROTC, he also backed out of a pledge he never meant to keep: to attend the "disreputable" University of Arkansas Law School.

His mother let the cat out of the bag:

"I never heard of such a thing...that Bill was going to study law at Arkansas. Why, all he ever talked about while he was at Oxford was that he wanted to go to Yale and take up law there. The only problem was that he didn't have the tuition, although I told him many times I would be glad to help him out.

"As it turned out, thank heavens, he got the scholarship. So that gave him another free ride."

His Mysterious Trip to Moscow

After spending the beginning of the 1969 Christmas recess from Oxford with some classmates in London attending a Yule concert in Albert Hall, Bill Clinton packed his bags and boarded a Soviet Airlines Aeroflot jetliner December 19 for a flight to Moscow.

He was accompanied by another Rhodes scholar, Jan Kapold, a Czechoslovakian, who got off the plane in Prague to spend the holidays with his parents.

Clinton remained aboard the flight and arrived in Moscow late that night. He made his way to the city's premier hotel, the National, where a room had been reserved. It can't be established who made the travel or accommodation arrangements for Clinton.

Two U.S. Congressmen, California Republican Robert K. "Bob" Dornan and Gerald B. Solomon, the Republican–Conservative-Right-to-Life Party New Yorker, and former Rhodes scholar classmate Cliff Jackson, the Little Rock attorney who wrote the letters about Clinton's attempts to evade the draft, all are of the same mind:

Because Clinton did not have a job, was not earning money, and, by his own admission, (supported by his English girlfriend Tamara Eckles-Williams) was always low on funds, Clinton's trip could have been financed many ways, but two stand out as most likely:

1. The Vietnam Moratorium, for whom Clinton worked in Washington and fur-

thered its cause by organizing Americans in Great Britain for two 1969 anti-Vietnam War rallies. The Moratorium held a rally in Moscow early in the New Year and, because of his loyalty to its cause, Clinton was invited to attend.

2. The KGB, the Soviet secret police and international spy organization that was the counterpart to America's CIA. Fomenting unrest in the United States for waging the Vietnam War, it wanted Clinton in Moscow to give impetus to the "peace rally" held there on January 2, 1970.

Clinton's activities in Moscow remain a mystery. He has never discussed with the media either that trip or his travel to at least one known "defector country," Norway. However, one phase of his visit to Moscow has been ascertained.

Clinton attended the January 2 peace rally and banquet held in the National Hotel's ballroom that had as guest of honor U.S. Senator Eugene J. McCarthy, the Minnesota Democrat who was defeated in 1968 by Vice President Humphrey for their party's presidential nomination.

There are no other details of Clinton's trip to Moscow, which presumably ended when he boarded another Aeroflot jet on January 4, 1970. That plane took him to Prague, where he stayed for four days with his Oxford classmate, Jan Kapold, and his family.

Jan's grandmother on his mother's side, Maria Smernova, the author's personal research at the Czechoslovakian Consulate in New York ascertains, was a founder of the Communist Party in that country just after World War II. She was its first president, a position she still held when Clinton visited Prague in 1970.

Maria's husband, Jan Smerva, was an intimate of Czechoslovakia's first president (premier), Klement Gottwald, who took office after the first post-war elections on May 26, 1946, which put the Kremlin-controlled party in power.

Twenty-four years and one week go by.

It is now Tuesday, January 11, 1994. Clinton is en route to Moscow for what is to be his third trip there in his lifetime. Clinton is president of the United States—and is heading for a summit meeting with Russian President Boris Yeltsin.

Enroute, he takes a side trip to Prague to fulfill an itinerary that calls for meetings with Czech leaders, a visit to a neglected fourteenth-century cemetery, and obligatory visits to other hallowed landmarks. Then he drops into a jumping nightclub for a friendly round of good fellowship.

During the evening, Clinton introduces to the tag-along Washington press corps a white-haired couple—the parents of the student who attended Oxford with Clinton. Without identifying them, he divulges that he had stayed with Jan Kapold's parents during his visit in January 1970.

President Clinton doesn't mention the *hospitality* accorded him by the other couple, Jan Smerva and Maria Smernova, who were by then dead.

At the end of his curious 1970 stopover on January 8, Clinton and his classmate depart Prague and returned to Oxford for the spring semester.

The question of how the trip was financed still lingers. Clinton—stung by California Republican Congressman Robert Dornan's charges during the presidential campaign that it was paid for by the KGB—briefly addressed the issue. He said he footed the bill out of his own pocket.

That explanation created a contradiction that he himself caused by what he had said so many times in the past—that he "had no money when I was at Oxford."

The 1969-70 excursion to Moscow, as shown, was only the first of the three journeys Bill Clinton took to the cradle of communism.

His second—and most important—journey would take place in mid-1991, significantly and very necessarily, as will be shown, less than four months before declaring his candidacy for the presidency.

Bill Clinton's Oxford years bear one final and lasting mystery—why hadn't he completed the third year of study to which he was entitled under the condition of his Rhodes Scholarship?

Oxford declined to release Clinton's transcript to the author's researchers in Great Britain. But interviews on campus with persons who were at the university when Clinton attended, revealed that this Rhodes scholar was *asked* not to return for a third year.

As best as the story pieces together, the Oxford regents were turned off by Clinton's aggressive anti-Vietnam War activities—and by his trips to Moscow and Prague.

They were said to have told him he would not be welcome if he returned.

Thus Clinton, who had already sewn up a scholarship at Yale—mainly by dint of being a Rhodes scholar—was able to return to the states, his head held high, and continue receiving an education on the cuff at one of America's finest universities.

During the presidential campaign, Clinton would say that "I wished I could have finished another year at Oxford" but Yale had beckoned.

He never gave the real reason for his abortive Rhodes scholar studies.

On June 8, 1994—a quarter of a century after he failed to complete his studies at Oxford—Bill Clinton returned to the legendary eighth-century locale to receive an honorary degree, a Doctorate of Civil Law, which is given to heads of state and royal families.

The honor was the first ever given to a U.S. president who attended Oxford. Previously, only one sitting president, Truman, and a future one, General Eisenhower, just after World War II, were honored with doctorates by the university.

No one mentioned Clinton's anti-Vietnam activities at the ceremony, but White House officials took an uneasy stance about the president's return to his alma mater. Communications director Mark Gearan said, "We knew that would be the story whenever we came here."

But Clinton got off lightly. The only reminder of his own notorious past at Oxford was a noisy demonstration outside the Sheldonian Theater where the ceremony was held. Hundreds of Oxford students, who started out protesting a variety of causes ranging from scholarship cuts to rent hikes, then also shouted some sharp barbs about Clinton's bumbling foreign affairs policies.

Hillary accompanied her husband on a brief tour of the campus, which included the two-room suite he occupied while a student—and where he entertained Tamara Eckles-Williams.

The *New York Times'* page one story on the Oxford visit, written by Maureen Dowd, began with perhaps one of its briefest, brightest, and all-telling lead paragraphs in its 143-year history:

"President Clinton returned today for a sentimental journey to the university where he didn't inhale, didn't get drafted, and didn't get a degree."

6

BILL AND HILLARY AT YALE LAW

"I'm Hillary—What's Your Name?"

Bill Clinton arrived on the Yale campus in New Haven with the heady knowledge that, just as at Oxford, he was on scholarship. His mother didn't need to pay his tuition as she had when he went to Georgetown University.

He hit the books as hard as he knew how and found himself enjoying classes almost as much as his off-campus life, which, to him, was another frolic.

With his charm, charisma, and gift of gab, Clinton grabbed off more than his share of girlfriends. Not that he had ever had much problem "making out" either in Georgetown, next to Washington, where the ratio runs five women to every man, nor at Oxford, where he set standards for philandering seldom seen in Britain since American GIs of World War II put the horns on. Even when he was dating Tamara Eckles-Williams, who believed he was seeing only her, Clinton was playing the field behind her back.

At Yale, it was no different. He was a swinger. Almost every girl he dated had been drawn to Bill because he'd flirted with her. That is, every girl but one.

Hillary Rodham returned to Yale for second-year law studies after a summer spent in the nation's capital working for the Washington Research Project founded by Marian Wright Edelman, a Yale Law School graduate and first black woman to pass the bar in Mississippi. In the years since, Ms. Edelman gained a national reputation as a civil rights lawyer, whose work merited a small feature in *Time* magazine in early 1970, when Hillary was finishing her first year at the law school.

Hillary had read that article. And when she learned Ms. Edelman was to lecture on campus the following week, she was excited. Her works were the very causes in civil rights that had become Hillary's primary focus after her experience with the Black Panther trial.

"In one of those strange twists of fate that enters all our lives if we're open to hear and to see them," Hillary was to say, "I knew right away that I had to go to work for her"

After the lecture, Hillary asked Ms. Edelman for an opportunity to take part in Washington on her research project during summer recess. The answer was, "Come on down—but the organization can't afford to pay you." Hillary found a way to get remuneration when she discovered Yale Law provided small grants to students engaged in civil rights legal work.

She went to Washington and was assigned to Senator Walter Mondale's subcommittee investigating conditions in migrant labor camps. She returned to Yale with a deep-felt compassion for the children suffering unmentionable hardships in the sordid environments she explored. She made up her mind to pursue a cause: the law and its application to the rights of children.

In early September 1970, students returned from summer recess and congregated on campus with the incoming first-year class. Registration would start soon, but now the order of the day was greeting old friends and meeting new ones.

The Student Center was the focal point for those social ententes. When Hillary Rodham entered the building, her attention was commanded by a handsome, long-haired, young man with a thick, black beard and a silver tongue. Listening to him talk as a group stood around him, fascinated by his tall tales, Hillary wondered who "this newly arrived law student with the Elvis Presley voice" was. She was mesmerized by the line he spouted:

"I come from Hope...that's the greatest hometown in Arkansas anyone could want to come from...it's the watermelon capital of the world...we grow the biggest watermelons you'd ever wanna see."

Hillary, who dated several law school students during the 1969-70 semester, wouldn't go out with another man from the next day forward. Not after her encounter the next morning with the glib newcomer in a Political and Civil Liberties class.

Hillary's adrenaline flowed every time she glanced across the classroom and caught the man from Hope gazing at her with a fixed intensity. After class, he followed her and remained hard on her heels as she went to her next study—at what she admits was a painfully slow gait. Although she thought she felt his hot breath on her neck, they didn't meet that day.

"I followed her into the hall," Clinton admitted, "but I got cold feet. I couldn't move myself to speak to her."

What was there about this girl with the waist-length, straight blonde hair and thick-lensed glasses that gripped him so?

For an answer, *Vanity Fair* quotes Clinton in an interview during the presidential campaign:

"I could just look at her and tell she was interesting and deep."

Hillary next encountered Bill when she dropped into the Yale Law School Library and saw him from afar in whispered conversation with another student. Bill Clinton's ear had been taken captive by a member of the *Yale Law Review*.

"This guy was trying to talk me into joining [the publication's staff] and telling me I could clerk for the U.S. Supreme Court if I were a member...and then I could go on to New York and make a ton of money."

The pitch was made because "they were trying to get southerners...they wanted geographic balance on the *Law Review*." But Clinton had no interest, saying, "I wanted to go home to Arkansas. It didn't matter to anybody [in his state] whether I was on the *Yale Law Review* or not."

While being wooed by the *Review*'s pitchman, Clinton was peering with inordinate interest down the long, narrow stretch of book depository where he had spotted a by now familiar vision.

"This sensational-looking blonde was at that far end of the building," Clinton was to say. "She was reading a book but she happened to look up and catch me staring at her. She stared back. She kept staring as I kept my eyes frozen on her. Then all at once she snapped the book closed and walked all the way down the library.

"She walked and walked and kept getting bigger and bigger because she was coming toward me—right to the table where I was sitting, where the guy who was trying to get me on the *Law Review* had sensed he wasn't going to recruit me and went back to bury his nose in his book."

Clinton, who said he had just "broken off with a steady girlfriend at Yale," recreated this exchange:

GIRL: Look, if you're going to keep staring at me, and I'm going to keep staring back, I think we should at least know each other.

BOY: No response. Just his face turning beet red.

GIRL: I'm Hillary Rodham. What's your name?

BOY: I...I...I...my name...is B-B-B...Bill...C-C-C...Clinton. I'm Bill Clinton...hi, Hillary.

"I was so embarrassed," Clinton recalled. "But we've been together, more or less, ever since."

From that day on, Bill Clinton and Hillary Rodham were to remain fast friends. When the romance began is their deep, dark secret. They don't talk about those early times at any length.

Hillary Rodham became Bill Clinton's girlfriend at Yale, but it wasn't her intention to have a serious relationship. She was an ardent feminist who sought a life of independence and a career unencumbered by marital ties.

"It was never in the game plan to grow up and fall in love with someone from Arkansas," she has said. "I had never known anyone from Arkansas."

Magnetized by his good looks, ready smile, charm, aristocratic bearing, and southern drawl, Hillary soon was won over. At first she couldn't see Bill in her future, yet she was drawn to him so compellingly that for the remaining three years at Yale, they were inseparable.

Christmas with Hillary's Folks

During summer vacation after their first year together at Yale, Bill and Hillary made it a point to continue dating although they had each returned to their respective homes. The pattern of study intermingled with the strong bond of friendship that grew between them continued. But this routine was often interrupted for Clinton, who had to work to earn pocket money.

He found clerical work with a law firm in New Haven and with a city alderman in Hartford. He also held a part-time instructor's job at a New Haven community college—and kept his hand in politics by doing volunteer work for the Connecticut State

Democratic Party.

Was it a serious romance?

Apparently neither Bill nor Hillary wanted to let the relationship go too far—in the beginning.

Clinton explained to *Vanity Fair*:

"I loved being with her, but I had very ambivalent feelings about getting involved with her." He told her flat out, "I'm really worried about falling in love with you, because you're a great person, you could have a great life. If you wanted to run for a public office, you could be elected, but I've got to go home (to Arkansas). It's just who I am."

No less than Bill, Hillary didn't want to be locked into a relationship that could stifle her career, which now seemed might be that of a children's rights advocate. She felt it was her mission in life to pioneer the rights of children older than 12 years. She proposed to legally confer authority on such children to make responsible decisions by themselves about their lives when parents or guardians were unable to do so.

Dorothy Rodham was the first to sense that her daughter had fallen for the "young man I met at Yale" when Hillary told her mother Bill would spend a few days of the 1971 Christmas holiday with them.

Clinton drove from Hot Springs in a low-mileage, second-hand, 1968 Buick provided by his step-uncle Raymond. The car replaced the 1960 Buick Bill's stepfather "lent" to Bill and that he ran into the ground during his Georgetown years.

The 600-mile journey to Park Ridge on Highway 61 was Bill's first trek over the ill-fated route his father had taken in 1946, going in the opposite direction. Some 460 miles from his destination, Bill pulled off to the side of the road, in Sikeston, Missouri. Here his father had lost control of his car on the rain-soaked highway, crashed, and was thrown unconscious into a ditch filled with water, to drown. Bill observed the scene with sadness, then proceeded to Hillary Rodham's home in Illinois.

When the front doorbell rang at the imposing, two-story, brick house at 235 North Wisner Street in Park Ridge, the woman who answered the ring found a tired, droopy-eyed, pallid-faced, young man who, in the words of Dorothy Rodham, "looked like he was on his last legs."

But that wasn't the only observation Hillary's mother made that early evening of December 23, 1971, a Thursday.

"I instantly saw the man who was going to end my daughter's days as a single girl."

"Hello, I'm Bill Clinton," he said with a smile.

"That's nice," Mrs. Rodham responded, trying not to scowl.

"The introductions were pretty chilly," confessed Hillary's mother in an interview with *Paris Match*. "To be honest, I sort of wanted him to go away. I knew he had come to take my daughter away."

Bill asked where Hillary was. Mrs. Rodham pointed to the stairs leading to the second floor.

"In her room, that's where she is."

Without so much as a "May I...?" Clinton dashed up the stairs to find Hillary.

"It dawned on me to ask myself what kind of a character he was," she recounted. "I knew nothing of him. But I don't know why I trusted him. He stayed a whole week. He slept in [son] Tony's room. My husband and I made sure he stayed in there."

When Hillary emerged from her room after a few minutes and led Bill downstairs to the living room, the thaw began to set in. His outgoing personality soon disarmed Hillary's mother. She was taken in especially by his smooth Arkansas drawl.

Before another nightfall, Bill had captured Mrs. Rodham's heart and soul.

"He walked in on me in the living room while I was reading a philosophy book." Mrs. Rodham was doing homework for an extension course she was taking at a Chicago area community college.

"When he asked me which philosopher I admired the most, I was startled to hear him deliver a dissertation on that thinker.

"He was absolutely brilliant," Mrs. Rodham rhapsodized, "and from that moment on, I loved him right away."

Christmas Day began after breakfast when the family and their guest gathered around the tree and opened gifts piled high under it. Later they gorged themselves at a dining room table that groaned under the weight of a banquet-sized dinner Mrs. Rodham prepared.

The next day, Sunday, Hillary took Bill on long tours of Park Ridge. In her little red Fiat she drove her beau to the park and took him on meandering walks. She introduced him to friends like Jeannie Snodgrass Almo, her high school classmate, and Betsy Johnson Ebeling, the other pal from pre-college days.

Hillary took Bill to Chicago to sightsee, to dine in a downtown restaurant, and to see a movie. But most of the time was spent at the Rodham manse, where Bill seemed to grow on the family, especially Mrs. Rodham.

"It was always the same subjects [that Clinton and Hillary talked about]," Hillary's mother recalled. "Arkansas! American society! They never stopped thinking. They were amazing. We could listen to them for hours on end because they spoke from their hearts, and they were really concerned with people. They had a very humanist vision of America."

When Mrs. Rodham had it firmly fixed in her belief that Bill would marry her daughter, she was impelled finally to ask what his plans for the future were after he completed studies at Yale.

"I plan to go back to Arkansas," was Clinton's response.

"Okay," Mrs. Rodham returned, "you'll go back to Arkansas to realize your ideals. But what about my daughter?"

Clinton didn't answer. He let the question pass with a wry smile. Hillary wasn't there to see Bill's reaction.

Waiting for Bill to Graduate

In the summer of 1972, just when they were about to return to Yale for Bill's second year of study and Hillary's third and final year, Bill convinced her to cut classes for awhile and accompany him to Texas. He wanted Hillary to participate with him in

U.S. Senator George S. McGovern's presidential campaign. Clinton, then "a long-haired liberal," was sold on the North Dakotan before he'd even won the Texas primary.

To his delight, Clinton's experience with Senator Fulbright's Foreign Relations Committee and with political causes in Connecticut served him well in the McGovern camp. He was named state coordinator, teamed with writer Taylor Branch to run the state campaign.

Branch, the Pulitzer prize-winning biographer of Martin Luther King, Jr., had taken an apartment in Austin for the duration of the campaign. He allowed Bill and Hillary to bed down there—just as they had begun doing in New Haven, when earlier in the year they moved into a rented house near campus.

In his first summer on his return home from Oxford, Clinton had spent a week on Martha's Vineyard with a group of young "thinkers" and political activists. Taylor Branch was one of that crowd.

One reason Clinton was so highly regarded in the McGovern campaign was his experience with the Connecticut Democratic State Committee. He had served as a coordinator in Joe Duffey's anti-war Senate campaign in the state.

A year later, according to Anne Wexler, who managed the campaign and then married Duffey, Clinton was asked to work in Maine Senator Ed Muskie's campaign for the presidency.

"We got most everyone in the room—except Bill," Anne Wexler recalled. "He said quietly, and firmly, that he was for McGovern."

Betsey Wright, then an active Democratic Party loyalist from Texas, remembered the impression Bill Clinton and Hillary Rodham made on her upon their arrival.

"He and Hillary came down from Yale," Miss Wright said. "I'd never been exposed to people like that before. I mean, they spent the whole semester in Texas, never attended a class—then went back to Yale and aced their finals. They were breathtaking."

Miss Wright admitted she was more impressed with Hillary Rodham's promise as a political animal, although she would later become Clinton's chief aide when he was Arkansas governor, then his presidential campaign manager, and lastly, a top assistant in the White House.

"I was kind of disappointed when Hillary married Bill," said Miss Wright, who also had been active in feminist politics. "I was hoping she'd run for office herself."

Taylor Branch disagreed with that assessment. Speaking to *U.S. News and World Report*, he made this observation:

"Whereas his purpose was so fixed, she was so undecided about what to do."

With Hillary working tirelessly beside Bill (she concentrated on registering Hispanic voters for the Democratic Party), the couple stuck it out until the end, when early returns signaled Republican Richard Nixon was going to bury McGovern. Then they departed Texas back to Yale to catch up on their studies.

"I came to realize early on during McGovern's campaign that his movement had lost touch with the Americans he was trying to win over," Clinton soberly reflected. "I believe in my heart of hearts that's the reason Nixon skunked him."

Hillary was to have graduated from Yale Law School in May of 1972 but opted to remain for another year so she could graduate at the same time as Bill.

During her fourth year, Hillary studied child development at the Yale Child Study Center. There she researched what was to become, in time, her highly controversial thesis on the rights of children.

Before graduation, Bill and Hillary were summoned to a conference with one of their law professors, Burke Marshall, the member of Kennedy's administration who had advised Hillary from her earliest days at Yale. Marshall was more impressed with Clinton for the picture taken of him with JFK than of his academic proficiency, which was commendable but not nearly as profound as Hillary's.

"The House Judiciary Committee is looking for a couple of bright-eyed youngsters like you to work for them," Marshall volunteered. "How'd you like to go there?"

The House was assembling a staff for its forthcoming impeachment proceedings against Nixon for his cover-up of the "plumbers" break-in at the Democratic National Committee headquarters in Washington.

Hillary accepted the challenge of the Watergate hearings; Bill did not. He'd been through the Washington legislative committee routine before and didn't want any more of it.

Going Their Separate Ways

"All I want to be is a country lawyer," he told Hillary. "I'm going back to Arkansas to become just that."

Hillary didn't head for Washington immediately. She received word from Burke Marshall's friend, John Doar, the newly appointed Special Counsel of the House Judiciary Committee, to stay put. She would not be needed for a while. Doar, a Republican who made his reputation as a lawyer during the civil rights era in the South, was chosen to head the committee's impeachment proceedings against President Nixon. The hearings were not to begin until mid-January 1974.

Meanwhile, Hillary learned about an opening for a staff attorney at the Children's Defense Fund in Cambridge. This was just up her alley—to be a children's rights advocate.

Hillary plunged into her work with a passion and soon had put together a powerful essay titled "Children's Rights" that was published in the *Harvard Educational Review*. Her paper advocated massive and immediate expansion of federal child-care programs. She made a quantum leap into a radical redefinition of the relationship between state and family. She advocated three measures to obtain those "rights":

(1) "the immediate abolition of the legal status of minority and the reversal of the legal presumption of the incompetence of minors in favor of a presumption of competence;

(2) "the extension to children of all procedural rights guaranteed to adults;

(3) "the rejection of the legal presumption of the identity of interests between parents and their children, and permission for competent children to assert these independent interests in court."

In effect, what Hillary Clinton espoused was that when parents and their teenage kids don't see eye-to-eye on who's the boss, the dispute goes into the hands of a judge.

Hillary's toils with the Children's Defense Fund ended at year's end. Then she was off to Washington to serve with the House Judiciary Committee Impeachment Inquiry Staff. Hillary was then 26 years old and had little experience as a lawyer since her work in Cambridge didn't engage her in litigation or court proceedings of any kind. Thus she was appointed *counsel*, a bottom-rung position on the committee for a lawyer, which lasted until Richard Nixon resigned the presidency in early August.

By then, Bill Clinton was in Fayetteville, Arkansas—not as a country lawyer, but as a $17,000-a-year instructor at the University of Arkansas Law School—the very institution he once deprecated as "disreputable."

When Clinton graduated from Yale Law School, he left one curious legacy behind. Although the fighting in Vietnam continued for a time, and atrocities such as the massacre of 347 South Vietnamese at Mylai and the killings of four students at Ohio's Kent State University by National Guardsmen shocked the nation, there is no evidence of any further protests on Clinton's part.

That raised questions during the presidential campaign among critics who wanted to know:

Why did Bill Clinton suddenly stop being a war protester?

Was it because he was too deeply involved in his law studies?

If so, how was he able to take two months away from classes in 1972 and work in George McGovern's presidential campaign?

Or had Bill Clinton shunned further protests and demonstrations because the No. 319 he drew in the selective service system's lottery on December 1, 1969, immunized him forever from military service?

The questions still hang. To this day, Clinton has not responded to critics who pose them.

How, they still ask, could Clinton stop beating the drums so precipitately against a war that he so dedicatedly "...opposed and despised with a depth of feeling I had observed solely for racism in America before Vietnam"?

7

THE LAND OF OPPORTUNITY BECKONS

Bill Cons the Law School Dean

Bill Clinton has often told the story of how he landed the job as an instructor at the University of Arkansas Law School.

While Hillary went off to Massachusetts to take up lawyering for the Children's Defense Fund, Clinton pointed his 1968 Buick toward Hot Springs. But as he neared Little Rock, an hour's drive from home, he remembered what a professor at Yale had told him—that the University of Arkansas Law School had an opening or two for instructors. He had suggested that Clinton apply for a position.

Bill stopped at a roadside rest on Interstate 40 and phoned the university. He spoke with the dean, Wylie Davis.

"Sir, I'm calling to tell you that I have my law degree from Yale and wish to fill one of the vacancies I hear you have at the school," Clinton remembers telling Professor Davis.

The dean listened but didn't seem especially anxious to prolong the conversation, until the caller went into this song and dance:

"Sir, I want you to know that I'm willing to teach anything I'm asked to teach. I like to teach. I like to work. I want to join the staff of your law school. I'm a native Arkansan. I was born in Hot Springs and lived there all my life. In fact..."

In fact, Bill Clinton told a lie. He was born in Hope.

Presumably Clinton took a deep breath and measured his words as he went on:

"You cannot know this but I was hell-bent to come to the University of Arkansas Law School. I was so sure I was going to attend that I joined the ROTC there. But things didn't exactly work out for me to fulfill my obligation. I won a Rhodes Scholarship and spent two years in England. And then Yale University offered me a scholarship, so I had to take that. You see, I didn't have a scholarship to Arkansas nor could I afford the tuition. And I couldn't ask my mother for it. She had done enough for me, putting me through Georgetown University."

What was it Bill Clinton wrote to Colonel Holmes while explaining why he turned down his commitment to serve in the University of Arkansas ROTC?

"I began to think I had deceived you, not by lies—there were none—but by failing to tell you all the things I'm writing now."

Does Bill Clinton's spiel to Dean Davis have a ring of historic precedent borrowed from his writing to Colonel Holmes three years earlier?

Clinton capped his sales pitch to Dean Davis with this plea:

"I'll do anything for you if you put me on your staff—and I don't care a hoot about tenure. I don't want tenure. That means you can fire me any time you want."

Professor Davis seemed convinced of Clinton's sincerity. Yet one thing bothered him.

"You're only twenty-six," Davis observed. "That's kind of young for an instructor in law school."

"But...but..." Clinton interrupted, "That's the story of my life. I've always been told that I'm too young for everything I've ever done!"

"All right, Bill," Davis said finally. "Come in and see me. I think you've sold me on you."

When Clinton arrived in Hot Springs that evening, he burst into the house and shouted the news that he was to be an instructor at the law school.

"Big deal!" his mother bellowed. "You're gonna work for twenty-five thousand a year?" (Actually, the salary was a shade over $17,000.)

"Yeah, ma, isn't that great?" he asked.

"Chicken feed!" she snorted. "Why you could make twice and three times that up in New York. Where are all those high-paying jobs you were telling me you were gonna get after you graduated law school? Eh...where are they? What happened?"

"Ma, I don't want that kind of work or to live that kind of life up there in New York," Bill protested. "I want my future to be in Arkansas. In Fayetteville I'll also be close to you."

"Rubbish!" shouted Mrs. Clinton. "Here we struggled all these years to put you through school, for ten years we stood behind you while you were being educated. What's the matter with you anyway? Doesn't money mean anything to you?"

"Sure, ma, it does. But I want to follow my instincts. My heart's set on teaching. That's what I really want to do."

And teach Bill did. But he wasn't the great teacher he thought he could be, or wanted to be.

His former students found Clinton lacking in some areas. They agreed he was a "swell guy, a fine human being"—but not a very good teacher. His shortcomings abounded.

"He would come to class unprepared for the lesson of the day," said one law graduate who took a course with Clinton. "He seemed to be more absorbed in politics, in his own ambition to run for public office."

****

Clinton had decided in mid-1974 to make a run in the democratic primary as one of four candidates for the U.S. House of Representatives in Arkansas's 3rd Congressional District. The incumbent was old-line Republican Congressman John Paul Hammerschmidt, who had held the seat since 1966. Hammerschmidt was elected easily the first time, riding the wave of anti-Vietnam protesters, and won reelection handily the next three times. In 1974 he was seeking his fifth term and didn't anticipate much opposition that time either.

He was in for a surprise. He couldn't have foreseen the challenge in store for him from a brash University of Arkansas Law School instructor.

Despite his shortcomings, Clinton held on to his instructor's job for two years. And to his credit, he did stir political ambitions in some of his students.

One of them, David Matthews, ran for state representative for Benton County, just outside of Fayetteville, and was elected. Another, Lou Hardin, a resident of Russellville, was elected a state senator, an office he still holds today.

One more state senator, Morril Harriman, was in one of Clinton's classes and couldn't believe he was the instructor.

"He was so young looking," said Harriman, who found Clinton diverging from the curriculum of "Agencies and Partnerships" and lecturing on a subject unrelated to the class program.

"He talked a great deal about Watergate," Harriman noted. "He had his students discussing the legal and philosophical issues behind the scandal.

"He was enthusiastic and dedicated and demonstrated a great deal of fairness," Senator Hardin pointed out. "He gave us the opportunity to tell him what we thought. It was a liberating and thought-stimulating class time."

But he was not much on the ball when it came to preparing his students' grades.

"I recall one semester when Clinton posted the spring class marks," Hardin said. "They went up on the board on Labor Day!"

Clinton's decision to challenge Representative Hammerschmidt for his congressional seat wasn't without complications. Before he could declare, three other Democratic Party aspirants jumped in, creating a primary contest he had never expected.

But Clinton got 44 percent of the vote, almost the combined total of his three rivals, State Senator Eugene "Gene" Rainwater, David Stewart, and James Scanlon. The outcome put Clinton into a runoff with Rainwater, who'd finished second with 26 percent.

Clinton routed Rainwater by grabbing nearly 70 percent of the votes. Now he faced the Republican incumbent Congressman Hammerschmidt in the November election.

The Clinton for Congress Committee worked feverishly to sell him in the Republican-dominated Fayetteville area, the state's northernmost region. Many of Clinton's supporters were high schoolers who couldn't vote. Yet they made spirited sales pitches for their hero to teachers, parents, and other voters.

Hillary Joins the Team

On August 8, 1974, 19 months into his second term, Richard Nixon resigned from the presidency after the Watergate cover-up did him in.

Hillary Clinton would soon be without a job. She could return to the Children's Defense Fund's main stand in Washington and man the ramparts at a higher level than the ground floor position she held before in Cambridge. But destiny—and her heart—

ruled otherwise.

By this time she had passed the bar and was a full-fledged attorney. That came about the previous summer during a break in the Watergate hearings when she capitulated to Bill's pleas and finally set foot in Arkansas for the first time.

Bill was waiting at the airport. Instead of taking her home to meet his mother at the family home in Hot Springs, he escorted her on a long and circuitous sightseeing tour. He was bent on selling her the idea of moving to Arkansas—and marrying him.

"We drove for eight hours," Hillary said in an interview with *Newsweek*. "He took me to all those places he thought were beautiful. We went to all the state parks. We went to all the overlooks. And then we'd stop at his favorite barbecue place. Then we'd go down the road and stop at his favorite fried-pie place. My head was reeling because I didn't know what I was going to see or what I was expecting."

Bill eventually took Hillary to meet his mother. She was also introduced to Jeff Dwire, Clinton's mother's third husband, whom she married in 1968, four months after second husband Roger Clinton, Sr., succumbed to cancer.

Dwire, a hairdresser who used to do Virginia's coiffures, was divorced with a daughter, Dianne, who was Bill's age. She was an attractive, well-spoken woman who met Bill for the first time at her father's civil wedding ceremony. Later she chatted with Bill at the reception in a Hot Springs restaurant, along with her brand new husband Buford Welch.

Dianne married just weeks before her father took the plunge with Bill Clinton's mother, shortly after Bill returned to Hot Springs following graduation from Georgetown. Dianne's husband was a well-to-do Texas oil company entrepreneur in Houston. Two years into the marriage in 1970, Dianne bore Buford a son named Jeffrey.

Shortly after his birth, Dianne brought Jeffrey to Hot Springs to show him off to her father and stepmother. In all the years that followed, a visitor to Bill's mother's home in Hot Springs was more than likely to be introduced to a bulging family photo album. Among the prints the guest would see was one of Mrs. Dwire taken in 1970, showing her holding four-month-old grandson Jeffrey in her arms and feeding him his formula. A later chapter will tell why displaying that photo brought considerable sadness to Bill's mother.

Bill's Losing Bid for Congress

After her visit with the Dwires, Hillary accompanied Bill to Fayetteville for an introduction to the University of Arkansas campus.

"This is breathtaking," Hillary gasped as she looked over the Razorback countryside and the community's stately Victorian houses on its tree-lined streets nestled in the foothills of the picturesque Ozark Mountains near the Missouri state line. She stayed at Bill's rented house for two weeks, boning up on questions she expected to find in the bar exam that she had decided to take in Arkansas.

Before she departed Fayetteville for the test being given in Little Rock, Bill took Hillary to meet Dean Wylie Davis.

"If you should want to teach at our school, just let me know," he said to Hillary, who had impressed him.

"Thank you," she responded without much enthusiasm. "I certainly will keep that in mind." She couldn't conceive of herself living in Arkansas at that time.

Bill then drove Hillary to the state capital to take her bar exam.

"What in the world are you doing here?" Hillary was asked by Ellen Brantley, who had gone to Wellesley with her. She was stunned when she heard her name during roll call in the lecture hall at the University of Arkansas Graduate Extension Center in Little Rock, where the bar exam was given.

Hillary told Ms. Brantley (today a Chancery Court Judge in Little Rock) that she'd been visiting Bill. She needed to be a member of the bar of some state to improve her standing at the Children's Defense Fund. Arkansas was as good as any.

Before leaving for Washington, Hillary accompanied Bill to Hot Springs for another visit with his mother. Then it was back to wind up her duties at the Watergate hearings, now as a full-fledged member of the legal staff of 40 lawyers, only three of whom were women. This was a time when Capitol Hill wasn't making much of an effort to employ women in key positions.

If during the 1992 presidential campaign one noticed an aloofness by the Clintons toward ABC network correspondent Sam Donaldson, chalk it up to an encounter one late afternoon when special counsel John Doar gave a press conference in the Capitol with Hillary Rodham in tow to assist him.

Hillary found herself being pursued by Donaldson who shouted at her, "How does it feel to be the Jill Wine Vollner of the Impeachment Committee?" Ms. Vollner was the very visible woman lawyer serving on the special prosecutor's staff. Hillary didn't take kindly to sexist cracks and she minced no words telling Donaldson that. She further cut him down to size with a lingering, angry stare, but she never attended another press conference.

No sooner had the Judiciary Committee folded its tent after Nixon's resignation than Hillary hurried back to her bedroom in the Washington townhouse where she'd been staying with Sarah Ehrman, who had worked with Hillary and Bill in the McGovern campaign in Texas.

Hillary had reached a decision about her future. She was going to Arkansas to teach beside Bill Clinton at the University of Arkansas Law School.

"I barely ever saw Hillary when she stayed with me," Ms. Ehrman acknowledged. "I just remember driving her at seven every morning to the Watergate Committee offices in an old converted hotel. We used to laugh and laugh about the absurdity of the life she was leading."

Conditions were trying. The staff worked late into the night.

"If we left by nine o'clock, that was early," Hillary said. "On those occasions when the staff enjoyed the luxury of leaving at that hour, we often went for a quiet dinner and a glass of wine in one of the Greek or Italian restaurants near the Capitol."

No plane or train would take Hillary Rodham out of Washington. She had too much luggage, plus a 10-speed bike. So her bags filled with her clothes and boxes bulging with her books were stowed in the trunk and the back of Sarah Ehrman's Buick, the bike firmly lashed to the rack on the roof, and away to Arkansas they went.

"I told her every twenty minutes that she was crazy to bury herself," Ms. Ehrman told the *Washington Post*'s Martha Sherrill. "'You are crazy. You are out of your mind. You're going to this rural, remote place—and wind up married to some country lawyer.'"

Ms. Ehrman hoped Hillary would stick it out in Washington. If not with the Children's Defense Fund, then with the capital's prestigious, top-rank law firm of Williams & Connolly, which had interviewed her and offered her the position "of counsel."

"She'd been either in the middle or the edge of everything," Ms. Ehrman said. "She was on the fast track to becoming a great legal star."

Now the fierce feminist who had proclaimed it was not in her "game plan to grow up and fall in love with someone from Arkansas," had not only done that—but also had given up her world in Washington.

As Judith Warner wrote in *Hillary Clinton: The Inside Story*, "The sense of her potential power, the thrill of her potential as one of the few women lawyers at the top agencies in Washington, was exhilarating. The idea of heading down to the second poorest state in the union, a backward state with few legal services and no legal activism, seemed like shooting herself in the foot."

Back in Park Ridge, Mrs. Rodham was mulling over her daughter's decision.

"I wondered if Arkansas would be so great for Hillary," admits Mrs. Rodham. "But you know? I've never told my children what to do. I had to rely on Hillary's judgment. There'd never been any reason not to."

But sometime later, when Hillary phoned again—Mrs. Rodham promptly did an about face. Not only did she tell sons Hugh Jr. and Tony what to do, but she also gave husband Hugh those same instructions.

She said they had an obligation to go with her to Fayetteville and join Hillary in Bill Clinton's campaign to unseat GOP Representative John Paul Hammerschmidt.

Although Hillary joined the staff at the University of Arkansas Law School to teach criminal law and to supervise a legal aid clinic, she found herself helping Clinton in his campaign.

Bill's campaign headquarters was in a small, creaking house on Fayetteville's College Avenue. He campaigned by touring the 3rd Congressional District in a battered, green, American Motors Gremlin. He spoke and shook hands with everyone he could corner.

When Hillary took time out to look in on the haphazard way Bill was running the campaign, she was appalled. She took command. Her talents as an organizer became apparent at once. She set ground rules for the election team and assigned tasks. It was at this stage that she summoned her family to do what they'd never done before: work for a Democrat.

Hillary's brothers, Hughie and Tony, became "sign hangers." They plastered the district with "Clinton For Congress" posters, putting them up on trees, lampposts, and any bare wall. Dorothy and Hugh Sr. manned the phones. It was a total family effort.

At Hillary's insistent urging, Clinton hammered away at his rival, adopting a no-holds-barred stance.

"He bears the stigma that's been cast upon the Republican Party by Nixon, who resigned the presidency in disgrace," Clinton proclaimed until his voice grew gravelly and hoarse—the start of a chronic problem during all his future campaigns when he overtaxed his vocal chords.

"And my opponent puts the interests of our state's interests far ahead of the interests of his constituents," Clinton went on, now in almost a breathless whisper.

Hammerschmidt struck back in booming tones. He cited Clinton's participation in George McGovern's disastrous bid for the presidency.

"He's a loser!" bellowed the Congressman. "He is also beholden to labor. Where do you think his campaign funds come from? From the forces of labor."

The election results for November 5, 1974, brought Democrats resounding victories over the country in an "off-year" election that saw the party's candidates swept into office.

But Clinton was a loser. Not a bad loser, yet a loser just the same. He gave John Paul Hammerschmidt a real run—and a solid scare. Clinton corralled 48 percent of the vote to the victor's 52 percent. It was a close call for the incumbent who locked horns with a "nobody" and almost got gored.

"Bill Clinton has made his mark as a brilliant law professor," crowed one of the state's leading newspapers, the *Arkansas Gazette*. "It is regrettable that Arkansas did not quite add its own extra momentum to the national Democratic landslide."

The article ended with a prediction:

"Bill Clinton very nearly made it to Congress, and surely he will be back in 1976."

A Rodham Becomes an Arkansan

Clinton returned to teaching at the University of Arkansas Law School from which he had taken a three-month leave without pay to do his politicking. When he returned to Fayetteville, Bill was supremely happy. For now Hillary Rodham was close to him as a fellow member of the law school's teaching staff.

When they were in their separate classrooms, it was strictly business. They lunched together whenever schedules permitted. Otherwise their relationship as sweethearts remained on hold until after class. They dined together almost every night, if not in one of the local restaurants, then the homes of friends such as Margaret Willock, Ellen Brantley, or Ann Henry, who were close to Hillary and always tried to make her feel at home.

Ms. Willock recalled that Bill always went out of his way to have Hillary socialize with his friends. One was Ann Henry's husband, Morris, chairman of the local Democratic Party. Others were on the faculty and lived in town with their families.

"He wanted her to like Arkansas, he wanted to marry her," Ms. Willock was quoted by biographer Judith Warner. "It was a great time in our lives. There was a lot of camaraderie. Bill loved to tell these Arkansas stories. We all did. And we used to eat a lot, sitting around [on] the floor of my living room, eating after ball games and talking till all hours. It was a good place to live, a good time."

Hillary herself spoke fondly of those times, during the 1992 presidential campaign.

"We had a wonderful life there," Hillary maintained. "The pace of life was so much slower, so much more open to long conversations with friends and dinners that went on for hours, when you talked about everything that was going on in our life and in the world. I miss that in our lives now."

While they taught at the university, Bill and Hillary lived apart. Fayetteville wasn't New Haven, where propriety and decorum were accepted and interpreted differently. Thus Bill and Hillary couldn't freely cohabit in the Arkansas college community as they had at Yale.

Nearly a year had passed since Hillary moved to Fayetteville. It was now July 1975. With time on her hands until classes resumed in September, Hillary took the opportunity in her summer sabbatical to be with her family, whom she hadn't seen at home since graduation from Yale.

Hillary told Bill she had to get away from him for a while, to be off by herself to think things out. He wanted to marry Hillary. And she felt that Bill was the only man for her. Yet she couldn't easily reconcile herself, much as she liked living in Fayetteville and enjoyed being with the friends she made there, to spend the rest of her life in that rustic setting.

Her dilemma would have been complicated had she known about Bill's ever-constant propensity for romantic entanglements.

Pretty Coed in Bill's Law Class

No longer were married students a rarity in post-graduate classes when University of Arkansas Law School instructor Bill Clinton convened his criminal law class on the Fayetteville campus for the opening of the spring semester that early February day in 1974. So it didn't strike him as odd to learn that the pretty coed seated in the first row of his class had a 25-year-old husband back in Little Rock.

Twenty-four-year-old Elvira Susann Jenkins married Dalton Miles Coleman in Little Rock on May 15, 1971, after completing her sophomore year at the University of Arkansas. At the time, Susann lived with her mother, Ruth, and stepfather, Alvin Tate DeMedicis, an army recruiter, in the southernmost Arkansas city of El Dorado.

When Susann enrolled for Clinton's class in criminal law at the U of A in Fayetteville, she had finally found the field to specialize in: law. She was magnetized by the legal profession after clerking for a Little Rock law firm between her junior and senior years. Until then she ran a checkered—but brilliant—scholastic course. She'd been a straight-"A" student in high school and maintained a high academic standing through college. However, Susann couldn't focus on a career goal until she tried her hand as a law clerk.

Now in Bill Clinton's class, Mrs. Susann Coleman seemed in her element. A beauty with dark hair and large, brown, bedroom eyes, she was easily the most attractive of the seven women in the class of 100 students.

Always with an eye for a pretty face and shapely body, Clinton appeared to seek common ground on which he and Susann could relate to each other—and start what was always on his mind: a relationship.

This happened in 1974 when Hillary Rodham was still in Washington, D.C., with the House Judiciary Committee. Although Bill had taken a serious interest in her at

Yale and during their McGovern campaign days in Texas, the distance separating them now inhibited their romance. The ambitious, fierce feminist that Hillary was, may have convinced Bill Clinton they likely had no future together so long as she remained so far away.

He was twenty-seven in that spring of '74. He had developed game-cock mannerisms when in the presence of women. His erect bearing, squared shoulders, inflated chest, large, jut-jawed head, pale blue eyes, and thick pile of black hair made him appear seven feet tall, instead of six-feet-two.

When he stood in front of the class, he commanded a mastery over the coeds and enjoyed their flatteries, spoken or unspoken.

In time, some would label Bill Clinton a sex maniac. As an instructor in that year of 1974 at the U of A Law School, Bill Clinton could succumb readily to primitive urges without saddening his home. He could not commit infidelities then, for he had not yet given his vows to Hillary. He would become a chronically cheating husband only after Hillary lost her job in Washington, joined the U of A Law School faculty, and married him in October of 1975.

What if a coed, such as Susann Coleman, who was married, committed adultery with her as-yet-unmarried "professor" in that spring of '74—would that constitute a blemish on Bill Clinton's escutcheon?

No answer can be provided. No record shows the question was ever asked of Bill Clinton.

All the Clinton archives reveal is a sketchy report about a purported dalliance with Susann Coleman.

The affair is said to have begun after the instructor found a common ground to make the student's acquaintance.

Clinton heard that Susann's father, like his own dad, Bill Blythe, had died before her birth. Blythe was killed in an auto accident four months before his son was born. Susann's father, Francis R. Jenkins, was also killed four months before his daughter's birth.

There was as much irony in Susann's father's untimely death as there was in the way Bill's dad died—he was thrown from his car, landed unconscious in a ditch filled with water, and drowned.

Susann's father was a front line soldier in Korea about to get a respite from action. He and a complement of 3,000 battle-weary G.I.'s were assembling on the edge of an airfield to board Army transports for a flight to Tokyo for rest and rehabilitation. All at once, a surprise charge by North Korean troops overran the defenses and inflicted severe casualties on the Americans. Frank Jenkins lost his life—and never saw his daughter, born to his wife, Ruth, on September 4, 1950.

There's no clear record of how far beyond the classroom Bill Clinton's association with Susann Coleman carried. But there are vivid road signs pointing unerringly to the pains Clinton has taken to destroy all traces of a relationship with his student.

The effort begins shortly after San Francisco private gumshoe Jack Palladino is retained by the Clinton For President Campaign Committee early on during the primaries. Palladino's mission was succinctly stated first by the *Washington Post* when it caught up with the story about three months after Palladino had wound up his assignments.

"The Clinton campaign is conducting a wide-ranging effort to deflect allegations about the Democratic nominee's private life and has retained a San Francisco investigator and lawyer to discredit stories about women claiming to have had relationships with the Arkansas governor."

No sooner had Clinton swept his draft-dodging story under the rug than the Susann Coleman scandal threatened in late June of '92. Just as he had won the primaries and was heading for the Democratic National Convention, Clinton got wind that the Susann Coleman story was to be aired. This was a more worrisome exposé than anything in the past. It carried elements of moral turpitude that unquestionably could harm his candidacy.

For months, a letter of unknown origin had made the rounds of newsrooms around the country. But for reasons unexplained, it was ignored.

Until Bill Clinton's campaign committee got wind of what Floyd G. Brown was up to.

Brown and his Citizens United organization had produced the "Willie Horton" ad that sank Michael Dukakis in the 1988 presidential race. Now Brown was reported to have completed a wide-ranging investigation of the Susann Coleman story—and was about to air it with paid TV commercials.

Clinton and his staffers, obviously panic-stricken, reached out and put Jack Palladino on the pad on July 1, 1992, with a swift $12,824.79 illegal payment out of campaign funds. The expense was listed for "legal services." The real reason the gumshoe was taken on was to be a "Bimbo Eruptions Buffer."

The shamus earned his money at once by taking the Susann Coleman story to "CBS Evening News."

Correspondent Eric Engberg and a camera crew were dispatched to Augusta, Georgia, to track down Susann's mother and stepfather. Alvin DeMedicis had suffered a stroke in January and couldn't be interviewed. Out of fear, shame, or whatever other unknown reasons, Susann's mother Ruth wouldn't face the cameras either.

Consequently, anonymous people were interviewed, people who had no personal knowledge about what the letter purported:

> *Susann and her husband Dalton Coleman left Little Rock abruptly in the summer of 1976* (shortly before Bill Clinton was elected State Attorney General). *The Colemans moved to Memphis, Tennessee.*
>
> (Bill Clinton by then had been married barely a year to Hillary Rodham.)
>
> *A short while later, Susann learned she was pregnant, Coleman said the baby couldn't be his and left his wife. She then went to stay with her parents in Warrenville, South Carolina.*
>
> *On February 15, 1977, in the seventh month of her pregnancy Susann Coleman is purported to have put the muzzle of a shotgun into her mouth and pulled the trigger.*

Her life ended just five months after her 26th birthday. She was buried in Warrenville's Pentecost United Methodist Church Cemetery.

The "CBS Evening News" segment on Susann Coleman aired on July 13, 1992—less than two weeks after Palladino was retained to be Clinton's "Bimbo Eruptions Buffer."

Anchored by Dan Rather, the presentation featured Engberg in a series of interviews with the unidentified know-nothings who protested Floyd Brown's "gut-level negative attacks" but said nothing about Susann Coleman's relationship with Bill Clinton—not even to establish that she attended the U of A and was in Clinton's criminal law class.

After citing the gist of the letter—that "Susann Coleman's suicide fifteen years ago followed a love affair with her law professor, Bill Clinton, that left her pregnant"—Engberg then concluded that "Susann's family asserts there is no truth to this, and reporters who investigated the anonymous letter found it to be a nasty hoax."

Neither CBS nor any other accredited news-gathering organization explored the many leads the anonymous letter provided. It clearly identified Clinton aides and associates at the time he was campaigning for Attorney General in 1976—when Susann Coleman was living in Little Rock—and described sexual relations between members of Clinton's staff and hanky-panky in other forms: including homosexual encounters among the staffers, even Clinton himself!

No one talked to the people named in the letter—except Floyd Brown. And he was getting the goods—until he was shot down before he could go public with his findings.

If Palladino achieved anything, he managed to put the lid on the most critical text in the letter, which contained charges that were never properly addressed:

"...The affair had cost her [Susann Coleman] her husband, her family, her self respect. Her heart was lost to the lover who rejected her and her baby. A mistress with child wouldn't fit in with his political ambitions—and his ambitions were large scale. His ambitions were of a national scope. His name was Bill Clinton..."

Eleven days after that broadcast, on July 24th, another illegal payment of $5,003.40 out of Clinton's campaign funds was mailed to San Francisco.

Plumber Jack Palladino was being rewarded again. He had plugged the leak that could have drowned Bill Clinton on the campaign trail.

But in the summer of 1975, Bill had no foreknowledge of the disastrous results of this ill-conceived romance. Back on the Fayetteville campus, Bill Clinton was suddenly heartened by the return of Hillary Rodham after two weeks' absence.

In Illinois with her parents, Hillary had discussed her brothers' education and a decision was reached for Hugh Jr. and Tony to attend the University of Arkansas, where Hillary would look after them.

By this time, Hillary had probably made up her mind about marrying Bill Clinton. Otherwise, why arrange to have her brothers at Arkansas?

Nevertheless, Hillary was to say that she was still undecided about settling down in Arkansas when she left Park Ridge to visit friends in Wellesley, Boston, New York, and Washington. Ostensibly the trip through the Northeast that summer was supposed to sound out her friends, sort of poll her pals about whether she should return to Fayetteville permanently.

Some told her not to go back. Others advised that was the only right decision she could make. In the end, Hillary's heart told her what to do.

"I didn't see anything out there that I thought was more exciting or challenging than what I had in front of me," Hillary told Gail Sheehy in an interview published during the campaign in *Vanity Fair*.

When Hillary returned to Arkansas, she was met at the airport by Bill Clinton who, as Hillary was to say, "looked like the cat who swallowed the canary."

She peered into his eyes and asked what he was up to.

"I have a big surprise," he smiled. "Remember that house you said you liked?"

"What house?" She was mystified.

She'd forgotten all about a casual remark she made one day, months ago, when she was cruising with Bill in his car along California Drive in Fayetteville. She'd been attracted to that house. She liked its big bay window, surrounded by a colorful flagstone facade that complemented a glazed red brick exterior.

"What's the big surprise?" Hillary wanted to know.

Tucking her under the chin, Bill explained softly. "I went inside and it's a real beauty. You're gonna love the beamed living room ceiling and the cute dining room and kitchen."

"Why are you telling me this?" Hillary asked.

"That I bought it for us," Bill returned.

"Bill!" Hillary fairly shouted, shaking her head in disbelief. "I only said I liked it...it had a *For Sale* sign in front, I know. But I didn't say anything about buying it."

"Well, I did," Bill cut her off. "So, there's nothing left to do but marry me...Will you?"

Hillary needed no further urging. She had made up her mind. She was going to marry this handsome, charismatic, smooth-talking *Arkie* who had first won her heart in the Yale Law School library five years ago.

A Rodham Becomes a Clinton

"Eight days before the wedding, I came down from Chicago to help them renovate. Everything had to be done—repainting, decorating, getting things organized. Hillary and Bill wanted to do the wedding dinner in that house. Just family. They had so many friends that they couldn't have invited everyone."

The words were spoken by Dorothy Rodham, who had helped Hillary and Bill ready the house for their wedding in the early afternoon of October 11, 1975, a Saturday.

As Hillary's parents and brothers stood in the living room beside the other invited guests—Bill's mother, Virginia; her husband, Jeff Dwire (whom she married after husband Roger Clinton died); and Roger Clinton, Jr., who was his half brother's best man—the Reverend Vic Nixon, pastor of Fayetteville's Methodist Church, performed the marriage rite during which the bride and groom exchanged rings that were family heirlooms.

"It was the simplest ceremony possible, but also the most beautiful, truly," Mrs. Rodham exulted. "To see these two brilliant students loaded with diplomas which could have brought them all the luxury and money in the world there, in Arkansas, in that modest house because they had dreams of realizing the ideals. It was moving."

In late afternoon, a second wedding ceremony was performed at the home of Morris and Ann Henry who, respectively, were Bill and Hillary's closest friends in that college town. The Henrys lived in a huge, Victorian-style house on two acres. And good thing they did. For nearly 300 people attended that wedding and reception.

Bill's invited guests included classmates and acquaintances from everywhere he'd ever been—hometown pals from Hope and Hot Springs like Carolyn Staley and Mack McLarty, Georgetown chums like Thomas Caplan, Oxford friends like fellow Rhodes scholar Robert Reich, and many others from the Yale campus and the local scene, including close acquaintances like Arkansas Attorney General Jim Guy Tucker.

Hillary had many pals at the wedding too—Betsy Johnson Ebeling, one of her childhood friends from Park Ridge; Sara Ehrman; Marian Wright Edelman of the Children's Defense Fund; and Betsey Wright. Miss Wright didn't want Hillary to marry Bill and live in Arkansas. She thought she should have stayed in Washington where, Betsey felt, she could have become president of the United States (a position some say she shares anyway).

The reception lasted well into the night. Eventually, Bill Clinton took center stage to address reporters from the *Arkansas Gazette*, the *Arkansas Democrat*, and other newspapers as well as from TV and radio. They had been invited not so much to witness the rites and to eat the Clintons' food, as to hear an announcement from the groom.

"We are gathered here today," smiled Clinton in a mocking play of words borrowed from the wedding ritual, "to witness the joining of two people..."

He let the last word dangle for a moment. Then, "...who'll be deeply involved in the political wars of 1976."

What office would he seek, reporters wanted to know? Would he try again to unseat Congressman Hammerschmidt?

"I don't know if I'll go for the House or...or seek the office of Attorney General of Arkansas."

An even broader smile creased his face now as Clinton glanced at Jim Guy Tucker seated at one of the tables. Guests and reporters gasped with surprise.

Tucker, who happened to be the state's attorney general, allowed himself to smile. Clinton had broken ground for Tucker's own announcement not to seek reelection in 1976 but, instead, to make a run for a House seat—in a district other than the 3rd that was represented by Hammerschmidt.

A longtime friend, Tucker had prevailed on Clinton not to tangle with Hammerschmidt again in '76 but to run instead for the state's fourth-highest office, behind governor, lieutenant governor, and secretary of state.

Bill Clinton didn't take long in announcing his decision about the office he'd seek. It would come just as soon as he and Hillary completed their commitment as instructors at the University of Arkansas Law School in the late spring of 1975.

But before that, there was the matter of a honeymoon. Bill and Hillary decided they were too involved as instructors at the U of A to take time out. But Mrs. Rodham differed with the newlyweds.

"I found some cut-rate tickets to Acapulco," she surprised everyone. "This honeymoon will be a family affair."

So Bill and Hillary went with Hugh and Dorothy and Hugh Jr. and Tony to the Mexican resort city on the Pacific's coast.

"Don't let anyone tell you that it wasn't romantic," Clinton was to quip. "It was every bit of that—but we also had gobs and gobs of fun with the Rodhams. It was something to remember forever."

8

ATTORNEY GENERAL CLINTON

Hillary Outshines Bill

It took hardly any time for Hillary Clinton to adjust to her new life in Arkansas, a land once known as the "Bear State," then the "Wonder State," and ultimately "The Land of Opportunity." An ironic nickname and certainly no more apropos than the misname it supplanted. For Arkansas was the second-poorest state in the nation behind Mississippi.

As yet, Clinton hadn't been handed a mandate from the voters to help Arkansas live up to its wondrous nickname. Yet his bride seemed to have made up her mind that she could make something of herself in Arkansas. She set about doing just that when she branched out from her teaching duties at the university's law school into the operation of a legal aid clinic and student-oriented involvement with prison inmates.

In fact, Hillary seemed to steal her husband's thunder. She got her name in the papers and on the six o'clock TV newscasts much more frequently than he. When 1976 rolled around, Hillary was making waves in Fayetteville that directed the spotlight completely away from her husband's political ambitions.

It was March, and Bill was still talking preliminarily about his plans to run for Arkansas attorney general with Morris Henry, the local Democratic Party chairman, and some of the state's party hierarchy. Not many higher-ups were convinced Clinton was the right candidate to fill incumbent Jim Guy Tucker's shoes. Some veteran officeholders like former Secretary of State George T. Jernigan and Assistant Attorney General Clarence Cash had also put their bids in for the office. And they seemed to have more clout statewide than the brash newcomer, who had scored well in a single Arkansas Congressional district but had yet to show his mettle in a statewide contest.

There was virtually no question that any Democrat on the ballot for that office would win the election. The Republicans, historically a poor show at the statewide level, were deemed unlikely to run a candidate of any strength. It wouldn't be the first time a Democrat ran unopposed for a statewide office other than governor.

As Clinton pondered his uncertain future, Hillary began making impressive achievements that soon commanded wide media attention. She had broadened her legal-service work into efforts to have state legislators pass a law requiring judges to rule from the bench whether evidence of a rape victim's prior sexual behavior was admissible before being presented to a jury. Although the bill didn't make it out of committee, Hillary Rodham stuck to her guns on this sensitive issue involving women's rights. She also single-handedly campaigned, with success, for the establishment of a rape crisis center, the first in Fayetteville. Furthermore, she instituted a program of education for women on sexual violence, a subject that had commanded little attention in the area until then.

Hillary had passed other impressive milestones by the time her husband received the Democratic Party's endorsement—along with the aforementioned hopefuls, George Jernigan and Clarence Cash—to buck heads in the attorney general three-way primary.

To some it seemed Hillary and Bill were vying against each other for attention in their respective independent careers, but that was not the case. Bill and Hillary seemed to be too much in love to play the game of career one-upmanship.

No one appeared more perceptive about Hillary's ambitions than her friend Carolyn Ellis. She offers a counterpoint to a theory advanced earlier by Betsey Wright, who at the time was working with the National Women's Education Fund and campaigning to elect more women to public office.

As one of Hillary's most ardent rooters for her to seek an elective post, Ms. Wright also was a political realist.

"As much as I wanted to see Hillary as a candidate for some public office, I had the understanding to know that people, especially in the South, had a low tolerance of marriages in which both spouses were elected officials. Of course, that was merely what I believed, not necessarily what Hillary wanted."

"Hillary was very much in love with Bill, but had to reconcile what ambition she might have with marrying him," offered Carolyn Ellis for counterpoint in Judith Warner's biography on the First Lady.

"She wanted to have her own independent life. She knew that he was going to do things political and go into public service, run for office. I think there was some fear on her part that she would simply be an adjunct to him. That was the traditional thing that we had seen up until that point. My response at that time was that she had no political base of her own, and she could do an awful lot down in Arkansas with her talent. I guess the only thing that surprised me is that it took her so long to go to Arkansas.

"Eventually she made an emotional decision. And she seemed so much more certain of herself once she went."

Was it a choice between following her heart or her head?

Indeed it was, and as Hillary told Gail Sheehy in the *Vanity Fair* interview, "I followed my heart...I just knew I wanted to be part of changing the world. Bill's desire to be in public life was much more specific than my desire to do good."

Bill's encouraging showing in his challenge to Congressman Hammerschmidt undoubtedly helped shape Hillary's decision to shelve any political ambitions she may have had and throw in her lot with Bill.

"While many aspects of my new surroundings were strange to me, I was quick to adjust to them and soon felt at home in that small-town environment that Fayetteville offered," Hillary was to explain. "I loved the law school, the staff and students, and the thought of Bill running for political office again."

Despite the frustration of his narrow four percent loss, Clinton oozed with confidence that he could take his opponent the next time. More than anything, he wanted to be Congressman Hammerschmidt's rival in the '76 election—to upset him in a year when political prognosticators were predicting nationwide Democratic landslides.

Cooler heads prevailed when Clinton sought soundings from his closest campaign advisers. One wise man consulted was Jim Guy Tucker, who counseled Clinton early on that he could depend on support from most of the estimated 100,000 voters he met during his campaign for Congress—if only he ran for a state office.

"You'll be a shoo-in for my job," Tucker said. "I'll bet you a bundle of C-notes the Republicans won't even come up with a candidate for attorney general, not even a sacrificial lamb to take his lumps in the election next year."

Clinton had enlisted a solid bloc of voters as the congressional election results demonstrated. He'd done nothing since last November to disenchant them. There was no reason to believe they would not be in his corner for the next round.

Typical of attitudes among Clinton converts was that of a rhapsodizing senior citizen from Johnson County:

"I think he's the greatest! I would vote for Bill for governor in an instant."

One problem with that. The incumbent, Democrat David H. Pryor, a former congressman, had just been elected governor. He had vast experience in government and was well known throughout the state. Clinton was a virtual unknown, except in that small northeast corner comprising the 3rd Congressional District. He'd be no match for a sitting governor certain to be seeking a second term in 1976.

Clinton risked facing odds too formidable to overcome. A loss in a primary run against Pryor could end his political dreams.

Moreover, in 1976, the 29-year-old Clinton could have barely fulfilled the state's minimum age requirement of 30 years for a gubernatorial challenge against a 42-year-old rival. The cry of "too young" would again haunt him.

"Why not save it for 1978?" Jim Tucker suggested.

Tucker had heard rumblings that Pryor didn't intend to serve more than two terms in Little Rock. He wanted to seek the U.S. Senate seat held by 78-year-old Democrat John L. McClellan since 1942. It seemed unlikely that the headstrong lawmaker, the second most senior member of the Senate, would seek a seventh six-year term. His 82 years in 1978 would have made such a run virtually prohibitive. As it turned out, McClellan died November 17, 1977, and Pryor, as governor, found himself in the catbird seat. He had only to appoint Kaneaster Hodges, Jr., to finish McClellan's unexpired term, then put himself on the '78 ballot for the seat.

That strategy also opened the way for the ambitious Bill Clinton's gubernatorial bid. But first things first.

Clinton's election as attorney general came about virtually by default. The waves he made early on in his campaign so overwhelmed the Republicans that they opted to allow the deadline for filing nominating petitions to pass.

The Democrats were going to win without a rival candidate on the November ballot.

At first, however, the rub was that Bill Clinton wasn't the only Democrat bidding for the office. Former Secretary of State Jernigan and Assistant Attorney General Cash also wanted a shot. That called for a primary.

Clinton's Easy Election Victory

Despite their extensive political backgrounds and higher visibility, Jernigan and Cash were no match for Bill Clinton, who by garnering 55 percent of the primary vote eliminated the need for a runoff—and became the next attorney general.

Even before they tendered their resignations "with great regret" to Dean Wylie Davis at the University of Arkansas Law School, Bill and Hillary journeyed to Little Rock over the Christmas holidays and found a residence in the suburb of Hillcrest. They found their "dream home" in a small but quaint and comfortable, rented, red brick house on the lower extremity of hilly, tree-lined L Street.

In time, they would furnish it with artifacts, paintings, and antiques acquired from the nearby shops and boutiques or from a trip Bill and Hillary took to Europe the following summer.

Bill Clinton was administered the oath of office on inauguration day in January 1977.

No sooner had the new chief prosecutor taken over than he replaced his predecessor's crew with a retinue of young, idealistic staffers who soon came to be known as the "bearded wonders"—after they were given free rein over day-to-day operations.

Clinton found a solid political base in the attorney general's office to prepare him for his next venture in politics. That preparation began just as soon as he sat behind the desk Jim Guy Tucker had vacated. The new attorney general now had his sights set on the governor's mansion.

Thanks to the scuttlebutt Jim Tucker whispered in his ear, Clinton could break ground early toward that goal. It helped to know what Governor Pryor's game plan was: He was using his office for a *halt*, much as a climber scaling a mountain spikes a *piton* into the rock and ties his rope to it for a breather before resuming his climb.

Pryor hammered his *piton* into the governor's office to rest before resuming his ascent to the next elevation, the U.S. Senate seat alongside the one formerly occupied by Clinton's hero, J. William Fulbright. Fulbright had been ousted by an upstart politico named Dale Bumpers, the Arkansas governor who had defeated the grizzled incumbent in a hard-fought 1975 primary and then swept the general election.

Clinton paid scant attention to his duties as state attorney general. He distanced himself from the day-to-day operations of his office and spent most of his time studying the maps, charts, and campaign strategies for the 1978 gubernatorial campaign. When he paraded around as the attorney general, he did so only out of an urgency to address causes popular to the electorate—to help win votes for the next election.

Meanwhile, Hillary Rodham, as she continued to call herself (a practice that did not endear her to most Arkansans), sought to further her career as a lawyer. But she found rock-ribbed resistance in Little Rock, where prestigious, powerful law firms did not hire women lawyers.

"I thought maybe I'd practice law when I got to Little Rock," Hillary complained to the *Arkansas Gazette* some years later when she was interviewed as first lady of Arkansas, "but there were not any women lawyers, period."

She settled for another teaching post at the University of Arkansas. This one was as an adjunct professor at the school's Graduate Extension Center in Little Rock, where just a few years ago she had taken her bar exam.

By 1977, Hillary was on the move once again. Her reputation as the pioneer of the university's legal-aid clinic in Fayetteville and founder of the city's first rape crisis center had not gone unnoticed by some members of Little Rock's dominant Rose Law Firm, the oldest in the state.

Hillary Was No Clothes Horse

Rose took her on its legal staff (the very day Bill became attorney general), making Hillary one of the few women who were "of counsel" in any of the state's top-flight law practices. As she had in Fayetteville, Hillary paid little attention to her personal grooming. She wore practically no makeup, let her long hair dangle loosely to her shoulders, and wore clothes more befitting a hippie than a college professor.

This continued despite disapproving glances from Rose's partners and the practically all-male office staff. But the day of reckoning came when the Rose Law Firm's only lady barrister was summoned for an introduction to a distinguished client.

"She was so mortified that she never forgot the experience," a feature in the *Arkansas Gazette* chronicled years later. For when she entered a senior partner's office to meet the client, she realized she was most inappropriately attired in orange slacks! The story goes on:

"Back in those days she was such an intellectual that she really paid very little attention to her appearance. That was not high on her list of priorities, and you'd see her around with her petticoats showing, and she just wasn't real put together. She was probably not as aware that people were noticing as she should have been. It takes a while to catch on."

Her decision to be better groomed played no evident part in President Jimmy Carter's decision to appoint Hillary to the board of directors of the Legal Services Corporation in Washington, D.C. This independent, federally financed corporation establishes guidelines and allocates funds to the nation's legal aid societies that afford legal services to indigent defendants in criminal cases.

While her appointment brought her back to familiar precincts in Washington, Hillary's primary stamping ground remained Arkansas. Here she made big moves with the Rose Law Firm but also branched out to tackle the problems of abuse, neglect, poverty, pregnancy, and drug dependence involving adolescents and teenagers. She helped establish the Arkansas Advocates for Children and Their Families, the first children's advocacy group in the state.

Hillary also distanced herself for a time from the predominant corporate cases in which the Rose Law Firm specialized and teamed up with leading Little Rock criminal defense attorney William R. Wilson, Jr., for different lawyering.

Wilson had been deeply impressed with Hillary two years earlier when she appeared before an Arkansas Law Association House of Delegates gathering and made an eloquent plea for funds to organize the first legal-aid program in Fayetteville.

"I remember one of the first things I told people when I litigated with her and against her," Wilson said in praise of Hillary, "was [that] she tries a lawsuit like a lawyer rather than like a woman.

"At that point in time [1977], some female lawyers relied on their femininity, and sometimes didn't get down to the business at hand. It was a style for chauvinistic times, and Hillary didn't have it."

Bill Gives Himself Good Grades

Bill Clinton didn't totally neglect his duties as attorney general before he was elected governor. He made waves whenever he deemed it necessary to impress the public. And he hit a few bull's-eyes.

The earliest targets struck by his legal punches were Arkansas's privately operated power and light companies, which Clinton charged were "gouging the workingman with their unconscionably high rates."

But Clinton seldom stopped touring the state in a frenzy of speech-making, all calculated to enhance his posture for the future.

Most often his speeches were nothing but thinly veiled campaign discourses touting his oft-dubious achievements as attorney general. So obvious were his intentions that at one pit stop a young boy stepped out of the crowd, greeted him by his first name, and shook Clinton's hand. The child, no older-looking than ten, asked:

"When you're governor, can I still call you 'Bill' or do I have to call you 'Mr. Bill'?"

Seemingly the question titillated Clinton, who patted the boy on the head and gushed:

"Yes, young man, you may still call me 'Bill.'"

Arkansas newspapers also were caught up in the phenomenon of Bill Clinton's travels and became his biggest boosters. One example can be found in the praise heaped on him by a newspaper in the Faulkner County community of Conway, a city with a population then of 10,000 in central Arkansas, some 30 miles north of Little Rock.

Clinton, observed the *Log Cabin Democrat*, was "an attractive, articulate political leader...whose record as attorney general has been studded with examples of hard work, consumer concerns, and a generally aggressive stance that has led him into a variety of situations with seeming zest."

The press appeared to have adopted a special affinity for him. Reporters and editors seemed averse to faulting him in any way. They found him smart and likable.

Encouraged by all this attention, Clinton went for the kill in the latter days of his first term by publishing his own "Attorney General's Report." This compendium of all his achievements in office—even the most dubious ones—only prompted more flowery encomiums from the *Arkansas Gazette*.

But neither that newspaper, nor any others in the state, ever carried a line about the way the report's printing and distribution costs were financed.

The money came out of Bill Clinton's campaign treasury. The report was put together to prepare everyone for his announcement that he was running for governor.

A thorough examination of his record then would have revealed he was not nearly as effective an attorney general as the report made him out to be. Many questions would have been raised about his self-portrayal as an innovative, progressive prosecutor—but no one bothered to query him.

Had his record been placed under closer scrutiny, he might have found his four opponents in the forthcoming Democratic gubernatorial primary more formidable than they proved to be.

Had his activities been further scrutinized—the activities away from the office—he might have found his future in politics less promising than it appeared.

9

THE INTERVIEW THAT LED TO SEX

Bill's Plea: "I Need T' See Ya," as Genn Dims the Lights

"I'd been hired by KARK-TV [Channel 4] in Little Rock [and] sent to the airport to get an interview with Bill Clinton, who was then Arkansas attorney general."

Speaking is forty-something Gennifer Flowers, a twenty-something reporter when she first met the state's top legal gun in 1977. At the time, Clinton was winding down his second year in office.

Gennifer Flowers, TV reporter, met Bill Clinton at Little Rock's Adams Field, where his plane had just returned him from yet another speaking engagement.

"I nervously approached him," continued the pretty, green-eyed blonde with a shape Venus would've been proud of, "and he looked at me and said, 'Where did they find you?' The way he said it was real flirtatious. I thought, 'Oh, my God, this is not what I need. I'm just trying to do my job.'"

The interview ended on a happy note. Gennifer Flowers returned to the studio, went on camera during the 6 o'clock news, and reported the gems she mined from her talk with the attorney general. The news editor must have been pleased for he assigned her again to the attorney general's office beat.

"Over the next couple of weeks, I saw him several times when I was covering news stories for the station," Gennifer went on. "He always made eye contact and it made me uncomfortable. He'd stare at me so much, other people began to notice."

Three weeks went by and Gennifer was sitting outside Clinton's office, writing on a pad, when he materialized before her.

"He...started to make small talk. Then he suddenly burst out, 'I really can't take this anymore. I need to see you.' He asked for my phone number.

"I kind of stammered, 'I'll have to think about it.' I knew he was married and I shouldn't have given my number to him. But there was something special about him. He was a very sexy man, and I couldn't help myself from being interested."

Over the next few days, the phone rang off the hook at Gennifer's pad in Little Rock's Oakwood Apartments complex.

"We'd talk about everything under the sun. In every call, he'd suggest coming over to my place. He kept asking when we could get together."

Clinton finally got his wish.

"Two weeks after the first phone call, he arrived on the doorstep of my apartment...We held hands and talked for hours, but when I said I thought he should leave, he kissed me goodnight."

Some three weeks more went by with such shadowboxing before she and Bill decided the preliminaries had gone on long enough. By then, "...we both knew we were ready to make love. He called to say he was on his way over, and I made sure the lights were low and soft music was playing. We sat and talked for a while and then we began kissing. He was such a good kisser—he has a real pretty mouth," Gennifer said as she parted the curtain shrouding her boudoir.

"One thing quickly led to another. And we tumbled onto my bed. He stayed about four hours that night and we made love several times."

The affair raged on into 1978.

"...he'd drop by my apartment as often as our schedules would allow. I began to fall in love with him, and he told me he was in love with me. Our lovemaking was always passionate—he told me this was the best sex he'd ever had. I wanted to believe that.

"He'd say he wished he could be with me always, and I believed that, too. I wanted him to spend the night with me, to watch him sleep, but he always said he couldn't."

Did that mean that after all the whoopee, Clinton preferred to go back to his own bedroom and let Hillary *watch him sleep*? That cannot be answered here inasmuch as President Clinton declined to be interviewed for this biography.

"I never felt he was struggling with his conscience about breaking his marriage vows," Gennifer said. "He just came on so strongly and I let my feelings take over. I thought he felt like I did, that we had something special going."

The relationship became so hot and heavy, according to Gennifer, that Bill would call her at the television station and they'd "talk for ages." This happened so often that it provoked a reprimand for Gennifer by KARK-TV.

"...it became so noticeable," she said, "the news director, who had no idea who I was talking to, would tell me to get off the phone."

The affair continued for several months into 1978, until Gennifer found the pressure of reporting too burdensome and quit.

"Since I was a little girl, I'd been a singer. I recorded my first record at age eleven. I wanted to get back to my first love. When I told Bill, he encouraged me. 'Do what you want,' he said. 'We'll be able to see more of each other.'"

Gennifer, who likes to think her voice is like Barbra Streisand's, landed a singing engagement at the nightclub in Little Rock's Camelot Hotel.

"One night Bill arrived with a bunch of people. I sang some numbers with a message for him, 'Since I Fell in Love with You' and 'What I Did for Love.'

"After I finished, I stopped by their table. Bill left for a few minutes and one of the women leaned over and said, 'Bill was staring at you the whole time.' She told me he'd been going on about how beautiful I was and began questioning me about him. I just passed him off as a casual acquaintance."

Later that year, after Clinton became the Democratic Party's candidate for governor, KARK-TV's sportscaster Rob Wiley took a leave of absence to work in Clinton's campaign.

"Bill told me one night Rob was answering phones at campaign headquarters when a woman called in and said, 'Tell Bill Clinton we know about his affair with Gennifer Flowers, and he'd better stop it.'

"When Rob passed on the message, Bill told me he laughed and said, 'I'm flattered anyone would think she'd have an affair with me.'"

Gennifer added, "Bill treated our relationship as if he were bulletproof."

Clinton also carried on with many other women, ranging from a former Miss America to a sleazy, coked-up prostitute, from women on his staff to women from all walks of life—including two other shapely beauties who also happened to work for Little Rock's Channel 4 as Gennifer had (later chapters will dwell on those affairs).

When Clinton's history of womanizing was exposed early on in the 1992 presidential primaries, Clinton took refuge in his bunker and let his campaign staff stammer and double talk in his defense.

When the press made it clear it was unwilling to accept those responses, Clinton came into the open and babbled, "Oh, that's old news in Arkansas...and they've [the women] been exposed for the trash they are."

That caused Clinton's close associates who knew about his extramarital meandering to shake their heads.

"Such effrontery in the face of all this overwhelming evidence of his longtime sexual involvement with not one, but literally scores of women," said one detractor, who felt Clinton was being "trashy" himself for hanging that label on his paramours. "Imagine that, gratuitously denigrating the women who provided him with their favors as 'trash!'"

Gennifer Flowers was perpetually amazed at Bill Clinton's stamina—especially when in 1978 he announced his candidacy for the state's highest office.

"He was out constantly speaking all over the state, staying up till all late hours of the night," Gennifer related. "Yet somehow he always managed to keep his rendezvous with me. I never ceased to admire his stamina. His sexual prowess was unbelievable, even when he'd come to my apartment moaning, 'My ass is dragging, Pookie [the nickname Clinton bestowed on Gennifer].'"

The Turkey Farmer's a Laugher

There may have been some raised eyebrows when an aging turkey farmer pronounced himself a candidate for governor in the spring of '78. But such oddball happenings were fairly routine in Arkansas politics. Besides, 75-year-old Monroe Schwarzlose had sent the electorate into paroxysms of laughter four years earlier when he tossed his coonskin cap into the primary race for state representative. He lost that bid, as he would the '78 bid for governor—and subsequent ones.

The other four gubernatorial aspirants in the '78 primary were lawyers: Randall Mathis, Frank Lady, Joe Woodward, and Bill Clinton.

Clinton needs no introduction. The others, however, were virtual unknowns outside Arkansas's local political precincts.

Mathis, 47, had been a Clark County judge and served as president of the Arkansas Association of County Judges. But his main interest was cattle ranching.

Lady, 48, once a state representative, was unsuccessful in the '76 Democratic primary for governor against David Pryor. Lady, like Mathis, had only a limited regional following, as his bid for statewide office two years earlier had proved .

Woodward, 48, had been an assistant attorney general (an appointive post), a trial lawyer, and a legislative assistant to Governor Dale Bumpers before he went to the U.S. Senate.

Woodward was the most formidable rival because his base for voter backing, other than the sitting attorney general's, was the widest.

Against these odds, Clinton won the primary of '78 in a historic sweep, capturing all but four of Arkansas's 75 counties and 60 percent of the Democratic vote.

How did he manage that?

The nickname Slick Willie that *Arkansas Democrat* editor John Robert Starr conferred on Clinton during his attorney general days wasn't undeserved. Many Arkansans detected a squiggly slickness in Clinton, yet didn't seem to be turned off.

One reason may be that, despite his four years at Georgetown, two years at Oxford, and his Ivy League law degree, Clinton came off as a local boy, an authentic Arkansan—and so were the people he chose to work around him.

Many advisers were friends and/or political allies. Some were former political opponents won over by his charm, charisma, and chutzpah. Above all else, all his supporters were from Arkansas. And in that state, such associations virtually guarantee the electorate's backing.

Arkansans are a people with particularly low expectations of government. Listen to Cal Ledbetter, Jr., a professor of political science at the University of Arkansas:

"People settled here originally to get away from government and taxes and other people—they wanted just to be left alone. So they don't expect much from their elected officials. They don't care if they're not too effective."

After Clinton won the primary, his campaign went into high gear, and Hillary Rodham campaigned by her husband's side. Though she remained an active litigator in the Rose Law Firm, Hillary took the time needed to bolster Bill's stock with the electorate.

Despite a strong, hard-hitting campaign by his Republican adversary, Lynne Lowe, voters seemed not to care that Clinton was "too liberal with his views on gun control...he doesn't want to strengthen the state's marijuana laws...and he's against capital punishment."

Hillary was criticized for using her maiden name and for "having no religion," because neither she nor her husband attended church.

Whispers of his philandering also wafted across the landscape as Gennifer Flowers' name, and other names, were bandied about as Bill Clinton's "women." But nothing slowed Clinton's momentum.

That momentum was not entirely his own doing. The Republicans allowed the election to be virtually a formality. They capitulated to Bill Clinton's bluster and bluff and even his *baseness*.

With the GOP's virtual abandonment of its candidate (it was unwilling to put up the big bucks that a gubernatorial campaign required) clean-living, honest, decent citizen Lynne Lowe was left wanting to cry when the ballots were counted. Clinton carried the election by more than 140,000 votes. He might have won by twice that margin if a substantial number of Arkansans had not decided not to vote. They suspected that Bill Clinton's campaign tactics were too slick, too well orchestrated and organized—and too pushy.

That pushiness became blatant exhibitionism even before the absentee ballots were counted. For Clinton wasted no time hiking off to Washington, D.C., for an audience with President Jimmy Carter. With his impressive *off-year* election victory, Clinton was now one of the National Democratic Party's "fair-haired boys."

Gennifer's Blue Election Night

It is well known that Gennifer and Bill carried on almost to the eve of Clinton's declaration for the presidency in late 1991.

Yet there were times, as Gennifer recalls, when she and Bill couldn't be together.

"The night he was elected governor was very tough," said Gennifer. Bill was with the woman he had promised to *love, honor, and obey*—at least he was with Hillary Rodham on that Tuesday of November 7, 1978, when the returns came in.

Gennifer sadly watched the election results on Channel 4 and "saw pictures of him and Hillary smiling and laughing."

Bad as she felt, Gennifer only had to wait until tomorrow for relief. Only a day or so later, Bill was back in the warm embrace of his mistress. It couldn't be any other way because, "...I couldn't give him up. Sex was wonderful with Bill. He introduced me to things I never did before, like oral sex. We made love all over the apartment, not just in the bedroom, on the floor, in the kitchen, on the couch—even in the shower."

Their affair had just passed its first anniversary at this point. It was to continue for another eleven years.

10

AMERICA'S YOUNGEST GOVERNOR

Fueling Rumors for a Presidency

No one was more aware of the national spotlight that shone on Governor-elect Clinton than the triumphant candidate himself after his landslide victory. He was soon to be the country's youngest governor and his future held a promise of brilliance.

Clinton relished that role. No sooner was the meeting with President Carter concluded than the newly elected governor arranged to open a state office in Washington (not so much to advance Arkansas's industrial and commercial interests, as he trumpeted, but to promote himself as a force in national politics).

Then he returned to Little Rock to prepare for his occupancy of the Georgian-style governor's mansion early in the new year.

Meanwhile, instead of preparing for the work ahead, Clinton went off to the National Democratic Party's mid-term convention in Memphis, Tennessee. Here he moderated a discussion on national health care, a forum that set the wheels in motion for his future role in national politics.

As the nation's youngest governor, Clinton attracted considerable press attention. He was dubbed "Arkansas's Boy Governor." His time as a media darling had arrived.

And he took full advantage of that status.

Even before his inauguration on January 10, 1979, Clinton's public relations people began spreading the rumor that should Massachusetts Senator Edward M. Kennedy defeat Jimmy Carter in the 1980 primaries and be the Democratic nominee for president, his choice of a running mate would be "Boy Governor" Bill Clinton.

Since politics is the science of exaggeration, pencil into the aforesaid scenario these bold strokes applied to the 1980 presidential picture: Should President Carter survive the challenge of the Chappaquiddick bridge survivor, he would dump his Vice President Walter Mondale and embrace Bill Clinton as his 1980 running mate.

That brings to mind a political categorization suggested by Clinton's moves. It was advanced sometime in the 1848–1903 lifetime of Paul Blouet, the French soldier and writer better known as Max O'Rell.

O'Rell wrote, "To be a chemist, you must study chemistry; to be a lawyer or a physician you must study law or medicine; but to be a politician you need only to study your own interests."

How well Clinton studied his *own interests!* In his haste to make the most of his "young man in a hurry" mien, he neglected to consult Article II of the U.S. Constitution, which states:

"No person except a natural born Citizen, or a Citizen of the United States, at the time of the Adoption of this Constitution, shall be eligible to the Office of President; *neither shall any Person be eligible to that Office who shall not have attained to the Age of thirty-five Years,* and been fourteen Years a Resident within the United States."

That applies to the Vice President, also. No way could Bill Clinton have been selected by Ted Kennedy or Jimmy Carter as a running mate in 1980—because he'd have been a mere 34 years old and constitutionally ineligible.

After seeding these rumors for his self-aggrandizement, Clinton stood on the steps of the statehouse on January 10, 1979, and took the oath of office as Arkansas's 40th governor.

Hillary Rodham, as the new first lady of Arkansas still insisted was the name by which she wanted to be addressed, held a Bible on which her husband placed his hand. He then swore to uphold the state constitution and serve to the best of his ability.

Hillary smiled broadly—and proudly. Her big, thick-lensed glasses atop the bridge of her nose were on their way out now. Soon she began wearing soft contact lenses that had finally been developed for commercial use.

The inaugural ball was held in Little Rock's Robinson Auditorium, an affair trumpeted as a "Diamonds and Denim" celebration. The public was invited to attend (that is, those with invitations) in dress of their choice. The options were that they could wear diamonds and formal clothes, or come with paste jewelry and Levis.

Hillary outdid her husband, who came simply attired in tuxedo and black tie. She was poured into a rose panne velvet gown designed by Arkansas's premiere designer, Connie Fails. It was a modified version of Hillary's wedding dress, ornamented with antique black lace, silk embroidery, and beads. Her neck was adorned with a 4.25 carat diamond that, like the $20,000 diamond in her broach, came from the only diamond mine in the United States, the Arkansas Crater of Diamonds State Park.

The Clintons were happy to end their tenancy at their L Street "dream home" they had occupied during Bill's two-year term as attorney general. They were moving into the rent-free governor's mansion, a two-story, red brick dwelling built in Georgetown architectural style and situated on a beautifully landscaped, six-acre tract in Little Rock's historic Quapaw Quarter. All around it, the homes abutting the stately grounds on Center Street were elegant Victorian-style homes along with a growing number of modern post-World War II dwellings, which shape one of the city's few racially integrated neighborhoods.

A cook and two servants comprised the mansion's staff when the Clintons moved in. Around-the-clock security was provided by the Arkansas State Police. Two troopers were on duty in eight-hour shifts to guard not only the mansion but the grounds that accommodate small guest houses.

When the Clintons moved in with their dog, Zeke, they also put a social secretary on the state payroll as part of the mansion's regular staff. But no social secretary could prevent Hillary from being pilloried early on after she let it be known she intended to continue being known as Hillary Rodham, not Hillary Clinton.

She was confronted by the *Arkansas Democrat* to explain herself. Hillary gave a series of explanations, none of which seemed to sit well with Arkansans.

At one juncture when asked how she wanted to be called, she snipped, "I'm the first lady, Bill is the first man, and Zeke is the first dog."

Soon after, she professed: "We realized that being a governor's wife could be a full-time job. But I need to maintain my interests and my commitments. I need my own identity, too."

After she was named in the *Arkansas Democrat*'s "Style" section that panned: "MS. RODHAM/JUST AN OLD-FASHIONED GIRL," Hillary took another route explaining why she insisted on being identified by her maiden name:

"I had made speeches in the name of Hillary Rodham. I had taught law under that name, I was, after all, twenty-eight when I married, and I was fairly well established."

Soon after he took office, Bill Clinton appointed Hillary Rodham to chair the 44-member Rural Health Advisory Committee. Her mandate was to develop a program to deliver adequate health care to the population in the state's small, rural communities. This appointment was the forerunner to Hillary's assignment 13 years later by her husband, the president, to head the administration's chief domestic initiative: reform of the nation's $800 billion health-care system.

Newsweek was to ask in its cover story early on after Clinton took office in Washington: "Hillary's Role: How Much Clout?" It answered its own question:

The "operation [in the Oval Office] isn't run by a 'he' alone...the administration is something entirely new in American political life. It's a Team Presidency whose own act has no script and whose political consequences are unknown." *Newsweek*'s Howard Fineman and Mark Miller then proceeded to quote Hillary "on her view of government's role—and, implicitly, her own. 'We are all in this together,' she declared, a comment that could apply as well to her and her husband."

In retrospect, it appears Hillary Rodham began practice for the "Team Presidency" as far back as 1979.

Promises He Can't Keep

In his inaugural speech, Governor Bill Clinton pretended to hear no call to higher office. He claimed his avowed intent was to move Arkansas out of its historic and endemic state of poverty—a task that could well take longer than one two-year term.

"We can fashion a life that will be the envy of the nation," he promised.

However, before long it was obvious that Arkansas still had a long way to go.

How did Clinton expect to reform one of the nation's weakest, most impoverished states?

He promised to improve education, heighten economic development, foster equal opportunity, help emotionally disturbed children, end abuse of power by government officials, give the aged and infirm needed assistance and, above all else, inject new life into the state's economy.

One of his first acts was to dump the members of the state's Arkansas Industrial Development Commission, an "ineffective and enfeebled" body, as Clinton called the

AIDC, before seating his own political cronies to run it for the governor's personal gains.

When Clinton axed its director, Frank White, he had no way of knowing he'd rue the day he signed that pink slip. For White would charge back two years later to make Clinton the nation's *youngest ex-governor.*

What did Clinton do in his first term to warrant his short-lived tenure in that office?

He installed three "hot-shot power brokers" as a triad who went by the names of John Danner, Rudy Moore, and Steve Smith. As top aides, they proved to be, in the words of *Arkansas Democrat* editor John Robert Starr, "three young, bearded, impractical visionaries [who] had not a shred of common sense among them."

They caused trouble for Clinton from the instant they became his "brain trust." In no time at all, Danner, Moore, and Smith had everyone in the state—from dirt farmers to bankers, blue collar workers to those in the professions, the rural poor to the wealthy landowners—hopping mad.

Clinton set out on the wrong foot with the state's motorists by doubling vehicle registration fees from the annual average of $15, and imposing onerous increases for auto transfer fees, and gasoline and tire taxes.

Clinton also clobbered homeowners and businesses with drastically increased property assessments and even steeper tax bites, arguing that Arkansas's roads had to be repaired and rebuilt. In no time at all, the saying all over Arkansas was: "Bill Clinton never saw a tax he didn't like."

Clinton renamed the Arkansas Industrial Development Commission. It became the Department of Economic Development. It's new focus put an end to efforts that were attracting industry to the state and promoted instead its varied agricultural exports and small farm and small business development.

That didn't sit well with Arkansans who, despite low-scale wages paid by the state's many large commercial employers, preferred to see a continued effort to proliferate such enterprises as the better of two evils.

The state's physicians also came down on Clinton for the network of rural clinics that the Rural Health Advisory Committee, under Hillary Rodham, had created. The clinics deprived doctors of their ability to minister to the needy without a sacrifice to their established fees. It was a very unpopular exercise.

Clinton and his administration stepped on more toes. But some of this was a mere pretense on the governor's part.

Timbermen strongly protested the governor's efforts to restrict *clear-cutting,* the practice of chopping down all the trees in a stand of forest.

The poultry industry objected to taxes it viewed as too oppressive to pay for road improvements that didn't totally address its routes to market.

Time will show these moves were shams. Clinton would soon bend over backward to help the International Paper Corporation cut down trees to its heart's content—for favors rendered to Clinton.

And the same would happen for Tyson Foods.

And then there were the public school teachers and educators who didn't welcome

Clinton's proposal for arbitrary dismissal procedures and competency tests before issuing teaching certificates.

In this, he was four-square.

But Clinton's efforts to be the "Education Governor" backfired in the legislature, where his proposal to consolidate the state's nearly 400 school districts to eliminate "duplicative and inefficient administrative structures" met with resounding opposition. He was forced to withdraw the plan.

Yet he steamrolled through the legislature a statute requiring the state's public school teachers to take—and pass—the National Teacher's Examination. Although the Arkansas Education Association didn't oppose the new law, many teachers deemed it to be unproductive, even counterproductive—especially in rural areas where local residents, many not even high school graduates, nevertheless were doing an effective job in classrooms, teaching such subjects as carpentry, electrical circuitry, other vocational subjects, and driver education.

Clinton's second year in office was no better than his first. Yet the same cannot be said about the turns fate had in store for the Clintons in their private lives.

Whitewater—an Ozark Mountains Boondoggle

Happenings on August dates in 1978 and 1979 make it appear that this was the best of times for the Clintons.

On August 2, 1979, Hillary learned she was expecting. The baby was due in mid-March of '80. The announcement that Hillary was to be a mother brought the Clintons the most goodwill since they had settled in the governor's mansion.

On that same date a year before, Bill and Hillary became part owners of a parcel of 230 acres of prime vacation land along the White River in Arkansas's Ozark Mountains.

It was an "investment" for the Clintons that would go largely unnoticed until the '92 presidential campaign. Then it would make some noise in the *New York Times* as a curious transaction. But it would simmer on the media's back burners until 1994, when it would come to a full boil on page one headlines as *Whitewatergate*.

In the beginning, Bill Clinton was winding down his term as attorney general and had three months left before he'd be elected Arkansas's 40th governor.

On that August 2, the Clintons became the beneficiaries of a surprising sweetheart deal.

Putting up no money that anyone knows of for the venture, the Clintons became equal partners with James B. McDougal and his wife, Susan, in ownership of that undeveloped 230-acre tract in the Ozarks.

McDougal, a 37-year-old well-to-do real estate operator and his wife, barely in her twenties, put up the purchase price reputed to have been around $100,000. However, mystery abounds about the purchase price.

Mortgage money amounting to $203,000 was borrowed by the corporation and secured by the land in June and August 1978—which was long *after* it was bought. It's believed the value of the property was greatly exaggerated to obtain those loans in a scheme called *land-flips,* a form of real estate hocus-pocus that will later be clarified for the reader.

Today, this transaction and all other matters bearing on Whitewater are the subject of inquiries by special prosecutor Kenneth W. Starr, and congressional committees.

Why the McDougals made the Clintons their partners, or why neither side ever openly discussed the dollar amounts of their respective investments, are two of the biggest questions.

However, from what has been seen of their income tax returns and from all appearances of the way matters materialized in 1978 and 1979, the Clintons found themselves in an enviable position. They likely faced no peril of losing money they hadn't advanced should their newly formed Whitewater Development Corporation fail.

On the other hand, if it succeeded, they would cash in on the 50 percent interest they were cut in for by the *blindly generous* McDougals.

Bill Clinton and Jim McDougal met in the summer of 1968. That was after Bill's graduation from Georgetown University and before his departure for Oxford.

U.S. Senator Fulbright, whom Bill clerked part-time for on his Foreign Relations Committee during college vacations, was running for reelection in 1968. Clinton volunteered his services in the lawmaker's campaign. He was assigned to work in the Fulbright Little Rock Reelection Committee's headquarters.

The office was run by Jim McDougal who took Clinton under his wing. The two became fast friends.

After Fulbright was reelected, the office was closed and the friends went their separate ways.

In the early '70s, McDougal left politics and joined his father's firm to dabble in real estate.

Meanwhile, Clinton made his way through Oxford and Yale, taught at the University of Arkansas Law School, married Hillary Rodham, was elected attorney general, and on that *lucky* August 2, 1978, Bill was not only poised on the gubernatorial threshold—but also found himself a partner with an old friend in a business venture that faced a promising future.

It's important to note that the 230-acre parcel that became Whitewater Development's property was initially owned by a private investor who bought it from the International Paper Corp., one of Arkansas's largest industries and its biggest owner of real estate by far.

International Paper had thousands of acres of verdant Arkansas woodlands, its most valued assets.

However, to realize profitability from idle forests, International had to be able to chop down trees and turn them into that lifeblood of its existence—*paper.*

It also needed to be able to sell off the land it had denuded for uses such as the one Whitewater Development planned: a mountain vacation retreat.

To do all this, International first had to get clearance from the state to chop down the trees.

The procedure is called *clear-cutting*—the practice of felling virtually *all of the trees* in a given stand of forest (but allowing just enough small clusters of woody perennials to stand so the land isn't totally shorn of its rusticity).

International Paper had found difficulty in getting then-Governor David H. Pryor to go along with the ploy. Pryor, an ardent environmentalist, had his sights set on a seat in the U.S. Senate and played hardball.

(Today, as noted, Pryor serves alongside Dale Bumpers as Arkansas's junior senator.)

Because of what happened after the Clinton-McDougal acquisition of those 230 acres, suspicions continue about the existence of a possible quid pro quo between International Paper and Whitewater's partners.

In fact, former special prosecutor Robert B. Fiske, Jr., has subpoenaed all the records bearing on the giant company's dealings with Bill and Hillary Clinton, Jim and Susan McDougal, the Rose Law Firm, and a bank called Madison Guaranty Savings and Loan, which will be introduced to the reader shortly.

Those documents were subsequently turned over to Kenneth Starr in early August, after he was picked by a federal appeals panel to supplant Fiske. The judges concluded that it was inconsistent with the independent counsel law to retain Fiske as an investigator of the Clintons, since he was a Clinton administration appointee.

What is eminently clear, as the record shows, is that International Paper found it easy to get permission to do wholesale *clear-cutting* once Bill Clinton took office as governor in January 1979.

The paper company found that in Clinton's early years as governor he could also be a great benefactor in an even more significant fashion.

For no sooner did he ease *clear-cutting* restrictions than the governor threw his support to special legislation that granted International Paper a multi-million dollar tax break!

But that isn't all the manipulating ascribed to Clinton.

Few have been privy to what happened earlier, when Clinton was still attorney general. That's when the deal was cut that enabled the Clinton-McDougal axis to buy its 230 acres on August 2, 1978. Bill then was still attorney general, but a shoo-in for governor 90 days hence.

The transaction was negotiated through 101 River Development, Inc., a local outfit that parceled the McDougal-Clinton tract from a much larger holding along the White River.

Few seemed to know—or care—that 101 River Development, Inc., originally bought the land from International Paper, which had thousands more acres in the area that it wanted to sell off, but couldn't find buyers.

Because there were no access roads to bring vacationers into this backwoods "paradise."

After Bill Clinton became governor, that ceased to be a problem. His moves would benefit not only International Paper—but the newly formed Whitewater Development Corporation as well.

Clinton began by firing the commissioners of the state's only two autonomous bodies of government—the Arkansas Game and Fish Commission and the Highway Commission—and put two cronies in place of the "old fogies" who were running those agencies.

First to go was the head of the Game and Fish Commission. Some basic background must be introduced to show why Clinton was compelled to give him the boot.

The big issue was the lack of a road to the tract that 101 River Development sold to Whitewater Development.

The old commissioner of highways had steadfastly declined to build "a road to nowhere," as he put it to the owners of 101 River Development:

"You guys bought the land. You're the ones who stand to make the big bucks when you sell parcels for vacation homes. So build a road to your property from the main highway yourselves. Don't ask Arkansas's taxpayers or the federal government to foot the bill for such a road."

After Whitewater Development had parceled its acreage in the Ozarks, the situation would be drastically altered. But not until after Bill Clinton was installed as governor.

Before then, when he was still attorney general, the corporation tried a futile end-around run on the Highway Commission. It offered the Game and Fish Commission a "sweetheart deal."

Whitewater was willing to "donate" a waterfront parcel along the White River to Game and Fish on condition that the commission build a boat ramp to serve the state's sailing enthusiasts.

Left unspoken was that the project would make the remaining Whitewater lots much more attractive in the enhanced sales brochures, which the Clintons and McDougals were anxious to have printed.

The commissioner of game and fish had no inkling of the true extent of Whitewater Development's underhandedness. He was merely relying on sound judgment to tell him this deal was no deal.

The commissioner couldn't see why he should take that land and build a boat ramp in the boondocks. Who could get to it—unless it was made accessible? And to do that, the Game and Fish Commission would have to ask the Highway Commission to lay down a road that it never wanted to build in the first place.

The Game and Fish Commission had no desire to go through those gymnastics because there were so many similar recreational facilities in the state, all easily reached over existing roads.

That was Whitewater's deception.

In offering the free land to the Game and Fish Commission for a boat ramp, the Clinton-McDougal development company was hoping to get its road!

The director turned thumbs down on the proposition not knowing that what Whitewater Development was really after was opening a path to its property so it could make a killing selling plots for vacation sites.

He also didn't know that Attorney General Bill Clinton and wife Hillary had a 50-50 interest in Whitewater.

But just as soon as inauguration day passed, the director of the Game and Fish Commission and his counterpart on the Highway Commission were given their education. They got the old heave-ho—so Bill Clinton could begin to work the first of his many conflict-of-interest scams on the people of Arkansas.

Minutes of a Game and Fish Commission meeting in January 1979, chaired by

Clinton's new appointee, show the donation offered by Whitewater Development was belatedly accepted.

With that, construction began on a miles-long access road from Highway 101 to the mountain retreat. Arkansans couldn't squawk too loudly about the deal, because the road was paid for by the Highway Commission out of the Marine Fuel Tax funds advanced by the federal government.

Even before Clinton became governor, evidence shows Whitewater's partners were hell-bent to make killings with their property.

Tract 7 serves as a beautiful introductory example of a *land-flip,* the instant big-profit realty transaction.

This attractive parcel was in the Ozark Mountains alongside a lazy mountain stream called Crooked Creek, which empties into the wondrously wide and rapidly flowing White River.

Only two months after Whitewater Development had been cleverly crafted into its earliest "bulletproof" configuration, the four-way partnership pulled off their first *smelly* deal.

That was on October 14, 1978.

On that day, the Whitewater partners sold Tract 7 to Chris V. Wade and Associates.

The Arkansas State real estate tax stamps affixed to the deed show a selling price of $2,000.

Yet a further transaction the next day indicates that Chris Wade sold the very same parcel to M. T. Bronstad, Jr., for $32,250.

This beautifully executed scam was one the Clintons and McDougals would pull again and again. As shown, *land-flips* involve assigning greatly inflated values to properties purchased at dirt-cheap prices—which invariably take lending institutions for a ride. Each time selling prices are inflated, the new owners qualify for higher mortgage financing.

Susan McDougal will be shown to be a master in this rip-off as she played hocus-pocus with Whitewater property and other investments. The plot involved a cast of shadowy characters, primarily friends, and relatives with different last names. This coterie sold parcels of land (or buildings) back and forth among themselves, pyramiding their gains into unconscionable profits.

Susan did wonders with this clever juggling act when she performed it with the bank her husband would soon be running, Madison Guaranty Savings and Loan. That *land-flip* was pulled with a commercial building in Little Rock that a lawyer bought in Susan McDougal's name for $45,000.

The same lawyer soon afterward sold the property to Susan's best friend for $95,000.

Best friend waited a couple of months before unloading the property on Susan's brother for $135,000.

Brother subsequently leased the block-long building to Jim McDougal. He occupied it for the newest Madison Guaranty offices—but not before brother took out a new mortgage on the building for $190,000.

Madison Guaranty, then a fledgling thrift, underwrote the financing each time.

The lawyer on the initial purchase was Jim Guy Tucker, who later gave Clinton his first big boost in politics by opening the door to the attorney general's office.

He would later succeed Clinton as governor in '92 after Clinton was elected president.

Hillary's Cockamamie Plunge into the Commodities Market

While Hillary appeared to steer clear of primary corporate cases, that isn't to say she wasn't steering herself toward primary corporate principals. One such animal was James B. Blair, Attorney General Bill Clinton's long-time confidante.

Like William Wilson, the criminal lawyer with whom she had dealings outside the Rose Law Firm's sphere, so did Hillary have an association with Blair. He was not only one of her and Bill's closest friends, but was also the primary lawyer for Tyson Foods, Inc., the nation's biggest poultry company, located in Springdale, Arkansas.

Eleven years older than Clinton, Blair was a partner in Crouch, Blair, Cypert & Waters, headquartered in Springdale, the center of Arkansas's thriving poultry industry.

The adviser to Tyson and some of the state's other poultry companies, his law firm also represented big trucking companies and the local utility.

Blair was also a power in state politics. He had run the ill-fated 1974 reelection campaign for Senator J. William Fulbright, Clinton's great benefactor, who was defeated in the Democratic primary by Dale Bumpers.

In the earliest days after the formation of his law firm, Blair personally became general counsel to Tyson's chairman and principal owner, Donald J. Tyson, whose company was founded in 1936 when his father trucked live chickens from Arkansas to Chicago.

Eventually, Blair left his firm and went to work for his friend Don Tyson. In time he would serve as a director of more than 20 Tyson-controlled companies across the country.

Blair also had his hand in the stock market. He began trading as far back as 1956 when he was 20 years old. Through the 50s and 60s, he dealt in commodity futures— a highly leveraged gamble of trading (*betting* is a more accurate way to put it) on whether the price of commodities on any given day will rise or fall.

An investor who climbs aboard this risky venture for the ride is on a roller coaster. The author is indebted to columnist Ray Kerrison, his former colleague on the *New York Post,* for this example of how trades can make or break an investor in commodities futures in one spectacular swoop.

His comments were made on March 21, 1994, after the *New York Times'* Jeff Gerth, Dean Baquet, and Stephen Lebaton conducted a months-long investigation of Hillary Clinton's financial dealings. Their findings were these: that James Blair counseled Hillary Rodham in commodities—specifically cattle futures—trading in 1977, and that the first lady then not only plunged into that activity whole hog, but went for a kill.

Kerrison is a "veteran of many gambling rackets," as he likes to describe himself.

The author remembers him best when he covered thoroughbred racing for the *Post* in the 80s. He was the most widely read and most successful newspaper handicapper of horse flesh in New York's history.

Kerrison discusses what it was like, in theory, to trade the way Clinton's wife began to do in 1978 three weeks before her husband, the attorney general, was elected governor.

"Hillary would have had to put up $700 to buy a contract of 40,000 pounds of cattle. At today's market price of 76.5 cents a pound, the contract is worth $30,600. If cattle prices go up a cent, she makes $400. If they go down a cent, she loses $400.

"This is a game to test the nerve of the most experienced gambler. For the Clintons, who had neither money nor experience, it is ridiculous."

Hillary Rodham's foray into this volatile commodities trading business was of short duration, but it would be talked about 16 years later and create some of 1994's biggest news stories.

James Blair's own experience in that market has been recorded by the *New York Times*:

"Mr. Blair's timing was impeccable [after he switched his trades from stocks to futures in the 70s]. In the tiny Springdale office of Refco, Inc. [Refco stands for Ray E. Friedman Company], a trading firm based in Chicago composed of a rag-tag group of brokers, some of whom had been small-town liquor salesmen and clerks, was making millions of dollars capitalizing on a stunning boom in futures contracts prices.

"The office's founder, a professional high-stakes poker player named Robert 'Red' Bone, was a 13-year Tyson executive who turned a knack for gauging odds into a small fortune."

Blair was similarly riding the crest of a heady wave when he helped guide Hillary to bet on commodities futures. He credits his own great success in those trades to his close friendship and lawyer-client relationship with Red Bone.

"I recommended to her that she open an account at the Refco office," Blair explained.

"I was on a streak, on a streak that I thought was very successful, and I wanted to share this with my close friends, as I did with my fiancee, as I did with my law firm, as I did with my children, as I did with my fiancee's children, and as I did with the person who was the best person at my marriage, which was Hillary, a tennis partner and friend."

Blair told the *Times* he steered Hillary Rodham into the cattle futures market because "I specifically was trading the cattle futures and thought I knew what I was doing...I'm damn good at it."

Trading records show that Hillary opened her account with $1,000 in Refco's office in mid-October 1978. Blair said he helped guide Hillary's trades.

"We discussed whether she ought to be long or short," a reference as to whether she'd bet on the rise or fall of commodity prices.

This creates a mystery, because Blair did not say which way he advised Hillary to go—*long* or *short* on traded commodities, such as cattle, or pork, or even foreign currency. All of them are the riskiest and most volatile of investments.

It's estimated that nearly 95 percent of investors lose money, betting either way.

Only a savvy trader, or one with special knowledge of a market, can turn a small stake into millions—as Jim Blair claims to have done.

"We [Blair and Hillary] discussed whether she ought to be long or short in her trades," Blair said without further amplification. "It was done in consultation. I gave her my best advice."

Nevertheless, Blair admitted that while he made "specific trading recommendations," Hillary always "determined the size of the trade."

Hillary also may—or may not—have made a decision that conceivably—but very unlikely—was of her own doing.

She opened another commodity trading account around the very time of Clinton's election as governor, with Stephens, Inc. This large brokerage firm in Little Rock was owned by Arkansas's wealthiest and most influential banking family, with branches and financial holdings throughout the world.

In 1978, the Stephenses ranked as Bill Clinton's biggest political contributors, along with the Tyson Poultry interests. This financial cornucopia grew with each ensuing gubernatorial primary and election campaign until Clinton's 1992 run for the presidency, when his coffers overflowed with Stephens' and Tyson's money.

What can be made of Hillary opening a second trading account at Stephens, a decision in which Blair swears he had no part?

Great mystery surrounds that move, which was initiated with $5,000 that Hillary plunked down to activate her commodity futures trading account at Stephens where she had previously made only small-scale stock investments.

Bill Smith, her Stephens adviser and broker, became her trader for commodities futures, too, making her bids through three market-specialist brokers.

In retrospect, it appears that Hillary, who had to scrape together that $1,000 to open her account in Refco, had made a quick killing with Blair's trades for her to have gotten her hands on $5,000 to begin dealing with Stephens.

The big question that must be asked is this:

What accounts for that curious second-account step by Hillary Rodham, a Jim Blair intimate, a Stephens family benefactor (not only through their political donations to her husband's campaigns, but also one of the Rose Law Firm's biggest and most influential clients)—and, above all else now, the wife of Arkansas's next governor?

Let's go to Ray Kerrison, the self-anointed "veteran of many gambling rackets."

Kerrison describes "mirrored trading," a practice in which the *profits* from a series of transactions in commodities trading, such as the cattle futures that Hillary chose to dabble in, are credited to one account.

But in the practice of taking *losses* in these self-same trades, the beatings in "mirrored trading" are recorded in another account.

From all the evidence at hand, it would appear Hillary used the good offices of Refco, with poker whiz Red Bone, as the broker of record for her profit-making.

While Bill Smith did Hillary's wheelin' and dealin' over at Stephens, no word came out of there to indicate that her losses weren't being entombed in that account.

What's the best thing that can be said about "mirrored trading," as Kerrison views it?

"This set-up is a familiar vehicle for transferring funds for *favors* [author's heavy emphasis], for *funneling funds abroad* [also author's stress], and *laundering money* [again, the same as before]."

Is that what Hillary Rodham was up to when she fashioned the appearance that she *played two ends against the middle?*

No way to tell just yet. All that's known about the Clintons at this stage of their lives is that they didn't have anything close to what it takes to play the commodity futures market.

Consider that their income as instructors at the University of Arkansas Law School was capped at $18,090 each in annual salary and that they took a beating when they went payless during the six months away from their teaching posts during Clinton's failed 1975 congressional campaign.

Also, Clinton's salary as attorney general of Arkansas in 1977-78 was barely $26,000 a year, before he moved up to the $35,000 bracket as governor at the beginning of 1979, a time when Hillary started making a respectable $46,000 per year.

It wasn't until 1981—more than two years hence—after becoming a partner at Rose Law that Hillary began to earn $100,000 per annum.

Does it make sense for a rank novice with no experience—and no appreciable capital—to plunge into the frenetic whirl of commodity speculation?

The reader will learn of the outcome, just around the bend now.

At the same time, Jim McDougal was making money hand over fist. But his gush of gold wasn't in the commodities market but in his father's real estate business—and he stood to mine new lodes now that good friend Bill Clinton was governor.

As well off as he was financially, McDougal incongruously took a Clinton appointment as low-salaried head of the State's Department of Economic Development.

Clinton would feel considerable heat after McDougal stepped in and changed the agency's focus from attracting industry to Arkansas to promoting agricultural exports, funding small farms projects, generating community development, and providing counseling to small business.

No one knows what Clinton had in mind when he put McDougal in as agency boss, a position he held only during the governor's first term. But in his later 10-year run as governor, Clinton would make the Department of Economic Development's multi-million-dollar treasury his personal kitty, dipping into it just as frequently as need be to finance trips abroad for himself and staffers—but most frequently to pay for his endless "bimbo excursions."

Meanwhile, let's not overlook that matter of Hillary's pregnancy.

Chelsea Is Born Prematurely

Bill and Hillary committed themselves to have the baby delivered by the Lamaze method. They attended classes, learned the procedure well, and were prepared to go through with the natural birth of their child. But all the training in the eight-week course on how to relax, control breathing, and other ways to facilitate delivery, went awry on February 27, 1980.

Just before 8:00 p.m. Hillary cried out in anguish. The labor pains began—three weeks early. Hillary told Bill she wanted to go to the hospital. A state trooper drove the governor's Lincoln limousine with the first couple to Baptist Medical Center in Little Rock. At the hospital, the contractions grew more frequent, the pain more unbearable. Shortly after midnight, the Clintons' gynecologist decided the baby had to be delivered by cesarean section.

Hillary was wheeled into the delivery room at 12:45 a.m. Minutes later a perspiring Bill Clinton, clad in a green hospital frock and a white surgical mask, exited the delivery room. In his arms he cradled a six-pound, one-and-three-quarter-ounce baby girl, whose name, Chelsea, had been selected by the Clintons during their European vacation the past summer, just after Hillary had learned she was pregnant.

"It was this glorious morning [in England]," Hillary told *Newsweek* during the '92 presidential campaign. "We were going to brunch and we were walking through Chelsea—you know, the flowerpots were out and everything. And Bill started singing, 'It's a Chelsea Morning,' the Judy Collins song."

Hillary described her husband's elation at becoming a parent:

"Bill was amazed by fatherhood. He was overwhelmed by it. I've heard him say that when he saw the child, he realized it was more than his own father could do."

At another time, Hillary would express her own great thrill in experiencing motherhood:

"I was so exhilarated to have given birth to Chelsea that I vowed to do everything possible for her and to have her above anything else in my life. My mother had done that for me and I never stopped being grateful for that. But that didn't mean I'd be a round-the-clock, stay-at-home mother."

Hillary's compulsion to make something of herself was still on the front burner. She had fretted for many months about becoming a partner in the Rose Law Firm. In fact, the pressure she was under trying to make the grade was said to have been the cause of her premature labor.

"When I told *Newsweek* that I would put Chelsea above everything else in my life," explained Hillary, "that didn't mean I would be staying home all the time." What she did tell the magazine was, "You never know in retrospect whether you did or didn't do exactly the right thing—stay-at-home mothers, gone-away mothers, all of us worry whether we should have done something differently than we did."

Determined to return to her office and duties as counsel at the Rose Law Firm, Hillary "put Chelsea above everything else" in her life—by placing the infant into the tender care of a pseudo nanny. Although a nurse by training, the woman retained to mind the Clinton's daughter was not legally covered under the regulations established by the Arkansas legislature for staffing the governor's mansion. To sneak a nanny in through the *back door*, the Clintons pulled a subterfuge by listing nurse Dessie M. Sanders as a "security guard" at a salary of $75 per week. Her compensation may seem low, but she only worked part-time—just for the hours Chelsea's career-oriented mother was away at work.

The tab for the nurse cost taxpayers $3,130 for the period of her employment, from March 4, 1980—a week after Chelsea's birth—to January 31, 1981, the day

Clinton left office at the end of his first term as governor. Most significant about this expense is that the Clintons did not file Form 2241, "Credit for Child and Dependent Care Expenses," which should have been attached to their Internal Revenue Service 1040 joint return for the year 1980.

They did make a claim for child care reimbursement in their 1981-82 returns, when Clinton was out of government service and in private practice. In those years they received a $400 credit for payments that averaged slightly more than $5,500 per annum for nursing care for Chelsea. In other words, when the Clintons occupied the governor's mansion, they benefited to the tune of some $7,000 that came out of Arkansas taxpayers' pocketbooks.

Arkansas State Auditor, Julia Hughes Jones, was interviewed at length on the Clintons' lavish spending habits, by Lisa Schiffren, a speechwriter for former Vice President Dan Quayle. Ms. Schiffren wrote the cover article, "Bill and Hillary at the Trough," in the August 1993 edition of the conservative magazine *The American Spectator.*

This is getting ahead of the story, but it is important to spotlight the *insatiable greed and avarice* that characterized the Clintons' seamy 12-year history as Arkansas's first couple.

"Remember Bill Clinton's much-touted 'lowest-in-the-nation' $35,000 governor's salary?" asks Ms. Schiffren in her article.

"That was merely his cash compensation—mad money. For the decade [actually 12 years all told] he was governor, all Clinton personal living expenses (including food, shelter, transportation, and entertainment), along with security, housekeeping, administration, utilities, etc., were paid out of various state funds. Including those expenses, the care and feeding of their humble governor cost taxpayers in the nation's second-poorest state more than three-quarters of a million dollars a year."

Two funds are cited in the piece that raise "interesting legal questions"—the yearly $51,000 food allotment and the annual $19,000 "public relations" fund, neither of which was subject to scrutiny by state audits.

In both instances, the governor appears to have shafted Uncle Sam by failing to make declarations or required disclosures about benefits reaped from over-generous food and PR moneys on which they deliberately avoided paying taxes.

Former IRS Commissioner Donald Alexander, who reviewed the Clintons' tax returns, concluded that not listing the $51,000 food allocation on their 1040's "probably constitutes a failure to report income."

Since they persistently failed to record such benefits through the years and right up to their tax filing for 1992, the last full year as Arkansas's governor and first lady, the three-year statute of limitations would not preclude the IRS from dunning the president and first lady for those back taxes—and the ones for the year before. Yet many close observers wondered when, if ever, the IRS would ask the Clintons to pay up—especially after Ms. Schiffren's exposé appeared not only in *The American Spectator* but also was reprinted in such widely read, large-circulation dailies as the *New York Post.*

A *second opinion* on the Clintons' dubious—if not outright devious—tax gymnastics is offered by Bill Goodman, chairman of the Arkansas Legislative Joint Budget Committee, which allocated the funds for the state's first family's living expenses.

"The nineteen-thousand-a-year PR fund is by all accounts taxable income," Goodman pointed out. "You have always had to pay a tax on that money, because it is an allowance, not a reimbursement."

Ms. Schiffren goes on in her *American Spectator* article:

"In 1989 the fund—earmarked for items as varied as fruit-basket gifts for constituents and political events that advanced Bill Clinton's career, not Arkansas business—became an issue with the legislature. Under political pressure and press scrutiny, Clinton finally began declaring the extra $19,000 as part of his income—as the law had always required."

The most telling discovery Ms. Schiffren made about the Clintons' tax returns is to be found in a matter that exploded when a congressional committee, during confirmation hearings for President Clinton's cabinet, unearthed the failure of Attorney General nominee Zoe Baird to pay social security taxes on salaries for domestic help (a baby-sitter in her case). She got an unceremonious heave-ho by Clinton—as did some later appointees who ignored the payment of such taxes on domestics they employed.

The big question that all this raises is this:

Did Bill and Hillary pay social security taxes on salaries they paid to nanny Dessie Sanders and to other Chelsea minders? These hired hands received between $1,000 and $1,500 per year from the Clintons, who continued to take the child-care credit until 1985, when they no longer applied for relief in this category.

The author poses the question for these reasons:

The Clintons owe the nation an explanation why their tax returns appear to show that the president and first lady live by a double standard. They laid down ground rules for *their* cabinet members (remember, it's a co-presidency), who must adhere to the strictest of guidelines and must pay social security taxes on employees who earn more than $50 in any calendar year's quarter. *Yet they themselves do not appear to have paid the taxes for the nannies who worked for them.* If they had, they then appear to have omitted the cardinal requirement in the preparation of their tax returns—they clearly neglected to list the employees' social security numbers. By failing to do so, the government is certainly unable to properly credit the Clintons' employees' accounts, and those people are deprived of their rightful share of social security in their retirements.

This question was put to White House Counsel Bernard Nussbaum on the phone by a researcher for the author. This was the response:

"President and Mrs. Clinton have complied with all of their social security obligations. Those records are being safekeeped in the White House, but—for reasons of principle—we are not going to release them."

In time Nussbaum would deny a similar request on yet another touchy, more nerve-rattling subject—Bill and Hillary's connection with the shady Arkansas vacation land enterprise. But when this turned into 1994's *Whitewatergate* headlines, the tax returns were finally released by the White House—and they raised more serious questions about the Clinton-McDougal partnership than ever before.

Hillary's Star Brighter than Bill's

Hillary and Bill had a double celebration when Chelsea was a month old. Besides their daughter's natal observance, Hillary had received word from the Rose firm that she was made a partner.

With the promotion came a substantial increase in salary—nearly $50,000. Bill Clinton was left by his wife at the *starting gate*, so to speak. The governor still had a $35,000-per-annum cap on his salary.

But Clinton had other concerns besides his wife becoming the rising star in their household. For his own political star was descending.

Clinton had not run the state the way he had promised. His brain trust—the three "bearded wonders"—had pulled the rug out from under him with their harebrained schemes. The populace was infuriated. Neither he nor his administration seemed able to do anything right.

When state revenues fell below projections, he was compelled to call a special session of the legislature to endorse a sleight-of-hand the brain trust devised to infuse money into the state's anemic treasury.

This was done by amending the quarterly collection procedures for employee tax withholdings from employers to a monthly basis. A "windfall" of some $40 million accrued to the state as a result. Half of those funds were channeled into teacher salary increases. This averaged out to a $1,200-a-year pay raise. But the $22,000-a-year Arkansas teacher was still the next-to-lowest paid educator in the nation.

Helping to accelerate Clinton toward his soon-to-be-status of ex-governor was the additional onus of scandalous mismanagement.

One appointee, James Dyke, director of the state's newly established Economic Development Department, apparently was a closet horticulturist. No sooner was he seated in his office than he placed a standing order for live plants—a $450-a-month expense item the governor evidently had no qualms endorsing.

The order was rescinded finally—after *Arkansas Democrat* editor John Robert Starr brought this botanical outrage to full bloom in his newspaper's columns.

Another of Starr's editorials was aimed at an energy department flunky who found a way to blow $2,000 by holding a "retreat" for his staff on the shores of peaceful, restful Lake DeGray.

Clinton defended that expenditure, saying "the money was well spent because the conference was long overdue and very much needed."

Starr found a more substantive target when he zeroed in on another of Governor Clinton's pet projects that, like so many before it, seemed destined to fail. The Special Alternative Wood Energy Resources Project (or SAWER, as it was called), provided employment to low-income Arkansans to cut wood and distribute it to the needy. But the *Arkansas Democrat* couldn't support spending $62,000 of taxpayer money to pay the hired hands SAWER put on its employment rolls.

Not after the newspaper discovered they produced only three cords of cut wood.

That was too much even for Bill Clinton, who fired the director Ted Newman.

Jimmy Carter Sinks Bill Clinton

The worst was yet to come. It happened on May 26, 1980, a day before the Arkansas gubernatorial primary. Some 350 Cuban refugees, "boat-lift people," as they were called, declared their independence from the 20,000 or so other detainees who had landed illegally in Florida ports to escape Fidel Castro's tyranny. To the dismay of residents in the western part of the state, the refugees were housed by the federal government at Arkansas's Fort Chaffee.

Because the refugees were criminals and degenerates Castro had encouraged to leave Cuba—the populace pushed the panic button after the 350 displaced Cubans sauntered out of the stockade. Governor Clinton reacted with what many thought was correct procedure. He ordered the state police to round up the escapees. This was accomplished over a three-day period—but not without some head-bashing with Arkansas State Police nightsticks, more popularly called "Billy Clubs" in honor of the governor.

Then Clinton mobilized 200 members of the Arkansas National Guard and dispatched them to Fort Chaffee to augment its skimpy army detail.

So far as Arkansans were concerned, Bill Clinton had made all the right moves. But he hadn't gone far enough. For when Clinton appealed to President Carter to move the Cubans out of Arkansas to a site in Pennsylvania, this advisory came from the White House:

"Because the refugees are from a warm climate, Pennsylvania's harsh winter weather is unsuitable for those people. It would subject them to extreme hardship. So Arkansas, where the climate is milder, is the only logical alternative."

The fact that the Cubans bolted the stockade the day before the May 27 gubernatorial primary had no bearing on the Democratic primary, which pitted only one rival against Clinton.

He was none other than turkey farmer Monroe Schwarzlose, the perennial "go-nowhere" candidate, now a hardy 77 years old and still hankerin' to win elective office. It was too soon for Schwarzlose to cackle about the Cuban crisis because it was only just developing. But he had other ammunition: the higher cost of auto registration, the inadequacy of efforts to bring more industry into the state, and, above all else, the SAWER scandal. Schwarzlose played this for all the mileage he could get. He appeared in a campaign photo beside a pile of wood he cut with his own two hands that was stacked higher and wider than the three cords cut by SAWER's industrious servants at a cost of $62,000.

Although they had laughed at him in previous political primaries, few found pleasure in ridiculing Schwarzlose's showing this time around. He received 31 percent of the statewide vote. If Clinton assessed the results with indifference, he couldn't really be blamed. For there seemed to be no obstacle in his path to a second term.

The Republican primary produced a clear winner: ousted Arkansas Industrial Development Commission director Frank White. He had spent his two-year exile from public service as an officer of a savings and loan association, stewing about his dismissal by Governor Clinton.

When White entered the political arena, he was steaming. He defeated Marshall Chriseman with votes to spare.

Yet the outcome must have buoyed Bill Clinton's hopes for reelection, for less than 10,000 GOP loyalists went to the polls. The traditional lackluster showing of GOP partisans augured another easy victory for the incumbent in November's election.

Clinton believed he'd resolved the Cuban refugee situation with his state police roundup and assignment of National Guard troops to fortify the beleaguered soldiers at Fort Chaffee. But that soon proved to be a mere Band-Aid applied to a festering wound.

His Black Beauty's a Migraine

Arkansans found a reason to rejoice in early September 1980. It was the heartening news from Atlantic City, where the annual Miss America Pageant was conducted.

A black Miss Arkansas had finished fourth in the finals. For Lencola Sullivan, whose svelte figure won her the swimsuit portion of the 1980 pageant, meeting the governor of Arkansas upon her return was a great honor.

Governor Clinton put a bouquet of roses in her outstretched arms—but that was not their last meeting. For soon after, the shapely miss, who hailed from the sleepy hamlet of Morrilton, a town of 6,000 along the Arkansas River, found herself employed as a reporter for KARK-TV.

That's the same Channel 4 in Little Rock where Gennifer Flowers had been a reporter.

While his sexual encounters with Gennifer hadn't stopped, Clinton managed to add Lencola Sullivan to a constantly growing gubernatorial stable of playmates.

These now were the final months of Clinton's first term as governor and, besides campaigning hard for reelection, he seemed to be making the most of the mix of politics and the high, good life behind Hillary's back. Yet in speaking with friends like Betsey Wright, one learns that Hillary apparently was quite aware of her husband's philanderings but chose to look the other way.

Many in the know are said not to have found reason to be saddened by Hillary's seemingly cursed *hurt-wife* role, for it was understood by a number of townsfolk of Little Rock and its precincts that Arkansas's first lady was able to experience solace in the companionship she found with a handsome, strapping, Rose Law Firm partner named Vincent W. (Vince) Foster, Jr.

Foster was more than a mere professional associate to Hillary. This 34-year-old lawyer, whose brilliance was his trademark, found success very early in his career when he was made a partner two years after joining Rose. That came after he graduated from the University of Arkansas Law School in 1971 and went on to score the highest grade on the bar exam that same year.

Twenty-eight years earlier, in 1951, when Bill Clinton lived in Hope with his grandparents, he and Vince Foster had attended Miss Mary's Kindergarten, where

Thomas F. (Mack) McLarty also was a pupil. Forty-two years later—in 1993—McLarty and Foster would become two of President Clinton's most-trusted aides!

But Vince Foster would command the biggest, boldest, blackest, and saddest headlines of 1993:

Suicide shocks the White House - *New York Daily News*
Death Mystery Deepens - *New York Post*

The mystery of Foster's death on July 22, 1993, appeared to have been resolved on June 30, 1994, when Robert Fiske's five-month probe concluded that Hillary's former law partner wasn't murdered, but took his own life.

However, many sources felt Fiske did not go far enough and took issue with the suicide theory. With Kenneth Starr's arrival, the hope in many quarters was that a more thorough investigation would ensue.

Foster and Clinton went their separate ways after those early years. Vince remained in the Arkansas hamlet of his and Bill's birth, while the future president moved to Hot Springs. Their close childhood friendship was to be rekindled after Clinton's election to state attorney general.

By then, Foster was in the eighth year of his marriage to wife Lisa and the father of two toddlers, Vincent III and Laura. Mrs. Foster soon began carrying their third child Brugh, who was born in 1977—two years before Hillary gave birth to Chelsea.

When Hillary joined the Rose Law Firm that same year, it was no secret in the state capital that Foster's influence greased the way for Hillary's hire. Two years later he helped elevate the governor's wife to a partnership in the firm.

The Clintons and Fosters enjoyed a reasonably moderate social life, visiting each other's homes and taking excursions together to formal dinners, to the theater and other functions, for the most part political. Foster was to become a "heavy hitter" for Clinton in his many campaigns in Arkansas—and especially in his 1992 run for the presidency.

If Bill didn't see Hillary some evenings, or Lisa didn't see Vince, it could be understood. For Hillary and Vince were specialists in similar kinds of civil legal work: commercial litigation, securities litigation, and professional liability litigation.

Nor was it surprising that they worked on the same cases at times—and during those times they often burned the midnight oil.

There was talk that the close rapport of Hillary and Vince behind the locked doors of the Rose Law Firm on those nights might be more than a mere professional calling. But those rumors never went as far as the much louder whispers about Bill Clinton and his floozies.

The author can report without equivocation that Bill Clinton's association with Lencola Sullivan, the "black beauty" of the Miss America Pageant, is just another example of this man's considerable charm—and audacity.

Yet not too long into the affair, which began in September 1980, the governor and the TV reporter found they could no longer have an extension on the amenities they were enjoying.

"Word of the affair was about to leak out," explained Larry Nichols, an official with the Arkansas Development Finance Authority. Nichols, then 31, was beginning to wonder what was happening to a slush fund set up with 200 million of taxpayer dollars that Clinton controlled. He was getting distinct vibes the kitty was being dipped into to finance a slew of the governor's pet projects, including an unending procession of sexual escapades.

Soon Clinton became aware that his encounters with Lencola Sullivan might begin to get a public airing:

"Suddenly she was whisked out of Little Rock and moved to New York. She departed for the Big Apple without having a place to stay or a job to go to," according to Nichols.

Nichols later detailed Clinton's caper with Lencola in legal papers he filed after the governor fired him from his Arkansas Development Finance Authority job as marketing manager.

"The governor used state funds on three separate occasions to travel to New York to see Lencola," Nichols stated in his $3.05 million libel and defamation suit filed on October 25, 1990, in Little Rock's U.S. District Court against his former employer.

The dossier on Lencola Sullivan, now 34 years old, bears two final update entries.

One item was submitted by John Rupp of New York's Tiger Employment Agency:

"She's been trying to get her big break in show business, but it hasn't been easy for her. She worked with us briefly as a placement director, but her heart was set on making something of herself in the entertainment world.

"Lencola doesn't want to think of herself as an ex-beauty queen. She will not accept the remotest suggestion that her future is behind her."

The second entry in the log kept on Lencola came in 1988, during Clinton's fourth term as governor. She returned to see her parents in Morrilton and jarred the populace out of somnambulance by showing up on the arm of popular entertainer Stevie Wonder.

"Stevie wanted to meet my parents and see Arkansas," she trilled.

Wonder let Lencola lead him to her church, where he thrilled the congregation with his rendition of three songs.

However, Lencola's run with Stevie Wonder turned out to be no more lasting then her earlier affair with Bill Clinton, once "word of the affair was about to leak out," as Larry Nichols put it.

With Lencola Sullivan "put in cold storage," Bill Clinton no longer had to fear that a scandal would mar his administration.

His main concern now was the pesky Cuban refugees who were at it again.

11

"I DIDN'T RUN IT RIGHT"

Arkansas's Cuban Rebellion

Only four days after the primary, the "prisoners" at Fort Chaffee rioted. Some 200 dissidents fled the stockade and bulled their way down Arkansas Highway 22, bound for the tiny community of Barling on Fort Smith's outer perimeter.

They were intercepted by Arkansas state troopers, who made short work of herding their quarry back to the "concentration camp," as opponents characterized the military compound.

Once again the governor called upon Washington to control the problem. His tone was more deferential than demanding. He was not so brash as to take on a head of state from his own Democratic Party.

To worsen the situation, President Carter sent a message to Clinton:

"Prepare to receive another ten thousand Cubans from other military installations around the country...they are being transferred to Fort Chaffee."

That was a slap in the face Clinton could scarcely challenge lest he be labeled a rabble-rousing, redneck governor.

That fall, Frank White's TV commercials cannonaded Clinton for allowing the Cuban situation to fester, but the hammering didn't end there. White's campaign war chest suddenly bulged with an uncharacteristic largesse of GOP funds notably in short supply in other elections. It even provided generous outlays of green for bumper stickers that read, "Cubans and Car Tags."

Whenever he was asked what Clinton should have done about the refugees, White's crisp response would be, "He should have sued the government when it announced it was settling the Cubans in Arkansas!"

White also hopped on Clinton for allocating nearly a million dollars to the Ozarks Institute of Eureka Springs. He claimed that was a pork barrel project aimed at "teaching rural residents to grow gardens."

No criticism was so harsh as the volleys White directed at Hillary Clinton, who he found was either "too snobbish or too ashamed to be identified with her husband's name."

In time, Hillary Clinton herself realized the problems she had caused by using her maiden name. That came after Bill lost his bid for reelection in 1980.

"I found that going by my name was a political liability," she said. "In any other state it would not have been so. But in Arkansas it certainly was an anchor around my husband's neck. So, after he lost the election and before he made his comeback, I gave it up because I concluded it meant more to the voters that I not be Hillary Rodham but appear before them as Hillary Clinton."

Using her maiden name instead of her married one was one of two complaints voters harbored against the Clintons in their personal life. The other was that the family appeared not to practice any religion. Bill was born a Baptist and Hillary a Presbyterian. But their upbringing wasn't tied to a serious dedication or concentration to religious worship. Even their wedding was a non-denominational, civil ceremony.

All that changed after Clinton lost the election and the Clintons heard the whispers that they were "heathens" in the eyes of Arkansans for not attending a church. Bill and Hillary, along with little Chelsea, became members and regular worshippers at Little Rock's Immanuel Baptist Church.

America's Youngest Ex-Governor

Perhaps the early polls that showed Clinton ahead by a comfortable margin caused him to drop his guard. He seemed to ignore Frank White's TV propaganda showing Cuban refugees helter-skelter over Arkansas streets, storming Fort Chaffee, and in other forms of uprising.

Pooh-poohing one of the campaign spots on the tube, Clinton turned to a gathering in the governor's mansion and cracked, "Do people really believe this crap?"

"Yeah, a lot of them believe it," Dee Dee Myers, the governor's press secretary, replied. "Why don't you strike back at that bum?"

"Yeah!" cried Hillary, jumping up from her arm chair. "They sure do believe it. Why don't you do something, Bill? You've got to give it back to White!"

Hillary said she wished she could do more for her husband as she had for his narrowly lost campaign against Congressman Hammerschmidt and his successful campaigns for attorney general and governor. But now, with motherhood and her own career as a partner in the Rose Law Firm commanding more of her time, Hillary couldn't go on the stump as frequently as she once had.

Her absence did not go unnoticed. Hundreds of letters of protest poured into the governor's office. The electorate was furious with Hillary's laid back attitude.

"What's the matter, Bill doesn't she love you anymore?" one typical letter-writer asked.

"Who does she think she is?" asked another. "Does she believe her career is more important than yours?"

The cannonading was deafening—and brutal.

Scores of voters wanted to know if the Clintons' marriage was "on the rocks." And repeatedly, the question was asked: "Why doesn't your wife take your last name?"

University of Arkansas Professor Cal Ledbetter, Jr., a friend of the Clintons who often offered his views on the way the state's political winds blew, had this opinion:

"It would seem that when she kept her own name, Hillary was telling the world she is the boss. People in all likelihood assumed that she wore the pants and was the stronger one in the family."

Arkansas Democrat editor John Robert Starr leveled his anti-Bill Clinton barbs in print almost daily with such demeaning name-calling as "Hillary Rodham is Bill Clinton's *backbone*" and "Bill Clinton is a *spineless* wimp alongside his wife." More than Frank White, more than the cascade of anti-Hillary correspondence, more than anyone else, Robert Starr is looked upon as the media mogul who fired the most damaging ammunition that shot down Bill Clinton on election day 1979.

Despite all of the many warnings, the governor remained supremely confident of reelection. The governor even got a big laugh out of being written for a speeding ticket when he was stopped doing better than 80 mph during a time when Arkansas was staging a safe-driving campaign on its state roads. This happened in the late months of Hillary's pregnancy, so Clinton cracked, "Maybe we should name our baby Hot Rod-ham."

That was no-no on two counts: the mention of Hillary's name and his apparent insensitivity to highway safety. It grated against the public and constituted a "double whammy" against the governor. Nothing he did for the rest of the campaign seemed to sit well with the voters.

The returns by nightfall on election day put Frank White into a comfortable lead and prompted him to quip when a reporter asked whether the voters were trying to send Bill Clinton a message, "I think they're sending a message that they want me to be governor!"

Elsewhere across the country, voters were sending President Carter a message: They wanted Ronald Reagan to be president.

And likewise in Arkansas, the people had spoken—nearly 840,000—and a plurality of more than 32,000 supported the challenger.

Wednesday, November 5, dawned and Clinton was a lame-duck governor.

Little Rock's KAAY-Radio's morning talk show host, Ray Lincoln, was the first to jest about Clinton's defeat.

"Mornin' folks. Guess who I ran into at the supermarket early this morning? Bill and Hillary...they were hunting for boxes."

The first upset in an Arkansas gubernatorial contest in more than a quarter century was not so much an expression of an electorate's yearning for change as a desire to rid themselves of a leader who had failed them in his promise to lead.

Clinton himself would admit that he reached too far, trying to accomplish too much for a people with a "leave-us-alone" tradition.

As the 39 governors who preceded him in office, Clinton had to overcome a host of formidable obstacles in his efforts to effect change. And, as the saying goes, he learned the hard way.

Or as Professor Ledbetter had put it, Arkansas was founded 150 years ago as a haven from strong government, excessive taxation, and too many laws. Vestiges of that tradition remain, and no one knew it better than Clinton brain-truster Steve Smith, who bemoaned the defeat with this post-election eulogy:

"We probably did too much head bashing in the first term. Part of it was that people like me on the staff were sort of smart [alecks], and angered a lot of people. We were after every dragon in the land."

But, above all else, Clinton's administration did not endear itself to the electorate descended from people who for a century and a half resisted change. Not since Winthrop Rockefeller had been elected governor in a major upset in 1966 had Arkansas been headed by a progressive with a bent to turn the state's fortunes around.

Rockefeller was followed by a procession of other revisionist governors. But given the built-in obstacles they faced from the people they were trying to benefit, their achievements never rose above the spotty. And while Clinton came into power a beneficiary of sorts of that evolving tradition of office, there were still many reforms that were needed but which he could not effect.

When Clinton took office in 1978, Arkansas ranked dead last or almost at the bottom in the nation in per capita income, unemployment rates, average weekly wages, teacher salaries, education, health insurance, and in a host of other categories.

According to veteran lawmaker John E. Miller, a member of the Arkansas house for some 35 years, Clinton tried to do a great deal for the state but "the perception was out there that he was going to do what he wanted without consulting anybody."

Clinton himself analyzed his shortcomings:

"I simply didn't communicate to the people that I genuinely cared about...I think maybe I gave the appearance of trying to do too many things and not involving the people as I should have."

His biggest failing was that he was looking out more for his own interests than for the people's—a characteristic that will cling to him like a second skin for all the rest of his political life.

Two years to the day from taking the oath of office in the house chamber, Clinton returned to face a joint session of the legislature with his wife and nearly year-old daughter held in her mother's arms. Now he was the defeated candidate and serving his last minutes as Arkansas's governor.

Shedding Tears over His Loss

The *Arkansas Gazette* recorded that poignant scene and Clinton's farewell address:

"It was an upstream speech, moving against the current of political fashion. But, as the governor remarked, Arkansas remains 51st—last—in the payment of state and local taxes.

"We pay less taxes than the people in any other state in the Union, not to mention the District of Columbia," Clinton told the lawmakers. "Accordingly, we are at the bottom in the level of public services in nearly every category, from teacher salaries to higher education to unemployment compensation. There is but one answer— broadening the tax base—and the state will have to come to it, sooner or later, meantime settling for the barest minimums in services expected in the American society."

The *Arkansas Gazette* tribute concluded with this sentimental sendoff to the outgoing governor:

"It is sad to see Clinton go, departing public life for an indeterminate period before the comeback campaign...that everyone knows is certain. We have always thought of Bill Clinton as something special. No one in Arkansas in modern times has been elected governor so young with so much promise. If circumstances joined with certain errors in political judgment to deny him the customary second term, inevitably Clinton has learned lessons that will serve him in the future."

Indeed he had learned lessons. He decided that, "The people gave me the message: You were too young, too arrogant, too ambitious, and too insensitive."

Hillary's Cattle Trades: $106,035 of Nonkosher Steer

Clinton had tears in his eyes during his address to the legislature, and again when he spoke to reporters who besieged him for comment about his tomorrows.

"I'll take life a day at a time," he said, reiterating what he told the press the morning after his election loss in November. "I've decided to practice law but I fully expect to make a comeback. I'm not a quitter."

This was the question being asked by the political pundits who had every expectation that Clinton would come roaring back for his old job:

"Can a political leopard like Bill Clinton change his spots?"

It would be two years before the answer comes.

Meanwhile, the Clintons went to live in an elegant, nineteenth-century-style house on fashionable Midland Avenue in Little Rock's upscale Hillcrest section.

In time the Clintons would be asked about this residence and to explain how they managed to put their hands on $60,000 up-front money to buy the house. Hillary would tell the press during the '92 presidential campaign that the house was purchased, in large part, "from savings and a gift from my parents."

Nothing could have been further from the truth.

The funds with which the Clintons paid for this sumptuous dwelling, which tax stamps show was sold for $110,000, came from the brokerage offices of Stephens, Inc., and Tyson Foods' major domo James Blair's broker Red Bone's Refco firm, which had handled Hillary's commodity futures trades from October 1978 to May 1980, when Hillary abruptly bailed out of the market.

Here's the *inside* on Hillary's activity in that volatile investment venture that has all the earmarks of *insider trading*.

Hardly a better example of this illegal and most unethical practice can be cited than the way Hillary plunged into this market in October 1978. It has every appearance of what became the insider-trading scourge of Wall Street's financial institutions and brokerages in the 1980s.

The signs were visible immediately after Blair began to *steer* Hillary on ways to play with *steer*: dabble in the cattle futures market and ride the tail end of the go-go years in the riskiest of all investment undertakings.

The bottom fell out of that market at the end of 1979, after Bill Clinton became a lame-duck governor and his wife had turned herself into a *self-made woman* with two successive *killings* in cattle futures trading before calling it quits.

Her first score came just after she "invested" in that market in October 1978. She earned $26,541 in a quick two months.

The next 12 months of 1979 continued to be gravy times for savvy traders—players who knew precisely when to ring the bell before prices rose or fell.

Hillary evidently kept the gong clanging right through those fruitful, yet always perilous times and, incredibly, into the first five months of 1980—without being blown away as so many investors had been after the market went into an end-of-year tailspin.

Then she pulled out—closing her accounts in Refco, Inc., which Blair had opened for her, and the shadowy Stephens, Inc., account in Little Rock, which Hillary herself launched with $5,000.

By that time, May 1980, Hillary had made another $79,494.

But that figure can't be reconciled by looking at the Clintons' tax returns and their reportable incomes, which actually amounted to a total gain of $106,035 over Hillary's 19-month involvement in commodity futures trading. Here's why:

Her financial profile for the 12 months of 1979 shows Hillary's net profit from trading amounted to $72,436. That figure is faithfully mirrored in the Clintons' joint U.S. Individual Income Tax Return for that year, prepared and mailed on April 14, 1980, just a day before the IRS's deadline for filing.

The Clintons' 1978 return also accurately reports Hillary's quick end-of-the-year two-month $26,541 killing.

Without argument, the Clintons' accountings from October 1978 to December 1979 cannot be disputed. They reflect that Hillary netted $98,977 over a 14-month period playing commodity futures.

Perfectly correct and truthful reports.

However, that still leaves an unaccounted $7,058 that Hillary had pulled down in the first five months of 1980 before bowing out of the commodities market, with the grand total of $106,035 for her 19-month gamble that was launched with a $1,000 ante.

It would take 14 years to fathom that mystery.

The bottom of the conundrum is reached after one moves to early 1994, a time the Clinton *co-presidency* has entered its second year—and writers like the *New York Time*'s Jeff Gerth, Dean Baquet, and Stephen Lebaton are exposing Hillary's strange machinations in the cattle-futures market, and the *New York Post*'s Ray Kerrison is going a giant step further.

"Hillary Rodham Clinton's $100,000 kill in the commodity market is so patently implausible that it cries out for official investigation by the Commodity Futures Trading Commission, which regulates the market."

Kerrison goes on to thread the tapestry of what has the "strong smell of *fowl* play" (Arkansas-based Tyson Foods is America's leading poultry producer) by challenging the CFTC to look into "questions that are crying out for answers":

How did Hillary make more profitable trades than losing trades—in a market where "the best and biggest traders might win [only] 30 percent of the time"?

Why did a newcomer to the business like Hillary open two accounts "when many professionals have only one"?

Who made the decision on what to trade and who called the trades into the brokerage houses—Hillary, Blair, or someone else?

How much of her own money did Hillary "put at risk to get into the game...did she put up $4,000, $10,000"?

[The White House will claim Hillary put up $1,000—a sum far smaller than commodities traders uniformly require from clients in such a risky business. They will withhold word about the other $5,000 investment until the Clintons' backs are put to the wall for explanations.]

And the biggest mystery of all, "if Hillary was so spectacularly successful that she could make $100,000 a year trading commodities, *why did she stop in 1979 and not take it up again?*"

Hillary's first—and only—word on the subject was that she got out because she was pregnant and couldn't tolerate the pressures of commodity trading. To her critics, that seemed far-fetched, for why couldn't she have let an expert like Jim Blair keep on handling her account? His almost flawless track record makes it seem the logical thing to have done.

Kerrison's conclusion on the mysterious trades is, "Hillary's $100,000 hit has the appearance of a *money transfer disguised as commodity profits.*

[Translation: This looks like money dumped into the Clintons' coffers for *services rendered*—or to be rendered by the next governor of Arkansas.]

"If the Clintons...refuse to release these transactions, her records and those of James Blair should be subpoenaed by the Special Counsel and/or the Commodity Regulatory Commission—before they are shredded." [The records were obtained by Bob Fiske in April 1994.]

"The bottom line here is that as James Blair worked with Hillary to make her rich in commodity trading, his other client, Tyson Foods, began reaping huge benefits from the state of Arkansas, governed by Bill Clinton."

While the author has yet to see the *real* records bearing on Hillary Rodham Clinton's odoriferous, and probably illegal tradings in cattle futures, other records, thanks to deep-digging reporters like Ray Kerrison, Jeff Gerth, Dean Baquet, and Stephen Lebaton, show that a real doozy of a *steer* may be in for a roping.

They don't mention Red Bone's unsavory past as a deceitful trader of commodities, whose forte had been illegal mirror trading. He was caught in the act not just once, but twice—once before his cattle trades for Hillary began, then again after he sold off for her.

Regulators disciplined Bone for trading violations, which included "parking" or "allocating" trades after arbitrarily determining whether his customers were winners or losers.

For example, if Hillary were one of his fair-haired clients fated to have a raft of winning trades (with an occasional losing one to make the account look kosher), that could have been the method by which she made her 10,000 percent killing.

If indeed Hillary had knowingly allowed Jim Blair and Red Bone—and perhaps the Stephens clan, too—to *allocate* other customers' winnings to her accounts and to *park* her losses in those of others, then she had committed the ultimate fraud.

If it can be proved that such a practice was followed—and she was aware of it—she would have committed a significant breach of trading rules and a serious violation of ethics.

According to Ray Kerrison, his study of commodities trading in the late '70s shows no speculator could make more than $400 profit on any day with one contract of cattle futures.

"If Hillary made $5,300 in one day," Kerrison reports, "Hillary would have had to buy 13 contracts.

And that would have involved 232 tons of beef valued at $280,000. There is no way that the commodity exchange or a broker would permit a novice speculator to control $280,000 worth of cattle with a skimpy $1,000.

"Not, that is, *unless a friend, guardian or partner guaranteed her investment.*

"And if some 'angel'—such as her mentor James Blair or her broker...Bone—did guarantee the investment, it would amount to a payoff."

Significantly, in this very area the White House has resolutely refused to release the details of Hillary's trades—it has released only a carefully selected partial history of that trading.

But in early April 1994, an increasingly garrulous press, frustrated by the games the White House was playing, sent in the B-52s. It was bombs away bringing the Clintons' personal lawyer, David Kendall, out of his bunker waving a white flag.

The Clintons gave Kendall the signal to release **all** of their returns since Bill had entered public life. Thus the four years from 1977 through 1980, which the White House zealously guarded, were put in the public domain.

And what should happen?

Eureka! Kendall has made a monumental *discovery.*

The Clintons' 1980 tax return has *an error.*

Kendall calls it an "oversight."

The IRS calls it a "damnable and outrageous rip-off."

Arkansas's first couple failed to report a $6,498 profit on Stephens account trades between January and May of 1980, when Hillary tossed in the towel for good on commodity futures betting. The actual gain was that $7,058 cited earlier, but broker fees reduced the net to $6,498.

To an IRS examiner visited by the author at the agency's Long Island offices in Smithtown, it appears to be "a damnable and outrageous rip-off." Apparently, they believed they could get away with that stuff because they must not be filing any *gains* with the IRS because, as the evidence seems to indicate, this account was maintained to reflect Mrs. Clinton's commodity trade *losses.*"

The agent suggested the Clintons finally breasted with the truth because "the special prosecutor has probably subpoenaed [he has indeed] the Stephens firm's records of the first lady's trades, and the conflict would soon become apparent when reconciling the gains and losses with the figures on the couples' 1980 tax return."

Kendall's disclosure also forced another confession:

Hillary hadn't stopped trading, as she claimed earlier, because she "did not have the stomach for it anymore and found it to be nerve-racking" after she became pregnant with Chelsea.

The statement that Hillary ceased all trading and closed her accounts in November 1979 wasn't true.

She continued to bet on cows, hogs, soybeans, and other commodities right through Chelsea's birth in February—all the way into May 1980. Only then did she close the accounts with Refco and Stephens.

In 1994, now that Bill and Hillary were caught with their hands in the cookie jar—much as they had been nabbed by the *New York Times* twice before with the double rip-off on their 1985-86 tax returns in the Whitewater caper—the pangs on their conscience apparently were too much to bear and moved them to atone for their sins.

They whipped out their checkbook in a gesture intended to denote magnanimousness, and scratched a $13,449 check to the Treasury Department and another $1,166 check to the Arkansas tax collector to cover their $6,498 "oversight" on which they should have paid $3,829 in federal and state taxes.

They allowed $10,786 above the figure owed to cover accrued interest for their 14-year shafting of Uncle Sam.

Besides revealing that Hillary made that $26,541 profit in 1978, the Clintons' tax return shows they also deducted $10,131 for interest payments to the Great Southern Land Company, a corporate entity controlled by Madison Guaranty's James McDougal—their partner in Whitewater Development.

The payments were to service two loans used to buy the 230 acres in the Ozarks, one for $20,000 taken out in June 1978, the other for $183,000, taken out in August 1978. Both loans carried a 10 percent interest rate.

No one paid much attention to those loans—until Jim McDougal called a press conference in Little Rock on April 12, 1994, to release Whitewater documents he had finally received from the White House. And then he unlimbered his fire at Hillary with both barrels:

"Hillary consulted with me about how to reduce her tax liabilities from her commodities speculation that earned her nearly one hundred thousand dollars in seventy-eight and seventy-nine.

"The only suggestion I had was that since we had accrued interest payable [on the Whitewater loans] which we had not paid, to go ahead and pay it previous to the due day of the note, to let the tax write-off fall in the year in which she had an extraordinary profit."

In short, McDougal recommended this ploy to Hillary as a tax shelter. This brought another immediate about-face by the White House, which had said the interest payments represented the "losses" the first couple took in their Whitewater venture.

"Yes," Dee Dee Myers reluctantly conceded when confronted with McDougal's claims. "The Clintons did use it to shield commodity profits...but they probably didn't get into it with that in mind.

"I mean, if you look at their tax returns, they offset interest in one investment with profits on another investment the way the tax code is set up...they got into it as an investment."

Tax experts agreed that interest prepayments are a proper method of sheltering income from another source—so long as the interest is actually accrued and paid in the year it's deducted.

But McDougal's revelations that the interest payments were part of a conscious tax-shielding strategy raised serious questions about the size of the deduction taken by the Clintons in '78.

"They would be entitled to that portion of the interest that related to them," the Associated Press reported after an interview with Atlanta tax lawyer N. Jerold Cohen, a former Internal Revenue Service chief counsel.

For, with the Clintons and McDougals jointly responsible for interest payments amounting to $20,000 annually, it is unclear how the Clintons could have accrued a $10,000 liability in just a half-year.

12

WIFE AND MOTHER PROBLEMS

He Becomes "Available Bill"

In retrospect, Bill Clinton might have survived Frank White's onslaught were it not for Ronald Reagan's whitewashing of Jimmy Carter in the Democratic Party's 1980 debacle.

But the national landslide wasn't the only force seasoned political observers calculated had cost Clinton the governorship.

White, a savings and loan president and a political novice, had hammered away at the higher highway imposts and the Cuban refugee problem. Yet Clinton maintained a lead in the polls until Arkansans cast their ballots on election day.

So why did Clinton lose?

Mostly because he found too many distractions along the way to fulfill the desires of the people who elected him to be their full-time governor.

His '78 victory made him an instant media darling. He was projected as one of the decade's rising political stars. His popularity even bowled over Democratic National Chairman John White, who inadvisably let it be known that Clinton was presidential timber and might make the ticket as early as 1984.

On the heels of such clamor, the National Conference of Democratic Governors elected him chairman and showcased his obvious oratorical skills in a nationally televised speech to delegates at the 1980 Democratic National Convention. But the delegates ignored the Clinton-for-vice-president talk, which the "baby boomer" governor's boosters had propagandized. The convention went for the incumbent Carter-Mondale team again.

After his showcasing in the national spotlight, Clinton hurriedly made himself over into "available Bill" for the TV networks whenever news programs needed comment or analysis on one political topic or another.

All this distracted Clinton from state business—and the voters were not unmindful of that. Some perceived the governor to be an unconcerned, uncaring, young whippersnapper who was using their state as a stepping stone to national office.

Of course, the universal resentment of Hillary Clinton for using her maiden name and for her seeming divorcement from his campaign for reelection never abated either.

So, despite the polls which had him out in front of his rival, Clinton was nosed out by Frank White. In his 52-to-48 percent margin loss, the defeated incumbent was repentant as he conceded the election:

"The people sent me a message—and I learned my lesson."

It was then back to Blackstone. Bill joined the law firm of Wright, Lindsey, and Jennings at a salary reputed to be a shade more than the $35,000 a year he made as governor.

Clinton gave his private practice even less attention than he had invested in his duties as attorney general. Now his mission was to return to the office from which Frank White had ousted him.

Clinton virtually began his campaign for the 1982 Democratic gubernatorial nomination before the paint for the lettering for his name on his door had dried. Barely three weeks out of the governor's job, Clinton went on TV and apologized for raising highway taxes and promised he'd serve the state of Arkansas and its people "more faithfully and diligently" if the voters ever returned him to the statehouse.

Meanwhile, Frank White did little to distinguish himself as governor. The months ground by, and he increasingly gave every appearance of being a disaster.

By late April 1982, a month before the gubernatorial primaries, White had failed to fulfill his 1980 campaign promise to bring more industry and jobs into Arkansas. His own appointees to the State Utilities Commission had approved a steep rate increase that cost consumers $130 million, while the gas and electric barons increased their profits by nearly 50 percent.

Ironically, among those lining his pockets was Thomas F. (Mack) McLarty, chairman and chief executive officer of Arkansas Louisiana Gas Company, the largest utility in the state. McLarty, Bill Clinton's childhood chum in Hope, who attended Boys' State and Boys' Nation as a high school teen with Bill, didn't suffer too harshly when Clinton was attorney general. An editorial writer mockingly suggested the state's first lawyer went out of his way to "cultivate" an anti-utility, pro-consumer image.

Now White went all out to give the utilities every spare nickel they could get out of Arkansas's residential and commercial customers. Politics, as it's practiced in Arkansas, makes no rhyme or reason—whether the player's a Republican or a Democrat.

Clinton was nearly as much a stranger at his law firm, Wright, Lindsey, and Jennings as before he'd been hired on with the title "of counsel." His prolonged absences occurred as he crisscrossed the state pleading with voters for a second chance, pledging that he would listen much more carefully to the voice of the people this time around.

"I made a young man's mistake," he came clean on the eve of the primary. "I had an agenda a mile long that you couldn't achieve in a four-year term, let alone a two-year term. I was so busy doing what I wanted to do that I didn't leave enough time to correct mistakes."

His public contrition was almost enough to win a majority in a crowded primary field of four. Clinton overcame the challenges of State Senator Ken Hendren and Congressman Jim Guy Tucker, his friend who had opened the door for Bill to run for his first public office as attorney general.

Total victory was denied Clinton by former Lieutenant Governor Joe Purcell. Purcell, who served under Clinton during 1978-80 and was a loser on the 1980 ticket with the governor, received enough votes to force a runoff.

Clinton then defeated Purcell by a substantial margin and prepared for what promised to be a bitter rematch with Governor White.

With his own campaign phrase, "You can't lead without listening," ringing over the length and breadth of Arkansas, Clinton found himself facing a tiger—or, more accurately, a man leading a leopard on a leash.

White went on television with a live, full-grown, jungle cat and reminded voters that neither the leopard nor the former governor was likely to change his spots.

White also stung Clinton for his stand on capital punishment, asserting that he would have executed even more criminals than he'd done—"if Clinton hadn't commuted the sentences of so many dozens of death row inmates."

Once again Clinton had to backpedal on his past record.

"I pledge to be more restrained in handing out commutations when I am governor," he declared.

Bill Invites the Bimbo Factor

Long before November's election, the rumor mills began to grind out reports about the "bimbo factor," which they stressed was nothing new for Bill Clinton, but his mistresses had not been given the attention they should have received in print.

One of the first to put her finger on the problem with Clinton and the women who chased him was his old friend Betsey Wright, who had known him since the McGovern presidential campaign in Texas.

Precisely when Bill Clinton's reported infidelities began has never been established completely. There were reports that he began "messing around" just as soon as he and Hillary returned from their Mexican "family honeymoon" to their U of A Law School teaching posts.

"Hillary's tolerance for some of his behavior just amazes me," said Betsey Wright in an interview with *Vanity Fair*.

"Bill was always very careless, out of an unbelievable naiveté. He had a *defective shit detector* [author's emphasis] about personal relationships sometimes."

Clinton tolerated "bimbos" and "groupies" who clung to him at virtually every campaign whistle stop, or even when he was on official business.

"They were on the streets, sidewalks, in choirs, singing at his church. They were in the walls here [the governor's mansion]. And nationwide!" Miss Wright said.

"We'd go to a National Governors Association meeting and there'd be women licking his feet. There were always so many women who were throwing themselves at him. And he was naive about that.

"They'd want to take photos, and he'd stand there with his arm around them and not understand that it was naive. They'd go, 'Governor Clinton, I want to meet you,' and then the batting of the eyes and the silly gaze and the brushing of the shoulders would begin.

"When Chelsea and Hillary would both go and do something together at night, or when they were both out of town, his idea of a really exciting thing to do was go to the movies by himself. Well, we had rumors all over the place before the movies were out about how he was really there for some secret rendezvous or something sad like that.

"His attitude was, 'I don't care. I'm not gonna let people rob me of going to the movies by myself if I want to just because they want to make up stupid things.'"

But according to Miss Wright, the rumors had enough substance to make his wife not only aware of his contretemps with the bimbos, but to be even tolerant and understanding of her husband's infidelities.

"I think," Miss Wright concluded significantly, "Hillary knew those women weren't important."

The Women Who Were Important

Clinton's extramarital liaisons were a distraction for Hillary, to be sure. They were also of considerable concern to his staff, who knew the problems the bimbo factor could cause the candidate as he stirred the pot for his comeback.

Yet, despite his infidelities, Clinton's political star seemed to be rising anew. The campaign began much earlier than any statewide political race in memory because Clinton wanted to show voters he had turned a new leaf.

It wasn't enough that Bill was rehabilitating himself with the voters. Hillary also was remaking herself into a different, more acceptable person to please the finicky Arkansas electorate. She stopped using her maiden name for the time being and also undertook a rigorous and relentless speech-making schedule, plugging her husband's proposed new programs, hitting his rival's shortcomings and failures in office, and in general being a one-woman whirlwind.

Hillary cut her hair and ditched her thick-lensed spectacles for the newly marketed soft contact lenses that afforded her a totally different—and more appealing—look.

Bill, too, began sporting a changed appearance. He had his barber shorten his locks so his ears showed. He got rid of the bearded brain trust that editor John Robert Starr found so reprehensible and replaced them with clean-shaven, older men as his counselors who commanded not only greater respect from the media, but from the public as well.

Seeing the change coming in the next election as early as the summer of '81, Frank White took off the gloves and began pounding the rival he had unseated in the last election. He hammered unmercifully at Clinton's "ultra left-wing liberalism," his inability to deal with the Cuban refugee uprisings, and other political shortcomings. Some of the governor's sharpest barbs were against Hillary.

"You can't wash the spots off a leopard," became White's battle cry. "It's still Hillary Rodham and Bill Clinton."

As the campaign boiled hotter, Bill could scarcely wait for Sundays to roll around—the one day he found surcease from the frantic, nerve-shattering road to election.

But his day of rest on that Sunday of June 28, 1981, was not his idea of the respite Bill expected.

The phone rang in the early afternoon at the Clinton's Midland Avenue home. His mother was calling.

"It...it...happened again," Virginia Dwire gasped in a halting, hesitant tone, according to a family source made privy to the conversation. "Another patient...how can I say it...expired...just like the last time."

This news at once suggested his mother was in for trouble at the hospital where she was a nurse-anesthetist.

Mrs. Dwire had to explain at length about the latest patient, for her cryptic opening instantly brought to mind a previous case. Clinton listened while his mother described the second fatality in the operating theater.

He could still recall the remorseless details of an earlier bungled anesthesiological procedure during abdominal surgery performed in 1978 on 23-year-old Laura Lee Slayton. At the time, Clinton was finishing his term as attorney general and campaigning for governor. He was a powerful political figure and his stature weighed significantly in the way the case was adjudicated then.

Laura Slayton was on the operating table under anesthesia when her oxygen supply, being administered by nurse-anesthetist Virginia Dwire, was abruptly cut off. Attending surgeons became aware at once of the need to restore oxygen and commanded Mrs. Dwire to do so. But she was unable to respond. The patient died before the routine surgery could be completed.

Following Miss Slayton's death, some doctors and others on the hospital staff openly offered reasons for feeling uncomfortable working with Virginia Dwire in the operating room. There were murmurings, however, that she was "an untouchable," that she had "immunity" and couldn't be dumped as the hospital's nurse-anesthetist. Her son was a powerful politician and was likely to be the next governor. Quachita Hospital wanted the state's generous financial grants to go on.

Nothing came of those grumblings. Mrs. Dwire endured in her practice even as other whispers persisted. Some suggested she was too much the lady about town, who spent more time on those rounds than her professional duty call permitted: making whoopee in Hot Springs nightclubs into the early morning hours, following the ponies for long, tiring afternoons at the racetrack, then attending to demanding duties at the hospital with a body perhaps fatigued, mind clouded, eyes heavy-lidded. But most of all, they said that at age 56, Bill Clinton's mom was "getting on in years" and suggested the hospital ought to consider putting her out to pasture.

Nothing of the sort happened. Mrs. Dwire remained as the hospital's chief nurse-anesthetist at a salary reputed to be in six figures. Even after Laura Slayton's estate sued the hospital and its nurse-anesthetist for negligence, Mrs. Dwire's position didn't appear threatened. Not even after the hospital shelled out a large payment in an out-of-court settlement with the victim's family.

Now, four years later, Bill Clinton listened to his mother describe a second death that occurred while she was administering anesthesia to a patient on the operating table.

This was a nightmarish turn Bill Clinton could ill afford at this critical juncture in his comeback gubernatorial campaign. To protect his flanks against possible adverse publicity, he asked his mother to fill him in on what happened.

13

TRAGEDIES IN THE OPERATING ROOM

Five Teenagers on a Toot

The two-lane, potholed kidney-buster zigzagging the 50 miles between the tiny lumber mill town of Dierks and the bustling city of Hot Springs doesn't rate even a trace on the Rand McNally. But for the five young people in the 1978 Ford Fairlane it was their highway to heaven. The well-worn, blacktop, federal road was taking them from their hinterland hamlet of 1,692 rawboned, backwoods Arkansans to the sophisticated Big Town, renowned for its reparative mineral springs and reconstructive night life.

Soon after their departure, the passengers broke out their Bud six-packs. If when they reached their destination they weren't potted, they were after their spree of all-night dancing and heavy drinking.

The dashboard clock told the homebound revelers it was 5:30 a.m. on that Saturday of June 27, 1981.

They soon realized they were lost. They had breezed into a rundown neighborhood of the city trying to find their way back to Dierks.

The sight of five intoxicated young whites—a couple in the car's front seat and three in the back—wasn't as offensive as the actions they were soon to take.

The identity of only two of the Ford's passengers is relevant to the story, the others' names are not.

Seventeen-year-old Susie Deer, a fun-starved high schooler, who'd dropped out of class just before Christmas of 1980 to have a child out of wedlock, hadn't been anywhere much livelier than Dierks. She had begged her 23-year-old aunt, Diane Brown Cox, to take her partying.

All tuckered out after her first real fling, Susie slumped back in the rear seat of the car and closed her eyes. Beside her sat Aunt Diane, and to the latter's right, her beau, his arm around his date.

It isn't clear who was doing what as the Ford cruised the 400 block of Grand Avenue, but the Hot Springs Police Department can say the merrymakers got in a shouting match with people on the street.

A beer can was hurled out the car window and nearly hit one of the disputants. That provoked the near-target of the can to shout a heated protest.

To which the thrower replied, "Oh, why don't you shut your ass, mother fuckin' nigger!"

To 22-year-old Billy Ray Washington and his young, black, neighborhood friends on a street corner on a hot summer night, hearing that profanity prompted an instant response.

At Billy Ray's feet lay a hand-sized hunk of broken sidewalk concrete. He picked it up and hurled it at the car. The slab flew through the passenger side's open front window. It was her good fortune that the young, mini-skirted occupant of that seat was snuggled against the driver, for otherwise it would have been she, not Susie Deer, who'd be screaming now in frenzied anguish.

The concrete projectile hurtled to the back seat and smashed against the dozing Susie's face, rendering her mouth and nose a bloody pulp. It was evident at once that, drunk as he was, the driver had to get his injured passenger to a hospital.

It was a minute or so past 6 o'clock in the dawning hours of Saturday when the Ford screeched to a stop outside the ambulance entrance of Quachita Memorial Hospital. Susie, blood gushing from her face, was half-walked and half-carried into the emergency room by the two men in the party.

Her condition commanded an alert to ready the operating theater for surgery, while a doctor and nurses sutured Susie's wounds and sedated her with a pain killer.

Prepared for Emergency Surgery

Upstairs, green-frocked nurses and doctors, one a plastic surgeon, scrubbed up and attended to other preparations for the patient to be wheeled into the O.R., or the "pit," in the parlance of the wise-cracking nurse-anesthetist standing aside the operating table readying her equipment.

For 33 years Virginia Dwire had practiced her craft since earning her credentials after two years of concentrated study at New Orleans nurses' school. She had since dedicated herself to her profession, as the hospital records show, with diligence and devotion—yet not without blemish.

For three hours, Drs. William Schuelte, James Griffin, and William Johnson performed their medical and plastic surgery specialties on the patient's face. They set the broken jawbone, reconstructed her torn and lacerated lips and mouth (restoration of her broken teeth was to come later), and stitched her gashed left cheek.

All the while, nurse-anesthetist Virginia Dwire hovered over the patient, monitoring the liquids flowing through the I.V. tubes inserted in her arms and stabilizing the windpipe supplying air to Susie's lungs.

Before her niece was wheeled out of emergency and taken to the O.R., a doctor had assured a weeping Diane Cox that Susie's injuries, grotesque as they seemed, weren't life threatening.

"She'll be perfectly all right," he told her.

Now, three hours into the operation, the surgeons were prepared to set the broken cartilage in her nose.

Dr. Schuelte directed Mrs. Dwire to remove the breathing tube supplying oxygen to the anesthetized patient's lungs from her nose and insert it in her mouth.

"I watched the procedure," the physician said. "She tried to slip the tube into the girl's mouth and feed oxygen down her lungs at least two times, maybe more."

As Mrs. Dwire struggled vainly to restore the supply of oxygen to the patient, Dr. Griffin admonished her:

"For God's sake, force air into her...she's showing signs of being starved for oxygen."

Death under the Knife

Bill Clinton's mother finally managed to insert the tube in a seeming correct position—but it was too late. The patient had suffocated.

"She stopped breathing," was how Dr. Schuelte put it.

Dr. Schuelte, who has since retired from medicine, recognized at once the need for cardiopulmonary resuscitation, as did the other physicians.

Taking turns effecting the CPR procedure, the doctors pounded and massaged Susie's chest for the next hour and three minutes, but couldn't restore her heartbeat. She was pronounced dead on the operating table.

The body was transferred to a gurney, covered with a white sheet, and wheeled to an elevator that took it to the basement. The remains were placed in a refrigerated crypt to await removal to the state medical examiner's mortuary on Monday for autopsy.

Arkansas law grants the medical examiner sole authority to arrive at an official determination of how a person died when the cause appears to be suspicious or undetermined. Because Susie Deer had been struck by a rock and expired in surgery, the cause of death had to be determined by Dr. Fahmi Malak, an Egyptian-born pathologist appointed to his $90,000-a-year chief medical examiner's post in 1979 by first-term Governor Bill Clinton.

Meanwhile, it fell to one of the doctors from O.R. to bear the news of Susie Deer's death to her aunt and the others, who'd been waiting long, anxious hours for some word about the progress of the operation.

Diane Cox and her companions weren't given specifics of the way Susie had died. They didn't hear the discussion among the operating room staff—after nurse-anesthetist Dwire departed the hospital. They spoke about the way she handled the air tube, the difficulties she encountered, incomprehensibly being unable to position the device properly in the patient's mouth, and her failure to respond to Dr. Griffin's commands to feed the patient's lungs with oxygen when her breathing became labored and asphyxiation was setting in.

They talked, too, about Virginia Dwire's past bungled anesthesiological procedure performed on Laura Lee Slayton in the same operating room in 1978. Miss Slayton had died in much the same way as Susie Deer—after the oxygen supply to her lungs was cut off and Virginia Dwire was unable to respond to the emergency.

When Susie was put to sleep by Mrs. Dwire, not she, not her aunt, not her companions who brought her to the hospital, were aware of the anesthetist's past difficulty in administering oxygen to a patient in O.R

Even the suit for negligence that Miss Slayton's heirs initiated in 1979, after her death, had not yet been adjudicated. It would not be for more than two years, when for reasons never made public, it was settled out of court. According to records on file in Arkansas State Supreme Court, Miss Slayton's estate received a payment of $90,000.

Because the case didn't go to trial, more extensive details of Laura Slayton's death remain under seal. All that's known of the way she died during surgery is this brief, official pronouncement from the hospital:

"While under anesthesia being administered by Virginia Dwire, the patient went into coma, her breathing became labored, and she expired."

Called a "Mother F——in' Nigger"

Susie Deer's death prompted immediate action by the Hot Springs police, who had earlier responded to the scene of the disturbance involving Billy Ray Washington, who told authorities, "Those dudes were making fun of me...they called me a mother fuckin' nigger, too...so I picked me up a rock and got between the bushes...then I threw it, tryin' to hit the car...I didn't know if it was gonna hit anyone or what, ya know."

Washington was released after interrogation. But as soon as Susie's death was reported to the police, homicide detectives were dispatched to his Grand Avenue neighborhood and Washington was arrested. The charge: negligent homicide.

Washington's family retained a young Hot Springs lawyer, J. Sky Tapp, to defend Billy. Tapp had been in practice just three years, yet he was determined to defend his client with all the wiles of a veteran lawyer.

"You threw that rock because you had reasonable cause after those foul-mouthed words were shouted to you," Tapp said to Washington. "I'm confident I can plea-bargain this and get you off with a light sentence."

Tapp had no more idea than Washington how Susie Deer died: that she did not succumb to the injuries inflicted by the rock Billy hurled at her, but by the apparent operating room negligence of an anesthetist. Tapp and Washington would not learn that fact until four months passed. It would be October before Tapp learned the truth and set out to seek redress for his client.

Tapp filed a motion on October 15 to remove Washington's plea, because Susie Deer's death wasn't caused by the defendant's negligence but "by other intervening circumstances." Neither the lawyer nor his client knew about the medical examiner's cover-up that absolved Mrs. Dwire in Susie Deer's death and placed blame on Billy Ray Washington.

Dr. Malak prepared his report on Monday, June 29, after his assistant, Jesse Chandler, the pathologist's chief investigator, claimed Susie Deer's body at Quachita Hospital and delivered it to the mortuary for autopsy. The report was reviewed—and approved—by Malak and Chandler's boss, Dr. M. Joycelyn Elders, the Arkansas Health Director who was subsequently rewarded by appointment to Surgeon General of the United States in the Clinton administration.

Besides the clothing the victim was wearing when struck by the rock, Chandler brought the hospital records to the morgue and turned them over to Malak. Those records included the doctors' reports and comments about Virginia Dwire's performance in the operating room.

Malak himself conducted pathology on Susie Deer's remains, then prepared the report on his findings. He ruled the cause of death was **"homicide...resulting from injuries suffered when struck by rock thrown by assailant Billy Ray Washington..."**

Incredibly, his report made no mention of the problem anesthetist Virginia Dwire had with the breathing tube, or of the concerns the doctors expressed about her ability to continue in her work.

Thus Billy Ray Washington, not told the victim died because of negligence in the operating room, and believing he killed her, went off to serve his time.

Bill's Mom Seizes the Records

"Let me tell you something, Sky...Billy Ray didn't kill that girl."

"Hey, Mr. Lawyer, listen to me...why don't you check out the hospital records and see who really killed Susie Deer."

Calls. Middle-of-the-night-calls. The phone ringing off the hook. Some pal trying to make his lawyer believe Billy Ray shouldn't be in jail?

It didn't take more than three such pre-dawn-hour awakenings to convince Sky Tapp he must indeed look at those records.

But someone had been to the state's archives ahead of him. Not that the records weren't available, but copies had been obtained previously—by somebody who shouldn't have been allowed even to look at them.

Virginia Dwire.

In light of Sky Tapp's discovery that Mrs. Dwire was given access to the autopsy report, the question had to be asked:

What kind of clout did Virginia Dwire have to be shown a report the State Crime Laboratory does not release to anyone except prosecuting and defense attorneys for evidentiary purposes in homicide trials?

Permission had to have come from the very top of the State Health Department—the office of the director, Dr. M. Joycelyn Elders. No inquiry was ever conducted to determine who ordered the release of the privileged autopsy report to the person who precipitated the patient's death.

Why would Mrs. Dwire want to see the report in the first place?

The answer from Mrs. Dwire herself was that she wanted to see the report because she "was worried." In time she would add, "I wanted to satisfy my own curiosity about Susie Deer's death."

Once her curiosity was satisfied, did Mrs. Dwire go public and offer herself in defendant Ray Washington's place?

Of course not. So Billy Ray Washington did time behind bars for a death the attending physicians in the operating theater had clearly laid at Mrs. Dwire's feet.

"Curiosity," as she put it, wasn't the only reason Mrs. Dwire was driven to illicitly obtain the autopsy findings.

She was compelled to get her hands on it because, at long last, she was being dealt with by the governors of Quachita Hospital. Obviously, she had to arm herself against the hospital's action that followed demands to give Mrs.Dwire her walking papers. Susie Deer's death was the last straw for the hospital's doctors.

Consequently, the Quachita's board finally ended Mrs. Dwire's association with the hospital by contracting for the services of Dr. Robert Humphries, the anesthetist at Little Rock's St. Joseph's Hospital.

But Mrs. Dwire wouldn't hear of it. She filed a federal antitrust lawsuit, charging the hospital's action created a monopoly in the state capital, since Dr. Humphries would then become the sole anesthetist in Little Rock. The suit was dismissed in 1984 by a federal judge. Shortly thereafter, word went around that Virginia Dwire had let her anesthetist's license lapse. This left her with only a registered nurse's certification to keep her hand in medicine.

When Virginia Dwire chose to cross swords with Quachita Hospital, she stirred a hornet's nest that brought a swarm of them not on her alone, but on her son as well.

She Reads *Racing Form* in O.R.

Before the antitrust suit was dismissed, the hospital's attorneys obtained depositions from Mrs. Dwire. In those cross-examinations, she was asked about her conduct in the operating room during Susie Deer's operation and her purpose in obtaining the medical examiner's report.

The questioning brought out an embarrassing series of responses.

• She was very greatly concerned with her performance in the O.R. during Susie Deer's surgery.

• While administering anesthesia, she often read the *Racing Form.*

• She also filed her nails when she was monitoring the breathing apparatus while her patients lay sedated and under the knife.

The lawyers also dredged testimony out of Virginia Dwire that in time would embarrass the governor and force him to lie repeatedly about his role in one of the biggest scandals of his long-running administration.

No one deserves more credit than defense attorney J. Sky Tapp. His efforts alone brought to light the duplicity and the cover-up Dr. Malak orchestrated, not by commission but by omission, to save Virginia Dwire's reputation and job. Dr. Malak spared her from the possibility of arrest, prosecution, and imprisonment for the very homicide charge lodged instead against Billy Ray Washington.

After Tapp received a favorable ruling on his motion to throw out Washington's plea, he subpoenaed all the doctors, nurses, police, and others involved in Susie Deer's case so he could establish through their testimony that Mrs. Dwire was to blame for the girl's death.

"But I then hit a roadblock," Tapp revealed. "All the witnesses indicated they would not readily cooperate. That suggested a huge expenditure for the defense to compel those I subpoenaed to testify. We'd also have to retain an outside medical examiner to expose Dr. Malak's duplicity in preparing his autopsy report.

"Billy didn't have that kind of money. And I was only in my third year of legal practice. I was against very powerful people who could cause me a powerful lot of trouble."

So, on advice of counsel, Washington went back to court, reentered his no-contest plea, and went off to serve the rest of his six-month sentence.

The hospital's lawyers weren't out to establish whether Dr. Malak bungled when he prepared the autopsy report on Susie Deer's death, which effectively exonerated Mrs. Dwire. By then they knew Malak's reputation well. He had compiled an appalling record of professional ineptitude—and was to become far more proficient in that deficiency as the years rolled by.

Nor did they care to know whether Malak prepared his report to curry favor with Clinton.

What they wanted was the bottom line:

Had Bill Clinton been in touch with Dr. Malak when he prepared his report?

Strange the doctors did not ask Malak the question but posed it, instead, to Bill Clinton's mother. Perhaps they didn't talk to Malak about Clinton because they had already heard Malak was saying he didn't know Mrs. Dwire was the highly placed politician's mother. Although later, Jesse Chandler, Malak's aide, would say he not only reported the problems in the O.R. to his superior—but also told him that the nurse-anesthetist involved was Clinton's mother.

Mrs. Dwire was evasive with her responses. The lawyers couldn't get her to say that Clinton—who at the time was in private law practice—had spoken with Malak. But they succeeded in getting her to admit that she discussed Susie Deer's death with Bill Clinton—something Clinton to this day refuses to acknowledge and insists "couldn't possibly have happened."

Mom Admits: "I Spoke to Bill"

Here's the verbatim question-and-answer exchange in the deposition:

Q. Do you know or have you heard whether Bill Clinton ever had any contact with the Medical Examiner [about the Susie Deer case]?

A. I have no recollection of it.

Q. Do you deny that that occurred?

A. I deny recalling it.

Q. So you're denying any recollection that your son, Bill Clinton, had contact with the Medical Examiner prior to the autopsy report being filed in the Deere [sic] case?

A. I do not recall at this time.

Q. Did you ever have any conversations with Bill Clinton about that?

A. Yes, I did.

When Mrs. Dwire was asked to divulge the substance of those conversations, her attorney objected on grounds that it would violate the attorney-client privilege. Some heated sparring followed between the lawyers, then the quiz continued.

Q. Have you ever consulted Bill Clinton as an attorney regarding the subject matter of the autopsy report in the Deere [sic] case?

A. Yes, I have.

Q. Did you do that before or after the autopsy report was filed?

A. I don't recall.

Writing in *The New Republic* magazine's edition of August 3, 1992, Mark Hosenball, a producer for television's "Dateline NBC," gave this report:

"The questions surrounding Deer's death lay buried for nearly a decade. What resurrected it was a public crusade against Malak for his incompetence in a variety of cases. Over a five-year period (out of his twelve years in office), Malak had been challenged in court at least seventeen times by other pathologists; the National Association of Medical Examiners says this is an unusually high figure. Malak's misjudgments became so notorious that a group of families formed a pressure group called VOMIT (Victims Of Malak's Incredible Testimony) to picket his public appearance and pressure the governor [by then, Bill Clinton was back in that office] to remove him."

Despite the great public controversy and VOMIT's impassioned pleas, the governor turned a deaf ear to all appeals to fire Malak. In fact when the demands grew loudest, he gave the medical examiner a hefty raise in salary—to $106,000, making him the second-highest paid official on the state's payroll.

There exist different levels of inferior individual effort, but Dr. Fahmi Malak's examples of incompetence set new standards for awfulness.

Dr. Malak was never at his worst than when he performed autopsies on the mangled remains of two 17-year-old high school chums found lying on railroad tracks in Arkansas's Saline County.

Kevin Ives and Don Henry had gone out in the early hours of a hot, August night in 1987. They planned to return to Don's house where Kevin would sleep over. But the understanding with his mother, Linda Ives, was that Kevin would phone and assure her he had arrived home with his friend and all was well.

"He won't be coming home," Kevin's mother said cryptically about his son after Don's worried father phoned about the boys. "I think he's dead," she continued, saying she had a premonition of the boys' deaths. When Henry asked, "How [did Don die]?, Mrs. Ives replied, "I don't know how. I think a train."

Mrs. Ives was correct in saying she didn't know how the boys died. She was wrong about the train. The train hadn't killed them—even though Dr. Fahmi Malak, who performed the autopsies in the state morgue in Little Rock, ruled the deaths accidental, caused by the train that ran over the two teenagers.

Mrs. Ives refused to believe her son and his friend "would be so dumb as to be on the tracks in the dead of night and let themselves be run over" by a slow-moving freight train on a steep, mountain grade and not be alerted to its approach by the loud groan of the diesel engine straining to pull 40 cars.

"Well, I just wanted my son's death investigated," Mrs. Ives said at a later time on "Dateline NBC," which aired a report titled "Family Connection." In this report Brian Ross asked, "Does the doctor [Malak] have something on the presidential candidate and his mother? Is there a family connection?"

Malak's Blunders Stir a Storm

The highly rated, weekly NBC-TV magazine co-hosted by Jane Pauley and Stone

Phillips, opened with an introduction by Phillips:

"This man's blunder as chief medical examiner caused an uproar in Arkansas and led to the collapse of a big murder case."

The cameras then showed Dr. Malak, scenes of protesters calling for his ouster, and a police photo of a murder victim whose suspected killer, as later segments of the broadcast established, had the murder charge against him dropped because of Malak's testimony in court.

State prosecutor Paul Bosson came on camera to say that Malak read the wrong lab slides the morning of the trial and his testimony caused the case to collapse.

Dr. Malak's botched efforts in the murder case didn't remotely compare with the incompetence he demonstrated in his handling of the autopsies of Kevin Ives and Don Henry.

The noise Mrs. Ives made over Malak's "accidental" ruling in the boys' deaths led to a grand jury investigation described by Brian Ross:

"...to the astonishment of experts who later conducted a second autopsy, Dr. Malak failed to notice clear evidence of beating marks and a stab wound. But Dr. Malak never admitted making a mistake."

Mrs. Ives' two-year crusade to have Malak's decision in the boys' deaths overturned and a murder investigation opened succeeded when a grand jury was convened in 1989 and concluded that it was not just a train accident. The boys had been murdered!

The competent pathology belatedly performed by other medical examiners determined that Kevin Ives and Don Henry had been beaten and stabbed before they were laid on the railroad tracks to have their bodies mutilated under the wheels of a half-mile-long freight train to cover the murder.

Fahmi Malak performed admirably for the killer or killers once more. They have yet to be apprehended.

After Mrs. Ives' courageous efforts to set the record straight on how the deaths were caused, calls were made to her home from all over Arkansas, from people who said Malak had bungled their cases.

"And what began four years ago, as a simple effort by one mother to get her son's death investigated," Stone Phillips told his viewers, "led to a big political controversy in Arkansas and a statewide campaign to get Dr. Malak fired, all raising a lot of questions about Governor Bill Clinton; about why, as more and more came out, the governor's office seemed to be defending and protecting Dr. Malak."

Clinton refused to be interviewed by "Dateline NBC's Brian Ross, but his presidential campaign committee faxed a statement to the producers:

"There has never been any connection between my mother's professional experiences and actions I have taken or not taken as governor of Arkansas, and I resent any implications otherwise...I do not have the professional knowledge necessary to judge the competency of a forensic pathologist."

Note the way that statement is cagily couched: "...actions I have taken or not taken *as governor of Arkansas.*"

At the time Bill Clinton's mother was involved in Susie Deer's death, when medical records and other data were obtained illegally for Mrs. Dwire's use, and at the time she admitted under oath she had spoken to her son, Bill Clinton *was not the governor*!

Another Slick Willie, eely attempt to slither away from a breast with the truth?

"Dateline NBC's" Mark Hosenball and Brian Ross think so.

So do the directors of Quachita Hospital.

As do the droves of viewers who responded with angry letters demanding Clinton come clean after the nationally broadcast TV show was aired during the height of the '92 presidential campaign.

A further indication of Clinton's effort to distance himself from the Dwire-Malak controversy is to be found in his claim that it wasn't the governor's decision to keep the doctor as the state's chief medical examiner for all the years he served in that office—despite the never-ending cascade of complaints against him. Clinton cited a state commission that supposedly is charged with overseeing the operations of the medical examiner's office. It was this commission that decided whether Malak was competent, Clinton maintained.

By taking refuge in this *fairy tale*, Clinton could not mitigate his own seeming dereliction in not removing Malak from his post. For, in the decade of the 1980s, the commissioners hadn't met more than four times—and never reviewed autopsy findings. They limited their inquiries to the way the medical examiner's *office* functioned.

The Malak-Dwire-Clinton Axis

While there's no hard proof—no memoranda, no tape recordings, no known or available records of any kind—to show the "Family Connection" that "Dateline NBC" set out to define, such documentation isn't required to establish that there's more to the *Malak-Dwire-Clinton Axis* than meets the eye.

"The only time I ever knew that Malak was involved in any way, shape, or form with anything Mother had ever done was that, when you said what you said."

That's Bill Clinton denying to *Arkansas Gazette* reporter Joe Nabbefeld that he discussed with either his mother or Malak any aspect of the Susie Deer case.

When Mrs. Dwire testified at the deposition-taking, she was under oath. She was facing several lawyers when she took that oath. And she clearly answered, "Yes, I have" when asked, "Have you ever consulted Bill Clinton as an attorney regarding the subject matter of the autopsy reporting the Deere [*sic*] case?"

Clinton's recollection about all of the above grew less categorical when his aide, Betsey Wright, issued a response to yet another question about the governor's involvement—or noninvolvement—in the case of the 17-year-old girl from the hamlet of Dierks:

"He did not represent [his mother] in the case of Susie Deer. Neither does he *recall* [author's emphasis] 'interceding' with Dr. Malak."

That is quite a turnabout after Clinton's earlier certitude that he didn't even discuss Malak or the Susie Deer matter with his mother or the medical examiner.

And quite a turnabout for Bill Clinton's mother, too, who in a 1992 interview with a weekly newspaper in Clinton's hometown of Hope made yet another flip-flop:

"Bill never knew about this patient [Susie Deer] and still doesn't. My lands, *I never talked to him about my patients* [author's heavy stress]."

Punishment: A Slap on the Wrist

This story has a happy ending.

Bill Clinton removed Dr. Fahmi Malak from his medical examiner's job.

And he "punished" the good doctor as severely as he claims he could—by shunting him off to the state health department to monitor venereal disease, putting him into a job that paid a mere $70,000 per annum for his incompetence.

And the governor came down like a feathered sledgehammer on Dr. Malak's expense account. He was to receive future reimbursement for travel only for trips taken strictly for business.

Clinton also placed severe restrictions on meal allowances. The state would pay only for the doc's meals on official out-of-town trips made on health department matters and which bore only on his new specialty: the control of venereal disease.

Some cynics suggested Clinton took this action against Dr. Malak only because he was thinking about his own future.

The governor waited all of three weeks following his *punishment* of the controversial doctor to announce his candidacy for the Democratic presidential nomination.

Some cynics feared, that if elected, Clinton might repent the action he took against Dr. Malak and appoint him to his cabinet—as surgeon general of the United States.

Instead, President-elect Clinton picked Malak's boss, Dr. M. Joycelyn Elders, under whose aegis Malak practiced his incompetence for a dozen years in the medical examiner's office.

In truth, Dr. Elders didn't come to be surgeon general without bearing some of the onus of Dr. Malak's botched autopsy on Susie Deer. For she was aware of her subordinate's incompetence and calls for his ouster. Yet she never lifted a finger to remove Malak despite a deafening cataract of criticism.

Her office also approved the illegal release of the tainted autopsy report to Mrs. Dwire when she was not entitled under law to receive it.

Still, Clinton's choice of Dr. Elders for the nation's top medical post was a fortuitous one, his critics chide. He could have done much worse with the likes of Dr. Malak.

14

BILL ROARS BACK,
BUT TROUBLES BREW

Hillary's Name Is a Hindrance

Dr. Fahmi Malak was not the problem for Bill Clinton in 1981 as he made his way around the state laying the groundwork for the 1982 gubernatorial race.

By the end of '81, Bill and Hillary had decided that their careers in private law practice should be placed on the back burner if Bill Clinton was to return to the statehouse.

Thus they took leave from their respective law firms 17 months before the election. But not before February of '82, with nine months to go before election day, did they begin campaigning in earnest.

Bill called a press conference and, with Hillary at his side cuddling little Chelsea in her arms, he officially announced his candidacy for governor.

While Bill attracted considerable interest among the reporters, Hillary commanded even greater attention. She made it a point to inform the press that from this day forward she'd call herself Mrs. Clinton.

That pronouncement didn't cause as much of a stir among the journalists as did Hillary's divergence from it later in the year. She left the campaign trail unexpectedly, returned to the Rose Law Firm, fetched her brief case, and hauled it into a Little Rock courtroom to argue an appeal before the bench on behalf of her office.

Embarrassment followed after reporters trooped to the courtroom and found the judge addressing her as "Madam counsel Hillary Rodham." When reporters confronted her as to why she went back to using her maiden name, Hillary stormed at them angrily:

"I don't have to change my name. I've been Mrs. Bill Clinton since the day we were married."

Further questioning caused Hillary to admit that, no, she had not legally changed her maiden name to her husband's—and, yes, she was still on the election board's registration rolls as Hillary Rodham.

The controversy wouldn't go away and suddenly mushroomed into a national *cause celebre*. The *Washington Post*'s correspondent in Little Rock primed the pump of widespread ridicule in a feature that prompted the unflattering headline, **CHANGING ALL THOSE CHANGES**.

Explaining, *once again,* why she now, at last, was going to change the practice of using her maiden name, Hillary said, "It became a kind of growing concern among [Bill Clinton's] supporters, who came to see me in droves, or called me on the phone and related story after story, and said, 'We really wish you would think about this.'"

Stressing that her husband had never asked her to stop using her maiden name, Hillary went on:

"I joked one time that probably the only man in Arkansas who didn't ask me to change my name was my husband—who said, 'This is your decision and you do exactly what you want.' And so I did. I just decided that it was not an issue that was that big to me when it came right down to it."

But in the next breath, Hillary advanced yet another explanation that she admitted was closer to the truth. This time she was speaking to the *Arkansas Democrat*:

"I kept my maiden name when I married because it was important to me that I be judged on my merits and that Bill be judged on his merits...but I was not at all prepared about the concern people expressed about this decision which we had made personally."

Bill's Mom Marries Her Fourth

Once Hillary Rodham adopted her husband's name on the campaign trail, the crowds warmed up to her. But not for that alone. She worked ceaselessly for her husband's election. She went all over the state to speak, and her style was a winning one. Many saw in Hillary's deliveries a warmth that Bill Clinton's speeches lacked. She also appeared better able to address issues, to put across her husband's proposed programs with greater articulation and persuasiveness.

Despite the goodwill she amassed for her husband, the 1982 gubernatorial race was not a happy jaunt for Hillary. Governor Frank White kept pounding away at her with no less venom than he was dumping on her husband.

With election day nearing, White blasted away while at the Arkansas Republican Convention in September:

"Bill Clinton cannot change his spots. You can't wash the spots off a leopard...it's still Hillary Rodham and Bill Clinton."

With that theme serving as his battle cry, Frank White headed into the midterm election oozing with confidence.

During the campaign, Bill Clinton's mother decided to end her ten years of widowhood. Her third husband of six years, Jeff Dwire, had succumbed in 1972 to the complications of diabetes.

For several years, Mrs. Dwire had been acquainted with Richard W. Kelley, a Hot Springs food broker. They dated with increasing frequency until one day in 1982 Kelley popped the question and Virginia, who was seven years younger than her 67-year-old swain, said yes.

Bill, Hillary, and Chelsea attended the private civil ceremony held on January 17 in Little Rock and celebrated afterward with a wedding supper in That Little Restaurant, where European cuisine was served and live music featured nuptial tunes. The fête was arranged by Clinton friends Dr. Thomas Jansen and Janet Honeycutt, the restaurant's co-owners.

Virginia Kelley settled into a comfortable life of retirement in Hot Springs with her new husband. She narrowed her interests to two: thoroughbred racing and taking the hour-long drive with her husband to Little Rock to "watch my little granddaughter grow up."

The Kelleys and Hillary's parents, the Rodhams, were all on hand in the Clintons' Midland Avenue house on election eve, November 2.

The results touched off Democratic Party celebrations throughout Arkansas. Clinton was declared the winner over incumbent Frank White with a 55-to-45 percent margin of victory.

During the holidays the Clintons packed their possessions and readied them to be lugged out of their Midland Avenue house. Soon after, on inauguration day, the moving van carted their possessions to Center Street and swiftly disgorged its cargo into the governor's mansion.

Later, the returning occupants were installed as Arkansas's 42nd governor and first lady in the packed statehouse chamber.

Clinton spoke glowingly about his plans to turn Arkansas around by beefing up education. He also promised to target legislative reforms on business and consumer affairs.

That night, a record crowd attended the inaugural ball in the State House Convention Center and spilled over into the grand ballroom of the recently opened Excelsior Hotel.

The crowd gushed as Hillary waltzed into the ballroom on the arm of her tuxedoed husband. The first lady was attired in a floor-length gown of Chantilly lace. The 4.25-carat Arkansas diamond, the centerpiece around milady's neck at the 1979 inaugural ball, now sparkled from its solitaire ring setting upon a platinum band on her hand.

Bill drew hearty laughter when he thanked his supporters for "coming to this nice little intimate party for a few friends." Then he escorted Hillary to the dance floor where they brought the house down by pirouetting to the strains of "You'll Never Know," played by the Betty Fowler Orchestra. Earlier, musicians had saluted the Arkansas governor and first lady on their arrival with the popular New Deal tune "Happy Days Are Here Again."

The only somber note had come earlier, during the inaugural ceremonies, when the Clintons had learned that Hillary's father, Hugh Rodham, had experienced chest pains and had been admitted to University Hospital for tests. After his condition was diagnosed as stable, the Rodhams—mother Dorothy and sons Hugh Jr. and Tony—attended the inaugural ball, as did newlyweds Richard and Virginia Kelley, and Clinton's half brother, Roger.

He's the Education Governor Now

Not many days later, Bill Clinton returned to the house chamber and delivered his

State of the State address before a joint session of the legislature.

Singling out education reform as his top priority, Clinton harped on a popular theme, for Arkansas had traditionally neglected its 371 school districts. In 1983 the state was paying its teachers the next-to-lowest salary in the 50 states. It was spending the least per pupil on education than only one state, Mississippi.

"Over the long run," Clinton told the lawmakers, "education is the key to our economic revival and our perennial quest for prosperity. We must dedicate more of our limited resources to paying teachers better; expanding educational opportunities in poor and small school districts; improving and diversifying vocational and high technology programs; and perhaps most important, strengthening basic education. Without competence in basic skills our people cannot move on to more advanced achievement."

Clinton didn't neglect other targets for legislative reforms, notably business and consumer affairs. But education remained his uppermost consideration.

His plan to raise teachers' salaries, provide more funds for educating pupils, and impose stricter requirements for teacher certification and academic achievement received widespread approbation. But his proposal to subject all public school teachers to a test of basic skills ran into a buzz saw of opposition from the Arkansas Education Association, which represented most of the state's teachers.

Despite the criticism, Clinton stuck to his guns and worked at a feverish pace with advisers and aides to shape what in time would become the controversial Education Reform Act. He hoped to present that package to the Arkansas legislature before the year was out.

Bill and Gennifer's Intermezzo

Meanwhile, it wasn't all work and no play for Governor Clinton. His affair with Gennifer Flowers had followed a course much like that of his political career. Just after Clinton surrendered the governor's office to Frank White in January 1981, Gennifer opted to pursue her singing career in Dallas, where opportunity beckoned.

For the next three years, their affair played an intermezzo. They met only occasionally while she was in Dallas. For a time, they saw nothing of each other. Gennifer had become a back-up singer with the Roy Clark country music ensemble. And the troupe went off on an extended tour of the United States, Canada, and Europe.

Upon her return, Bill and Gennifer carried on a long-distance liaison with stolen moments at the Excelsior Hotel on her visits to Little Rock, or idyllic, passion-filled evenings in Gennifer's apartment in Dallas, where Clinton often traveled under the pretense of "state business."

Gennifer has fond recollections of her resumed liaison with Clinton.

"The first time I went home [to Little Rock], Bill said I should take a room at the Excelsior. A lot of functions were held there, so he felt no one would question his being [at the hotel].

"After not seeing him for weeks at a time, when we did get together, it was wonderful. We'd dive into bed—and talk afterward."

Although they were living miles apart—a six-hour drive between Little Rock and

Dallas—the distance didn't inhibit their affair.

"A couple of months might go by before I'd see him, and then we'd get together twice in as many weeks. He'd come to Dallas *on business* and would sneak away to meet me.

"I was singing at the Pyramid Room in the Fairmont Hotel. Bill'd come to see me. If I hadn't had my career, I don't think I could ever have settled for being the 'other woman.'"

But Gennifer's recall about her career taking up slack in her secret affair with Clinton isn't how her best friend, Lauren Kirk, remembered it. Gennifer and Lauren, a Dallas Realtor/interior designer, shared a two-bedroom, $500-a-month apartment in Texas's leading metropolis for two years, from late 1983 through the end of 1985.

"Back [early] in 1984, she told me she was in love with someone called Bill who was breaking her heart," Lauren related. "That didn't mean anything to me. Who could this Bill from Arkansas be?"

It didn't occur to the roomie to ask Gennifer who her lover was. His visits to the apartment were discreet, and every time he was on his way, Lauren had to take her leave.

"Anytime he was to drop by, he'd phone. There'd be a long conversation. It didn't irritate me that she spent half her lifetime on the phone because we each had our own separate lines. But when she was finished talking with him, she'd come out of her room and say, 'That was Bill...now, Lauren, he's on his way...would you mind going somewhere?'"

In one of several interviews Lauren Kirk gave, she described in intimate detail the atmosphere Bill Clinton found in Gennifer's boudoir on his first visit early in 1983. Speaking to the *New York Post*'s premier gossip columnist, Cindy Adams, Lauren made this revelation:

"Her bedroom was made for sex. King-sized bed. Black satin sheets. Black satin spread. Zebra drapes and a canopy. She had candles and room fragrances. She went to the scent shop for those aromatic rings you stick on lampshades so they'll emit a fragrance. She put on special bedtime makeup, mascara and everything, and gorgeous negligees.

"Honey, she did it right. This girl should really write a book on romance because the way she prepared for bed was like a Gloria Swanson ceremony."

It wasn't until a long time after her initial introduction to the nondescript person named Bill that Lauren learned that Gennifer's man from Arkansas was its governor.

"When she told me it was Bill Clinton, I didn't pay much attention," said Lauren. "I'm not that much interested in politics.

"But every time he'd come into town, she'd get all excited, and when he left she'd be very depressed. I'd tell her it was silly to be involved with a married man. But he was very charming and she was blinded by him."

Gennifer, according to Lauren, half-expected Clinton would leave his wife for her.

"She wanted to believe that because he told her he wanted to be president. That gave Gennifer's ego a boost because she was just zany enough to believe she could become the first lady of the land."

"We Elected the Wrong Clinton"

By mid-1983, Hillary's role as Arkansas's first lady all at once was extended.

"We have talked about this subject more than any other issue," Clinton addressed a packed news conference in the statehouse. "This will guarantee I'll have someone closer to me than anyone else."

He had just named Hillary chairperson of his newly formed Arkansas Education Standards Committee, a body committed to reform the state's public schools. Just recently, the National Commission on Excellence in Education issued a report on "The Rising Tide of Mediocrity In Schools" and in its report, "Nation At Risk," listed Arkansas students pathetically below the national average in reading and mathematics.

Although Clinton was warned against appointing Hillary to the committee for fear that his administration would be accused of nepotism, such criticism didn't materialize. Hillary left the starting gate at full gallop, which pleased even her most outspoken detractors.

"One of the principal problems we face in our state, and apparently in the country, is that we are not expecting enough of ourselves, our schools, or our students," she told the *Arkansas Democrat*.

"We have an obligation to challenge our students and to set high expectations for them. Rather than setting minimum standards, we should set expectations and urge schools and districts to aim to achieve those expectations and not to be satisfied with meeting some artificial minimum."

While at first she appeared laid back, acting predominantly as a moderator at committee discussions, she eventually emerged as its most influential member. She so dominated the group that it came to be known as the "Hillary Committee."

Her agenda was written into a paper that prompted her husband to call an extraordinary session of the Arkansas Legislature in November 1983 at which he urged passage of the controversial Education Reform Act. The bill not only mandated the testing of teachers and imposed stiff requirements on school administrators to maintain acceptable accreditation, but also required all eighth-graders, beginning in 1987, to pass a high school entrance examination in no more than three tries before they could pursue a higher level of study. Then, to stem the staggering 30 percent high school dropout rate, school attendance was made compulsory until age 17.

By then, the legislators knew that the proposals Clinton advanced at the special session weren't his but had been hammered out by Hillary. She had brought that program to their attention at a committee hearing in late August. She told the lawmakers that the state must give its teachers better salaries to attract more competent instructors.

"We are looked upon as having too many teachers who are incompetent," she declared. "Whether that is fair, whether that is accurate or true, we are going to have to come to terms with the perceptions that they were. The problem and the perception had to be dealt with together."

Hillary also insisted that Arkansas had to accept its first sales tax increase in more than a quarter century so that the administration's proposed program could get off the ground.

The legislators gave Hillary a standing ovation. Observed standing in the hall outside the meeting room was Bill Clinton. Hillary nodded to him to come in and take a seat. He sat next to Senator Nick Wilson, a Democrat from Pocahontas. The governor wore a steady smile as he listened to his wife field questions and fire answers back for the better part of two hours.

Many legislators wondered whether the smile was sincere or a put-on—after Representative Lloyd George, another Democrat from Danville, finally burst out in admiration of Hillary's presentation:

"I think we've elected the wrong Clinton!"

Hillary swallowed hard. "No," she protested, "the work's too hard."

Lloyd George picked up on Nick Wilson's remark that Hillary "carries a lot more weight with the legislators and a lot of people out there in the state than Bill does."

Nudging Clinton playfully, George cracked, "I think when we prepare those bumper stickers that say 'Clinton For Governor,' we should make it clear that they say, 'Hillary, That Is'!"

Again Hillary swallowed hard. "Oh shush!" she burst out with a broad grin. "You're always getting me in trouble at home."

A Slick Chick Named Perdue

About this time, the governor was purported to be entangled with yet another former beauty queen. This one was to claim she first encountered Bill Clinton in 1973, before his marriage to Hillary.

The alleged affair was kept under wraps until July 17, 1992, halfway into the presidential campaign. Because Sally Perdue's account dwells upon this particular time of Bill Clinton's life, it must be chronicled here, the period when this one-time beauty queen from Arkansas claims the affair took place.

Cutting a still-lithe, attractive, and shapely figure despite her 53 years, Sally Perdue, who hailed from Pine Bluff, appeared on the ABC-TV "Sally Jessy Raphael Show" and informed the studio audience she had been Arkansas's 1958 entry in the Miss America Pageant—the second beauty queen linked to Bill Clinton. Lencola Sullivan was the first.

Like the Misses Sullivan and Gennifer Flowers, who were journalists for KARK-TV in the state capital, Miss Perdue also had been a television reporter, with Little Rock's PBS (Public Broadcast Service) station in the early '70s.

"I've known Bill or known of Bill, I guess, since 1973," Miss Perdue said on the TV show. "I was from Arkansas. I was very visible, had a television show and worked for a PBS station that was funded by the legislators. So I spent a lot of time in the senate. I worked for the state senate for a while, so I was around all those people. And there was an attraction, I guess [between her and Clinton], from the very beginning."

Despite that "attraction," Miss Perdue says no romantic interest developed with Clinton until 10 years passed. That came in August of 1983, she purports, at the very time when Hillary and Bill were busy hammering out the education bill.

By then, Sally Perdue persisted, she had been infuriated by a bad-mouthing that

Rand McNally, the map maker, gave her hometown of Pine Bluff, calling it "the second-worst place in the United States to live."

Miss Perdue was living in a Little Rock condominium at the time. Her proximity to the statehouse, she explained, prompted her to get in touch with Bill Clinton to enlist support from his office for development of a railroad historical society to improve the image of her Arkansas backwater community.

Unlike the long, warm-up stage in his affair with Gennifer Flowers, Miss Perdue said Clinton scored with her the night he went to her condo to discuss her ideas.

"Right from then it was a fun and games relationship," Sally professed. "Bill's driver would drop him off in a park near my condo and he'd sneak in through a back patio to have it with me for an hour, two hours, three hours—but never all night."

Each time, when Clinton was satisfied, said Sally Perdue, "he'd flick the patio lights on and off to summon his driver."

In the interview on the "Sally Jessy Raphael Show," Miss Perdue engaged in this exchange with her hostess:

RAPHAEL: Would you say you were the pursuer or would you say he was the pursuer?

PERDUE: I think it was a mutual...I think he saw in me maybe something that was a little different from your Arkansas woman.

RAPHAEL: Now, was he married at this time?

PERDUE: When I first met Bill, he was not [married] in seventy-three, but...

RAPHAEL: No, when the affair took place?

PERDUE: Yes. And I...I certainly accept full responsibility for that. I was not married. He was married.

RAPHAEL: Did it disturb you that this was a married man?

PERDUE: No, it did not disturb me because it was an affair of the moment. I was not looking beyond that.

RAPHAEL: Where did the sexual side of the affair take place?

PERDUE: In my condominium in Little Rock.

RAPHAEL: Did you go to dinner together and public places?

PERDUE: No, we were never seen publicly.

The relationship began to "sour" after "it got beyond a physical attraction and turned into a mental challenge," Sally told the other Sally before the TV cameras.

"I told Bill I was considering running for mayor of Pine Bluff. But he pooh-poohed my ambition. He said, 'The Democrats will destroy you [in the primaries].'"

That exchange ended their last evening together. The three-month relationship, as Sally Perdue put it, was "stone daid."

Seven months later, in May of 1984, Sally Perdue went on, she encountered Clinton at a University of Arkansas alumni function in Little Rock.

"I was the enemy by that time," lamented Miss Perdue. "He treated me like I was yesterday's dog's dinner."

Sally Perdue harbored no ill feelings toward Clinton.

"I never loved him. We were in it for the fun and games. And serious conversation was not to be brought up...I really don't think that Bill is saying what he thinks women want to hear."

There is one major flaw in Miss Perdue's story that Sally Jessy Raphael and other interviewers who latched on to the 53-year-old former beauty queen failed to recognize.

How could she have met Bill Clinton in the statehouse while she spent "a lot of time in the senate...[to be] around all these people...and there was an attraction [with Clinton], I guess, from the very beginning"?

In 1973, Bill Clinton had just graduated from Yale Law School and went off to Fayetteville to teach law at the University of Arkansas for the next two years.

Clinton did not step an official foot in Little Rock's statehouse until he was elected attorney general and began serving his term in January 1977—some four years after the date Sally Perdue claims they had their first encounter.

This flaw probably also caught the eye of Capital Cities Broadcasting, the parent company and owner of ABC. The show, taped before its airing, was abruptly canceled without any explanation and replaced with one of Sally Jessy's reruns.

Coke Probe in the Gov's Mansion

"Bill, I've come to tell you something not very pleasant and you may not want to hear it...but I must tell you about it."

Speaking was Colonel Thomas (Tommy) Goodwin, the head of the Arkansas State Police, appointed to his post by Governor Bill Clinton. The time Goodwin came to the governor's office bearing bad tidings is said to have been mid-summer of 1983.

He brought a visitor's log maintained by his state police, who served as security at the governor's mansion on Center Street. One of the entries that Goodwin showed Clinton read, "Roger and girl in," and the time noted was 7:25 p.m. on June 6, 1983, which referred to the arrival of the governor's half brother at that hour. He was accompanied by an unidentified female.

The log also recorded Roger going to the guest house at 9:20 p.m. But there was no mention of what happened to the girl.

Roger was also shown to have departed the guest house at 10:41 a.m. the next day. But the record again didn't show what became of his companion.

"Bill," Commander Goodwin then continued, "your brother is in deep shit. He has come to our attention in a sting operation we have going with the Federal Drug Administration...and the task force has filmed Roger selling cocaine to an informant."

The colonel paused for a moment, as he was to later describe his encounter with the governor. Then, "What do you want us to do?"

The conversation was reported in part by Joe Klein in *New York* magazine's January 20, 1992, edition.

"Do what you normally do," Klein quoted Clinton after he interviewed the then-presidential candidate, adding that the governor knew "it meant his brother would remain under surveillance for at least another month while the police tried to roll up the rest of the drug network."

"'I couldn't tell my mother, or her husband, or my brother. It was a nightmare,' Clinton recalled.

"'But it was the right thing to do. He had a four-gram-a-day habit. They said if he hadn't been in incredible physical shape, he would have died.'"

Thus Governor Bill Clinton had been informed as early as mid-summer of 1983 that his half brother was mixed up in illicit drug activity. In time he would flatly—and vehemently—deny he was aware of Roger's criminal excursions until early 1986—after Roger and one of Bill Clinton's closest political allies and benefactors, investment entrepreneur Dan R. Lasater, were arrested, indicted, prosecuted, convicted, and sentenced to prison as drug traffickers.

Bill Clinton's private life was now commanding almost as much, if not more attention than he was able to give to his office.

One thing Clinton could not escape: The gubernatorial mansion was not in his complete control, nor in Hillary's. And soon, the Clintons will lose all management. It will become a bawdy house, a shooting gallery, and a den of iniquity all rolled up into one—without anyone in charge.

15

THE CLINTONS' DEN OF INIQUITY

Bill's Half Brother's a Cokehead

The governor's mansion is guarded around the clock by the Arkansas State Police. Virtually all visitors are required to sign in and out, although the troopers make exceptions for family members and their guests.

"They just look the other way when one of Bill's or Hillary's relatives drop by," said Rodney Myers, a former close friend of the governor's younger half brother, Roger.

Myers is no longer a friend of Roger's because Myers ratted on him for turning the governor's mansion into a den of iniquity that featured out-of-control cocaine and sex orgies—under the very noses of the state police, who looked the other way and never reported the incidents to their superiors.

Since Roger had begun his visits to the stately, Georgian-style mansion, the air around the premises had become pregnant with the feeling that every time the governor's "little brother" walked into the white-columned dwelling he was carrying a time bomb with him.

Governor Bill Clinton apparently did not take the warning sounded by state trooper boss Tommy Goodwin too seriously. For Roger Clinton continued on his merry way, dropping into the mansion whenever the mood moved him—bringing women and, as it will develop, all sorts of illegal drugs. All this while Bill and Hillary Clinton were elsewhere in the mansion.

To many, it seemed inconceivable that Bill Clinton wasn't able to do something about his half brother's years-long, severe drug habit before it was brought to his attention by Commander Goodwin.

"Roger was in his teens when he became involved in the drug scene that was to lead to his downfall," Rodney Myers was quoted. "He was the great concern of his big brother, Bill, who was trying to straighten him out but didn't succeed."

Branded the "black sheep" of the Clinton clan in his early teens—Roger was said by Hot Springs sources to have been hooked on cocaine when hardly out of adolescence. He was purported to have launched his criminal career at 15 by selling drugs to his childhood chums.

Bill Clinton was 22 years old when he went off on his two-year pursuit of Rhodes scholar's studies at Oxford University. He left his widowed mother and 12-year-old half brother happy in the knowledge that they were no longer subjected to the violence he endured when he was Roger's age. Cancer had claimed Roger Clinton, Sr.'s life and an unaccustomed serenity settled upon the once-melancholy household.

But, except for a brief spell in 1969, when he spent part of his vacation between first and second year study in England with his mother and brother, Bill couldn't conceive of what life was really like at home.

It was a curious life that mother and son were living while Bill was away. Bill couldn't—or didn't want to—see how his teenaged brother was finding it increasingly difficult to shake off the traumas of his earlier childhood.

While Bill supposedly tried to straighten out Roger's involvement with drugs when he was a teenager, the evidence shows he failed totally in his efforts.

Nor was Bill able to assess his mother, Virginia's, oddish existence: weekdays spent from dawn to dusk anesthetizing patients in the hospital operating theater, nights devoted to the frenetic life she shared with her late husband in Hot Springs' nightclubs—and being unable as a widow to do without that intoxicating convention. Then came weekends at the racetrack and its betting windows, or immersion in a therapeutic hot tub at a mineral springs spa, or to do whatever else Virginia's mood moved her to.

Certainly his mother's prolonged absences from home must have influenced the drift young Roger took in his critical teen years, years whose importance was all too apparent to Bill Clinton when he told *New York* magazine writer Joe Klein that, as children of alcoholics, he and Roger had two options for their future: *become governor or a coke dealer.*

Bill Clinton's concession probably pained him to make, but it was reflective of a reality the man who became governor conceded on his own behalf and on behalf of the half brother who indeed became a "heavy" cocaine peddler.

When Roger Clinton, Jr., drifted into the world of drugs is something neither his brother nor he has discussed willingly. Nor can it be connected even tenuously to Bill Clinton's own involvement in the drug scene that he reluctantly owned up to early on during the '92 presidential primaries.

"I tried it a couple of times," Clinton professed about smoking marijuana when he attended Oxford. "I literally didn't like it and never did it again."

Clinton said he was 22 when he took his drags on pot because, as he put it, "I did what most everybody else did over there."

At that time Roger was 12 years old, and if Clinton didn't smoke a reefer following his return to Arkansas in late spring 1970, no link can plausibly be connected to his brother's addiction and the cankering results that followed.

No official record exists, so far as is known, to give a researcher a precise insight when and where Roger Clinton entered the drug scene. Yet his involvement both as a cocaine addict and peddler in his teen years is a generally accepted "fact" in Clinton's old Hot Springs neighborhood.

Drug Busters Eye Roger Clinton

So far as is known, Roger came under suspicion only after the formation of the Organized Crime Drug Enforcement Task Force in the late spring of 1983. This body was eventually staffed by members of the Federal Bureau of Investigation, Federal Drug Enforcement Administration, the Arkansas State Police, the Little Rock Police Department, and the North Little Rock Police Department.

The joint investigation was supervised overall by U.S. Attorney Asa Hutchinson of the Western District of Arkansas and U.S. Attorney George W. Proctor of the Eastern District. It was a heavy-duty, statewide crackdown on drug trafficking and the hunters were out to bag big game.

There's no question that the investigators' antennas shot up in July 1983 when they spotted Governor Clinton's younger brother, Roger, huddling with Sam Anderson and Curtis Lee "Chuck" Berry in what was perceived to be a drug transaction. This was the very first case of substance logged in the task force's file.

While Roger needed no introduction to the agents on the stakeout, Anderson and Berry weren't known to them. But as they'd soon learn, Anderson was a 39-year-old Hot Springs lawyer and Berry, 38, was employed as a chauffeur for Dan R. Lasater, the owner of Lasater & Company, one of the state's leading financial houses, with headquarters in Little Rock.

What interested the probers after the stakeout ended that day was to learn that Lasater was one of the governor's best friends and one of his biggest campaign contributors. What didn't show up in the early stages of the inquiry was the sudden gush of business Lasater & Company began experiencing as an underwriter of state bond issues just as soon as Bill Clinton regained office.

A preliminary tabulation for the first six months of Clinton's second term showed Lasater & Company was given $110 million in bond underwritings for the newly formed Arkansas Development Finance Authority. Clinton established the ADFA after he regained office as a way of attracting industry and commerce to the state.

He had lost his interest and affection for the little farmer and small business. The *big businesses* had Clinton wrapped around their fingers now.

The task force agents who watched Roger Clinton's meeting with Sam Anderson and Chuck Berry on that June afternoon suspected a drug transaction had brought them together. But they couldn't establish that with any certainty. They hadn't brought surveillance cameras or other equipment to record the scene. All they saw at this rendezvous was a handshake between Anderson and Berry after what appeared to be an introduction by young Clinton.

That was all it was, as authorities would later establish. Roger Clinton introduced Chuck Berry to Sam Anderson that day as a drug connection in Hot Springs who could sell him all the cocaine he'd ever want. All that Anderson required was $125 up-front cash for every ounce of "nose candy" he delivered.

As a matter of routine, the names of the three people who met that afternoon near the racetrack in Hot Springs were put through an FBI identification records search. Roger Clinton and Sam Anderson showed no "priors"—meaning they had never been arrested for a crime.

But the return on Curtis Lee "Chuck" Berry was a stunner.

Roger's Pal Is a Murderer

The FBI profile on Chuck Berry showed that he was a paroled killer who'd been sentenced to 10 years imprisonment in 1973 for the cold-blooded robbery-murder of a Little Rock nightclub owner.

Much mystery surrounded the case at that time, when Roger was 16 going on 17 and living in Hot Springs.

Both Chuck Berry and the man he blew away with a fusillade of five .38-caliber bullets fired at point-blank range were veteran troublemakers. David "Pete" Mack, Jr., the 42-year-old nightclub owner, had been in hot water with Little Rock police for years.

Pete's Place, on 610 West Ninth Street, was the scene of numerous shootings, stabbings, and gambling law violations since Mack took it over a half-dozen years before.

Police Chief Gale F. Weeks repeatedly petitioned Pulaski County Prosecutor Jim Guy Tucker to file a public nuisance suit against Pete's Place. But the pleas fell on deaf ears.

Reports prevail that Jim Guy Tucker, *who succeeded Clinton as governor of Arkansas and today continues in that office*, "was in somebody's hip pocket" to have allowed the crises at Pete's Place to fester.

Meanwhile, the police department itself came under a strange scrutiny after Jim Guy Tucker inexplicably instigated an investigation by the Fred Myers Private Detective Agency. The scenario approached Keystone Cops dimensions when private eyes were observed by Little Rock cops tailing their department's vice squad detectives on their rounds. Tucker tried to justify this comedy by saying he was out to "catch police taking payoffs at Pete's Place."

Tucker's investigation had also enlisted the services of the discredited Curtis Lee Berry—the pistol-packing, paroled killer—as an "undercover operative" to gather information on alleged police payoffs at the nightclub. Obviously, law enforcement had no compunction in using Berry as an informant despite his extensive—and still mushrooming—police record. As recently as the previous January 4, Berry was arrested for assault with a gun and fined $54.50. In March 1972, he was arrested for robbery and again fined $54.50. Both cases were handled by prosecutor Jim Guy Tucker's office.

Chuck Berry killed Pete Mack on April 13, 1973, after he went to Pete's Place at 1:10 a.m. and got into an argument with him. Berry pumped five bullets into Mack's chest and abdomen and ran. But he didn't get far. Little Rock Patrolman George Hirrell captured Berry in a doorway he tried to use for refuge.

On September 19, after a trial that ended with his conviction of second-degree murder, Berry was sentenced by Circuit Court Judge William J. Kirby to 10 years in prison.

During the trial, Berry, who is black, as was his victim, testified that he feared Mack or members of the police department vice squad would have him killed for his role as an informant and for having agreed to testify before the Pulaski County grand jury about payoffs to law enforcement people at Pete's Place.

In the aftermath of this long-ago courtroom saga, several matters still cry out for an explanation. That is because of Chuck Berry's association with Bill Clinton's brother, Roger, in 1983, after the Task Force operatives observed him introducing the ex-convict to Hot Springs attorney Sam Anderson, Jr., a boyhood chum of Clinton's.

What prompted Chuck Berry to suspect that Mack, or the vice squad, had targeted him for death?

Berry's trial centered extensively upon the activities of the 1971-72 administration of then-Pulaski County Prosecutor Jim Guy Tucker, who launched the investigation into purported police payoffs at Pete's Place. Tucker was subpoenaed and testified that he enlisted Berry as an informant and paid him $10 a night during December 1972 for his undercover work. Berry testified that he used the money to gamble and buy drinks.

Many Arkansans arched their eyebrows when Phillip McMath, a prominent lawyer, was retained to defend Berry along with two other top-of-the-line legal eagles, State Representative Henry J. Ostrloh and Leo Vehik, a former deputy prosecutor under Jim Guy Tucker who'd gone into private practice.

Why did a down-and-outer with an unsavory past like Curtis Lee Berry command such high-priced legal talent to conduct his defense? the public asked.

No answer. Nor had the *Arkansas Democrat* received a response when it declared, "The central question in the case is how Mack knew, if he really did, that Berry was an informant and had talked to the grand jury."

Great mystery clouded the case when Deputy Prosecutor Jimmy Patton, another member of Jim Guy Tucker's former staff, testified that Berry's undercover work couldn't have been compromised because *Tucker took the files of the case with him when he left office.* Tucker had been elected attorney general the previous November. "...*Took the files with him...?*" Of course! This is Arkansas!

Thus the question of who, if anyone, informed David "Pete" Mack that Curtis Lee "Chuck" Berry was tattling on him to authorities remained unanswered.

The above is prelude to Bill Clinton's own first election success in 1976, when he was handpicked by Jim Guy Tucker, Jr., to succeed him as attorney general on the Democratic ticket.

In 1990, after serving in other elected capacities the previous 14 years, Tucker became Governor Bill Clinton's running mate and on November 6 was elected lieutenant governor.

On January 2, 1993, when Clinton was inaugurated president, his old benefactor, Jim Guy Tucker—warts and all hanging fire from his curious role in the Pete's Place murder saga—succeeded his own hand-picked protégé as Arkansas's 43rd governor.

The Most Powerful Husband-Wife Political Partnership

"This was the golden age of Bill and Hillary Clintons' reign over the state of Arkansas," wrote Judith Warner in *Hillary Clinton: The Inside Story.* "They were frantically busy. Hillary's typical day, after work at the law firm, might include a conference, a cocktail reception at the governor's mansion, a museum-exhibition opening, and a dinner party, with her first meal (besides a vending-machine lunch) eaten at nearly ten o'clock at night. Often for dinner she merely sneaked hors-d'oeuvres in the kitchen during an official reception. Time with Bill was hard to catch. Hillary might wait up late at night for him, if she could. Otherwise, they saw each other while riding together in the limousine between events.

"They made every effort they could to find time together to relax and reconnect. Making personal time was essential to Hillary. It was so easy to be devoured by the governorship, to have no time left for a married life, a personal life, a social life..."

It's not necessary at this juncture to relive Governor Clinton's late-night excursions that kept him away from the governor's mansion for such lengthy periods as to make it impossible to have "time left for a married life, a personal life, a social life..." with wife Hillary.

In time, the wear and tear on Hillary as a wife and mother would take its toll. But not before she endured several more years of her husband's unfaithfulness, at times under her very nose.

The "golden age of Bill and Hillary Clintons' reign" didn't reach its zenith, as Ms. Warner implied in her book, after the 1986 election when Clinton was reelected to his fourth term and Arkansans assertedly had gotten a "two-for-one" deal at the polls. They had begun their rule as a husband-and-wife team as early as Clinton's first term. That was the beginning of their Ozark Mountains real estate venture that paved their path to one of the most powerful husband-and-wife political partnerships—and biggest political scandals—in state government. That scandal made 1994's headlines and is still being investigated by the special prosecutor and Congress as 1995 dawned.

16

A GOVERNOR OF COZY ACCOMMODATIONS

Bill Wins Some, Loses Some

Bill Clinton's second term as governor had a difficult launch. Much as he expressed a desire to better the lives of Arkansans, his programs met rock-hard opposition from the state's legislators.

For openers, Clinton introduced a utility reform package to the legislature that proposed electing members of the Public Service Commission, instead of letting the governor make the appointments. This gave authority to the PSC to deny utilities rate increases in times of economic difficulty.

The utilities opposed the bill on the laughable grounds that appointed commissioners were free from political pressures and were better able to safeguard consumers' interests than elected ones.

To convince the Insurance and Commerce Committee in the house to pass his bill, Clinton conveyed an elected PSC official from North Dakota to address the lawmakers. He told them that an elected PSC in the Sioux State was a commercial success and that North Dakota's utility rates were lower than in Arkansas.

The powerful utility interests, led by Arkansas Power and Light lobbyist Cecil Alexander, railed against House Bill 453, calling it "the most damaging" of all utility reform legislation. The Arkansas Chamber of Commerce allied with the utilities, warning that Clinton was trying to harm economic development and choke the state's business climate.

The measure finally died in committee.

Some say that no one was more delighted with the outcome than Governor Bill Clinton himself, the measure's most ardent proponent. For, had it passed the legislature and he was compelled to sign it into law, his best friend, "Mack" McLarty, the Arkansas-Louisiana (ARKLA) gas utility's majordomo stood to lose most by having elected PSC members overseeing utility rates. Without the governor's influence on the commission's members, whom he handpicked, how would ARKLA continue to flourish?

Clinton had yet to be targeted for the harsh criticism that PSC members were getting for their hefty allowances to both Arkansas Power & Light, the electric utility, and ARKLA, the natural gas supplier in the state. But the governor, sensing the public would inevitably blame him for the proliferating rates, publicly supported an elected PSC—a move he was confident could never happen because of the widespread opposition expected from the states' big business establishment.

"It's amazing to me the influence the utilities have on the Insurance and Commerce Committee," moaned Governor Clinton in what was perceived to be mock frustration. "I mean, we had an election in which utilities were a major issue, and now it's like we never had an election."

By this loss, Clinton (and McLarty) won big.

The next measure that appeared to give Clinton an Excedrin headache was House Bill 220. It sought to raise highway taxes for trucks entering Arkansas from other states. The measure, proposed by his own Highway Commissioner, Henry Gray, advocated upping the existing 73,000 pounds weight limit on trucks to 80,000. A companion measure, House Bill 192, covered repairs for the wear and tear on highways that heavier trucks would cause. The measure raised highway licensing fees for trucks, giving the state an additional $2.5 million to cover upkeep for the roads.

At the close of the legislative session, Clinton proclaimed the highway legislation as "a major accomplishment." Yet he drew catcalls from political watchdogs who chastised him as a "double-crosser," who said he was not a "flexible mediator" as he claimed to have been, but was a "fence-sitter" during the heated legislative battles waged on both bills.

Clinton's next legislative goal was the betterment of education in Arkansas. He was encouraged to take vigorous steps toward that goal after the Arkansas Supreme Court, responding to a suit by 11 of the state's school districts, ruled that Arkansas could no longer use the method by which the state's educational system was financed. The high court found that poor school districts were receiving a disproportionately small amount of assistance, and the wealthier ones benefited from the disparity.

Clinton immediately hopped on the court ruling by calling for a special legislative session to deal with Arkansas's education situation. He promised to push for a tax increase to pay for the improvements in classrooms.

"To put it bluntly," Clinton declared, "we've got to raise taxes to increase our investment in education. Arkansas is dead last in spending per child, and the Arkansas Supreme Court has just ordered us to spend more money in poorer districts to improve education there."

Clinton then outlined a program with a $17 million price tag.

"I hope to be able to convince you that we have to raise the money for education if we ever hope to get out of the economic backwater of our country, that this expenditure can bring greater economic opportunities to us, and that my program will do just that."

With a month to go before the legislature returned to tackle his agenda, Bill Clinton may or may not have been aware of developments being logged by the Organized Crime Drug Enforcement Task Force.

Roger's Drug Deals Mushroom

Clinton's half brother, Roger, was now a central figure in the probe. He became a *prime* target at the beginning of September 1983. Roger had not yet taken his seemingly permanent residency in the governor's mansion when the federal/state snoopers keyed on a Columbian emigré living in New York. He attracted attention by carrying cocaine from Brooklyn to Little Rock.

The man, named Maurice Rodriguez, in what appeared to be pure coincidence had become involved with one of Roger Clinton's ex-girlfriends, Lana Crews, who was from Hot Springs. Lana went to New York to attend drama school in early 1981. She met the 23-year-old Rodriguez and became his live-in girlfriend.

Soon afterward, she found that her lover "had access to large quantities of cocaine." A convenient discovery, for it enabled Lana's friends back in Hot Springs to benefit from her relationship with Rodriguez through shipments of the drug to them. The first to gain was the beau who succeeded Roger Clinton in Lana's affections back home, 22-year-old Russell Ray Crump.

Later, when Crump and others in the conspiracy were busted, he would tell how the "mule in New York" supplied him and others with cocaine:

"Rodriguez sent most of the stuff in small quantities by Federal Express...I sent payments to Rodriguez by Western Union."

The payments amounted to $2,000 for an ounce of coke.

Roger Clinton's involvement came about after Rodriguez journeyed to Little Rock, rendezvoused with Crump, and together went to a party at the home of "Jodie Mahoney," as he was known to them at the time. Roger Clinton was at the party and was introduced to Rodriguez by his old friend Crump.

Jodie Mahoney, authorities were to determine, was Joseph K. "Jodie" Mahony III, the 23-year-old son of State Representative Joseph K. "Jodie" Mahony, Jr. At that very time, the legislator was pressing hard for Governor Clinton's education reform legislation. Hillary Clinton was constantly in touch with Mahony, pressuring him to lobby the house for favorable action on the bill.

Young Mahoney, as Jodie spelled his name, for the shortest time had attended Hendrix College in Conway, Arkansas, with Roger Clinton, who went there for an even briefer period. Mahoney lived with his divorced mother. She was Assistant U.S. Attorney Shirley Bartley, who lived at 4 Crestmont Drive in suburban Little Rock's upper-income community of Robinwood. She was on the staff of U.S. Attorney George Proctor, who headed the Justice Department's office for the Eastern District of Arkansas—and was one of the top officials behind the joint task force drug investigation.

Before he made the governor's mansion his more-or-less permanent residence, Roger Clinton had lived with Jodie Mahoney in Robinwood, until January 1984.

In his statement to the grand jury at a later time, Russell Crump described the scene at the Crestmont Drive party in September 1983:

"When I arrived, Roger was in an upstairs bedroom weighing out some cocaine on a tri-beam scale. Lana and Maurice were downstairs in the game room.

"[During the party] Maurice told me that he would be staying at Jodie Mahoney's home."

Two months later, in November 1983, Rodriguez again journeyed to Hot Springs and stayed with Jodie Mahoney.

"At this time," Crump's sworn testimony went on, "Maurice told me that Roger was going to New York with him to pick up an unspecified quantity of cocaine...Roger and Maurice returned to Little Rock around the end of the first week in December 1983...Maurice told me he had sold Roger all the cocaine that Maurice hadn't kept for himself.

"...During the third week of February 1984, Maurice told me that if I flew back to New York with him to pick up ten to fifteen ounces of cocaine for Roger, he would deduct fifteen hundred dollars from what I owed him."

Crump said he accompanied Rodriguez back to the Big Apple, obtained nine ounces of coke from Rodriguez' brother, Tony, then concealed the bag of drugs in his coat pocket on the return flight to Little Rock. He and Maurice were on their way then to rendezvous with Roger Clinton, whom Crump said he phoned at the governor's mansion on landing at Adams Field Airport.

"Roger arrived at my apartment [in Little Rock] at about three-thirty p.m.," Crump swore. "Maurice gave Roger the package containing the cocaine, and Roger opened it for inspection."

After that transaction, Rodriguez left Little Rock and didn't return again until late March 1984. By then Roger's moves were under round-the-clock surveillance.

"It was at this time that Maurice told me Roger owed him sixteen thousand dollars for cocaine Maurice had fronted Roger with," Crump testified. "...Maurice collected only ten thousand dollars before he left."

Bill's "Closest Political Ally" Is a Drug Trafficker

Eight thousand of that sum was said to have been provided by Dan R. Lasater, the 40-year-old Little Rock millionaire investment banker and one of Governor Clinton's biggest campaign contributors, whom Clinton often described as "my closest political ally."

Reports would surface showing Clinton was totally aware of the financial assistance Lasater provided Roger, yet it would be more than three years from these early stages of the investigation before the governor would belatedly admit knowledge of this "political ally's" role in the drug probe and the financial bailout he provided to Roger Clinton.

Lasater was just now coming into the inquiry as a target.

Meanwhile, Lasater & Company continued receiving more and more bond underwritings for the Arkansas Development Finance Authority, a plum that was putting millions of dollars into Lasater's coffers, enabling Bill's good friend Dan to open branch offices elsewhere in the state and to become one of Arkansas's most affluent citizens. Lasater was able to acquire several other holdings, a result of Bill Clinton's largesse in naming him underwriter for the bulk of the state's bond business. Lasater purchased a horse farm in Summerfield, Florida, acquired a string of thoroughbred race horses, and bought a controlling interest in a restaurant chain that included Black-Eyed Peas Restaurants in Little Rock and Memphis, and the Dixie Cafe in Atlanta.

His $8,000 bailout of Roger Clinton came only after learning that he was threatened by Rodriguez, "who told me he was going to break my legs and get my brother and mother if I didn't cough up the money I owed him."

Authorities said no inference of a relationship should be drawn between the drug traffickers and Jodie's mother, Shirley Bartley, the federal prosecutor. She had moved out and gone to Washington for a year at the time the drug activity was recorded at her house.

She left just before the first cocaine deal was transacted in the house. Ms. Bartley had been summoned to the capital by the U.S. Department of Justice's Advocacy Institute. She was one of two federal prosecutors handpicked nationwide to coordinate the training of assistant U.S. Attorneys from all around the country.

Ironically, one of the areas of instruction was narcotics enforcement!

In the Chicken King's Hip Pocket

"After a year of his second lease on political life, Clinton looks stronger than he has been since his first legislative session in 1979. He has three groups of unalterable foes—the truckers, utilities, and teachers—but in each instance the fights have proved to be a net advantage for him."

Such was the assessment of *Arkansas Gazette* columnist Ernie Dumas in early February 1984 about the first half of Clinton's second term. Clinton had fulfilled only part of his campaign promise to give truckers the extra weight load they wanted to carry on the highways. He'd also reached a dubious compromise with the highway commissioners which did not win the truckers' hearts. They demanded more concessions.

The summer of 1984 was Bill Clinton's opportunity to shine for the first time before a nationwide television viewing audience. Only a month from his 38th birthday and still the nation's youngest governor, Clinton was summoned by the National Democratic Committee to speak before the national convention in San Francisco that opened July 18—less than four months before Arkansans were to vote for a governor.

The 1984 Democratic primary had not produced a formidable challenger to Clinton. Only the perennial candidate, turkey farmer Monroe Schwarzlose, and two unknowns, Kermit C. Moss and Lonnie Turner. Clinton relegated his rivals to memory by capturing 70 of the state's 75 counties. Clinton claimed that the 64 percent of the popular vote he received was a vote for his "referendum on education."

Arkansas Republicans nominated Jonesboro contractor Woody Freeman to oppose Clinton in November. A member of the state's Board of Higher Education, Freeman promised to work even harder than Clinton promised to improve education in Arkansas.

In San Francisco, Clinton spoke after a film clip was run in the smoke-filled convention hall that featured highlights from the presidency of Harry S. Truman, whom he had been asked to eulogize. Clinton found currency in Truman's presidency in the 1940s that applied to the 1980s.

"He'd remind us that 1948, like 1984, was a time of change, when new realities required new ideas and a willingness to stand up to interest groups both within and outside our party when the public interest demanded it. He'd tell us you can't please everybody in tough times and you shouldn't try."

Bill, accompanied by Hillary, remained for the duration of the convention, which nominated former Vice President Walter Mondale and New York Congresswoman Geraldine Ferraro.

The tab for the Clintons' five-day stay in San Francisco was picked up by the Democratic Party. Transportation was reportedly provided by poultry baron Don Tyson, chairman of the mammoth $4 billion-a-year Tyson Foods, Arkansas's largest business employer. Tyson and his family not only were heavy contributors to Clinton's campaigns, but also frequently furnished free rides to the governor and his wife in company planes.

Time magazine referred to this "cozy accommodation as an example of the frequent chumminess between southern governors and major industrialists." Correspondent George J. Church pointed out that Clinton "has been notably reluctant to fight the state's industries on environmental issues."

Writing in the April 13, 1992, edition of *Time*, Church noted, "Clinton has done virtually nothing to hinder clear-cutting on the 82% of Arkansas forest land that is privately owned."

Although Clinton backed a plan by the U.S. Forest Service to restrict clear-cutting, that was "nowhere near enough to please such environmental groups as the Sierra Club, which has filed suit."

Further evidence of Clinton's willingness to reach cozy accommodations with corporate interests was his do-nothing attitude toward the dangerous pollution caused by the poultry industry, Arkansas's most dominant. The industry was dumping tons of dried chicken excrement, known as litter, or droppings, on croplands in the northwestern part of the state.

"We're well past the land's capacity to accept the waste," contended Robert Leflar, a Sierra Club official. Leflar and other leading environmentalists feared the litter would seep through porous limestone and contaminate streams and groundwater.

"Clinton in 1990 appointed an animal-waste task force," reported George Church in his *Time* article entitled "How Clinton Ran Arkansas," with the subhead, "He won more battles than he lost but rarely upset special-interest groups in the process."

The Question of a "Crude Payoff"

Church wrote, "...a favorite tactic: his first move in almost any crisis is to appoint a task force or study commission, but it has yet to recommend any [positive action]."

The *Time* piece also raised the question of a "crude payoff" for Clinton's reluctance to clamp down on industrial polluters. But it pointed out that environmentalists "generally doubt" kickbacks are involved. What they believe in this case is that Clinton "genuinely—though in their view, mistakenly—fears that strict environmental regulations will cost the state badly needed employment."

Upon returning from San Francisco, Clinton was forced into making a critical decision involving a potentially steep rate increase that suddenly confronted the Arkansas Power & Light Company. A Federal Energy Regulatory Commission ruling had made it liable for a 36 percent share of construction costs for the Grand Gulf nuclear power plant in Mississippi. AP&L threatened to seek a 40 percent rate hike for its customers in the state.

Clinton went on record opposing the decision to assess AP&L for the Mississippi plant and threatened to create a public power authority to take over the utility. When AP&L struck a compromise with Mississippi Power and Light that reduced the share of construction costs to the Arkansas utility to 17 percent, Clinton still stood against the decision. He said AP&L should have to pay nothing.

Never "No" to Special Interests

Many viewed his stance as another of Bill Clinton's bluffs, designed to make it appear he was protecting the interest of Arkansas's ratepayers, when in fact, he wasn't so much the crusader as a pawn for special interest groups.

Time summarized this characteristic:

"Setting realistic priorities and putting together the coalition to achieve them are obviously skills a president must possess. But some of Clinton's critics wonder if a president should not also be a bit more of a crusader than Clinton has proved himself. In their view, the governor has been a bit too quick to settle for what he could get, a bit too reluctant to antagonize actual or potential supporters."

Little Rock attorney Tom McRae, who challenged Clinton in 1990 in his final Democratic gubernatorial primary, saw him as a political chameleon who "never wants to move until he takes a poll—he has retreated where he didn't have to."

Time then asked, "Could Clinton take on the special interests that have been blocking needed legislation on a national level any more effectively than he has stood up to special interests in Arkansas?"

The magazine answered its own question through correspondent George Church, aided by reporters Michael Riley and Richard Woodbury reporting from the field, respectively, in Atlanta and Little Rock:

"The situations of course are not fully comparable: Clinton would presumably come to power with a mandate for change and would wield far more power in the Oval Office than any governor—and especially a governor of Arkansas—ever can. Nonetheless, it is a troubling question that Clinton has not yet put to rest."

Roadblocks to a Third Term

His confrontation with the AP&L dilemma wasn't the only impediment to Clinton's third term of office. The Arkansas Education Association began making louder noises against the teacher-testing law. President Peggy Nabors let it be known the AEA had every intention to challenge it in court. Meanwhile, it stepped up its "teacher alert" commercials on Arkansas radio stations to warn educators about the flaws and pitfalls it saw in the administration's teacher-testing plan.

Clinton also came under attack by Thomas McRae, his old nemesis. The president of the Winthrop Rockefeller Foundation called a press conference in late September and castigated Clinton for neglecting Arkansas's industrial development. Charging that Clinton "has had his head under a rock," McRae went on to say the state's industrial development policy was like "a blind hog rooting in the brush and occasionally finding an acorn."

Clinton countered by announcing he was working on a proposal to energize the state's industrial development program, and would submit it to the legislators in the 1985 session. McRae called this a "Slick Willieism," because Clinton was presumptuous enough to assume he'd be the governor in the next term.

Woody Freeman, his Republican opponent, also made waves.

On the campaign trail, he promised not to raise taxes, as he predicted Clinton would do once reelected. Freeman pointed out that his rival's Industrial Development package that called for job-training programs, development financing, and a scheme to launch a nationwide recruitment for industry to settle in Arkansas would cost the state a fortune and needlessly burden the taxpayers.

Hillary's role as a procurer of state business for her employer, the Rose Law Firm, also came under heavy fire. As the second-largest law firm in Arkansas, Rose by now had cornered a disproportionately large share of contracts. Rose also was one of the leading representatives of bond underwriters (besides Lasater & Company) doing business with the state.

Hillary's feeble defense: "I don't share any of the money my firm earns from state contracts and I receive no fees from representing bond underwriters [who do business with the state]." Yet she commanded a six-figure paycheck from her partnership in the law firm—plus other lucrative perks.

While Hillary was still actively involved in trying to better Arkansas's educational standards, she was severely criticized by Erwin Davis, a Republican gubernatorial hopeful who lost the party's nomination to Woody Freeman. Davis accused Clinton of violating the state's nepotism laws by appointing his wife to head the Education Standards Commission.

That argument lost its steam after the Arkansas Press Association's first Headliner of the Year Award went to Hillary for the successes she gained with her educational reform efforts.

Hillary's role in private practice as a highly visible and influential lawyer and its appearance of a conflict-of-interest because of the significant part she played in her husband's administration, drew this comment from the *Washington Post* during the '92 campaign:

"Rarely in American politics have married partners played such interconnected public roles," wrote *Post* staffers Michael Weisskopf and David Maraniss in their Sunday March 15 edition. "...and the convergence of legal and political power in the Clinton family poses several problems for them."

This criticism had been sounded on and off for more than a dozen years—since Clinton's first term. Even during the two years he was out of office, Bill and Hillary continued unabatedly to exercise that influence and power—putting the Big Lie to their insistence that they didn't crisscross each other's businesses.

It was, as the *Washington Post* concluded, "a curious intersection of politics and private interests" by the couple who subsequently moved on from their "small town, politically inbred [and corrupt, as other sources have described Little Rock] capital" to the White House.

Add to all this the accusation Bill Clinton faced from one of Little Rock's most populous ghettoes. It was contained in a newsletter fired off by a Little Rock restaurateur and black activist, Robert "Say" McIntosh.

McIntosh accused the governor of having had orgiastic affairs with some of the area's hookers—and to have fathered a mulatto child.

- 17 -

A JOGGIN' MAN'S ORGIES

Along Seedy Hookers' Row

Little Rock's seedy "Hookers' Row," as it's called, is the last place that a governor of Arkansas would be expected to visit—unless he were touring the inner-city ghetto to proclaim rehabilitation for the neglected slum.

Apparently that wasn't his mission in 1984 when the 38-year-old Clinton allegedly ventured into the red-light district, unescorted and unprotected by the state police charged with providing round-the-clock escort.

Clinton was said to have materialized in that repellent neck of the woods in a pair of white sneakers, maroon running shorts, and a body-hugging, knit black sweatshirt. Although the locale was only shouting distance from the governor's mansion, Clinton was in a world apart from those cozy quarters and the still-sleeping wife that he left at the crack of dawn.

What sent Clinton jogging into that drug-ravaged skid row cannot be ascertained. But what happened that early morning after Clinton encountered three young black women strolling along Spring Street has been certifiably reported and therefore cannot remain under the rug any longer.

It begins with kinky sex involving that triad of street princesses, gravitates to an orgy in Bill's mother's country home, and continues into a lengthy relationship with one of the tarts, a drug-addicted woman of easiest virtue who claims Clinton was overly generous with his payments for the favors she and her fellow hustlers provided him.

The cover on the profligate governor's encounters with the hookers was blown by Bobbie Ann Williams, a coked-up, 33-year-old, poverty-stricken ghetto mother of three—who claims one of her children was fathered by Bill Clinton. The sex, Mrs. Williams attested, was accomplished without the protection of condoms.

Bobbie Ann said Clinton didn't use "protection" because he "just didn't like them."

"There's simply no doubt that my little Danny is Bill's son," she insisted in a 1992 interview, as she put her arm around her light-skinned, seven-year-old son she affectionately called "my loving, mulatto baby."

"Just look at his face," the mother went on. "He looks just like his daddy. When my baby was born, he was white as any white child. I told myself then, 'This is Bill Clinton's baby. I know it is.'

"And the older he got, the more he started looking like his daddy Bill."

Even the Times of London Knew

Bobbie Ann's account wasn't the first to cast light on Clinton's purported extra-marital affairs and reports that he fathered children out of wedlock. Such rumors had been circulating in Arkansas for years.

Many of the state's newspapers had printed those allegations, but it wasn't until Clinton announced his candidacy for the presidency that stories crossed the state line and landed in leading dailies such as the *Washington Post*, *Chicago Tribune*, *Newsday*, and *Los Angeles Times*. Even the *Times of London* and *London Telegraph* carried items about Clinton's profligacies with black women.

Just when Clinton let it be known in late 1991 that he had no intention of keeping his vow to serve out the fifth term as governor and tossed his hat into the ring for the presidency, Arkansas's leading black activist and Little Rock restaurateur Robert "Say" McIntosh had a handbill printed with a startling headline:

"The Hottest Thing Going" Bill Clinton's D*** ["Dick," meaning penis] Will Keep Him From Running For President Of The United States Of America."

A picture of Clinton appears to the left of the headline with the caption: "Super Stud."

The text reads, "Please help me raise money to take care of black baby, 'the black sheep of the family.' This baby is by a black woman."

A cherubic, curly-haired, smiling youngster who is Bobbie Ann Williams' son Danny appears to the right of the text, which continues:

"This picture is furnished by Righteous Rev. Tommy Knots.

"Rev. Knots is an aide to Hillary Clinton at the Rose Law Firm…after he did a six-month investigation. God told him to bring it to me."

Upon crediting the Almighty for that secular miracle, McIntosh swears to heaven upon this earthy postscript:

"All Clinton is willing to do for the mother is to keep her out of jail and prison [for violation of prostitution laws]."

The pamphlet makes a further reference to Clinton, but the chronicler diverts into a seeming non sequiter:

"During the 1980 election, Clinton agreed to pay me $25,000.00 to have Yarnell's Ice Cream Company manufacture my pie mix."

As the author was to learn, Knots's statement was meaningful. Hillary heard about stirrings Knots was making about the mulatto baby and reported it to her husband—who then offered to bankroll the manufacturer of the minister's "pie mix." This move kept Knots's lips sealed for the election, but Knots held a grudge when Clinton thumbed his nose at him after the polls closed. He vowed to "get him" the next time Clinton ran for office.

Knots's accusations were given further airing by Bobbie Ann Williams who described her street encounter with the governor that early morning some eight years before.

"I was twenty-four [in 1984] and was working as a prostitute at the Johnson apartment building on Seventeenth and Main Street when I first met Bill," she asserted.

"Me and some girls were walking around Spring Street near the governor's mansion when we saw him come jogging down the street in a tight T-shirt.

"I was dressed real sexy in this tight little skirt, a halter top nothing under it, and a wig with curls.

"The other girls were pretty excited. They knew about the governor's jogging trips. He'd pick you up right there on the street.

"My friends and me were disappointed by the governor that day. He just stopped to talk to us.

"But about three days later, we saw him again. This time, he picked me—and said that he knew a place where we could go have sex."

Oral Sex behind the Hedges

Bobbie Ann said the governor had her meet with him nearby, behind a row of hedges paralleling the roadside. She said he asked her to perform oral sex on him, which she claimed she did after asking to be paid $60.

"When it was done, he gave me two hundred dollars," she related.

"He talked all the time I was doing it [performing oral sex on Clinton]," remembered Bobbie Ann. "Then after he was done, he pulled up his pants and ran off jogging.

"A couple weeks later, he said he wanted to have an orgy. He said that he'd pay four hundred dollars apiece. There was me and two friends—and we jumped at his offer.

"That was a lot of money for us in those days. He said he'd pick us up in a white car on the corner of Main Street at seven o'clock that night.

"We were waiting when this big white car—it wasn't a limo, but it was a big car with tinted windows [Clinton's official state transport, a Lincoln Town Car]—drove up and stopped beside us."

The man behind the wheel was a state trooper assigned to guard the governor.

"We just ran to the car, opened the door and got right in the back with the governor," Bobbie Ann went on. "He knew that we liked to drink Hennessy cognac and he had a bottle and some glasses with him.

"He was really nice. He made us drinks and we talked and laughed. He was a funny guy. He liked saying dirty things—but they were funny.

"We called him Bill right from the start. He was like any other man. He wanted just one thing: sex. The only difference was that he paid more money—a lot more. And all we had to do was what he told us.

"And he paid us right there in the car. That made us feel real good because we didn't have to wait for our money."

Bobbie Ann didn't need to consult a road map to retrace the journey she and her two sisters in sin were taken on by the Arkansas state trooper and his distinguished passenger.

"We left town on the John Barrow Road and traveled about an hour [all the way to

Hot Springs, a 60-mile drive] to this little house in the woods.

"The house wasn't a big family place or anything. It was kind of small with a fireplace and a small bed. But it was pretty inside and nicely decorated.

"The driver stayed outside smoking cigarettes. When we got in, we all just took our clothes off. Bill smiled and flopped down on his back on the bed, just laying there, stretched out naked."

"He Watched Us Girls Make Love"

"He liked looking at us," Bobbie Ann recalled. "We all three crawled into bed with him and started playing around. We played like that for a long time, changing positions. He liked using all the dirty words he could think of for the woman's body parts. And we could tell he liked it when we talked dirty to him.

"He also watched us girls make love to each other. He told us what to do. That really got him turned on."

"Finally, he was ready for straight sex and tried using a condom, but he took it off.

"'I just don't like scumbags,' he said.

"I didn't care. It didn't matter to me. I guess that we didn't think much about it. We were done in about three hours—and he surprised all of us with a fifty dollar tip apiece. We were really happy, and we giggled all the way back to Little Rock."

This story was told in its entirety for the first time in early 1992 by the weekly tabloid *Globe*—after it'd been stung by the rival *Star* with its exclusive on the governor's steamy, years-long affair with Gennifer Flowers and his sexual exploits with a half-dozen other feminine charmers.

"We sent a team of reporters to backtrack on everything that Bobbie Ann Williams told us," said Phil Bunton, the editorial director of the 1.5 million-circulation *Globe*. Editor Dan Dolan assigned staffers Ken Harrel, Bob Boyd, Stan Wulff, Bob Temmey, and George Hunter to investigate every aspect of the prostitute's story.

"Before we did anything," Bunton stresses, "we had Bobbie Ann take a lie-detector test. She passed it not once but twice. Then we proceeded from there."

The reportorial team established that the governor indeed had a white car. In fact, all his cars were white. And they were large, long-chassied, eight-cylinder Lincolns.

"Then our reporters followed Bobbie Ann's directions to the house in the woods," Bunton continued. "They found Barrow Road was the fastest way to get to the house she described—and discovered it was the home owned by Clinton's mother."

A green, wood-frame cabin with a wood-shingle roof, the residence overlooked picturesque Lake Hamilton and a 30-foot dock jutting out into the placid waters. No boat was tied up there, but all around on the grounds lay fishing paraphernalia. Behind the house was piled a cord or more of firewood. The grounds were shaded by giant trees and protected from intruders by a chain-link fence.

A conflict would arise in 1994 about the use—and ownership—of this cabin.

Ostensibly, it had been purchased in 1981 or earlier to serve as a retreat for Bill when he was a first-term governor and as a getaway for his mother from her year-round residence, the family's old Hot Springs home.

This information comes from his mother's account in her recently published autobiography *Leading With My Heart: My Life*, written with James Morgan for Simon & Schuster, which went on sale Mother's Day.

As she unfolds the details, Bill's mother, Virginia Kelley, who died January 4, 1994, affords her son an opening to use her words from the grave as a crutch in a lame attempt to help him limp past the Whitewater mess.

But it doesn't work after Clinton calls a televised White House press conference the evening of March 24 and resorts to his dead mother's memoirs to escape the heat over the size of the loss he said he and Hillary sustained in Whitewater.

By then the topic was on everyone's lips, and the Clintons had been exposed as tall-tale tellers when they claimed they took a $68,900 bath in Whitewater.

His meeting with the press was forced on Clinton after the first couple had been pressured relentlessly to speak more forthrightly about that loss. Clinton promised to release tax returns that "would prove *I* did nothing wrong" in that failed real estate investment.

Note the use of the first person *I* instead of the collective pronoun *we*. Why was Clinton distancing only himself from suspected wrongdoing?

At only his second press conference since taking office, Clinton astonished everyone by admitting he had drastically overstated his and Hillary's "losses" in Whitewater. They did not lose $68,900, he fessed up. The figure was inflated by about $22,000—"because I had forgotten that I used the money to help my mother buy a cabin."

Of course he was referring to the Lake Hamilton cabin where he had the orgy with the three skid-row hookers. The president didn't mention that diversion. He did expand on the $22,000 he claimed to have given his mother.

Bill Sees the Light...Belatedly

"I was wracking my brain to remember my investment," and then he saw the light "the past few days.

"I was reading and fact-checking the galleys for my mother's autobiography and realized then that I had borrowed that money to help her buy a home, that I didn't invest that [sum] in Whitewater."

Many publishers were asking what utterly advanced methods had Simon and Schuster developed which enabled it to go to press, bind the book, and send out copies to reviewers just two weeks after galleys were still being fact-checked.

In the book, Clinton's mother says she and Richard Kelley were married January 17, 1982, and both had wanted to live on Lake Hamilton. Mrs. Kelley took her husband to look at the house Bill used as a *retreat*.

"Actually, calling it a 'lake house' is giving it more credit than it deserves," she writes forthrightly. "It was a small piece of property with what amounted to a cabin on it...across the road from our property were several mobile homes. Dick wasn't exactly impressed."

But Mrs. Kelley explains that they thought about expanding the cabin and "Bill, who never had spent much time there, asked Dick if he'd like to buy his share. Dick jumped at the opportunity."

Neal Travis, who writes the "New York" gossip column for the *New York Post*, leafed through a copy of Mrs. Kelley's memoirs and questioned whether Clinton could depend on what she wrote to get him off the Whitewater hot spot.

The book "raises, rather than answers, questions about the $20,000 Clinton says he borrowed in 1981 to help his mother buy a home.

"This is where the questions arise:

• "When did Clinton and his mother buy the cabin at the lake? It possibly *was* in 1981, but Mrs. Kelley seems to imply she and her son had owned it for a longer term than that.

• "How much did the cabin cost? At that time in the Whitewater development itself, about $13,000 would build a comfortable home.

• "Clinton says the $20,000 he borrowed and, in turn, lent to his mother was to 'help' her buy a home, implying she was putting some money in, too—and implying the cabin by the trailer park cost *more* than $20,000.

• "Mrs. Kelley says her new husband 'jumped' at buying Clinton's share of the cabin. How much did he pay for that share?"

Travis, a former colleague of the author's at the *Post*, as were so many others cited in these passages as sources, comes to a conclusion about Clinton's attempt to lean on his late mother's words to blow away Whitewater's ill winds:

"By any reckoning, this sounds like the most expensive little house in Arkansas. Sure, a presidential log cabin fetches a premium, but this one wasn't log, and Bill Clinton wasn't president."

The *Globe*'s reporters, who gained surprisingly easy access to the cabin after introducing themselves to Clinton's mother, informed the author that the house could be called "modest" at most.

Mrs. Kelley was home because she couldn't be at the racetrack. This was Sunday, the oaters day off.

"On entering, the reporters found the interior had wood-paneled walls, plush leather furniture, and a display on its walls and shelves of many trophies and pictures of the governor.

A conflict arose during the reporters' visit to the Lake Hamilton cabin regarding Clinton's appearance there.

Mrs. Kelley was quoted:

"Bill never comes to this house. I've told him not to try and visit me here because he doesn't have time with his busy schedule. I go to see him and sometimes we meet halfway."

However, Mrs. Kelley's claim was disputed by her immediate neighbors, Darlene Lewis and Effie Kirby.

"Bill uses his mom's place to get away from all the stress that he's under," said Effie Kirby. "We've seen him come down here a lot when Dick and Virginia are away from the house."

Chimed in Darlene Lewis, "That's because we've become friends with his driver, Buddy Young. Buddy's a big ol' state trooper who mostly stays outside and comes and talks to us."

The eyewitness to this scenario was speaking about Captain Raymond (Buddy) Young, chief of Governor Clinton's security detail.

Darlene Lewis, the next-door neighbor, had told us that Buddy Young didn't enter the cabin when Clinton was entertaining his sexual playmates, because he obviously wanted privacy.

Neither neighbor hinted at any hanky-panky occurring in the residence, where Bobbie Ann Williams said the governor could have made her pregnant—but if not on the day of the orgy she described, then on one of the 12 or more other times.

One of the other times was reported to have been a liaison on a cool November evening in 1984, when Clinton settled into a room at the downtown Little Rock Holiday Inn.

While he waited for one of the "uniformed pimps" from his state police security detail to arrive, the governor poured himself a jigger of Hennessy cognac in the presence of another trooper and sipped the drink slowly.

Soon a feathery knock on the door signaled the arrival of Bobbie Ann Williams. The trooper opened the door, admitted her, then took his leave.

Behind the closed door of his suite and alone with her, Clinton poured Bobbie Ann a drink and crossed her palm with $200 for a couple of hours of heavy sex.

Afterward, Bobbie Ann Williams was escorted out of the hotel by the trooper who had conveyed her to the Holiday Inn. He drove her back to her skid row beat. Meanwhile, the other trooper went to the desk and checked out "William Clay," the name in which the suite was booked. Clinton slipped out the back entrance, again unnoticed, and was taken in the second trooper's car back to the governor's mansion, where Hillary was asleep.

Whether Bobbie Ann conceived the mulatto baby she bore some nine months later on this November night or on one of the other occasions is of no great matter. Facts show that she had the baby.

During Clinton's 1990 bid for a fifth term, detractors showed up at rallies with small glass vials and signs that read, "Just a few drops, Bill."

They wanted blood samples to prove the paternity of Danny Williams. None were ever obtained then—as none were obtained on earlier occasions when Bobbie Ann's supporters besieged the Governor's mansion as well as the statehouse.

Bobbie Ann was anxious to give her interviewers chapter and verse about the pregnancy.

"I was still working the street into the fourth month I was carrying Bill's baby. And Bill got a special kick out of having sex with pregnant women. He said that pregnancy makes gals hotter.

"When I told him that he was the father of my baby, he just laughed. He rubbed my big belly and said, 'Girl, that can't be my baby.'

"But I knew it was. I just had this kind of woman's feeling that this was his child."

The boy's dirt-poor granny was convinced of that, also, but was reluctant to discuss it.

"I told Bobbie Ann to keep her mouth shut as she could destroy Clinton's career in politics, and for doing that, he might then destroy her," said 53-year-old Sylvia Howard.

Bobbie Ann's 29-year-old sister, Lucille Bolton, was much more forthcoming.

"When she told me she was carrying Bill Clinton's baby, I was very skeptical," professed Lucille. "I didn't believe Bobbie Ann. But then I saw that little baby in University Hospital. He was white. That's when I started believing my sister. And as Danny got older, he started to look more and more like the governor."

Danny's Mother's Put in Pokey

Shortly after Danny's birth, his mother was jailed on prostitution and drug charges and Lucille became the boy's guardian.

Today, little Danny lives in poverty in a ramshackle, two-story home in Little Rock. He sleeps on an old, torn mattress on the floor and eats in a kitchen whose refrigerator and cupboards are often bare.

"I was so furious over the situation that I went to the governor's mansion last year to talk to Clinton about Danny," said Lucille. "But I couldn't get past his aides, who listened to my story and then sent me packing."

"They took my name and address and asked me some questions about the boy, but I never heard another word from them," stated Lucille, who passed both lie-detector tests given by the *Globe*.

Bobbie Ann's husband, Dan Williams, who knows the child couldn't be his because he's black, was likewise frustrated when he tried to get relief for Danny.

"He drove up alongside the governor while he was jogging and told him about the boy," Lucille explained about Williams' action. "Clinton's reaction was shocking."

"Dan said the governor pulled out a roll of hundred dollar bills and threw it in the window of the car. Then he just kept jogging."

Not the *Globe*, nor any other publication, could get a comment from Clinton's campaign about Bobbie Ann Williams' claims. The governor's press secretary, Susan Whiteacre, would only say, "There is no comment to be made."

Bill Clinton had nothing to offer. He wouldn't even sit still for any questions about his widely heralded mulatto baby.

Paternity can't be proved so long as blood tests of the principals haven't been taken for comparison, so no other way exists to affirm the truth of Bobbie Ann's claims.

Thus rumors persist about Clinton's relations with prostitutes—and about Danny and other illegitimate children.

Black activist Robert McIntosh was left to utter the last words on the subject:

"Bill Clinton has been with enough black women to cast a Tarzan movie. And he's got a little black son out there living in poverty."

18

TUMULTUOUS TIMES IN BILL'S THIRD TERM

More Scandals for Him to Bear

Bill Clinton was running for reelection as governor in 1984 when, in early August, Arkansas State Police Commandant Tommy Goodwin was once again the bearer of bad tidings. The conversation wasn't taped, but sources inside the governor's office revealed anonymously what they said they heard Clinton and his police boss discuss—and also what they heard on the recording Goodwin assertedly played for the governor.

"It doesn't look good, Bill," Goodwin is said to have informed Clinton. "Roger's going to be indicted."

The words stunned Clinton.

"He was left speechless," is how one source described the governor's reaction. But the news that Bill's cokehead half brother was going to be charged as a drug trafficker couldn't have come as great surprise. After all, Goodwin had alerted Clinton to that likelihood more than a year before when he told him that Roger was being investigated by the joint task force.

Perhaps Clinton's silence was due to his concentration on the recordings Goodwin brought with him. Tape recordings—a total of 12 made between May and June 1984 on a Nagra recorder/transmitter that Roger's friend Rodney Myers had body-packed into the governor's mansion.

The unintentional confessions from Roger's mouth not only incriminated him in the furtive drug conspiracy with Russell Crump, Maurice Rodriguez, and others, but also in a far more sinister complicity in similar illegal activity that involved "close political ally" Dan Lasater, and the governor's mansion itself. The following FBI-Arkansas State Police transcript was revealing:

MYERS: Hey, Rog, did you ever take women over to your brother's place to screw?

CLINTON: Yeah. There was the mansion and the guest house. Oh, they love it. Just fucking love it. There's so much cunt in this town. Too much cunt in this town.

MYERS: Good Lord. That's a fucking good life. Get over to the god damn governor's mansion and fuck yourself to death.

Precise dates and times when Roger Clinton entertained his girl friends haven't been furnished by authorities. The FBI characteristically declined comment. The Arkansas State Police, whose director serves at the pleasure of the governor, categorically denied any knowledge of hanky-panky, either in the mansion or guest house, whenever Roger and his pals, and their coke, padded down with Bill and Hillary lolling about "upstairs" as gracious and seemingly disinterested hosts.

Whether the governor and first lady were aware of Roger's liaisons no one seems to know, or wants to tell.

However, those in the know paint a purple portrait of partying during many of Roger Clinton's visits, when he was accompanied by loud and boisterous women friends.

"It was like a Roman orgy," said one informant. "The food and drinks served up to the revelers from the kitchen was one thing—like, you'd think Arkansas was the horn of plenty and it didn't matter the Clintons were dishing up all that grub and booze to little brother and his horny friends which was being paid for with the people's tax dollars."

Bringing in Broads for the State Troopers

Another source reported that Roger and his visitors "had all-night screwing sessions with alternate partners and X-rated video cassettes running on the TV all the while to keep them aroused and stimulated for non-stop sex."

This informant remembered more:

"The smoke alone from all the pot they smoked gave me a high when I was eight rooms removed from the party—and my door was closed!"

Was marijuana the only narcotic in use when Roger and his gang were living it up in the governor's mansion?

"Why not ask me if they were doing coke?"

Were they?

"Like it was going out of style. Snort, snort, snort—all night long!"

Where were the state police? Didn't they do anything to stop the illegal behavior? Did they report to their superiors about such goings-on?

"Hah," laughed one insider. "The visitors were bringing broads for the cops—so why should they put a stop to a good thing?"

Visitor logs maintained by the state police do not mention wild partying. They are quite sketchy. They show that Roger Clinton stayed at the mansion or guest house no fewer than 36 times between February 7, 1983, and January 13, 1985. Some log entries simply—yet tellingly—note that he was accompanied by "a friend," "a girl," and in some instances "females."

When log entries were occasionally more detailed, Roger was shown either to have stayed "downstairs" in the mansion itself or in "the guest house."

However, most records consisted of a two-word entry. "Roger in." Several failed to mention the time he left.

When shown a copy of the log with that notation, one of the snitchers said,

"'Roger in' meant exactly that. It was cop code to kiddingly indicate that Roger *got in.* In other words, that he made out with his bimbo."

Was that *it,* so far as the Arkansas State Police's involvement in the mansion's security was concerned—to avail themselves of the services of the "broads" the "visitors were bringing…for the cops," and to maintain a log that recorded the times little half-brother Roger "made out with his bimbos"?

Not quite.

Just as Bill Clinton was winding up his first year of the presidency, an explosive article in the January 1994 edition of the conservative magazine *The American Spectator* reopened the old story of his adulteries, but with a new, nasty twist.

David Brock is the writer of the latest *American Spectator* bombshell, entitled "His Cheatin' Heart," a jarring account of how nearly a dozen Arkansas State Police troopers were used as *pimps in uniform* to feed their boss's insatiable sexual appetite.

Brock has impeccable journalistic credentials as an investigative reporter for *The American Spectator* and as author of the recent blockbusting Free Press book exposé, *The Real Anita Hill.*

In unveiling the previously untold story that he gathered in a three-month investigation, Brock went after a dozen or so troopers known as the "palace guard."

He hit pay dirt when he landed four troopers willing at long last to blow the whistle on the sordid partnership of sexual hanky-panky that existed between the governor and his security guards.

Two troopers consented to let their names be used, two declined. But all of their roles in roping women for the governor's clandestine sexual nourishment were iterated at great length in Brock's *American Spectator* piece.

Willing to be identified were Troopers Larry G. Patterson, 49, a 26-year veteran of the force, and Roger L. Perry, 44, who served 16 years.

The other two troopers who spoke with Brock (and with reporters of the *Los Angeles Times,* who got on the story just about the time Brock began his probe) did not want their identities revealed, but it is the author's duty to introduce them as Danny Ferguson and Ronnie Anderson.

According to David Brock's long investigation and further findings of a corresponding four-month probe by *Los Angeles Times* reporters William C. Rempel and Douglas Frantz, the evidence conclusively points to a more shocking service that the Arkansas State Police performed while acting as Governor Clinton's security force.

Citing Troopers Larry Patterson and Roger Perry, Rempel and Frantz came to this conclusion:

"The troopers, who were on Clinton's security detail for several years while he was governor, describe a pattern of deception and indiscretions and say that he required them as state employees to go beyond their duties as bodyguards to help him conduct and hide these" [the "new details about extramarital affairs that caused a crisis in Bill Clinton's campaign for the presidency"] as revealed in the *Times'* front page story of its December 21, 1993, edition. It should be pointed out that the *Times* finished in a near dead heat with the *American Spectator* in reaching the nation's newsstands. Regardless, the bottom line in both publications was the same:

"The troopers are lawmen who knew the then-governor intimately—even, by their own accounts, as confidants. They drove him around the state, answered his phone and did errands, as well as protect him. They shared many private moments with him, joked with him, ate with him and became his shield from the public.

"The troopers also shielded his infidelities, they allege, from his wife, Hillary Rodham Clinton, as well as the public.

"It was that part, the troopers said, that they came to resent, along with what they regarded as an increasingly cavalier way Clinton began to treat them."

That "cavalier" treatment began only after Clinton was elected president and troopers Patterson and Perry looked to Washington for the kind of reward for his silence that was afforded to Captain Buddy Young—a $92,300-a-year job as a regional director of the Federal Emergency Management Agency (FEMA) in Texas.

Before Clinton and his family left Little Rock for the White House in January 1992, according to Perry, the president-elect asked him what sort of federal job in law enforcement he might want—it is presumed the same offering was advanced to Patterson.

But when requests went to the White House for such beneficent treatment, they were met by a wall of silence. The troopers resented this. They contended they served virtually full-time as Clinton's "intermediaries" in arranging and concealing his extramarital liaisons—by frequently picking up and delivering gifts from Clinton to his women, often driving him in his Lincoln Town Car to rendezvous at various love nests, and performing other "pimping services."

"We were more than bodyguards," Patterson told the *Times*' William Rempel and Douglas Frantz. "We had to lie, cheat and cover up for that man."

Their sensational accounts may never have seen the light had it not been for the President's old Oxford classmate—and latter-day nemesis—Little Rock attorney Cliff Jackson. He's the Cliff Jackson who, during the 1992 campaign, blew the whistle on the candidate as a draft dodger by disclosing details, through letters he wrote to friends from the English university, of the evasions Clinton took to avoid serving in the military during the Vietnam War.

Snubbed by the president for federal employment, Patterson and Perry began batting around the idea of collaborating on a book about their experience. That led them to the offices of two Little Rock lawyers.

One was their ex-boss, former director of the Arkansas State Police, and a onetime FBI agent, Lynn Davis.

The other was Cliff Jackson.

It was Jackson who brought the matter to a head after he introduced the troopers to David Brock and to William Rempel and Douglas Frantz. The reporters conducted many hours of separate interviews with Patterson and Perry, who revealed Bill Clinton's modus operandi in "giving Hillary the slip so that he could shack up with his women."

"Each trooper described incidents on the night shift at the governor's mansion in which Clinton would come down after midnight and say he was going for a drive," the *Times* reported. It added that the troopers on duty at the residence had standing orders on those occasions to call the governor on the cellular phone "if the lights came on in his wife's bedroom [Bill and Hillary often slept in separate bedrooms, so he had no fear on those occasions of disturbing his wife when he was sneaking out of the mansion]."

But Hillary knew of her husband's profligacies, and no one was more aware of that than the cheating governor. So Clinton had an arrangement with the troopers to protect himself if his wife woke up in the middle of the night, peeked into her husband's bedroom to see if he was in the arms of Morpheus or had gone off to be in the arms of "another one of your sluts," as she referred to them.

Hillary on Bill: "The Sorry Damn Son of a Bitch!"

One night his worst fear was realized. Hillary awakened, checked her husband's empty bedroom, and asked Perry where Clinton was.

"He went for a drive in my car," Perry responded. "He wanted a breath of fresh air."

"The sorry damn son of a bitch!" Hillary screeched.

Just as soon as he was out of earshot, Perry grabbed Clinton's ear on the cellular phone—at one of his mistress's boudoirs—and told him about developments.

"I remember exactly what he said," Perry recalled. He said, 'God! God! God! God! God!'"

The *Times* reports the consequences:

"About 10 minutes later Clinton drove through the mansion gates at top speed, screeched to a stop outside the kitchen door and hurried inside without closing the car door, according to Perry. Perry said he went out to close his car door and overheard a loud, angry exchange between the couple.

"Later that morning, Perry continued, he went in and cleaned up the kitchen where he found a cupboard door broken from its hinges and debris scattered around the floor."

Patterson described an incident that took place in the parking lot of the governor's mansion one late night with a cosmetics salesclerk from a Little Rock department store. The woman had driven there in her car and Clinton got in. Unaware of the security camera nearby, the governor and his visitor went into action.

As a family newspaper, the *Los Angeles Times* sanitized the report from its reporters Rempel and Frantz to:

"...[Patterson] said in his affidavit and in interviews that he observed on the security monitor Clinton and the woman in a sex act."

David Brock's account of the same incident in the *American Spectator* hits the bull's-eye.

He speaks of a woman who peddled fragrances by day and had an aromatic evening encounter with Clinton at a time when he was enroute to the annual reception of the Harrison County Chamber of Commerce. Clinton asked Patterson, who was driving the governor's Lincoln, to make a detour into a deserted parking lot of daughter Chelsea's school, Booker Elementary. There the trooper found the sales clerk, parked nearby as Clinton walked to the waiting vehicle.

"I could see Clinton get into the front seat and then the lady's head go into his lap," Patterson is quoted in *American Spectator*. "They stayed in the car for 30 or 40 minutes."

The Spectator's version was more explicit in yet another episode:

"...the same woman drove up [into the governor's mansion parking lot] in a yellow and black Datsun or Nissan pickup truck and asked to see Clinton. The governor came out of the residence and climbed into the front seat of the truck which she parked in an area off the rear drive.

"This time Patterson said, with a gleam in his eye, he got an even clearer view of the sex act by aiming a remote-controlled [video] camera with a swivel base mounted on a 30-foot pole in the back yard of the house right into the truck. The image was projected onto a 27-inch [TV] screen in the guard house.

"'He was sitting on the passenger side and she was behind the wheel. I pointed the thing directly into the windshield, and watched on the screen as the governor received oral sex,' Patterson said.

"As this act was occurring, Chelsea's baby-sitter at the time, Melissa Jolley, drove into the compound."

Realizing that she would usually drive right by the area where the pickup was parked on her way to the guest house, where she lived, Patterson intercepted her, told her there was a security problem on the grounds, and instructed her to drive by a different route, go in her house, and stay there.

David Brock goes on to quote Patterson:

"When they were done Clinton came running over to me and asked, 'Did she see us? Did she see us?' I told him what I'd done and he said 'Atta boy.'"

Patterson was privy to a great deal of the first family's private doings, as on that Sunday afternoon in the late 1980s when Bill and Hillary were tiffing in "highly colorful language" in the mansion's kitchen. The first lady was beefing about her inadequate sex life and her words were being picked up by the audio monitor on the back porch, aside the kitchen window.

"I need to be fucked more than twice a year," Patterson heard Hillary complain.

At times, Hillary carried her frustration almost into the open, and often at public events. Once, according to Patterson and other troopers, Bill had chatted at length with an attractive woman. After he returned to a fuming Hillary's side, she was overheard to rasp, "Come on Bill, put your dick up. You can't fuck her here."

But Hillary's complaints may have been a bit much—in light of her own apparent *association* with law partner Vincent (Vince) Foster. The same Foster who, special prosecutor Robert Fiske has now concluded, took his life on the banks of the Potomac after he moved to Washington to serve as a top White House aide.

"According to all of the troopers," David Brock reports in *The American Spectator*, "whenever Clinton left town, no sooner would he be out of the mansion gates than Foster would appear, often staying in the residence with Hillary into the wee hours of the morning."

That takes the relationship somewhat further than this author advanced in an earlier chapter, when Hillary and Vince were "burning the midnight oil at the Rose Law Firm."

"One of the off-the-record troopers drove Hillary and Foster to a mountain cabin in Heber Springs, maintained by the Rose firm as an out-of-town retreat for its lawyers, where the two spent significant amounts of time alone."

Patterson and Perry knew not only of the liaisons at the Heber Springs hideaway, but also once even eyeballed Vince and Hillary in a car stopped for a light on a Hot Springs street—and "observed [them] embracing and open-mouth kissing."

Brock also reports the two lawyers were seen in a "compromising position" at the Little Rock French restaurant, Alouette's, at a gathering also attended by Foster's wife, Lisa, and Hillary's husband, Bill.

"While seated at the restaurant's bar, outside the dining room, Patterson said he observed Hillary and another woman from the Rose firm, Carolyn Huber, come out to the bar for a private chat. Soon thereafter, Foster emerged from the dining room on his way to the men's room.

"He came up behind Hillary and squeezed her rear end with both hands. Then he winked and gave me the 'OK' sign," Patterson is quoted by the reporter. "On the way back, Huber was turned away, and Vince put his hand over one of Hillary's breasts and made the same 'OK' sign to me. And she just stood there cooing, 'Oh Vince, Oh Vince.'"

Carolyn Huber, a fourth member of the Rose Law Firm (beside Webb Hubbell, Vince Foster, and William Kennedy III) to become a White House staffer, with the title "assistant to the president," said she didn't attend such a gathering at Alouette's.

Patterson also told the *Spectator* about other of Clinton's long-term mistresses whom the trooper counted from the time he came on as security guard at the governor's mansion in 1987.

In addition to Gennifer Flowers, Patterson listed "a staffer in Clinton's office, an Arkansas lawyer Clinton appointed to a judgeship, the wife of a prominent judge, a local reporter, an employee at Arkansas Power and Light...," and the cosmetic salesclerk at the Little Rock department store.

Some of these women were discussed earlier in this book and in sworn affidavits that Larry Nichols provided in his federal lawsuit against Bill Clinton.

The author will further explore Clinton's—as well as Hillary's—intimacies with the opposite sex in coming passages. In Clinton's case, this will carry forward right up to the day he is elected president and even to the last hour before he leaves Little Rock for Washington.

But for now, other matters must be attended to.

One is naming some of the other Arkansas State Police troopers who manned the ramparts at the governor's mansion Besides the aforelisted Larry Patterson, Roger Perry, Danny Ferguson, and Ronnie Anderson, troopers who also pulled security duty at the mansion were Frank Tappin, Derrick Flowers (no relation to Gennifer), and Bob Walker, and their supervisors Lieutenant Carl Kirkland and Corporal David Donham.

As already shown, the officers commanding this contingent were Colonel Tommy Goodwin, commander of the state police, and Captain Buddy Young, chief of Clinton's security detail—the selfsame "big ol' state trooper" Clinton's mother's neighbor

Darlene Lewis found such a friendly conversationalist.

The other matter of an even more exigent nature is half-brother Roger Clinton and the trouble brewing all about him, and of how that suddenly becomes a matter of great concern to the governor.

Hidden Mike Foils Roger

Clinton had not received really hard evidence of Roger's entanglement with narcotics in his initial briefing by trooper commander Tommy Goodwin. So he did not seem overly troubled by the revelations then. But when Goodwin returned to the mansion to let the governor hear the tapes of the secretly recorded conversations between Roger and Rodney Myers, the friend who became a government informer to save his own skin after he was busted as a drug dealer, Clinton was devastated.

Those tapes, which initially were in the custody of federal investigators, became available to the Arkansas State Police late in the year. Clinton then was able to hear for himself how deeply Roger was involved in sleazy goings-on in the mansion and of his drug activity with the governor's political ally/big money man Dan R. Lasater.

The trusty Nagra recorder/transmitter, strapped to Myer's skin under his clothing, was all it took to catalog the incriminating evidence of Roger and Lasater's unmistakable partnership in drug deals. The government suspected that such a conspiracy had existed for some time, but until then it lacked the hard evidence. The dialogue between Myers and young Clinton was transmitted to an FBI listening post in an unmarked car parked on Center Street, barely out of sight of the governor's mansion.

Roger blew what he had come to believe was his most precious cover—the governor's mansion, where, ironically, his drug deals were being guarded 24 hours a day by the state's supposedly unsuspecting police. Supreme confidence led Roger to unknowingly thrust his own head into the noose. By blabbing freely into the hidden mike on no fewer than those dozen occasions, Roger set himself up—and Lasater as well.

When he began unburdening himself to Rodney Myers, Roger Clinton had taken his leave of Jodie Mahoney's place in Little Rock and had become what seemed like a full-time resident in the mansion. The authorities picked up Roger's trail there just as he entered negotiations to sell a quarter pound of cocaine for $10,000. According to a joint task force report that would surface into the public domain from the Arkansas State Police files on August 2, 1984, his dealings were with Little Rock druggie Russell Crump and the New York mule, Maurice Rodriguez. That was the first "hard evidence" authorities nailed down against the conspirators.

As the lawmen determined, when young Clinton met Rodriguez at Jodie's party in September 1983, Roger by then was freely snorting cocaine and looking to make a score as a trafficker after he seemed to have become irrevocably hooked on the drug.

To give himself a front, Roger took to singing with a Little Rock rock band called, most appropriately, Dealer's Choice. But his deepening commitment to cocaine soon led him to the Big Apple.

"I had all I needed in New York City," he recalled in a 1992 interview in Los Angeles, where he was dispatched to jump-start a new life that his big brother forced him into after Roger served prison time.

"I had friends, I was dating several girls, and I had a lot of money," Roger's narrative went on. "Then all of a sudden—boom!

"I met this guy who's offering me the same thing, except I won't have to work hard for it. Shoot, all I had to do is sit around and do cocaine."

Roger body-packed the white powder and carried it in his pockets and luggage through airports in New York, Atlanta, St. Louis, Chicago, and wherever else his master directed him to mule the junk.

"It was easy," Roger was to say after the ax fell and he was put on the witness stand. "You put it in your jacket, walk through this little security clearance, and you're home free."

"And I had nothing to fear because I was an all-American type."

Half Brother's Indicted as a Druggie

When August 2, 1984, dawned, Bill Clinton had to face the electorate with an explanation of his *black sheep brother.*

On that day the federal grand jury sitting in Fayetteville didn't seem to care that Roger Clinton's brother was the governor of Arkansas. The *Arkansas Democrat's* front page headline told it all:

DRUG CHARGES NAME BROTHER OF GOVERNOR

The story went thusly:

"Roger C. Clinton of Hot Springs, the 26-year-old younger brother of Gov. Bill Clinton, was indicted Thursday [the same day as the story broke] by a federal grand jury on five counts of distributing cocaine and one count of conspiracy to traffic the drug.

"Governor Clinton called a news conference to say it was 'a time of great pain and sadness for me and my family.' After reading a two-paragraph statement in which he said drugs were a curse which has reached epidemic proportions,' Governor Clinton immediately left the governor's conference room at the state capital without taking any questions."

The story further reported, "Roger Clinton wasn't available for comment Thursday."

Strange that the press couldn't locate Roger, who was right down the street from the governor's office, holed up in the executive mansion.

The governor's brief statement concluded:

"I love my brother very much and I will try to be of comfort to him, but I want his case to be handled exactly as any other similar case would be."

Bill Clinton couldn't say otherwise. For the case was in the jurisdiction of United States Attorney Asa Hutchinson. A federal matter, it was totally immune from any State of Arkansas influences or "fixes."

Hutchinson, whose office in Fort Smith handled all federal investigations and prosecutions for the Western District of Arkansas, didn't offer the names of others involved in the inquiry. They had not yet been charged by the grand jury.

Following young Clinton's indictment, Little Rock narc-big Russell Crump and New York mule Maurice Rodriguez reportedly became "leery of Roger Clinton because he was *hot*," meaning that his indictment caused his accomplices to suspect he was going to become a canary.

No one yet knew about the "singing" Roger had done for Rodney Myers' body recorder.

That Roger Clinton was playing the role of informer certainly appeared likely after prosecutor Hutchinson asked U.S. District Judge Oren Harris, sitting in Hot Springs, to postpone his arraignment. That was a sure sign a plea-bargain was in the wind.

Roger Clinton was finally arraigned before Judge Harris on August 22—the same day Russell Ray Crump and Maurice Rodriguez were arrested by FBI agents in Boston. Soon after, Crump turned state's evidence. He gave authorities a full statement about the drug conspiracy that began after he met Lana Crews, Roger's ex-girlfriend—a conspiracy that continued through her association with Rodriguez, the launch of cocaine shipments via Federal Express, payments through Western Union, and the cattling of the white powder in the Little Rock home of Jodie Mahoney, the son of Representative Joseph K. "Jodie" Mahony, Jr., the Arkansas legislator.

During the proceeding, Roger Clinton's mother sat in the front row in the courtroom. She wept uncontrollably as her younger son stood before the bench and listened somberly to the charges read by Judge Harris.

Finally, when the court asked how he wished to plead, Roger responded in a firm voice, "Not guilty!"

His plea, however, was confined only to Roger's drug dealings between May 24 and July 1, 1984, which reflected merely one aspect of the conspiracy with Crump and Rodriguez. Nothing signaled in the court papers of additional drug dealings with Crump, Rodriguez, and Hot Springs attorney Sam Anderson, Jr., the governor's bosom buddy since boyhood days. Those charges were held in abeyance while authorities attempted to define the role others played in the conspiracy.

A prime target of the investigation continued to be Dan R. Lasater and some Lasater & Company employees, including his previously identified ex-convict killer chauffeur, Curtis Lee Berry. Additionally, a well-known former state senator and nine other suspects were targeted but would not have their day of reckoning for many months to come.

Meanwhile, the governor headed toward the end of his second term.

Clinton's a Third-Term Governor

During the campaign, Republican challenger Woody Freeman promised not to raise taxes and to run state government like a business.

"I will correct Clinton's mistakes and bring about the repeal of the tax on heavy trucks," Freeman told voters as election day closed in. "This election will be a referendum on Clinton's entire tenure in office."

But the electorate didn't respond favorably to Freeman's flowery oratory. For when the polls closed on November 6, Clinton's promises for job training programs, finance development, and a nationwide effort to recruit commerce and industry to invest in Arkansas was what the public bought.

In one of the smallest voter turnouts in years, Clinton amassed a formidable 63 percent in statewide balloting that returned him to office in a breeze.

His victory at the polls not only gave him a third term, but also prompted Clinton to press the legislature for passage of teacher testing, which had been unsuccessfully challenged by the Arkansas Education Association in a lawsuit filed just before the election.

"I can't believe that a court of law would really rule that it is unconstitutional to determine the basic learning skills of a teacher and to require those who don't have those skills to improve in order to stay in the classroom," Clinton orated.

The victorious governor hammered hard at the Arkansas Education Association's "overreaction" to the entire teacher-testing issue.

"The leadership of the AEA sort of chose to make this their last stand and act as if it were the most important issue that had ever occurred in the whole history of time," Clinton said. "It undermined their ability to fight for their own pay increases in special session, or for any substantive improvements."

Roger Cops a Plea: "I'm Guilty!"

Bill Clinton could hardly savor his third-term victory before news out of Hot Springs savaged him with screaming front page stories in the state's dailies, and television and radio newscasts.

ROGER CLINTON PLEADS GUILTY TO DRUG CHARGES

That headline in the *Arkansas Democrat* broke three days after Bill Clinton's victory at the polls and just 48 hours after the balloting became official.

Roger had copped a plea before U.S. District Court Judge Harris.

With tears streaming down her cheeks, Virginia Kelley again took in the courtroom proceedings from her seat in the front row, surrounded by friends and relatives. Her son, free on the $5,000 bond she had posted for him at his August 14 hearing when he pleaded innocent to five drug charges, sat in a seat two rows behind Mrs. Kelley. Roger seemed nervous. He alternately glanced up at the ceiling, straight ahead at the American flag behind the judge's bench, then down at the floor. Seated beside him and trying to lend comfort was his stepfather, Richard Kelley, who had married Roger's mother in 1982.

Reporters had expected the governor of Arkansas to be in the courtroom to demonstrate brotherly support, but he was nowhere to be seen. Bill Clinton was distancing himself from the debasing family event. His office offered this "cop-out," as some called it.

"The governor is out of town," said a press secretary, Joan Roberts. "He will not be issuing a statement."

Roger Clinton's revised plea confessed guilt to two specific drug deals. One occurred the previous June 29 in the parking lot of Little Rock's Raintree Apartments—not far from the Governor's mansion—where Roger had bought a bag of cocaine from his "main men," suppliers Russell Crump and Maurice Rodriguez, then transported the drug to Hot Springs and sold it to undercover state police.

He also pleaded guilty to a charge that he sold a gram of coke to a police informer on June 20 for $150. This transaction took place at 111 Bridgeview Lane in Hot

Springs, an apartment authorities had set up as a "sting" operation.

Roger Clinton reportedly believed he had a fighting chance to beat the rap of cattling drugs after the federal grand jury returned its five-count indictment against him the previous August 2. He had no idea how solid the government's case against him was.

Not only did U.S. Attorney Hutchinson have the audio tapes Rodney Myers recorded, but the drug enforcement undercover sleuths and FBI agents on the case also augmented that with a further damning catalog.

"We not only have substantive proof of both incidents that Roger Clinton pleaded to, but we have plenty of video," Hutchinson told reporters after the hearing ended and Roger was allowed to continue his freedom on the same $5,000 bond.

But it wasn't until after Roger's two collaborators, Crump and Rodriguez, were arrested in Boston that the case became ironclad against him. On August 22, Crump came clean and gave his account of the conspiracy that began in early 1981 after Crump met Lana Crews.

Before Roger Clinton left the courthouse after he pleaded guilty, prosecutor Hutchinson let it be known:

"There is no agreement regarding sentencing. That is left entirely to the discretion of the judge."

But Roger Clinton had cut a deal with Hutchinson. He would, in time, deliver to the feds Bill Clinton's "political ally" Dan Lasater and other conspirators. Roger's arias would spare him the punishment Uncle Sam would have had in store for him had he remained silent: a maximum of 15 years imprisonment in the federal slammer and a $25,000 fine.

Judge Harris ordered a pre-sentencing investigation of Roger Clinton and his two accomplices and said he'd sentence the defendants in January. He also would dispose of the three remaining counts against Roger before passing sentence.

When Roger Clinton emerged from the U.S. District Court after his arraignment on that November 9th, he could offer only three words to reporters.

"I feel fine," he said, then walked to the parking lot with a smile and waved adieu to the press.

Barely a week went by before Roger Clinton's name was back on the front pages. He was indicted anew as a drug trafficker. This time the federal grand jury meeting in Fort Smith indicted not only him and his cohorts in the Little Rock drug capers, but also brought new charges against Hot Springs attorney Sam Anderson, Jr., the governor's longtime chum.

Anderson was hit the hardest. He was accused of making cocaine buys from Roger Clinton, for the most part, and some others from Roger Crump and Maurice Rodriguez. Unlike the other three accused druggies, Anderson would maintain his innocence and elect to stand trial.

Clinton Begins His Third Term—with a Heavy Heart

The following January, Bill Clinton, accompanied by wife Hillary, who held four-year-old daughter Chelsea by the hand, stood before a joint session of the legislature and took the oath of office administered by the new Chief Justice of the Arkansas Supreme Court, Jack Holt, Jr. The judge was the nephew of the late Frank Holt, who'd given Clinton his first taste of Arkansas politics when he employed him as an aide in his gubernatorial campaign.

After taking the oath Clinton addressed the lawmakers:

"I think we have an opportunity coming into this new legislative session to make the same sort of commitment to the economic development of our state, to increasing our capacity to bring jobs to our people, that we made to education the previous two sessions. And if we view the two as two sides of the same coin, and if we muster that amount of dedication and concentration, I think we can have a great legislative session and lay another great cornerstone in the future of our state."

Clinton then asked the legislators to join him in working for the future of Arkansas:

"I believe as strongly as I ever have believed anything that, starting two years ago, we began a movement to put this state into the front ranks of the states of this country and that we will stick with it. If we will stick with the education program and develop an economic development program that is second to none in America, there is absolutely no reason we cannot do something that all generations of past Arkansans have not been able to do. That is, to bring our state out of the backwaters of American economic conditions."

In mid-afternoon Clinton returned to the capitol building's steps as he'd done after two previous swearing-in-ceremonies and delivered his inaugural address before a crowd of nearly 3,000, many stomping their feet for warmth in freezing 30-degree weather.

"We must believe in ourselves and our ability to shape our own destiny," he declared. "Too many of us still expect too little of ourselves and demand too little of each other because we see the future as a question of fate, out of our hands. But the future need not be fate, it can be an achievement."

Days later, Clinton handed the Arkansas Legislature an imposing, dictionary-sized, bound booklet. It contained copies of 80 proposed bills. The package zeroed in on economic development, improvements in education, control of crime, and regulation of utilities.

The massive number of bills was viewed as somewhat onerous. It was suggested by some of her detractors that the idea of bunching them all into one huge bundle was Hillary Clinton's.

"She was trying to choke the legislators by having them swallow that giant pill," said one critic.

"Who's running this state?" asked another. "Is it Bill or Hillary?"

The governor's proposals were topped by a catch-all measure to create a state agency to issue tax-exempt bonds to finance his programs and development projects. The bulky package was aimed at "blindsiding the legislature," critics complained, by having the lawmakers mandate the state's three major retirement systems to invest at least five percent of their assets in Arkansas.

Clinton envisioned a $400 million windfall accruing for financial backing of his economic development proposals.

None of his measures met stiffer legislative examination than the education bill. At times it seemed the pressure applied by the Arkansas Education Association and its supporters would win over the intensive lobbying by the governor.

In the end, House Bill 616, the measure drawn up for the AEA to skirt the court's action and repeal the teacher-testing law, was defeated. That meant that Bill Clinton would get his way: the teacher basic skills tests would be administered beginning March 23, 1985.

19

RAISING ILLEGAL FUNDS FOR CLINTON'S CAMPAIGNS

Bill Becomes a Beggar Drumming Up Business for Rose Law

During the '84 campaign, Bill Clinton may have used more funds from his political war chest than he or his reelection committee had counted on. That came to light on April 4, 1985, when Jim McDougal, riding on a heady high in the savings and loan business, made a strange move to help his Whitewater partner ease the financial crunch in which he found himself.

Investigative reporters William Rempel and Douglas Frantz of the *Los Angeles Times* sniffed out the curious deal—10 years later—as Clinton begins to wallow in the most explosive issue of 1994: the Whitewater Madison Guaranty S&L scandals.

Rempel and Frantz uncovered a caper Clinton pulled in '85 that had gone largely unnoticed for its unethical, if not highly criminal configurations.

Jim McDougal set the scene for the episode:

Clinton is returning from an early morning jog, winded and sweaty. It isn't clear whether his short breath and perspiration were worked up on his run or because, as he is often known to do, he pretended to jog when he actually went for a shack at Gennifer Flowers' pad—or to some other bimbo's.

With no concern about Jim McDougal's desk chair, which is upholstered in fine-grain leather, Clinton plops into it with his soaking-wet shirt and shorts clinging to his body, then proceeds to cry him a river of economic woe.

He gripes about how tough things are in making ends meet. McDougal gets the drift. He knows when his arm's being twisted.

"I asked him how much he needed, and Clinton said, 'About two thousand a month.'"

This from a man whose own salary may be a pitiable $35,000—lowest pay by far of any governor in the other 49 states—but who has a wife pulling down better than $100,000 a year.

McDougal swings into action.

After all, isn't Bill Clinton his main man up at that big ol' statehouse—where with a stroke of his pen he could give International Paper Corporation a multi-million-dollar tax break?

And in return to receive, even before the ink from his Waterman has dried, and at a fraction of its worth, a beautiful 820-acre parcel of prime vacation land for further Whitewater Development exploitation?

Seeing how he, Susan, and his partners, the Clintons, could come out so far ahead in the game of corruption and graft that his pal the governor is playing in office, what harm for McDougal to let a couple of grand come out of his Madison Guaranty once a month. After all, it isn't even his money—it belongs to the depositors!

Thus McDougal immediately commands $2,000-a-month payments to go to the Rose Law Firm as a "retainer," although there's a suspicion today that the payments were consigned for direct delivery to Hillary.

The bottom line comes from Jim McDougal:

"I hired Hillary because Bill came in whimpering that they needed help."

McDougal would soon have a crying need for Hillary, her Rose Law Firm, and a much-needed provenancer at the gubernatorial stand. Jim has taken Madison Guaranty to the well once too often—it won't be long before the boys from the Federal Savings and Loan Insurance Corporation descend on him for an accounting.

The question of whether Hillary or Rose Law pocketed that $2,000 "retainer," which today sounds more like a euphemism for *payoff*, is a deep, dark secret. But it's a secret that may not remain obscured for much longer—despite recent denials that Clinton "had nothing to do with those payments," voiced by Dee Dee Myers, the White House press secretary and chief "damage controller."

A onetime McDougal associate recalls vividly that Clinton had "everything in the world to do with the payoffs. Because "Bill used to pick up the checks on his morning jogs."

The incident has remained frozen in Jim McDougal's mind because of his concern about the damage he feared Clinton could conceivably do to his leather chair that morning.

"I worried like hell that he'd stain the damn cowhide with his sweat," is a direct quote from the former banker and manipulative real estate wheeler-dealer.

The year 1985 is vital in Kenneth Starr's inquiry for another reason. It's also the start of a long period about which a lot of questions have been asked—but never answered adequately. In fact, they have been totally ignored by Bill Clinton, who is the central figure in those matters.

They culminate with a mysterious $300,000 *business* loan that will soon be taken out by Susan McDougal from the Small Business Administration.

The genesis of the transaction goes back to Jim McDougal's relationship with David Hale, a quiet, soft-spoken, 52-year-old pro in the Arkansas politics that became his bag when he was 18 years young.

At that age, he sat in smoke-filled rooms and listened, mesmerized, to ex-Governor Orval Faubus discourse on his *misunderstood* political career.

While he attended the University of Arkansas, Hale was president of the campus's Young Democrats and a member of the executive committee of the National College of Young Democrats.

In 1961, he was at John F. Kennedy's inauguration and sat next to celebrated thrush Lena Horne at the inaugural ball. A dozen years later, as a young lawyer in Little Rock, he was elected president of the National Junior Chamber of Commerce.

Then came his connection with Governor Bill Clinton who, in 1979 during his first term, appointed Hale to the bench of one of the just-established small claims courts throughout the state. Hale presided at the one in the Little Rock area, the Pulaski County Municipal Court.

That same year, Hale established a small investment firm, Capital-Management Services, Inc., a private lending company backed by the government's Small Business Administration.

Although Hale's outfit, by law, could lend only to small businesses, that's not how things turned out when his lawyer, Jim Guy Tucker (governor of Arkansas today), entered the scene.

Back then, Tucker had established himself as low man on the totem-pole in the McDougals' purchase of that $45,000 building that almost overnight became a $190,000 *land-flip* gem for the banker and his wife.

Interviewed by the author's researchers, Hale recalled that in the fall of 1985, Tucker, still in private legal practice, invited him to a meeting with Jim McDougal. They met at Castle Grande, a low-cost residential development that was one of the banker's Little Rock real estate investments. Hale recited the details:

"He told me something like, 'We're going to need your help.' I don't remember the exact words, but I'm certain that McDougal used the phrases 'political family' and 'clean up.'

"To me, that was meant to say that I had to help clean up things for members of the political family."

Hale says he wasn't exactly sure who the members were, but he sort of got the drift—that it was going to be a *bailout for someone in high political office.*

Yet at first, it hardly seemed so to him.

For Hale was asked to advance McDougal a small business loan to pay for one of the banker's own most speculative—indeed, off-the-wall—investments: the purchase of land at Franklin Delano Roosevelt's summer retreat, Campobello Island. Surrounded by the chill Atlantic's waters between Maine and New Brunswick, this is where the New Deal president went swimming as a young man and contracted paralyzing polio.

McDougal committed himself to a $4 million binder on the property, on which he planned to build a resort. How much thinking had gone into the project isn't clear.

Unlike the Ozark Mountains, where a friendly and very giving governor could manipulate the construction of a road to *nowhere*, there was no one of comparable influence in that easternmost corner of America to improve the travel time to the site McDougal bought—a nearly four-hour drive from the nearest airport.

Moreover, James Ring Adams noted in the February 1994 edition of *The American Spectator*: "...roaring tides twice a day opened a mile of mud flats between waterfront lots and the ocean."

After granting the first loan for McDougal's bailout, Hale quickly advances a second one through his SBA-backed loan firm.

This financial emancipation is more in line with what he guessed at the outset his loans were to be used. That advance of big bucks—$45,000—is made to Stephen A. Smith, a political scientist with a polling firm, The Communications Company of Little Rock.

Smith, Clinton's administrative assistant during his first term, 1978-80, was out of that job after Frank White unseated Clinton.

Smith quickly rebounded. He became president of Madison Bank & Trust. This is the bank in Kingston that Jim McDougal bought in 1980, which formerly did business as the Bank of Kingston.

This is also the bank that advanced Hillary Rodham that curious $30,000 loan for construction of the model house at the Clinton-McDougal Whitewater project in the Ozark Mountains.

The game of name-switching continues when, still in 1980, MB&T loses its identity after it's swallowed up by Jim McDougal's newly formed Madison Guaranty Savings and Loan.

In this merger, Stephen Smith is retained as an officer but undergoes a personal title change. He is metamorphosed from president of MB&T to vice-chairman of Madison Guaranty Savings and Loan.

The Government Regulators Begin to Smell a Rat

It should be noted that, unlike commercial and savings banks, which are controlled by the federal government—and supervised closely by the Federal Deposit Insurance Corporation (FDIC)—thrifts (savings and loans) operate under charters issued by the individual states.

While the feds cannot step in and exercise direct authority over S&Ls, they can exert plenty of influence. If warranted, they can close any thrift in the land—simply by yanking the indemnity the thrifts' deposits receive from the Federal Savings and Loan Insurance Corporation (FSLIC).

In the mid-'80s—before it declared itself bankrupt in the midst of the scandalous, trillion-dollar, nationwide S&L debacles—the FSLIC backed the thrifts' deposits under the aegis of the Federal Home Loan Board.

This overseer of S&Ls is modeled after the Federal Reserve Bank. It has the same number of regional banks, thirteen of which are committed to dispatch examiners to look into the affairs of the S&Ls, just as the FDIC's financial watchdogs do with commercial and savings banks.

Soon, the FDIC, theoretically out of arms-reach control—yet still a *big brother*— over the S&L landscape, spotted something askew in the Kingston Bank's acquisition by Jim McDougal.

Its suspicions were aroused by the swift conversions Kingston had undergone. It was of little concern to the regulators when it went to Madison Trust (still a bank, subject to FDIC controls).

But when it was removed from federal regulators' rigid hands-on controls after McDougal took it into the softly regulated S&L arena, questions had to be asked.

What was McDougal doing pulling that stuff? the FDIC wanted to know as it examined the records and outstanding debtors' notes left behind by the Bank of Kingston.

The examiners scratched their heads in bewilderment as they traced how Jim McDougal was operating before the Kingston acquisition and after his merger with Madison Guaranty.

What raised their eyebrows was the incomprehensible way that some of Kingston's problem loans were shifted by McDougal to Madison Guaranty Savings and Loan's newly opened ledgers.

Remember, Jim's start-up of Madison Guaranty was greased by a $70,000 loan from the empirical Stephens family's Worthen Bank. His initial shares in Madison, without any recorded increase in value, enabled this clever, real estate manipulator, a Johnny-come-lately in the world of finance, to secure an additional loan of $142,000 from Worthen.

All of this borrowing would have seemed to make Worthen the potential owner of Madison by way of foreclosure, should McDougal default on those loans.

Add to this scenario's maze the further complication of a $390,000 loan from Union National Bank of Little Rock, advanced earlier-on that enabled Jim McDougal to close on the purchase of Madison Bank & Trust, the former Bank of Kingston.

Clear?

If it isn't, the reader's in good company. A lot of folks can't follow these convolutions in high finance that are now in the hands of special prosecutor Kenneth Starr and Congress to untangle.

One of Starr's more enlightening discoveries may come out of his research into Union National Bank's 1993 merger with the granddaddy of all big Arkansas financial houses, Worthen Bank.

Union's records, followers of McDougal's business transactions suggest, may hold a treasury of discoveries about the way Jim wheeled and dealed his way to the top in Arkansas's banking community.

Or the big eye-opener could even come out of Starr's exploration of the loans we now have David Hale industriously making at McDougal's behest, right into the following year, 1986.

But long before then, Clinton—hardly past the midway point in his third term as governor—had begun preparing to run for a fourth term in '86. Indeed, he was looking forward anxiously to that prospect, for the legislature had just amended the length of service in that office from two to four years.

As Clinton began drafting his campaign plans, he heard disturbing soundings. He was to face a primary challenge from former four-term Governor Orval Faubus, by then a creaking, 76-year-old warhorse, yet a name to be reckoned with in Arkansas where he once ruled like a segregationist demi-god.

If Faubus's challenge wasn't enough in the '86 pre-election gymnastics, Clinton felt as though he were being double-whammied by the return of an old foe, Frank White, once again the GOP's candidate on the November ballot.

McDougal doesn't recall the exact words, but he seems fairly certain of what Clinton told him:

"Look, Jim...I kinda need ya he'p...the money in my political war chest is down low...I'm gonna have ta have a hefty infusion of long green."

By that time, McDougal was in a bind. The federal examiners from Texas had been through his Madison Guaranty records and didn't like what they found. They told him he'd better tighten up on the fast-and-loose ways he was making questionable loans—and shore up Madison's threadbare vaults with some of that same green paper Clinton wanted.

This may have been February 28, 1986, but so far as McDougal was concerned, it was still December 25, 1985. Unlike Santa Claus, David Hale hadn't gone back to the North Pole after his Christmas rounds. He was still in Little Rock.

Only a week or so ago, McDougal had asked Hale for a $150,000 advance from Small Business Loan Administration funds. The loan, perfectly illegal since McDougal was *big business*, was approved. But Hale wanted time to find a way to put up that money without arousing suspicions at the SBLA.

He had worked things out twice before for the banker when he anted up the loans for McDougal's Campobello bailout and Stephen Smith's personal financial emancipation, both of which had nothing to do with *small business* either.

Hale's curiosity had been aroused only slightly when he made those advances. But he didn't ask questions. McDougal's words, "political family" and "clean up," carried a vague message for Hale: Bill Clinton could likely be the one presiding as the patriarch of that "political family." But he couldn't know for certain.

Then came February 28, and Dave Hale could no longer have any doubt. He was standing outside the statehouse and who should nudge him with a wink and a question?

The Cat's Out of the Bag! Clinton's the Big Borrower

"Whadda ya say, Dave, ol' pal, you're a-gonna he'p out Jim McDougal, aren't y'all?" Clinton rasped to the bewildered Dave Hale.

Hale now *knew for certain* that Bill Clinton was very much the "political family" that McDougal spoke of.

In that brief encounter, Hale replied, "Oh sure, Governor. "I'm gonna go along with Jim on that matter. Don't you have a care in the world about that."

If it occurred to Hale to ask himself what business Clinton had asking about a loan that McDougal wanted for Madison Guaranty, Hale doesn't say.

All he knew at the time was that Madison Guaranty seemed to him to be a solid operation. Jim McDougal had assured him of that when he applied for the $150,000 loan:

"The federal examiners are coming up from Texas, and I've gotta balance accounts. No problem, you understand. But I'm in a slight bind because there's a shortfall of ready cash to balance the books perfectly."

Hale had no way of knowing that one of the Federal Home Loan Board's 13 regional regulatory banks, the one closest to Little Rock—the Home Loan Bank of Dallas—had already dispatched its examiners to Little Rock and pored over Madison Guaranty's books.

Madison Guaranty's situation was far more serious than McDougal led Hale to believe.

Thus, being in the dark and with the little poke in the ribs he got from Clinton, Dave Hale gave Jim McDougal those 150 *big ones* from funds out of his SBLA-backed financial service.

Not many days following that February 28 encounter with Clinton, Hale received a call from McDougal on a matter that would soon complete Dave's education in power politics. He was invited to drop by Castle Grande, the residential development in Little Rock that recently had become one of McDougal's real estate investments-turned-sour.

"Jim said he wanted me to meet the governor," Hale revealed in the interview for this book. "So I drove to Castle Grande and walked into the office there, where I found Clinton and McDougal in rapt conversation.

"They were discussing the challenge Clinton faced in the coming election from [ex-Governor Faubus and] Frank White."

Bill Clinton's campaign would need a lot of *scratch* to knock off Faubus, should he enter the Democratic primary, and to ward off White's challenge as a GOP rival in November.

Clinton and McDougal got down to cases rapidly.

"How's this gonna work?" Hale asked after being told $150,000 was needed to resuscitate Clinton's near-comatose war chest.

McDougal had the answer.

"We'll put it in my wife, Susan's, name."

"Can that fly?" Hale inquired.

"Hey, we can make anything take off," McDougal snapped, turning to Clinton with a wry smile and a knowing nod.

Clinton rubbed his hands for a moment, then issued a nervous caveat:

"Just remember this, guys...my name can't show up on any of this stuff...don't forget that."

That was fine with Hale, but he wondered about Susan McDougal's ability to repay a loan as large as $150,000.

Odd that Clinton needed the same amount of money McDougal had to have when he put the touch on Hale in behalf of Madison Guaranty?

It didn't occur to Hale at the time that it was anything more than a coincidence.

The only concern that crossed Hale's mind was whether Susan McDougal had the ability to repay the loan that Jim wanted to replenish Clinton's campaign coffers.

"Oh, no sweat," McDougal said. "We'll put it into her advertising company...you know, make it to 'Susan McDougal dba [doing business as] Master Marketing.'"

Poor Dave Hale didn't have the foggiest notion that Susan's company was strictly a one-woman operation and that her assets of symmetrical body and pleasant face constituted the firm's entire holdings.

Hale said he'd accept Master Marketing as security, but he must first run a credit check on the company to determine its financial profile.

That caused Clinton and McDougal to rear back in obvious discomfort and descend into a deafening silence. Until Clinton offered, "Look, Dave, I'll personally provide security on the loan."

"What kind is that, Governor?" Hale asked in a respectful voice.

"Well, I have a nice tract of valuable land up in Marion County," Clinton responded. He referred to Whitewater Development's 230 acres that he co-owned with Hillary and Jim and Susan McDougal.

Hale didn't need a map to tell him what Clinton was talking about, and he was quick to comment:

"That may not be the end of the world, Governor, but it sure as hell's a place to go if you wanna see the last outpost of civilization."

No last word on a deal was reached at that meeting, which Hale remembers lasted no more than 20 minutes. Hale left Clinton and McDougal without a further word from either man.

It would be some time before Hale talked with Clinton again. But he spoke with McDougal in just a short time, when McDougal phoned Hale's office on or about March 1, 1986:

"Dave, you know that hundred and fifty thousand that you're supposed to lend *Susan* [the code name for *Bill Clinton*]?"

"Yes, what about it...I'm just in the process of drawing up the check."

"Hold on, Dave...don't cut that one."

"Why not?"

"Because...well...err...*Susan* says to...uh...err...make it out...for...for...three hundred thou..."

"What! Why?"

"Because that's what *Susan* says she *Frank*-ly needs to do the *White* number...you know, the TV commercial we talked about."

To an eavesdropper, that might sound like a deal Susan McDougal was working on for her Master Marketing agency—but not to David Hale.

The message's peal was clear to Capital-Management's *patsy*—who, in time, would also be the *fall guy*.

But not for seven more years. Not until after the Whitewater scandals began burning like the fires of hell all around the Oval Office—when President Bill Clinton's Justice Department pushed the panic button and reached for the *hot line* to the U. S. Attorney's office in Little Rock:

"Nail David Hale's ass—right away!"

The call was made to Paula Casey, who happened to be an old acquaintance of Clinton's. But she also happened to have integrity, a quality missing in all too many of Clinton's other acquaintances.

Ms. Casey had been appointed U.S. Attorney in Little Rock by old friend Bill Clinton on August 10, 1993.

Duty-bound, Ms. Casey proceeded with her instructions from the Justice Department in Washington. She convened a grand jury and obtained the indictment on September 23, thus conforming to the Clinton White House demand that such action was to be taken "at all cost and at once."

For the next four months, according to her many colleagues, Ms. Casey wrestled with her conscience about going through with David Hale's prosecution. She had known Hale for many years as an "honorable and fair-minded individual."

So on a day soon after Robert Fiske was appointed special prosecutor to probe the Whitewater-Madison Guaranty mess, Ms. Casey decided to turn over David Hale's case to Fiske, who has since turned it over to Kenneth Starr.

"I felt it was the only thing I could do," she was quoted by an aide. "I decided to recuse myself from the case."

Hale Vows: He'll Send Bill and Hill to Prison

Prior to Ms. Casey's decision to wash her hands of his prosecution, Hale had tried to go on a fast track to a reduced charge. He was willing to plead guilty to misrepresenting a loan to his company as "paid-in-capital," when no such transaction existed. Yet he found no relief. There were no takers to his offer. Then out of the blue, he found his old friend, Paula Casey, despite her execution of his White House-engineered indictment, to be a godsend.

With the special counsel handling his case now, Hale felt emancipated. He was certain his testimony to the special prosecutor's grand jury would accomplish his original aim: put the screws on President Clinton for the double cross he pulled on him!

"I know that my testimony is going to land Clinton behind bars before he finishes his term as president!" Hale told one of the author's researchers. "He has no way of weaseling out of the corner I have him in. He's doomed! And so is Hillary!"

The last thing Hale wanted was to take a fall for the bad loans he made to McDougal and Clinton, which helped Madison Guaranty to go under in 1989 when the FSLIC closed in and took over the thrift.

In short, his Capital-Management became insolvent only after Jim and Susan McDougal did their big numbers on him with defaulted loans taken in the name of Bill Clinton's campaign chest.

Hale had an inkling that Clinton would put the screws to him just as soon as he was elected president. For a year, Hale had figuratively held his breath—after Jeff Gerth's exposé about Bill and Hillary's involvement in Whitewater and Madison Guaranty was published in the *New York Times* during the '92 campaign.

Back then, Hale was warned by a friend that if Clinton was elected and the Whitewater-Madison issue ever got hot, Dave would be a target for prosecution.

Hale had every reason to believe the friend. He knew that the $300,000 loan advanced to the McDougals had not made its way into Clinton's campaign treasury.

He learned that about three months after making the loan, when he ran into Clinton again. The encounter, Hale recalls, was at Little Rock's University Plaza Mall.

"Clinton spots me, comes runnin' over, and he looks like he's fit to be tied. He almost screams at me:

"'Have you heard what that fuckin' whore Susan has done?'

"I'm about to answer that I haven't heard, but there's nobody to respond to. Clinton just rushes away without waiting for my answer."

Dave Hale had no idea what Clinton was referring to at the time—but then he learned that Clinton had never seen any of that money; it was plowed into Madison Guaranty in a vain effort to stop it from becoming another casualty in the epidemic of nationwide S&L failures.

All the issues related here are targeted by the twin investigations now under way, or soon to begin, in the Whitewater-Madison Guaranty scandals.

However, Special Counsel Starr and congressional probers aren't the only ones interested in rooting out the truth about those long-ago, shadowy happenings.

The Resolution Trust Corporation, not mentioned thus far, is also engaged in probings of its own and, as matters stand today, these investigators could turn into the most fearsome of all for the White House's main occupants.

Principally, the RTC has set its sights on activities by Clinton's 1984 gubernatorial campaign committee, which it views as a prime suspect in the criminal probe of Madison Guaranty.

An introduction is in order.

The RTC is a creation of the Treasury Department, designed to be a non-political investigative arm or, as it's now called, a "clean-up agency" in the half-trillion-dollar nationwide savings and loan collapse.

It's mission is conducting inquiries into the thrift failures and, where warranted, lodging criminal and/or civil charges that must then be turned over to the Justice Department for adjudication or prosecution.

Sometime in October 1993, the Clinton White House received the first disturbing vibes about the RTC's progress in the Madison Guaranty S&L probe. It learned that no fewer than 10 criminal charges had been formalized against individuals involved in the case—and that Bill and Hillary Clinton would be "witnesses" earmarked for questioning on related matters.

It's not known who revealed this information to the White House, but there's one known leak that has since become a raging cataract.

It involves Roger C. Altman, a former Wall Street investment banker and college friend of President Clinton's, who wrote himself into the scenario that same October.

Altman, the deputy secretary of the treasury, admitted making tracks to the White House to conduct a series of "briefings" for Bill and Hillary's top aides.

"I went there to update them about certain matters" in the RTC investigation, is how he put it.

The first "seminar" is said to have been held in the presence of the president and first lady, but neither has stated what was learned from Altman. Hillary has been completely silent on the matter, while all Clinton will say is that he cannot remember any of the *who*, *what*, *when*, *why*, and *how*'s of the meeting, only the *where*—that it was in the White House.

Later "briefings" were held in January and February.

The public might never have learned of these get-togethers had it not been for Altman's inadvertent statement at a House Banking Committee hearing. He blurted that he had talked with White House people about approaching statute of limitations deadlines threatening to terminate the progress of the RTC's investigation unless they were extended.

Altman was widely criticized for these briefings because, in effect, he had consorted with the "enemy." Prosecuting agencies don't divulge their hands in matters bearing on the targets of their probes.

Republicans charged Altman's contacts might have compromised the Treasury's inquiries into Madison Guaranty.

White House *damage controller* Dee Dee Myers protested "the contacts and conversations were not of any substance," yet she didn't say what information was advanced or which staffers were at the "briefings."

Altman, 47, quickly seems to have sunk in his standing with the Clinton Administration after the firestorm that followed his breast with the truth.

He suffered another setback after he went to Harold Ickes, the recently hired White House deputy chief of staff, and announced he was removing himself from all RTC activity. He failed to tell Ickes that before recusing himself, he took on former U.S. Attorney Jay Stephens to investigate for the RTC aspects of the Madison Guaranty failure—and its connections with Whitewater.

Stephens, who was the chief prosecutor for the Washington, D.C., area, was fired in January 1993, along with almost all Republican U.S. attorneys, after Clinton took office. It's a routine happening when a new administration comes to Washington.

Instead of taking his dismissal lying down, Stephens went public and charged his firing was designed to stall the ongoing Justice Department corruption probe of Representative Dan Rostenkowski (D-IL), the recently resigned chairman of the House Ways and Means Committee. He was indicted for fleecing the House Bank with bounced checks and of committing other improprieties.

Rostenkowski is one of Bill Clinton's leading congressional supporters. He's ridden herd on every administration bill in the House and shepherded most of them to a favorable vote.

When the Chicago lawmaker was embroiled in a bitterly contested primary in March 1994, the president ignored his advisers and vigorously campaigned for Rosty, who managed to overcome his rivals' challenges—although he's not in the clear insofar as the Justice Department charges are concerned. He turned down a plea bargain and opted for a trial.

So when Ickes and George Stephanopoulos, the president's 34-year-old whiz-kid senior adviser, learned independently on February 24 about Stephens' new role with the RTC, they were infuriated.

One White House source says, "Harold and George had catatonic fits" when they found out about Stephens.

"They couldn't conceive of how Altman, who went to school with Clinton, could be so insensitive as to hire a prober for the RTC who's been so outspoken as Stephens has been against the president."

Another source offers this suggestion:

"This was Altman's way of getting even because he was told the president would have nothing more to do with him for tattling about the RTC briefings. He heard he didn't have a prayer of ever taking Lloyd Bentsen's place, should the treasury secretary leave his post.

"In short, he was dead meat."

Of course, the RTC is supposed to be an independent government agency and free from White House influences.

Yet Ickes and Stephanopoulos didn't look at it that way.

Stephanopoulos is a past master of pulling strings and working fixes, since he learned those techniques at the knee of his mentor, Bill Clinton, during their Arkansas days.

Ickes is viewed by many as being far more adept with the fix than George because, now in his 60s, he was the steward for nearly nine years of New York's corrupt Local 100 of the Hotel and Restaurant Employees International Union, which for two decades was dominated by the mob.

He came to the Clinton administration in January 1994 with the heavy stench of "fixer" trailing behind him—and with the tell-tale onus of having been denied a clean bill of health from the FBI. The G-men weren't happy with Ickes's performance as overseer of Local 100.

An independent private investigator—said to have been paid out of White House funds—was retained to give Ickes the sanitizing needed to pass congressional muster for his White House job.

So it should come as no surprise to find Ickes and Stephanopoulos on the phone on February 24 in what the White House describes as a "conference call" with Altman and Treasury Chief of Staff Joshua Steiner.

What did Ickes and Stephanopoulos say to Altman and Steiner?

White House sources tell the *New York Post* that they "inquired about the possibility of having Stephens taken off the case.

"They backed off after being told [by Altman and Steiner] that nothing could be done."

The *Post*'s Washington correspondent, Thomas Ferraro, goes on to note in his story, "Stephanopoulos and Ickes said *they cannot recall suggesting that Stephens be replaced* [author's emphasis]."

Note that Ickes and Stephanopoulos haven't denied that they asked for Stephens' removal. In typical *Clintonesque* style, they simply *cannot recall.*

Time is quick to get on top of the story. The magazine quotes an administration official:

"Based on the facts, we believe [special prosecutor] Fiske has developed...it's possible that at least one, and perhaps several, indictments [involving possible obstruction of justice] could [be] issued."

Ickes remains silent about what he said to Altman and Steiner.

Stephanopoulos made a contrite admission:

"I was puzzled [by the hiring] and blew off steam over the unfairness of that decision. Because Jay Stephens had accused the president of improper interferences in an investigation."

Stephanopoulos claims all he wanted was to learn about the circumstances that led to Stephens' hire—but he doesn't explain why he, a senior White House official, deems it correct to confront the Treasury Department's chief of staff about a decision bearing on an independent regulatory/enforcement agency such as the RTC.

"I wish I hadn't gotten angry," Stephanopoulos laments. "But I was just trying to get information."

Evidently special prosecutor Fiske wasn't impressed with the responses. For he promptly slapped George and Harold Ickes with subpoenas to testify before the grand jury.

But what they testified to appeared to get everyone off the hook, for Fiske's findings failed to nail them to the mast. The story before congressional probers could have a different ending. The solons on the Hill don't have ties to the Clinton Justice Department as "independent counsel" Fiske had--nor his successor Starr.

Meanwhile, the other big news in Washington was the RTC's conclusion that there may have been wrongdoing in Clinton's gubernatorial campaign fund-raising activities.

The investigators' primary focus is on an April 4, 1985, fund-raiser Jim McDougal held to help Clinton pay off a $50,000 personal loan for that campaign—actually, as it will later develop, raising money that wasn't really needed because Clinton had adequate funds in his treasury at the time.

This is in addition to inquiries to determine the ins and outs of the "fund-raising" McDougal was involved in when he took out some $600,000 in "loans" from David Hale's SBLA firm for the "political family."

In a referral to the Justice Department—the first visible action of a criminal nature taken by the RTC—the Treasury Department's probers let it be known they are trying to determine how much of Madison funds were diverted to the '84 gubernatorial campaign *with the knowledge of campaign officials.*

The RTC people haven't yet addressed campaigns other than 1984's to determine how legitimate their contributions may have been. Such inquiries are seen as a certain outgrowth of the attention initially being given to the political fund-raising activities for '84.

The RTC's probers seem to have gone into high gear only after former U.S. Attorney Jay Stephens came aboard.

Stephens, whom Ickes and Stephanopoulos purportedly tried to uproot as an RTC investigator, appears to be zeroing in on heavy-duty areas—such as, for one, determining why certain Madison Guaranty funds ended up in the Clinton Campaign Committee's treasury after passing through various accounts of Jim McDougal's thrifts.

Or why certain funds have gone through a Madison Guaranty account in the name of the Whitewater Development Corporation—the Clinton-McDougal real estate venture.

Most significantly, the referral names Hillary Rodham Clinton as a witness who must be questioned about whether there's a relationship between at least one of the fund-raising activities—specifically for 1984's campaign—and Hillary's legal representation of Madison before state regulators appointed by her husband.

Suspicions about her were raised by the $2,000 "retainer" McDougal paid Hillary and/or her Rose Law Firm after Clinton extracted those payments from the banker during that early morning jog reported earlier.

Jay Stephens doesn't let it rest there. He comes up with a second RTC criminal referral said to name the Clintons as "potential beneficiaries" in the diversion of Madison Guaranty funds to the Whitewater Development Corporation.

In the wake of these referrals, the Clinton White House is at a loss to provide coherent responses.

"The Special Counsel's looking into this," says Dee Dee Myers. "There is no further comment."

"I'm totally unaware of these allegations," comments Betsey Wright, Clinton's former chief of staff.

Asked whether she's received a subpoena from Fiske to talk about the campaign contributions, Ms. Wright declines to say.

Asked whether the campaign records have been turned over to the special prosecutor, Ms. Wright replies, "The records documenting contributions from the 1985 fund-raiser cannot be located."

How familiar!

Here's the wind-up on this issue:

• His aides acknowledge Clinton didn't really need the $150,000 loan for his '84 campaign, but he wanted the money to take no chances with a Ronald Reagan landslide expected to sweep the nation. Of course, Clinton won handily, defeating GOP rival Woody Freeman with 63 percent of the vote.

• Madison Guaranty overdrafts were written on the account of Flowerwood Farms, a McDougal-owned company that was actually one of a dozen "shell corporations" used in a check-kiting scheme to funnel money out of Madison.

• Loans made to the real estate ventures of Charles Peacock, a director and Madison borrower, also trickled into the Clinton campaign coffers. The probers will want to know why Peacock gave the '85 Clinton fund-raisers a batch of $3,000 checks, one of which bore the name of Ken Peacock, his then-24-year-old son, who protested that he never contributed to Clinton and knows nothing about the contribution credited to him.

• Another name on a $3,000 check is that of former Senator J. William Fulbright, who is currently too ill to comment, and that of Dene Landrum, now dead.

• Of greatest interest will be determining why $10,500 worth of checks written to the Clinton campaign in February and October 1985 caused overdrafts in the Whitewater account at Madison and at Master Marketing, which was Susan McDougal's "advertising agency"—now considered just another "shell corporation."

All of the above checks were deposited in the Bank of Cherry Valley, whose records Bob Fiske subpoenaed and passed on to Starr.

Under 1985 Arkansas law, the maximum donation a candidate could accept from a contributor was $1,500 per election.

It's clear that Bill Clinton—or at the very least his election committee—paid no heed to that law.

Moreover, the state's law required that a campaign also report the name of the bank, the amount of the loan, and the name of guarantors for personal loans donated to a campaign. While the '85 campaign documents may be missing, as Betsey Wright claims, other sources say they know that there were no such listings in those records.

Stay tuned for latest developments in your daily newspapers, radio and TV newscasts, and weekly magazines.

Meanwhile, let's return to January 1985.

Clinton has begun his third term as governor, and he's asked the legislators to join him in working for the future of Arkansas.

But he first faces some disturbing distractions.

20

MORE FAMILY MIGRAINES FOR BILL

How Can Bill Not Remember?

On January 27, 1985, Governor Clinton could breath a deep sigh of relief. That day Judge Harris passed sentence on Roger Clinton: two to five years imprisonment. That meant he'd be out of circulation for at least a year before he could be considered for parole—a period the governor could look upon as a respite from more scandal.

Although by now Roger had stopped dealing in drugs, he had not broken the habit. He was, according to the testimony of Little Rock drug therapist Karen Keller, snorting coke at least sixteen times a day.

"His cocaine habit is getting close to a lethal dose," she told the court.

Judge Harris sentenced Roger to the Federal Correctional Facility in Fort Worth, where he was ordered to undergo treatment for drug dependency. But his confinement in Texas would soon be interrupted.

It was February when Roger Clinton did an encore in the U.S District Court in Hot Springs. This time he materialized there with barrister Sam Anderson, Jr., Bill Clinton's longtime chum. It was not a client-attorney relationship that brought them before Judge Oren Harris, who only three weeks earlier had sent the governor's sibling off to Fort Worth to begin drying out. If he had not chosen to turn state's evidence and testify against Sam Anderson, Roger Clinton would have been sitting in the dock alongside the lawyer, who now faced the music as a defendant in a courtroom that'd been on his beat as a barrister in better times.

Sam Anderson's trial is significant because it standardizes the many sides of truth that President Clinton relies upon when diversity of testimony is needed to serve his best interests.

It didn't take long for trial prosecutor Asa Hutchinson to establish Anderson's misdeeds:

•   Paid Roger Clinton $4,000 for two ounces of cocaine that was delivered on November 21, 1983.

•   Took a shipment of three ounces of *snow* on December 11, 1983, and coughed up $6,000 to the governor's brother for it.

•   Paid $4,000 for more coke from Roger on December 19, 1983.

•   Made a like payment on January 4, 1984, for another batch of the white powder.

- On January 26, 1984, paid $10,000 to Roger for one of the largest coke deliveries so far made.

But the eye-opener at this trial was the name Dan R. Lasater, which surfaced for the first time on the public record in connection with illicit drug activity.

For openers, Gina Canada, a prosecution witness, named Lasater as a drug dealer. She also described the banker as being Roger Clinton's "angel"—advancing a "very substantial amount of money" to help bail him out of the financial crunch he found himself in with Crump and Rodriguez.

Then Anderson himself took the stand in his own defense and testified that Roger Clinton had told him the Arkansas state police "were looking to sting me, Rodriguez, and Lasater."

But Clinton himself put Lasater in cold storage by telling the court that his brother's "political ally" had advanced him $8,000 to pay off Rodriguez, who had "threatened to harm the governor and our mother."

All of the above is offered to point out what Bill Clinton should have known by reading the newspapers but, instead, pleaded ignorance to so he could distance himself from the troubles of two people who'd been closest to him in the past.

Of course, this experience must have been traumatic. But many critics cannot condone the way Clinton handled himself during the crisis involving his closest brother and his best friend.

Despite his brother's arrest, prosecution, and guilty plea in the first months of 1984, followed by his sentencing on January 27, 1985, Governor Clinton claimed he didn't know until August 1986—18 months later—about Dan Lasater's involvement in the cocaine ring. Clinton claimed he first learned of it two months before Lasater and ten co-conspirators were indicted by the federal grand jury in Little Rock on October 24, 1986. Moreover, he asserted, he had no inkling at all that his brother was implicated.

Clinton also maintained he was unaware that Roger had testified at Sam Anderson's trial, even though Little Rock's two daily newspapers carried prominent stories about the drug case and mentioned both Roger Clinton and Dan Lasater—as well as Governor Bill Clinton.

To believe Clinton, one must believe that the governor and his staff weren't interested in news stories about him—that such headlines as **Brother Says Clinton's Safety Feared**, which topped the story about Rodriguez' threats against the governor and his mother, were not read by them.

To all of that, Clinton's old nemesis, former Governor Frank White, cried "Rubbish!" He offered an explanation:

"Colonel Tommy Goodwin [the Arkansas State Police commandant] told me as early as 1983 that Lasater was under investigation as a cocaine distributor and that the probers were also looking at Roger Clinton's role in the caper.

"So I say Bill Clinton had to know about the Lasater investigation as early as 1983. Too many people knew about it for him to be totally unaware. It's just not possible."

As was shown, Clinton indeed was informed about the drug probe in 1983.

In a *New York Post* exposé of March 24, 1992, Mike McAlary offered insights into the Lasater situation:

"...just as it strains credulity to hear Bill Clinton deny that he had an affair with Gennifer Flowers, and that the would-be politician didn't know his own draft number two days after it was pulled, it now strains all belief to hear the Arkansas governor say he didn't know about Lasater's involvement with drugs."

McAlary draws on this quote taken from a published interview with Clinton in the *Arkansas Gazette* on October 31, 1986, after Roger and Lasater had been put on ice:

"I honestly don't remember [when Lasater first told the governor about his troubles with drugs]. But I'm guessing that he told me about it probably right *before* [author's emphasis] he testified in the trial [there was no trial, for Lasater and his co-conspirators would all take the short cut to prison by pleading guilty]. Or maybe we discussed it *after* he testified [again, Lasater never testified]. But it probably would have been about that time."

Four days before he spoke those words in the governor's office, on October 27, 1986, Clinton insisted, "The state hasn't done any business with Lasater since I became aware of the investigation [in August 1984, just before the indictment of Lasater and the other 10 for cocaine violations, by a federal grand jury in Little Rock]."

McAlary quickly retorted, "Clearly this is an untruth...in fact, yesterday [Monday, March 23, 1992], Clinton's campaign released this statement: 'Governor Clinton learned about Lasater's loan [to Roger Clinton] in February 1985, during the trial of Sam Anderson, Jr.'"

Whoever issued that statement from the governor's presidential campaign office apparently hadn't gotten the high sign to issue another lie.

The author's investigation shows that shortly after Anderson's trial ended with his conviction and sentence to three years' imprisonment, Bill Clinton, still clinging to loyalty for Dan Lasater though his number was up, feverishly lobbied lawmakers to OK his pal for the contract to sell the multi-million dollar bonds to develop the state police communications network.

Of this, more shortly.

Two Giant Steps for Education

March 1985 was a very good time for Governor Bill Clinton and First Lady Hillary Clinton.

By the beginning of that month it was clear that the Arkansas Education Association would be unable to derail Clinton's teacher-testing law. Pressure on the legislature to repeal the unpopular measure had waned by then. The most serious challenge had come a month before when some 3,500 Arkansas teachers marched on the capital, demanding that the legislature stop the "testing madness."

One speaker at a rally, teacher Johnnie Sheeler of Arkadelphia, directed her remarks to the architect of the measure:

"Pardon me, Governor while I get personal. My teaching career is personal to me...I do not intend to take any test to keep something I already have. And yes, Governor, I take your insults personally. It's time all Arkansas took your insults personally."

Despite the protests and a call by the Arkansas Education Association to boycott the tests, only 1,623 of the state's 26,700 certified teachers were no-shows on March 23. A 94 percent turnout of 25,077 complied with the new law, took the tests, and enabled Arkansas to be the first state to test teachers for competence without regard to their years of service.

Before the test was administered, Little Rock's KARK-TV received a copy of the exam from an anonymous source. That touched off reports that copies of the test had gone into the black market. Clinton promptly ordered the Arkansas State Police to investigate. The inquiry hit a dead end, but the Arkansas Department of Education voiced the view that the integrity of the tests had not been compromised.

The exams were given and 10 percent of the teachers failed to demonstrate sufficient competence in basic reading, writing, or mathematics skills. Remedial instructional programs and retests were ordered for those who failed in the different areas.

The AEA again vowed to continue opposing testing. It maintained that the practice weakened teacher morale, took away respect for the profession from the public, drove good teachers out of the system, and made it all but impossible to recruit teachers from other states.

Clinton stuck to his guns on the teacher-testing procedure—and watched with satisfaction as his wife commanded attention with her own pet project: HIPPY.

That was the acronym for Home Instruction Program for Preschool Youngsters. Originated at Hebrew University in Jerusalem during the 1960s, HIPPY was designed to prepare pre-school children of immigrants in the basic skills required to tackle education programs offered in public schools. The premise is to have mothers prepare their children at home.

"Half of all learning occurs by the time a person is five," Hillary explained in an interview with the *Arkansas Gazette*'s Charles Allen. "There are instances…where people from very terrible situations rise above them and do well. But those are the exceptions, and most people will have the kind of impoverished, often neglectful backgrounds that we see so often among many of our children today just come into school with so many problems that it's very difficult to deal with. So a good pre-school program, whether its center-based or home-based, is one of the smartest investments.

"What HIPPY does is to provide a very structured way for mothers to interact with their children. A lot of other programs are well meaning, but they basically put too much responsibility on the mother. If the mother knew what she was supposed to do, she would do it."

One of Hillary's harshest critics, *Arkansas Democrat* editor John Robert Starr, saluted her not only for the educational reform she initiated with her committee, but also for the long-ranging benefits she caused to be advanced by the HIPPY program. After more than a dozen years, an estimated 2,000 young students had proceeded through that pre-school training agenda. The program was still going strong after the Clintons took occupancy of the White House.

It'd Be Fun to Run for President

The euphoria growing out of the success of the teacher-testing program had hardly subsided before Governor Bill Clinton had a new conquest to rejoice over.

The *Atlanta Constitution-Journal* informed neighboring Georgians that the state next door had a possible candidate for the 1988 presidential race. Since Ronald Reagan was prohibited by law from seeking a third term, the obvious Republican contender was Vice President George Bush.

What was Governor Clinton's reaction to a possible race against the former CIA chief and World War II aerial combat hero?

"It would be fun even if you lost," Clinton responded to the question posed by reporter Raad Cawthon. "It would be a challenge to go out and meet the people and try to communicate your ideas and bring the different parts of the country together."

Cawthon had interviewed Clinton after his impressive reelection to a third term the past November and his reemergence as a star in national Democratic Party affairs. Asked to clarify the statement by the *Arkansas Gazette*, trying to play catch-up journalism on the *Atlanta Constitution*'s scoop, Clinton expanded on his presidential thoughts:

"You know how it is...a reporter comes here...and the one thing all reporters ask about is whether you want to run for president someday. And I told him, yeah, I'd thought about it. I think all politicians have thought about it—even if just in their wildest dreams."

In the next breath, Clinton told the *Gazette* he'd most likely run for governor again in 1986, when a new state law extending the term of Arkansas's constitutionally elected officials to four years would go into effect.

Not many days later, Clinton tendered a personal invitation to *Gazette* political reporter John Brummett to attend a reception for "a gathering of dear friends" at the governor's mansion.

The affair, in effect, was Bill Clinton's way of announcing his candidacy for a fourth term in 1986.

"I will stay the course," Clinton began in a brief address to the assemblage on the Tuesday afternoon of July 23. "I have asked people of this state to commit themselves to a decade of dedication. Over and over again I have asked you to work for the future. Over and over again you have responded, and today I can do no less.

"I cannot ask you to stay the course if I am willing to leave office before our programs are fully implemented...I want to stay home and finish the job."

During the gathering, Clinton was observed in a quiet corner with one of the guests, where they spoke in hushed voices. The fact that the guest was Little Rock mortgage banker Dan Lasater raised a few eyebrows. The rumor mill by now had caught up with the information the governor had received from Arkansas State Police Commander Tommy Goodwin—that Lasater was mixed up with Roger Clinton in drug deals.

Bill's Deal with the Bad Banker

The probe of Dan Lasater, followed by his indictment, conviction, and incarceration, wouldn't conclude for another two years. Nevertheless, as the evidence clearly shows, Governor Clinton was totally aware of it at this time. Indeed he had been privy to those facts nearly from the day of their inception—that investigations had been undertaken against both his half brother, Roger, and his best friend, Dan Lasater, for drug trafficking.

What did the governor and his suspected drug dealer pal have to say to each other on that July 23 afternoon social?

The question was murmured by many who watched the unscheduled get-together. There can be no doubt that the man who controlled Lasater & Company was putting the squeeze on the governor for yet another plum. This one was the installation of the massive state police communications system, a $30.2 million state bond deal that was hanging fire.

Former Governor Frank White told the author's researchers that since Clinton first took office in 1978, Lasater's bank had received assignments from the state to sell more than $664.8 million worth of Arkansas bonds for construction of state projects. Those transactions netted Lasater approximately $1.6 million in brokerage fees.

"The benefits to Lasater were monumental," White asserted. "He was able to branch out his business to far-off Chicago and other locales. He was able to buy a chain of restaurants, a string of thoroughbreds, and a horse farm in Florida. Bill Clinton helped to make Dan Lasater a multi-millionaire."

Lasater had received virtually no state business during White's 1980-82 term.

That afternoon the topic uppermost on both the governor and the banker's agenda must have been the new state police communications network. The $30.2 million project would line Dan Lasater's pockets with another $750,000.

But why hadn't Governor Clinton awarded the bond sale contract to his friend by now?

Because the legislature was balking at that expenditure and had refused to pass it. Nevertheless, Bill Clinton conducted a relentless campaign for its passage in the spring and summer of 1985. Legislators remember the feverish lobbying Clinton conducted.

"He talked to me," Legislator Lloyd George said, recalling being summoned to the governor's office. "He talked to me and said, 'George, why aren't we going along?'

"I said, 'I don't know—it costs so much." To which George remembered the governor pressing on relentlessly until "He really sold me on it."

Much as Bill Clinton felt impelled to push as vigorously as he could for passage of the police communications network, developments elsewhere were to intrude on his programming.

21

IS THIS ANY WAY TO RUN ARKANSAS?

Off and *Bumming* for a Fourth Term

After announcing his intention at 1985's July social to seek a fourth term in 1986, Bill Clinton got national exposure in early August by journeying to Boise, Idaho, for the National Governors' Association Conference. An opportunity for a moment in the sun came after Clinton was chosen to arbitrate a simmering dispute with Republicans. A fund-raising letter sent out with President Ronald Reagan's signature had angered the Democratic governors, who were severely criticized in the text over voting ethics.

Clinton mediated the dispute that resulted in a GOP apology and the scrapping of a second mailing of the offensive literature. Before the meeting closed, the Arkansas governor was elected vice chairman of the NGA, an honor that assured him the chairmanship at the next convention in 1986.

With this latest honor going in tandem with his election to the chairmanship of the Southern Growth Policies Board in July, Bill Clinton seemed very much a man on the move in the national political scene.

As the year wore on, Clinton drew up a travel log for an excursion to the Far East he described as a "trade mission," a term many of his critics called a *euphemism* for *boondoggle*. Hardly a year ever passed that the governor wasn't off on an all-expenses-paid trip to some far-off land that he billed as a "trade mission," purportedly to drum up investment by foreign countries in Arkansas's commercial and industrial development. Arkansas was far below the national average of recorded benefits growing out of such taxpayer-funded travels by state officials.

This outing by a 13-member delegation was to Tokyo and Osaka. The fruits of that travel were hailed by Clinton as "a great success." While no new business was drummed up for the state, a well-fed and well-rested Bill Clinton and his entourage returned from the mission with glowing reports about the high marks accorded Arkansas by the Sanyo Corporation. Sanyo already had a television assembly plant in eastern Arkansas in full operation for years and had no plans to infuse a greater input into the state's economy.

However, "We were told that the company is very pleased with the way the factory is functioning here," Clinton boasted. "And they extolled the hard-working people who work for them and the close working relationship Sanyo has developed with the state government."

Not all Arkansans were ecstatic over their governor's annual journeys abroad, which brought back merely a gush of platitudes and plaudits but no profitability.

One memorable adventure, a two-week trip to Europe, cost Arkansas taxpayers more than $25,000.

Clinton's critics frequently complained that the trips hadn't brought the rosy results he always claimed they had.

One detractor was Sheffield Nelson, chairman of the Arkansas Industrial Development Commission (AIDC) in 1987 and 1988, and the unsuccessful challenger to Clinton in 1990. Nelson pointed out that at least one foreign investor Clinton claimed to have locked into an agreement had, in fact, declared intentions to open a plant in Arkansas *before* the governor went on his trip.

But Clinton put down Nelson's assertion when asked whether his journeys were justified.

"Absolutely," he retorted. "They are very, very hard work. The idea that this is some kind of extravagant vacation paid for by taxpayers is nuts."

On that earlier trip to the Continent, Clinton maintained, "It was routine to work until after midnight and then rise again before six in the morning."

However, whenever AIDC officials were asked to release the names of the companies Clinton contacted, the response was always the same:

"We can't do that because it would hurt our industrial recruiting efforts."

Despite all, Clinton received high praise for his efforts to sell his state in foreign lands from Bob Lamb, chairman of the Arkansas State Chamber of Commerce.

"After Bill opens foreign doors," said Lamb, "the state's regular industrial recruiting team [AIDC] gets the opportunity then to work them one on one."

Lamb also thought a banquet Clinton tossed for executives of 20 European firms with plants in Arkansas was a good idea. The banquet cost Arkansas taxpayers $2,100 and featured a menu of lobster salad, asparagus, whitefish with broccoli, potatoes, cheeses, orange dessert, coffee, and petits fours.

"That's the biggest boondoggle I ever seen," complained former Governor Orval Faubus, who was beginning to make louder noises about challenging Bill Clinton in the 1986 Democratic primaries for the gubernatorial nomination.

When the aging Faubus let it be known that "I'm definitely making plans" to enter the race, Clinton responded with a wise-guyish, "Wonderful!"

The Clintons Rip Off Uncle Sam

All wasn't nose-to-the-grindstone politics for Bill and Hillary Clinton in 1985. A major diversion continued to be tending to their holdings in the Ozark Mountains vacation property.

One of the significant findings by the *New York Times'* investigation of that enterprise was that Bill and Hillary had played gymnastics with their 1984 Internal Revenue Service joint tax return by claiming a $2,811 deduction for "interest payments" on the $30,000 loan Hillary took out from partner Jim McDougal's Madison Guaranty Savings and Loan Association in 1978.

Actually the payments the Clintons claimed to have made on that loan on that year's tax return—as well as on IRS Form 1040 for the following year of 1985—had been made by Whitewater Development, the corporation formed to buy the land.

But no one smelled the falsification in the filing until the *New York Times*' Jeff Gerth exposed the Clintons' manipulations in the Ozarks venture during the presidential campaign. Gerth pointed out the sleight-of-hand to Susan Thomases, the Clintons' lawyer, who was burdened with having to explain the Clintons' double-jabbering. The response was a reluctantly admitted, "It is clearly an error." Incongruously and deceptively, the lawyer blamed it all on preparers she described as "professional accountants in Arkansas."

The Clintons got away with that pair of back-to-back false filings and faced no punitive action because the statute of limitations gave them refuge from penalties and prosecution.

"Since the filing error occurred more than three years ago," wrote Jeff Gerth in the *Times*' front page story, "under Internal Revenue Service regulations, the Clintons are no longer liable for the taxes."

Gerth then went on to report, "The Clintons' lawyers say they are reviewing all the Clintons' tax returns and the other records relating to Whitewater, trying to determine what steps they might take."

So far as is known, no steps of any kind were taken. But a spokesman for the IRS in Washington sent up a signal worthy of note:

"We are looking into the Clinton returns for later years."

This is not the last word on the Ozark Mountains caper.

Bill! Your Stepsis Robbed an S&L!

"Why'd he wait all this time to tell me about such a thing!"

Bill Clinton's voice that morning of Friday, August 9, 1985, was shrill. He was raging at press secretary Joan Roberts, who had Don Bankston, an attorney with a practice in Richmond, Texas, on the phone. Sources in the governor's office from that era identified Bankston as a "big wheel" in the Fort Bend County Democratic Party.

A Don Bankston, who the author has been assured is the same Don Bankston said to have made that 1985 call to the governor's office in Little Rock, will play a crucial role in the closing days of 1992's presidential campaign and in the outcome of the election. What he would do then, as many political analysts agree, probably spelled the difference between victory and defeat for Bill Clinton against incumbent President George Bush!

That portrayal of Dan Bankston will unfold later. But since we are examining 1985 at this juncture of the narrative, and it is the genesis for the Texas lawyer's later actions, we'll first fill in the earlier details from the recollections of witnesses at the scene in Clinton's office on August 9.

Speaking from his law office in Richmond, 30 miles down the pike from Houston, the caller conveyed this troubling message to the governor's office:

"I've got a client that I'm defending in a criminal action...she robbed a bank at gunpoint...she claims to be related to Governor Bill Clinton...she keeps saying it to me over and over...I don't know what to think...I thought you'd like to know."

An agitated Bill Clinton had taken the phone. He kept the receiver to his ear for some six to seven minutes. As he listened, his face paled and he appeared to tremble at what the voice on the other end was saying.

Dianne Dwire Welch, the stepsister who entered his life in 1969 when her father, Jeffrey Dwire, married the twice-widowed Virginia Cassidy Blythe Clinton, had been arrested for an armed bank robbery pulled the previous March 15. She was grabbed several days after the holdup, which was staged with a 16-year-old friend of Dianne Dwire Welch's 15-year-old son, Jeffrey.

(The reader met Dianne in an earlier chapter when she visited her father and stepmother in Hot Springs in 1969 to introduce the Dwires to her infant son, Jeff, just born in her recent marriage to Texas businessman Buford Welch.)

Clinton was told that Don Bankston successfully plea-bargained a second chance for Dianne, who also was charged with the holdup of a doughnut shop after the bank was robbed.

The court placed a great deal of weight on the fact that Dianne had no prior criminal record. Thus the mandatory 10-year prison sentence she faced was set aside by the judge and Dianne was placed on probation for the next 10 years. This probation carried strict guidelines: If she failed to remain on her best behavior for the entire probation period, the least infraction of the law automatically subjected her to arrest and incarceration—for 40 years!

That was the gist of the story Clinton listened to that day. He didn't care to learn any more about the crimes, nor to hear what Dianne's circumstances were. Just as he distanced himself from half-brother Roger Clinton, campaign benefactor Dan Lasater, and childhood pal/lawyer Sam Anderson, Jr., on learning they were in the eye of a drug bust, so did Clinton now seem not to want any truck with the gusts of scandal blowing up from Texas.

Dianne Dwire Welch was no longer "family," so far as Bill Clinton was concerned. His connection to Dianne, he was heard to say, ended after Jeff Dwire, his stepfather No. 2, a diabetic, died in 1974 after a long illness growing out of complications from the disease.

Clinton delivered the eulogy at the funeral that Dianne attended with her husband Buford Welch. Clinton did not see Dianne again in the intervening 11 years after his stepfather's death in 1974. However, there was one further contact with his stepsister.

"That came in 1975, a year after my father's death," Dianne Dwire Welch said in 1993. "He phoned me to discuss a matter regarding my father's estate. That was the last time I spoke with him."

Bill Clinton's efforts to distance himself from Dianne did not end as he thought it would when he gave the receiver back to Joan Roberts and voiced his rage at this development, then finally made a thumbs-down gesture accompanied by a loud, "Whew!"

The case was not closed, as the governor would learn to his dismay.

Sis: "Why I Became a Bank Robber"

"I was very unhappy in my marriage," Dianne Dwire Welch explained. "My husband's business…was doing badly and he kept me very short of money. He wouldn't give me any money for clothes."

Her unhappy marriage led Dianne to take up with a young man, a Colombian in his 20s named John Rodriguez. The affair didn't have a happy ending. Dianne fell into despair and decided to end her life.

"I swallowed thirty Valium pills and hoped that would end everything for me," Dianne said in an interview with a researcher for this author. "But before I passed out, I became wary of dying and phoned Buford and told him what I'd done."

Her husband summoned help and Dianne's stomach was pumped in the hospital. After she was discharged, her state of mind didn't improve. She still needed money and decided to pull a stickup.

"I went to a Houston pawnshop and bought a Colt automatic. Then with a sixteen-year-old kid who was a friend of my son, Jeff, who agreed to be my partner in crime, we drove to a bank in Sugarland [another Houston suburb] and robbed the bank."

The "hit" was on the Gold Coast Savings and Loan office, just across the street from a sugar refinery where Dianne had once been employed.

"I walked up to the teller's cage and pointed the gun at the woman behind the counter. I ordered her to sit down in her chair while the boy who was my partner went behind the counter and helped himself to the money in the teller's cash drawer."

The teller, Jessie McClure, would later tell police that Dianne had threatened her by demanding, "Get this cash drawer opened or you get a bullet in the head."

In her statement to police, Dianne insisted the gun had no bullets in it.

Fleeing the scene of the holdup with $902, Dianne and her teen confederate staged another stickup that night at a Houston doughnut shop. They sweetened the pot with another $150 from the cash register.

On March 22, Dianne was arrested—as was her 16-year-old accomplice. The Fort Bend County Sheriff's Office tracked down Dianne and her partner in crime after viewing the tape in the Gold Coast Savings and Loan office video camera.

Fellow workers in the sugar company processing plant identified Dianne, and Deputy Sheriff Craig Brady, joined by Sugarland Police Department Detective Howard Kiecke, went to Dianne Welch's small apartment in Houston. They found her living with the lover who had replaced her husband, Buford Welch, after they separated. The lawmen identified him as John Rodriguez, a native of Colombia, 23, and 16 years younger than his mistress.

Dianne was arrested. Within the hour, so was her young accomplice.

Attorney Dan Bankston entered the picture as Dianne's legal defender. His first action was to ask for a conference with Fort Bend County Assistant District Attorney Ralph Gonzalez. Bankston was prepared to have his client plead guilty. He wanted to avoid a trial that would lead to certain conviction and long-term imprisonment.

"I wasn't looking to fill up the county or the state's jails," Gonzalez conceded to the author. "Inasmuch as Mrs. Welch didn't have a *prior* [police record], I was willing to negotiate for a settlement that would keep her out of jail, but at the same time give her every reason to hoe the straight and narrow." That would save the taxpayers of Texas the cost of imprisonment over a 10-year period.

"There was no problem in working matters out with her lawyer," said Gonzalez, who left the prosecutor's office after Dianne Welch's case was adjudicated and went into private practice in Richmond.

Dianne Dwire Welch appeared before Judge Charles Dickerson in the Fort Bend County Courthouse, just down the street from the bank she hit.

Whether or not Dianne—or her lawyer—paid strict attention to the court's injunction cannot be answered here. But a question arose over whether or not the law under which the sentencing was imposed had been clearly spelled out to the defendant and her counsel. The issue was over the mandatory 40-year prison term for any criminal infraction during the 10-year probation period.

None of this mattered to Bill Clinton. So far as he was concerned, his brush with stepsister Dianne's troubles was over and done. She had gotten out of doing time in prison and Clinton could sweep the problem under the rug and return to the agenda taking priority over all else: winning next year's election so he could become Arkansas's first four-year-term governor.

Women, Women, and More Women

Bill Clinton must have first realized that his top aide was being scrutinized too closely about the perks the governor was suspected of procuring, after Wooten Epes caught his deputy, Larry Nichols, nosing into the affairs of the Arkansas Development Finance Authority.

While this situation didn't flower into full bloom until 1989, the events leading up to it had their beginnings in the mid-1980s, roughly the period we are examining now.

Most disturbing to Clinton was learning about his ADFA marketing manager's inordinate curiosity about a slush fund set up with 200 million of taxpayer dollars—and how the fund was being dipped into to finance a slew of the governor's pet projects. These ranged from an unending procession of sexual escapades to a future undertaking: a bid for the presidency.

What signals (call it body language) betrayed Larry Nichols' probing into his boss's business aren't clear. But eventually Bill Clinton was enraged to learn that his deputy was gathering string on the ADFA's president—the governor's closest ally and "bag man"—for orchestrating backdoor stratagems that profited Clinton many thousands of dollars a week.

The ax wasn't lowered on Nichols until mid-October of 1990. And in less than a fortnight—on October 25—Arkansas would be rocked by a $3.05 million libel and defamation of character suit filed by Nichols against his former employer.

In Nichols' account, yet another beauty contestant figured in Clinton's private life. This time it was Arkansas's gift to the 1982 Miss America Pageant, Elizabeth Ward. She brought home the crown to her native Russellville at the very time Clinton was campaigning for reelection.

The statuesque Arkansas Tech student won her title in Atlantic City on September 12, 1981. In a locale and time frame that Nichols didn't specify, yet insisted in sworn testimony, Clinton made Elizabeth's acquaintance and soon after allowed it to proliferate into a "shameless, red hot entente."

"She used to have a friend drive her to a meeting point where Clinton's car would be waiting," asserted Nichols. "She'd get in beside him and they'd take off. A couple of hours later, the friend would pick her up at the same spot."

A born-again Christian, as she described herself in her application to the pageant, Elizabeth Ward didn't list among her hobbies for the Miss America judges the posture of volcanic eroticism ascribed to her by Nichols. She said she was into things like "hog-calling, chopping wood, auto mechanics, and weight-lifting."

The beauty queen, 21 when she was crowned, became so enamored of the governor that she recorded a radio commercial endorsing him in his bid for a third term in 1984.

"The governor would be great for Arkansas," she piped in a commanding, articulate southern drawl no porkers on a hog farm ever heard.

Her romance with Clinton ended in due course and Elizabeth left Arkansas to find happiness with a man she married later in California.

"She had to leave Arkansas," Nichols said, "because her affair with Clinton got too hot to handle."

Another Clinton heartthrob Nichols identified was Deborah Mathis, a reporter for the *Arkansas Gazette*. Evidently the governor wasn't turned off by Miss Mathis when she originated the label "Hillary the Hun" in a feature story she wrote about his wife.

Miss Mathis softened the sting by praising Hillary for the "tough way she took on a political cause."

The newspaper article on his wife apparently hit a note of approbation in Bill Clinton for, according to Nichols, he was soon involved with the reporter, who was then in her early 30s.

There weren't many details on the governor's relationship with this journalist, but that didn't detract from the impact of Larry Nichols' accusations.

Nichols also claimed to have watched from his vantage point at the Arkansas Development Finance Authority as money flowed out of its treasury and was funneled to the governor's office—whenever he snapped his finger for "some loose change," as Clinton assertedly wisecracked whenever he needed cash to entertain one or another of his paramours. Finally Nichols could no longer tolerate Clinton's antics and decided to do something about it.

But not before January 1989, when Nichols began making waves about the governor's meanderings. What Nichols logged in his dossier were "confirmations of what I heard about the governor..." in those earlier days. For example, "Several times I saw him coming out of the governor's mansion jogging. He'd go for about half a block and a state police car would be behind him.

"As soon as he was out of sight of the mansion, he'd get into the car to go to an apartment complex nearby. He'd be in there for about forty-five minutes, then come out, get into a police car, be dropped a block from the mansion, then run back in."

The continuing rumors floating about in 1985 about Bill's womanizing made Hillary so unhappy that she reportedly was ready to end the marriage.

Therapy for Bill and Hillary

Wiser heads prevailed and influenced Hillary to induce Bill to undergo psycho-therapy with her.

Those sessions were not as beneficial to Bill as they were to Hillary. During his period of soul-searching, Bill appeared to descend into periods of depression and ex-treme moodiness. Some saw what has been termed "a tendency to be self-destructive because he viewed himself as a failure."

But Clinton eventually pulled out of the morass and the marriage survived. Hil-lary herself was to talk straightforwardly about that difficult period of her marriage, during the '92 presidential campaign.

She spoke not only more openly but also much more frequently than Bill about the years of their troubled marriage. She almost admitted that she considered divorce.

She came closest to such a confession in an interview with David Frost. She stopped just short of spelling out the word d-i-v-o-r-c-e. Frost had asked if that was ever considered during the difficult times of their marriage. Hillary responded, "Not seriously...no, no...I mean...I never doubted and I know he never did either, that not only do we love each other, but that we are committed to each other. That love was something so much a part of us that it was impossible to think of ending or cutting it off or moving beyond it."

Later during the campaign, in a talk with *Glamour*, Hillary refined her words:

"Bill and I have always loved each other," she offered in a tone that smoothed the rough edges and hesitation that framed the interview with Frost. "No marriage is per-fect, but just because it isn't perfect doesn't mean the only solution is to walk off and leave it. A marriage is always growing and changing. We couldn't say, 'Well, this isn't ideal' and get a divorce. I'm proud of my marriage. I have women friends who chose not to marry, or who married and chose not to have children, or who married and then divorced, or who had children on their own. That's okay, that's their choice. This is my choice. This is how I define my personhood—Bill and Chelsea."

Betsey Wright, who was perhaps most aware of Bill Clinton's infidelities, gave this explanation to biographer Judith Warner:

"They both wanted their marriage. They went through the hard work it takes to get beyond that. It was not an open marriage [as it would be suggested that it was for a time, by *Arkansas Democrat* editor John Robert Starr in a 1992 article].

"It's not that they sit around and tolerate each other running around," Miss Wright continued. "It takes really hard work *to heal the wounds in a relationship following infidelity* [author's emphasis]. It's like medicine, and it's like therapy, physical ther-apy and mental therapy, and they went through that, and it was worth it.

"And I think their marriage is stronger for it. I think that they, in the process, were able to articulate what was valuable about each other, and you know, I have a lot of friends whose marriages are solid, but it's routine. And it's not routine to Bill and Hillary. With them, it's almost a fresh, new commitment."

The Clintons indeed made a *fresh, new commitment* after they faced the biggest problem in their marriage: Bill's infidelity.

"We just had to deal with the issues in our marriage and work them out," Hillary told *People* magazine.

They may have worked out the "issues" in their marriage, but the biggest one, infidelity, cannot have been resolved at the time Hillary and Bill made their peace. For there's ample evidence to demonstrate that Clinton didn't abstain from extramarital involvements during any of the years that followed. He was hooked on one woman or another right up until the day he announced his candidacy for the presidency. And afterward—right down to the day before he moved into the White House.

Many close to the first family maintain that Hillary and Bill came to an arrangement to have an "open marriage," whereby he would continue to play around—and she would be free to engage in extramarital activity whenever she so desired.

Many of their friends spoke about such an arrangement. Several well-informed sources, such as John Robert Starr of the *Arkansas Democrat* and Gail Sheehy of *Vanity Fair*, also advanced that suggestion. We'll return to that premise later.

And Then There Were These Women

Despite psychotherapy and an agreement to make their marriage viable again, Bill Clinton doesn't appear to have altered his behavior. He pursued his extramarital relations with no visible evidence of even the remotest compliance to that pact.

Larry Nichols seems to have made it his duty call to focus on the details of Clinton's affairs. He rounded up witnesses to corroborate his charges, and Nichols suggested that if Bill Clinton were Bill Clinton's lawyer, he'd do well to counsel copping a plea.

These women are among the witnesses he called:

Sherry Wright, owner of the Something Special Boutique.

Beverly Lindsey, an Arkansas Democrat and state coordinator of Walter Mondale's 1984 campaign against President Reagan.

Helen Van Berg, who was to be asked to describe incidents at a condominium complex in Hot Springs.

Beth Coulson, an Appeals Court judge appointed by Clinton.

The last word hasn't been heard in this lengthy litigation. Since 1990 it has gone a roller-coaster course of delays, adjournments, dismissals, and reinstatements to the court calendar.

As if this legal headache wasn't enough, Clinton was hit by another lawsuit, one demanding payment of $20,000 in "hush money" the governor was said to have promised Little Rock restaurateur Robert McIntosh.

McIntosh claimed he was hired by Clinton as a "Mr. Fix-it" to derail Larry Nichols' efforts to expose the governor's secrets about favors he received from both the ADFA and his women.

"I was promised twenty-five thousand dollars by Clinton to show up wherever Nichols was speaking and brand him a Republican mole," fumed McIntosh. "And I did a good job. But all he paid me was five-thousand dollars. He still owes me twenty thousand and won't put it up. That's why I'm suing him."

And that is also why McIntosh went public and blew the whistle on Clinton's affairs with prostitutes by printing handbills about his mulatto child.

Of the six women Nichols linked intimately with Clinton, only one rebelled against the charges. She was the governor's press secretary, Susie Whiteacre, who succeeded Joan Roberts in that post and who, Nichols maintained, was still having an affair with her boss.

"Clinton uses state police to transport him to his secret rendezvous with Susie," Nichols claimed.

Susie Whiteacre maintained a discreet silence about the charges except to issue one terse comment:

"You can talk to my lawyer. That man [Nichols] is a liar."

Her attorney, Bill Wilson, agreed:

"The allegations about Susie Whiteacre in that lawsuit are false and Larry Nichols has admitted to my client he was mistaken about her. Nichols was quick to respond.

"I have not seen nor spoken with Susie Whiteacre since I was fired on the flimsiest excuse: that I was making unauthorized phone calls," Nichols protested. "As for what her lawyer shoveled out—well, that's what he's paid to do."

Another Clinton press aide, Mary Ellen Glynn, who was at his side during the primary campaign in New Hampshire when the legal fur began to fly in Little Rock, loyally came to her employer's defense:

"The charges are ridiculous."

Susie Whiteacre must not be confused with Susann Coleman, the student in one of Bill Clinton's classes at the University of Arkansas Law School who became pregnant and purportedly committed suicide.

One woman Nichols did not identify, but merely described as a member of Clinton's staff, also allegedly "became pregnant and had an abortion" as a result of an affair with Bill.

While Helen Van Berg was listed by Nichols as a witness to testify about incidents at a Hot Springs condo, Nichols didn't zero in on those details as much as he did the goings-on at another condo, near the governor's mansion.

John Kaufman, manager of Quapaw Tower, a sprawling, red brick, balconied, 12-story condominium complex, was considerably annoyed by the effrontery and arrogance he complained were exhibited by Clinton, then just a newly elected governor, according to Nichols. That conduct occurred during what unmistakably was his longest-running affair—the 12-year go with Gennifer Flowers.

Nichols cited Clinton's early experience with Flowers when he padded down in her Quapaw Tower apartment before she departed for Dallas.

Supporting Nichols' account about the "open-door policy" Clinton was afforded at Gennifer's pad was John Kaufman.

"We had considerable trouble with Clinton," explained Kaufman. "The main problem was with his car that was always parked out front where that's not permitted.

"The car would pull up late in the evening and park in the unloading zone. The governor would get out, go into the complex, and stay anywhere from one to four hours. He visited between ten and twenty times. His driver would stay in the car.

"On at least three occasions, my security guard had to tell the chauffeur to park in the lot like everyone else. I was told by tenants Clinton was visiting Gennifer Flowers. When Gennifer moved out, he never came back."

Raunchy Love Outside a Laundry Room

Some of Bill Clinton's encounters with women border on the ribald, as this one with a well-known rock groupie appears to have been.

Connie Hamzy of Little Rock prides herself in having had affairs with the likes of Don Henley, David Lee Roth, Keith Moon, and Huey Lewis, to name but a handful of rockers she says were her lovers.

What of Bill Clinton?

For the answer, Connie Hamzy takes us back to the Riverton Hilton Hotel in Little Rock. It's August 1984, just as the voice of Miss America beauty Elizabeth Ward is pleading over the airwaves for votes for the incumbent governor.

The city's temperature rose to an uncomfortable 100-plus degrees in the shade, but Connie wasn't feeling the heat much. She was in the refreshing water of the hotel swimming pool.

"I was just lounging around the pool when a man in a blue suit walked up to me. He said, 'Hi. I work for Governor Clinton. The governor would like to meet you.'

"I had on this teensy-weensy purple bikini, so I said, 'I can't meet the governor. I don't have any clothes on.'

"He just laughed and said, 'That's why he wants to meet you.'

"So I followed him into the hotel. Governor Clinton was standing in a hallway with his bodyguard and another aide. The three men quickly excused themselves.

"Clinton said, 'You looked so good lying out there by the pool that I just had to meet you. You really made my day.'

"I thanked him and he said, 'Where can we go? Do you have a room here?'

"I explained that I just live nearby and sneak in to use the pool now and then.

"I suggested he get his guys to book us a room under an assumed name, but he said he really didn't have time for that. Then he suggested we try sneaking into one of the banquet rooms on that floor.

"So we walked down the hallway, fondling each other and trying every doorknob. They were all locked except for one that led to the laundry room. He didn't think we could go in there because people were inside.

"Then he asked how long I'd be at the pool and said he'd try to come back. He asked how he could get in touch with me. I told him I'm in the phone book.

"He kissed me and left."

Clinton did not get in touch but Connie occasionally "bumped into" the governor.

"He was always very friendly," said Connie. "But there had always been too many people for us to get together."

At one of their encounters, Connie reminded Clinton of their initial meeting. She was astonished to hear him say that he hadn't sent anyone to fetch her, but that she initiated the meeting.

"That's just ridiculous," Connie demurred. "First of all, I didn't even know he was in the hotel. Besides, I'm a rock groupie. Politicians are not my thing. But I have to admit, I was willing to do him when he asked me."

These examples of Bill Clinton's promiscuity and his continual escape from exposure and censure speaks volumes about Arkansas's attitudes and mores toward its leaders.

That easy attitude appears to be mirrored by Clinton's publicists. These political flacks paint Clinton as a concerned father who checks daughter Chelsea's algebra by fax when he's not nearby. They venerate him by projecting Hillary at his side as a reminder to the unsuspecting masses that she's been his loving wife for almost 20 years.

One editor in Little Rock, who properly chose anonymity, gave Clinton a vapid endorsement for his womanizing:

"If Hillary Clinton doesn't mind, why should anyone else care?"

Does that explain why local newspapers gave their favorite native son such an easy ride?

Republican Sheffield Nelson, who lost the governor's race in 1990 to Clinton, offered a more profound and sobering outlook during the presidential sweeps.

"His playing around and all the other messy things he's involved in may not hurt him in Arkansas—and, in fact, they haven't bothered him so far. But it certainly won't satisfy the national press."

But had the nation's media really buckled down to find out what Bill Clinton was all about? Or had they merely given just a lick and a promise to the rumblings of each scandal whenever it surfaced, then dropped it like a hot potato and continued their honeymoon with the Democratic Party's "walking time bomb," as he has been characterized?

The bottom-line summation came from John Robert Starr, the *Arkansas Democrat*'s editor who called on Clinton to own up to what everyone around him could see: his shame.

"Deep in his heart," said Starr, "Clinton knows he can never answer these questions to the satisfaction of the American people."

22

THE FOURTH-TERM, FOUR-YEAR GOVERNOR

Early Heading into Campaign '86

The New Year dawned on that Wednesday, the first day of 1986, with Bill Clinton looking more and more like a Democratic contender for the 1988 presidential nomination.

More fuel was poured on his already brightly burning political fires when he was invited to appear on television's "MacNeil-Lehrer News Hour." Sounding more like a presidential aspirant than ever before, Clinton took swipes at President Reagan's sixth annual budget proposal that called for another increase in military spending and a reduction in domestic programs amounting to $40 billion.

"This [trillion-dollar] budget essentially says again that you get better defense if you spend more money," Clinton drawled before the TV cameras. "Everything else is better if you spend less money."

He came down heavily on deficit spending and decried the "mortgaging of our children's educational future, because that only undermines efforts to reach economic excellence."

He laced into proposed cuts in farm programs, law enforcement, aid to cities, as well as scheduled reductions in financial assistance for college students.

"I think we have to keep moving forward in things that are critical for the economic future of our country and for human decency at home."

Clinton hammered hard at the point that 40 states, including his own Arkansas, were forced to raise taxes to revive programs previously funded by the federal government that were victims of budget cuts.

Meanwhile, Clinton's campaign kitty was virtually filled for his run for a fourth term, the first four-year incumbency for a state executive since before the turn of the century. As in his last two races, Clinton received bountiful contributions from Arkansas Power & Light executives, Tyson Foods, and a $3,000 check from drug-trafficking kingpin Dan R. Lasater who, in the governor's own oft-voiced words, "is my best political benefactor."

Lasater could well afford to part with half of one percent of the $750,000 profit he made from the sale of $30.2 million worth of bonds for construction of the Arkansas State Police communications network. The legislature had capitulated to Clinton's relentless lobbying and had reluctantly approved the expenditure.

Clinton then immediately awarded the lucrative bond deal to Lasater & Company—despite knowing that Dan Lasater not only was a prime target in the ongoing investigation of the Organized Crime Drug Enforcement Task Force, but also was due to be named as a key figure in an upcoming federal grand jury indictment. The charges were to cite once again the governor's half brother, but this time as an unindicted co-conspirator. At this stage, Roger Clinton was back in the Fort Worth Federal Correctional Facility after testifying at the drug trial of Bill Clinton's boyhood friend, Hot Springs lawyer Sam Anderson, Jr.

Anderson was found guilty and sentenced to three years in a federal penitentiary. Disbarment from further practice of law was automatic.

Roger Clinton experienced swift rewards for his testimony at Anderson's trial. Just as Russell Crump had been sentenced to serve only a year at the Fort Worth federal lockup for having blown the whistle on Roger and Maurice Rodriguez, so Roger benefited from being a prosecution witness against the Hot Springs lawyer. Judge Oren Harris sentenced Anderson to serve the same three-year term imposed on Rodriguez.

Roger Clinton breathed the fresh air of freedom on January 29, just when brother Bill was honing his attack on President Reagan on the "MacNeil-Lehrer News Hour." The Federal Parole Commission dispatched the 28-year-old Roger to a Dallas halfway house. He was released from prison on condition that he take part in a "special drug aftercare program."

If he kept his nose clean in that rehabilitation facility, Roger was told he could look forward to a parole hearing on April 25.

Not more than a fortnight after Clinton's MacNeil-Lehrer appearance, former Governor Orval Faubus let it be known he was thoroughly convinced that he would challenge Clinton for the Democratic gubernatorial nomination.

After Arkansas political analyst Jerry Russell suggested that Faubus had a "definite intention" to be a candidate but couldn't say when he'd announce, the septuagenarian politician was asked how viable he believed his candidacy could be.

"That all depends on how many people Bill Clinton has made mad," Faubus cracked. Then came the follow-through on March 20 when the old governor said he wanted to be the new one. Admitting the contrast between a 76-year-old political warhorse like himself and the 39-year-old Clinton was marked, Faubus insisted he was ready to tear off the gloves.

"Some say I have an uphill battle in this race I am entering," Faubus crowed in a feisty voice. "I was reared on a mountainside. Whenever I sought the top, I had to climb. When I was away from home in the valleys, the way home was always uphill. If this is an uphill battle, so be it."

Faubus was asked whether the electorate would hold it against him for having barred blacks from entering Little Rock High School in 1957 in defiance of the U.S. Supreme Court school desegregation ruling:

"That's nearly thirty years ago. What we need to be concerned with now—all our citizens, rich or poor, country and city, black and white, or whomever—we need to be concerned with the here and now, the benefit of ourselves, and the progress of our state."

Bill Clinton hardly seemed to care about what the old political infighter was saying. For other concerns suddenly loomed on the horizon.

Stepsister's in a Big Drug Bust

The caller from Fort Worth on that mid-April day was the last person Bill Clinton wanted to hear from. It was more grim tidings about his stepsister, Dianne Dwire Welch, whose reemergence into his life loomed like a bad soap opera.

"Dianne's really gotten herself jammed," the informant is reported to have told Clinton. "She's been arrested in a major drug bust...her 16-year-old son and four others were rounded up with her while they were negotiating a drug deal in a Rosenberg [Texas] shopping center parking lot."

Attorney Don Bankston, the Fort Bend County Democratic Party's "big wheel," was not Dianne Welch's defense lawyer this time. Instead, a lawyer named Matt Leeper, Jr., was representing Clinton's stepsister in her latest bout with the law.

Clinton was told that soon after entering the first year of her 10-year probation in the bank and doughnut shop armed stickups, Dianne began fraying at the edges. With no income and no one to turn to for financial rescue, she began to smoke marijuana and snort cocaine until her remaining funds petered out. To feed the habit, Dianne turned to peddling drugs in Houston saloons. Her dependence on drugs was so extensive that she could find no way out other than to try to make "a big score."

With her son Jeff in on the caper, Dianne and four accomplices went to a shopping center parking lot to consummate a deal for the sale of 50 pounds of marijuana. A team of Rosenberg Police Department cops headed by officer R. C. Thurman closed in on the suspects, who'd been under surveillance for some time. They were all arrested.

Judge Charles Dickerson, who'd released Dianne on parole in 1985, threw the book at her this time. After revoking her probation, he sentenced her to 45 years imprisonment, 40 years to be served for the bank and doughnut shop robberies and the remaining five years on the drug charges.

Her son, a first offender, was released on parole.

A few weeks after sentencing, Matt Leeper dropped out as Dianne's defense counsel. He had made preliminary motions for a review of Dianne's sentence by the Texas Court of Appeals, but abruptly severed all ties with his client after, in his own words to the court, "Dianne threatened defense counsel with bodily harm."

While still in the Fort Bend County lockup prior to being shipped out to serve her time in Texas's tough Mountain View Prison in Gainsville, Dianne also threatened to do a number on police officer Thurman, who arrested her.

In both instances, according to a county jailhouse informant, Dianne boasted she could have her Colombian live-in lover, John Rodriguez, kill the lawyer and policeman.

Bill Clinton could breathe easier with Dianne salted away in Gainsville. With such a long prison term ahead of her, it was unlikely that his stepsister would ever emerge again as a skeleton from the Clinton family closet.

Yet in May 1992, an event would occur in the life of Dianne Dwire Welch that shook the Democratic Party's presidential candidate down to his very toes. We'll recount that event when the narrative reaches that later time.

Frank White Haunts Bill Again

Former Governor Frank White waited only a few days to spring his own surprise after Orval Faubus announced as a candidate for the Democratic nomination. White, a lifelong Democrat, had switched to the Republican Party in 1980 to make his successful run against incumbent Governor Bill Clinton.

"When a governor gets too much power, it breeds arrogance, and arrogance breeds corruption," White declared when he entered the race on April Fool's Day.

But the Arkansas Education Association wasn't fooling when it broke the tradition of withholding endorsement of a candidate until after the primaries.

"We don't feel like the candidates in the Democratic primary for governor were committed to the issues that are of concern to teachers," explained AEA President Edward Bullington.

He was referring to Clinton, Orval Faubus, and a little-known aspirant named Dean Goldsby.

"They never even laid a glove on me," Clinton quipped after he breezed to victory with 60.5 percent of the vote. Faubus limped home with 33.5 percent, a result that wrote finis to the political career of the former four-term governor. Goldsby wasn't even a factor in the race with an unimpressive six percent.

White faced three opponents in the GOP runoffs and emerged the clear winner with 61.9 percent of the vote.

"I'm happy that the Republican primary ended the way it has," Clinton remarked. "I look forward to a campaign against Frank White."

He'd rue the day he said that. Because in this campaign it would not be just a Frank White vs Bill Clinton encounter. It would be Gay White vs Hillary Clinton. And Frank White vs Hillary Clinton, as well.

Meanwhile, August brought two developments: one happy, the other unhappy.

In the first instance, Bill Clinton again performed for a national audience when he attended the National Governors' Association Convention and was elected chairman. Addressing the gathering, Clinton once more sounded like a presidential hopeful, as he had earlier in June when he served as co-chairman of the association's Task Force on Welfare Reform that met in Washington, D.C.

Though the governors did not endorse the proposals advanced by the Reagan Administration, they agreed that the nation's welfare system needed restructuring. Speaking for the other members of the task force, Clinton advanced three major objectives as requisites for a viable welfare system:

1. Put welfare recipients back to work.
2. Strengthen family bonds and responsibilities.
3. Ensure adequate health care for young children.

Two months later, at the Governors' Association Convention, the newly elected chairman once more sounded like a candidate when he addressed the assemblage:

"Today I come as the first of the over-the-hill baby boomers to ask: Can we make America work again for her people? I believe we can, but only if we find ways for Americans to be able to work and have work. We must face squarely our responsibility to make Americans more competitive from the ground up and to reverse the tide of lost human potential in those who have fallen through the cracks of what I call America's leaky bucket."

Back in Little Rock he received heartening news: his brother Roger was released from the Dallas halfway house on two years' probation. But that joy was short-lived. For almost as soon as the governor held a small welcome-home family celebration, Roger quickly demonstrated that *old habits are hard to break.*

Exile to Hollywood for Roger

Roger Clinton was letting drugs control his life again.

His first jam with the law came when state police stopped him for a traffic infraction and found a .22-caliber pistol tucked under his feet in the car. They found also another gun in the vehicle and a quantity of Quaaludes (tranquilizers).

Roger could have been sent back to the slammer if he'd been prosecuted and convicted on the gun possession charges. But the state police was headed by Governor Clinton's appointee, Colonel Tommy Goodwin, who had alerted his boss about Roger's drug activities in the past.

It is undetermined whether or not influences were wielded in Roger Clinton's case.

However, the arresting cops couldn't provide "adequate corroboration" to prosecute Roger as federal authorities had done. So he beat that rap.

Not long afterward, Roger—on a toot—brawled with the manager of a Hot Springs nightclub where he'd worn out his welcome with what authorities described as his "rowdiness and foul mouth." He was arrested, but threw himself on the mercy of the court, which had the power to revoke his parole and return him to finish the remainder of his unserved drug felony sentence in a federal prison.

The state judge ordered Roger into an alcohol rehabilitation center and tacked three more years onto his parole term.

By now, Bill Clinton couldn't tolerate the distractions Roger was causing in the governor's office—and, more worrisome, in the forthcoming presidential race he appeared to have his heart set on entering.

Bill Clinton decided to get his troublesome brother out of Arkansas. No one could have agreed more with that tack than Hillary. The last thing she and Bill wanted was to have Roger occupying the governor's mansion with the menagerie he called his friends and smear the place with a fresh tarbrush of scandal.

That was when the good offices of Harry Thomason and Linda Bloodworth-Thomason entered the picture. Two of the Clintons' best friends, this husband-wife team from Arkansas had gone to Hollywood and become top television producers. Among their long-running series were "Designing Women" and "Evening Shade."

The Clintons prevailed upon—indeed begged—the Thomasons to take Roger off their hands. Here is how a family friend described the approach:

"The Clintons have been close to the 'Designing Women' bosses for years. They used their clout to get Roger in. It was easy for Hillary to pick up the phone and get Roger fixed up with a job."

Roger was handed a job and a title, "production assistant and musician." To say this employment was served up to Roger on a silver platter would be precisely correct. For no sooner was brother Bill elected president, than Roger was buried under a gush of gold.

It reminded folks of the way Billy Carter became a national phenomenon after his brother, Jimmy, was elected president. All Billy had to do to collect his six-figure income while his brother occupied the Oval Office was sit beside a potbellied stove in a general store, tear the lid off a beer can, and gab with the townspeople.

But Roger Clinton's role was different from Billy Carter's. He went from stirbird to Hollywood hotshot before he made his first million. He got there the hard way—he earned it.

"They were kind enough to offer me the opportunity, so I took it," he explained. "I am a production assistant, but I work sixty hours a week. In the evening, I work in a band called POLITIX.

"...We play before the tapings of 'Designing Women' and 'Evening Shade,'" Roger went on to describe the musical combo's duties on the stage where the TV shows are produced.

It wasn't all that easy for Roger before Bill and Hillary exiled him to the film capital.

"I had thought about taking my life," Roger related about the time when he was in deepest trouble. But he took his punishment instead and now wants his feelings known:

"I'm good all over again. The thing that woke me up is freedom. Plain and simple—freedom."

Gennifer Meets Hillary

On October 11, 1986, Bill Clinton observed two milestone events that grew out of his long, varied, and intimate experiences with the opposite sex. He turned that Saturday night into an occasion for a double celebration: his 11-year marriage to the former Hillary Rodham and the return to Little Rock of Gennifer Flowers. Her four-year residence in Dallas had tried the lovers' endurance as they shuttled between Arkansas and Texas.

Clinton chose to celebrate the two events simultaneously on that Saturday night, with the governor's mansion as the stage.

On that night, the governor didn't wear his jogging shorts and sneakers, as he often had when rendezvousing with Gennifer. He showed up nattily attired in a pale blue linen suit, blue-striped white shirt, and a plain blue silk tie. Hillary, as guests recall, came in a floor-length gown of Chantilly lace much like the one she wore at the 1983 inaugural ball.

Gennifer Flowers' presence was duly noted by a small knot of astonished insiders in an assemblage where most guests weren't aware that the beautiful singer, who had come to perform at the gala, was the mysterious woman all Arkansas had been talking about. When she was introduced, even those who knew who she was shared the view of those who didn't: Gennifer Flowers had come to entertain them with songs accompanied by a small rock band.

Coming out of their collective stupefaction after Gennifer Flowers' appearance in a red cocktail dress adorned with a generous splash of shiny silver beads, the know-it-alls began to wonder: was Arkansas's first lady unaware of who the guest vocalist *really* was? Or, as developments soon suggested, was she totally onto the role Gennifer played in her husband's secret life?

"I knew she knew," Gennifer Flowers would say in 1992, after her 12-year affair with Bill Clinton had run its course. "Hillary avoided looking at me all night long. I felt peculiar being there, but I didn't want to disappoint Bill."

The highlight of the evening—more precisely described as a "perilously close call"—occurred in a second-floor hallway where Bill had steered Gennifer for some out-of-bounds monkey business.

"Come on, nobody's in there...let's go in and get a quick one off," Gennifer said Bill pleaded with her.

They were standing outside the men's room.

"'You're crazy!' I almost screamed out. 'What if Hillary should catch us?'"

"'Oh, you worry too much,' Gennifer quoted Clinton's protest. 'She'll never be the wiser.'

"Just then, who should come sauntering along the hallway?" Gennifer asked.

"It was Hillary. She passed us with her gaze straight ahead, walking like a zombie. She didn't acknowledge Bill, and she seemed to want to regard my presence even less."

That was the sum total of Gennifer Flowers' experience in the governor's mansion. Once, at the outset of her affair with Clinton, she had briefly entertained the hope that she could replace Hillary as the mansion's mistress. It didn't take Gennifer long to reconcile herself with reality: she could never succeed Hillary in Bill's life.

And, after her encounter with Hillary, Gennifer also reconciled herself with another reality: she could never return.

But that episode didn't write finis to their affair. If anything, Gennifer's return to Little Rock only stepped up the tempo and heightened the passion of their liaison.

As for Hillary's cold-eyed reception of the "other woman's" presence in the governor's mansion that night, Gennifer Flowers had this candid reaction for her former Dallas roomie Lauren Kirk, who reported it to *New York Post* syndicated gossip columnist Cindy Adams:

"That tight-ass bitch, she cut me dead!"

To which, Lauren Kirk replied, "Well, no wonder. What do you expect? You're sleeping with her husband."

"Yeah, and I'll keep on doing it," said Gennifer.

Educating Chelsea on Politics

Something must have told Hillary Clinton that the 1986 campaign was going to be a barn burner. All that the first lady will own up to in retrospect on *Campaign '86* was her awareness that Bill was facing two rivals in the Democratic primary. That made her decide to have a heart-to-heart with Chelsea, who was now six. Writer Judith Warner described that discussion in *Hillary Clinton: The Inside Story*:

"Chelsea was too big now not to understand campaign slurs on TV, too little to realize they weren't necessarily true, but old enough to know that rock-slinging hurt. Hillary and Bill decided they had to begin to educate her in the seamier side of political life."

Hillary embroidered on this parental concern:

"When I saw we were going to have a primary campaign in 1986, Bill and I talked to her at dinner, telling her that sometimes in political campaigns, people say mean and untrue things about other people. And her eyes got real big, and she said, 'Like what?' And I said, 'Why don't you pretend to be your daddy?' She was six years old. 'Why should you be governor?' And she said, 'I should be governor because I've done a good job.' And I said, 'Okay, but somebody running against your daddy will stand up and say, 'Bill Clinton has done a terrible job, he doesn't care about anybody, he's a bad person.' Her eyes just got huge. And she said, 'Why would they say that?' And I said, 'Because they want people to vote for them.'"

It was a mean campaign, no doubt about that.

Hillary appeared to be the object of the greater bashing because she not only had to withstand Frank White's blows, but his wife Gay's as well.

"Hillary Clinton is a first lady who shamelessly uses her vicarious role as first lady of Arkansas to direct business to herself and her partners in the Rose Law Firm," Gay White would say.

Husband Frank picked up on the theme:

"Hillary Clinton has benefited financially to the tune of five hundred thousand dollars from the bond business her law firm has done with the state."

White asserted that Rose had been either bond or underwriter's counsel on every bond issue by the Arkansas Development Finance Authority. That agency not only played a role in the governor's economic-development program for the state—but was also the till Bill Clinton dipped into whenever the mood moved him to finance "missions" to foreign lands. Or to cover the cost of his many romantic escapades.

Clinton conceded that his wife benefited financially from the business the Rose Law Firm conducted with the state. But he denied a conflict of interest existed.

During the year, Hillary had added several prestigious honorary titles to her growing list. Among them was her appointment to the William T. Grant Foundation Commission on Work, Family and Citizenship, and the Winthrop Rockefeller Foundation (with a substantial grant) to develop programs that help "at risk" children with social, psychological, or economic problems and to study "Youth and America's Future."

But the appointment that helped Hillary Clinton become a wage earner with an income more than three times her husband's $35,000 base salary was her appointment to a third board of directors, that of the Arkansas-based conglomerate Wal-Mart, Inc. As with all her other directorships, Hillary received a $5,000 check for each of the several meetings the directors held annually.

All of this brought a challenge from Frank White to release figures bearing on the bond business Hillary conducted with the state. In a moment when perhaps Bill Clinton wasn't of a mind to remember the two illegal $2,811 deductions he and his wife claimed as interest payments on their Ozark Mountain enterprise on their 1984 and 1985 IRS 1040s, he offered to make public his and Hillary's joint tax returns, provided Frank and Gay White disclosed theirs.

The Whites didn't respond and the Clintons were home free. Had White forced the issue, Bill and Hillary would have been caught in their larcenous manipulation of figures. If those returns were opened to scrutiny in 1986, they would have been unable to find refuge in the three-year statute of limitations. All of this was exposed in the *New York Times* article by Jeff Gerth on the Clintons' Whitewater Development scam—and which in early 1994 had erupted into a full-blown "Ozarkgate" scandal.

Now Lasater's in the Wringer

The campaign trail grew rockier for Bill Clinton on September 18 when his brother, Roger, made the headlines again. This time he was called upon to testify before the federal grand jury in Little Rock. The panel heard testimony from witnesses summoned by Assistant U.S. Attorney Terry Derden, the director of the Justice Department Drug Force in Arkansas. The jury was reported *honing its talons* for what Frank White lightheartedly referred to as "the Dan Lasater scalp hunt."

Despite U.S. Attorney George Proctor's refusal to comment, reporters were able to paint a portrait of the proceedings behind the grand jury's locked doors. A clue to the direction the inquiry was taking was gleaned earlier in the week when the grand jury returned a six-count indictment for distributing cocaine and possession of a firearm against junkie Curtis Lee "Chuck" Berry. Berry was the friend Roger Clinton had introduced to lawyer Sam Anderson, Jr., an episode that had launched him on his ill-fated career as a drug merchant.

Berry is better remembered as the stoolie who worked in the mid-1980s for Pulaski County Prosecutor Jim Guy Tucker who succeeded Bill Clinton as governor in 1993. Berry shot to death tavern owner David "Pete" Mack, Jr., in a crime that put the assassin on ice for 10 years.

Berry came out of prison to serve as a chauffeur for mortgage banker Dan Lasater. That employment had ended only recently. Lasater was the focus of the grand jury's investigation.

Among those summoned to testify were Joni Anderson, a big cog in Lasater & Company's Chicago branch office, a post to which she succeeded after an internship in the bank's Little Rock headquarters. Other Lasater employees were also called before the jury, but their identities weren't disclosed.

Bill Clinton was asked about Roger's involvement in the latest drug probe and gave this response:

"The grand jury investigation is the result of evidence uncovered by an ongoing joint state-federal drug operation. I was very supportive of the state involvement."

Clinton acknowledged that he was also aware of little brother's connection with the case.

"Roger told me he had been subpoenaed to testify, that he was going to cooperate, and he was not the target."

The governor withdrew into his shell when informed that the probers had also called Joni Anderson, whom Clinton knew from her pre-Lasater days as a Little Rock television reporter.

"I wasn't aware that she was asked to testify," he begged off. "I can't say anything more. I don't think it would be appropriate for me to say anymore at this time."

Frank White must have seen the handwriting on the wall for Dan Lasater, because all at once he lashed out at Clinton for his "favored friend" treatment of the banker.

Addressing a Conway Kiwanis Club luncheon, White attacked Lasater as "one of Bill Clinton's biggest financial backers, and because he is, his firm has underwritten six hundred and forty-nine million dollars in bonds for the Arkansas Development Finance Authority." Then he threw out a challenge:

"Bill Clinton, can you show anybody else that's received any more? Not that I can think of. So don't tell me this administration can't be influenced…I think Dan Lasater has a very tight hold over the governor's office and is benefiting from it."

Clinton let Wooten Epes, the ADFA boss, do the explaining. Epes pointed out that as many as seven companies had been involved in underwriting all the issues. The lead underwriter had always been a New York firm, which he didn't name. He also said that White's firm, Stephens, Inc., where the GOP challenger was vice president for public finance, "had participated in every bond issue the authority had ever made." He did not, however, offer a dollar amount for the total business White's firm corralled. White was to say that Stephens "received only a pittance of the fee that Lasater & Company earned."

It was difficult to determine what had gone through Epes's mind when he let on that Lasater & Company had underwritten $837.5 million worth of bonds since 1983. That was $88.5 million higher than the figure Frank White cited!

Uncle Sam Clobbers Bill's Political Pal

October 25, 1986. Only nine days left to election day. What a time to run the story in the *Arkansas Democrat* under the screaming, page one headline:

Lasater, 10 Others Charged

Here's the way the newspaper's Patrick Casey and Tyler Tucker presented the story that broke the day before:

"Investment banker Dan Lasater, George E. "Butch" Locke, and David A. Collins, partners in the defunct Little Rock bond house Collins, Locke and Lasater, Inc., were among 11 people charged Friday by the U.S. attorney's office with cocaine violations.

"Locke, a former state senator from Hamburg was charged with conspiracy to violate a federal law and illegal use of a telephone to facilitate a drug transaction.

"Lasater and Locke—along with Curtis Lee "Chuck" Berry, Lasater's former chauffeur, James Brainard of Little Rock, also a former Lasater employee, and Berl D.

Clayton, Jr., a Little Rock real estate broker—were charged with 'conspiracy to distribute and to possess with intent to distribute cocaine.' If convicted, they could be sentenced to 15 years in prison and fined $250,000.

"Indicted for possession of cocaine by the grand jury which was meeting this week at Little Rock, were Keith Peterson, a former University of Arkansas basketball player who worked for Lasater, George Jeffries, a local investment banker, and Larry Kelly, a Fort Lauderdale, Fla., investment banker."

Then followed the punch line that was said to have left Governor Bill Clinton screaming, "Why the hell do those bastards pull such shit just before the election! Jesus H. Christ!"

This is how the paragraph that offended him read:

"Roger Clinton, the younger brother of Gov. Bill Clinton, was named as an unindicted co-conspirator in an indictment that cited Mitchell Wood of Little Rock, an industrial training manager with the Arkansas Department of Education, with conspiracy to possess cocaine for distribution."

The story than went on to stress emphatically, "U.S. Attorney George Proctor said Gov. Clinton was in no way involved. 'Absolutely not,' Proctor said. 'There is nothing that would pull the governor into this.'"

Proctor offered this last word:

"Politics did not play a role in the timing of the indictments," despite the fact that the election was just 10 days away, on October 24, when the grand jury findings were handed up to U.S. Magistrate John Forster, who arraigned the defendants the next day. The case was assigned to U.S. District Judge G. Thomas Eisele, who was to listen to pleas and preside at a trial—if there should be one.

But the likelihood of a lengthy court jousting was nil—especially after prosecutor Proctor stated that Lasater and Locke would plead guilty.

Despite All, Arkies Go for Bill

Election night, Tuesday, November 4, 1986, was over before the ballots were half-counted. Bill Clinton overcame all the adversity of the campaign and soundly trounced Frank White, 64 percent to 36 percent.

In his victory speech, minutes after Frank White conceded, Clinton put his arm around Hillary and thanked her for her loyal support.

"I'm proud that she made this walk with me tonight," he said in a voice faintly gravelly. He was beginning now to show the onset of throat problems that had bothered him in the past. The same trouble would plague him in the 1992 presidential race, when he was constantly speaking in a voice that, more often than not, was hoarse, and frequently seemed like he was about to lose it.

"I think when the history of our state is written," Clinton went on about his wife, "no one will prove to have done more to advance the cause of our children and the future of this state than she has."

Clinton continued his speech:

"In our one-hundred and fiftieth year, I believe with all my heart our best years are ahead of us. The tough campaign is over and now it's time for the hard work to begin on our problems and our opportunities. It's time for all of us to pull together as a family."

In 1986, Texas held the biggest birthday party of the year when it celebrated the 150th anniversary of its independence from Mexico. The Texas Sesquicentennial Commission, based in Austin, sanctioned some 10,000 events for the occasion. This included the World's Largest Rattlesnake Roundup in Sweetwater, Buccaneer Days in Corpus Christi, a specially commissioned ballet in La Port, tributes to the oil boom-towns in Odessa and Abilene, a reunion in Mexia of German prisoners of war held in Texas during World War II, and innumerable ethnic festivals, art fairs, and barbecues.

As Bill Clinton voiced in his victory speech, Arkansas was also celebrating its 150th birthday in 1986, but even there Texas dominated the news. Organizers in Ar-kansas complained that many people didn't even know about their own state's sesqui-centennial.

If Governor Bill Clinton had failed to make a splash for the Land of Opportunity's own sesquicentennial, many said, it was because he was diverted by a whole host of other interests.

Others said Clinton couldn't be blamed because he didn't expect to lead Arkansas much longer. He had his eye on the White House.

Case Closed, Lasater's in Stir

Dan Lasater stood before Judge G. Thomas Eisele in Little Rock's U.S. District Court on the morning of Friday, December 18, 1986, a broken man. Moments earlier, the court had sentenced co-defendant 35-year-old Donald G. Bradley, who was em-ployed by Lasater's banking house. He had faced a maximum 20 years imprisonment and a $35,000 fine on his guilty plea to conspiring to buy 1.5 pounds of cocaine in Florida and to selling cocaine in pound quantities (to Lasater and others in the con-spiracy).

Judge Thomas gave him eight years in prison.

Now it was 43-year-old Lasater's turn. His violations of the drug laws were pun-ishable by sentences totaling 15 years and a $250,000 fine.

Judge Eisele ordered Lasater to serve two and a half years in prison on his guilty plea to "conspiracy to distribute and to possess with intent to distribute cocaine."

As U.S. marshals approached the defendant and tapped him on the shoulder, La-sater extended his hands to allow his jailers to snap the steel bracelets on.

Seconds later, he was led out of the courtroom on his way to federal prison.

The Dan Lasater case has now been officially closed. But this will not be the last that we'll hear of Bill Clinton's "closest political ally" and biggest political benefac-tor.

That time would come after he had been paroled, when Governor Clinton would do one last favor for his old pal.

23

MISTRESSES QUEER BILL'S '88 RUN

Bill Won, but Hillary's Boss

Bill Clinton began his first four-year term in office after the swearing-in ceremony by addressing a joint session of the legislature. Afterward he delivered his State of the State message from the capitol steps to about 3,000 cheering supporters, a sight the governor was growing accustomed to.

Clinton spoke extemporaneously. He described the feeling that came over him when he met the approaching dawn of a new day to prepare for his installation:

"...I confess I found myself this morning—I woke up at four-thirty—more awestruck by the opportunity, more humbled by the responsibility, more grateful for the chance to serve than in any previous time."

Arkansas Gazette columnist John Brummett described the start of the governor's fourth term as a "two-thirds mandate" from the electorate to rule over Arkansas for the next four years.

Clinton sounded as though he had read Brummett's piece, which made a stab at analyzing the meaning of the governor's 64 percent plurality:

"Pure, unadulterated power is what he has now."

If only Brummett had looked back at Clinton's past half-dozen years at the helm of Arkansas's government!

During that time, Clinton had amassed a record that didn't lend itself to easy summary. Yet the evidence was that Clinton already had exerted considerable *pure, unadulterated power* in each of his three previous terms.

Clinton also exercised what many viewed as a willingness to reach cozy accommodations with corporate interests—whenever those arrangements suited his own interests. A generous contribution by a big business to a Clinton campaign was all it took sometimes for him to ignore that particular industry's defoliation of Arkansas's environment.

Incongruously, Clinton also appeared comfortable adopting a regressive tax structure that worked against his state's growth and well-being. While he created more jobs, he did so all too often by allowing industry to pollute Arkansas's land, air, and water.

His welfare reforms also suffered from a lack of follow-through, despite a wide consensus that the programs were well conceived. He appeared to be occupied so much with other interests that the state business at hand most often stayed on the back burner.

Clinton seemed not to care that his goals weren't reached—so long as his own welfare wasn't affected.

His accomplishments in improving education standards won justified—but excessive—praise. Yet very little of the progress was of his own doing. Hillary was the quarterback who steered most of the reforms through the legislature. Still, the school system that ranked among the worst in the nation when Clinton took office in 1978 continued to lag near the bottom in most national ratings through four terms in office. The situation improved by mere fractions of percentages in Clinton's remaining years as governor.

While Clinton made gains in improving race relations in a state whose name was once synonymous with segregation, black officials in Arkansas had no reason to rejoice over his performance. They conceded that he created opportunities for greater minority employment, developed a more favorable climate in which minority businesses could operate, and spearheaded other reforms for minorities. Yet Arkansas remained one of only nine states without a law banning discrimination in housing rentals and sales. It was one of only two states—Alabama was the other—that had no civil rights bill barring racial discrimination in hiring and promotion.

It was no illusion that blacks and other minorities had not fared well during the Clinton years. The record shows they were seldom as well off as blacks and minorities in other southern states. Moreover, his administration also came under frequent criticism for failing to provide legal protection and improved economic conditions for blacks. Clinton blamed the legislature.

"They didn't do right with the bills I proposed to them," he whined.

Clinton never responded directly to critics who chastised him about his practice of steering his administration's economic development efforts into predominantly white northwestern Arkansas. While state officials vehemently denied the charge, they couldn't satisfactorily explain why most of the state's economic growth in recent years had been in areas outside the poverty-ravaged Mississippi Delta.

A *New York Times* study found that northwestern Arkansas was settled by the bulk of newcomer firms because the area had a better-educated work force and was already populated by the state's premier companies such as Tyson Foods and Wal-Mart Stores.

Dave Harrington, the latest director of the Arkansas Industrial Development Commission and a Clinton appointee, offered a response to why most of the state's industrial and commercial expansion was in the northwestern tier:

"In the industrial recruitment business, anyone who understands has to see the public sector cannot take companies where they do not want to be. You take them where they've asked to be taken or to an area that has the criteria that they've asked for."

When Clinton's 1986 trip to Japan bore its first fruit some three years later, a contingent of black state legislators strongly protested the manner in which Tokusen USA was steered to Conway, a predominantly white city 27 miles northwest of Little Rock, to open an assembly plant.

Harrington defended the move.

"Tokusen was not steered away from black areas," the AIDC director insisted. "The records will show that race played no part in the company's decision to put its plant in Conway."

Clinton Won't Bare the Records

When the *Arkansas Gazette* asked to look at those records, Harrington balked.

"To make them public will harm Tokusen's competitiveness," he protested.

The newspaper sued the state to gain access to the documents.

Clinton made a speedy end run to the legislature and slipped the lawmakers a hastily written bill that significantly tightened the state's Freedom of Information Act. The measure was then passed by the legislators who, as their detractors complained, probably had as much to hide from the public as Clinton and his administration.

Consequently, the *Arkansas Gazette* obtained a meager number of documents out of the voluminous records. These, the newspaper found, "were only the most innocuous portions of the files kept on the Japanese company."

Clinton was freer with other records. He never hesitated to routinely release state demographic data comprising the racial makeup of cities and counties to businesses contemplating moves to one of those locales.

Harrington defended that practice.

"It becomes important to a certain extent," he said. "When people are looking to the area they want to live in and the types of employees they want, it's important that you give them a personality and a makeup of the community, providing that it is not always negative. In some cases it's very positive."

While the Clinton administration made some effort to help black businesses and tried to create jobs for African Americans and other minorities, poverty persisted at shamelessly high rates among blacks in the rural counties of southeastern Arkansas's Mississippi Delta. Correspondent Steven A. Holmes noted in a *New York Times* exposé, "There, illiteracy and joblessness remain stubbornly high, and at least one county has an infant mortality rate higher than that of French Guiana, Malaysia and Cuba. Even Mr. Clinton's admirers among blacks complain that his administration has yet to materially improve the lives of blacks in the Delta."

Jimmie L. Wilson, a black state representative from that area, gave Bill Clinton far lower grades than the governor gave himself during the presidential race. Clinton claimed the number of the state's unemployed blacks decreased by 34.8 percent from 1983 to 1990 and took credit for that "improvement."

"Clinton appointed just a few token Negroes to various boards," Wilson said. "But he knows full well how to go into African American churches, get in the pulpit, and sound like a black Baptist preacher.

"But in the final analysis, eastern Arkansas has fared no better under Clinton than it did under previous governors."

Lending weight to Jimmie Wilson's assessment was the U.S. Bureau of Labor Statistics. Clinton campaigned his way to the presidency by claiming he performed *miracles* for blacks and other minorities in Arkansas.

True, this federal agency concurred that Arkansas's black unemployment rate had decreased by 34.8 percent, as Clinton boasted. However, the joblessness among blacks *nationwide* fell by a heftier 37.6 percent in that same period.

Contradicting Clinton's assertions that he'd done much to elevate blacks, Arkansas's 17.5 percent black unemployment rate was actually higher than for several other southern states, such as Alabama, Louisiana, and Mississippi.

Typifying the quality of life for African Americans under Clinton's 12-year rule of Arkansas, is the all-black community of Lake View that borders the Mississippi. The town was founded in the 1930s under President Franklin D. Roosevelt's visionary New Deal. The purpose was to give Arkansas's economy a desperately needed shot in the arm to help it emerge from the Great Depression. Ninety black families were settled in Lake View. Each was given 40 acres of land and two mules.

Today, Mayor Leon Phillips calculates that only five of those families still own their farms.

"And they're barely hanging on," Phillips said. "Most of the black families lost their farms in the last ten years [while Bill Clinton was governor]."

"How are the community's 609 residents making ends meet now?" Steven Holmes asked the mayor.

"Welfare, man, welfare," Phillips responded unhesitatingly.

Bill Favors Educated Blacks

Clinton's record does show that he made an effort to better the plight of educated blacks. He appointed a greater number of blacks to boards, commissions, and departments than his predecessors. He picked African Americans to serve in such influential posts as chief financial officer of the state, health commissioner, and head of the Department of Social Services.

Clinton gets even higher grades for bettering race relations in the justice system. "That's because," as Clinton gloated, "those bums in the house and senate didn't have any voice to interfere with my choice of picking judges."

The *New York Times*, in another in-depth study by correspondent Neil A. Lewis, found that Clinton had appointed a substantial number of blacks to serve on the various state courts—and elevated at least five blacks to the state's seven-member Supreme Court and the Court of Appeals.

The appointments were made despite the fact that all judges, in compliance with Arkansas's constitution, must be elected. The governor figures in the selection of judges only after vacancies occur, such as when a jurist dies or leaves office.

While Clinton could claim he advanced Arkansas's race relations in the judicial system, many lawyers in the state frowned upon the unseen but key role Hillary Rodham Clinton played in determining appointments.

In '92, these same voices expected that the Clintons' practice in Little Rock would carry to the Oval Office—and that Hillary would be as deeply involved in naming judges to the federal bench as she had been in selecting jurists for the state's courts.

A review by the *Times*' Neil Lewis of Clinton's appointments to the state's judiciary and regulatory boards and commissions—totaling several hundred, or virtually all of the officials presently holding such posts in Arkansas—spotlighted one dominant feature about the method of selection:

Clinton picks only "candidates [who] fit into the governor's network of friends and political allies."

A judge who didn't owe his job to the governor, yet insisted on anonymity, corroborated that evaluation in the *Times*:

"Almost all of these lawyers he has put on the bench have some political connection or are just friends of the Clintons."

John Ruston Pagan, a law professor at the University of Arkansas, said he was "dismayed by the governor's apparent indifference on questions of judicial philosophy." Pagan, also an Arkansas state senator, said he often spoke with Clinton about legislation affecting the courts.

"I have never heard him express any opinion about legal philosophy," Professor Pagan said. "We talked for hours at the governor's mansion one night, and he talked extensively about the role of the courts on a procedural level. But I haven't ever heard the governor express any views about the proper role of courts in society."

While conceding that Clinton had made some "stellar appointments" to the state's two top courts—supreme and appeals—Pagan refused to allow the *nepotism* factor, inherent in so many of the governor's appointments, to cloud the issue.

One notable example of using the justice system to reward his—or Hillary's—friends and political allies was to be found in Clinton's appointment of Webster "Webb" Hubbell as acting chief justice of the Arkansas State Supreme Court for six months in 1984. Hubbell was a senior partner, along with Hillary, in the Rose Law Firm.

Hubbell also was one of the Clintons' closest friends. And when Clinton became president he named Webb Hubbell assistant attorney general, the No. 2 position in the Justice Department. In effect, Hubbell became the head man at Justice, filling the vacancy created by the resignation of Richard Thornburgh, who stepped down in the last days of the Bush administration to make an unsuccessful run in Pennsylvania for the U.S. Senate.

Using the courts for patronage became a headache for Clinton in 1986, after he selected Beth Coulson, a lawyer in Perryville (and a "very, very close friend," as she has been authoritatively described), to finish an unexpired term on the court of appeals. Mrs. Coulson's name wasn't on the list of 11 women recommended for their high qualifications for the post by the Arkansas State Bar Association.

Clinton ignored such protocol with regularity. He was true to form when he picked the wife of a wealthy oil dealer, one of his most giving contributors, for the high court. Mrs. Coulson proved an embarrassment when she sent correspondence on court-letterhead stationery to the Workers' Compensation Board, urging a favorable ruling for a former client.

The *Arkansas Democrat*, which always bent over backward to thwart Clinton, blew the whistle on Mrs. Coulson. Chagrined by the exposé, the justice apologized for her lapse of ethics. When her term ended, Clinton felt no compunction about using his influence to have Mrs. Coulson's name placed on the ballot for another judicial seat because, as the record shows, she still was his "very, very close friend!"

She was then soundly thrashed at the polls.

Clinton Eyes the Oval Office

Not many days after his fourth inaugural, Bill Clinton delivered another voluminous bound volume of proposed measures to the legislature. As in the previous year, many felt that Hillary had the big hand in shaping the 214-page outline of the governor's agenda for 1987-88.

Clinton, who had frequently hinted he was preparing to propose a "modest" sales tax increase, shied away from that unpopular notion this time. While his programs were deemed impossible to enact in toto without a hike in the sales impost, Clinton played it coy with the lawmakers:

"It won't be easy for you to vote for this plan. I know that. Maybe you'll have a better one. But so help me, when we walk out of here, when this session is over, let's say, 'This will be the time when we were most alive, because we did our duty and we secured the future of this state.'"

While Clinton whipped up the legislature, his mind and heart were elsewhere. He was about to become "a man very much in a hurry." He was looking toward the 1988 presidential race against Vice President George Herbert Walker Bush.

In mid-February of '87, Clinton flew off to Washington and mounted the rostrum before a professional group promoting greater cooperation between educational institutions and business.

"American students are not on the same educational level as their foreign counterparts," he told his listeners.

"Most disheartening is the decline in the number of students who can demonstrate higher literacy skills…although almost all U.S. students easily meet the lower literacy standards of a generation ago, a majority do not meet today's higher standards."

Clinton called for a complete restructuring of the nation's educational system:

"For decades, policy makers have focused their attention on minimum standards. But there are limits to what we can accomplish with minimums: oriented policies, and their effect upon teachers and administrators may sometimes be to prevent excellence as well as mandate minimum performance."

Clinton sounded as though he aspired to be the "Education President," which was one of the 1988 presidential campaign themes George Bush sounded a year later.

A fortnight then passed. Clinton returned to Washington for the annual National Governors' Association convention. As the NGA's chairman, Clinton presented the group's findings on welfare reform to President Reagan. The program proposed that welfare recipients enroll in work programs and called for increased spending for education and job training.

At a White House press conference conducted with New Hampshire Governor John Sununu, who would later become President Bush's chief of staff, Clinton discussed the proposals:

"We want to create a program that is fundamentally a jobs program. We want to move the person [on welfare] toward independence."

After Reagan endorsed the requirement to have welfare recipients enter mandatory work programs, Clinton presented the package to the House Ways and Means Committee for introduction at its forthcoming hearings on welfare reform.

Before he left Washington, Clinton was cornered by reporters and asked whether he intended to run for president. He responded, "I see that [New York] Governor Mario Cuomo has declined to be a candidate. That makes it simpler for someone like me to run. Finishing second in Iowa or New Hampshire is better than a third-place finish. It looks good for people who thought the candidates would be Cuomo and (Colorado U.S. Senator) Gary Hart."

When he returned to Little Rock, reporters for the *Arkansas Democrat* and *Arkansas Gazette* plied Clinton with questions about his statements in the nation's capital.

"I don't think a sitting governor could enter into a campaign like that unless the people thought it was a good thing, unless they supported it," he offered.

In effect, Bill Clinton was scrounging for a people's mandate to run for the presidency.

"The people would have to feel it's something they were proud of, something they wanted," he went on. "Not one hundred percent, but a significant percentage would have to feel that."

But the Democratic presidential field wasn't building up as a two-man race between Clinton and Hart. Arkansas U.S. Senator Dale Bumpers was making noise about entering the '88 Democratic primaries, but soon his press secretary, Matt James, released a statement that withdrew Bumpers from contention.

"It would mean a total disruption of the closeness my family has cherished, and if victorious, much of that closeness is necessarily lost forever," Bumpers' statement went.

With the Arkansas senator out of the race, Clinton faced only one real challenger in this early pre-primary period when potential candidates felt their way about and tried to make up their mind.

Colorado Senator Gary Hart stood out as the overwhelming early favorite for the Democratic nomination. But then came a startling turn.

Hart had been tailed by a team of reporters from the *Miami Herald* who caught him spending a weekend in his Washington town house with a Florida model, Donna Rice, while his wife was away in Colorado. The story stirred controversy not over Hart's character and judgment alone, but also opened to question the proper limits of the press to probe a candidate's private life.

Hart's situation was not unlike the one that would confront Bill Clinton five years later, in 1992, when the Gennifer Flowers scandal would erupt. Similarly, Hart treated his relationship with Donna "as if he were bulletproof"—the very words Gennifer Flowers used to describe Clinton's attitude toward her.

Thus a "bulletproof" Hart went out to sea one night aboard a luxury yacht, appropriately named *Monkey Business*, on a heading to Bimini in the Bahamas. It was disclosed that Donna Rice and another couple were aboard. The story prompted Hart to withdraw from the race. Although he later filed for the New Hampshire primary, his chances were greatly diminished. He quit the race on May 5.

The Democrats took another pummeling after potential candidate U.S. Senator Joseph R. Biden of Delaware was disclosed to have cribbed—without attribution—some of his most ringing rhetoric from British Labor Party leader Neil Kinnock, and had been disciplined for plagiarism as a student at Syracuse University Law School.

Finally, after *Newsweek* magazine revealed that Biden misstated his academic attainments as a college undergraduate and in law school, he formally withdrew from the race.

By that time, Bill Clinton was invited to the Democratic National Convention in Atlanta, to be held in July 1988, and was asked by former Massachusetts Governor Michael Dukakis to place his name in nomination for the presidency. By then a year would have passed since Clinton himself bowed out of the '88 presidential sweeps.

Fear Taxes Bill's Conscience

The decision was announced at an hour-long news conference in Little Rock's Excelsior Hotel grand ballroom on the afternoon of July 15, 1987.

For more than a week, preparations had been under way to accommodate more than 300 reporters who wanted to hear what everyone expected would be Clinton's declaration of candidacy.

Signals had pointed to such an eventuality. One of the clearest was the moving of Hillary's parents Hugh and Dorothy Rodham from their longtime Park Ridge home in Illinois into a commodious Little Rock condo. Their daughter offered this explanation:

"We moved them here so they can be close to their granddaughter."

With the Rodhams nearby to watch over the Clintons' seven-year-old, Bill and Hillary were free to embark on a vigorous and exhausting countrywide presidential campaign.

But there'd be no such run now.

Clinton addressed the reporters in the Excelsior's ballroom with tears in his eyes:

"I had promised myself a long, long time ago that if I was ever lucky enough to have a kid, my child would never grow up wondering who her father was."

Clinton said he made that promise because he had seen the children of many politicians grow up under intense pressure.

Before he threw in the towel, Clinton had traversed the length and breadth of the country, feeling out the electorate's mood toward him. After 34 trips to 20 states, he returned to Little Rock convinced "we had a chance to run well.

"It is certain that we would have been taken seriously and it's entirely possible we could have won. Thousands had volunteered to work in a Clinton campaign. And total strangers had offered to give up their jobs to help get me elected."

Scores of supporters and volunteers from around the country, prepared to be campaign workers, descended on Little Rock on Monday and Tuesday expecting to hear the governor announce he was running, and to help launch his campaign.

When the stunning declaration came, Clinton's words were drowned out for long seconds by cries of "Oh, no!" and "Why, why, why?"

With Hillary sobbing while her husband spoke, Clinton discussed at great length his reasons for turning down the opportunity to run for the nation's highest office.

"I think there are worse things than going to your grave knowing that you lived putting your child first," Clinton said.

"I need some family time," he went on. "I need some personal time. Politicians are people, too.

"I feel like I'm at the Iran-Contra hearings. 'What do you know and when did you know it?'" Clinton continued, mimicking reporters' attempts to pinpoint when he reached his decision.

"I think, very frankly, one of the reasons I would have had an excellent chance to win is Hillary," Clinton concluded, before turning the podium over to his wife.

Dabbing at her still tear-filled eyes with a handkerchief, Hillary addressed the gathering, her voice choked:

"When I tried to think about this my mind shut down. It is very hard to think about running for president of the United States. I really had to work to think about it."

Max Brantley, editor of the *Arkansas Times*, who found Clinton's statement "shocking and...very moving," wrote a colorful portrait of the scene that sent shock waves of the kind Arkansas perhaps never felt before:

"The room was jammed with network TV crews and people from all over the country. And most of the people and friends of Bill's and political associates in the room fully expected him to announce that he was running for president. It was one of the most moving talks he had ever given. He didn't speak from notes, he spoke from the heart. It seemed a really genuine performance. It seemed regretful on his part and deeply felt, and it seemed that he had a high purpose. I guess it was the picture of a politician forgoing a chance to do something that clearly, from the day I met him, I knew he was destined to do. It seemed a selfless kind of decision."

A selfless kind of decision?

Hardly!

The truth is, Bill and Hillary Clinton had been terrified by a report that the *Arkansas Democrat* had readied a "blockbuster" about the governor's infidelities and was preparing to explode it with a page one "splash," much as the *Miami Herald* had done with Gary Hart.

The exposé was reportedly timed to hit the newsstands at an hour that coincided with Clinton's announcement of his candidacy.

For days the Clintons had been on tenterhooks, fearing that something of that sort would derail their carefully charted road to the White House. That feeling grew after several disturbing episodes.

Just days before the big press conference, Clinton spoke on the phone with Gary Hart. He commiserated with the Coloradan over the attention his affair with Donna Rice had commanded in the press. During that exchange, Clinton wondered what one had to do to gain a public's absolution for past indiscretions.

Afterward, Clinton went to a ball field and watched Chelsea, then a first grader at

Little Rock's Forest Park Primary School, play in a soccer game. Sitting beside him was the *Arkansas Times'* Max Brantley.

"What I'd like to hear," Clinton said haltingly while expanding on the theme touched upon in his conversation with Gary Hart, "is there a point ever in a person's life, a political person's life, when the things you've done in the past are forgotten?

"There's nobody in the world who hasn't done things they weren't embarrassed about. Aren't you ever forgiven? Aren't they ever allowed to be in the past?"

Back at the gubernatorial mansion, Hillary was reported "ready to scratch Bill's eyes out." Betsey Wright had given her all the reason to tremble at the prospect that there was truth to the report the *Arkansas Democrat* was preparing to go with a story about Clinton's extramarital shenanigans.

"I don't see Meredith Oakley's column in the *Democrat*," Betsey had observed. "I wonder what the paper's got her doing."

That made Hillary conclude—as Miss Wright ostensibly had—that the columnist wasn't doing her political pieces because she'd been detached by her editors to prepare the dreaded story.

Miss Wright's perceptiveness had always been viewed by the Clintons as a "super quality," one that impelled them to seek her out to run the campaign that defeated Frank White; then they persuaded her to stay permanently as Bill's closest adviser.

Miss Wright met Bill and Hillary in Texas during George McGovern's campaign. They grew to be fast friends. She accepted Clinton's offer to become his "eyes and ears" after she helped him regain the governor's office in 1982. Together with Joan Roberts as Clinton's press secretary, the day-to-day business—dealing with legislators, state officials, and others—was almost always left in their capable hands.

As the now-mysteriously missing *Arkansas Democrat* political columnist Meredith Oakley would write another time, Betsey Wright and Joan Roberts, along with Hillary Clinton, had "kept the administration on an even keel since [Bill Clinton] regained the office in 1982."

Clinton himself had gotten what he deemed to be "straight goods" after talking to a reporter phoning from the rival *Arkansas Gazette*:

"Bill...I hear the *Democrat*'s gathering string on you and they're readying a story to blow you out of the water."

The informant concluded, as Betsey Wright had, that Meredith Oakley must be the reporter digging up the story, since her "Politics 1987" column hadn't been running lately.

Actually, no such preparation was ever in the works, according to Meredith Oakley herself. The columnist said she temporarily stopped writing her "Politics 1987" column after being asked by her editors to work on a "special assignment."

"The truth is...that the *Democrat* had no such story, either in the works or in the can." Meredith Oakley said.

In the irony of all ironies, Bill Clinton had been psyched out of running for the presidency in 1988 by the fear that his extramarital affairs were to be opened to the treatment Gary Hart received for his own adultery.

Fear—"the tax that conscience pays to guilt," as eighteenth-century physician George Sewell put it—drove Bill Clinton to the biggest miscalculation of his life.

24

CLINTON, THE CONSUMMATE POLITICIAN

The Clintons' Long, Hot Summer

After his announcement, Bill Clinton submitted to many news conference post mortems on why he chose not to run for president in '88. However, the public found it hard to decide which of the many reasons he gave was nearest the *truth*.

He said the "15 contested elections" he'd been through in the past 13 years had left him "aching, literally, for having a more normal, personal family life." Although Clinton was on the November ballot only seven times, he was in six primary contests for his party's candidacy.

His seven-year-old daughter came up again as a factor in his decision. His purported conversations with her made it seem he was chatting with a teenager.

"When I first talked to Chelsea about my possible candidacy, she told me, 'Daddy, that's a great honor.' And she assured me that she could 'handle it' during the times I was gone for long stretches at a time, campaigning."

Then Clinton went off for three or four nights in succession. "Daddy," he quoted the seven-year-old, "you know, this isn't such a good idea."

Asked by a reporter how old Chelsea would have to be before he'd run for president, Clinton blurted, "Eight."

Pressed whether he would accept No. 2 on the presidential ticket, Clinton shook his head with disdain. "I'd first try to talk the nominee into getting someone else," he said, again evoking his sense of familial duty.

Would he accept an appointment in the new administration should the Democrats defeat George Bush? Clinton responded with no enthusiasm. "I've given no thought to that." But he vowed to continue his work with the National Democratic Organization and travel in its behalf as extensively as in the past.

Clinton became edgy when prodded about whether he'd be concerned about an intense scrutiny of his personal life. He was particularly irked when asked if his decision to quit before the race started had anything to do with reports about his womanizing. He said that possibility didn't even enter his mind. Yet in the next breath, "But, I thought about it a lot and we debated it a lot." He then added cryptically, "I had decided how I'd handle questions like that."

Clinton shrank away from further discussion of his infidelities. "I don't want to talk about that any more because I'm not a candidate," he said, an edge in his voice.

His last word on the subject appeared a month later. In an interview by E. J. Dionne, Jr., for the August 16 edition of the *New York Times*, Clinton summed up his position:

"Mentally I was 100 percent committed to the race but emotionally I wasn't."

The decision, he insisted yet again, was based solely on family considerations. Recalling the uncertainties of his own childhood, he reiterated that he feared the distractions and burdens of a presidential campaign would be detrimental to Chelsea's well being.

Then Clinton left the glare of the national spotlight and buckled down to business-as-usual in the statehouse. All at once he was beset with an assortment of headaches.

One of the most painful was a decision by the U.S. Supreme Court in a Pennsylvania case that cast doubt on the constitutionality of Arkansas's weight-distance tax on large trucks. Legislators were divided on whether to charge three cents or two cents a mile for rigs using the state's highways. Clinton stood firm for the three-cent impost, but the lawmakers split the difference and passed a two-and-a-half-cent tax. This proved to be merely a stopgap measure.

Hillary's Clout Keeps Growing

Meanwhile, Hillary Clinton's work at the Rose Law Firm was going at full gallop. By now she had pushed all the right buttons that gave her law partners full access to the state government. Rose and Hillary exercised one power play after another. They obtained unprecedented sanctions for environmental standards from the state Pollution Control and Ecology Commission. They lobbied to protect the powerful poultry industry against strict regulations on animal waste. They wrote and rewrote the rules by which corporations hobble and hog-tie their voiceless shareholders.

Rose's greatest benefactor in all of the above instances—and scores of others—was the state government, which fell into the deplorable practice of issuing nonbid contracts to Hillary's law firm.

One of the juiciest plums for Rose was a $115,000 fee to represent the Arkansas Public Service Commission in the ongoing nuclear power plant dispute with Mississippi. The commission's members were all Clinton appointees.

Rose earned another $175,000 for bond counsel services performed for the Arkansas Development Finance Authority. Curiously, Rose had not been assigned bond counseling work from the state until Hillary moved into the higher echelons of the law firm and began using her muscle.

Hillary's work at Rose was just one phase of her professional life. As cited earlier, she had led task forces for her husband, including the 1983 panel that reformed the public education system and enabled Arkansas to become only the country's second-worst state in the field of education.

Additionally, she was often a witness at legislative hearings on issues dealing with schools and children. The Children's Defense Fund was her *baby*. She nursed it so close to the breast that many felt she harbored an even greater passion for the CDF than for her own child.

By the fall of '87 when Arkansas was still close to being the bottom-rung state in education, despite commendable gains, Hillary was even more in demand on matters scholastic. U.S. District Judge Henry Woods appointed her to a committee charged with finding a way to eliminate racially identifiable schools. The target was every school with a black enrollment of 75 percent or greater.

Attention had turned to Hillary because of the influence she exhibited in getting her husband to set tough education standards. Additionally, there was the much-touted teacher testing, which wasn't all that tough in the view of highly placed educators. Its inherent weakness was that teachers who flunked could take it over and over until they passed.

One area in which Hillary could do nothing was in bettering scores achieved by Arkansas's high schoolers on standard college tests. The stats on this remained painfully stagnant. A dismaying 60 percent of the state's students who made it to college required remedial instruction once on campus. Yet the widespread consensus was that the schools had improved and the Clintons, Bill and Hillary—or the *Billary administration*, as it was now being called—deserved much of the credit.

About the time she took her assignment from Judge Woods to count the black population in schools, Hillary was appointed by the American Bar Association as chairman of a newly organized committee of 12 members shaping the lawyers' Commission on Women and the Profession. Her committee held hearings and sought to sort out problems women encountered in law offices, the courts, and in other areas where they performed as counselors-at-law.

"Hillary was able to stimulate all sorts of construction developments within the association that have significantly changed the course of the constituency of the association," praised ABA president Robert MacCrate, who appointed Hillary to the commission. "The ABA was pretty much a male-dominated old boys' club. Hillary brought about a greater participation of women in our organization. People have told me that the best appointment I ever made was naming her the chairman of that commission."

Politics and Private Interests

"It is an axiom of life in Arkansas that most people who want something out of the state will at some point solicit support from the governor's office, where Bill Clinton runs the show, or from the Rose Law Firm, where Hillary Clinton is a partner. Or quite often both. The power line here runs 14 blocks from the red brick Rose building up to the pillared state capitol."

This assessment was advanced by *Washington Post* reporters Michael Weisskopf and David Maraniss in the March 15, 1992, edition, just as the presidential primaries were heating up. The article went on:

"Rarely in American politics have married partners played such interconnected public roles, and the convergence of legal and political power in the Clinton family poses several problems for them as they seek to move on from this small town, politically inbred capital to the White House."

At the core of these discussions were questions being asked over the years—but never answered directly or honestly—about the political favoritism Hillary bought for her firm's legal clients, and the apparent conflicts of interest for her husband, the governor, whose appointees regulated many of the business and financial institutions Rose represented.

While friends and supporters found nothing awkward about the intertwining business dealings that crisscrossed those 14 blocks separating the Rose firm from the statehouse, others didn't agree that it was all an innocent but unavoidable coincidence, as claimed by Clinton adviser Diane Blair, a political science professor at the University of Arkansas.

"If you are going to be a high-powered lawyer," said Professor Blair, "it would be pretty hard to separate yourself from the economic power of the state."

Critics complained that by merely listing Hillary Clinton as a partner, Rose's clients gained undeserved or excessive clout in their dealings with state government.

"If you want something special in this state, you go to the Rose firm, said Sheffield Nelson, the Little Rock lawyer who, in 1990, would run against Clinton. In 1988, Nelson had just ended a tour with the Arkansas Industrial Development Commission and was credited by many with knowing whereof he spoke.

Hillary Clinton always hit hard at the backbiters by claiming she didn't represent clients before the state government. But why, then, would she say she declined her share of Rose's fees for such cases—a statement disputed by her own husband, who conceded Hillary did benefit financially from those power ploys?

The stance of arms-length association didn't fly with the wife of Jim McDougal, the old friend who brought the governor and his wife into the curious Ozark Mountain real estate deal in the late 1970s.

Susan McDougal, also a partner in the Ozark venture, stated flatly that Hillary played a significant role in saving the McDougal-owned Madison Guaranty Savings & Loan from insolvency and possible bankruptcy. This occurred after the Clintons pulled out of the vacation land deal and walked away, not only with their entire "investment," but also, as the record reflects, a "magnificent profit."

"Hillary Clinton actively did the solicitations in the effort to increase its ratio of capital to assets, as federal regulators were pressuring the bank to do," Mrs. McDougal went on. "The Rose firm then petitioned the state securities commissioner to approve in principle a plan by Madison to issue preferred stock as a means of acquiring the additional capital to take it out of its bind."

In the initial pleading to the commissioner, just appointed by Governor Clinton, Hillary Clinton was listed as one of two lawyers to contact for particulars on the case. Reports were rife at the time that the securities chief's predecessor wouldn't go along with the scheme either and was forced out of his post by Hillary's husband, to be replaced by "a rubber-stamp puppet."

More Hanky-Panky in the Ozarks

Busy as she was drumming up state business for the Rose Law Firm's clients,

Hillary didn't neglect "sideline ventures." She reentered the Ozark Mountain's business excursion in early 1988, after the buyer of the Whitewater Development Corporation's model house went into bankruptcy, stopped making payments, then died.

Hillary bought the house back from the estate of the buyer for $8,000 and a short time later, the records reflect, she resold it for $23,000.

The picture of what went on here is much clearer than the many out-of-focus results developed earlier, when the *New York Times'* Jeff Gerth had to rely upon New York lawyer Susan P. Thomases to explain the sinuous deals the Clintons transacted in their Ozark outing. The records of later aspects of the story are not the questionable ones Mrs. Thomases showed to Gerth.

The reporter examined local, state, and federal tax returns that brought out an extraordinarily convoluted picture of the Clintons' manipulations in high finance. As previously noted, the Clintons pulled fast ones on Uncle Sam with their 1984 and 1985 federal income tax returns. They not only juggled figures, but finagled and rigged them—and placed the blame on the tax preparers. At their worst then, the Clintons *countenanced* dishonest accounting procedures that bordered on the criminal.

But the deal Hillary entered in 1988, which brought the model house back into her portfolio, has the appearance of being aboveboard—although the figures at first blush suggest it wasn't. The reason: While Hillary paid $8,000 for the Ozark property and sold it for $23,000, she and Bill reported only a $1,640 capital gain on their 1988 federal joint tax return.

Though Hillary realized a $15,000 profit from the deal, her net gain was significantly smaller, $2,000. For she purportedly paid off the balance of the $13,000 debt that Whitewater was obligated to meet after the buyer of the property entered Chapter 11 bankruptcy proceedings and ceased making payments.

The Clintons could provide seemingly justifiable arguments for the $1,640 figure entered on their '88 Internal Revenue Service 1040 form. It is not an unreasonable amount to claim from the $2,000 that Hillary accrued after Whitewater's debt was paid. The unaccounted $360 could have been the closing costs on the resale.

When Hillary unloaded the house, it broke the Clintons' last visible ties to their Ozark Mountains adventure. But it didn't end their association with Jim McDougal and his Madison Guaranty Savings & Loan empire. It finally fell on hard times—as had most of the nation's free-wheeling, irresponsibly managed S&Ls. That's when Clinton pulled out all the stops to have the State Securities Commission extricate McDougal from his jam.

Clinton could do no less for his old pal. For McDougal had made Bill and Hillary his partners when neither of them invested any money to speak of in the Ozarks venture. So they had little to lose if it failed, but had it succeeded, they could have cashed in on the 50 percent interest they were cut in for by a blindly generous McDougal.

Or was that generosity just an insurance policy for the future? Had McDougal foreseen the looming savings and loan scandal descending upon his Madison Guaranty thrift empire? Who but Arkansas's most omnipotent legal and political powerhouse could better defend McDougal if, God forbid, such an occasion arose? For that's a combat few survive, since federal regulators are programmed to chew up sinners and spit them into prison with a deplorable lack of heart.

These questions are no more likely to be answered than those Jeff Gerth posed to Bill and Hillary Clinton and their attorney Susan Thomases. Nor can one expect Jim McDougal to feed a fire that has already burned him with indictment, arrest, and prosecution for fraud. But those questions could be answered—now that special prosecutor Kenneth Starr is probing. Or, if he doesn't come up with satisfactory responses, the congressional committees are certain to do so.

For whatever reason McDougal made his generous Whitewater grant to the Clintons, we can say that Bill and Hillary "owed him one."

Thus the Rose Law Firm was committed to represent the savings institution when it was threatened with closure by federal regulators, who found it to be insolvent. Hillary, riding shotgun for her firm, went to the State Securities Commissioner's office seeking relief.

Bill and Hillary Rescue the S&L

Hillary's plea fell on deaf ears, for the commissioner couldn't see the viability of McDougal's proposal to stave off a Chapter 11 filing. He wanted to thwart bankruptcy through an infusion of new funds into Madison Guaranty by an issue of nonvoting, preferred stock.

That would mean McDougal could grab the investors' funds, play with them to his heart's content, and leave his benefactors no say in how their money was used.

So Clinton fired the commissioner and put another in place who went along with the scam. Even after a Securities Department lawyer tried to halt the deal, he was told to keep his nose out of it.

Did either Bill Clinton or Hillary Rodham Clinton ever address that episode, which is documented fact?

No, they did not.

As recently as March 8, 1994, Clinton continued to maintain that neither he nor Hillary conspired to commit such illegalities to save Madison Guaranty from its ultimate fate—insolvency and failure.

"I do not believe for a moment that she [nor he] had done anything wrong" Clinton professed. "If everybody in this country had a character half as strong as hers [and his], we wouldn't have half the problems we've got."

That statement brought a reaction from Senator Alfonse D'Amato, the feisty New York Republican who called for congressional hearings until the Democratic majority in the upper house caved in and agreed to give *Whitewatergate* the scrutiny the minority membership was demanding.

What was D'Amato's response to Clinton's attempt to drape a halo around himself and the first lady? "That's the problem!" he grumbled.

Try as he might, Clinton couldn't douse the flames licking all around him and Hillary.

One reason: That $2,000-a-month retainer Clinton extracted during his morning jog from McDougal to retain Hillary and/or the Rose Law Firm to look after Madison Guaranty's interests.

Another reason: The identification of the new Securities Department commissioner, whom Clinton appointed to grease the way for Madison Guaranty's bailout. The appointee was Beverly Bassett, who not only happened to have a brother, Woody Bassett, Clinton's finance chairman, but also didn't give up her ties with her law firm, Mitchell, Williams, Selig, Jackson & Tucker.

Does the last name on the law firm's letterhead ring a bell?

It should! That's Jim Guy Tucker, whose past has been extensively chronicled in preceding pages and whose present status is Arkansas's governor; he took Clinton's place despite the fact that he played the lead role in Susan McDougal's $45,000-to-$180,000 land-flip scam.

The old adage, *it's all in the family*, was never more apropos than in this Clintonesque opera.

What further proof is needed to show Hillary got her way with the Securities Department (not with McDougal's nonvoting stock plan, but two alternatives of her own that breathed temporary life in Madison before the roof finally caved in in 1989)...proof that the "fix" was in and Hillary and Bill were the prime movers in the illegality?

Let's look at the solid and validated documentation of a letter—a letter Beverly Bassett wrote that contains her approval of the deal to rescue Madison Guaranty, over her signature!

It's written to the Rose Law Firm.

And it's addressed "Dear Hillary"!

Both proposals to save Madison Guaranty were advanced by Hillary Clinton, as counsel of record for Madison—repeatedly assisted in researching the law by her firm's senior partner Webb Hubbell!

With that new life breathed into it by the Clintons' intervention, the thrift was able to enjoy a longer-than-deserved run. But McDougal couldn't extricate his banking empire from the pits, despite all of Hillary Clinton's efforts.

Federal regulators finally stepped in and took Madison Guaranty out of McDougal's hands, leaving him a broken man. A federal grand jury indicted him for fraud and he was prosecuted in Little Rock's U.S. District Court.

Diagnosed to be suffering manic depression, he was nevertheless adjudged competent to stand trial. Although acquitted, he had little reason to rejoice.

In the interviews he conducted with McDougal, Jeff Gerth found him to appear "stable, careful, and calm" as he described his relations with the Clintons. The banker told the *Times*' reporter that sometime in 1991, the governor phoned a mutual acquaintance "to ask whether Mr. McDougal harbored any hostilities."

Gerth wrote further: "Mr. McDougal said Mr. Clinton also suggested that he might be able to find a job for him."

When Gerth confronted Clinton with McDougal's claim, he would not discuss that conversation—as he had declined to talk about any aspect of his dealings in Whitewater Development or McDougal. The Clintons directed all inquiries to their New York attorney, Susan Thomases.

Mrs. Thomases told Gerth that Clinton had told her about an earlier conversation he had with McDougal, who allegedly asked the governor for a job. McDougal, asserting he had no animosity toward Clinton, said the governor never called back to discuss his request for employment.

Despite extensive legwork, Jeff Gerth couldn't nail down what became of the bulk of Whitewater's existing records.

McDougal maintained that, at Bill Clinton's request, the file was delivered to the governor's mansion.

When asked about that, Clinton insisted that many of those records have "disappeared."

Therefore, many questions about their curious involvement in the baffling Ozark Mountains venture will likely remain unanswered forever.

The Pain Won't Go Away

After the *New York Times* story broke on March 7, 1992, reporters caught up with Bill Clinton on a one-day, whirlwind Texas tour. He was trying to sew up the Lone Star State's 196 delegates, the biggest primary prize of the next week's Super Tuesday contest.

Clinton immediately challenged the *Times'* claim that he and Hillary were at little financial risk because McDougal heavily subsidized the real estate venture.

"The truth is that we lost more than twenty-five thousand dollars—never made a penny on it," Clinton said. Later, he hiked that figure nearly $10,000—and still later was embarrassed by his own IRS filings that made him a big exaggerator.

His 1984 and 1985 joint-income tax returns didn't support his claims.

Nowhere on the Clintons' 1984–1985 returns is there a reported business loss amounting to any Whitewater losses. All the returns show is that Bill and Hillary Clinton reported joint income of $111,000 and $102,000 for those respective years, and that they paid federal taxes of $22,260 and $18,791 for each of those years.

Bill and Hillary Clinton walked away clean from the Whitewater fiasco, but the man who bankrolled them suffered not only financial ruination, but also was left, in the end, to agonize over his involvement with two people he miscalculated to be friends.

Jim McDougal had a few last words on the subject:

"The pain from my association with the Clintons will never go away."

Jim McDougal's affliction may likely bring even greater hurt for Bill and Hillary Clinton in the second year of their presidency. For two separate probes into the dealings involving Whitewater and Madison have been instituted by federal authorities. The heat generated by the inquiries was being felt at the White House by mid-1994 as Congress also was readying a probe into the mess.

Yet, in a way strikingly like past performances, President Clinton was whistling a tune of innocence and putting on a mindless show of arms-length distancing from reality:

"We did nothing improper and I have nothing to say about it."

The White House press office reacted as it had during the campaign when the issue was raised.

"It's an old story," spokeswoman Dee Dee Myers protested. "The president is not a subject or target of an investigation. That is clear. It is something that was well reported during the campaign."

True enough. It was well reported by the *New York Times*. But that publication was hamstrung from unearthing the entire truth about the Clintons' involvement in the convoluted partnership. The Clintons escaped the pain others suffered.

One of the victims, besides the most-seriously wounded investor, Jim McDougal, was identified in fresh uncoverings of evidence as David Hale, the former municipal judge in Little Rock who became a small business loan administration official and was indicted for defrauding the Small Business Administration on the $300,000 loan scheme to bail out Madison.

Hale unsuccessfully tried to fend off the grand jury charges by offering to blow the whistle on the "financial activities of Arkansas politicians," then turned an accusing finger at Bill Clinton following the rebuff:

"The former governor and others pressured me to make Small Business Administration-backed loans to help get bad loans off the books of McDougal's failing thrift."

Now the trial's been put off in the trade-off with special prosecutor Robert Fiske, as described at length earlier.

As an outgrowth of the probe Fiske launched, the Rose Law Firm's senior partner Webster L. Hubbell reluctantly conceded that Hillary had done "some work for Madison Guaranty but not a major share." Pressed for details, he inexplicably cited "confidentiality of attorney-client relations" and withdrew into silence.

Hillary Clinton herself repeatedly refused to comment on Madison Guaranty matters. She absolutely declined to define the role she played. And she refused to say when she stopped profiting from the Rose firm's representation before the state on other matters, such as the multi-million dollar windfall from the sale of Arkansas Development Finance Authority bonds.

Meanwhile, with the David Hale case hanging fire and threatening to burn the president and first lady, the White House saw fit to put its two cents in with another defense of the first couple—obviously *damage control* in its sleekest form.

George Stephanopoulos went to bat for his boss and said "Bill Clinton had no role whatsoever in the Madison Guaranty S and L failure. Nor was he involved in any matter that may have concerned his wife as an attorney at the Rose Law Firm."

Hillary's press secretary, Lisa Caputo, took this tack for her boss:

"Our view is that Hillary Clinton, when a lawyer at the Rose Law Firm, acted with the utmost integrity and professionalism. I have no reason to believe otherwise."

Could Miss Caputo have said anything differently?

Hillary acted with *integrity and professionalism*?

By whose standards? By what yardstick?

Miss Caputo offers no proof whatsoever with even one case that can make her point.

One especially noxious case that involves Hillary Rodham Clinton must be cited to demonstrate her *integrity and professionalism*.

This scheme enabled the first lady to rake in thousands of dollars in Rose Law Firm partnership profits—income that to this day continues to pour in even as she conducts America's business from the West Wing.

Struck behind locked doors, this multi-tentacled deal involved the precipitate inflation of real estate values and sale prices of 45 nursing-retirement homes in Iowa.

The details on this transaction were revealed from across the Atlantic by yet another newspaper—*The Sunday Times* of London.

The charges focus on a set of deals in 1989, just as Hillary's man was preparing to announce for the presidency.

The deals involved homes for convalescents and the elderly that were bought and sold by Texas financier Bruce Whitehead. The newspaper found that in the transactions, the price is jacked up from $47 million to $92 million in *just in one day*!

According to the *Times*, the Rose Law Firm called the shots all the way and caused the value of the homes to skyrocket.

This was done through a series of sales, to so-called "shell companies," which gave Rose's clients an instant profit of about $10 million, the newspaper states.

The deal stuck it to Mercy Health Initiatives, the ultimate owner of the homes, which was forced to bear millions of dollars in additional debt and compelled to raise health care costs.

The wheeler-dealers behind those manipulations also got their hooks on $86 million in tax-free bonds from the Iowa State Finance Authority. Later, Iowa tax assessors determined that at least one of Whitehead's shell firms wasn't entitled to state tax breaks.

The denial was based on a decision that one particular Mercy Health affiliate was not a charitable venture deserving such tax relief.

That decision caused Mercy Health to raise rates even higher.

Representative Jim Leach, the Iowa Republican so critical of the Clinton administration and who called for a congressional investigation into the Clintons' co-ownership of the Whitewater Development Corporation, is quoted by the *Times* in a critical view of the nursing home deal:

"What appears self-evident is that the nursing home sales increased the cost of health care."

The *Times*' investigation also reveals that William Kennedy III, the fourth Rose Law Firm partner to have tagged along with Hillary Clinton, Vincent Foster, and Webster Hubbell to Washington, spearheaded the Iowa scheme.

The story says he "had full knowledge of every step of the Iowa transactions [because he was involved in most of the manipulations]...and Hillary Clinton also knew precisely what was going on."

Lastly, the *Times* quotes an unidentified lawyer at Rose:

"All partners were aware of all deals and they all shared in the profits [from the Iowa nursing-retirement homes]," which caused many convalescing patients and the elderly to pay 14 percent higher fees for services provided.

Trudging to Little Rock, the *Times*' investigative team turned up legal sources who informed them that the Rose Law Firm could have made up to $500,000 on the turnovers, with Hillary purportedly having pulled down some $15,000 for herself.

Although Hillary denies any part or knowledge in this obvious flimflam, the *Times* not only concludes Hillary pocketed the 15 g's, but also that she couldn't be telling the truth about her noninvolvement.

As a partner in the law firm, it would be impossible for Hillary not to have been aware of this deal—one of the biggest going for Rose at the time.

Besides, a Rose lawyer flatly states she <u>was</u> in on it!

The newspaper voices the view that the Iowa transactions "demonstrated the same sort of price-gouging and unconscionable profiteering" the first lady has been complaining about in the medical profession and in the pharmaceutical and insurance industries, while "trying, in the righteous pose she's taken" to peddle health-care reforms for the nation.

The lawyer for the Iowa tax assessors, Frank Pechacek, tells the *Times* he places the blame for the convoluted mess totally on the Rose Law Firm. He states, "While not exactly illegal, there is a big difference between making a reasonable profit and ripping off someone."

The passel of legal minds the White House has recruited from Rose's ranks continues to cause eyebrows to lift, higher than ever in fact, after the *Sunday Times* exposé.

These are the sort of lawyers the president chose to conduct America's most sensitive legal business.

When Kennedy joined the lineup on the Hubbell-Foster-Rodham team to perform their now-you-see-it, now-you-don't talents on the same controversy-riddled field, one could suggest that they had carried playmaking one better than Tinkers-to-Evans-to-Chance.

But make no mistake.

Hubbell-to-Foster-to-Rodham-to-Kennedy was a very different kind of *American Pastime*.

Webb, Vince, and Hillary had one last hand in the Madison Guaranty failure, which has been almost totally ignored by the media.

What a Blunder! Government Retains the Rose Law Firm!

The author is duty-bound to bore through the wall of deception and lies they have built around themselves and expose Hubbell, Foster, and Mrs. Clinton for what they were as partners in the Rose Law Firm and in the savings and loan scandals: double-dealing, conflict-of-interest manipulators.

Two cases scream for a grand jury investigation.

Both have their genesis in the actions taken by Webb Hubbell as the law firm's top litigant in Rose's savings and loan portfolios.

In each instance, Rose represented the Federal Savings and Loan Insurance Corporation in efforts to recover depositor losses that ran into the millions as a result of mismanagement on the part of S&L operators.

The FSLIC doesn't have lawyers on its staff to litigate against people who've taken it to the cleaners, as Dan R. Lasater did when he took an Illinois bank, the First American Savings and Loan, in the Chicago suburb of Oak Brook, down the tube.

When the FSLIC decided to move against Lasater—the Clinton intimate and imprisoned drug trafficker—to recoup $3.3 million in depositors' funds the bank lost through mismanagement, the government agency chose to fight Lasater on his home turf, Little Rock.

The obvious choice for legal representation in the arena was the Rose Law Firm, based in the Arkansas capital with a reputation as one of the state's most prestigious litigators.

Two strange things happened on the way to court.

Webster Hubbell always had a lock on handling virtually every one of Rose's savings and loan portfolios. Yet for reasons never brought into the open, and which scream for explanation, Hubbell didn't pursue the FSLIC vs Lasater suit—although he had helped in soliciting the government agency's business for his law firm on that case.

The call went to Rose partners Hillary Rodham and Vincent Foster. They are said to have been summoned at the time from one of their *retreats* at the law firm's Ozark Mountains *cabin in the sky*, the facility maintained for the R&R of Rose's hard-working barristers such as Hillary and Vince, whose laborious toils into the late hours of the night have already been recited.

No sooner did they return than Hillary and Vince huddled with Dan Lasater in discussions that are nowhere to be found in a public record.

When they emerged from the dark, they announced that a deal had been struck with the defendant.

He agreed to put up $200,000 in settlement of his $3.3 million obligation. That was paying back less than a thousandth of a cent to each of America's 250 million potential taxpaying citizens whom Lasater cheated through his theft of the $3.3 million.

What was wrong with the deal?

Just this: Dan Lasater had only recently been sprung from the federal pen after doing a two-year stretch for drug trafficking.

Lasater was a *family intimate*, acquainted not only with Bill's half brother, Roger, and their mother, Virginia Kelley, but also very much so with Hillary.

When Hillary stepped in to bat for the United States Government and was entrusted to sue Lasater in the name of America's taxpayers, who but the key players in this legal drama had any inkling that her adversary was one of her husband's best friends?

Or that he'd be handled with the softest of kid gloves and have that $3.3 million suit settled for a paltry $200,000?

Would it be out of turn to ask whether this is one of the most blatant cases involving conflict of interest?

There's not even the slightest clue as to how Hillary and Vince Foster reached that settlement with Dan Lasater.

No word at all whether or not the Rose Law Firm's legal team even tried to determine how much of Lasater's ill-gotten gains from drug trafficking might be stashed in cold storage, or even if they were able to determine what real assets of his could be recouped when they struck the deal with him.

Or why neither Hillary nor the Rose Law Firm informed the FSLIC of her close relationship with Lasater, clearly a conflict of interest that was withheld from the plaintiff.

A spokesman confirms that the FSLIC did not know of Hillary's friendship with Lasater when she took the case.

Certainly Kenneth Starr cannot ignore the easy settlement worked out with Lasater, either. Nor can he not acknowledge a third Rose lawyer's representation of the federal thrift regulators in another case: <u>Federal Deposit Insurance Corporation vs James McDougal</u>

That's the case the Rose Law Firm sent Webb Hubbell to litigate for the government, which sought to collect $10 million, the token amount the FSLIC was to shell out to Madison Guaranty Savings and Loan's depositors left holding the empty $50 million bag that once was in the thrift's vault. Federal regulators finally closed the thrift down in 1989.

His day of reckoning comes after McDougal, ably assisted by his Whitewater partners, the Clintons, had taken the thrift belly-up despite last-ditch efforts by the governor and his wife to keep it afloat.

Then it became Webster Hubbell's turn to be McDougal's angel. As a friend of Jim's, which Webb happened to be, it should not come as a surprise to find the $10-million suit the FSLIC brought against the banker was settled for ten cents on the dollar.

Remember, again no one at Rose told the FSLIC about Hubbell's old ties with McDougal—another blatant conflict of interest violation.

That left the Loan Bank of Dallas, the FSLIC, and the nation's taxpayers taking a $9-million bath.

Hubbell's efforts earned the Rose Law Firm a neat $400,000 legal fee and left the plaintiff netting less than $600,000 since, as the record shows, Webb Hubbell never spared expenses in cases he litigated. Padding expenses became Webb Hubbell's nightmare. For he was clobbered so mercilessly in the press with those charges, that on March 14, 1994, he threw in the towel and walked out of the Justice Department, ending his brief career in Washington—and what conceivably could be his career as a lawyer.

For the day after he submitted his abrupt letter of resignation, the Rose Law Firm let it be known they had filed an ethics complaint against Hubbell.

In his resignation letter, Hubbell said, "After a thoughtful weekend, I believe that my continued service will not be as effective as it has been; that the distractions on me at this time will interfere with my service to the country and the president's agenda; and that my family, although totally supportive, is being harmed."

Hubbell's resignation severed the main link the Clinton White House had with the Justice Department. Hubbell had been the eyes and ears for the Clintons in keeping tabs on Janet Reno.

With Webster Hubbell shot down and Vincent Foster shot dead, the Clinton White House and the Rose Law Firm lost two of its formidable showcase legal talents. Only Hillary and Kennedy remain. But their future, to say the least, seems uncertain.

25

LOOKING OUT FOR NUMBER ONE

Ethics Laws Are Not for Clinton

In February 1988, Bill Clinton was in his eighth year as governor and the second year of a four-year term. That made the 41-year-old officeholder one of the state's longest-serving governors.

It began to appear that Clinton was turning a democratic government into what many feared was almost despotic rule.

He began by advancing a comprehensive ethics and disclosure law for public officials. A law with every appearance of having been chartered principally, if not wholly, to benefit himself, Hillary, and the Rose Law Firm.

The code, as ultimately hand-crafted by Clinton and his so-called *Gang of Three*, protected them all from ever having to publicly disclose their arcane Ozark Mountain and Madison Guaranty S&L deals. They were immunized further from openly accounting for any of their numerous other, always questionable business transactions.

For more than 150 years, since it became a state, Arkansas had gotten along without an ethics law for public servants. That frequently gave state officials an unfair advantage over the public. It fostered corruption and led many government workers into believing they were duty-bound to extract as much money as they could for their services to the state.

Bill Clinton began laying the foundation for an ethics code as far back as June 9, 1987. He appointed a commission to write the proposed law to cover all state officials, as well as lobbyists currying favors from lawmakers and other influential government employees.

Before the code was enacted into law, Clinton led the Arkansas general assembly and the state's estimated 2,455,000 residents to believe he was acting in their best interests by formulating the state's first comprehensive ethics and disclosure standard. But after a sequence of political circumventions, the initial law was quietly altered by Clinton, aided and abetted by the very people he wanted protected. They fashioned a legal haven for themselves that exempted them from the rules applied to other public officials. The changes create the perception that the only interests the governor had at heart were his own and those of his allies.

As the ethics committee formulated the law originally, all government officials—

including elected public servants such as the governor—were required to disclose *certain assets and sources of income*. Under that guideline, Clinton was required merely to list his wife as an employee of the Rose Law Firm and state only that she derived her income from that source.

The original legislation also contained a comprehensive conflict-of-interest clause requiring all state employees to make full disclosure, with precise details, when their duties involved them in "the taking of an action or the making of a decision that may cause financial benefit or detriment to him, to a member of the public servant's family or a business in which he or she is an officer, director, stockholder owning more than 10 percent of the stock of the company, owner, trustee, partner or employee, which is distinguishable from the effects of the action from the public generally or a broad segment of the public."

The precise language on reporting requirements read:

"[All affected public servants] shall: prepare a written statement describing the matter requiring the action or decision and stating the potential conflict."

No record reflects Bill Clinton's reaction to the bill, as drafted by his ethics commission. The governor received the bill around the Christmas holidays. He let it sit on his desk until late January 1988, when he called a special session of the legislature merely to introduce the proposed ethics code.

The bill ran into a buzz saw from the instant it landed on the legislators' desks. The house attached 19 amendments before clearing it for a vote. Then it was finally passed, overwhelmingly.

The senate found the proposed ethics code far less palatable. A raging debate ensued, and more than 30 changes were incorporated into the bill. By then any semblance to the original was purely coincidental. And the senators weren't through yet. They began talking about writing their own version of the legislation.

Senators didn't like the provision that called for the formation of a permanent ethics commission. Nor did they see any merit in requiring lobbyists to fully account for what they spend while wooing legislators and public officials. The upper house further wanted a one-man Office of Ethics Counsel and no disclosure statements from lobbyists. That clashed sharply with the position the lower house had taken.

The impasse between the house and senate resulted in an adjournment of the special session. Precisely what the governor wanted. The general assembly had played into Clinton's hands, or as the *Arkansas Gazette*'s Bob Wells commented on February 7, "If the special legislative session had been a movie, Governor Bill Clinton couldn't have been a more brilliant director, jumping in at just the right moment...to shout 'cut.'"

Clinton was now free to carry out what was on his mind all along: To put the matter of an ethics code in the hands of the voters. But they wouldn't get a crack at any of the proposed legislation previously debated. Clinton was to fashion a bill designed to create the special immunity he sought all along for himself and his pals.

The language for his ethics code was to be structured by the Rose Law Firm's ablest counselors: his wife, Hillary, and Rose's senior partner and Clinton's future assistant attorney general, Webb Hubbell. They called on Little Rock attorney Scott

Trotter to assist them—but very surreptitiously.

Clinton had long planned to have his ethics code passed not by the knowledgeable legislators, but by the *know-nothing* public. *Know-nothing* because, unlike the legislators who have the entire text of a proposed law in their hands to study, the voter is shown only a two-line, 25-word extract in the polling place instead of the thousands of words written into the measure. How, then, with such a paucity of words, could the electorate know that *Slick Willie* was putting another one over on them?

In a seeming dress rehearsal for the public forays he would make to win support for his agendas after he became president, Clinton mounted a drive with petitions for signatures to put the ethics code on the ballot in the November 1 election. His campaign workers amassed the necessary 50,000-plus signatures by the July 8 filing deadline.

Bill Clinton could now stuff the ethics code he and his *Gang of Three* had formulated down the voters' throats and, by their approval of it at the polls, would give him the legal cover to hide every detail of the secretive, powerhouse deals he and Hillary were conducting along that 14-block stretch between the Rose Law Firm and the statehouse.

The *New York Times*' Jeff Gerth identified the role Clinton played in eviscerating a once-meaningful Arkansas ethics code:

"Governor Clinton's revised version of the house bill retained the disclosure requirements for legislators, but deleted it for the governor, other elected officials and the appointed officials in state agencies and commissions.

"The version favored by Governor Clinton, which exempted these officials...[had the practical effect] to exempt Mr. Clinton from any possibility that he would be responsible for reporting in detail any actions or decision on his part that affected the clients of his wife or the Rose Law Firm.

"With this language out of the legislation, Mr. Clinton also did not have to wrestle with the potentially complex legal question of which of his wife's or the firm's activities would require disclosure—a potential quagmire of complex and debatable judgments."

When Gerth's story broke in the March 27, 1992, *Times*, Clinton's press office quickly issued a "damage-control" statement attributed to the then-presidential candidate:

"The reasons for dropping that particular provision had nothing to do with possible problems for me, my wife, or her law firm, a subject which no participant recalls ever even arising in countless conversations on the ethics bill."

Hillary Clinton's role in the Rose Law Firm and the business she conducted on its behalf with the state, coupled with questions about the income she derived from her partnership in Rose, was an issue in every gubernatorial campaign—and continued to be in the Democratic presidential campaign in 1992!

At that moment, former California Governor Edmund G. Brown, Jr., was loudly calling it a conflict of interest for Hillary Clinton to work for a firm that did business with the state of Arkansas!

The Clinton campaign protested that nothing the governor, his wife, and the Rose

Law Firm negotiated was prohibited by Arkansas's ethics laws, and that they made public information beyond what was required by law.

More misrepresentation. For neither the Clintons nor the Rose Law Firm ever disclosed any information about deals they hammered out for their clients with the state. Of course, their assertions that they abided by the Arkansas ethics code were true. As rewritten by Bill Clinton and the *Gang of Three*, it did not cover them or oblige them to make disclosures.

Playing Slick Willie to the Hilt

Clinton himself tried to justify what he'd done:

"The original law passed by the house was too broad, and that did not address the state's most serious ethics problems in a simplified way to assure approval of the ballot initiative by the voters, once the ethics package had stalled in the senate.

"We were determined to propose to the people an act that dealt with the most serious problems (unregulated and undisclosed lobbying of the state legislature); that was clear and comprehensible and could not be easily distorted by those opposed to any ethics reform; that applied to all 'public servants' (such as citizen volunteers on local boards and commissions); and that was tough enough to clean up the problems while still succeeding with the voters on election day."

Clinton was now playing *Slick Willie* to the hilt, distorting the applications of the ethics code. "All public servants" were not covered under the conflict-of-interest sections of his ethics code. Only members of the legislature were.

Jeff Gerth's efforts to get straight goods out of Webster Hubbell and Scott Trotter were just as futile.

Like Clinton, Hubbell and Trotter said they had no recollections of why the deletion of "all public servants" in the ethics law ultimately was made, or why mandatory disclosure was limited only to the Arkansas legislature.

"It's not logical," concluded Trotter.

Trotter had every right, as a right honorable lawyer, to say that.

Because the Clintons and Hubbell, the *Gang of Three*, deleted the obligation of "all public servants" to account for their actions—behind Scott Trotter's back!

The final word on the ethics question came from Bill Clinton.

"I have gone far beyond what state law required or what my predecessors had done in disclosing information regarding potential conflicts of interest," the governor said. "It was I who asked the Rose Law Firm to exclude my wife from her salary any share of revenues for work the firm did on behalf of the state."

If we are to believe that what Clinton said is gospel, that would surely put to rest the universal belief that Hillary Rodham Clinton wears the pants in the family.

The *know-nothing* electorate, going into the voting booths *blind as bats* about the ethics law on the ballot, cast their approving vote and made it the law.

Bill Puts His Audience to Sleep

The summer of '88 produced one of Bill Clinton's biggest political embarrassments. He had accepted the invitation to Atlanta from former Massachusetts Governor Michael Dukakis to place his name in nomination for the presidency at the Democratic National Convention.

Virtually everyone agreed that the speech Clinton gave was one of the most boring and ill-conceived ever given at national political convention.

He claimed he stayed up that night until 5:30 a.m. drafting the speech and believed he had it fine-tuned for the 15 minutes allotted for its delivery.

But when Dukakis's aides pored over it, they redid portions. With the lengthy inserts and adds, it almost doubled.

As Clinton mounted the podium, he was supposed to be accorded the same spotlight treatment that Texas's Ann Richards and the Reverend Jesse Jackson were given—a dimming of the lights. That didn't happen. Clinton blinked blindly and uncomfortably into the glare.

Then, just as he was about to deliver the address, the loudspeakers on the podium brought the audience to its feet, applauding and cheering the cry, "Jesse! Jesse! Jesse!"

Oops! Someone played the wrong tape!

By the time order was restored and Clinton began to speak, he was taken aback when the 25,000 delegates and spectators applauded and cheered every time he mentioned Dukakis's name. The interruptions were magnified by spontaneous demonstrations. In frustration, Clinton finally took the crowd to task.

"Now I want you to calm down so I can tell the rest of the country why they should want Mike."

This was greeted with boos and catcalls. Beads of perspiration rolled down the angry speaker's face. Unbeknownst to him, after the speech extended beyond the time the TV networks scheduled for it, NBC and ABC had cut to other coverage of the convention.

"I am afraid," commented John Chancellor, "that one of the most attractive governors just put a blot on his record."

Clinton brought the house down near the end of his 33-minute spiel as he uttered the words, "And now, in closing..."

As he left the podium to half-hearted applause with some catcalls mixed in, Clinton was trembling visibly.

Oblivious to the Dukakis partisans on the podium, Clinton stormed past them, muttering to his security detail, "That...motherfuckin' Greek son-of-a-bitchin'...bastard!"

Someone tried to shush him but Clinton wouldn't hear of it.

"I'll destroy that cocksucker!" he ranted. "He tried to ruin me politically by fuckin' up my speech...I'll kick the dirty fuckin' Greek's ass in...if I can only get my hands on that cuntfaced asshole!"

Finally Clinton was escorted out of the hall to his hotel where he finally settled down, and—as some reports put it—a woman he had appointed to a high judicial post in Arkansas was seen entering his suite and staying for several hours.

Next day, reporters asked Clinton for comment on his debacle. "It was just one of those fluky things…a comedy of errors…I guess," he stammered. "Like in good Roman tradition, I fell on my sword."

The coup de grâce on Clinton's marathon speech was delivered by Johnny Carson on the "Tonight Show" when he deadpanned during his monologue, "The surgeon general has just approved Bill Clinton as an over-the-counter sleep aid. What a windbag!"

26

CLINTON GOES FOR A RECORD FIFTH TERM

Bush and Hillary: They Debate!

"You know, Mr. President, we're at seventeenth or eighteenth in the whole world in infant mortality."

"Hillary, whatever are you talking about? Our health-care system is the envy of the whole world."

"Not if you want to keep your child alive to the year of his first birthday..."

That give-and-take took place during the 1989 Presidential Education Summit at the University of Virginia in Charlottesville. The exchange was between Hillary Clinton and George Bush.

Bill Clinton was delighted to attend the summit as a principal participant, but wife Hillary came suffering from a handicap: She had much to say about health care, yet she wasn't allowed to participate in the dialogue. Her husband had been invited to the summit. She went along only as a *spouse*.

Yet when the opportunity suddenly opened for her to speak, after she was seated at the president's table, Hillary made the most of it.

Bush had the last word at the luncheon after Hillary told the president, "I'll go back to my room tonight for the statistics and have Bill give them to you tomorrow..."

Bush cut her off abruptly. "I'll get my own statistics," he snapped.

The following day, Bush approached Hillary's husband.

"Here, Bill," he said, handing Clinton a note.

The message from the president: "Tell Hillary she was right."

Upon returning to Little Rock, Bill Clinton found himself still confronted by a dilemma: whether to run or not run for a fifth term in 1990. His advisers were many. Their opinions were varied. Some said yes, run. Others said, don't run because you ought to prepare for the 1992 presidential race. The fence-sitters said to just wait and see how the wind blows next year.

Although the governor's election of 1990 was still more than a year off, Clinton was anxious to reach a decision. Part of his quandary was caused by bickering in his own administration between Hillary and Betsey Wright, Clinton's powerful chief of staff.

"There is a serious difference of opinion in the governor's office between Betsey and Hillary," said political consultant Jerry Russell of Little Rock. "Betsey doesn't think Bill ought to run for reelection and Hillary thinks he ought to run."

Russell's remarks were made during a panel discussion at a joint meeting of the Arkansas State Chamber of Commerce and Associated Industries of Arkansas on November 8, 1989, at the Arlington Resort Hotel and Spa. He attributed the report to an unidentified lobbyist.

By this time, Betsey Wright, known as the *Iron Maiden of Bill Clinton's administration* had been missing from the governor's office for nearly four months. She had taken leave in July, ostensibly to take a long-delayed vacation. But as the weeks passed into months, rumors grew into full-blown stories in such newspapers as the *Arkansas Democrat*. The paper's political columnist Meredith Oakley was the first to write, in the October 23 edition, "If you're looking for Betsey, she's gone. Probably for good."

Miss Oakley asked Clinton about Betsey:

"She is taking a genuine vacation away from the day-to-day work." But then he added cryptically, "I don't know whether she'll come back or not."

Miss Oakley offered an assessment of Betsey Wright that cut to the heart of the matter:

"Although Wright's competence was seldom questioned, her authoritarian style of management reportedly caused frequent personality conflicts with others who work in the governor's office.

"She also got crosswise with a number of important legislators, specifically Senators Knox Nelson and Nick Wilson, who have complained privately that she did not always make them and their constituents feel welcome in the governor's office."

Hillary Clinton for Governor!

If a falling out with Hillary precipitated Miss Wright's departure, that was ironic indeed. For when Betsey met Hillary and Bill in Texas during the McGovern campaign in 1972, she at once took to the articulate and worldly Yale law coed. She believed that Hillary's potential for a political career was far greater than Bill's. She had continued to feel that way right to the end.

In fact, it was rumored that Miss Wright floated the talk that threaded its way around Arkansas in mid-summer of '88: that Hillary might run for governor in '90 instead of her husband. Significantly, neither of the Clintons did anything to derail that talk. And as recently as August of '89, Clinton was giving interviews saying Hillary would be "terrific," "wonderful," and "unbelievably good" as governor.

Yet he declined to state flatly that his wife was ready to run if he stepped down. "I'm not going to speak for her," he said. "That's not my business...if Hillary wants to run, that would have a big impact on my own decision [about running for reelection]."

The *Arkansas Democrat*'s Meredith Oakley further stoked the rumors:

"She wouldn't be the first strong, capable, brilliant woman to stand aside for a weaker, less capable, brilliant husband."

The rumors multiplied and Hillary was now said to be ready to make the run. But during the 1992 presidential campaign she denied any such thing had crossed her mind.

"Since I was in eighth grade, people have been urging me to run for public office," Hillary told *Glamour* magazine. "People think that because I care so much about public issues, I should run for office myself. I don't want to run for office. In 1990, when it looked as though Bill might not run for governor, I had dozens of people call me and tell me to run. But it just wasn't anything I was interested in. An elected official has to deal with many things—I see the way Bill does it. Seven or eight different things in one day. And he's good at that. What I see for myself is a role as an advocate."

Had Hillary considered a race, she might have been advised that many Arkansans don't go for outspoken, aggressive, and domineering women who stand on their own two feet and tell the world who they are and what they stand for. They consider such women "threatening."

All else aside, Hillary could never project the lovable *puppy dog warmth* that so endeared her husband to Arkansans.

Please, Bill, Don't Run Again

Clinton's indecision was based not so much on fear that he would lose the race as a concern over the state legislature's prickly disenchantment with him since the failed February special session that took up his ethics bill. His end run of the general assembly with the rewritten version grated on members. Clinton's new bill—facing certain passage in the November election—held every legislator of the house and senate accountable for the least appearance of a conflict of interest—while the governor was completely off the hook.

Even if he won the election, Clinton felt his effectiveness would be significantly diminished. His legislation would likely be deep-sixed with far greater frequency than in the past. The general assembly had already shown hostility by holding up several of Clinton's bills, while others died in committee.

Clinton then got into a cat fight with legislators, whom he called back into session once again in the late fall. When he addressed the combined houses, he was contrite. He said he had changed his mind about a controversial sales tax increase to fund his education and drug-reform programs. He proposed, instead, a surcharge on cigarettes and tobacco products and whiskey that, as Clinton calculated, would bring in $21.6 million in additional revenue.

Nevertheless, the legislators thumbed their noses at Clinton. Not once, but four times! And with the final defeat of their governor's proposal, the general assembly ended its special session and went home to await the November 7 election day results.

Despite a massive advertising campaign by a powerful lobby group called The Committee Against Higher Taxes, Clinton's ethics and disclosure bill passed with a better-than-60 percent voter approval.

"This bill has been a passion of mine for ten years," Clinton told *Arkansas Gazette* reporter Mark Oswald. "The voters' mandate is just a big step forward in the quality of government in Arkansas."

Clinton didn't discuss what that bill meant to him, to Hillary, and the Rose Law Firm.

His mind was on a different agenda, the one preoccupying him all along.

"Bill, you should think about it and think long and hard about running again. You're not getting anywhere with the legislature. I have no doubt that you can run and be reelected. But I don't believe you can be effective in office with a hostile house and senate. You'll be hurt and it won't sit well for your future in politics. I'm thinking of the presidency."

This advice came from a dear friend and former aide, ex-State Assemblyman Rudy Moore, who by that time, in late 1989, was back in private legal practice.

State Representative David Matthews was another confidante known to have whispered in the governor's ear:

"Don't run for that unprecedented fifth term, Bill. You'll be doing well to take a high-profile position with the National Democratic Committee instead.

"I truly believe you have a chance to be president of the United States—but not this soon. Your time will come in the late nineties. By then, the nation will be tuned into your wavelength on what must be done for education in this country and standing ready to support your other brilliant programs."

Despite the advice Clinton was receiving from intimates despairing over his troubles with the legislature, he was bound to his admitted affliction of being a young man in too much of a hurry. Clinton nevertheless whistled this tune publicly in the darkest moments of his political life:

"I will say this: The last three months have been very good. I've enjoyed them. I'm at peace no matter what happens."

His Fourth Term Scorecard

Clinton's performance in his fourth term was producing some laudable gains on the issues he had emphasized: education and the economy.

He could point with pride to the way the state jumped from near last to third in the share of its budget spent on education. Moreover, the proportion of high school students entering college rose from 29 percent in 1981 to better than 50 percent in 1990—although a large majority still had to take remedial courses for acceptance in collegiate curricula.

His innovations in upgrading Arkansas's social fabric and the people's skills— namely the teacher competency tests, a law prohibiting high school dropouts from being issued drivers' licenses, boot camps for first-time drug offenders, and state-business partnerships to promote and teach literacy—all merited recognition by his fellow governors, who selected him as the 1990s' most effective state leader.

Nevertheless, Arkansas continued to be last of the 50 states in environmental protection and worker safety. And one of only two states still without a civil rights law.

Clinton turned the other way when it came to the greening of Arkansas and purify-

Proud mom Virginia's life-size toddler, 1950. (Arkansas Democrat-Gazette)

A trophy for Hope's most beautiful baby, 1947. (Arkansas Democrat-Gazette)

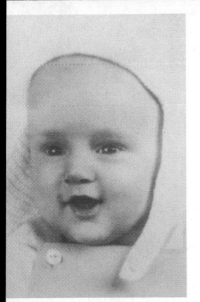

lliam Jefferson Blythe IV, his first picture months, 1946. (Arkansas Democrat-zette)

Ride 'em cowboy at Miss Mary's Kindergarten, 1951. (Arkansas Democrat-Gazette)

All dressed up for Easter, 1
(Arkansas Democrat-Gaz

Growing up with stepdad Bill Clinton, 1953.
(Arkansas Democrat-Gazette)

Taking part in the American Legion's Boys' Nation, 1964. (Arkansas Democrat-Gazette)

...nd his Hot Springs High School chums,
... (Arkansas Democrat-Gazette)

...(far left) plays his saxophone in the school band, 1963. (Arkansas Democrat-Gazette)

Meeting President Kennedy in the Rose Garden, 1964. (Arkansas Democrat-Gazette)

Heading for Sunday church services with half-brother Roger, 5, 1961. (Arkansas Democrat-Gazette)

At 18, mom's big boy has grown up, 1
(Arkansas Democrat-Gaz

Ready for graduation exercises on the Hoya campus, 1968. (Arkansas Democrat-Gazette)

All dressed up to get an education at Georgetown, 1965. (Arkansas Democrat-Gazette)

U.S. Senator Barry Goldwater counsels Bill on duties of a summer clerk with the Foreign Relations Committee, 1966. (Arkansas Democrat-Gazette)

Good showing in race for Congress but not good enough in his first political campaign, 1974. (Arkansas Democrat-Gazette)

Boning up for his Rhodes scholar's tests, 1968. (Arkansas Democrat-Gazette)

Tootin' his sax at Oxford, 1969. (Arkansas Democrat-Gazette)

ring Arkansas Attorney General Jim Guy Tucker
y the governor) campaigns for his successor,
. (Arkansas Democrat-Gazette)

His face clean-shaven, he woos and wins Hillary
over, 1975. (Arkansas Democrat-Gazette)

ely congratulations for Arkansas's newly elected attor-
general, January 1977. (Arkansas Democrat-Gazette)

Headquarters of the Rose Law Firm, where Hillary practiced her trade for 16 years, 1977. (Arkansas Democrat-Gazette)

Hillary's friend and benefactor, Vincent Foster, Jr., at Rose Law, 1977. (Exclusive photo by Mark Wilson, Arkansas Democrat-Gazette)

The state capital in Little Rock where Bill will spend 14 years of his political life, 1977. (Arkansas Democrat-Gazette)

Bill is sworn in for his first term as Arkansas's governor, January 1979. (Arkansas Democrat-Gazette)

Clintons' new home is the magnificent governor's mansion, January 1979. kansas Democrat-Gazette)

The governor-elect takes Hillary to church to give prayerful thanks for the victory, November 1978. (Arkansas Democrat-Gazette)

Hillary sports a new look to help Bill regain the governor's office, 1982. (Arkansas Democrat-Gazette)

Bill and Hillary lobby their causes in the state capital, 1 (Arkansas Democrat-Gaz

Arkansas's first lady enjoys the company of the nation's first lady, Rosalyn Carter, 1980. (Arkansas Democrat-Gazette)

's mom, Virginia (right), after marrying her fourth, Richard Kelley (left), celebrates with wedding guests in a Little Rock aurant, summer 1984. (Arkansas Democrat-Gazette)

Bill introduces Chelsea to the voters as he campaigns for his third term, summer 1984. (Arkansas Democrat-Gazette)

lsea goes to the state fair, spring 1983. kansas Democrat-Gazette)

Bill and Hillary take Chelsea on the campaign trail again, fall 1984.
(Arkansas Democrat-Gazette)

Bill and Hillary at the January 1985 Inaugural Ball.
(Arkansas Democrat-Gazette)

Bill makes a pitch for
the NAACP vote, fall
1984. (Arkansas
Democrat-Gazette)

Hillary and Chelsea, a loving mother-daughter number, 1986. (Arkansas Democrat-Gazette)

Bill comforts Roger after his arrest as a drug trafficker, 1985. (Arkansas Democrat-Gazette)

Her mom watches Chelsea in soccer game, 1987. (Arkansas Democrat-Gazette)

The Clintons and Kelleys on an outing, (from left to right) Richard, Virginia, Roger, Bill, and Hillary, winter 1988. (Arkansas Democrat-Gazette)

Hillary looks after Chelsea, a growing girl of eight, fall 1988. (Arkansas Democrat-Gazette)

The Clintons continue campaigning tirelessly, summer 1988. (Arkan Democrat-Gazette)

y wipes a tear away as Bill explains
he won't make '88 presidential bid,
July 1988. (courtesy of National
Broadcasting Company)

Wannabe President Perot, the Yellow Ross of
Texas, 1992. (from the author's collection)

Bill tells Johnny Carson how he put Democratic National
Convention audience to sleep with his speech, November 1988.
(courtesy of National Broadcasting Company)

Vince and Lisa Foster on the town with Bill and Hillary, 1992. (Arkansas Democrat-Gazette)

Gennifer Flowers has it all on tape: "Bill and I had a twelve-year affair, 1992. (from the author's collection)

Bill and Hillary dance the night away at the Inaugural Ball, Januar 1993. (World Wide Ph

Press aide George Stephanopoulos has a secret or two only fe president's ear at cabinet meeting, April 28, (official White House p

ing its environment. He had an overriding need to live up to his campaign promises to attract more investment in Arkansas, bring in more business, and create new jobs to counter one of the nation's most horrendous unemployment rates.

Clinton continued to grant businesses an inordinate number of environmental easements. This left him with no record whatsoever as an "ecology governor." But by ignoring the state's land, air, and water resources—and by pushing through the legislature an estimated $150 million in tax breaks since 1983— Clinton had hit a jackpot.

Arkansas's economy expanded by 29 percent during Clinton's terms in office, five percentage points ahead of the national rate. The state also doubled the growth rate of the four states in the West South Central Region. Its job and income expansion slightly outpaced the nation's and region's average.

All in all, Clinton's performance as a 10-year governor as 1990 approached received mixed reviews from his state's most pugnacious watchdogs.

One of those who kept closest tabs on Clinton was Ernest Dumas, the *Arkansas Gazette* columnist.

"He really has changed attitudes about the importance of a good education in this state. He's really wrestled with the flight of low-skill jobs to other countries. He's been less effective in some other areas, like in attacking the state's regressive tax code and forcing the coal-burning utility plants to clean up their act.

"But the expectations were so high, his talents so awesome. We expected miracles. We've had to settle for just good works."

Another journalistic observer, David Osborne, saw Clinton in another light—cast against the problems inherent in the state itself:

"The fact is, it's hard to accomplish much in a poor state like Arkansas. If you improve education too much, people take their skills elsewhere. If you don't bribe businesses with tax breaks, they can easily leave, too. In that context, Clinton has done pretty well.

"Although the state still lags behind most of the nation in economic development and educational achievement, Arkansas now has a reputation as one of the more innovative state governments."

The biggest rap against Clinton coming from his enemies—and a few of his friends—was that he was shifty, hard to pin down, and tried too hard to please.

Sheffield Nelson described how he saw the real Bill Clinton:

"He's a political chameleon. He changes colors to convince people he's what they want him to be."

We'll return to Sheffield Nelson shortly when he challenges Bill Clinton's bid for a fifth term as governor.

The Crime He'd Fight Fells *Him*

A few days after Bill Clinton had said he was at peace with himself and rejoiced over the good he saw in the past three months, he was stung by a challenge from a totally unexpected quarter.

"The decade of the nineties holds for Arkansas great opportunity. That opportunity can and will be realized if we have a governor who is a leader."

Saying those words 12 years after Clinton's one-term exercise as one of the state's least effective attorneys general, was his successor in that office, Steve Clark. He announced his candidacy for Clinton's job.

Among the programs Clark proposed to make Arkansas realize its great potential were ones Clinton had promised but was unable to deliver: new road construction funded by a five-cent gasoline tax, an education initiative that would pay college or vocational training tuition for students with acceptable grades and good behavior, and $1,000 across-the-board raises for the state's public school teachers.

Clark's proposals have a ring of familiarity, for those three programs, couched in different language, Clinton proposed for the nation when he entered the race for the presidency.

Clark also offered to establish the first state agency on aging for Arkansas's large and ever-expanding elderly population.

Clark promised not to be soft on crime as Clinton had been during his dozen years in office.

"I'm going to be tough on crime," Clark said. "I will be a leader who can win the war on drugs. We're not going to win just by building prisons, prisons, prisons."

But the only "crime" Clark managed to battle was the one he committed with sloppy personal bookkeeping. While Arkansas officeholders weren't required to file precise documentation for expenses, they were required to monitor their spending. Clark allegedly neglected to file adequate statements and became the focus of an inquiry by the state's Legislative Joint Auditing Committee—a probe reportedly instigated by the governor's office.

By the time Clark tried to atone by writing the state a check for $4,000, his candidacy was no longer viable. Clark called a press conference and read from a prepared statement:

"After much reflection and discussion with my family and friends, I have reached the conclusion that the mistakes in my expense records and subsequent news coverage about those mistakes have virtually destroyed my ability to run an efficient and effective campaign for governor."

His retreat stymied by reporters whose questions he didn't want to answer, Clark skedaddled to a roof exit in the capitol building. He didn't jump off as some feared he might. He merely bounded to another flight of stairs and escaped.

With Clark out of the picture, Clinton was faced with one remaining challenger for the Democratic nomination, if he decided to run for a fifth term.

Down to the Last Democrat

Tom McRae was that adversary. The grandson of a 1920s' governor, long-serving president of the Winthrop Rockefeller Foundation, and a frequent Clinton critic, McRae formed a 76-member statewide campaign committee "to help elect a new face as governor." Holding a broom in hand, McRae made this promise at a rally:

"I'm going to sweep Arkansas government clean. I'll brush away the rhetoric, the career politicians who can do nothing but live off the fat of the land."

McRae's high-flown language probably did not send shivers up Clinton's spine. McRae had no political record to speak of. Moreover, Clinton had yet to declare his candidacy. Was he going to go for that fifth term, or not?

Then in a surprising development, Clinton's old friend, Jim Guy Tucker, who had urged Clinton to replace him as attorney general in 1976, declared his candidacy for the gubernatorial nomination. Tucker, who had fulfilled his ambition to serve in Congress, was in the House a brief time before returning to private life. He now wanted to make a comeback to politics.

"I think he's had a good ten years as governor," Tucker exhorted. "But I think that's long enough."

However, despite an impressive opening splash, Tucker took only a few serious strokes in what concededly was an upstream swim, then climbed out—even as Clinton was still to be heard from.

Tucker, who had made $65,000 as a congressman, $26,500 a year as attorney general, and stood to have a $35,000-a-year income as governor, opted instead for the lieutenant governor's post that paid a measly $14,000.

But could Tucker have known what his old pal Bill Clinton had in mind for the future?

Speculation about that future was now running out of hand. Clinton's name was being bandied about for a possible candidacy for the House of Representatives, for the U.S. Senate—and even the presidency. But Clinton put a halt to the speculation by calling a press conference in the state capital.

Clinton's opening statement caused eyebrows to lift.

"I must tell you that the fire of an election no longer burns in me," he began.

Was this the end of Bill Clinton's political career?

Had he decided he'd had enough as a public servant and now, perhaps, at long last was to fulfill the first of his life's ambitions—to be just "a country lawyer"?

Standing at his side, in a black, two-piece, turtle-necked dress with onyxlike buttons and a four-strand pearl choker around her neck, Hillary Clinton smiled at her husband as he turned to her expectantly. Always his rock of support, Hillary offered an approving nod.

"I'm aware of the concerns expressed by many that I've been in office too long," he went on. "But we're going to be real careful to reach out in every county in this state to find new people to be part of our family so that none feels excluded from the appointments and nobody feels excluded from other decisions of the governor's office. And we know there is always the problem of arrogance of power, and we are bending over backwards to be as humble as we can in this campaign."

Translation: Bill Clinton was going after a fifth term as governor!

But the road to the November election was paved, as never before, with serious criticism from many former supporters.

When he went to New Orleans in late March to accept the chairmanship of the Democratic Leadership Conference, opponents raked him for taking time away from his state duties to mess with national politics.

No sooner had he returned to Little Rock than Clinton felt a blast from *Financial*

World magazine, which ranked Arkansas 41st of the 50 states in financial management practices.

Clinton argued that the publication didn't understand the state's budgeting process
and claimed that "Arkansas has one of the most tightly controlled budgets in the nation."

Left unsaid was that the state—unlike the country—was legally prohibited from
deficit spending and that the governor and legislature cannot do otherwise than maintain a tight rein on budgets.

Another slap at Clinton came when the AFL-CIO declined to endorse him in that
1990 gubernatorial race—the first time it had failed to support him.

In a resolution drawn up at their Arkansas annual convention, Clinton was condemned for turning his back on labor.

"...[He] has deceived us with broken promises of support for Workers' Compensation, right-to-know and other beneficial legislation. [He has] tricked us on taxes and
has further rigged the tax system against workers with more special interest exemp-
tions and loopholes."

When called to address the convention, Clinton whined that he was just a poor
victim of the legislature.

"The most appalling suggestion of all is that I somehow tricked you on taxes and
tax reform," he protested. "I raised this issue and we lost [in the legislature]. And
what was the response? Bill Clinton jumped off the tank on tax reform."

The resolution had also accused Clinton of securing a $300,000 loan guarantee for
a plastics firm "to be used to build an inventory as strike protection." Clinton claimed
this was brought on by the company's biggest customer, the Ford Motor Company.
Ford threatened to terminate its contract with the firm unless it stocked a two-month
inventory of parts as a hedge against possible strikes.

"My job is to save jobs," Clinton declared defensively about that minority-owned
business with 410 employees. "I don't ask you to agree with me. Just put yourself in
my position."

Although the resolution rapping Clinton was withdrawn after he addressed the
convention (after a debate was threatened on the floor) he didn't escape a tongue-
lashing by the AFL-CIO's President J. Bill Becker. Standing before the assembled
membership in the packed hall, Becker blasted away:

"That Bill Clinton will pat you on the back and piss down your leg. He just
twisted the facts to suit himself."

Hillary at Her Very Worst

During the summer of '90 Clinton was off to Washington again. This time to deliver a report to Congress bearing on a study of the Mississippi Delta. His remaining
rival in the primary, Tom McRae, took the opportunity to do a number on the governor.

McRae and Clinton had agreed to debates, but so far none had occurred. While
Clinton was in Washington, McRae called a press conference:

"When my rival doesn't debate me, it's only right that I ask him questions and provide the answer myself."

McRae raised four issues: first, why Arkansas's teachers were the lowest paid in the nation—seven years after the Clintons' education reforms were initiated and a penny hike in the state sales tax was passed to pay for higher salaries.

Secondly, he wanted to know what Clinton was doing about a dioxin contamination in Jacksonville and thirdly, whether he was favoring lumber interests by "going soft" on *clear-cutting* restrictions. Finally, McRae demanded, did Clinton intend to serve out his new term, if reelected, or was he going to enter the 1992 presidential race?

"Those are the four issues that I would raise, but since the governor is not here, I would give him at least an opportunity to respond."

Laughter crackled across the room as McRae pointed to a life-sized nude caricature of the governor, hands clasped over the parts of his anatomy viewed by so many women behind Hillary's back, clothes scattered at his feet. A caption read: *THE EMPEROR HAS NO CLOTHES.*

McRae had no idea he was about to be coldcocked by Hillary Clinton in a scheme, the author's investigation has determined, that was hatched with Bill on the telephone from Washington the night before. Informed ahead of time of McRae's stratagem, Clinton gave Hillary the go ahead to defuse it.

No sooner had McRae asked a rhetorical question and was set to answer it for Clinton, than a voice broke out from the phalanx of newsmen at the press conference.

"Do you really want an answer, Tom?" the *Iron Lady Of Little Rock* cried out. "Do you really want a response from Bill when you know he's in Washington doing work for the state? That sounds a bit like a stunt to me."

McRae, a gentle man with impeccable credentials after serving 14 distinguished years as chairman and director of the Rockefeller Foundation, was disarmed. He stared, mouth agape, at Hillary, who stepped forward attired in a houndstooth tweed blazer, turtleneck, and pearl earrings. The huge Clinton campaign button pinned to her sweater was a dead giveaway that she was there to perform for the TV cameras.

Hillary pulled out a four-page prepared statement and read encomiums for Clinton carried in the Rockefeller Foundation's reports over the years. The paper targeted the very areas in which McRae was criticizing Clinton: education reform, the environment, and economic development.

Much of the praise, it later developed, originated with Hillary herself—since she had served on the foundation's board!

"I went through all *your* reports because I've really been disappointed in you as a candidate," Hillary continued "and I've really been disappointed in you as a person, Tom."

Recovering from the shock of a surrogate's unscheduled defense of his rival, McRae laced into Hillary, taking healthy swipes at her husband that left her silent and red-faced.

McRae conceded he had either written "or approved" the reports, and granted that Clinton's record was "good in a number of areas":

"The issue is not whether Bill Clinton has done good things, but whether someone else should be given a chance to run this government…shouldn't somebody else be given a chance to try? If the best he can do is last, then it's time for someone else to give it a try."

With a look of disdain for the still-embarrassed Hillary, McRae went on:

"Bill Clinton has been a failure. State education over the past decade has been in decline. Arkansas teachers are still the poorest paid in the nation…Bill Clinton still has done nothing to live up to his 1986 campaign pledge to clean up the dioxin spill at the Vertac site in Jacksonville, and…"

McRae paused to give Hillary his steeliest stare before talking directly to her:

"…you know, Hillary, that the Federal Environmental Protection Agency has listed that site as one of the worst cases of contamination in the country…and, moreover, I want to know why Bill's record is so poor as well in halting the incineration of toxic wastes…"

In a small voice, Hillary listed Bill's accomplishments. She admitted problems still remained, and that much more had yet to be done to better Arkansas's last-place standing in education. Finally, she implored McRae:

"For goodness sake, let Arkansas stand up and be proud. We've made more progress than any other state except South Carolina, and we're right up there with them."

No one asked Hillary what she meant when she said "we're right up there with them [South Carolina]," whose teachers averaged $27,076 or $5,067 more than Arkansas educators were paid in the 1989-90 school year.

McRae closed his rebuttal:

"It's not that we're not making progress…it's that we're staying the same."

The spectacle over, reporters besieged McRae and Hillary.

Would the candidate call Hillary Clinton's outburst as rudeness.

"On one level, yes," he said firmly. "I think that her coming out, in a political strategy sense, it makes some sense. You send her out there, she knows the issues and she doesn't have an accountability—and she takes me on. That's fine."

Then with a snide look at her, he continued:

"And she's probably more popular than her husband."

Hillary was asked what occasioned her to drop in on the press conference. She said she "might have heard about it" while at a luncheon of the North Little Rock Sertoma Club that day, where she spoke. But she claimed she'd forgotten all about McRae's press conference—until she arrived at the statehouse and "a reporter brought it to my attention."

And the four-page backgrounder on her husband? How did that materialize so conveniently?

"Oh," she replied, "I had brought that with me to the Sertoma Club…" to guide her in the address she gave on her husband at the civic club luncheon.

Had she spoken with Bill about McRae's press conference?

"Oh, no," she answered, "but I will now." She said she was furious about the nude caricature of her husband and was "going to tell Bill about that."

Bill Breezes into His Fifth Term

On the Republican side, Sheffield Nelson, the former director of the Arkansas Development Finance Authority, faced Sonny Robinson in the GOP primaries.

Robinson, who had given up his congressional seat to run for governor, was a formidable opponent. Robinson had impeccable Republican credentials, more so than Nelson, who had renounced his lifelong membership in the Democratic Party—ala Frank White in 1980—and campaigned as a newly born Republican.

On primary day, Clinton finished on top of his Democratic rival Tom McRae with votes to spare, and businessman Sheffield Nelson handed Congressman Robinson his first political setback.

Robinson pinned the blame for his defeat on Clinton. He charged the governor "meddled" in Republican politics "by asking Democratic Party loyalists to cross over and vote against me in the primary."

Many people sympathized with Robinson and agreed that Clinton's campaign workers had every reason to ask their followers to cast ballots for Nelson, the significantly weaker of the two GOP hopefuls.

Many political analysts felt Robinson could have beaten Clinton in the November election. As it turned out, Clinton defeated Nelson by a smaller margin—57 percent of the vote—than in any of his previous four gubernatorial races.

Ironically, Clinton's victory was aided by a friendly Circuit Court Judge, John Plegge, who kept the lid on one of the biggest scandals ever suppressed about the governor: More of Clinton's womanizing and the illegal use of state funds for his personal needs.

The charges became full-blown in the $3.05 million libel and defamation suit by Larry Nichols, the fired marketing manager of the Arkansas Development Finance Authority whose reports about Clinton's affairs with women have already been chronicled.

In his complaint, Nichols identified six women—including Gennifer Flowers and Arkansas's 1981 Miss America Elizabeth Ward—as Clinton's sexual partners.

But the charges, filed two weeks before election day, didn't become public until after the polls closed. Judge Plegge sealed the papers on an application for relief by Nichols' former boss, ADFA chairman David Hargis, who labeled the allegations "obnoxious."

The author's investigation into the circumstances surrounding the court action leaves little doubt that had Bill Clinton's people not bushwhacked Congressman Sonny Robinson, and Judge Plegge hadn't suppressed the public's right to know about their governor's behavior, Bill Clinton wouldn't have been reelected governor, or elected president.

The GOP's loser, Sheffield Nelson, conceded the election:

"The people said they wanted Bill Clinton for four more years, and I don't think it would have made any difference who was against him. He was just that strong."

A fine concession speech but inaccurate. As already shown, Bill Clinton would most likely have lost had his factotums not robbed Sonny Robinson of his rightful votes in the primary, and had Judge Plegge not prevented Larry Nichols from airing his charges against the "shameless candidate."

27

THE MAKING OF THE PUPPET PRESIDENT

Clinton's Last Arkansas Hurrah

Bill Clinton's inaugural address was a 21-minute oration given despite efforts by some members of the legislature to recess the session or shorten the agenda. That was in deference to the pall that hung over America brought on by the uncertainty of whether war would break out in the Middle East.

Even as President Bush teetered on the edge of unleashing the United Nations forces massed in Saudi Arabia, Clinton said that nothing that happened in the Persian Gulf should "undermine our responsibility to build this new future."

About 700 onlookers crowded into the Capitol rotunda at noon to hear the speech by the fifth-term governor, who was to be the longest-serving in state history. Inclement weather forced the ceremony indoors from the Capitol steps.

Clinton's old political benefactor, Supreme Court Justice Jack Holt, Jr., administered the oath of office. Hillary stood by her husband's side, and he placed his hand on a Bible held by 10-year-old daughter Chelsea.

Earlier, Clinton had given a 28-minute speech in the general assembly that outlined some of his legislative proposals. Twice, applause interrupted the address in which he proposed four legislative programs:

• *Education.* Specifically, teacher raises of $4,500 over the next two years, to increase the $23,000-a-year average salary that put the state dead last in teacher pay in the nation (this after 10 years of "education reform" masterminded almost entirely by First Lady Hillary Clinton).

• *Better Medical Care.* Again, a program shaped virtually single-handedly by Hillary. She would take on a similar responsibility on a far grander scale when she moved to the White House. Arkansas's medical care plan was widely scorned by tax-weary opponents. They feared it would bankrupt the state and send it into permanent medical disability—as many more were to fear about the nation's fate with the Clinton administration health-care reformation.

• *A Far-Reaching Program of Expansion for State Highways and Bridges*, along with a reduction of paperwork required in obtaining car tags. It included a mandatory seat belt law, which Clinton called "a social decision because those who do not die [in vehicular accidents] become wards of the state."

- *A Comprehensive Plan for Solid Waste.* "Our biggest headache," as Clinton called it. The plan would deny pollution permits to companies *with bad records in other states.* "We should hold people responsible for what they have done," said Clinton (Tyson Foods, the state's worst polluter and Clinton's biggest political contributor and patron was home free, because this giant of the nation's poultry industry does all its *plucking* polluting in its home state.)

The rotunda crowd outdid the general assembly on the applause meter. Clinton was interrupted 14 times by the people who elected him on his promise: "I will serve out my full term...I will not seek higher office."

The crowd included some of Clinton's closest friends and family: his mother, Virginia Kelley; her husband, Richard; Hillary's parents, Hugh and Dorothy Rodham; brother Roger; and the governor's former chief of staff, Betsey Wright, who after leaving the statehouse had become head of the Arkansas State Democratic Party.

Betsey had tears in her eyes—but those eyes didn't acknowledge the presence of First Lady Hillary Clinton, standing at arms-length—when Betsey embraced her former boss.

"I think he has not only a very coherent plan for the state, but he talks about it with such heart," said Miss Wright. She couldn't have known that plans to announce for the presidency were already solidified in Bill Clinton's mind—and that he awaited the "go-ahead" sign from a far-off confederate, soon to be introduced in this narrative.

At precisely 9:25 p.m., 3,000 guests from across the state who packed Governor Bill Clinton's fifth inaugural ball applauded and cheered for the man of the hour.

Beaming and quipping, "Is everyone having fun?" Clinton stood momentarily at the huge double doors that were open to admit Arkansas's first family into the State House Convention Center. Bill escorted Hillary and Chelsea into the ornate, red-carpeted hall, draped for the occasion with sheer canopies on which patterns of light and spangles flashed.

Huge video screens on opposite sides of the stage offered a view of the arrivals throughout the huge hall. A moment of silence was observed for Arkansans in the Persian Gulf while the screens were taken over by fluttering flags as North Little Rock's teenaged Amberly Wohner sang the national anthem.

Few, if any of the inaugural crowd could tell that Hillary had not worn a new gown but, instead, selected a favorite dress "which I have not worn as much as I would like." The black outfit, a Black Tie creation the first lady bought at Barbara/Jean's in Little Rock, was cut low in the back, decorated with silver beads, and had a waltz-length chiffon skirt.

There was nothing "old" for fast-growing Chelsea, who wore a floor-length gown her mother described as "every little girl's dream of a dress." Hillary explained to the *Arkansas Democrat*'s high-profile editor Phyllis D. Brandon that it was sewn by family friend Pat Quails.

Hillary had the traditional first dance with her husband to Woody Herman's sedate "Early Autumn," played by the Little Rock Jazz Machine and highlighted with a sax solo by Stan Getz.

The first daughter, her hair in a French braid, had the second dance. The song this time was a bit jazzier, "Sittin' on the Dock of the Bay," played by the Groan-Ups.

The crowd followed out to the dance floor—and found security tighter than ever. More troopers of the Arkansas State Police were present than at any previous inaugural ball.

Although those attending the convention center ball paid $25 a ticket, others shelled out $100 to be at the nearby Democratic Party benefit reception on the mezzanine of the Capitol Hotel. Two of four former governors were able to attend, Orval Faubus and Dale Bumpers. David Pryor, now a U.S. senator, and Sid McMath, who was down with the flu, didn't show.

The gala was hosted by Betsey Wright, the party chairman. She appeared happy to be in her new element, away from the headaches and heartbreak of the governor's office.

Paula Puts Bill Behind 8-Ball

Little Rock's Excelsior Hotel was mentioned earlier as Bill Clinton's preferred love nest for his encounters with Gennifer Flowers when she was singing in Dallas and didn't have a pad of her own in Little Rock. Whenever she dropped into town, they met there, where Bill and Gennifer "jumped into bed and talked afterward."

The Excelsior doesn't hold such fond memories for Mrs. Paula Jones, the former Miss Paula Corbin, a former employee of the Arkansas Industrial Development Commission.

The bad taste left in her mouth for the Excelsior stems from an experience Paula had on May 8, 1991, four months into Bill Clinton's fifth term as Arkansas's governor—five months before he was to announce his candidacy for president.

Paula had done all she could to erase that episode from her mind and was doing mighty well at that—until she was hit in the solar plexus by State Trooper Danny Ferguson's story of the pimping he and other troopers had done for Bill Clinton all through the '80s, and almost to the eve of his inauguration in January 1993.

Although the stories in *The American Spectator* and the *Los Angeles Times* didn't give enough detail about her experience to clearly identify Paula, the mere fact that her first name was mentioned was traumatic.

"That's outrageous!" Paula screamed to her husband in their Southern California home, where they have been living in recent years. "There's my name, *Paula*, larger than life, splashed all over in print—having me going to Bill Clinton's hotel room, then afterward the stories have me telling a trooper that I 'was available to be Clinton's regular girlfriend if he so desired me to be.'"

Implying, as the stories did, that she had sex with Clinton, in Paula's words, "is a false, malicious, and outrageous suggestion."

Feeling "humiliated and exposed," Paula decided she must seek redress. She set out to confront the trooper who identified her in the stories.

Although only her first name was mentioned, that was still enough for people to know who was being talked about—people like her former co-worker, Pamela

Blackard, in the Arkansas Industrial Development Commission, where Paula had worked for three years.

Others who would know: her good friend, Debra Ballentine; Paula's husband, Steve Jones; her mother; her two sisters; and the people Paula suspected had heard about her experience with Clinton from one or more of the few who were privy to the story.

Paula was put out so much because when she reported her experience—the one and only time she encountered Clinton in a hotel—she described it in a totally different light from the news stories.

"I never had sex with Clinton...that was my story then and that's my story right now," Paula insisted, as she rolled up her sleeves on a frigid February day of 1994 and prepared to give the president of the United States the kind of heat that British journalist Peter Hutchins, of the London *Daily Express* suggested could be in Clinton's future:

"*...if anything similar had happened to a major British politician, he would now be out of office.*"

Although the White House categorically denied Paula Jones' claims, why was its army of lawyers, all through the remainder of 1994, trying to suppress the yarn and to silence her?

The anwer's coming. But first, the story.

"You have nice curves and I love the way your hair goes down your body."

Soon-to-be president Bill Clinton had just loosened his tie and taken 27-year-old Paula Jones' hand in his. He pulled her toward him in his suite in the swank Excelsior.

Lights Are Dimmed for Paula

Paula had just been brought to this cozy nook, where the lights were dimmed and sweet music played softly. Only the sensuous-smelling fragrance that Gennifer Flowers released on such occasions was missing from this romantic setting.

For what Clinton had in mind, fragrances weren't needed.

It was 2:30 p.m. when Paula was first approached that day of May 8. She was seated at a desk, serving as receptionist for the Arkansas Industrial Development Commission, which was participating in the third annual Governor's Quality Management Conference at the Excelsior.

The AIDC (also known as the Arkansas Development Authority, or ADA), the reader will recall, is a Bill Clinton creation to drum up business investments for his dirt-poor state. But, as shown earlier, the governor reconstituted this previously legitimate arm of government to serve another purpose: to provide him with a bottomless font of *ready cash* and to finance illicit outings.

A while back, Paula Jones was Paula Corbin who had lived in a tiny town outside Little Rock called Lonoke (population 4,123). Here she faithfully attended church three times a week—twice on Sundays, once on Wednesdays, and even went at other times for revival meetings.

Paula was reared in a house where Bible Belt beliefs were always the first order of the day. Her father, Bobby Gene Corbin, who earned his living as a clothing factory worker, was a Nazarene preacher who often took his three daughters along on his travels, to recite Bible verses and sing hymns.

When Paula was 18, in 1985, her father collapsed and died of a heart attack while playing piano at a church service.

Paula then pitched in at home almost full time, tending to household chores to help her mother, Delmer, a bouncy, ebullient 64 today, and a nose-to-the-grindstone widow. When her husband passed away she took a job in a sewing factory in order to help support Paula and her two older sisters.

All three Corbin girls disliked high school, but Paula stuck it out, graduated by the skin of her teeth, then attended Capital City College in Little Rock for a brief spell.

Time passed. Paula Corbin married Steve Jones, a Northwest Airlines ticket agent, and became Paula Jones. They settled in the state capital and Paula landed a receptionist's job with the AIDC.

Still more time went by. Then one day, at the age of 24, Paula decided to advance her station in life. She heard about an opening in the governor's office and told herself that was just what she needed. She went for the job.

She was surprised to find that this governor *personally* conducted interviews with job-seekers!

No decision was reached on Paula's application that day, according to sources that furnished the details of the encounter. Bill Clinton cordially shook her hand, thanked her for dropping by, and assured her she'd be hearing from him soon.

That person-to-person encounter between Paula Jones and the governor has not been confirmed. Paula declined to comment about this account after her court suit seeking $700,000 in damages for sexual harassment and violations of her civil rights was filed at the U.S. District Court in Little Rock.

However, if that meeting hadn't taken place, then what would have prompted Clinton at a later time—prior to the Excelsior Hotel incident—to call out, "Hello, Paula...lookin' good," when he passed her in the statehouse rotunda?

Witnesses—including one of the then-governor's state trooper bodyguards—recall Clinton greeting the shapely AIDC employee in that manner. Certainly it would appear they had been introduced before.

But the sexual harassment issue didn't take shape until the Governor's Conference on May 8.

This was a time when Bill Clinton was no longer having it with Gennifer Flowers at this hotel—because his longtime flame had been distancing herself from him. She was also blackmailing him to get her a state job, which he would soon do—after bumping a dozen other more qualified civil servants out of the line of hire (all the details of this are still to come).

On this Wednesday afternoon, when she least expected anything out of the ordinary to happen, Paula was at her desk in the hotel, chatting with co-worker Pamela Blackard. Then, who should appear before them but a big, burly hunk in the uniform of the Arkansas State Police. He introduced himself to the receptionist behind the desk as Trooper Danny Ferguson:

"Ma'am, ah b'lieve y'all are Miss Paula Jones, em ah right, li'l lady?"

"You shuh are, suh," Paula replied, before quickly correcting the trooper with a smile. "But ah'm not a Miss...ah'm a Missus."

Ferguson paid no mind. He knew the governor didn't care whether the chicks he was sent to fetch were feathered with a Miss, a Mrs., or a Ms.

With her marital status duly established, Ferguson made his mission known. The governor wanted to *interview* Paula in his suite. To *brief* her about the duties she'd be required to perform—once she was hired.

Her hopes high, her heart pounding from the excitement of hearing this news, Paula got up, rapidly fixed her makeup, and breathlessly accompanied Trooper Ferguson to the governor's suite.

Paula had no concern about leaving her post because Pamela Blackard had agreed to mind the store until she returned.

According to Paula Corbin Jones, who was interviewed by two of the author's researchers, Clinton didn't come on strong with her at the outset.

"When I first entered the hotel room, Clinton chatted with me about my job. Then we talked about Hillary and the projects she was working on."

But soon Clinton edged into his advances.

"[After] we talked for a few moments," Paula remembers, "he proceeded to take my hand and then loosened his tie.

"He pulled me over...I pulled back. He tried a second time and started to get closer to me against a chair."

After she pulled back a third time, Clinton tried once more to have Paula cuddle next to him. Then, "He started to put his hand on my thigh [under Paula's culottes] and slide it up my leg. I pushed him back. I got away...it was humiliating...you're supposed to trust somebody like that or I would've never went to that room."

Does such resistance deter Clinton from further exploration?

"It certainly does," Paula sighed relievedly. But she wasn't out of the woods yet.

Clinton had other angles to work on Paula.

He unzipped his fly, loosened his belt, dropped his pants, and exposed himself through the opening in his briefs, according to Paula's charges contained in her 20-page brief that was filed by Little Rock attorney Daniel Traylor, who had been Paula's lone legal eagle—until Clinton reached out for heavyweight Robert Bennett to defend the president's *honor*.

Then Traylor did some reaching out of his own and roped into his corral two of the East's heaviest buckaroos in the criminal field, Joseph Cammarata and Gil Davis. Many observers believe Paula's legal team may be more than an even match against the likes of a Robert Bennett—especially after he was unable to get 18-term Congressman Rostenkowski out of his career-destroying bind before the Justice Department hit him with a 49-page, 17-count indictment for misusing more than $660,000 of government funds over two decades.

Some legal watchers see Bennett facing a similarly difficult situation with the charges Paula Jones has shaped against Clinton.

"He asked me to perform a type of sex that doesn't require me to remove my clothes," is the blunt way Paula put it in explaining Clinton's "harassment" of her in the hotel suite. She shivered at the very thought of the sight of the future president in the shocking state of undress that she described so lucidly.

"But I refused to do what I was asked to do...and I said I needed to get back to my work station," Paula went on.

In her interview with the author's researchers, Mrs. Jones did not describe a further attempt by Clinton to get his way. But from what she said in another interview, it appears there was more to the story than what was widely interpreted to mean was merely an *obtuse reference* to oral sex.

During an April 6, 1994, telephone interview on National Empowerment Television's "Other Side of the Story" program, hosted by Reed Irvine, director of the Washington-based press watchdog *Accuracy in Media*, Paula was more blunt:

"He wanted me to 'kiss it.' That's the words he used."

That's not all that happened. There's more if one is to peruse the sworn affidavit Paula's lawyers filed in the U.S. District Court for the Eastern District of Arkansas (Western Division).

In the action "to obtain redress for the deprivation and conspiracy to deprive Plaintiff of her federally protected rights," as the court papers state, Paula swears that after Clinton slid his hand under her culottes, "he also bent down to attempt to kiss" Paula's neck.

"What are you doing?" Paula demanded to know and "tried to distract Clinton by chatting with him about his wife."

After some small talk, the sworn document alleges "Clinton then approached the sofa and as he sat down he lowered his trousers and underwear exposing his erect penis and asked Jones to 'kiss it.'

"There were distinguishing characteristics in Clinton's genital area that were obvious to Jones.

"Jones became horrified, jumped up from the couch, stated that she was 'not that kind of girl' and said, 'Look, I've got to go.'

"Clinton, while fondling his penis said, 'Well, I don't want to make you do anything you don't want to do.'

"Clinton then stood up and pulled up his pants and said, 'If you get in trouble for leaving work, have Dave [Harrington, a supervisor] call me immediately and I'll take care of it.'"

Clinton's last words to Paula as he zippered his fly: "You are smart. Let's keep this between ourselves."

Of course Paula, who now says "I didn't get the job but almost got the works," went back to her station and gasped out the account of her harrowing experience to Pamela Blackard. The author wasn't present to hear that conversation and must rely on Ms. Blackard for a report:

"Just as soon as Paula returned, she stated that the governor had made unwelcomed sexual advances and expressed embarrassment, horror, grief, shame, fright, worry, and humiliation."

Ms. Blackard's not the only person to whom Paula spilled her tale of woe. Good friend Debra Ballentine also heard what happened from Paula's lips.

"[That same day] Paula told me that she rebuffed three separate unwelcomed sexual advances by the governor."

Paula also confided in her mother and two sisters about her experience.

Sister Lydia Cathey, 29, said Paula came to see her the night following her confrontation with Clinton.

"She was in tears," Lydia recalled. "I comforted her as she told me what happened. She was scared he would come back to her again and worried that she would lose her job."

Time would prove Paula was justified to be apprehensive about her future with the AIDC. For other than three small, *mandatory* cost-of-living raises, she received only one minuscule routine wage hike that peaked her annual wages to less than $200 a year over her starting salary of $10,270.

Paula, who took time out to give birth, returned to her job, but then threw in the towel in February 1993, when she moved with her husband and son to California.

The media made much of circulating stories suggesting Paula was short on *credibility*, alleging that she had been compromised by right-wing groups to strike at the president.

"I think she's being used," is how pricey barrister Robert Bennett put it in his first public utterance that officially launched his $400-an-hour defense of the president. "The incident never took place...this case is about money and book contracts."

In contrast to what Lydia Cathey said, older sister Charlotte Brown, 33, had a far different recollection of what she claims Paula told her about the encounter with Clinton.

"She seemed amused, not traumatized," Charlotte said. "She confided in me that she *smelt* money either way it went."

The author's own investigation of the Paula Jones case has turned up one wrenching—and highly significant—oddity that may explain Charlotte Brown's stance.

Charlotte Brown's husband, Mark, a heavily tattooed, bearded, and beefy individual, once worked as a disc jockey at the Little Rock nightclub B. J.'s Star-Studded Honky Tonk.

Brown added his two-cents' worth by claiming Paula Jones' charges of sexual harassment are just so much hogwash.

"Paula is always coming on to men," he said. "She flirts with them no end."

In a 2,000-word *People* magazine cover story titled "The President's Accuser," Mark Brown is quoted: "'Paula loves dressing real provocative. Hot damn, I'd have probably propositioned her myself.'"

The story, published in the May 23, 1994, edition, was produced by nine staffers (four in Little Rock, one in Memphis, three in Los Angeles, and a writer in New York, aided and abetted by additional bureau reports).

While this huge team of journalists faithfully recorded the fact that Mark Brown indeed was a disc jockey at B. J.'s Star-Studded Honky Tonk, it failed to note the most significant fact—that Bill Clinton patronized the club for years with his floozies!

Did Mark Brown know the governor as patron?

People's people don't say—yet the six-page spread very prominently displays photos of Charlotte and Mark Brown, one taken of them by Nina Berman of Sipa Press on assignment for the magazine, and another taken by Chelsea Clinton!

Arkansas's first daughter happened to be at a 1990 Christmas tree lighting ceremony with her father. And with camera and flash in hand, Chelsea snapped the *tell-all* photo showing a smiling Bill Clinton holding a toddler in his right arm, and his left hand on the shoulder of another tyke standing in front of him.

A rotund woman attired in a choke-collar, two-piece suit-dress is standing on Clinton's right, and a bearded man in a leather jacket with a black patch worn over his right eye is on Clinton's left.

The caption under the picture identifies the couple, the children's parents:

"Paula's sister and brother-in-law, Charlotte and Mark Brown."

Does the old adage that a picture is worth a thousand words apply in this instance? The author's research bears out that it does.

For it developed that Hillary Rodham Clinton, Arkansas's first lady, refused to pose in the photo with Mark Brown because she not only was aware of Brown's role at the nightclub, but also of her husband's frequent patronage of the place—where she knew he did much of his catting!

While *People*'s nine staffers failed to cite any of these facts in their story, they didn't let pass the opportunity to echo Mark Brown's derisive ventings about Paula, in their own derogatory words that describe her appearance while working at the AIDC:

"Her short, tight, dresses and habit of wearing her hair in a knot on the side earned her the nickname Minnie Mouse among security guards at the State Capitol."

Paula not only unburdened herself of the Bill Clinton abortive oral sex experience to her two co-workers and two sisters, but she also told husband Steve about the governor's improper advances and proposition.

Jones' advice: "Honey, just forget it. Chalk it up to experience and don't go near that womanizing bastard again. You should have known better—you've heard the kind of reputation he has with women in this state. Just stay away from a bum like that."

Paula followed Steve's advice and, for all intents and purposes, erased the incident from her mind—until *The American Spectator* and the *Los Angeles Times* exploded their "Troopergate" stories, which shook up Paula more than the California earthquake would do a few weeks later.

So infuriated was Paula that she set out at once to seek a retraction from the trooper, who wasn't identified by name in the stories, but who she vividly remembered introducing himself as Danny Ferguson.

Paula knew her way around, so she went to the Little Rock law offices of Clinton nemesis Cliff Jackson, Bill's Oxford classmate and whistle-blower on his desperate draft-evasion daring-do's.

Paula wanted Jackson to point her in Ferguson's direction. She had read that Jackson was guiding the troopers' destinies after urging them to go public about serving as Clinton's "whoremasters."

Jackson told Paula that going after Ferguson for a retraction wasn't the way to go. At least not yet. He recommended that she hook up with Daniel Traylor.

Paula found Traylor had a better idea.

"Let's shake up Slick Willie with a letter," Traylor advised. He wrote it and sent it to the White House:

> Dear Sir:
>
> I represent Ms. Paula Jones. Ms. Jones complains of your conduct at a meeting with her in a private room at the Excelsior Hotel...during her workday on Wednesday, May 8, 1991, in connection with the Third Annual Governor's Quality Management Conference. Today Ms. Jones will probably characterize your conduct as the equivalent of on-the-job sexual harassment but will refrain from an explicit description as to afford you an opportunity to publicly apologize and take responsibility for your actions.
>
> On a related matter, Ms. Jones also complains that her good reputation has been defamed by your former bodyguard, Arkansas State Trooper Danny Ferguson. You may refer to page 26 of 'Living With the Clintons,' *American Spectator*, January 1994, for his derogatory statements. Because you have personal knowledge that would discredit Trooper Ferguson's account and restore Ms. Jones to her good reputation, she is requesting that you publicly do so.

Traylor didn't miss a trick. He enclosed a seven-point, sworn and signed affidavit in which Paula socked it to the president with the specifics of their encounter, then left him to mull it over—by reading it in the newspapers before Press Secretary Dee Dee Myers and Communications Director Mark Gearan could mount their damage control rebuttals.

In her affidavit, Paula made it clear that unless Clinton complied with her demands, she would sue him. For in 1991, he was Arkansas's governor—and thus her *supervisor*.

Sexual harassment is a violation of the law.

"It's just not true," protested Dee Dee Myers.

"The incident never happened...the president was never alone in a hotel with her," argued Mark Gearan.

Dee Dee didn't say what part of Paula Jones' story wasn't true. Certainly she didn't call the whole story a lie.

Gearan's explanation was puzzling in that he said Clinton wasn't alone *in a hotel* with Paula. A curious way to put it, since no one is ever *alone in a hotel*, which always has people in it. Why didn't Gearan address himself to attorney Traylor's specific statement that Clinton's meeting with Paula took place *in a private room*?

How the *Washington Post* Killed Paula's Story

The *Washington Post*, which had won a Pulitzer Prize for its early disclosures on

Watergate, may have had an idea that it could win another journalistic trophy after reading the *Troopergate* stories in the two aforementioned journals.

It was by no means sold on Paula Jones' story after she recited her experience with Clinton at a press conference attorney Daniel Traylor called on February 11, 1994. In fact, the newspaper not only relegated the report to its "Style" section, but also belittled Paula's account as an "eruption...of Mount Bimbo."

Then under the direction of *Post* executive editor Leonard Downie, a major investigation of Paula Jones' charges was launched. Three reporters were assigned to the probe which, from what the author determined, was designed to deep-six the accuser by dredging up all the dirt about her from the past that would discredit her.

The only reporter's name that's important in this account is Michael Isikoff's. But for the record, the others were Charles Shephard and Sharon LaFraniere.

Not surprisingly, the reportorial team's first stop was the offices of Daniel Traylor, who was delighted to be told the *Post* was going to conduct the investigation.

For by then, Traylor had the sworn affidavits of the six people in whom Paula had confided about her experience with Clinton—plus a seventh, notarized statement from Trooper Danny Ferguson, attesting to his role in the caper (admitting that he picked up Paula at the reception desk on Clinton's command and took her to the governor's suite).

Convinced that the *Post*'s inquiry would confirm what he knew about Paula's experience with Clinton, Traylor gave the reporters his word that "my client will not cooperate with other publications until your newspaper has had ample time to complete its investigation."

Consequently, Isikoff was granted an exclusive interview with Paula and her husband on Saturday, February 12, the first of many the reporter and his colleagues would have with her.

Traylor also provided the names of the seven people whose testimony he had taken as corroborators of Paula's tale.

Isikoff himself had a hour-and-a-half lunch with Debra Ballentine during which she reported in exacting language about Paula's recital of her experience.

Then he interviewed Pamela Blackard, Paula's co-worker at the AIDC. Isikoff had been urged to speak to Ms. Blackard at any cost.

"I wanted this reporter, above all else, to talk with her," Traylor said. I wanted him to understand for himself that Paula couldn't have invented that story in the ninety steps it took to get from the room back to her work station. And why would she?

"I knew there was nothing in her background that would remotely suggest she would make up this kind of story."

The *Post* reporters did that background search with a vengeance.

They interviewed Paula's six former employers, all leads supplied the team by Traylor.

"They contacted each employer and got either the boss's or her supervisor's opinion about the kind of worker she was, about her punctuality, her attitude in the workplace, and the reason for leaving that job.

"All the evaluations were highly favorable, most complimentary—including her supervisors at the AIDC where she had worked for three years.

"They also interviewed her high school principal, teachers, fellow classmates, and even her boyfriends of those days, as well as some of her casual dates.

"They also unearthed the fact that she went to a junior college for a while to gain experience on computers and improve her secretarial skills.

"They did a thorough and most intensive research, trying to find anything that would cut either way—to discredit her story or to help support it."

Traylor didn't know that the *Post* wasn't exactly looking to make Paula's story stand up. He learned of that only after February passed into March and the lawyer found himself under increasing pressure from the media to let them interview his client.

"They were arguing that it was a mistake to give an exclusive to just one newspaper when it was the duty of all publications to let the public know about Paula's ordeal."

Finally, March 24 dawned—"Bloody Thursday," as Traylor dubbed it.

"I had a confrontation with Isikoff. I told him I had given him a reasonable period to gather information about Paula and to run his story as the *Post* saw fit.

"But that was the rub. The *Post* didn't want the story to run. Mike Isikoff, Charlie Shephard, and Sharon LaFraniere had prepared a full-page account, a real blockbusting story, as best as I could determine from what was said.

"I got the distinct impression the *Post* would never run it. Isikoff assured me that Thursday he'd go back to the office and 'fight for the story to see the light of publication.'"

"Bloody Thursday," to be sure!

It was Michael Isikoff's blood that spilled—all over the newsroom of the *Washington Post*. He really did fight for the story. So valiantly, so forcefully, so insistently that he was suspended for two weeks!

The suspension followed an exchange of some last words—during a raucous shouting match—with national editor Fred Barbash, whom Isikoff is said to have pinned to a wall.

Isikoff's exile ended April 4, and he returned to work in a newsroom whose staff he found was "ninety-eight percent in favor of publishing the Paula Jones piece."

But the story was still impaled on the spike where stories that are "killed" end up.

Why did the *Post* not run the story?

No clue is forthcoming from publisher Katharine Graham's commandos, but there may be something more behind this report than meets the eye.

During its lengthy investigation, the *Washington Post* questioned the White House, Traylor revealed.

"They were furnished, as I understand it, an alibi by Clinton, and they checked it out."

But, incredibly, the alibi didn't cover the most significant time—2:30 p.m. on Wednesday of May 8, 1991.

He Gets Programmed for the Job

Hardly a month had passed after he dropped his pants and exposed himself to Paula Jones, and Bill Clinton was to be found at Little Rock's Adams field with Hillary and Chelsea.

After interviewing Max Brantley, editor of the *Arkansas Times* magazine, who was also at the airport that early June day, one comes away believing Bill Clinton had no intention whatsoever of paying attention to the business of governing Arkansas in his fifth term.

Brantley and his wife had taken their children to the airport to see them off to summer camp, as had Bill and Hillary Clinton, each holding a hand of 10-year-old Chelsea, who stood between her parents smiling.

"I remember speaking with Bill at the airport that day," recalled Brantley. "He left me with the distinct impression that he was on the verge of a decision about whether or not he was going to make a stab for the presidency in ninety-two.

"I do know that Hillary was pushing him to run. But I didn't imagine that they were thinking about winning then. They were simply out to test the waters of that presidential campaign for the future, to build up recognition."

Indeed, how could Bill Clinton have believed he—or any Democratic aspirant—had a prayer against George Bush? With the election 17 months away, the president's approval rating had climbed to 82 percent in the euphoria following the end of the Gulf War.

Nevertheless, Max Brantley decided that Hillary was obsessed with having her husband back out of his promise to the people of Arkansas not to seek higher office after barely beginning to serve his fifth term.

The *real* Hillary Clinton had yet to be discerned by people outside of Arkansas. Those folks already had a good look at what made their first lady tick. Yet nothing appeared in print about what kind of person Hillary was until midway through the presidential primaries. The *New York Times* then published the quotes of two elderly women who volunteered to assess the "Hillary Problem," as it came to be known.

"She's only interested in being with a winner," said one senior citizen, 71-year-old Bernadine Elliott. "And believe me, if he doesn't get elected, she's going to dump him. Mark my words."

"That's right," echoed 69-year-old LaRoux Tanner, "she'll dump him."

People in the Clinton camp itself became leery of Hillary Clinton. Betsey Wright was one. The truth has finally been learned about her actions. She had urged Bill not to run. Then she had a falling out with Hillary and quit cold when she was told her advice wasn't needed.

The days ahead would show that Hillary Clinton was a "very aggressive woman," "overly ambitious," and "truly the power behind the throne." In short, she had Bill Clinton "dancing to her tune."

The above quotes were gathered by the "Arkansas Travelers," friends of Bill and Hillary who worked the presidential campaign trail for the candidate. They encountered voter after voter who would never cast a ballot for Clinton so long as he had a wife so "scary and who'd dominate him should he occupy the Oval Office."

Days after the scene just described at the airport, Bill Clinton returned to board a plane to Washington, D.C., to catch a trans-Atlantic flight to Germany. He was weighed down by two large suitcases and flanked by two husky, uniformed, state troopers, his bodyguards, who helped him board the plane, but did not accompany him on the flight.

"How odd," onlookers remarked. No one could remember when Clinton had traveled abroad without his omnipresent Arkansas State Police bodyguards.

He was traveling solo now because his agenda was *top secret*. He was off on two of the most important missions of his life, and he wanted no one to clearly know what he was up to.

One appointment was in the most elegantly jeweled precincts of Germany's fabled Black Forest.

The other engagement was to forge a compact within the shadows of the Kremlin in Moscow.

The therapeutic mineral waters gushing from the earth in Hot Springs, Arkansas, are inarguably as ancient as those flowing out of the ground at Baden-Wertenberg in Germany's Black Forest.

The springs in Arkansas were first seen by white men when Hernando de Soto's expedition arrived in 1541. Not until the 1700s did the French and Spanish begin availing themselves of the warm waters' healing powers.

By contrast, the twenty-nine hot springs of Baden-Baden had been known to the Romans before the advent of Christ. Since then, the vaporous waters that leave the ground at a scorching 150 degrees had been used by the German nobility between the fourteenth and seventeenth centuries. In ensuing years, the renowned waters have been visited by people from all over the world.

Baden-Baden is the posh locale Bill Clinton visited in June 1991. He hadn't gone there to draw comparisons between the German spa and the one in his home state. According to the governor's office, he was there to attend the 37th annual Bilderberg Conference.

This is an informal, *secret* organization, formed in 1954 by Prince Bernhard of the Netherlands, reportedly to encourage more dialogue and closer ties within the Atlantic Community of Europe and North America.

The organization claims "secrecy is demanded so as to encourage frank discussions by persons whose positions otherwise would restrict full expressions of their personal view." Consequently, the identities of those attending the gatherings are never made known. They are referred to only by their own press releases or by reporters camped at a distance from the meeting sites, always off-limits to both press and public.

Over the years, the Bilderberg Conference has attracted many highly placed critics who protest that the organization

- sets itself above governments.
- manipulates global finances and imperiously establishes rigid and binding monetary rates around the world.
- *selects political figures whom the conference decrees should become rulers*

of nations—and also targets those whom it wants removed from power.
- decides which countries shall wage war upon others.

"The Bilderbergers are powerful enough to pull the rug out of one nation and to pave the way for the rise of another," said a scholar intimately acquainted with the Bilderberg modus operandi.

"An example is the way the conferees decreed the impoverishment of South American countries for many years. Now they've done an about-face and are building up those lands.

"They are above government. They dictate terms and run the world the way the Bilderberg brain trust decides it should be.

"It is incomprehensible how so many highly placed people of influence can be sucked into this secret society's orbit to participate in their closed-door planning sessions that ordain drastic and historic changes to create a *new world order to be controlled by the most powerful of the global bankers*," says the scholar.

A partial roster of influential Americans who have attended Bilderberg Conferences includes Arthur Hays Sulzberger, president and publisher of the *New York Times*; C. D. Jackson, vice president of Time, Inc.; George F. Kennan, former ambassador to the Soviet Union; Eugene R. Black, president of the International Bank; Gabriel Hauge, economic adviser to President Dwight D. Eisenhower; David J. McDonald, president of the United Steel Workers; David Rockefeller, chairman of the Chase Manhattan Bank; and former Secretary of State Henry A. Kissinger.

Meetings are generally held semi-annually and participants, as some of the aforementioned names indicate, represent selected public officials, economists, professionals, publishers, industrialists, labor leaders, and people of influence from virtually all walks of life.

Prince Bernhard himself uniformly issues the invitations to about 90 to 100 persons on a personal basis, after screening by a conference steering committee. Expenses, met by private funds, are unrestricted and allow for participants' security personnel and aides. Only invited delegates are permitted to attend the closed door meetings. Their entourages are not allowed into the sessions.

Conference sites are selected on a rotation basis, changing from one country to another, in the most exclusive and extravagantly appointed setting of the host nation. For example, the first session held on United States soil, in 1957, was at Georgia's posh St. Simons Island, where the hotel ballroom was transformed into a resplendent, mirror-image, miniature United Nations chamber.

That conclave drew among others, recognized when they arrived at the airport, former New York Governor Thomas E. Dewey, Britain's Lord Chancellor Viscount Kilmiur, German Chancellor Konrad Adenauer's top aide Kurt Kiening—and Senator J. William Fulbright.

The 1954 launch of this society—which has since come to be regarded as "the most exclusive club of the Western establishment"—was held in the Dutch town of Bilderberg, from which its name was derived.

Meetings are always held in an atmosphere of utmost security. Each delegate is sworn to secrecy, pledging never to divulge what is discussed or to identify others who attend.

Clinton himself upheld this rule by failing to divulge the name of a single person at the gathering—including that of Virginia's Douglas Wilder, the only other governor there.

On June 3, Clinton's press secretary, Mike Gauldin, issued a news release saying the governor was going to the conference "dealing with international affairs" and was joining 100 political leaders and professionals from North America and Western Europe in the German resort city.

The invitation, according to the press release, was tendered by Vernon E. Jordan, former president of the National Urban League and a prominent Washington, D.C., lawyer.

Gauldin emphasized that the governor's expenses for the trip were being paid by the "American Support Group" (none of whose members was identified) for the Bilderberg event, scheduled for Thursday through Sunday, June 4-7.

"Of particular interest to Clinton," Gauldin said, "are trade and economic development opportunities for Arkansas" that loomed under Germany's recent unification.

Curiously, Gauldin did not mention a two-day side-trip to Moscow that Clinton would take after the Bilderberg Conference.

As frequently happened later during the presidential campaign of '92—and after he occupied the White House—Clinton and his spokespeople often seemed deceptive about his activities when they came under scrutiny. In this instance, the trip to Germany got underway with no fanfare whatsoever other than that terse press release. The governor left Little Rock on June 3 under the most secretive circumstances. The press never got wind of it until Gauldin's announcement was issued long after Clinton took off.

June 3 separates Bill Clinton by 122 days from October 3, 1991, when he would announce his candidacy for the presidency, and was five months removed from the day he began a fifth term as governor and vowed he'd serve a full, four-year term.

Whether Clinton intended to throw off the public can be judged by how details about the Moscow trip were *managed* by Gauldin and others on the governor's staff— and even by Slick Willie himself!

One early curiosity that struck everyone familiar with Clinton's habits was that he flew to Baden-Baden unattended by his Arkansas State Police bodyguard. He wasn't even accompanied by one member of the Arkansas Industrial Development Commission, who were always found in the governor's company on every one of his nine earlier excursions to foreign lands, trips unvaryingly billed as "searches for jobs and investment by companies" in Arkansas.

Why Clinton chose to go it alone this time was explained by another spokesman:

"The reason he didn't have a staff member with him was due to limited space and limited provisions. The sponsors asked that they (the invitees) not bring staff members with them."

As pointed out earlier, the Bilderberg Conference gives invited delegates carte blanche expenses, so heads of states, for example, who cannot possibly travel without security and staff, can feel free to attend without having to pay expenses for their retinues out of their government's or personal funds.

Besides manipulating the facts about Bilderberg travel expenses, the governor's staff also offered no explanation on Vernon Jordan's role in the invitation.

Curious that Prince Bernhard should designate an American civil rights leader to invite the governor of Arkansas, when rigid organization protocol always called upon the Netherlands' ruler himself to invite delegates supposedly nominated by the screening committee to attend the conference.

The paucity of information about this significant trip for Governor Bill Clinton can be attributed to Clinton himself!

Details of the way the Bilderbergers operate are to be found in chapter 43.

More Double-Talk about the Trip

By stressing that the governor's expenses weren't being charged to the state, Gauldin touched on a perennial sore point with Arkansas's electorate. For Clinton had been widely criticized for his frequent "globe-trottings" in the guise of "drumming up business and investment for Arkansas."

In his first 10 years as governor, Clinton made nine recorded overseas junkets to such locales as Tokyo and Osaka in Japan; Taipei, Taiwan; Dusseldorf and Munich in West Germany; Florence, Italy; Helsinki, Finland; Brussels, Belgium; and London, England.

On those journeys, Clinton dipped unhesitatingly into funds of the Arkansas Industrial Development Commission and his own office to foot the bill for travel, lodging, food, entertainment, phone calls, and other sundry expenses.

However, Clinton's trip to the Bilderberg Conference did not become an issue in 1991 since it was assertedly paid for by the "American support group."

What did become an issue was the so-called two-day, "side-trip" to Moscow.

It wasn't until June 9, when he was already in the Soviet Union, that his office let it be known Clinton had flown to Moscow:

"The governor has left the Bilderberg Conference in Germany and gone to the Soviet Union, where he was invited to meet Ambassador John Matlock, Jr., in Moscow."

The State Department in Washington swiftly issued a denial that Ambassador Matlock had "invited" Clinton to the Soviet capital.

"Ambassador Matlock did not ask Governor Clinton to visit the Soviet Union," declared State Department spokeswoman Margaret D. Tutwiler. "Mr. Matlock merely invited the governor to stay for dinner as a matter of courtesy after he dropped into the American embassy *unannounced* and *introduced himself.*"

Clinton's staff did an about-face with facts that, even then, were couched in half-truth.

"The invitation to visit Moscow was tendered by Mrs. Ester Coopersmith (a Washington, D.C., philanthropist and former U.S. Representative to the United Nations during President Jimmy Carter's administration)," asserted a subsequent damage control Clinton press office dispatch.

Mrs. Coopersmith and a group of other American benefactors arranged the trip to

Moscow, said Gauldin, to deliver antibiotics to the Soviet government for children burned in the Chernobyl nuclear power plant disaster.

Even with that revised explanation, the story still didn't hold water. For in the next breath Gauldin said, "The Governor had planned the trip to Moscow [before he left for Baden-Baden], but it was not confirmed until after he had left."

Clear?

That statement failed to answer the question of why the governor's office didn't say a word about Moscow until the trip was nearly over and didn't issue a clarifying statement until *after* Clinton returned to the U.S.

Nor did it explain this further contradiction:

"On Monday [with the Bilderberg Conference ended and while still in Germany], I was on a plane back [to Frankfurt, presumably to catch a flight to Washington to attend a soon-to-be-held Democratic National Committee fund-raiser].

"I ran into an old friend [Mrs. Coopersmith] who was delivering humanitarian aid to the Soviet Union and she suggested that I tag along to meet the U.S. ambassador, and visit a country I hadn't seen in twenty-one years."

That's the story from Clinton's own lips several days later to some 55 big Democratic Party contributors looking to back a 1992 presidential candidate. He addressed them after his plane landed in Washington late Tuesday afternoon, June 9. The gathering of heavy political hitters heard Clinton at a 40-minute, closed-door meeting.

How did Clinton's trip to the Soviet Union from Sunday night of June 7 to late Tuesday afternoon of June 9, a 48-hour visit, *really* come about?

Menu from a Chinese Restaurant

Offering more than the choices given in Column A and Column B of a Chinese restaurant menu, Clinton's scorecard provides four picks to decide how his "side-trip" to the Kremlin evolved:

1.   The governor went to Moscow at the invitation of U.S. Ambassador John Matlock.

2.   The invitation to visit the Soviet Union was tendered by Mrs. Ester Coopersmith, the former UN ambassador, *before* Clinton left for the Bilderberg Conference.

3.   He was asked to go to the Kremlin before he departed for Baden-Baden, but the trip was up in the air because the plans "weren't finalized" yet.

4.   Clinton didn't know about Mrs. Coopersmith's humanitarian journey in behalf of the Chernobyl victims until he bumped into her at the airport in Frankfurt, and it was only then, at the last minute, that he decided to join her.

Clinton and his staff aren't content to have it one way. At times they prefer having it two ways. Sometimes even three ways. Given their druthers, they would even prefer having it four ways!

One thing was certain: Bill Clinton had dropped in, then dropped out of Moscow, without any press coverage of his mission.

When he told his audience in Washington that Mrs. Coopersmith's last-minute invitation in Germany afforded him opportunity to "visit a country I haven't seen in twenty-one years," he was alluding to the previously mentioned trip he took to Moscow in 1969-1970, while finishing his second and final year as a Rhodes scholar at Oxford.

During the '92 presidential campaign, when accounts about his draft status and unceasing efforts to avoid military service were raised by President Bush, reports surfaced suggesting Clinton had sought asylum in one or another of several foreign countries as a way to avoid the draft.

Clinton, the stories said, had been prepared to renounce his American birthright and defect—just so he could avoid serving in the military.

While it took many weeks during the presidential campaign to own up to his role as an anti-war activist, Clinton finally came partly clean because he could not duck the issue as he had so deftly succeeded in doing previously.

During his 1982 comeback gubernatorial campaign against former Governor Frank White, White had declared at a rally in Horsehead Bend, "Bill Clinton never ran anything in his life except anti-war demonstrations."

When that statement was thrown up to Clinton, he responded, "I have no idea what he could be talking about...Frank White is getting desperate in his bid for reelection."

Familiar words?

On October 9, 1992, President Bush suggested that Clinton's anti-Vietnam War activities as a student would make it difficult for him to lead this country's military forces as president. On ABC-TV's "Good Morning America," Bush made this declaration:

"This is something I feel strongly about and I think it impacts on how you'd react as the commander in chief."

Campaigning in Kansas City at the time, Clinton took time out from the stump to respond, "I don't know what he's talking about...George Bush is getting desperate in his bid for reelection."

But soon, Clinton could no longer hold onto his insistence that he *never* staged anti-war rallies.

10 Years Later: "Yes, I Protested"

"My protest activities," Clinton conceded when compelled to face reality, "were against the policy of the government, not against my country."

The earliest hint that Clinton might begin to level about his past anti-war activities came when *Arkansas Gazette* editor John Brummett asked him if he ever led anti-war protests. Clinton's response:

"I was around them [the anti-war demonstrations] but I didn't lead any protests."

On the heels of that concession, Clinton's campaign spokeswoman, Betsey Wright, rushed in to rehabilitate the candidate's resurrected denials of 1982. Despite her falling out with Hillary, Miss Wright had by this time joined the governor's bandwagon in her capacity as chairman of the Arkansas Democratic Party. She claimed his statements "weren't contradictory if applied to former Governor White's *specific wording* of the allegation—that Clinton '*ran*' an anti-war demonstration."

Then she quickly paralogized:

"Clinton never organized *an entire* anti-war demonstration *to my knowledge*...he merely had *helped organize* a London religious service in opposition to the war in 1969. He wasn't the only organizer or the leader of it.

"He was one of the people who organized that service. I think that was the only activity he organized or was an organizer of."

Then sucking in a deep breath to attack the press for being so insistent that Clinton come clean about his experiences as a demonstrator, Miss Wright fumed, "This is red-baiting crap that you are playing here. This is just nit-picking, silly little stuff you are into."

She called Frank White's 1982 allegations "silly hyperbole."

At about that time, Clinton himself spoke with the publication *Spectrum Weekly*:

"I have nothing to hide concerning my anti-war experience. My opposition to the war was well known.

"I've never hidden what I felt about it or what I did. I think I was right...I attended *two* anti-war rallies, *one* in Washington and *one* in London."

Haunted by Voices of the Past

What was it Clinton wrote to Colonel Eugene Holmes in the 1969 letter? After admitting he joined the Vietnam Moratorium in Washington, D.C., Clinton confessed he went to "...England to organize the Americans here for demonstrations Oct. 15 [1969] and Nov. 15 [1969]."

How many demonstrations in England?

One, as Betsey Wright—and Clinton—inaccurately stated?

Or *two* demonstrations as Clinton himself confessed in his letter to Colonel Holmes?

Betsey Wright again: "Bill Clinton's organizing consisted of coordinating travel for Oxford students to attend the demonstrations. He didn't organize the demonstrations."

Ms. Wright had no way of knowing when she defended Clinton that Colonel Holmes would angrily rise from retirement to put the lie to Clinton's lies about his double-dealings with the draft, the ROTC, and his vigorous anti-war activities.

The author wasn't the only journalist to inquire about Clinton's loyalty to his country. The Associated Press, the Hearst Newspapers, and the American Broadcasting Company asked the same questions.

These organizations were besieged with suggestions that a search through State Department files might turn up evidence Clinton sought to renounce his citizenship during the Vietnam War. The three services filed Freedom of Information Act requests with the State Department for Clinton's passport file and personal records.

The requests were spurred by reports that an American on a Rhodes Scholarship at Oxford had written to the U.S. Embassy in London, expressed his deeply troubled feelings about the Vietnam War, and professed that he was toying with the thought of renouncing his citizenship.

After reporters ran into a dead end at the embassy, their editors filed the necessary documents in Washington.

Assistant Secretary of State Elizabeth Tamposi—a Bush political appointee whose father was an important Republican fund-raiser—phoned the embassy in London with instructions to search the files for that evidence.

When the embassy reported it had no records of such correspondence from Clinton going that far back, to 1969–70, Miss Tamposi and aides Michael Brennan and Steven Monehan journeyed on Friday, October 30, to the National Records Center in suburban Maryland and obtained dossiers on Clinton.

Miss Tamposi then took the records to her home for the weekend. She brought the records to the State Department on Monday, November 2, and subsequently returned them to the records center.

What, if anything, was in the records has never been revealed. In fact, there was hell to pay for the searches—which included a look at Clinton's thrice-widowed mother, Virginia Cassidy Blythe Clinton Dwire Kelley's, passport files.

Upon learning of the activity by the State Department, a furious Bill Clinton, appearing at a rally in Seattle, fumed, "Now it turns out that the State Department was not only rifling through my files, but was actually investigating my mother—a well-known subversive. It would be funny if it were not so pathetic. This is a crowd so desperate to win that they have forgotten the purpose of power in a democratic government is to help people and to lift them up."

Senator Al Gore, campaigning in Macon, Georgia, as Clinton's running mate, called for a personal apology from President Bush:

"This is an outrage...absolutely despicable tactics...government by smear tactics..."

Bush responded to the storm—after the election—by firing Miss Tamposi.

Meanwhile, none of the questions about Clinton's purported attempt to seek citizenship in another country were answered. Nor did any details of his trip to the Soviet Union come to light before the election.

But, following interviews by the author with his Oxford classmates, a partial itinerary of Clinton's trip to the USSR was shaped, revealing that he participated at a peace rally sparked by Senator Eugene McCarthy and some further insight into the balance of his agenda, again as reported in chapter 5.

Bill Has a Buddy in the Kremlin: The New KGB Boss

Bill Clinton was more forthcoming about his 1991 trip to Moscow than he was about his earlier one.

Brushing off a suggestion that he took the trip to pick up "foreign policy credentials" for a presidential campaign, Clinton maintained that he merely went along with Ester Coopersmith, who was bringing medical aid for the children of Chernobyl.

"By going to Europe and the Soviet Union," Clinton declared, "I learned about governmental and economic events that will ultimately affect Arkansas."

The governor praised German and USSR education systems, and the "openness" in the Soviet Union, but was dismayed by the "economic distress" and "instability."

Clinton said he spent considerable time in Moscow's landmark McDonald's fast-food restaurant, where up to 60,000 Muscovites dine daily.

He also supped with Ambassador Matlock on Monday, June 8, and was introduced to Soviet Interior Minister Vadim Bakatin, a candidate in the following Wednesday's Russian presidential election.

"I met Mr. Bakatin on Tuesday and spoke with him for an hour and a half—that's something I could never imagine happening during one of my own campaigns," Clinton said.

"People in the Soviet Union crave the type of democracy we take for granted. It was absolutely fascinating to see them embracing what we take for granted [the election]."

An out-of-favor, liberal Communist and minister in soon-to-be-deposed Soviet President Mikhail Gorbachev's cabinet, Bakatin didn't win the election. Boris Yeltsin did. But in the wake of the failed August 1991 coup, Bakatin was among the reformers who came out on top. He was appointed to head the former Soviet Union's dreaded secret police!

The KGB's files certainly contained profiles and biographies on many thousands of Americans—including what must be voluminous data on Bill Clinton. How could the KGB not have opened such a file on a young man who stood so vocally against the very war the USSR deplored and who visited their country as a messenger of peace?

The *Arkansas Democrat*'s headline points out succinctly the important connection Bill Clinton made with Vadim Bakatin:

Clinton has powerful buddy in U.S.S.R.—new head of KGB

Last words on Bill Clinton's 1991 journey were offered by Cliff Jackson, the Little Rock attorney and Clinton's Oxford classmate, who provided information about his 1969-70 trip and earlier told about the president's many attempts to beat the draft:

"I have a pretty good idea what significance to attach to that meeting with the new KGB boss and Clinton's announcement that he was running for the presidency, which came just 85 days later.

"I wouldn't hesitate to bet the sucker, after being endorsed by the Bilderbergers for the presidency of the United States, Bill Clinton had his KGB file purged to give him the clean bill he needed to make his run for the White House.

His Mom: "Bill, My Cancer's Worse"

Not long after returning from his trip, Bill Clinton answered a call from his mother. She was the bearer of distressing news.

Two years earlier, Virginia Kelley had had a radical mastectomy and had been holding her own since, only to learn now that cancer was detected again and she required renewed treatment by her oncologist, Dr. Tim Webb.

Dr. Webb declined to comment because, he said, "I have not been given permission by the family to discuss the case."

However, other sources would discuss Mrs. Kelley's illness with the author's researchers and willingly let their names be used.

One of those is her husband's son-in-law, Clay Farrow, who is married to Richard

Kelley's daughter from a previous marriage.

Another is Dr. William R. Mashburn, the Garland County (Hot Springs) coroner who also would speak on the history of Bill's mom's bout with the disease—after her death from its complications on January 5, 1994.

What Farrow and Mashburn said about the recurrence of the cancer, around the middle of 1991, suggested that Dr. Webb was able to control the spread of the cancer for the next two years, until about June 1993, when her condition began to deteriorate.

Whether Webb used experimental drugs, chemotherapy, or both could not be learned. But this much can be reported:

"It was clear to us in the family that she took a definite turn for the worse six months ago," explained Farrow in the interview after Mrs. Kelley's death.

"But she didn't talk about it, in the sense that she did not want to acknowledge it was a problem. However, it was clear that something ratcheted up, that suddenly she was getting more aggressive therapy."

Mrs. Kelley was receiving transfusions of platelets, the tiny fragments in blood that hasten the clotting process. Often platelets fall to dangerously low levels when a disease such as cancer spreads to the bone marrow and destroys the very cells that form platelets.

Ironically, the side effects of anti-cancer drugs can also cause a drop in the number of platelets, which is what is said to have happened during Virginia Kelley's treatment by Dr. Webb.

This information does not come from the oncologist but from Dr. Mashburn, who described the workings of platelets and their effects on the human body.

Despite the weakness and fatigue she suffered, Mrs. Kelley continued to go to nearby Oaklawn Race Track and also traveled to other favorite haunts, most often with husband Dick.

"She was going somewhere every ten days or so," Farrow continues to report. "She was quite active despite a level of illness that would probably slow down ten people, and she was the one person [who] did not slow down."

At the track, she spurned favored treatment after her son was elected president— just as she had when he was elected to his first term as Arkansas's governor and all terms since.

"We had asked her if she'd go up to the private club," said track manager Eric Jackson. "She said, 'All my friends are in the grandstand. I'm staying there.' And that's where she's sat forever and a day."

When Virginia and Dick flew to Washington to spend Christmas '93 at the White House, she was so exhausted on arrival at National Airport she had to use a wheelchair to reach the waiting limousine, according to son-in-law Clay Farrow, who also made the trip.

"But she did not resort to a wheelchair to get about in the White House, although walking anything more than one hundred to two hundred feet fatigued her."

After she returned home on Air Force One and played host at the cabin for her son until his departure, Mrs. Kelley and her husband were off to Las Vegas for the New Year's holiday.

Mrs. Kelley was no stranger to that gambling mecca. The country first became aware of her affinity for betting on a night during the presidential campaign when her son was being interviewed on "Larry King Live." She phoned the studio—from Nevada—and told Clinton she was there "for politics, not casinos."

Cracking a broad smile and chuckling, Clinton teased her while a worldwide audience was tuned in. "That's your story, mother—and you stick to it."

Virginia Kelley was to be seen one last time on TV—on New Year's Eve, when her eyebrows were highlighted by a heavy pencil that gave her an uncanny resemblance to Broadway showstopper Ethel Merman, whose bombast the president's mother almost always exuded.

Virginia's Last Hurrah with Barbra Streisand

The last TV shots of Mrs. Kelley were occasioned by her presence in the sold-out crowd at the Las Vegas nightclub where Barbra Streisand gave two spectacular New Year's Eve concerts, her first in many years.

Virginia and Dick first caught the action at the casinos—the president's mother tried to empty the slot machines, her favorite pastime in Vegas—then they attended both ends of the Streisand double-header.

Between the acts, Barbra—one of Bill Clinton's favorite entertainers and a frequent guest at the White House—sat with the Kelleys, chatting animatedly with the president's mother. Barbra's mother was also in the group.

The first mother continued to get all she could out of life when she returned to Hot Springs and dropped into the Saw Mill Depot restaurant. This was Tuesday, January 4, a day when she also stopped off to see Dr. Webb and was told to return the next day for another transfusion of platelets.

"She was showing us pictures of the Barbra Streisand concert," says Patti Painter, the bookkeeper at the restaurant. "It was her, Barbra, and Barbra's mother. She said she was going to come in Friday and show us the rest of them."

But Mrs. Kelley wasn't able to keep that appointment.

Dr. Mashburn relates that the president's mother, after her treatment by Dr. Webb on Wednesday when she received what was to be her last transfusion of platelets, left his office and went home.

That evening, she told a friend, "I am as fatigued as I ever get," according to Dr. Mashburn, who described Mrs. Kelley's last hours.

After dinner—she didn't eat much because her appetite was almost nonexistent—she watched her beloved University of Arkansas basketball team on television. They were playing arch-rival Mississippi. The Razorbacks, who were riding at the top of the heap in the National Collegiate Athletic Association ratings, defeated Ol' Miss 87–61 (and went on to win the 1993 NCAA Championship, their first ever).

Mrs. Kelley was delighted by the game's outcome, but was in dire straits. Dick had taken her temperature and she had a high fever. He tucked her in bed and phoned Dr. Webb, who advised Kelley what medicine to give his wife.

"A little after midnight," Dr. Mashburn said, describing the desperate events that unfolded in rapid succession, "Mr. Kelley checks on his wife and finds that she has stopped breathing.

"He phones nine-eleven.

"Paramedics respond.

"The [Garland County] sheriff arrives shortly thereafter.

"They find she is beyond aid.

"I am notified and arrive to find that Virginia is dead."

Clay Farrow picked up the story:

"Dick Kelley then called the president. Moments later, Bill phoned me and asked that I go to his mother's home.

Another Autopsy Gives Clinton the Edge

"We all knew she was failing, but none of us thought that she was going to sleep and die Wednesday night—and that's the surprising shock to the family."

Although Mrs. Kelley's immediate cause of death couldn't be determined—only an autopsy could pinpoint the reason—Dr. Mashburn ruled out a post mortem and filled out the death certificate as any attending physician at the death bed would do.

"I have stated on the autopsy report that the underlying cause of death was cancer of the breast of about four years' duration," he said about an autopsy he *did not perform* out of respect for the president, who appointed Dr. Mashburn to his post when governor.

Bill Clinton seemed to command the everlasting loyalty of pathologists who owed their jobs to him. Dr. Fahmi Malak's faithful dedication to Clinton in another matter relating to his mother has already been reported. Mashburn offered an explanation of why he didn't perform the autopsy before coming to a conclusion about the cause of Mrs. Kelley's death:

"We could sit down with a pathology text and guess forever what that was—a pulmonary embolism, pneumonia, congestive heart failure, or stroke."

After receiving the call about his mother's death, Clinton summoned White House Chief-of-Staff Mack McLarty. Lights in the executive mansion burned until dawn. By then, it was decided Vice President Gore would take Clinton's place and deliver a noontime foreign policy address at the University of Wisconsin's Institute of World Affairs.

Shortly before Thursday noon, Clinton, red-eyed and somber, boarded a helicopter on the White House lawn—after Hillary gave him a big hug and rubbed his back in a comforting gesture. He was shuttled to Andrews Air Force Base to have Air Force One fly him to Hot Springs.

Hillary and Chelsea caught a later chartered flight that brought them to Clinton's old hometown in time for Saturday's 9:00 a.m. funeral in the Hot Springs Convention Auditorium and a 1:00 p.m. interment in Rose Hill Cemetery in Hope, where Virginia was raised and gave birth to Bill.

The convention auditorium was selected because the Clinton family's Baptist Church couldn't accommodate the more than 1,000 friends and personages expected to attend the last rites.

In office less than a year, President Clinton on this day, Friday, January 7, 1994, was obliged to make his third journey to Arkansas for a funeral.

The previous spring, he and Hillary went to Little Rock for the last rites conducted for her father, Hugh Rodham, who died after a stroke. Then in mid-summer, they made a sad return to pay their respects to their beloved friend Vincent Foster, Jr.

Today, the first couple were in Arkansas to pray for the repose of Bill's mother, Virginia Kelley's, soul.

28

"I WANT TO BE YOUR PRESIDENT"

Damage Control, Hillary Style

No one was more aware than Hillary Clinton of the land mines that her husband must avoid once he began the road to the White House.

It was now a matter of days before he'd formally announce his candidacy, from the steps of the old statehouse in Little Rock. The date was firmly set in Clinton's mind—October 3, 1991.

From the way the press lit into Gary Hart over his dalliance with Donna Rice, Hillary had every reason to feel uneasy about the going-over reporters from the nation's newspapers and magazines were likely to give Bill once they caught up with the tales of infidelities.

Arkansas newspapers had never paid much attention to them. But once Bill stepped into the national spotlight, Hillary could visualize the headlines about her husband's womanizing that Larry Nichols alluded to in his multi-million dollar federal court suit. That story the *Arkansas Democrat* and *Arkansas Gazette*, the state's largest newspapers, largely let pass.

Hillary drew upon a plan of damage control that became the blueprint for the future whenever the Clinton presidential campaign ran into the snag of potential scandal. She decided to air some of the family's dirty linen.

She hung out the first pieces of laundry at an early fall breakfast in Washington, D.C., a territory Hillary deemed most inappropriate for her husband's presidential campaign headquarters, although it was being promoted as such by many of Clinton's advisers. Hillary demanded to have the show run from Little Rock. She felt comfortable and safe on home turf. The clatter of the many skeletons in Bill's closet were likely to be quieter there than in the nation's capital.

Hillary foresaw no other problem but infidelity to upset Bill's quest. His failure to serve in the military didn't concern her. She had never paid much mind to the draft evasion charges periodically aired by rival candidates.

These stories were inevitably resurrected before every election, then quickly laid to rest until the next. Moreover, Hillary had a misconception about the seriousness of Bill's experience with the selective service issue. She learned the full truth during the *Wall Street Journal* exposé during the presidential campaign. Bill had never leveled with her about his circumventions to stay out of uniform. Hillary knew none of the details.

Those matters were never discussed at home. They were memories locked up in the deepest recesses of Clinton's mind. Or so we have been led to believe. Earlier we heard both Clinton and his mother say they always were able to "put away anything unpleasant" and profess an inability to summon recollections of it. Bill treated the draft issue the same way he handled memories of the suffering he and his mother endured over the years at the hands of his brutalizing stepfather.

He simply never spoke about it!

Although Clinton didn't wish to discuss his infidelities with Hillary either, he was compelled to over, and over. She demanded that he do so. That is, until Hillary realized in psychotherapy—in sessions with a University of Arkansas psychiatrist—that her husband's marital unfaithfulness was an incurable weakness, indeed a disease. From that understanding evolved the "open marriage" compact discussed earlier. Through it all, Hillary appeared to be standing loyally by Bill, always shielding him from the stares of those who would exploit his vulnerability to other women.

So on that fall day in Washington, Hillary took the bull by the horns and pressured Bill to speak candidly on the big question on many people's minds:

Can Bill Clinton survive those stories of adulterous affairs that've been circulating in Arkansas for so many years?

Gary Hart went down after he was caught in just one extramarital indiscretion. How can Bill Clinton weasel out of the mess he's in? How many women has he been accused of bedding down during his marriage? Is it six? Or is a dozen closer?

A recent story in an Arkansas newspaper had alluded to the Clintons' "open marriage." Hillary had wanted to sanitize the air before it became polluted with more allusions to Bill's affairs. But she didn't yet have a reason to go public.

One came along that sent her into immediate action—or reaction. A *USA Today* poll of its readers had found that 39 percent would probably not cast their votes for a candidate who'd been cheating on his wife behind her back; yet a resounding 65 percent would vote for him—"if the wife had been made aware of her husband's infidelity."

Hillary chose a setting made to order for her damage control. It was the National Press Club breakfast, where Clinton had to face some of the biggest guns in Washington's journalistic commune. A membership that includes David Broder, Morton Kondrake, Frank Barnes, Dan Rather, Larry King, Helen Thomas, Ted Koppel, and many other household names.

With Hillary seated beside him at the head table and urging him to speak forthrightly about their marriage, Clinton went to the dais and told the breakfast audience.

"Our marriage has not been perfect...but we have worked hard to stay together...and we're proud of our union.

"We are committed to our marriage and its obligations, to our child and to each other. We love each other very much. Like nearly anybody that's been together twenty years [his marriage to Hillary had just entered its 16th year], our relationship has not been perfect or free of difficulties. But we feel good about where we are. We believe in our obligations and we intend to be together thirty or forty years from now, regardless of whether I run for president or not."

Clinton drew in a deep breath, exhaled, and concluded his statement to a rousing round of applause.

"...And I think that ought to be enough!"

After the breakfast, Hillary hurried for the exits. She had to catch a flight to Little Rock to attend an open house at daughter Chelsea's school. But she couldn't board the plane before encountering reporters at the airport, who asked the inevitable question:

Did she think she herself could be a viable candidate for president?

"That may be," Hillary smiled nervously, "but I'm not the candidate. You know who is the one in this family, so carry the ball to Bill."

The reporters then went after Bill for his view on whether his wife could make a viable candidate for president.

"If she should run," Clinton rasped, seeming uneasy at the question and appearing not to grasp its import, "I would gladly withdraw."

Yet the question evidently registered with significant impact on Clinton, for he was soon to present a new perspective:

"Two for the price of one. Buy one, get one free. If I get elected president, it will be an unprecedented partnership, far more than Franklin Roosevelt and Eleanor.

"They were two great people, but on different tracks. If I get elected, we'll do things together like we always do."

Bill Clinton was speaking like an announced candidate, which he wasn't. But the time when he would be one was not far off.

Meanwhile, it was upstairs to the hotel suite that he and Hillary shared the night before. Now alone, Clinton dialed a familiar number in Little Rock.

Conversation with Gennifer

He wished to speak with Gennifer Flowers. The conversation, fully reported in a later chapter from Flowers' tape recordings, is condensed here to focus on Clinton's announcement for the presidency that follows shortly.

Clinton tells Gennifer that he's in Washington and is tired. He has been traveling a lot on planes. Now he's about to return home. Yes, he's very close to his announcement for the presidency. Gennifer is beside herself with glee.

"I would love to see you go," Gennifer trills. "Oh, I'd love to see you be president. I think that would be wonderful. I think you'd make a—a damn good one. I don't like Bush. I think he's a sneaky bastard [laughs]. He's two-faced. I'd just love to see somebody get in there for a change. Really make a difference. But uh...it's like I told you before. Whatever you need me to do, just let me know."

Clinton responds, "I will."

The exchange continues, with Gennifer speaking first:

"Remember a long time ago when you called me and said that if you announced for...well, it was back the first time you were going to announce for..." (She is referring to 1987 when Clinton backed away from a race against Vice President Bush because he feared the *Arkansas Democrat* would do a Gary Hart number on him.)

Clinton had playfully cut off Gennifer before she was able to complete the sentence with the word *president*.

"Governor," Clinton interjected whimsically.

"No. President," Gennifer responds, laughing [and says something that sounds like "shithead"]. "And you said [sounds like "shit"] 'Gennifer, [I] just wanted you to know that there might be some reporters or something out there [when he was leaving her apartment after a session in the sack]. And you said, 'Now, uh, you be sure to [sounds like "shit 'em," as both laugh] say, 'There's nothing to the rumor.' And I said, okay, I...well I shouldn't even say this to you, probably embarrass you. Do you remember what I said to you?"

Clinton responds, "No. What'd you say?"

"I said," Gennifer returns, laughing hysterically, 'you eat good pussy.'"

"What!" Clinton gasps.

"I said," Gennifer persists, unruffled, "I had to tell them you ate good pussy and you said, 'Well, you can tell them that—if I don't run for president,'" Gennifer bursts into more uncontrollable laughter.

In the morning, Clinton was off to Little Rock. He was ready to let the world know what kind of a president he intended to be.

"If reelected, I will not run for president in 1992."

Running on that pledge, Bill Clinton was resoundingly returned to office by Arkansas. He was not to serve even nine months of his fifth term before he backtracked on his promise.

On October 3, 1991, Governor Clinton strode out of the statehouse and stood on the high-tiered steps before a huge crowd of enthusiastically cheering supporters:

"I am proudly announcing my candidacy for president of the United States of America."

Clinton then launched into a scathing indictment of Republican domestic policies over the past decade as he promised to "restore the American dream for the forgotten middle class."

The governor, now 45 and his hair slightly streaked with gray, offered himself as someone who could "reinvent government," steep it in the values that Americans hold dear, and shape it into a vehicle that would bulldoze the problems plaguing the nation—ills ranging from economic decline to rampant crime.

"I promise an administration that will broaden opportunity for all Americans through better schools, more college scholarship programs, generous tax breaks for the middle class, and a healthier economy."

Clinton stressed that "my style of government will expect more from all Americans—from the welfare recipients who I will want to see seek work, to the corporate executives who will face an angry president if they engage in the excesses of the 1980s."

The candidate, who'd taken the position in recent years that the Democratic Party must recast its message if it is to reclaim the middle class, advocated a more active, problem-solving federal government—but not the stereotypical kind that Democratic presidential aspirants had proposed and which left them open to clobberings by Republican candidates in the past three elections.

"A Clinton administration won't spend your money on programs that don't solve problems and a government that doesn't work," said the candidate, whose run for the presidency was seen by many as validating the Peter Principle, which observes that people tend to rise to the level of their incompetence. After nearly a dozen largely dreadful years of mismanaging Arkansas, he was now bidding to do likewise for all the other 49 states.

"The Republicans have washed their hands of responsibility for the economy, for education, for health care, and for social policy," Clinton said. "Instead of leadership and vision, they offer only neglect and selfishness and division."

Clinton found the perfect setting to expound on the Republicans' record on race relations. In one of those historical ironies that often color southern politics, the ancient statehouse on whose steps he now stood had been the site of two conventions in 1861. Both led to the state's secession from the Union just before the outbreak of the Civil War.

"For twelve years, the Republicans have tried to divide us, race against race," Clinton declared. "Here in the shadow of this great building, all of us know all about race-baiting. They've used that old tool on us for decades now. And I want to tell you one thing: I understand that tactic, and I will not let them get away with it in 1992."

His audience roared its approval, caught up in the excitement of the moment: the first time in history that an Arkansan had tossed his hat into the presidential ring.

He's "Me, Too" on Foreign Policy

Clinton didn't have much to say about foreign policy. He could only tip his hat to George Bush's recent arms control initiatives and say that he, too, would "keep America strong and safe from foreign danger and promote democracy around the world."

Then going to his "strong suit"—his "domestic expertise," as he often referred to it—Clinton argued that America's strength must begin at home, with "the core American dream of education, home ownership, and decent jobs. There is where the nation is now imperiled.

"Middle class people are spending more time on the job, less time with children, and bringing home less money to pay more for health care and housing and education. The poverty rates are up, the streets are meaner, and even more children are growing up in broken families. Our country is headed in the wrong direction, fast. It's falling behind, it's losing its way."

Embracing a staunch, populist theme, Clinton promised to "preserve the American dream, restore the hopes of the forgotten middle class, and reclaim the future for our children."

He wanted to make it clear that "I'm not out to soak the rich. I wouldn't mind being rich myself. But I do believe that rich people should pay their fair share of taxes. For twelve years, while middle-class incomes went down, the Republicans raised taxes on middle class people. And while the incomes of our wealthiest people went up, their taxes were lowered. That's wrong, and the middle class needs a break."

Midway in his discourse, Clinton tried to resist labels pinned on the four Democrats who declared their candidacies before he had. They were Iowa Senator Tom Harkin, a *liberal*; Virginia Governor L. Douglas Wilder, who bordered on the *conservative order of fiscal responsibility and compassion*; former Massachusetts Senator Paul Tsongas, a *pro-business liberal*; and Nebraska Senator J. Robert Kerrey who, like Clinton, had positioned himself as a *future-oriented, fresh-thinking Democrat willing to challenge the establishment*.

(Former California Governor Jerry Brown, a *middle-of-the-road liberal* who'd become a member of the so-called "six pack," had yet to announce his candidacy, but would soon.)

"The change I seek, and the change that we must all seek, isn't liberal or conservative," Clinton emphasized. "It's different and it's both...most Americans care little about such distinctions and simply want policies that work."

Clinton's speech didn't ignore his "deprived" childhood. He closed on the sentimental note that he came from a "poor family" background, but a hopeful one. He spoke of his father's death before he was born and praised the grandparents and great-grandparents he had lived with as a young boy while his mother was away training to be a nurse-anesthetist.

"Its a long way from that," Clinton said softly, almost in a choked voice, "to the children in the streets of our cities who have to worry about being shot going to and from school, who do bullet drills at school, and go home and worry about their parents' drug abuse."

He gazed briefly up at the white pillars reflecting the antebellum architecture of the old South. He was flanked by daughter Chelsea, now approaching 11, and wife Hillary, now 44 to her husband's 45 years.

"I tell you, by making common cause with those children [from the inner-city ghettoes], we give new life to the American dream."

There it was. Bill Clinton was now a presidential candidate. He had disregarded David Matthews' advice to forego a fifth term and instead seek a high-profile job that would give him "a chance to be president of the United States in the late 1990s."

Likewise, he hadn't taken Rudy Moore's counsel not to run for governor because he "couldn't be effective with the legislature."

Bill Clinton had suffered reverses in his dealings with the legislature during his fourth term. He was certain that four more years of playing hardball with the lawmakers could ruin his chances for higher office. Yet he needed the prestige of being an incumbent governor in order to launch his candidacy for president. So, he went after that enabling fifth term giving this assurance to the voters:

"If reelected, I will not run for president in 1992."

After his announcement that he *was* in the race, Bill Clinton was viewed, more than ever, in the light his detractors saw him: he was Slick Willie.

Hillary Also Enters the Race

The Clinton campaign was to be masterminded by the one the newshawks had singled out as a candidate in the unofficial presidential sweepstakes—Hillary Clinton. As soon as the announcement was made, she began rounding up a bunch of hometown pals from Park Ridge to work in the campaign.

"I don't trust those quacks Bill has as his advisers to get him off the ground in this do-or-die drive for the White House," Hillary was overheard to say. "I'm calling in my friends to jiggle the nerve centers that'll elect my Bill to the presidency."

Hillary's friends descended upon Little Rock, got their marching orders, and then spread out over the landscape.

While people like James Carville, George Stephanopoulos, Dee Dee Myers, Betsey Wright, and other advisers carried the Clinton banner into the upcoming presidential primaries, Hillary Clinton led the charge.

She had the first and last word about anything and everything that the candidate was to do. Bill Clinton was the puppet and the head puppeteer was Hillary Clinton.

All eyes were on Hillary, admiring her commanding presence. Reporters were soon asking a familiar question: "Why isn't Hillary running for the office instead of Bill?"

Features were written suggesting Hillary might be her husband's running mate. She was also mentioned as a possible appointment to the cabinet. But Hillary soon popped those trial balloons.

"I'm not interested in attending a lot of funerals around the world," she protested, implying that No. 2 on the ticket, whomever that might be, was bound to have no greater role in Clinton's administration than his predecessors had.

Of course, Hillary could not serve in the cabinet. She was prohibited from holding a high-level appointive position by the Federal Salary Act of 1967. The law was enacted to preclude appointments that smack of nepotism, such as Robert F. Kennedy's designation as attorney general, made by his brother, President John F. Kennedy.

According herself the role of puppeteer in her husband's campaign was to prove providential. For, like the famed Pinocchio, whose nose grew with every lie, Bill would repeatedly encounter the threat of meeting the fate the puppet sustained in the book.

Clinton fortunately had Hillary to prevent that happening to him in "the dirtiest show on earth," as the '92 presidential campaign came to be known.

Hillary's damage control ability was soon to be put to the test.

29

THE PATRICK BUCHANAN FACTOR

"Hey Pat, You're My Kind o' Guy!"

On a cold, clear New Hampshire day, Tuesday, December 10, 1991, Bill Clinton waltzed about in his office in the state capital of temperate-zoned Little Rock before breaking into a jig.

He danced to the accompaniment of vigorous hand clapping.

That's the best news yet!" cried Clinton to Dee Dee Myers, just appointed manager of his campaign.

Others of his staff at this unusual Saturday session applauded lustily.

Just a while before, the news had trickled from Bill Clinton's "third world attaché case," as he called the portable radio/tape recorder on his desk:

"Patrick J. Buchanan sounded a battle cry of 'America First' today, proclaiming 'the administration has failed to promote cultural difference in the country,' and has formally challenged President Bush for the Republican presidential nomination."

The 53-year-old conservative syndicated columnist, television commentator, and lecturer had plunged into the nation's first primary contest:

"When we say we will put America first, we mean also that our Judeo-Christian values are going to be handed down to future generations—not dumped onto some landfill called multi-culturalism."

The former White House aide to Presidents Richard Nixon, Gerald Ford, and Ronald Reagan addressed some 300 reporters and supporters jammed in the lobby of the state legislative office building in Concord.

"I'm entering the race because my friend George Bush, our president, and the Republican Party have deserted the principles of conservatism, the cause to which I belonged since the day I was born."

Bush wasn't heard from. The February 18 New Hampshire primary was still more than two months away.

The New Hampshire primary would be followed by many more tests, but none as meaningful as the Sunbelt contests on Super Tuesday, March 10, to be tailed by the delegate-rich races in the industrial Northeast and Midwest. Then would come the crucial New York vote on April 7 and the closing contests of June 2 in California and New Jersey.

By then, a clear favorite should have emerged in each of the major parties' contests. Then it would be off to the four-day Democratic National Convention in New York's Madison Square Garden, starting July 13, and the Republican Party's big gathering in Houston's Astrodome, opening its four-day session August 17.

The morning after Buchanan's challenge to the incumbent president, Clinton was in the state capital, his bags packed for a flight to Washington, D.C., to take part in the first televised debate for Democratic presidential candidates.

At his desk, the governor thumbed through the *Arkansas Democrat-Gazette* (the *Arkansas Democrat* recently swallowed the *Arkansas Gazette* in a merger), hurled the newspaper aside disdainfully and reached for the *Washington Post*, according to a confidante at that morning's get-together.

"Yeah!" he wheezed. "This is a real newspaper! The goddam *Gazette* story on Buchanan's challenge to Bush doesn't amount to a hill o' beans."

Then Clinton began reading aloud, interrupting every now and then to inject his comments (in bold type to follow):

"'It's time for Washington to face the rising economic power of Japan,' Buchanan said, 'and the rise of a European superstate...' **Hey, this guy's just what the doctor ordered...hear what he's saying:** 'They intend to make the twenty-first century of Europe or Asia...' **Boy, there goes Bush's foreign policy experience advantage down the drain.** 'We must begin to prepare for the new struggle already under way...' **Oh, Pat! You're a dream come true**."

With Buchanan's theme out in the open, "Put America First," Clinton at once felt comfortable that he no longer needed to defend his barren background in foreign affairs. "Except for the little experience he gained at the International House of Pancakes," quipped one critic.

"While Bush and Buchanan slug it over foreign affairs, I can concentrate on domestic policies and beat both their brains in," Clinton exulted as he hurried to catch his plane. He kept one eye on Florida where, on that day, December 15, Democrats were conducting a nonbinding presidential straw poll among the six announced hopefuls to determine which candidates would successfully mobilize party activists for that state's March 10 primary.

An hour or so before an opening primary debate on the NBC network, Clinton received heartening word in his hotel suite in Washington. He had won the Florida straw poll by a wide margin—with 950 votes, or 54 percent—in the first test of strength against his five rivals. Harkin took 31 percent and Kerrey 10 percent, while Tsongas corralled less than 2 percent and Wilder a bit better than 1 percent of the vote. Brown's tally defied calibration—he received just 4 votes of the 1,775 cast.

During the debate that night, moderated by Tom Brokaw, most every candidate managed to grate on his rivals.

Clinton tried to stay above the fray but couldn't keep his voice from rising when he felt compelled to ward off an attack on his proposal for national service.

"I will create a domestic peace corps...not a mandatory program but a way to help the middle class go to college...you will see that people are aching to do this. It is a wonderful idea."

Citing his experience as governor for 12 years—longest-serving in the nation—

Clinton trumpeted further: "I worked on the receiving end of the Reagan-Bush revolution, trying to get and keep good jobs, educate people, serve social problems like health care and energy problems. And I just had to realize that the middle class would keep going downhill, poverty would keep exploding and people would never be what they ought to be unless we had a national strategy to regain our economic leadership."

If anyone found this talk boring, Jerry Brown enlivened the debate when he ignored Tom Brokaw's admonition—not once, but twice!—not to solicit viewers for campaign funds.

Brown asked the audience to call an 800 number to find out where they could donate sums—"nothing over one hundred dollars, please" to his campaign. The former California governor shouted down Brokaw each time he protested, then criticized NBC because "this network's owner, General Electric, gave millions of dollars to political candidates."

His Women Catch up with Bill

In New York, Roger Wood, president and publication director of the *Star*, and his editors gleefully raised their glasses to each other at the vest-pocket-sized horseshoe bar in The Pub, the small watering hole in the Marriott Hotel across the parking lot from the magazine's offices at 666 White Plains Road in Tarrytown.

On that late afternoon of Tuesday, January 21, the last of the copy for the magazine's cover story had cleared the news desk, and next week's January 28 edition was ready for the press. Wood and his editors were celebrating one of their biggest scoops, which carried a stunning headline:

FORMER AIDE CHARGES IN COURT: DEM FRONT-RUNNER HAD AFFAIR WITH MISS AMERICA

The *Star* exclusive's lead paragraph opened with a startling revelation:

"Bill Clinton, the Democrat's leading candidate for the White House, had a hot affair with a former Miss America and at least four other women. These are stunning charges made in a lawsuit against the married Arkansas governor that could scuttle his presidential ambitions."

The balance of the story ran along the precise lines reported in earlier chapters.

The public didn't have to wait until Monday morning, January 27, when the magazine went on sale. The newspapers, as they always do, pirated advance copies the previous Thursday, when editions began rolling off the presses in the *Star*'s five printing plants in the United States and Canada. Friday's papers carried the story, but they didn't go ape over the disclosures after learning that this was a twice-told tale back in Arkansas.

The *Star* had been tipped off about the $3.05 million libel and defamation of character suit against the Arkansas Development Finance Authority by its former marketing manager. Larry Nichols filed his lawsuit October 25, 1990, after he was pink-slipped for sticking his nose in the operation of the ADFA's secret slush fund, which helped Clinton support his lustful lifestyle.

The suit, as reported earlier, was paid scant attention in Arkansas newspapers.

Soon after, interest in Nichols' allegations faded. But the *Star* saw great possibilities in reviving the story. This was no longer a tale of profligacy by the governor of a backwater state but of a candidate seeking the highest office in America.

"My dear boy," Roger Wood told *Star* reporter Steven Edwards, "I am dispatching you to Little Rock to open the biggest can of worms in Bill Clinton's life. In your hands will rest the future course of this presidential race. Go to it, young man!"

A dauntless Scotsman and a recent graduate of Sorbonne University in Paris, Edwards took his instructions from a newspaperman whose nose for news was legendary. For Wood had been editor of the most flourishing publications on either side of the Atlantic. In his native England, he'd been editor of the *London Daily Express*, one of the world's largest circulation newspapers. After Australian media giant Rupert Murdoch brought him to America, Wood presided over the launch of the *Star* as a supermarket tabloid, then took the helm at the *New York Post* and increased its circulation from 400,000 to nearly a million, before returning to the *Star* and giving it a large measure of respectability by converting it to a magazine that is now pushing a 4 million weekly circulation.

But the Clinton people had the idea that the *Star* was still another tabloid newspaper. A trashy one, at that.

"The *Star* says Martians walk on the earth and people have cows' heads," Clinton ridiculed.

Clinton hadn't read such stories in *Star*. The supermarket tabloid *Weekly World News* scooped the magazine on both yarns.

While *Star* was also *scooped* by the daily press on its own exclusive, it was the "finest way to get scooped," as Roger Wood put it. "It should happen to us every week."

That was how it would be over the next few weeks. The *Star* would put together a series of exclusive stories on one of the governor's mistresses, Gennifer Flowers, and would see the story break each time on the Friday before the magazine hit the newsstands the following Monday. But with that advance publicity—the newspapers and electronic media all gave the *Star* credit for the scoop—the editors could rub their hands in glee. Circulation went through the roof each time they were *scooped*— because the *pirates* were restricted by copyright laws from too much copycatting.

The stories in the other publications merely served as the pièce de résistance that drove the masses to their supermarket checkout counters and magazine racks to soak up the whole story from the "trashy tabloid." That characterization was advanced by Clinton and one member of his staff, who dreamed up the idea to cozy up to *Star* newsmaker Steven Edwards down in Little Rock and conjoin him with Gennifer Flowers.

Yes, indeed, it was the Clinton camp that figuratively took Edwards by the nose and delivered him into Gennifer Flowers' welcoming embrace.

Like Water off a Duck's Back

After Friday, January 27's headlines broke with the juicy details of Clinton's extramarital affairs with some of the state's most exotic beauties, there was unease in Clinton's campaign headquarters.

At that time, Clinton was mushing through the New Hampshire snow on his first campaign swing through the state. Evidently the news hadn't reached him yet, for when reporters confronted him with the *Star*'s sensational story, he was visibly shaken. After he regained his composure, Clinton blasted the account as "trash" and an "absolute lie."

For the rest of the day, he looked drawn and edgy and kept repeating "trash" and "absolute lie" every time he was asked about the report.

Meanwhile, campaign aides sought to paint the explosive charges as "political dirty tricks." They contended that the Republican National Committee was "trying to promote those rumors" as it purportedly had the "Willie Horton" story during the 1988 presidential campaign that heavily damaged Michael Dukakis's challenge to George Bush.

To lessen the sting of the scandal, one of Clinton's campaign lawyers distributed an affidavit on the Friday the story broke. It was a sworn statement signed by the lawsuit plaintiff, Larry Nichols, retracting the allegation that Clinton staffer Susie Whiteacre had an affair with her boss, the governor.

Curiously, the lawyer who distributed that affidavit to the media didn't explain why he waited until the evening that the *Star*'s story reached the nation's newsdesks to obtain the affidavit from Nichols. More than a year had gone by since the suit was filed, with Ms. Whiteacre's name prominently listed in the papers that carried stories of the suit.

More curious was Clinton's seemingly swift recovery from the firestorm of media reports on his affairs. For just an hour after the stories broke, he was able to appear smiling before the cameras of WMUR-TV, an ABC affiliate in Manchester.

When the evening news reporter asked him, "Governor, did you ever have an extramarital affair?" the smile remained frozen on his lips:

"If I had, I wouldn't tell you!"

The response reminded viewers of Gary Hart's answer when asked by the *Washington Post*, and again by the *Boston Globe*, whether he had ever committed adultery.

"I don't have to answer that question," he stammered. And a few days later—after he was caught again in Donna Rice's company sailing off to Bimini—he was dead meat in the Democratic presidential primary race.

In Clinton's case, the flap that erupted a month before New Hampshire's primary, at a time when he had risen in the polls to top the Democratic pack, would damage his standing—but not fatally. He would survive this scandal—and others that would dog him all the way to the Democratic National Convention.

The *Star*'s story was followed by another volley from Little Rock, fired by the recently elected co-chairman of the Arkansas Republican State Committee, Sheffield Nelson, who ran against Clinton in the 1990 election for governor.

"Clinton has never answered the charges about his affairs with women," Nelson protested. "Wouldn't a simple yes or no answer it?"

Had he answered *yes*, he'd have destroyed the image Hillary was trying to fashion for him: a clean-cut, wholesome, family man. A *no* would brand him a liar because, if the public was not yet convinced of Clinton's many dalliances, they soon would be—when Gennifer Flowers went public.

30

THE HOKUM BEHIND GENNIFER'S TALE

Steering Gennifer to the *Star*

Weeks before *Star* magazine tarbrushed Bill Clinton with Larry Nichols' story, the people around the candidate were having fits. They heard rumors that Gennifer Flowers was about to blab about her 12-year affair with the most promising of the five Democratic Party aspirants to the presidency.

Two factors spurred that rumor about Gennifer Flowers. Make that two rumors *galvanized* that pair of factors.

Both stemmed from the two people closest to the nightclub singer: Her best friend and former roommate, Lauren Kirk, the Dallas real estate agent/interior designer, and Gennifer's mother Mrs. Mary Hirst.

Though living miles apart, what these women were saying entered the pipeline to the governor's office in Little Rock and burned his campaign aides' ears.

"I've tried to tell Gennifer for years that she should come out with the story, but she didn't want to wreck his career...but now I think she's prepared to go public."

That was what Lauren Kirk is purported to have been overheard saying. Gennifer's mother was likewise heard to remark, "Gennifer was always evasive with me when I asked questions about Bill Clinton...but no longer. She confided in me that she was going to talk to a magazine."

Which magazine?

Gennifer wasn't certain which way to go with her story. But while she was undecided, Bill Clinton's people, looking out for his best interests, selected the *Star*. Here's the story behind that story.

Just after the first of the year (1992), Christopher Bell, a reporter in Huntsville, Alabama, who freelances for *Star*, tipped off the news desk about Larry Nichols' long-dormant federal suit against the Arkansas Development Finance Authority. Bell was assigned at once to pore through the federal district court records in Little Rock and do a story for the magazine.

Word got back to Clinton's camp that someone was "messin' around with that Nichols stuff." The governor's people were furious. But then they developed enough information from the underground finally to tell them the *Star* was doing the story. They breathed a collective sigh of relief.

"Who the hell pays mind to what that trashy supermarket tabloid prints!" Dee Dee Myers is known to have said. "Let them run it...we'll tell them that it's all garbage."

And that's precisely the way it developed.

Confident that Nichols' story would not go far, a staff member on Clinton's campaign team, aware that Gennifer planned to tell her story to a magazine, offered a way to get maximum damage control out of this far more explosive situation.

"Hey, let's tip off the *Star* that Gennifer wants to sell her story," said this top strategist. "If that supermarket rag bites and gets her to sing, the story'll *implode*. Nobody will believe it if it appears in that sleazy tabloid."

The first story trolled from the Nichols' court files by Chris Bell and published in the *Star*'s January 28 edition, fell on its face. No sooner did the dailies run the story on the 24th, than Clinton's campaign team pooh-poohed the allegations of womanizing as the fabrications of a disgruntled former state employee.

Clinton's press secretary, Mike Gauldin, told the *Washington Post* that Nichols was merely looking to make a fast buck out of his suit. He had no intention of letting it go the distance. Gauldin claimed that Nichols phoned him and asked that they meet at a highway truck rest. There, Gauldin claimed, Nichols offered to drop the suit for a house and $150,000.

Then Clinton trashed Nichols as a head case.

"It's a totally bogus lawsuit," said the governor during his swing in New Hampshire's primary campaign. "This guy was fired for making illegal phone calls and tried to bribe me into giving him money, and I just wouldn't do it."

Nevertheless, mainstream reporters had a job to do, so they prodded the governor persistently. Did he sleep with those women, they wanted to know? And, as already cited, his wise-guyish cracks, "If I had, I wouldn't tell you," kept him on his feet.

Not a denial. Nor the response one might expect to hear from a presidential candidate who'd just begun airing TV commercials proclaiming him to be Mr. Clean, *an antiseptic and wholesome family man.*

Yet Clinton's noncommittal stance left him a survivor. The story died quickly, and when the *Star* hit the newsstands the following Monday, it seemed only supermarket customers on line at checkout counters were cackling about Clinton's womanizing.

The time between Friday, January 24, and the following Monday, January 27, when the *Star* went on sale, the Clinton think tank shifted into high gear in its endeavor to sell Gennifer on the idea of taking her story to the *Star*. But how could that be arranged without implicating Bill Clinton?

A $100,000 Publishing Tour de Force

Star reporter Steve Edwards' arrival in Little Rock solved that problem. No sooner had he entered the Flaming Arrow Club, where Gennifer was doing her singing, and asked the bartender, "Do you know Gennifer Flowers?" than Edwards was pointed towards John Hudges, seated at a table nearby.

The bartender had been directed by the bar's owner, a friend of Clinton, to "help that reporter if he asks about Gennifer Flowers."

Hudges was state GOP chieftain Sheffield Nelson's press secretary. He also once worked at Little Rock television station KARK, where Gennifer reported the news in a beat that led to her first encounter with then-State Attorney General Bill Clinton.

"Certainly, I know Gennifer," Hudges retorted. "We're friends."

When Hudges learned who Edwards was and that the *Star* was looking to score with Gennifer's story, that scenario seemed heaven-sent.

That's precisely how Gennifer Flowers and *Star* magazine were mated.

Edwards performed the rite. The clincher was a $100,000 dowry that no self-respecting paramour could refuse—especially after her experience standing in unemployment lines.

Although Gennifer was working in a $17,000-a-year state job that Bill Clinton pulled strings to get for her, she was being buffeted by the fallout over the job she was hired to perform and was convinced she would soon be pink-slipped.

Although she was still singing at the Flaming Arrow on and off, there was no guarantee she'd work steady. After her name surfaced in passing in the *Star*'s first story, the nightclub's manager told Gennifer that if the notoriety surrounding her didn't subside, she could go elsewhere.

What other choice did Gennifer have than to tell Edwards, "My dear boy, I will fly with you to New York just as soon as I pack a suitcase"?

As Gennifer dashed off to her apartment to prepare for the trip, Edwards stayed behind at the Flaming Arrow.

"'My dear boy,'" he mused, smiling at Gennifer's use of his editor's favorite expression. "I think she'll get along just jim-dandy with Roger Wood. They speak the same language."

While we wait for Gennifer to return so we can accompany her to *Star* territory, let's backtrack to the hush-hush piece of work Bill Clinton pulled to get his sweetie a job with the state of Arkansas.

That previously unheralded scandal began September 4, 1990, shortly after Gennifer had ended her 12-year role as Bill Clinton's mistress. The end came without acrimony, just an understanding that the affair was all over.

It all started with a phone call. And if you suspect an element of blackmail at Gennifer's end of the line, you won't be the first.

"Sit Tight, I'll Get You a Job"

"Any chance of a job?"

Gennifer Flowers was desperate on that Tuesday, the day after Labor Day. She was singing at the Flaming Arrow, but her engagement wasn't putting bread on the table.

"I need some daytime work, Bill," she said. Can you get me a job with the state?"

"Sit tight, my love, I'll look into it right away," he responded.

A few days passed. "Gennifer," the voice came over the phone to his old paramour's Quapaw Towers apartment, "do you have a pencil? Write this down."

The name was that of Judy Gaddy, one of the governor's special assistants.

"She'll fix you up," Clinton assured Gennifer.

On September 11 the phone rang.

"I'm leaving a state employment application for you with the guard at the capitol building," Judy Gaddy told Gennifer Flowers. "Fill it out and return it to me in the governor's office. I'll look it over and make certain it's worded properly."

The application was for a position as "Multi-Media Specialist" with the Arkansas Heritage Department.

After a few weeks Gennifer wondered whether she'd ever hear from the governor's aide.

Her patience was rewarded. Gennifer was summoned for an interview at heritage for an opening in the Arkansas Historic Preservation Program. Because she hadn't listed experience she could not truthfully claim in public relations and with computers, she wasn't hired.

Next day, Friday, February 23, 1991, Gennifer dashed off an angry letter to Bill Clinton. In it she came close to playing the badger game. Since she hadn't found work with the state, she felt she had no alternative but to file a lawsuit against a Little Rock radio station for having aired a report linking her and the governor romantically. The source of that story was Larry Nichols, who'd filed his multi-million dollar lawsuit against Clinton and the state, and had revealed the identities of the several Arkansas beauties he said the governor wooed with taxpayer dollars.

Gennifer followed up the letter with a phone call.

"Bill!" she exclaimed, "I'm furious. I didn't get the job and I can't understand why it went to someone else. What are you gonna do about it?"

"I'm pissed, too" he responded. "Don't worry...I'll stay on top of it from now on."

Whether Clinton suspected Gennifer's language had a peal of blackmail isn't known. But the letter, followed by the phone call, certainly brought results.

****

Don K. Barnes, chairman of the Arkansas Board of Review, faced what seemed a routine challenge in his department. Veteran unit supervisor Clara Clark was in line for a promotion, but budgetary problems were holding up her advancement.

Yet a game plan to play musical chairs in that office was in place. When Mrs. Clark moved up, her position would be filled by Charlette Perry, a longtime secretary, who was black. Her job, in turn, would be taken by an eligible applicant from the official hiring list of the state of Arkansas, an *equal opportunity employer*.

But because the "fix" was in by now, the order of hire was about to be shuffled, despite the fact that Barnes had received clearance for the promotions from Bill Gaddy, director of the Employment Security Division, who had administrative control over the Board of Review, or the Arkansas Appeal Tribunal as it's also called.

The last thing Barnes expected after he'd worked out the plan with his superior was to hear from Gaddy's wife, Judy, the governor's administrative assistant who, at Clinton's direction, tried, but failed, to place Gennifer Flowers with the Arkansas

Heritage Department.

"I have someone Bill Clinton wants to see given work," she told Barnes. "Can I send her to you?"

"Put her through the state merit testing system first and we'll see how she shapes up," Barnes responded. He was not happy with the pressure from the governor's office—but it wasn't the first time he'd had to contend with power politics from that quarter.

On March 21, Gennifer filled out an application for the merit system on which she listed "Administrative Assistant II"—a classification that more than qualified her for Clara Clark's position of "Unit Supervisor II."

Some chicanery figures in the shaping of that application before it was submitted to Board of Review chairman Don Barnes.

The application Gennifer completed that day wasn't the first she filled out. A few days earlier she'd been told about the opening with the Board of Review and was handed a state application by Mrs. Gaddy, who also had a heart-to-heart talk with the governor's former pillow mate.

"Because of your close relationship with this office," Gennifer was told, "we have to be careful to do things in a proper manner so no awkward questions arise."

Mrs. Gaddy went out of her way to assist Gennifer in filling out the application.

"No," the governor's aide admonished when Gennifer stretched her brief employment experience at KARK-TV to a two-year job, from 1976 to 1978. "You don't do that."

Mrs. Gaddy told her that office experience counted, not the work she performed for the TV station, which was reporting.

"The more office experience it looks like you've had, the better," Gennifer was told. She was handed another application and a copy of the job qualifications for Administrative Assistant II that was open at the Board of Review.

"Word it properly," Mrs. Gaddy instructed. "Then return the application to me."

Gennifer was not above altering the shape of facts after the many hints she received not to shortchange herself when describing her qualifications for employment.

She switched her job title from "Membership Director," the position she claimed she once held with the Dallas-based Club Corporation of America, and made it "Director of Public Affairs." That conformed to the qualifications required for the Administrative Assistant II position she was now applying for.

Jazzing up Her Application

Gennifer jazzed up the application by claiming experience not only in public relations, but also in computer usage as well. Neither of those workplace skills had been listed in her first employment form. Because, in fact, she had no such skills.

When Gennifer handed in the revamped application on March 21, she was told there was no immediate opening for Administrative Assistant II. Yet a number of administration officials, from the governor on down, knew a spot was about to open for Unit Supervisor II, just as soon as the budget bugaboo was squared away.

Gennifer added public relations and computers to her experience because her sporadic office experience, as a matter of record—and by her own admission—amounted to less than three years. She didn't remotely qualify for the job she applied for—unless the fix was in.

If anyone doubts that Clinton pulled strings to get Gennifer Flowers placed on the state payroll at $17,520 a year, those doubts should evaporate after this evidence:

Don Barnes received the initial phone call from Judy Gaddy commanding him to find a job for Gennifer at the appeals tribunal. The order came straight from the governor.

Obviously, Mrs. Gaddy already knew about the vacancy, most likely having learned about it from her husband, Bill, the tribunal's overseer.

Gaddy insisted he never told his wife about any vacancies. Yet he admitted he was aware as long ago as 1990 that Gennifer was looking for a state job.

To get her that patronage post mandated deception at the Arkansas Board of Review. Barnes had to override departmental policy and allow outside applicants in addition to those already employed by the department—staffers such as Charlette Perry, who led the office crew as the most qualified to step into Mrs. Clark's shoes.

Only after the appeal tribunal's eligibles were eliminated could Barnes turn his search to "outsiders" to fill the new post. That's the way the rules say it should be. But in Bill Clinton's administration, the game is played by the standards he set to suit himself.

Just days after she'd filed her application, Gennifer was summoned for the interview in Barnes' office. Present also was Randy Wright, the appeal agency's chief referee. She left the meeting without a commitment that the job was hers.

This prompted Gennifer to phone Bill Clinton at the governor's mansion and whisper, "This job'll be fine. I just want to make sure the same thing won't happen again—that it'll be given to someone else."

"No problem," Clinton shot back. "I talked to Barnes. It's a done deal."

Thus Gennifer got her foot in the door at the Board of Review. And on June 11, she sashayed all the way inside the appeal tribunal's office, her richly endowed body still svelte after a dozen years of strenuous bedroom sports with Bill Clinton.

That era, just a memory now, nevertheless was providing a meal ticket for Gennifer Flowers in her first day on the job as an Administrative Assistant II.

Though that's not the same job as Unit Supervisor II, the position Charlette Perry expected to fill after Clara Clark's promotion, it didn't matter to her that Gennifer Flowers entered the Board of Review work force in the newly created post of Administrative Assistant II. Mrs. Perry saw through the charade.

"The governor's people kicked a supervisor upstairs, denied promotion to the employee recommended to take her place, and they re-classified the job so it could go to an outsider," she protested.

On the day when Gennifer Flowers reported to work at the appeals board, Charlette Perry filed her complaint with the State Grievance Review Committee, made up of state employees enlisted from the various government departments.

Mrs. Perry contended that state officials changed the title of the job and attached unnecessary special duties in an obvious move to exclude qualified candidates in favor of Gennifer Flowers.

More Lies to Cover the Gov's Fix

No one could blame Bill Clinton for squirming during the hearings that opened October 9, 1991—just six days after announcing his candidacy for the presidency. Clinton dreaded the fireworks, for he'd been in touch with Gennifer Flowers and what she told him wasn't good.

"From day one when I started working at the tribunal, Charlette Perry wouldn't speak to me. She just can't be placated," Gennifer told Clinton.

"Clara [Clark], who stayed on a few weeks to teach Gennifer the ropes before going to her new job] is trying to explain to her that it isn't my fault she wasn't promoted, but Charlette just turns a deaf ear to her."

Judy Gaddy had informed Gennifer that Mrs. Perry filed a grievance, but that didn't seem to matter—until she received a summons from the review committee to give sworn testimony as a witness at their hearing.

"Bill! Bill!" Gennifer cried into the phone in panic. "They want me to testify *under oath*. They're investigating."

"Don't worry," Clinton consoled her. "Don will take care of it. I'll run it down."

At the hearing, Gennifer was a frightened calf when called to testify with her hand on the Bible.

"I loved Bill Clinton, but I wasn't going to jail for him," Gennifer later told the *Star*. "He told me to deny that we were lovers to protect his political career.

"But I wasn't going to stand in front of a grievance board under oath and lie for him. No way I'm going to jail for perjury."

At the hearing, Gennifer did her best to weasel out of the spot she was in. But she didn't succeed.

Preceding her to the witness chair were Don Barnes and Randall Wright, the appeals tribunal's head. They testified that Gennifer had scored ninth among 11 candidates who took the phony merit test given to camouflage what already was a fait accompli—nevertheless, they maintained she was still better qualified for the job with the appeals tribunal because of her experience in public relations and computers.

A memo Wright prepared for the grievance committee also gave Gennifer the edge over inside candidates.

But Gennifer proved to be her own worst enemy.

Although Barnes had testified that Gennifer had satisfactorily detailed her familiarity with various computer systems during her interview, Gennifer, in her own testimony was unable to name any computer on which she'd worked, other than a Lanier word processor she had used as a reporter at the television station.

She didn't help her defense when she lied and said that 80 percent of her job entailed "supervision" over a dozen secretaries who process appeals for unemployment benefits—then testified that another of her duties in the office was answering phone calls from the public, hardly a supervisory function.

When *Newsday* staff correspondents chased down the story and interviewed Barnes, he told them a key recommendation for Gennifer Flowers came from Bill Gaddy.

He had allegedly worked with her for six months in 1972 at the State Department of Finance and Administration. But Gaddy denied ever giving Flowers any such reference.

The Next President Lies, Too!

Gennifer's own discrepancies were glaring.

In her March 21 job application, she listed herself as Director of Public Relations for Club Corporation of America from 1982 to 1984. Yet in the earlier job form submitted to the Arkansas Heritage Department, she claimed she was Membership Director for the Dallas firm. Nor did she post any computer experience in that application as she had in the later one.

In both applications she stated that she had an associate degree from the University of Arkansas.

But the school had no record that such a degree was conferred on Gennifer Flowers.

Barnes assured the committee during the hearing that he and others at the Board of Review checked Gennifer's qualifications and references. Later, however, he told *Newsday* he couldn't explain why discrepancies about her past hadn't been discovered earlier.

A partial answer was provided by Shirley Thomas, an assistant director at the State Health and Human Services Department, who sat on a special committee that investigated the hiring of Gennifer Flowers in 1990.

"There was some misrepresentation of qualifications, and verification of those qualifications was not done to my satisfaction," she stated bluntly.

"There was favoritism. It was a very serious infraction. There certainly was not an adherence to state procedures."

At the hearing, Gennifer never breathed a word about the help from Judy Gaddy and others that had landed her the job. Asked under oath how she heard about the position, she testified, "It was advertised in the newspaper and I had heard through the [state] personnel department."

Barnes, present in the hearing room when Gennifer testified, didn't offer to contradict her even though, as he told *Newsday*'s Timothy Clifford and Shirley Perlman, her responses "didn't click."

Only much later, when the hearing was history, did he admit that Gennifer's testimony constituted "perjury."

Clinton's own involvement in the duplicity and lies is incontrovertible. All of the quotes attributed to the president were taken from Gennifer Flowers' telephone tapes she made in conversations with him. The voice, unmistakably, is Clinton's.

When she described her appearance before the committee and told Clinton that she wasn't prepared for the question about how she learned about the job, she told Clinton her response was that she heard about it from "personnel." At which point, Clinton complimented her: "Good for you!"

Gennifer Flowers and Bill Clinton could celebrate, even though the grievance committee's ruling went against Gennifer and in favor of Mrs. Perry:

"In the case at hand, the agency was unable to convince the committee of any overriding need for an employee skilled in 'public relations' and computer operations to the extent that the maxim of internal hire should be breached...emphasis upon the 'public relations' aspect of the job was excessive and beyond that necessary for an administrative assistant."

The committee recommended that Charlette Perry be awarded back pay and promoted to a position with comparable pay. But the committee's rulings weren't binding—and Don Barnes brazenly rejected them, citing "prior disciplinary issues" with Mrs. Perry.

Bill Clinton didn't have to call in Dr. Fahmi Malak to perform the cover-up like he performed for the governor's mother. He kept Gennifer Flowers in the job, wasting thousands of dollars of Arkansas taxpayers' money for the needless exercises just chronicled.

However, January 29—just before the *Star*'s story broke on Clinton's 12-year affair with Gennifer—the roof fell in on her. Declared AWOL after a three-day absence, she was fired.

Gennifer couldn't attend to her duties at the Arkansas Board of Review because she was in Tarrytown giving the *Star* the poop that almost—but not quite—tripped up Bill Clinton's march to the White House.

Gennifer's Aria Breaks Crystal

Political mavens were split on whether Larry Nichols' allegations of hanky-panky in the January 28 *Star* would hurt or help the candidate.

"Obviously it's going to hurt him," said New York political analyst Martin McLaughlin. "There's a segment of the population that doesn't want to worry about an adulterer in the White House—and I suspect it might be his segment in the Bible Belt."

Democratic media expert Bob Squier took the position that what looked like a mess early on could actually benefit Clinton in the long run.

"This gives him an opportunity to get something which has been burbling around underneath his campaign up to the surface—and to deny it," suggested Squier.

Still, Bill Clinton didn't flat out deny he had affairs with the women the magazine identified.

Nevertheless, the subject quickly evaporated from the front pages. Clinton once again seemed free to resume his role as "Mr. Clean."

But then the next *Star* ran Gennifer Flowers' own, first-person story in its February 4 edition, a story cannibalized by the dailies and blasted on their front pages on January 31.

The *Star* carried that story, after the by now *forty-something* nightclub entertainer sang her aria for Steve Edwards and colleagues Lisa Arcella and Marion Collins while closeted in a plush suite at the Tarrytown Marriott Hotel.

The story opened by highlighting these damning points about the romance while it simmered over a dozen years:

"Clinton cheated on his wife Hillary with Gennifer from 1977 until 1989, sometimes meeting her for sex several times a week.

"Told her he loved her—and called her 'Pookie.'

"Jogged from the governor's mansion to her apartment for sex—which was often so passionate that she kidded him he wouldn't have the energy to run home.

"Cried when Gennifer told him their affair was finally over."

Presented with the charges, Clinton vehemently denied that he was a womanizer and denounced as "trash" Gennifer's claim that he slept with her for a dozen years. He took refuge in what he called his three most important virtues: "integrity, family, and service." Yet this seemed a strikingly inadequate response for Gennifer's racy details.

"Sometimes Bill would jog the couple of miles from the mansion," to her apartment in the Quapaw Towers, then later to another condo not far from the governor's mansion.

For a dozen years, their Vesuvian romance flourished and set every bone to shuddering and flesh curling with intimations that the unholy bedlock would last forever.

They did it in every available venue, from Gennifer's condominium boudoirs to a medley of hotel rooms, and almost carried their coupling into the men's room of the governor's mansion, while Hillary prowled nearby corridors, coiled and ready to strike and catch them *en flagrante delicto* in the john.

Their romance crossed city, county, and state lines. It endured lengthy separations that pained them both so much at times that they couldn't last another moment apart from each other.

All the while, Gennifer knew that Bill would never divorce Hillary to marry her—no more than Bobby Kennedy would have divorced Ethel for Marilyn Monroe, or JFK would have dumped Jackie for the likes of Mafia call girl Judith Imoor Campbell Exner or Angie Dickinson.

Gennifer resignedly accepted the fact that Bill'd never leave Hillary for a working girl like her. In accepting what had to be, she recited a timeworn litany to justify being the "other woman":

"Thirty minutes of wonderful was better than a lifetime of so-so."

For Gennifer Flowers comforted herself in the belief that her lover was her very own hunk—and that she was his one and only outside the conjugal bed.

"He told me he had the best sex with me. He didn't talk much about his wife and I rarely asked him about her. I didn't want those precious hours spent with me talking about her.

"I thought I was giving him something he wasn't getting at home."

Bill Says, "Just Keep Denying It

She believed it would continue forever. But Gennifer Flowers never figured that her man could be the sort of sleazebag he was all at once made out to be by Larry Nichols, after his lawsuit made the headlines.

Was it possible, she asked herself—that what "her" Bill had been doing to her, he had also been doing all along to former Miss America Elizabeth Ward, to former Miss

Arkansas Lencola Sullivan, to *Arkansas Gazette* reporter Deborah Mathis, to his press secretary, Susie Whiteacre, and to yet another woman on his staff, whom he even made pregnant?

"When I heard the rumors that Bill had been with other women, I was devastated. I didn't believe it. He'd always told me I was the only one, and I believed him. Not once did he ever hint he was seeing someone else. He called me and insisted there wasn't a shred of truth in the allegations. He just laughed about it. He said, 'One fella told me I had good taste.'

"I pressed him. 'What about these girls, Bill? Why are they on the list? I know who they all are. Is any of it true? Tell me, please.'

"He adamantly denied everything. 'It's a pack of lies,' he said. 'I told you a couple of years ago, one time when I came to see you, that I'd retired (from having sex with other women)—and now I'm glad I have, because they've scoured the waterfront. I have talked to Elizabeth Ward maybe three times in my whole life...I don't know how she made the grade. At least Lencola Sullivan is a friend of mine. I've never slept with her, but she does come to see me...so I can see why [she was named].'

"When I started work as a news reporter with KARK-TV in Little Rock in 1977 I knew very little about the business. Only one person at the station was helpful to me, another reporter, Deborah Mathis. In 1986, Bill casually asked one day if I had been in contact with her. 'I wouldn't tell her anything,' he advised.

"After the Nichols suit was filed, I called Deborah. 'It's garbage,' she said forcefully. I don't know whether they ever had anything going between them.

"Since these other women were named, my world has turned upside down. My mother was so angry when she found out, and I'm so tired of hearing about what a dummy I was to stick by him.

"I guess deep in my heart I hoped he'd marry me one day. I used to have this fantasy: If Bill got into the White House and was a great president, then maybe nobody would care if he was divorced.

"I wanted to believe so badly that what I shared with Bill was different, special...but I just don't know anymore.

"And Bill, he thinks he can get away with it.

"All he has to do, he says, is to keep on denying everything."

THE PETAL IS OFF THE FLOWER(S)

Shaking up the Staid Waldorf

The dark glasses came off and she faced the world from a lectern at the Waldorf-Astoria Hotel just after her proclamations of relations with Bill Clinton were aired in the *Star*. No one could foretell what was in store for the historic and stately inn on New York's glamorous Park Avenue. Gennifer Flowers had hooked a tape recorder to her phone in early December 1990 and kept it on until early January 1992—long enough to gather the proof that detached Clinton from his pious pose as an honorable married man to the polar opposite.

A banquet room at the posh Park Avenue retreat was jam-packed with press people as Gennifer was introduced. Press kits, containing an 11-page, typewritten transcript with "extracts from telephone conversations between Governor Bill Clinton and Ms. Gennifer Flowers," were distributed.

Following the preliminaries, the session got down to the nitty-gritty of why the *Star* had arranged the live media event:

To play the most significant portions of the tapes Bill Clinton's paramour had made of her conversations with the governor between December 1990 and January 1992.

****

Early on in a conversation Gennifer recorded with him, Clinton sounds greatly concerned about the muck Larry Nichols stirred with his suit for damages. So he counsels Gennifer on ways to respond to reporters if they question her.

"If they ever hit you with it, just say no and go," Clinton advises in a conversation of September 23, 1991. "There's nothing they can do. I expected them [the press] to look into it and come interview you. But if everybody is on record denying it...no problem."

In his naiveté, Clinton goes on to "comfort" Gennifer:

"If no one says anything, then they [reporters] don't have anything...they don't have pictures."

"Gennifer is no chucklehead," the author was assured by one of her closest chums. "I'm not making any promises, but you just wait and see if Genny doesn't spring a video on the guv showing him in the sack with her."

Is that a promise?

"All I say is, you aren't dealing here with a ninny. Gennifer's got the smarts. She prepared for the fall Bill let her in for after he denied he had that 12-year fling and called her 'trash.'

"I'm sure she's more'n likely taken very good care of Number One. I think the audio is only her first volley. The best is yet to come."

Bill Clinton may not be home free after all from dreaded *full exposure* by Gennifer Flowers. For on May 25, 1994, even as the Paula Jones controversy raged, the president's old flame emerged from the shadows and made a startling appearance at a New York hotel.

And with a toll-free 800 number to place orders, Gennifer offered her audience a titillating audio cassette package: Not merely the 10 minutes of her conversations with Bill Clinton cited in the *Star*'s exposé, but a 60-minute exchange, along with a complete transcript of the dialogue.

Additionally, she let on that she had a letter from Bill (contents not divulged), which she claimed would put the lie, absolutely, to Clinton's denials that he ever had an affair with Gennifer.

Gennifer said she audiotaped the phone conversations with her longtime lover because friends warned her she'd have to protect her own skin should a scandal brew. She became concerned after reporters approached her with questions that "sounded scary." That concern is never more evident than in a conversation recorded in September 1991, just before Clinton announced for the presidency.

Gennifer informs the governor that reporters are trying to find out about their relationship. She's afraid and unsure of how to handle the situation.

"I hate to put you in harm's way," rasps Clinton, who then asks Gennifer to inform him whenever she's approached.

"I want to know every time...it enables me to run traffic and see what else is going on. Call me here, at the mansion."

When the conversation turns to Larry Nichols' lawsuit and the other women he's been linked to, Clinton denies he slept with anyone else. That prompts Gennifer to quip, "Well, I can't speak for any of the others, but I can tell you there's no one who eats a muff better than you."

Clinton chuckles at that reference to the high rating ascribed to his proficiency in oral sex, then discusses an Associated Press newsman's approach on the subject of his sexcapades.

"When Bill Simmons read that list to me [the six women alluded to by Larry Nichols], I said, 'God, Bill, I kind of hate to deny that.'"

Gennifer comes back with a laugh:

"You know what I said to myself [when she read the list that was made public after the lawsuit was filed in court]. 'Well, at least he's an equal opportunity lover.'"

That was a reference to Lencola Sullivan, an African American and one of the beauties Clinton wooed. She was Miss Arkansas of 1981 and fourth runner-up in that year's Miss America Pageant.

Clinton then informs Gennifer that her name made the list because a doorman at the Quapaw Tower apartments spotted him sneaking in.

"That scumbag spread that all over town," snorts Clinton.

The conversation ends after Clinton says he wants to help Gennifer and expects her to continue calling him with any news.

"I really want to talk to you," he purrs in a seductive whisper. "I really want to see you. I'm sorry you got involved in this."

Gennifer's Pink Slip's Showing

A few weeks go by and Gennifer buzzes her old beau on October 17—14 days after he's become a presidential candidate—to report that she was fired from the nightclub, the Flaming Arrow, because of the bad publicity over her involvement with Clinton.

"That's Republican harassment trying to break you and me," Clinton responds, annoyed. He says he'll use his muscle on the club owner to get her job back.

On December 11, 1991, Clinton phones and learns from a greatly shaken Gennifer that someone has broken into her apartment and gone through her things, probably looking for something that links her to Clinton.

A stunned Clinton asks tremulously, "Are you missing any personal papers or anything…a checkbook or phone records?"

In an agitated voice, Gennifer snaps, "No, why would I? You usually call me."

After both calm down, they talk at length about the presidential campaign. He tells her that the Republicans believe he's the only Democrat with a chance to beat President Bush.

The conversation then drifts to Gennifer's Tai Kwan Do lessons.

"Is it keeping you in shape?" he wants to know about the oriental self-defense program Gennifer is enrolled in.

"It's toned my little butt up so good," she laughs. "I love it."

After more banter, Clinton tells Gennifer to call him back after 11:00 p.m. at home—the governor's mansion.

Nothing like a nice tête-à-tête with an old girlfriend before hitting the sack beside Hillary.

****

In none of Gennifer Flowers' audiotapes of her conversations does Clinton sound more *presidential* than when he expresses concern that the scandal swirling around them could cause him to lose the nomination to handsome Nebraska Governor Bob Kerrey, a war hero who lost part of a leg in the Vietnam War.

"He's single, won the Medal of Honor, and looks like a movie star," grunts the governor enviously. "Because he's single, nobody cares who he's screwing."

On January 16, 1992, a dozen days before *Star* broke the first story of his involvement with her, Bill Clinton left two messages on Gennifer Flowers' answering machine to phone him.

She did not return the calls.

She was through talking with Bill Clinton.

All further talking would be done in Tarrytown.

And the tapes, which were authenticated by computer-certified tests conducted by Truth Verification Laboratories in White Plains, just down the pike from Tarrytown, would do most of that talking for Gennifer.

Here, courtesy of Roger Wood, president and editorial director of *Star*, is a verbatim transcript of excerpts from the conversations between Bill Clinton and Gennifer Flowers. Though the telephone taps ranged over the period between December 1990 and January 1992, the most significant dialogue was recorded between September and December 1991.

FLOWERS: Are you there? Sorry about that. Mother was...wanted me to get her a glass of water. See that was another thing. See, my parents are here, and I'll tell you what, the last thing I needed was to...

CLINTON: Have that happen...

FLOWERS: ...have that happen 'cause my mother would get very concerned and worried and so far, you know...

CLINTON: If they ever hit you with it just say "no" and go on. There's nothing they can do.

FLOWERS: Well, I will. But I mean, I...you know...she's my mother and you know how mothers can be.

CLINTON: They don't want to hear it at all.

FLOWERS: Well, she would just get all in a tizzy about...about it and, uh, so I thought, "Good God, that's all I need." Cause they [a reporter and a crew from TV's magazine exposé show "A Current Affair"] met me in the parking lot at the Quapaw Towers. I was going in to sing [at the Flaming Arrow nightclub] I didn't say anything. I just went in the door and...uh...he tried to come in one time and John Cain, who's the manager there...and a ballsy guy...made him go on...

CLINTON: Who was it...what channel?

FLOWERS: I don't know...uh...okay it's on channel eleven, whatever that is...CBS [actually the Fox network]...I don't know the guy's name...uh...at any rate, I had booked some more jobs there in December, and...uh...John has asked me not to come back...he says he really doesn't want...'cause see, that's the third...the *Dallas Morning News* also called there and...uh...

CLINTON: They didn't hassle you there?

FLOWERS: No, they didn't but "Current Affair" had not called beforehand, either for someone to call them back...they just showed up...and, anyway, then Wednesday there...there was a grievance filed in my office when I got the job...by a girl who felt like she should have gotten it...a black girl named Charlette Perry. And they called me as a witness. So I go in and...uh...nothing big came of it...it's just that they were questioning me about how I found out about the job and said well...that personnel said there would be a position and then...uh...and they told me it would be advertised in the newspaper...it was...and then I pursued it from there.

CLINTON: Good for you.

FLOWERS: Well, it caught me off guard 'cause...I...I at first I just didn't know...I just didn't expect that, for some reason. I thought about a lot of things, about my qualifications, and all that business...but I didn't think about that.

CLINTON: Yeah.

The transcript continues after Gennifer tells Bill she went to see her mother and gives the reason.

Now Her Mother Gets Flak

FLOWERS: Okay…and then the next thing that happens and the reason I went to my mother's is that my mother gets a phone call. This has all happened to me last week. I'm going to tell you…I am a nervous wreck.

CLINTON: Your mother got a call?

FLOWERS: My mother gets a call from a man who won't identify himself and tells her, 'Boy, you ought to really be proud of your daughter.' And goes on and on, and of course my mother now…you know…is not one…she's not gonna take this shit from this guy and says, 'Now, look…' you know she's telling him, 'Don't call'…and he says…and he says to her, 'Well, I think she'd be better off dead' and hangs up the phone…are you there?

CLINTON: A long-distance call…do you think?

FLOWERS: My mother said it sounded…now here's the thing, Bill…my mother's name…isn't Flowers.

CLINTON: So somebody had to know…

FLOWERS: Somebody, yeah, somebody had to know to ask for that name.

CLINTON: Republican harassment trying to break you and me.

FLOWERS: Oh, listen…I'm not going to break…but I'll tell you what I've about decided is that I really would like to leave here.

CLINTON: Just leave town?

FLOWERS: Yeah, my mother is in [Missouri]…one of the reasons I have stayed here as long as I have.

CLINTON: Oh, wow…

FLOWERS: We had a little bit of a scare recently 'cause she has a spot on an X-ray and she…went and had it checked again…and it wasn't cancer…Bill, what I'm afraid of…is that if somebody in the press finds out that I'm working for the state.

CLINTON: Yeah…

FLOWERS: And I just…don't know. I'm, of course, I…I'll have to tell you…I'm…uh…about to cry because my nerves at this point after this week…I'm a pretty strong lady…but I've been through a lot.

CLINTON: But the people at the place were from "A Current Affair"?

FLOWERS: That's what John [Cain] said…I just headed for that door…I…uh…I said, 'Leave me alone, this is absurd.' He started sticking that thing and I knew…I mean that's a private club and I didn't think they would follow me…but here's the thing…I have to have these singing jobs to survive. I'm only making…uh…seventeen thousand, five hundred on this job, Bill.

CLINTON: You mean this guy won't hire you anymore?

FLOWERS: I don't blame him. He's getting telephone calls from these people…the last time he said, 'Gennifer, I don't want any problems.'

CLINTON: So what did you tell him? Did you tell him there's nothing to it?

FLOWERS: I did...I said, 'John, I have nothing to do with this...it isn't true...I was hoping it wouldn't come to this...I'm glad...uh...mmn...to hear this. I just hope they just go away...I didn't have a chance to tell you about the *Dallas Morning News*.

CLINTON: No, but I figured they'd just try and run it down.

FLOWERS: That guy's name...was George Kempell and that was the night before the day you announced [for the presidency] Anyway, I would really like to leave Little Rock.

CLINTON: How can I help?

FLOWERS: I don't know anybody anywhere, to speak of...I have mixed emotions about it because...uh...I consider this [Little Rock] my home.

CLINTON: Not only that...I mean this is just crazy...there's not going to be any stories...mmn...no one has said anything.

FLOWERS: The only thing that concerns me at this point is the state job.

CLINTON: Yeah, I've never thought about that...but as long as you say you've just been looking for one, you'd check on it...*if they ever ask if you talked to me about it...just say no* [author's emphasis].

FLOWERS: I would...but here's the thing...I have to consider, too...I have to...umm...go in to work every day there and if these people start talking to the press...

CLINTON: Have they been nice to you there?

FLOWERS: Yeah, they have been...but I just want you to know what's going on...I'll be glad to hang in there.

CLINTON: Has the...ahh...the grievance committee ruled yet?

FLOWERS: No, not that I know of...I forget the guy's name but...Don Barnes [chairman of the Arkansas Board of Review, who, on Clinton's orders, shuffled the rules of hire and put Gennifer in the job that should have gone to Charlette Perry].

CLINTON: Is he happy with you?

FLOWERS: Oh, sure. I'm good at what I do, Bill...but...uh...when this guy was trying to beat up on me a little...I found that curious...how I found out about the job...but maybe at this point I'm paranoid.

CLINTON: You don't want me to get this guy to reconsider?

FLOWERS: What guy?

CLINTON: The guy at the Flaming Arrow [who threatened to fire Gennifer]...it wouldn't be...uh...through me...but I have a lot of friends there.

FLOWERS: No, I'd rather just leave that alone for now...but if things...uh...might stay quiet...

CLINTON: He might change his mind...err...and I'd rather it be his idea.

FLOWERS: Yeah...and my parents...they're gonna be here...well they're leaving Wednesday morning and they were at the club tonight. And they'll be there tomorrow night which, you know, parents do. And I thought, "Oh, please Jesus, don't let those people [reporters and photographers] be out there."

CLINTON: I'm just sorry that you ever had to put up with that [sounds like shit].

FLOWERS: Well, you know, to be real honest with you, I'm not completely surprised. I didn't think it would start this quickly. But I think, Bill, you're being naive if you think that these other shows like "Current Affair" and, oh, what are some of the others, uh...?

CLINTON: Well, I thought they...

FLOWERS: "Hard Copy..."

CLINTON: I thought they'd look into it. But, you know, I just think a crazy person like Larry Nichols is not enough to get a story on the television with names in it.

FLOWERS: Right. Well he better not get on there and start naming names.

Bill Asks Gennifer to Lie—Again

CLINTON: Well, that's what I mean. You know, if all the people who are named...deny...that's all. I mean, I expect them to come look into it and interview you and everything, uh. But I just think that if everybody's on record denying it, you've got no problem.

FLOWERS: Well, I don't think...I don't think it...I don't...well, why would they waste their money and time coming down there unless someone showed 'em some interest? See, they weren't there tonight.

CLINTON: No, no. See, that's it. I mean, they're gonna run this Larry Nichols thing down. They're gonna try to goad people up, you know. But if everybody kinda hangs tough, they're just not going to do anything. They can't.

FLOWERS: No, they can't.

CLINTON: They can't run a story like this unless somebody said, "Yeah, I did it with him." I'll tell you what. It would be extremely valuable if they ever do run anybody by me, you know...if they ever get anybody to do this, just to have, like I told you before when I called you...is to *have an on-file affidavit explaining that, you know, you were approached by a Republican and asked to do that.*

[Is Bill Clinton attempting to coerce Gennifer Flowers to commit perjury in a sworn statement and be party to a cover-up?]

FLOWERS: Mm hmm. Well...

CLINTON: The more I think about it, you should call him [the TV magazine reporter, "Current Affair's" Steve Dunleavy, the "Crazy Australian" and "Mr. Blood and Guts," as he's been variously labeled, and the author's colleague on the *New York Post* for six years] back [and say you] just don't know.

FLOWERS: Well, I think that...well, are you going to run?

CLINTON: I want to [run for president]. I wonder if I'm just going to be blown out of the water with this. I don't see how they can [have overlooked it] so far.

FLOWERS: I don't think they can...

CLINTON: Oh, they don't, if they don't have pictures.

FLOWERS: Mm hmm.

CLINTON: Which they [can't have of] anybody, and no one says anything. Then they don't have anything. And arguably, if someone says something, they don't have much.

FLOWERS: If they could blow you out of the water, they would have already blown you. I really believe that. Because I believe that there are various ones that have been trying pretty hard lately. See, like that "Inside Edition." Uh, there've probably been other sources too [pause]. So...I don't think so. I honestly don't. That's my gut feeling. I would tell you if I did [pause]. So, I don't think...I honestly don't. But...you may know more about...

CLINTON: How do you like holding [my] future in [your] hands? Do you like that?

FLOWERS: Yeah [laughs]. No. Well, if it's positive, I do, you know. I mean, 'cause I want you to...I would love to see you go...oh, I'd love to see you be president. I think that would be wonderful...but, anyway, I think...I think we're okay for now.

CLINTON: We have to watch as we go along.

FLOWERS: Well, you're, uh, you know, from the feedback I'm getting around as about various things that are going on with what you're doing. I'm getting very positive feedback.

CLINTON: Yeah, there's no negative except this.

FLOWERS: This is the only thing?

CLINTON: And there's no negative to me running except this and even if I was...as a matter of fact it might be better for me to lose the primary. I might lose the nomination to Bob Kerrey because he's umm...got all the Gary Hart/Hollywood money and because he's single, looks like a movie star, won the Medal of Honor, and since he's single—nobody cares if he's screwing...[laughs].

This is the end of the first two of the most significant tape recordings made by Gennifer Flowers of her telephone conversations with Bill Clinton.

The next exchange occurs on Monday, December 16, 1992, when Clinton phones Gennifer from Washington, D.C., the night before he participates in the first TV debate with his five rival Democratic Party presidential primary candidates.

FLOWERS: Hello?

CLINTON: Gennifer?

FLOWERS: Yes.

CLINTON: It's Bill Clinton.

FLOWERS: Hi, Bill.

CLINTON: Hey, I tried to call ya. I can't believe I got ya.

FLOWERS: Well, when d'ya try to call me?

CLINTON: Last night. Late.

FLOWERS: Well, I was here.

CLINTON: Did you take your phone off the hook?

FLOWERS: Well, I did. I...well, I've been getting some hang-up calls.

CLINTON: Oh.

FLOWERS: ...and at one point I took my phone...I, well I didn't take it off the hook. I just, uh...

CLINTON: Turned it off?

FLOWERS: Yeah.

CLINTON: Oh, that's what it was. I called...I started calling soon as I got home [a Washington hotel] last night and I called for a couple of hours.

FLOWERS: Well, sorry I missed you.

CLINTON: [Shit]...I was afraid I screwed up the number or something. And I kept calling.

FLOWERS: Well, are you...you got a cold?

CLINTON: Yeah. Oh, it's just my...every year about this time I...my sinuses go bananas.

FLOWERS: Yeah, me too.

CLINTON: And I've been in this stupid airplane too much, but I'm okay.

FLOWERS: Well, good. The reason I was calling [Gennifer doesn't say when she phoned Bill in the tape's transcript] was to tell you that, uh, well a couple things. Uh, this last Wednesday, someone got into my apartment.

CLINTON: Hold on a minute.

FLOWERS: Okay.

[Long pause]

CLINTON: Okay, I got it.

FLOWERS: Are you in Little Rock?

CLINTON: No. I am going to be there tonight, late. I'm in Washington now and...

FLOWERS: Well...

CLINTON: I'm going to Dallas and then I'm coming to Little Rock.

FLOWERS: Uh, well.

Bill: Cuomo "Acts like" Mafioso

CLINTON: So, somebody broke in your apartment?

FLOWERS: Well, yeah. Well...there wasn't any sign of a breakin'-in, uh, but the drawers and things...there wasn't anything missing that I can tell. But somebody had...

CLINTON: Somebody had gone through all your stuff?

FLOWERS: ...and gone through all my stuff.

CLINTON: You think they were...but they didn't steal anything?

FLOWERS: No, no. My jewelry...I had jewelry here and everything, it was still here.

CLINTON: You think they were trying to look for something on us?

FLOWERS: I think so. Well, I mean...why, why else? Um...

CLINTON: You weren't missing any...any kind of papers or anything?

FLOWERS: Well, like what kind of papers?

CLINTON: Well, I mean, did...any kind of personal records or checkbooks or anything like that? Phone records?

FLOWERS: Do I have any?

CLINTON: Yeah.

FLOWERS: Uh unh. I mean, why would I?

CLINTON: I don't know. I just...

FLOWERS: You...you usually call me, for that matter. And besides, who would know?

CLINTON: Isn't that amazing?

FLOWERS: Even if I had it on my phone record...oh, well, I guess they might be able to say, "Oh, well, you were in Washington on this date and maybe at that number and connect that but...

CLINTON: Well...

FLOWERS: See, you've always called me. So that's not a...

CLINTON: I wouldn't care if they...you know, I, I...they may have my phone records on this computer here [in the governor's office], but I don't think it...that doesn't prove anything.

FLOWERS: Well, that...that's true. But I just want to tell you about that.

CLINTON: Wow.

FLOWERS: Let me tell you something positive.

CLINTON: What?

FLOWERS: Um, I heard, uh...I've heard a couple of people say...one had been to San Antonio, the other had been to Los Angeles...and they both said that they were, uh, that all they heard out there was "Clinton, Clinton, Clinton." So...

CLINTON: Really?

FLOWERS: Yeah. So I thought that was exciting.

CLINTON: We've worked so hard.

FLOWERS: I know you have, but I...that may not be a lot. But I mean that's a...I think that's a good indication.

CLINTON: Well, no...most people think, you know, that except for [New York State Governor Mario] Cuomo, I'm doing the best right now and, uh...we're leading in the polls in Florida...without Cuomo in there. But Cuomo's at eighty-seven percent name recognition and I have fifty-four percent. So...I mean...I'm at a terrible disadvantage in name recognition still. But we're coming up and...so I...we're moving pretty well. I'm really pleased about it.

FLOWERS: Well, I don't particularly care for Cuomo's, uh, demeanor.

CLINTON: Boy, he is so aggressive.

FLOWERS: Well, he seems like he could get real mean [laughs].

CLINTON: [sounds like "dirty and lowdown"]

FLOWERS: Yeah...I wouldn't be surprised if he didn't have some mafioso major connections.

CLINTON: Well, he acts like one [laughs].

FLOWERS: Yeah...he comes off that way to me on television.

That last exchange caused Cuomo to hit the ceiling. At that time Cuomo had a good chance of getting his party's nomination but declined it. Clinton later apologized for his part in that slur against Cuomo's Italian heritage.

CLINTON: [About to say something but Gennifer still wants to have her say]

FLOWERS: The only thing that concerns me, where I'm concerned at this point is *the state job*.

CLINTON: Yeah, I never thought about that. But as long as you say you'd just been looking for one [and not say she got the job through the governor]. *If they ever ask if you've talked to me about it, you can say no.*

[Clinton is now counseling Gennifer to perjure herself in sworn testimony before the labor grievance committee hearing Mrs. Perry's complaint, to save Clinton's derriere.]

FLOWERS: All right, darling, well, you hang in there. I don't mean to worry you. I just...

CLINTON: Baby...I just want to know those things and...if I can help you, you let me know, darling.

FLOWERS: Well, when you can help me is if I decide I want to get the heck out of here.

CLINTON: All you need to do is let me know...

FLOWERS: Because I don't know...I don't know where to turn. I really don't. I mean my contacts have just sort of fizzled in Nashville. It's been a long time, and I don't know, I don't know anybody.

CLINTON: Listen, honey. I'll help you.

FLOWERS: Okay. Well, I'll...I'll be back in touch. And, uh, you will let me know if you know anything I need to know about.

CLINTON: I will.

FLOWERS: Okay [laughs].

CLINTON: Goodbye, baby.

FLOWERS: Talk to you later. Bye.

32

THE NINE LIVES OF BILL CLINTON

Into His Bunker, like Saddam

After transcripts of the taped conversation he had with Gennifer Flowers were released at the Waldorf-Astoria, front runner Bill Clinton pulled a Saddam Hussein and dove for deep cover, vanishing from public view for a week.

He didn't emerge until February 2, seven days after Gennifer's revelations were splashed across the front pages of the nation's tabloids and broadsheets. He was then seen in a bashful, "family-man" reappearance at the Little Rock YWCA. He was with daughter Chelsea for a father-daughter party. After they returned to the governor's mansion, Clinton claimed his 11-year-old only child taught him to play a card game called "Spite and Malice."

"It is a game which is quite appropriate for the last few days," Clinton rasped dryly. After stumping New Hampshire for a month, his throat was sandy.

At that moment, besieged by scandal, Clinton pretended to be more concerned about his weight—"I'm getting fat as a wood tick"—than the fate of his campaign, even though he could claim with a straight face, "The money merchants are still combing the back alleys."

It was hard to tell whether the "tabloid terrorism," as the explosive sex scandal sagas were called, had tempered Clinton or left him burned. He insisted that his opponents would not succeed in turning his recent confessions of past troubles in his marriage into a political noose.

"Most people down deep inside always want to do better, and most people down deep inside know that we're all imperfect, that even the very best lives are a daily lifelong struggle for integrity, for continuing to do better," Clinton said the next morning. He spoke from the back seat of a car taking him to the airport for the return flight to New Hampshire and more politicking.

"Remember that great story about Oliver Wendell Holmes in his nineties, and a law clerk asked him why he was straining his eyes reading an old dog-eared copy of *Plato's Republic*? And he said, 'I'm doing it to improve my mind.'

"I feel that way about character. It's about the continuing search for belief and conviction and action and the ability not to disappoint yourself as well as others. It's a lifelong process. And I think that people know that different folks have different difficulties to deal with, but they identify with people who seem to be on the journey."

Clinton now seemed a stark contrast to Gary Hart, after he was exposed for his affair with Donna Rice. As he returned to the hustings, Clinton did not cringe as Hart had whenever he was asked to have his picture taken with an attractive blonde.

This became evident when Clinton trooped through the streets of Hampton and photographers had a field day snapping him beside a gorgeous blonde with a black puppy.

Clinton was on his best behavior now. Though he was in no hurry to cut his conversation with the young woman, he didn't revert to character. Rather than fondle the blonde, he cuddled her puppy.

In that tour of New Hampshire, and in campaign swings through New Jersey and Arkansas, his campaign took on the ghostly aura of a theatrical event being staged for different audiences.

The *New York Times'* Maureen Dowd offered her observations gleaned on his tri-state swing.

"The professed feeling among aides," said Miss Dowd, "was that Mr. Clinton has triumphed in the first round against the tabloids."

Then the reporter turned the spotlight on Republican hatchet woman Mary Matalin's longtime boyfriend who was breaking ground for George Bush's rival, and offered, "The Clinton campaign was a din of spin. James Carville, the fast-talking gonzo strategist wearing jeans with holes so large his underwear was leaking out in the back, pinned reporters to their chairs with a wall of words:

"'In Washington, you get stories that this is a beleaguered campaign. WOW! No! No! No! People in Washington are not people. They're human beings and all, but they're not people. Washington is never right about anything. Even a broken clock is right twice a day. Look at the polls—have you ever seen a front-runner get out of a race?'"

"Sniveling, Hypocritical Dems"

As presidential candidate's spokespersons go, Mary Matalin's verbiage was given a big edge over Jim Carville's homily. He got far less mileage than Mary's far more widely traveled harangue:

"Sniveling, hypocritical Democrats: Stand up and be counted—on second thought, shut up and sit down."

That was not a bad suggestion for Carville to take. He would at least have plugged the "leak" in the back of his pants reported by Miss Dowd who, despite Carville's optimistic offering, went on to note, "But in Washington, Democratic Party leaders and elected officials were very nervous and fearful that there could be another slipper yet to drop.

"Could one more disclosure tilt voters against the candidate?

"Is there a subterranean Puritanism that public opinion polls are not picking up right now?

"Democrats and Republicans are divided about whether Mr. Clinton has been fatally wounded, or whether he has shrewdly inoculated himself."

The *Times* writer noted further that Clinton's Democratic primary rivals were "frantic at not being able to get any traction from his troubles [and they] grew sharpest as the week wore on."

She cited the outburst by former New Hampshire Senator John Durkin when he introduced Senator Tom Harkin at a Manchester labor rally: "I don't care much about Bill Clinton's infidelity to [his wife]." Harkin stressed what concerned him most was Clinton's poor record in dealing with Arkansas's "environment, working people, and the middle class."

The other senator in the race, Nebraska's Robert Kerrey, a divorcé, also addressed the defensive posture the Arkansas governor took after the scandal about his affairs broke in the *Star*. Clinton had implied that to work out a troubled marriage, as he admitted his had been, was morally preferable to parting.

"I reject the pious notion that one is either perfect or divorced," Kerrey protested to the *Boston Globe*.

Clinton was quick to protect his flank, rebutting, "The only point I tried to make is that having said that it's okay for divorced people to be president, we shouldn't go in the other direction and say if you've ever had troubles in your marriage and you want to run for office, just forget it.

"But I was never negative on Bob Kerrey for getting divorced. As a matter of fact, when my mother remarried my stepfather, I was against her doing it. I think sometimes divorce is not only appropriate, it is the only sensible thing to do in life."

As the primary season progressed, Clinton appeared to gain confidence that he could overcome his infidelity factor. He began suggesting that voters would relate to his confession of imperfection.

"Have you heard that song 'I Ain't Going To Worry No More' by Ray Charles and Ronnie Milsap?" Clinton asked reporters traveling on his small passenger jet rented for the campaign. He broke out with a few bars from the song in his raspy timbre, a condition that soon shunted him to the sidelines after a physician ordered him to shut up for a few days and rest his voice.

"That should be our campaign song," Clinton said after his vocalization. "As long as there's moonlight in Virginia, there ain't nothin' to worry about."

Right in his own political family a different, but no less hopeful, view of Clinton's confession was offered by his poll taker, Stan Greenberg:

"So long as voters believe the candidate hasn't lied and that his marriage is real, they will not turn on him."

Greenberg then beamed the spotlight on Hillary:

"Mrs. Clinton [in vivid appearances on television in campaign commercials] is fostering the image of a genuine marriage, which goes to further my belief the public will not turn on her husband."

Along the way, Clinton gravitated into a stream-of-conscience self-tribute—but not before he saluted the *dragon lady*, as his wife was increasingly being referred to by his campaign aides.

"I'm not sure people aren't right when they say Hillary is the one who ought to be running. You know, we like each other. You can watch me watch her speak sometimes, and I've got the Nancy Reagan adoring look. I think she's one good argument for voting for me."

Then he launched into what-might-have-been, had he not tried his level best to make the marriage survive.

"If the choice for us is my having gotten a divorce a couple years ago and being single and going up to New Hampshire and winning and being free of this almost unbelievable set of behaviors to which I and my family and our friends have been subjected, but ultimately being nominated and going on to the White House, or just going home to the rest of my life with her and Chelsea, I think now everybody in America ought to be able to see why I would choose to go home."

The Comeback Kid

Then, making one of his rare references to the embarrassment his wife has faced over the revelations of his womanizing, Clinton said, "I think she's just been extraordinary. One of the reasons that I guess I'm in elected office and she isn't is she's always wanted to guard her privacy much more, and I've always kind of hated to have to discuss some of the things that we have discussed in the last few weeks. If I learned anything it's like every other challenge that I've ever seen on her face, she was able to rise to it."

All this moved Jonathan Alter to report in the January 20 edition of *Newsweek,* "Without a single real vote yet cast, Clinton has already won the first primary, the one that takes place in the State of Mind, where the chattering class of reporters and Democratic Party activists live.

"These folks are important: they create 'spin' and 'heat' and factors that don't need quotation marks, like money.

"Perception often becomes reality."

Three weeks later, after the stories about Clinton's infidelities had run their course, *Newsweek's* Eleanor Clift added her view:

"Gary Hart would have given anything for the support Clinton got last week [after the last words about the scandals made the printed page].

"Truth is, the press is willing to cut Clinton some slack because they like him— and what he has to say.

"He is a policy wonk in tune with a younger generation of Democrats eager to take the party beyond the liberal stereotype."

At this stage, Bill Clinton was beginning to look like the "Comeback Kid."

33

SURVIVING SELF-INFLICTED WOUNDS

A Letter Returns to Haunt Bill, the Draft Dodger

Just before the New Hampshire's Republican and Democratic voters cast ballots in the first-in-the-nation primaries on February 18, the Clinton campaign was rocked by the seismic shocks of another scandal.

Clinton was suddenly stung by an old soldier who never died—or faded away. He was retired Army Lieutenant Colonel Clinton D. Jones, the one-time recruiting officer at the University of Arkansas ROTC. It'd been 23 years since they had seen each other, but Jones had read and heard all he could stand about Clinton's response to charges that he had staged anti-war rallies and avoided the draft. With a straight face, Clinton maintained that he voluntarily dropped a draft deferment that was given to him to continue his college education. He said he felt "a moral obligation" to do so after some of his high school classmates were killed in Vietnam.

Of course, that wasn't true. As we know, Clinton had manipulated the lottery, manipulated Colonel Jones, and manipulated his superior, Colonel Eugene J. Holmes, director of the ROTC at the U of A. Holmes had the last word on giving the future president a deferment—after he committed himself to serve in army greens upon finishing studies at Oxford.

Clinton had come to Holmes and Jones on bended knees, begging to be admitted to the ROTC—*after* he had received his draft notice to report for induction into the army. Of course, he never told *that* to the colonels. Had he come clean, he'd have been told no soap, you're in the army now—go and serve your country, buster!

Or as Colonel Jones put it, "If he had not deceived me, I would have urged rejection of his application to the ROTC and he would've been in the army."

Jones, who became aware of the letter only after he culled the ROTC files some time after Holmes put it there, made a copy and, upon his retirement, took it home along with other records.

Over the years, items in newspapers about Clinton's advances as a politician kept Jones abreast of the man he came to despise, not only as a draft dodger, but as a cheat and double-crosser.

Finally, Jones was moved to action—just before the New Hampshire primary— "because I wanted to let the country see the kind of man who is seeking the presidency." Infuriated by Clinton's insistence that he had not evaded military service, Jones let fly the truth. He released the letter Clinton wrote to Holmes. (The full text of the letter appears in chapter 5.)

Clinton was devastated. Coming on the heels of Gennifer Flowers' blistering revelations, his character was brought into wide disrepute. He suffered a sharp drop in popularity. Yet it didn't knock him out of the primaries. For he finished a fairly respectable second to Paul Tsongas in the February 18 inaugural test among Yankee voters. Bob Kerrey, Tom Harkin, and Jerry Brown followed in that order in their bids for Democratic delegates.

An acerbic message from the quill of columnist Murray Kempton after the '92 New Hampshire primary, berated Clinton's surprising finish:

"...I am in one of my periodic fits of patriotism and ridiculously affronted by an electorate that would allot twice as many of its ballots to a draft escaper as to a winner of the Congressional Medal of Honor [Kerrey]. If we must go on casting our votes for irrelevant reasons, let them at least have some tincture of romance."

In the GOP race, President Bush scored mightily against the upstart Patrick Buchanan for the state's 23 Republican delegates.

Despite his poor finish in New Hampshire, Senator Kerrey held a commanding lead in the race for delegates because he had topped the field in the kickoff February 10 Iowa caucus. He took the liberal state's 49 Democratic delegates in a close duel with Senator Harkin and headed with high hopes toward the March 10 Super Tuesday balloting, the monster primary day when 11 contests were to be waged from Massachusetts to Hawaii.

With 783 delegates up for grabs, Clinton—still flying but his wings clipped by the sex and draft scandals—was poised to lasso a herd of delegates closer to his home turf, in the Georgia and Maryland primaries where the combined numbers totaled 163 delegates.

Still, even in the deep South, Clinton couldn't shake his detractors. Kerrey, wounded in Vietnam, headed to a veterans' event in Atlanta where he was joined by Georgia's fiery Secretary of State Max Cleland, his top ally and a Vietnam triple-amputee.

Cleland, no less so than Kerrey, had not been reluctant in the past to paint Clinton a draft dodger. He did so again at the gathering of ex-GIs at the American Legion Convention. So did another Kerrey supporter, Vietnam double-amputee Lewis Puller—the late author of the acclaimed autobiography *Fortunate Son*—who voiced bitterness over Clinton's plea for sympathy for his professed "personal anguish" over Vietnam.

"I'm tired of these Rhodes scholars coming out of the woodwork and trying to seize the moral high ground," railed Puller. "To me, personal anguish isn't Bill Clinton writing a letter but a mother who lost her son."

Seeking to turn Georgia's large population of military veterans against Clinton, Kerrey roared, "Had he wanted to go and serve his country, he could have."

Then Kerrey's senior adviser, Bob Shrum, went on the offensive:

"Clinton is the classic case of the emperor having no clothes. He walks down the street and there are all those people who don't want to say out loud what they see, which is that he has nothing on—nothing at all!"

Kerrey again trained his sights on Clinton when he addressed a rally of college undergrads.

"I answered the call in Vietnam," Kerrey said. "Bill Clinton should not be the nominee of our party because he will not be able to win. The Republican Party knows how to exploit every weakness, to lay bare your soul."

Clinton, who didn't see himself as a factor in the earlier Maine caucus, was correct in that assessment. Tsongas emerged the clear winner and Jerry Brown the runner-up. His third-place finish disheartened Clinton and his backers, yet he still held the hole card. He led all his rivals in organization and financial backing. His trip to the Bilderberg Conference in Baden-Baden assured him of this support.

Senator Harkin, who fared poorly in New Hampshire and Maine, also didn't do well in South Dakota's primary, held two days after the balloting in the Pine Tree State. Spokeswoman Lorraine Voles let it be known the Iowa senator was "paring down" his campaigning: he was confining himself to thrusts in Minnesota and Idaho in the March 3 seven-state primary races, along with a brief foray into Maryland.

After Five Losses, Bill Bounces Back

Jerry Brown, whose showing in South Dakota was the poorest of all the Democratic candidates, lost eligibility for federal matching funds. But it was much too soon to write him off. His determination to win was boundless. He felt he could stay in the race even without a nickel in his pocket.

Clinton had not won a single one of the five presidential preference contests thus far and had yet to see light at the end of the tunnel when the seven-state primary races began Tuesday morning.

But by day's end of that March 3, he had scored an impressive regional victory in Georgia, taking 57 percent of the vote to Tsongas's 24 percent. Brown took 8 percent in the balloting; Kerrey, 5 percent; and Harkin, 2 percent; to trail the state's uncommitted slate of 4 percent.

In a tighter Maryland contest, Tsongas was the winner, defeating Clinton 41 to 34 percent, while Brown, Kerrey, and Harkin trailed in single-digit figures.

By winning the mid-Atlantic state, Tsongas called himself "The Breakthrough Kid," a reminder of the label Clinton put on his second-place finish in the New Hampshire primary after being deluged by all that bad press.

"This proves," Tsongas said cheerfully, "I'm not just a New England regional hero."

Tsongas also pulled off a convincing showing in the Utah caucus, which gave him 34 percent of the vote to Brown's 28 percent and Clinton's 18. A third triumph in the Washington State caucus gave Tsongas a total of 100 delegates.

Despite his second-place finish in the Maryland primary and third-place showings in Utah's contest, where Tsongas and Brown tied for nine delegates each to the Arkansan's five, Clinton still had a comfortable 88-delegate lead over the former Bay State Senator, thanks to his triumph in Georgia, where he also cornered a large share of the black vote.

The balloting in Colorado and Utah gave Jerry Brown new life, after his discouraging third-place finishes in Georgia and Maryland.

On a day when Democrats from the Potomac to Pago Pago in American Samoa held four primaries and three caucuses, the mixed results fell short of indicating the eventual winner of the party's nomination.

At this point only 383 of the party's 4,288 delegates were allocated to the six-pack, as the five candidates were still incongruously called.

Actually it was not inconsistent for the media to label the Democratic presidential hopefuls the six-pack, for at the start there were a half-dozen candidates when Virginia Governor L. Douglas Wilder was being counted. But he declined to make a run for the nomination and allowed the field to dwindle to five before it became a six-pack again after Lenora Fulani was counted as a candidate.

Miss Fulani was the left-wing hopeful who entered the New Hampshire primary with credentials as a Marxist and New York psychotherapist. But she wasn't welcomed by the Democratic Party because she declined to participate in the debates. After receiving 283 votes in New Hampshire, she aligned herself with the New Alliance Party and wasn't to be seriously heard from again.

Despite setbacks in the Northeast, Clinton was in the catbird seat with Super Tuesday just around the corner. In that March 10 showdown, 11 states were up for grabs. And the grabbing seemed to favor the womanizing draft evader whose character flaws hadn't harmed him in the southern states of Tennessee, Louisiana, Mississippi, Missouri, Oklahoma, and Texas.

Others holding contests on that most critical day of presidential primary balloting were Massachusetts, Rhode Island, Delaware, Florida, and Hawaii. Tsongas was seen as a hands-down winner on his Bay State's turf and its neighbor, the Ocean State.

The early betting on Super Tuesday favored Clinton to emerge with a lead in delegates, but still without a clear mandate that he could win outside his home region.

Of incidental interest thus far were the Republican Party's primary results. President Bush was clobbering Pat Buchanan by better than 2–1 in most contests, although the upstart, 53-year-old conservative, who had never held elective office, approached a 40 percent showing in Georgia to establish that his 37 percent share in New Hampshire was not a fluke.

With the seven-state March 3 primaries behind them, the Democratic front-runners headed on a frantic, pre-Super Tuesday round of campaigning. Two of the less successful contenders, Kerrey, 48, and Harkin, 52, sat it out in Washington and pondered their political futures.

"Yesterday was not a great day," moaned Kerrey's Florida coordinator Paul Pazella after the Nebraska senator canceled appearances in that delegate-rich state. "If the campaign goes on—and it's a big if—it won't be in Florida, because TV commercials are too costly here."

Harkin's Florida coordinator Steve Leisman sounded a similar lament:

"We're still the underdog, but this thing is far from over. Super Tuesday is not going to be pretty, but we'll do it. As I see it, Tom'll have stronger showings in Saturday's [March 7] South Carolina contest and the March 17 Michigan primary.

Leisman didn't mention that Arizona and Wyoming were also holding primaries on March 7, and Illinois' contest for Democratic delegates was being held the same day as the showdown in Michigan.

Here it was March 4, and after 10 primaries and caucuses, the results for the Democratic nomination process were as muddled as ever. As *New York Daily News* political correspondent Susan Milligan put it, "The results...further defied the early conventional wisdom about the five candidates.

"Clinton, an early front-runner, was once thought to be politically dead following allegations of an extramarital affair and questions about his efforts to avoid the draft.

"Tsongas, with his lackluster style and bout with cancer [which he insisted he had licked] was believed unelectable.

"Brown, carrying the old 'Governor Moonbeam' moniker from his early political days, was also written off."

When Brown announced his candidacy in late 1991, comedian Jay Leno joked "Poor Jerry Brown. The only people who'll vote for him are stuck in that Biosphere experiment."

Kerrey's Out, Clinton Climbs

Reporter Milligan noted that Kerrey and Harkin "were initially believed to be strong contenders," but now seemed ready to throw in the towel to make the primary dwindle down to "The Big 3" and "The Fading 2," as the headline on her *Daily News* story clarioned.

It took two more days for Bob Kerrey to bow out of the race. He did so with grace, a smile and, as *New York Post* Washington Bureau Chief Deborah Orin put it, with "the Kennedyesque humor that his fans had hoped to see more often while he was still running."

Addressing a Capitol Hill news conference, Kerrey declared, "I feel a little like the Jamaican bobsled team—we had a lot of spirit but, unfortunately, we didn't get a lot of medals.

"Paraphrasing the late Lou Gehrig, you may have heard I got some bad breaks, most of them self-inflicted. But today, I consider myself the luckiest man on the face of the Earth."

Kerrey's departure—after failing to win even one of the 215 delegates up for grabs in Tuesday's runoffs—was without rancor for the front-runner. A few days earlier, he had said Clinton was unelectable and "would get opened up like a soft peanut."

Dismissing his criticism of Clinton as "political hyperbole," Kerrey said that "the only unelectable politician running for president of the United States is George Bush." He added, "If he [Clinton] is the nominee, I will campaign feverishly to make sure he wins the election in November."

On March 7, Clinton lengthened his lead over Tsongas by trouncing rivals in a South Carolina landslide and received a bonus with a caucus victory in Wyoming.

With nearly 72,000 voters—or 63 percent—casting ballots for him in the Palmetto State, and a narrow victory, but a victory nevertheless, over Brown in Wyoming, Clinton headed into the heptathlon of southern primaries on Super Tuesday.

Clinton finished behind Tsongas in Arizona's primary and second to Brown in Nevada's race, yet even when he wasn't winning he was picking up delegates. He rounded up 15 in Arizona and 5 more in Nevada, giving him a grand total of 240 delegates to Tsongas's 118.

Meanwhile, President Bush, after easily defeating not one, but two Republican rivals in the South Carolina primary, was riding high.

"We're eight and oh and headed for Super Tuesday," said Bush as he looked ahead to those 11, critical Republican primaries on March 10.

Buchanan, with only 26 percent of the vote to Bush's 66 percent, was visibly disappointed. But he let campaign chairman Robert Teeter do his eulogizing.

"After tonight, nobody can doubt that President Bush is going to be the Republican nominee," Teeter predicted in a written statement.

The third candidate in the GOP race was former Ku Klux Klan *grand dragon* David Duke, who received 10,347 votes.

The weekend "tune-up" for Super Tuesday also put an end to Senator Tom Harkin's hopes. He called a news conference in Washington and, sitting not far from where Kerrey announced his withdrawal from the race, did likewise.

Tuesday, March 10, Bill Clinton scored grand slams in the southern primaries, overcame Tsongas's serious challenge in pivotal Florida, and overshadowed the Massachusetts candidate's victories in his own region.

Although Tsongas carried his state and Rhode Island, as expected, and finished in a tie with an uncommitted slate in Delaware's caucus to become that state's top candidate, the 368 delegates in his column after the 11-state sweepstakes paled alongside the 753 Clinton backers claimed in mid-March.

With 2,145 delegates needed for nomination at the Democratic National Convention, Slick Willie was a third of the way to his goal.

In contrast, President Bush was more than halfway to the GOP nomination.

With the Deep South wrapped up, Clinton hurtled toward the next week's critical battle with Tsongas in heavily industrialized Illinois and Michigan. Undeterred by Clinton's gains, Tsongas didn't seem to mind his underdog role. Striking a combative stance in his hometown of Lowell, the son of Greek immigrants addressed a gathering of supporters:

"Super Tuesday was meant to eliminate somebody like me. Well, I'm still here."

In Illinois, Clinton opened his campaign for 164 Democratic delegates with a whirlwind tour of Chicago. He stumped America's third-largest city for black votes and the support of key leaders in the city's precincts populated by minorities.

He kept an eye on Illinois' next-door neighbor, Michigan, with its nearly as rich 131 delegates.

Clinton's arrival in Chicago was marred by the *New York Times* story about the Ozark Mountains/Whitewater land deal, the questionable relations with former aide James McDougal, and his failing Madison Guaranty Savings and Loan bank that Hillary Clinton represented before regulators appointed by her husband.

Shaken by the disclosures and vehemently denying that all was not kosher, Clinton tried a strategy that at once came under fire. He ordered a "review" of the land deal "to settle the question once and for all." He chose James Lyons to conduct the inquiry.

"That's the wrong person for the job," complained Cornell University professor Charles Wolfram, an expert on legal ethics. "They shouldn't appoint friends. They should appoint disinterested people.

"Surely there must be somebody known to be honest and not a friend."

Wolfram said an academician or a judge would have been a far more appropriate choice than an old pal like Lyons.

"It's impossible to say if there were ethical improprieties in the Clintons' deal based on what has been made public so far," continued Wolfram, whose counsel on legal/ethical matters is solicited by the American Bar Association.

"There's plenty to raise questions, and so there's an absolute need to know what the facts are before one can reach a conclusion about the deal."

James Lyons' inquiry died aborning.

More Dark Clouds of Scandal

Even before the echoes from the Ozark Mountains explosion died, another ethics flap rose to haunt Clinton, just when he had begun to bask in his political resurgence.

The New York Times was after him again, this time for "secretly exempting himself" from the Arkansas ethics law that he rewrote. The law required legislators to disclose their own or their families' finances in matters dealt with in the legislature, matters that could have the appearance of conflict of interest.

Clinton quickly conceded that he removed "public servants" (such as himself and his wife as governor and first lady of Arkansas) from the measure, but denied that he did so to shelter himself and Hillary from public scrutiny.

"I initiated the bill," said Clinton, admitting that, as originally drafted, it covered public servants including himself. "But when it failed to pass, I initiated a referendum that exempted public servants because the term covered local officials who opposed the measure."

Clinton added, "If I wanted to get myself exempted why would I try to pass the bill in the first place?"

The explanation didn't fly for Jerry Brown, who complained, "His story raises new concerns. Clinton's carved out a little exemption for himself and his wife...and he's giving us an excuse that he couldn't do otherwise.

"Boy, this guy's real smooth!"

Brown didn't let up on Clinton. Just as the front-runner went courting Chicago's black communities, his nemesis struck again.

"Let's hear from Bill about his membership in all-white golf clubs," Brown said snidely. "I think he's got a lot to explain—and not just to say, 'Oops.' He made a mistake for eleven years, because that's how long he's been going there."

Actually, records showed that Clinton was an honorary member of *three* all-white clubs in Little Rock. One is the Pleasant Valley Country Club, where a reception in 1991 was boycotted by 12 members of the Arkansas legislature because the club had no black members.

Brown wasn't the first to cite Clinton's membership in all-white organizations. The *Boston Herald* and *New York Post* published stories about his affiliation with golf clubs that exclude blacks.

After the stories broke, Clinton's press people insisted he had no problem with those situations because he didn't set the ground rules for membership.

This prompted Virginia Governor Doug Wilder, the nation's only black governor, to explode:

"It's inconceivable that Clinton would recreate in a club that openly discriminates against blacks and other minorities."

Wilder, then added tartly, "Governor Clinton, a man besieged with stories about his personal life in the past few months, has taken to lecturing Americans about personal responsibility [in campaign speeches, particularly about welfare].

"All I can say to Governor Clinton is, doctor, heal thyself."

Clinton did not respond to Wilder's tongue-lashing, but after the National Association for the Advancement of Colored People protested his play on the fairways of the Country Club of Little Rock, he did a mea culpa.

"They don't have any black members yet," he said, squirming. "I shouldn't have done that. I won't play golf there again until they integrate."

Despite the adverse publicity, Clinton won an easy double-header in the Illinois and Michigan primaries to build a commanding delegate lead over his two rivals. A lead that should have made him the presumptive Democratic nominee against President Bush.

Clinton carried Michigan with better than 51 percent of the vote and sewed up 74 of its delegates. He won by the same percentage in more populous Illinois, and picked up 107 delegates. That gave him a total of 944 delegates, closer than ever to the 2,145 needed for nomination.

In another year, Clinton's impressive victories in the two key Midwest states would have ended the race. Party leaders, anxious to halt the internecine wars and rally behind a favorite son to challenge an incumbent president, would have thrown their support to the front-runner.

But this was 1992, and few in the Democratic Party hierarchy were willing to write off either Paul Tsongas or Jerry Brown. Picking up 46 delegates with 26 percent of the vote in Illinois put Tsongas ahead of Brown, whose 15 percent of the vote commanded only 11 delegates. But in the race next door, Brown reversed the situation. He picked up 37 delegates with 26 percent of the vote, and Tsongas brought up the rear with 17 percent and 20 delegates.

The results sent Tsongas and Brown off to campaign stops in New England for the March 24 Connecticut primary. They came away from the Illinois-Michigan fray with nothing to brag about. They picked up exactly 57 delegates each.

Though Clinton's spoils were much more bountiful—181 delegates—he could not assume they entitled him to the same consideration front-running candidates were given in years past. With New York, New Jersey, Pennsylvania, California, and smaller western states still to hold primaries, the party's mahatmas were not yet prepared to anoint Clinton.

The aforementioned states with upcoming primaries were treacherous turf for a southern candidate. Memories of Georgia's Jimmy Carter came to mind—of how, for example, he failed to carry California in two primaries and two presidential elections in 1976 (when he was elected over Gerald Ford) and 1980 (when he lost to Ronald Reagan).

Jerry Brown was the party bosses' big reason for not rallying behind Clinton. Brown's showing in Michigan, where he attracted the labor vote, was a big plus for him. Also in his favor was his boundless rhetoric that could rally voters in the other industrial states and fill them with misgivings about "a pretty boy from the South" like Clinton.

A further consideration—an overriding one—was that Clinton had been so badly riddled by scandal. Even his own staff, as shell-shocked by the disclosures as the party's leaders, could hardly start a new day without asking, "Is there anything more to come?"

The answer: Yes more was coming.

A Kinder, Gentler Pat Buchanan

The Republican primaries in Illinois and Michigan followed the script that President Bush had written on all the other battlegrounds—he swamped Pat Buchanan in both states.

Before the president swallowed up 76 percent of the vote in Illinois and 67 percent in Michigan to give Buchanan two of his worst primary defeats (he scraped bottom in Illinois with 22 percent and 25 percent in Michigan), Bush had 711 delegates wrapped up, with only 1105 needed for nomination.

Buchanan, who won no delegates in either the Illinois or Michigan primaries, had a mere 46 in his column, but he vowed to continue his campaign to Connecticut, North Carolina, and California. However—just short of admitting that defeat was inevitable—Buchanan let it be known he was yanking ads attacking the president.

"Only celestial intervention" can stop Bush's march toward renomination, Buchanan conceded. "But we think we have tremendous influence still.

"Mr. Bush is stronger because he's been moving in our direction...this campaign is clearly strengthening the party for the fall."

Buchanan's remarks prompted White House spokesman Marlin Fitzwater to remark, "The administration still considers Buchanan the opposition. However, if he's going to be a kinder, gentler candidate, why, that's fine.

"On the other hand, we hope it doesn't make him a better candidate, because we still want to beat him wherever he tries."

No sooner had Bill Clinton set foot in Connecticut than he was beset with fresh charges of wrongdoing. This double-barreled slam came from an "exclusive" that broke simultaneously in the *Los Angeles Times* and the *New York Post*. Both newspapers had investigated Clinton's dealings with convicted drug dealer Dan Lasater, for whom the governor lobbied to award millions of dollars of state bond contracts. Both newspapers raised serious questions about the propriety of having done business with Lasater, who was mixed up with Clinton's half brother, Roger Clinton, and was busted with him in the cocaine scandals.

In the *New York Post* story, writer Mike McAlary, who investigated the case for more than a month, asked, "So why does Bill Clinton do business with a man everyone else in his state knows to be involved with cocaine?

"Why does Bill Clinton take campaign contributions from a person being named as a target on the front pages of newspapers?

"Why does he fly on the guy's planes?

"And finally, years later, why does Bill Clinton pardon Dan Lasater?"

McAlary provided no answers but quoted the presidential candidate who said he was "prepared to lead the nation's fight on drugs.

"As is Clinton's custom in dealing with questions about his past, the governor denied all wrongdoing in the case yesterday. But political experts say this clearly documented story about a governor's lobbying on behalf of a drug dealer—and Clinton's decision to grant Dan Lasater a conditional parole two years ago—will only heighten doubts about the Democrat's electability. Some believe this new controversy may even doom Clinton's campaigning."

It almost did!

Readers straddling the New York-Connecticut state line had a bonanza of stories on this scandal. Besides McAlary's account in the *Post*, one could turn to the *Stamford Advocate* and read the *Los Angeles Times*' version of the subject, since both newspapers are members of the Times-Mirror Company media family and share each other's top stories.

Clinton, the overwhelming favorite in pre-primary polls, was stunned by Jerry Brown in the Connecticut showdown, one of the campaign's first significant upsets. Brown came away the victor with 62,718 votes, or 37 percent of the total ballots cast, while Clinton received 59,569 votes, or 36 percent. The final results were narrow-gapped, to be sure, but they indicated voter doubts about Clinton: not about his ability to be president—but about his character.

That complaint was expressed in the Nutmeg State's exit polls. Voters said they did not believe Clinton had the honesty and integrity to be president.

Clinton might have gone over the precipice had Connecticut voters been told in more detail what he'd done back in Little Rock just before he announced for the presidency.

The "conditional parole" McAlary glossed over in his piece needs explanation.

His good friend and financial backer, Dan Lasater, received the governor's pardon in Arkansas. That didn't cause a stir because excesses and corruption were everyday occurrences there. Arkansans were used to political head-bashings, torture and burnings, evidence tampering and destruction, false imprisonment, large-scale bribes, and government-sponsored cover-ups.

Did Governor Clinton have grounds to issue that pardon to the felon Lasater?

Clinton's flacks shaped the following press release to a gullible Arkansas citizenry:

"Mr. Lasater wishes to instruct his young son in the use of firearms. In order to do so, he must have a pistol permit. That was the sole purpose of giving Mr. Lasater the pardon."

That may have been the "sole purpose," but it achieved a great deal more for the governor's great political benefactor. With his criminal record wiped clean, Lasater's voting privileges were restored. He could also apply and receive state licenses for any endeavor he wished to pursue. Without the pardon, he could not have returned to the banking business as he did following his release from prison—to become one of the nation's worst offenders in the S&L scandals.

However, one thing Clinton could not grant his friend, even as governor, was to wipe the slate totally clean. Since Lasater was prosecuted and brought to justice by the federal government, his conviction and incarceration remained on Uncle Sam's books.

But that could change overnight—should the 42nd president decide to grant his old benefactor total absolution.

Paul Tsongas: Another Casualty

Clinton took his defeat with a light heart.

"We had a small setback in Connecticut tonight," he told a packed room of supporters at Manhattan's landmark Gallagher's Steak House. "But we've come to New York with our guns blazing. No one's going to take this election for granted."

For Jerry Brown, his upset of Clinton was energizing and elevating.

"This is a change," he exulted at a Manhattan union hall rally where he had watched the results on TV. "It's not the end of the story. It's just the second or third chapter. There is more to come."

More was to come. But it would come from a two-horse race. Just before the Connecticut primary, Paul Tsongas, who just a month before led the Democratic pack after winning the New Hampshire primary, bowed out. He lacked funds to match Clinton's heavy TV advertising in the crucial New York primary.

"The hard fact is that the nomination process requires resources," Tsongas told a news conference at a Boston hotel. "And last evening it was clear that we did not have the resources necessary to fight the media war in New York."

Ironically, even though he announced his withdrawal from the race four days before the Connecticut primary, Tsongas won 33,131 votes, or 20 percent of the total cast.

The result buoyed him and some of his supporters. It raised hopes that he could return to the primary wars if his financial situation improved. But it didn't, and in time Tsongas made it clear he was no longer a candidate.

After more than a week of heavy-duty campaigning, New Yorkers went to their polls on Tuesday, April 7. Bill Clinton won the Empire State's Democratic primary by tallying 393,903 ballots, or 41 percent of the state's total.

Jerry Brown received 252,383 votes, 26 percent, and left the state with 67 delegates, compared to 101 delegates for Clinton.

The state's remaining 76 delegates went to Tsongas, relegating Jerry Brown to third place.

Many saw the ballots for Tsongas as a protest vote against Clinton's many trespasses.

Did Bill Clinton have anything to say about the voters' doubts about his character?

"Yes I do," he said. "I'm not interested in whether they love me or not. I want them to respect me and to want me to be their president. I think time will take care of it."

Yet voter concern was focused around respect and not love. For 46 percent of Democrats questioned in New York's exit polls doubted Clinton had the integrity to be president.

How Clinton won the black vote in Illinois, Michigan, and New York is a mystery. Especially after a major rhubarb with the Rev. Jesse Jackson. The flap came shortly before Senator Tom Harkin dropped out of the race.

David Stanton, an anchorman for WIS-TV, the NBC affiliate in Columbia, South Carolina, innocently started the controversy during a taping of interviews with Clinton by several reporters from TV stations around the country on a one-hour satellite feed from Little Rock.

Stanton began his interview by saying to Clinton, "Let me ask you first about a report we're getting this morning that the Reverend Jesse Jackson is going to be campaigning with one of your opponents, Tom Harkin, here in South Carolina on Monday. How do you think that might impact on the primary race?"

A dark frown creased Clinton's eyebrow as he replied, "I don't know and I have no reason to believe that...he certainly has never indicated that he was going to do that...what are they going to campaign about?"

Stanton replied, "They're just going to be barnstorming across the state. Jackson's aides say *that does not indicate an endorsement of Harkin* [author's highlight]. But the Harkin camp, of course, says that that does say something about Jackson's feelings on the race. But you don't know anything about that?"

"No," snapped Clinton, who seemed considerably put out. After the interview, Clinton turned to staffers and, apparently under the impression the cameras were shut down, began brutalizing Jackson. Much earlier in the campaign, Jackson insisted he was maintaining a neutrality in the primaries and would endorse no candidate until the convention picked the nominee.

"That is not what we want," Clinton began annoyedly. "We want him not involved at all."

Obviously now, Clinton could not know that Phoenix television station KTSP, which was to interview him next, had its camera trained on the governor—and tape was rolling. The crew from the CBS affiliate in Arizona had been taping earlier interviews by other TV news teams to run a check on its equipment. So KTSP's cameras and microphones were still in operation.

"It's an outrage," Clinton suddenly burst out. "It's a dirty, double-crossing, back-stabbing thing to do to me." He hissed and spat out his words now as he stabbed the air angrily with his forefinger.

"There's only one person can be hurt by this...I mean, I want you to say, listen, I came to that guy's house at midnight. I have called him. I've done everything I could. For him to do this to me, for me to hear this on a television program is an act of absolute dishonor."

His face flushed with anger, Clinton railed on.

"Everything he had bragged about, he has gushed to me about trust and trust and trust...I want Wilhelm to try to shut it down!"

Clinton was referring to his national campaign director, David Wilhelm. The tirade continued.

"...I mean, you know if he wants to talk to me, fine. But this is a terrible way to find out about it...he owed it to the rest of us...he certainly owed it to me."

This was Governor Bill Clinton at his worst—a ruthless politician with a hair-trigger temper.

One of the two most telling commentaries about Clinton was his assessment of Jesse Jackson at the very outset, when the presidential hopeful met Jackson in Little Rock, hat in hand, seeking his blessing before announcing that he was making the run in '92.

"That was in October of 1991," recalled Trooper Roger Perry, who was on the scene in the governor's mansion during the meeting. "I'll never forget what Clinton turned and said to me just after Jackson left the room.

"He snapped, 'That Jesse's a smart dude—but I can no more stand that mother-fucker than I can Mario Cuomo.'"

Clinton's rage at the Phoenix TV station about Jackson's seeming favoritism toward Tom Harkin became volcanic when, to his mortification, he learned that the CBS camera and microphones had recorded his entire diatribe.

Dave Howell, KTSP's news director turned thumbs down when Clinton's flacks beseeched him to "kill" the "bootleg."

"Can't do that, sir," Howell countered politely but firmly. "You see, you were in a studio with a microphone. And we live by the credo the camera is always running and that the microphone is always on. That's live television. You appear clearly not to be familiar with that...sir."

Falling Out with Jesse Jackson

That would not be the last that KTSP would hear from the Clinton camp. Nor did it take long for Clinton to hear from Jesse Jackson.

"It would seem to me that Clinton panicked and went out of control...we should not let the campaign to be diverted onto these side issues," Jackson sermonized.

"I am disappointed with his overreaction. I am disappointed by the tone of his blast at my character. I feel blindsided by what I saw and heard him say.

"I'm not angry at anybody, but I see clearly he panicked and went out of control...I am disturbed by the tone of the blast at my integrity, my character."

Clinton's rivals didn't pass up the opportunity to be heard either.

Tsongas suggested Clinton's comments were unpresidential:

"I think the American people want a president who's cool under fire and that kind of instinctive, angry, emotional outburst I don't think is appropriate."

Brown recalled that this wasn't the first time Clinton "put his foot in his mouth when he thought the cameras and recorders were turned off."

He was referring to Clinton's remarks in a conversation he thought was "off the record and not for attribution" when he told an interviewer what he had earlier murmured into the phone to Gennifer Flowers: "That [New York Governor] Mario Cuomo...acts like he's a Mafioso."

True to form, Clinton had excuses ready for his Jackson flap.

"I didn't fly off the handle," he said. "I just used strong words to describe how I felt at that moment."

Clinton said he phoned Jackson and "It's fine between us. There's no point in spending any more time on it in the campaign."

But more time was spent on it. KTSP-TV aired the "bootleg" tape—but not before station manager Larry Klein was inundated by calls from Clinton's campaign strategists.

"They did everything they could to talk me out of going on the air with the tape," Klein said. "They even threatened subpoenas and everything else to stop us."

Clinton spokesman Chris Dorvall admitted calls were made but denied a subpoena was threatened.

"All we did was call and say, 'Are you going to use it and why?'"

Klein's answer was, "Why are we going to use it? Because it's news and that's our business, N-E-W-S."

****

Buried on the back pages during the New York campaign were the outcomes of four other Democratic contests.

On March 31, delegate-poor Vermont held town caucuses and gave 14 delegates to Jerry Brown, who welcomed them "in this very tight race." Brown had stopped in Vermont for a few hours of campaigning a day or so before the primary, Clinton had not.

Vermont added to Brown's momentum from Connecticut. But that advantage was soon counterpointed by Wisconsin and Kansas, after their majority votes for Clinton kept his juggernaut machine on a roll.

Wisconsin gave Clinton 35 delegates; Brown, 29; and noncandidate Tsongas, 18. Kansas blew Clinton's rivals away by handing him 27 delegates after voters allowed him 51 percent. Tsongas, with 15 percent of the vote, netted 6 delegates, and Brown a paltry 2.

A significant aspect of the Kansas primary was its protest vote—14 percent of the electorate, including Governor Joan Finney, marked the box on their ballots signifying "None of the above." Mrs. Finney had wanted New York Governor Mario Cuomo to run.

Now, with more than half the state elections completed, Clinton had a formidable lead of well over 1,300 delegates. Still, with less than a thousand delegates to go, Clinton wasn't home free.

Nor was he free of ancient ghosts, stirred by lingering questions about his past, which returned as they seemed to do with periodic frequency, to remind him of another curse of his own making.

Yet, each time the threshold of political extinction was approached, he rose,

Phoenix-like, from the ashes and lived another day, but then only to face another ghost.

It would not be unreasonable, then, to assume that the Clinton campaign brain trust blew its collective mind when *Playboy*, the magazine whose logo promises "Entertainment For Men," proudly proclaimed the forthcoming issue of May 1992 would feature a lady with a proud historic past and a promising future.

The subject, the press proclamation said, would be available for interviews on a date set not only to coincide with publication of the magazine—but also with the April 7 New York primary. The site chosen for the press bash was Little Rock.

The grave concerns of Clinton's staffers were without foundation. For *Playboy*'s editor, Christy Hefner (Hugh's daughter), had no intention of embarrassing Clinton with text to detract from the exciting pictorial of one Elizabeth Ward Gracen.

Of course, the sexual exploits of Bill Clinton and Elizabeth Ward Gracen, nee Elizabeth Ward, the former Miss Arkansas and 1982's Miss America, were not reported in the *Playboy* spread in the way they were earlier in this text.

Nevertheless, the panic the *Playboy* announcement caused the Clinton campaign points up the damage control that Hillary instituted to keep her husband squeaky clean in the public's eye.

34

PUT-DOWNS FOR "HILLARY THE HUN"

When Hillary Was Told, "Bug off!"

Hillary Clinton was expected to make a big splash alongside husband Bill in the presidential primaries. But she scored too few points to be of help. Her pushiness turned people off. The backlash began to hurt Bill.

"I think you'd better be laid-back for a while," James Carville told Hillary with unaccustomed bluntness. "I have to bring up what Richard Nixon said about you."

"That fink! What did Tricky Dick have to say about me?" Hillary demanded to know.

"He looks upon you and Bill as co-candidates," Carville replied. "And he said that you, being a strong wife, make your husband look like a wimp."

"He said that!"

"That's not all he said. He also said, 'Hillary pounds on the piano so hard that Bill can't be heard.' And his last word on the subject is, 'You want a wife who's intelligent, but not too intelligent.'"

Before Hillary could find her tongue, Carville put in the final word.

"Hillary, you just bug off and lay low. If you don't, you'll have to be satisfied with just being the *first lady* of Arkansas. Period."

Nixon wasn't the only one turned off by Hillary's incursive iron-handedness. NBC-TV's Tom Brokaw watched, nonplussed, after Clinton swept a tier of southern states in the Super Tuesday primaries. Without even an embrace or handshake for her husband, Hillary rushed past him and mounted the stage.

She raised her hands high above her head, fists clenched like a triumphant prize fighter. Then she spoke into the microphone while Clinton looked on from the floor in stunned silence.

With nary a reference to the *real* victor, whom she referred to as "the messenger," Hillary proceeded to exhort as though she were the victor.

"We believe passionately in this country and we cannot stand by for one more year and watch what is happening to it."

A bemused Tom Brokaw let the audience applause die down. Then he cracked,

"This was not just an introduction. This was a speech by Mrs. Clinton."

That same aggressiveness was apparent again after Clinton swept the Illinois primary. TV cameras at campaign headquarters again recorded the victory celebration. As on Super Tuesday, Hillary surged up to the stage, leaving Bill in the background sheepishly awaiting the end of his wife's long and labored introduction.

"Hillary left Bill looking like a hanger-on hungering for home-baked cookies," wrote the *New York Times*' William Safire. His column spoke of Hillary committing "usurpation of a candidate's strength."

In an earlier "On Language" column that appears weekly in the *Times*' Sunday magazine, Safire tore into Nancy Reagan on that same theme. But in 1987, he defined the former first lady's intrusions into her husband's office affairs as "interference." His conclusion then, as in 1992, was the same: a politician's wife's overbearingness leaves her husband "weakened and made to appear wimpish and helpless."

Even *Vanity Fair* wrote that Hillary leads people to believe there is "something a little scary, a little Al Haig-ish about her."

Hillary's impact on her husband's presidential campaign was so negative that, midway through the primaries, a public opinion poll taken in early April showed her approval rating had dropped to 49 percent, whereas a month before it hovered at the 65 percent level.

Everyone, it seemed, was taking swipes at Hillary, "The Lady Macbeth of Little Rock," as the *American Spectator* labeled her. She was compared with Eva Peron and called the "Winnie Mandela of American politics."

Richard Bond, chairman of the Republican National Committee, characterized Hillary as "that champion of the family" who "has likened marriage and the family to slavery" and is anything but a "champion of the family."

Hillary Clinton certainly was far from championing family values when she dealt with the rumors she said she despised talking about.

She took that route in the May 1992 edition of *Vanity Fair*—fully three months before the *New York Post* made headlines out of a tiny footnote in a book, *The Power House*, published by St. Martin's Press. The *Post* sensationalized the episode with this page one headline:

Mrs. Clinton Spreads Rumor about Bush's girlfriend
HILLARY GOES TABLOID

Written by celebrated author Gail Sheehy, the piece reported that Hillary Clinton was infuriated by what she viewed as a double standard: that reporters had no predisposition to investigate rumors about Bush's private life, yet had the effrontery to delve into her husband's.

Miss Sheehy quotes Hillary Clinton:

"I had tea with Anne Cox Chambers [owner-publisher of the Cox media empire and one of America's richest women] and she's sittin' there in her sun-room saying, 'You know I just don't understand why they think they can get away with this— everybody knows about George Bush.'

"And then Chambers launches into this long description of, you know, Bush and his carrying on, all of which is apparently well known in Washington.

"But I'm convinced part of it is that the Establishment—regardless of party—sticks together. They're gonna circle the wagons on Jennifer [Fitzgerald] and all these other people."

Miss Sheehy, a contributing editor at *Vanity Fair* and author of several best-selling books, also interviewed Mrs. Chambers and wrote that the communications heiress told Hillary, "I don't understand why nothing's ever been said about a George Bush girlfriend—I understand he has a Jennifer."

The article raised hackles all across the country. Newspapers editorialized that people who live in glass houses, as Hillary Clinton certainly did, shouldn't throw bricks—especially when they could boomerang.

Neither the president nor first lady protested Miss Sheehy's story as they were to do in August after the book written by former CNN reporter Joe Trento's wife, Susan, was published.

At that time, Barbara Bush blew her top about the footnote in *The Power House* when she was interviewed on television's "NBC Nightly News."

"The day we start letting lies run a campaign, instead of talking about the issues, is the day we're in sad shape," fumed the first lady. "And I think the press ought to shape up right now

Mrs. Bush and the Hillary Sleaze Factor

Earlier in the interview, Mrs. Bush criticized journalists for reporting that Bill Clinton had an affair with Gennifer Flowers:

"I said that about the other sleaze issue, too. I thought it was outrageous that people printed what a woman got paid to say. I thought that was terrible. And I think the press ought to pull themselves up and look at what they're doing and behave themselves. They are taking the campaign and putting it on a level that it should not be.

"I mean...our foreign friends say to us, 'What's happened to your country?' And it's true. The media has got to start printing facts, not lies."

Bush himself did not protest the story that he had had an extramarital affair until reporters confronted him with the *New York Post*'s headline during a news conference with Israeli Prime Minister Yitzhak Rabin at the president's Kennebunkport home in Maine a day after the story ran.

"I'm not going to take any sleazy questions like this," Bush sneered outside his summer retreat. "I am very disappointed that you would ask such a question of me, and I will not respond to it. I haven't responded in the past, and I think it's..."

After a momentary pause to catch his breath, he exhaled:

"...an outrage!"

That was the second time in less than 24 hours that Bush exploded over a question on his "adultery." The night before, in an Oval Office interview broadcast live on "Dateline NBC," Bush refused to say whether he had ever had a "prurient" affair.

"I'm not going to take any sleaze questions," Bush snapped at reporter Stone Phillips. "You see, you're perpetuating the sleaze by even asking the question, to say nothing of asking it in the Oval Office.

"And I don't think you ought to do that and I'm not going to answer the question."

Until that moment, Bush had never responded directly to the allegation about his supposed extramarital affair. But his son George addressed it for a *Newsweek* reporter during the 1988 presidential campaign with this rejoinder:

"The answer is N-O!"

Even as Bush fended off further questions at Kennebunkport, deputy campaign manager Mary Matalin took a strong swipe at *The Power House*. Appearing on CBS-TV's "This Morning," she said, "The Democrats have been peddling this trashy book to many reputable newspapers, who have all rejected the opportunity to reprint this trash. Furthermore, these accounts have been checked out for twelve years by every reputable news organization in the country and have been found unfounded, ungrounded. They're total trash."

Miss Matalin's broadside flushed out Susan Trento's husband from his fallout shelter to answer criticism of his wife's book.

"The president of the United States owes the public an explanation, not a tantrum," thundered the investigative reporter, who stated he was one of the sources for the information on Bush's alleged 1984 Swiss Alps affair with the English-born, sixty-ish Jennifer Fitzgerald. Trento, employed at the time by CNN, said he obtained the information from former U.S. Ambassador Louis Fields, who died in 1988.

Joe Trento, who routinely used a tape recorder in his interviews, didn't produce voice corroboration of the rumor he passed on to his wife. Nor did he explain whether or not, out of a sense of duty to his employer, he offered the report to the TV news show at the time he heard it from Fields.

The last word had not been heard from the Clintons in the matter of sleaze.

After George and Barbara Bush vented their outrage at the rumor concerning the president, a voice from afar was heard murmuring a whisper of understanding.

"I don't approve of it. I didn't like it when it was done to me, and I don't like it when it's done to him."

That was Bill Clinton commenting on the accusations made about Bush in *The Power House*.

Hillary was hard on Bill's heels to repent for having succumbed to the urge to "go tabloid" with Gail Sheehy in *Vanity Fair*, as the *New York Post* put it.

"Nobody knows better than I how painful discussions of rumors can be," were the words Hillary used to show contrition. "I wouldn't want anybody else, and I certainly don't want the Bush family, subjected to that."

Bush campaign spokesman Tony Mitchell commented, "We certainly would be pleased if, in fact, the Clintons have drawn the right personal conclusion about the reckless and irresponsible nature of her [Hillary's] statements to *Vanity Fair*.

"We hope this campaign will be properly focused on who has the leadership, the experience, the ability and the character to address the challenges facing the American people."

Hillary was defended by Democratic Party consultant Bob Squier, who didn't officially support any candidate during the primaries. He suggested that if the Clintons wanted the issue on Bush's marital infidelity out, they wouldn't have resorted to a monthly magazine as their sounding board.

"Her comments sound like the kind of frustration one would feel when one is being dealt with unfairly, and that, in fact, is the situation," said Squier.

"The bottom line is the Clintons have had to answer the Gennifer question and George Bush has yet to answer the Jennifer question with a J."

Gail Sheehy Outwits the Lady Macbeth of Little Rock

In her eagerness to dull the sting her words inflicted, Hillary recalled, with an air suggesting it had just come to mind, that her remarks were "off the record." But how could she have supposed that they were?

"It was a private conversation," Hillary said. "My point is, even if it were, I should not have responded, and it was done in the most difficult of times of the experience that Bill and I went through."

Miss Sheehy took issue with Hillary's recollections. She had reviewed the subject's quotes about Bush's alleged affair as recently as March 26 in a final interview.

"I wanted to give her an opportunity to elaborate or correct anything she thought was imprecise," Miss Sheehy explained. "She recalled it. She looked uncomfortable, but she didn't deny it or ask to change anything."

The interviewer also stressed that she couldn't tell whether Hillary was trying to get the Bush rumor out to warn Republicans to back off on further questions about her husband's character.

"Whether this was Hillary the wife or Hillary the clever strategist and litigator talking, I couldn't say," offered Miss Sheehy.

That wasn't the first time the writer had to respond to Hillary's bluster about the story.

Before the ink was dry on the advance copies of *Vanity Fair* that reached newspaper offices in New York, Hillary was besieged with calls to a New York hotel, where she was staying with her husband. She declined to speak to callers, but her friend and so-called "ultra-liberal" campaign aide, Susan Thomases, offered to speak for Hillary:

"The article contains a garbled version of a private conversation on an issue that is neither new nor relevant."

Miss Sheehy hit the ceiling when she heard that.

"We discussed this in two taped interviews and I independently confirmed it with Anne Cox Chambers," she retorted. "Like any political person, she wanted to get the story out, but she didn't want it traceable to her."

Miss Sheehy recalled her first interview with Hillary, in January, when "a terrible shrug went down [her] face just after an aide rushed in and informed her that the three networks were leading with Gennifer Flowers' press conference called by the *Star* magazine in the Waldorf-Astoria after it published the story of her 12-year affair with Clinton. Her taped conversations with Clinton were also being broadcast."

Miss Sheehy recalled that Hillary phoned her husband, who reportedly responded that he wasn't concerned because no one would believe his ex-flame.

Bill and Hillary were later given air time on CBS-TV's "60 Minutes" to deny the affair ever happened, and to sermonize that Gennifer Flowers *made it all up* for the

$100,000 she was paid to tell the story.

Gennifer did receive $100,000 and other perks from the *Star*—but the Clintons never proved that she *made it all up*.

Miss Sheehy's article dwelled on matters other than Hillary's claim that Bush had an affair with Jennifer Fitzgerald. A large part chronicled Hillary's wish to clutch Gennifer's throat and demand she tell the truth.

"If we'd been in front of a jury I'd say, 'Miss Flowers, isn't it true you were asked [if you had an affair with Bill Clinton] by the AP [Associated Press] in June of 1990 and you said no?'" Of course, she had. Clinton told her to deny everything—and Gennifer followed orders because she wanted a cushy state job.

Anita Hill's Hillary's Heroine

On the road to the nation's first co-presidency, Hillary went from her cookie-baking configuration to beating the pans for controversial law professor Anita Hill. Hill, Hillary said, had "transformed consciousness and changed history with her courageous testimony" in Senate confirmation hearings for Bush U.S. Supreme Court nominee Clarence Thomas.

The woman most likely to advise her husband, if he became president, on whom to appoint to the Supreme Court proclaimed, "All women who care about equality of opportunity, about integrity and morality in the workplace are in Professor Anita Hill's debt."

Miss Hill had thrown the hearings into disarray when she charged Thomas sexually harassed her while she was employed by him in his early practice in law.

All this brought *New York Post* editorial page editor Eric Breindel to comment, "It's hard to imagine a more forthright endorsement of Anita Hill's effort to destroy Justice Clarence Thomas.

"Obviously, Mrs. Clinton is entitled to her view of Anita Hill's contribution. Equally obviously—given the key role Mrs. Clinton is playing in the national campaign, and in view of her penchant for public policy pronouncements—it's reasonable publicly to take issue with her.

"It's our hope, moreover, that people who do so aren't constantly derided by the Clinton campaign as 'low-roaders' picking on Governor Clinton's wife. Hillary Clinton is very much her own person. She makes speeches in her own name; she writes serious articles; and it's been made clear that she'll have a policy-making role if Governor Clinton is elected."

Breindel's editorial continued:

"Isn't it appropriate to expect Mrs. Clinton to respond personally to her critics—on issues ranging from Anita Hill to her essays on children and the family to her work as head of the radical-left New World Foundation? Whatever happened to classic feminism?"

Hillary Clinton does not come off well in this *Post* mortem.

"With respect to Anita Hill, Mrs. Clinton's admiration places her in a decided minority. The Hill supporters may be vocal. But poll after poll demonstrated that a majority of Americans thought Anita Hill was lying...ordinary Americans—in great numbers—saw Hill as a fraud. This was no less true among women than it was among men.

"Never mind that it's been demonstrated that she was lying when she described herself as a pro-Bork Republican, that she was lying when she claimed to have left the Wald Harkrader firm in D.C. entirely voluntarily and that her specific testimony about Clarence Thomas turns out to have been riddled with inconsistencies. Right now, Anita Hill is enjoying her 15 minutes of fame."

After taking the American Bar Association to task for "seeing fit to give Hill an award...[and] has transformed itself from a national professional association into a highly politicized entity," Breindel accused the ABA of not wanting to "face the fact that substantial holes" existed in Hill's story—"nor, apparently, does Hillary Clinton [want to face that fact]."

A time will come, concluded Breindel, "when more is known about Anita Hill, her testimony about 'sexual harassment' will go down as one of the taller tales in American history."

That time soon came—when author/investigative writer David Brock blew the University of Oklahoma Professor out of the water with his 1993 book *The Real Anita Hill* (Free Press).

The real issue as Breindel saw it, was not Anita Hill, but Hillary Clinton.

"What does Mrs. Clinton mean when she says Americans owe a 'debt' to Anita Hill's performance? Where does Bill Clinton stand on these issues?

"Governor Clinton's standard response—'How dare you attack my wife?'—seems profoundly evasive and unsatisfactory."

Breindel's editorial conclusion is echoed in Gail Sheehy's observation in the *Vanity Fair* article, that Clinton is a man dependent on strong women. She then quotes an unidentified family member [suspected to be his mother] for this gem:

"Bill Clinton has always deferred to women to fight his battles."

Betsey Wright, Clinton's longtime chief of staff and staunch defender, is quoted as saying her employer is "careless about appearances":

"The frustrations I went through in the seven years of being his chief of staff, of watching the groupie girls hanging around and the fawning all over him. But I always laughed at them on the inside, because I knew no *dumb bimbo* [author's highlight] was ever going to provide him all of the dimensions that Hillary does."

Tracking Down the Bimbo Factor

Betsey Wright's observation may be deeper than its impression on the magazine page. For there is testimony by Sally Perdue, for one, (not authenticated by any means) that Bill Clinton's attraction to her was more physical than cerebral.

The word *bimbo* may have first been expressed in connection with Bill Clinton by Betsey Wright. But it wasn't the last time that slur for a fast and loose woman would be mouthed by the Clinton campaign.

As cited earlier, the 10-member investigative firm headed by crack San Francisco private eye Jack Palladino had been hired early on in the Clinton campaign to investigate and discredit women like Gennifer Flowers and Sally Perdue, among others, who came forward with kiss and tell stories about the candidate.

A Clinton spokesman [it is not clear whether it was Betsey Wright] said the firm's objective was controlling "bimbo eruptions." In short, any woman saying she'd gone to bed with Bill Clinton was a "bimbo."

Palladino could stop some blabbermouths, but not all. He had no way of muzzling Congressman Robert Dornan, the California Republican who labeled Clinton "a draft-dodging, womanizing son of a bitch."

Those introductory words, rising from the well in the House of Representatives were not recorded in the *Congressional Record* of August 5, 1992, but the feisty, gravel-voiced lawmaker was logged in the official congressional register for the remainder of his thoughts about Clinton. They were provoked by Congresswoman Patricia Schroeder (D-Colorado) who took exception to President Bush's vetoes on bills dealing with family planning:

"Well, thank goodness for Bill Clinton because he is one Bill that the president cannot veto," said Mrs. Schroeder, "and we know he is going to be a lot more enlightened on this and appoint people who are in touch with the twentieth century and not living in the nineteenth."

To which Dornan used up the minute Speaker Thomas A. Foley allotted him for rebuttal:

"Well, well, well, well, here we go again, Mr. Speaker, discussing politics in the well of the House, bashing our president and praising Governor Bill Clinton. Let me tell the gentlewoman from Colorado something:

"We all know the Gennifer Flowers story was true. I've heard the tapes. Believe me, there is not a newsperson in the whole world who's heard the audio tapes or read the hard copy who believes Flowers was merely 'a friendly acquaintance,' Clinton's laughable term of endearment."

After proclaiming that Gennifer was to appear in the November "election issue" of *Playboy*, Dornan lashed out:

"How utterly weird. If this man Clinton is elected, my colleagues, your high school kids and junior-high school kids will certainly have a super-negative role model in the White House, because of what his own senior guru, Betsey Wright, calls 'bimbo eruptions.' Mr. Speaker and colleagues, character is an issue, maybe the key issue."

Then Dornan hit the candidate in one of his most vulnerable spots:

"I hold here the draft dodger's December 3, 1969, letter to Colonel Eugene Holmes, at that time commander of the University of Arkansas's ROTC."

(The entire letter, reproduced in chapter 5, was entered into the *Congressional Record*, but not before Dornan prefaced its introduction with a raking speech.)

"Mr. Speaker...I ask permission to put into this House's permanent historical record, Governor Clinton's whining and dishonorable letter...admitting that he deceived that army officer [Holmes] in order to cause a third, repeat a third, young Arkansas man, repeat *man* [author's highlight], to replace Clinton in the draft quota for Hot Springs. The other young heroes stepped forward for the dodger in June 1968 and

April 1969. Read it and weep, loyal Americans."

Dornan iced the cake with George Bush's deputy campaign manager Mary Matalin's snidely worded series of questions faxed to media across the nation the weekend of August 1-2:

"Which campaign had to spend thousands of taxpayer dollars on private investigators to fend off 'bimbo eruptions'?"

The memo read, "Sniveling hypocritical Democrats: Stand up and be counted—on second thought, shut up and sit down."

The 38-year-old Miss Matalin, a protégé of the late GOP Chairman, Lee Atwater, who had a reputation for hardball politics, further rubbed it into Bill "I never inhaled" Clinton:

"Which candidate...admitted there was a deliberate 'pattern of omission' in his answers on marijuana use?"

It isn't known whether Miss Matalin got any flak from her longtime beau, (and future husband) James Carville, 48, Clinton's principal campaign manager, but she did get reproved by the White House, from where the president sent the message that he didn't want to engage in the "sleaze business," and directed his campaign staff not to hit below the belt.

Miss Matalin came perilously close to an apology when she sent a follow-up fax:

"It would appear to some that I might have violated, at least in spirit, the president's dictate to the campaign that we avoid references to Governor Clinton's personal life.

"I regret if the tone of my statement left the wrong impression in that regard."

Later, when informed of Bush's disavowal and Miss Matalin's lukewarm expiation, solemnly dispatched but most likely widely unread, Clinton spokeswoman Dee Dee Myers, offered, "That's fine with us."

Tammy Wynette Zaps Hillary

It was not "fine" with Tammy Wynette when Hillary Clinton defended herself against questions about her strong influence on her husband's politics and failed for once to give her stock response:

"Should I have stayed home and baked cookies and had teas?"

Hillary instead singled out one of the country's most beloved country-western singers to compare herself with:

"I'm not some little woman just standing by her man, like Tammy Wynette."

That reference was to the hit song "Stand By Your Man," one of the biggest hits in the First Lady Of Country Music's far-ranging repertoire.

Almost before the words were out of her mouth, Hillary had to bear one of the biggest put-downs of the campaign.

"I resent Hillary Clinton's remarks and I want her to know she owes me an apology for what she said," Miss Wynette protested.

Tammy Wynette was watching the January 26, 1992, run of CBS's "60 Minutes" when Hillary Clinton made the remark.

Bill's affair with Gennifer Flowers had just exploded in the news, and Hillary had hit the road in a panicky surge to rehabilitate her husband's image. Mike Wallace's widely watched show was her first stop, to be followed the next Thursday by an appearance on ABC-TV's "Prime Time Live."

"I was stone stunned." Miss Wynette said after she fired off a fast fax to Clinton campaign headquarters.

"Mrs. Clinton, you have offended every woman and man who loves that song—several million in number," the megastar declared.

"How dare you! With all that is in me, I resent your caustic remark. You have offended every true country music fan and every person 'who has made it on their own' with no one to take them to a White House.

"I would like you to appear with me on any forum, including networks, cable, or talk shows and stand toe to toe with me. I can assure you, in spite of your education, you will find me to be just as bright as yourself.

"I will not stand by and allow you or any other person to embarrass, humiliate, and degrade me on national television and print without hearing from me."

The fax was transmitted to Colorado, where the Clintons were campaigning. It was received by a gap-jawed Hillary Clinton, trudging the snow-covered, Rocky Mountain State's campaign trails with Bill.

Tammy's husband and manager, George Richey, also took umbrage at Hillary's distractive statement. Hillary, Richey found, was defending "a remorselessly unsalvageable husband to unnecessary excess."

Hillary's reported reaction was to turn red-faced, roll her eyes, and slap her forehead. She issued an apology, in all likelihood whipped up by a campaign blurbist, that dripped, "I didn't mean to hurt Tammy Wynette as a person. I happen to be a country-western fan. If she feels like I've hurt her feelings, I'm sorry about that."

Richey responded to the original remarks on "60 Minutes" calling them "an unforgivable insult," then faxed his own two cents to the presidential candidate's *designing woman*:

"It was totally off base. It embarrassed Tammy, who believe me, is not a little wallflower that'll stand anything."

After receiving a copy of the apology, Richey dashed off another message to Hillary: "Sorry, that's not good enough."

Then Richey faced a gaggle of journalists.

"This is totally unsatisfactory," he snapped about Hillary's response. "Tammy expects an apology on national TV for what Hillary Clinton said.

"Believe me, this is no fun, but I've got no doubt we'll hear from them."

Meanwhile country music fans all across the nation were up in arms over Hillary's intemperate remarks. Nowhere was this more evident than in Nashville, where scores of women phoned radio talk show hostess Devon O'Day on WSIX-FM.

"They went nuts," said Miss O'Day. "They were one-hundred percent with Tammy."

Is there a bottom line to this story? Did Hillary apologize to Tammy on national TV? Did she dare take the challenge and go "toe to toe" with the country-western star? No further questions, please.

35

WHO IS THIS ROSS PEROT FELLA?

Bimbo Eruptions False Alarm

"Bill Clinton wants to make it known that there is no truth whatsoever that there was a relationship between himself and Elizabeth Ward, the 1982 Miss America, who will be featured in the forthcoming issue of *Playboy* magazine.

"The Governor met Miss Ward when she was a contestant, as he does meet all Miss Arkansas finalists for the Miss America Pageant. Reports of an affair are totally without foundation, and Miss Ward herself denies any intimacy with Bill Clinton [totally denied by Elizabeth's response]."

That statement was issued after the panic button was pressed by Clinton campaign strategists who couldn't wait to get their hands on advance copies of the magazine's May edition. Although the bare-all, eight page spread might have made some folks in Arkansas blush, Clinton didn't have that much to fear from the text.

However, some *Playboy* readers—and Bill Clinton, too, after reading the text (and perusing the territory he is said to have previously explored in person)—may have found a problem with Elizabeth's response to the *Big Question*:

"Have I slept with this person? I don't believe that's anyone's business. I have certain boundaries about what I reveal about myself, and I respect other people's boundaries as well."

The text coursing through Elizabeth's nude and semi-nude photos also explains why this "lapsed born-again Christian who underwent a lot of therapy" because of her bad experience as a Miss America, decided to do the buff routine.

Now edging 32, married, living in California, and using the stage name of Elizabeth Ward Gracen, the lanky former beauty queen wanted to "make a splash" and jazz up her acting career.

In the meantime, the primaries continued.

****

On April 15, Clinton won 41 of Virginia's 78 pledged delegates, Brown took five, while 32 were uncommitted. Added to the Democratic front-runner's total were four delegates who could be counted with the 34 he previously won in Missouri's convoluted, three-stage caucus procedure.

At this point, Clinton had 1,324 delegates to Brown's 271. Tsongas's 529 delegates were frozen and no additional ones were being counted since he had suspended his campaign. Clinton now needed 821 more delegates to reach the magic number of 2,145 for nomination.

Meanwhile, a menace from Texas began to loom large for Bill Clinton, and even more so for George Bush.

A billionaire from Dallas, a corporate action figure and cowboy philanthropist named H. Ross Perot agreed to run for president as an Independent—provided his supporters got his name on the ballots in all 50 states.

Outside of Dallas, Perot was known for his wealth and dramatic exploits, including an unsuccessful 1969 attempt to fly 26 tons of food to U.S. prisoners of war in Hanoi, and a commando raid he organized in 1979 that freed two of his Electronic Data Systems employees from Iranian captivity.

His blunt denunciations of politics-as-usual had, in a relatively short time, gained Perot significant nationwide support. Exit polls taken after the April 7 New York primary and three other states' primaries—Alaska, Kansas, and Wisconsin—indicated 22 percent of Republican balloters in those races and 25 percent of Democratic voters preferred Perot to President Bush or Governor Clinton.

Newsday staff correspondent David Firestone was sent to Dallas to see what made Perot such a threat to Bush and Clinton. The reporter found, "Within Texas...Perot has always had a...complicated relationship with the public. Over the years, Perot has given many millions to Dallas's concert hall, its leading medical center, its food banks and charitable institutions. Much of his generosity is conducted without fanfare, such as his assistance to the families of several police officers injured in the line of duty. But he remains an outsider to the city's power structure, and a dubious curiosity to its burgeoning minority communities."

Clinton Whistles "Dixie"

After strong showings in the Virginia caucus and the Missouri balloting, Bill Clinton could whistle "Dixie." For along with southern states such as North Carolina, West Virginia, Kentucky, Alabama, and his own Arkansas, he was favored to grab the lion's share of the 336 delegates they were electing. That meant Brown, given no chance below the Mason-Dixon Line, could challenge Clinton only in the two remaining delegate-rich states of Pennsylvania and California, which held 169 and 348 respectively.

Long before Californians were to go to the polls on June 2, two explosive events occurred.

On April 27, in an interview with *New York Daily News* feature writer Daphna Barak, the Rev. Jesse Jackson declared that he wanted to be Bill Clinton's running mate.

"There is a time that a leader should keep his private thoughts to himself and surprise...we won't be eliminated this time. We can't be. Every action has consequences.

"We are ready for any opportunity to serve but we are ready if we are ignored or rejected…if I am rejected this time, I am prepared to react."

Then in what she described was spoken in a rising voice, Miss Barak quoted the minister:

"I think Clinton is a secure enough person to choose me as his running mate. I haven't seen any sign of him being intimidated by me. There is a mutual respect between us.

"When he was really at a low point, when he had to cope with the Gennifer Flowers situation, I didn't attack him. Instead, I suggested we pray together…I was continuously generous toward him. Although you remember, everybody remembers, how vulnerable he was."

Jackson's pitch posed some thorny questions because he was still shunned by some moderates and Jewish voters after his remark of a decade before that New York was "hymietown." But Jackson didn't see it that way.

"I've got the experience and I've got the votes…I see myself as a running mate for the Democratic Party.

"I have campaigned for the nomination [for the presidency] two times, and you know what? I got…more votes than any candidate could get this time, and I didn't get only black votes. So if the issue is who got more votes, I should be the next running mate" because, Jackson contended, many blacks had chosen not to vote for either Clinton or Brown.

No sooner had the fallout from this explosion cleared than California was rocked by the deadliest riots of the century. They broke out the afternoon of April 29, a Wednesday, almost immediately after a jury returned with innocent verdicts for four Los Angeles Police Department cops in the videotaped Rodney King beating—a black man the cops savaged with nightsticks, fists, and feet as he lay on the ground helpless.

The riots over three days left 58 dead, 2,383 people injured (228 of them critically), more than 12,000 under arrest, and in excess of $700 million in damage from looting, pillaging, and arson.

Initially, the White House said it would not play politics with the riots, but then in an about-face blamed the explosion on 1960s Democratic policies and "the liberal Democratic Congress."

The riots triggered the hottest campaign rhetoric thus far.

Speaking from the distant outpost—and safety—of Little Rock, Clinton asked churches nationwide to take time to reflect on the bloody upheaval.

"It's time for reconciliation," Clinton said. "Racism and violence only beget more racism and violence. We must come together to search our souls for forgiveness and tolerance."

The White House condemned Clinton for trying to "play politics with this," then President Bush asked the Justice Department to intensify its investigation of police conduct in the King beating. Bush aimed his angriest comments at the rioters.

"The mob brutality, the total loss of respect for human life, was sickeningly sad," Bush lamented.

Jerry Brown returned to his home turf to "help cool down emotions" and called for federal indictments in the King case—which ultimately were returned by a grand jury.

Patrick Buchanan, by now hopelessly behind Bush in the delegate race, said the president wasn't being tough enough in ending the "orgy of looting, arson, lynching."

Even as the fires raged in Los Angeles, Clinton and Bush romped to easy victories in the Pennsylvania primary, then both took the bulk of the delegates from their respective parties in Indiana, North Carolina, Ohio, and Washington, D.C., all on the same Tuesday of May 5.

A momentary diversion occurred when Clinton had to take time out from the campaign trail to hear about some developments in Texas—strictly a family affair.

More Stirrings from Bill's Bank Robbing Stepsis

"I want to tell you that Dianne's been granted a hearing," the caller, reported to be big Texas politico Don Bankston, informed Clinton. "It appears she may be getting out of stir—and it conceivable could be troublesome for you."

Clinton's response was said to be, "Stay on top of it, Don, baby, and keep me informed."

The last thing Clinton wanted to hear at that stage of the campaign was a late update on his stepsister Dianne Dwire Welch's situation.

Despite Clinton's overwhelming victory in the Keystone State, half its Democrats who bothered to vote said they wished they had another choice. Still, exit polls found 64 percent of Pennsylvania Democrats saying they believed Clinton had the integrity and character to be president—a significant improvement from New York where only 49 percent did.

The latest primary votes came in the wake of a stunning Times-Mirror Newspapers poll showing a virtual three-way dead heat nationally, with Bush at 33 percent and Clinton and Perot each at 30 percent.

How might these standings have changed had the national media paid attention to a backwater state magazine, *Arkansas Times*, which came out with a cover story just as the Times-Mirror Newspapers poll broke?

How shocked would the nation have been to read that story and to learn that Governor Bill Clinton had tolerated a drug-smuggling Contra's conspiracy to ship arms, under President George Bush's aegis, as well as under the previous administration of Ronald Reagan?

The story behind that story is a deeply rooted plot of intrigue, mystery, cloak-and-dagger operations, and monumental, widespread cover-ups. A plot that, had it seen the light in a major newspaper or television newscast, could have spurred a congressional probe—a happening that still cries for such an inquiry because it is said to continue to this day.

36

THE BUSH-CLINTON-CONTRAS DRUG PLOT

Why Didn't the Press Touch It?

Bill Clinton's friend Max Brantley's *Arkansas Times* broke a cover story in his monthly magazine with this headline:

BAD COMPANY

Arkansas's most notorious drug smuggler testified about his links to Colombia. His ties to Washington have yet to be explained.

The story begins:

"It has been 10 years since cocaine smuggler Adler Berriman "Barry" Seal moved his massive operation to Arkansas, and six years since Seal's personal plane—the same one he used to run drugs—was shot down in Nicaragua, just months after Seal was murdered in Baton Rouge."

The lead paragraph conveys a succinct recitation of well-known Arkansas history of the most sordid sort. But the article, written by investigative reporter Mara Leveritt, wasn't intended to be an archival rehash of the past. A thorough reading of the piece suggests it was published as a double-edged sword. In fact, it takes only two paragraphs before the rapier does its intended deed.

One side of the blade lodges against the throat of incumbent President George Bush.

The other rests upon one of Bill Clinton's broad shoulders, postured to knight the Arkansas governor for his heraldic, hands-off virtue in a scandal that had been tainting his administration for more than 10 years.

Ms. Leveritt doesn't hesitate to direct the finger of blame away from Little Rock and point it at Washington, D.C. The theme is quite clear: the commerce in crimes committed on a small but strategic patch of real estate on the Arkansas-Oklahoma state line was *not* in the purview of the governor.

"For years Seal had used his plane [a Lear jet], which he based in Mena [the Intermountain Regional Airport] and affectionately called The Fat Lady [Seal himself weighed more than 300 pounds], in the service of Colombian drug lords," the *Arkansas Times* story went.

"But when The Fat Lady went down in Nicaragua, she wasn't carrying cocaine. She was loaded with military supplies for the Nicaraguan Contras. And the people paying for her flight were not Colombians; they were American covert operatives with direct ties to the office of then-Vice President George Bush at the White House."

Ms. Leveritt accomplished in one short paragraph what millions of words of testimony had failed to sort out over months, indeed years of Iran-Contra hearings by the Congress of the United States. She had immersed Bush in the boiling cauldron that the Iran-Contra scandal had become. Yet she offered no corroboration for that dipping.

Bill Clinton couldn't have found a more welcome ally and friend than Max Brantley, who edited that copy and splashed it as the cover story of his publication.

The *Times'* writer appears to have specialized in mythology. For its chronicles about the airport at Mena virtually confers an innocence akin to sainthood upon the nestor of Arkansas. Clinton is freed from all complicity in the state's worst-kept secret. As early as paragraph nine, at the top of the column on page 24, he is anointed *William the Innocent* as the *Arkansas Times* story continues:

"While criticism has been leveled at Gov. Bill Clinton for his failure to adequately investigate Seal's 8 years at Mena, the more serious questions surrounding the case lead not to Little Rock, but Washington."

This is the first time that Bill Clinton's name appears in the 3,500-word story. It's also the last time. Nowhere else does the marathon opus tell what, if anything, Clinton did to stop the illicit drug trafficking activity at Mena. Nor does it hint at involvement on Clinton's part in the attendant money-laundering schemes the article says happened under the watchful eyes of the governor's very own Arkansas State Police. Nor is there a clue as to what Clinton did to halt the shipment of arms out of Mena to the Nicaraguan rebels.

Nor does the article even identify the state police chief, Colonel Thomas "Tommy" Goodwin—to show what, if any, role he played in keeping his boss, the governor, informed of his helplessness to stop the activity, since President Bush, the FDA, the FBI, the CIA, and other branches of the federal government assertedly prevented local authorities from interfering with the ongoing conspiracy.

Nor does the article touch upon huge payoffs Clinton allegedly demanded—and received—for his hands-off policy, which the author will detail shortly.

How Could Clinton Not Know?

To believe that Tommy Goodwin had not informed Bill Clinton about such matters suggests the top cop also didn't frequently tell the governor about his little brother, Roger, and friend/benefactor Dan Lasater's deep involvements in the Arkansas drug scene.

There's positively no question that such activity went on in Mena and that it was known by law enforcement agencies when Bill Clinton was governor. But they turned their heads the other way—for 10 years, at least!

It is all the more scandalous to find that Clinton countenanced that illicit activity for more than a decade—and did nothing to stop it! Such a posture is nothing less than criminal.

The *Arkansas Times* makes it obvious that its article is intended as a hatchet job on Bush when it fails to quote Bill Clinton's defense of his inaction in allowing this grotesquery to fester for so long.

The article dwells on four key questions that should have been answered by Bill Clinton—but which are left hanging without rebuttal.

"For instance," as the article puts it,

• "Seal's smuggling activities, which were among the largest in the nation's history, were known for years to federal agents. But he was never stopped. Why?

• "When Arkansas officials tried to investigate Seal and bring the smugglers to justice, federal officials thwarted them at every turn. Why?

• "Why, after Seal turned informant, did federal agents put him in a position where he was certain to be murdered? They knew his former associates had put out a contract on his life. Yet, though he refused protection, they ordered him disarmed and set free. He said he felt like a sitting duck, which he was.

• "And why does the Bush administration to this day refuse to cooperate with investigators trying to probe the relationship between the White House, the CIA, and the Drug Enforcement Agency, and smuggler-operatives like Barry Seal?"

The author doesn't intend to withhold opinion on this highly controversial matter. He feels duty-bound as an investigative reporter not to do so. His experience as such for more than a half century, prompts him to ask another series of questions:

Why, during the campaign, didn't *squeaky clean* presidential candidate Bill Clinton ask of the *villainous* George Bush:

• Mr. President, why didn't you put a stop to the shipment of drugs to the airport in Mena in my state of Arkansas?

• Mr. President, you had full knowledge that Lieutenant Colonel Oliver North organized transshipments of arms to Contras out of the airport in Mena in my state of Arkansas, and you did nothing to stop this. Why?

• Mr. President, my information also has it that North hooked up in this clandestine network with CIA chief William Casey, who referred the colonel to retired Army General Richard V. Secord who then, acting as a for-hire contractor, found pilots to make the secret air drops over Nicaragua, flights made by America's premier drug smuggler Bobby Seal, among others, a man you yourself recruited for this dirty work when you were vice president. Why did you allow this activity to continue for so many years at the airport in Mena in my state of Arkansas, but did nothing to stop it? I wish to hear you respond, sir! Why?

The author faxed Ms. Leveritt's questions to the White House on May 20, 1993, to the attention of President Clinton's press secretary, Dee Dee Myers, with a note:

> I am writing on the subject published in the May 21, 1992, edition of the *Arkansas Times* regarding the use of the airport at Mena for covert activities bearing on smuggling of drugs and arms in connection with the Contras.
>
> The foregoing questions were raised by the writer, Mara Leveritt, whose cover story, titled "Bad Company," explored the operation at Mena

and cited criticism that Bill Clinton endured 'for his failure to adequately investigate' that activity.

Essentially, the story maintains that President Bush, the FDA, the CIA, and other Governmental agencies thwarted the Governor from conducting such an investigation.

I will be deeply indebted to you, Ms. Myers, if you or a member of your staff can advise me whether or not during the '92 campaign Governor Clinton asked President Bush any of the four questions that I culled from the *Arkansas Times* story? If yes, I would like to know when and where one or another of the questions may have been addressed to the incumbent.

The author did not receive a response that day.

That was understandable, for Dee Dee Myers was up to her eyeballs in an imbroglio with the press, trying to explain why the Clinton administration had fired the entire staff of the White House Travel Office and given the job to a 25-year-old presidential cousin, who was to make travel plans through a for-profit Little Rock travel agency.

Ms. Myers was being shelled by reporters' queries demanding justification for the sudden dismissal of seven highly popular veteran employees—ones whose primary functions in several presidential administrations were to charter flights and hotel rooms for the press on presidential trips and commercial travel by White House staff. Turning the Travel Office over to Clinton's cousin's agency was the first attempt by the Billary co-presidency to introduce their own brand of boondoggling in Washington.

Dee Dee Can't Stonewall This Author

The author waited a long time without hearing a word of response to his questions from President Clinton's office.

That silence did not stonewall the author, who turned to other sources to clear up the mystery of Bill Clinton's "failure to adequately investigate Seal's years at Mena," as the *Arkansas Times* stated so forthrightly.

One of the most provocative—and telling—sources of information was Lawrence T. Patterson, founder and publisher of *Criminal Politics*, known as "The Magazine of Conspiracy Politics." Patterson's Cincinnati-based publication devoted its entire issue of November 1992 to critiquing the election. Separate articles covered such topics as "The Making of the 42nd President—How it Really Happened," "The Clinton Acceptance Speech," and "The Clinton Cocaine Connection," with a sidebar story on "Brother's Conviction."

The lead story was on the cocaine connection. Its thrust was to respond to the *Arkansas Times* article, "Bad Company."

"Since 1982 when the Seal operation arrived in Mena, Arkansas," the article begins, "Clinton was assigned the responsibility of covering for the CIA's selected transshipment point...Clinton's immediate contact was CIA agent, Vice-President

George Bush, a former director of the CIA—and life-long CIA operative.

"The cover-up," the article goes on, "continued through Clinton's campaign for the presidency to his selection and nomination by the Bilderberg Society in June 1991 at Baden-Baden, Germany. There is every probability that drug shipments are being funneled out of the United States from Mena...even as we publish this story."

Patterson's magazine ran a front page cutout of the *Arkansas Times* to exhibit the "Bad Company" headline. Three photos spread across its columns, head shots of Barry Seal, George Bush, and the head of Colombia's infamous Medellin Cartel, Jorge Luis Ochoa.

"The *Arkansas Times*...explained the existence of a national drug transshipment center operated by the CIA under George Bush's direction with Barry Seal as day-to-day operations manager [and of the way] Seal used many aircraft. The largest, however, was a whopper: a huge military transport, an Air Force C-130."

Adler Berriman "Barry" Seal was born in Baton Rouge, Louisiana, July 16, 1939, and took flight lessons at age 17. Seal soon demonstrated a jauntiness that was to be his trademark in life. He flew to out-of-town high school football games while his classmates took the bus or made the trip in their cars.

Upon graduation, Seal enlisted in the army and was to claim he served in the Special Forces, the elite combat unit whose members participate in covert operations. After a two-year hitch, Seal returned to Louisiana and tried college for a year. His penchant for flying took him into the Air National Guard. By 1972, at 33, he turned to commercial aviation and flew Boeing 747s for TWA as the nation's youngest airline pilot.

Seal left TWA in 1976 to become a full-time flyboy drug trafficker. When he testified before the President's Commission on Organized Crime in October 1985, Seal described his work both as a drug runner and as a U.S. undercover operative working for the CIA. He said he turned to the world of drugs because it "...was so simple, so lucrative. The money involved was incredible."

Seal said under oath that he flew about 100 drug flights into the United States between 1976 and 1986 and was never intercepted by authorities. Each load, he said, ran between 600 to 1,200 pounds. Before 1980, he transported marijuana; afterward it was the much more profitable cocaine.

He raked in somewhere between $60 million and $100 million just for the $3.5 billion worth of cocaine he muled into the U.S. in his last three years as a drug trafficker.

Arkansas State Police records were released to the *Arkansas Democrat* in late 1989, when the newspaper's Rodney Bowers was writing a four-part series about Seal's activities as a drug smuggler and government informant. The articles ran in early December of that year. The reporter cited heretofore secret data that revealed that the Arkansas State Police learned of the way "Seal was able to conceal his earnings by creating dummy corporations, through which he 'laundered' his drug money."

Clinton Stonewalled the Probes

Yet authorities did nothing. The report out of the state police files indicated that all levels of law enforcement—from the local Sheriff's Department of Polk County, where Mena airport is located, to the state police, the FBI, the DEA, and Internal Revenue Service—all had a bead on Barry Seal's operation.

"They were all eager to put a stop to the drug smuggling," *Criminal Politics* asserted, "but Bill Clinton's office as well as federal officials stonewalled them every step of the way."

Lawrence Patterson, besides publishing and editing *Criminal Politics,* is chairman of his own political action committee, The Silver Dollar Pac, and a non-profit charity organization, The Center For Financial Freedom. His attention to the discussion of the Bush-Clinton-Contras story was shared by the Fox Television Network's news magazine, "A Current Affair," which had programmed a broadcast for April 21, 1993, an episode entitled "Airport '92—The Clinton Connection."

The documentary, hosted by Maureen O'Boyle, was the first TV program to show an interest in the Arkansas drug connection to the Iran-Contra scandals.

Early in '94, CBS took a crack at the story, but it, too, died on the vine. "Current Affair's" investigative reporter David Lee Miller did super legwork on the story. Teamed with a camera crew, he proceeded to Little Rock and beyond, until his nose for news led him to the Intermountain Regional Airport in Mena.

The author obtained a transcript of the broadcast. It clearly indicates that, from the interviews Miller conducted, state police, IRS agents, and other law enforcement officials were reluctant to discuss the situation at Mena. Clearly, they felt their own safety would be jeopardized if they went on the air and divulged what they knew of the conspiracy.

Writing in *Criminal Politics*, Lawrence Patterson addressed the issue of fear:

"They are very aware that they are dealing with a horrible conspiracy of sinister and massive proportions—which traces right up to the Oval Office of *George Bush* and the governor's office of *Bill and Hillary Clinton.*

On the air, reporter Miller flatly stated that both Bush and Clinton cooperated in covering up cocaine smuggling and illegal CIA espionage and arms shipments to the Contras out of Mena.

The story's fulcrum is a young Arkansan named Charles "Chuck" Hendricks, who was taken in by the excitement of working with the CIA at the airport in Mena and flying with Barry Seal's C-130 transport carrying arms to Nicaragua and cocaine on the return flight.

On one excursion, according to information developed by "A Current Affair," Hendricks's routine changed and he went on a flight out of Mena bearing arms to Angola. That was the young soldier of fortune's last journey. The plane crashed and he was burned beyond recognition.

In his investigation, Miller turned up Hendricks's parents. They found it inconceivable that no explanation about their son's death came from Governor Clinton's office, despite their pleas on the telephone.

Finally they wrote a personal appeal to Clinton himself.

A staffer wrote a response.

"...This is a case that fell outside of the purview of the Clinton administration."

David Miller concluded that, inasmuch as Barry Seal's cocaine smuggling operation at Mena had been so thoroughly ignored by Clinton and his lawmen, the "purview of the case" consequently fell under the responsibility of President George Bush.

But Miller got nowhere trying to learn more about the case from the White House. Miller told the author, "A good part of the show was put together by a local production company headed by Frank Sneps [Sneps wrote a lengthy piece on the situation for New York's avant-garde weekly, *The Village Voice*, but the big dailies ignored its revelations].

"The case was not only apparently ignored by [Clinton, but also by] George Bush even though he had been the drug czar in the Reagan administration. Nor did charges of the cover-up stop in Washington...in 1988, a deputy [Polk] county prosecutor, Chuck Black in Mena, tried and failed to interest Governor Clinton in the case."

Miller predicted Mena "could be the biggest political scandal of the election...a cover-up that could threaten both presidential front-runners."

It didn't turn out that way. The silent treatment the case received in the press was an ear-splitting din. Consequently, it never became an issue.

Seal's Fate's Sealed by a Judge

Barry Seal's fate was sealed by a Louisiana federal court after the IRS, in 1986, seized his home, two boats, numerous planes, real estate, and other property in lieu of $29.4 million in unpaid taxes, interest, and penalties for 1981–1983. The IRS arrived at that figure based on his disclosures at his drug trial in June 1985 in Florida.

Seal beat the rap at that trial after the government inexplicably dropped its charges against him. Seal then got jammed on related charges in Baton Rouge, where he was sentenced to five years probation and fined $35,000. But the judge then immediately released Seal to a halfway house.

The terms of his release called for Seal to report each day at specified times to the halfway house. *But he was ordered to have no bodyguards or carry arms for protection.*

Consequently, on February 19, 1986, Seal was gunned down as he arrived at his appointed hour at the halfway house, run by the Salvation Army.

Three Colombians, members of the Medellin Cartel, did the number on him. They were captured a short time later, prosecuted, convicted of first-degree murder, and imprisoned for life.

But the smuggling operations at Mena did not cease with Seal's death. In fact, *Criminal Politics'* Lawrence Patterson maintained, "The conspiracy continues into 1993 and the presidency was a payoff to Bill Clinton. The most dangerous aspect of this [situation, is that] the new "Commander in Chief" and First Lady...will follow the orders of the conspiracy in order to stay in office.

"Obviously, to avoid humiliation and disgrace...they will do *exactly* as the conspiracy directs them.

"It is clear that the conspiracy will continue to be run from the offices of David

Rockefeller and his son David Rockefeller, Jr., and, of course, the offices of Henry Kissinger [all names associated with the all-powerful secret society, The Bilderbergs, which anointed—and programmed—William Jefferson Blythe Clinton IV to be the 42nd president of the United States.]"

****

Just before this book went to press, the author received information that the Arkansas State Police had compiled a 30-volume investigative report on the Iran-Contra drug-arms operation at Mena.

One of the most explosive statements in the report was that Governor Bill Clinton himself "personally managed the money-laundering operations of this scheme after he turned the Arkansas Development Finance Authority into a giant *Laundromat* for the CIA's drug money."

The author was told that Clinton "was so much on the take, demanding under-the-table payments for sanitizing the drug money at the ADFA before it went to pay for the Contra's arms, that his 'angels' (the CIA) became disenchanted over that greed of his..."

Although the flights continued for another few years at Mena after late 1986, they were greatly curtailed then, according to the report, which one of the author's informants said was "squelched" by Clinton himself.

"To thwart Clinton's wholesale shakedowns of the CIA," the author was told by sources conversant with the Arkansas State Police report, "a substantial portion of the operation was shifted [from Mena] to a small, out-of-the-way airport in Mexico. There the Mexican government agreed to permit the operations and, quite surprisingly, the officials south of the border, who have the reputation of being *on the take*, made no demands, such as Bill Clinton did, for under-the-table money..."

A still later development came along on June 29, 1994, when *Wall Street Journal* editorial page writer Micah Morrison dispatched a first-hand report from Arkansas, which was given a four-column spread on the op-ed page under the headline "Mysterious Mena."

This report tied Bill Clinton inescapably to the Iran-Contra drug-arms operation at the Intermountain Regional Airport.

The story quoted the most responsible sources, who forged a damning link between America's president to the crimes committed at Mena through his old pal and buddy—drug-big Dan R. Lasater, "my closest political ally," as Clinton referred to him.

The scoop that Micah Morrison came up with paints this scenario of Clinton playing his big hole cards at Mena:

"Charles Black, a prosecutor for Polk County, in which Mena is located...said he met with Governor Clinton in 1988 and requested assistance for a state probe.

"'His response,' Mr. Black said, 'was that he would get a man on it and get back to me. I never heard back.'"

The White House, which was asked similar questions (through the unanswered fax the author transmitted to Dee Dee Myers in early 1993), saw fit this time to respond to the *Wall Street Journal*'s request for an accounting. This was what Morrison got out of spokesman John Podesta:

"[He cited] a state government offer of $25,000 to aid a Polk County investigation, an offer long under dispute in Arkansas. 'The governor took whatever action was available to him,' Mr. Podesta says. 'The failing in this case rests with the Republican Justice Department.'"

Damage control being practiced at its most blatant worst? Of course. For Podesta—no more so than Dee Dee Myers (who may be on her way out after the recent cabinet shuffle put Leon Panetta in charge of the Mack McLarty White House staff)—does not answer the key question raised by the author in his communication of last year:

Why didn't Bill Clinton level an accusing finger at the Reagan and Bush administrations during the campaign and implicate them in the Iran-Contra drug-running operation?

What better reason could Clinton have wanted than to KO George Bush's candidacy with this fact?

That he was well aware of that is implicit in Micah Morrison's story: "In 1991, Arkansas Attorney General Winston Bryant presented Iran-Contra prosecutor Lawrence Walsh with what Mr. Bryant called 'credible evidence of gunrunning, illegal drug smuggling, money laundering and the governmental cover-up and possibly a criminal conspiracy in connection with the Mena Airport.' Seventeen months later, Mr. Walsh sent Mr. Bryant a letter saying without explanation that he had closed his investigation."

The author, who has cited numerous demands for a deep-digging probe of this matter by former special counsel Robert Fiske, received in the immediate aftermath of the latest disclosures in the *Wall Street Journal*, advice from his sources that spelled out certain problems if the investigation was handled by Fiske.

Fiske was appointed by Attorney General Janet Reno; thus he may be too close to the Clinton White House to adequately investigate "Mysterious Mena," as the *Journal* labels the situation. It was stressed by those who oppose an inquiry by Fiske that the matter is better left up to Congress to investigate—just as it did the Iran-Contra arms-to-Central America scandal.

"That's the only way to go," one source told the author. "Get the whole mess out into the open at public hearings on the Hill. Then we'll find out how deeply *this* president is involved in those illegalities."

Fiske's findings in Vince Foster's death and his exoneration of the Treasury Department's Roger Altman's briefings of the White House staff were said to confirm the belief by many that Fiske, despite his affiliation to the GOP, was beholden to Bill Clinton by dint of his connection with International Paper.

Kenneth Starr's appointment severed all ties between the White House and the office of the special counsel.

Micah Morrison also raised the specter in his story that the drug trafficking and arms shipments at Mena have a much more extensive and ominous connection with Bill Clinton: "There is even one public plea that [Fiske] should investigate possible links between Mena and the savings-and-loan association involved in Whitewater.

The plea was sounded by the Arkansas Committee, a left-leaning group of former University of Arkansas students who have carefully tracked the Mena affair for years."

How much closer can one come in forging the Mena-Bill Clinton-Dan Lasater-Barry Seal link than this? Does it not heighten the believability of the late word the author received from the explosive 30-volume investigative report: that Governor Bill Clinton "personally managed the money-laundering operations of this scheme after he turned the Arkansas Development Finance Authority into a giant *Laundromat* for the CIA's drug money"?

Morrison's narrative carries the money-laundering one logical step further—to Madison Guaranty Savings and Loan.

The *Journal*'s investigator also touched on the edges of what the author cited at great length in earlier passages—that "the hectic activity [in Mena] came to an abrupt halt in February 1986—the month Barry Seal was killed."

Of course, Morrison does not suggest that Clinton's greed for a share of the laundered drug money prompted the conspirators operating at Mena to shift the bulk of their activity to Mexico. Or that there could be a shred of truth to the very latest, still more tenebrous report—that Governor Clinton dispatched a team of plainclothes Arkansas State Police to New Orleans, where Barry Seal was slain, "to find out where he stashed all those millions of dollars..."

Micah Morrison ends his piece by giving President Clinton the only breathing room his story provides: "Of course, it all may be just a coincidence, and perhaps Governor Clinton did not even know that drug smugglers, the CIA and the DEA were operating in his backyard. Perhaps he did not want to know. After all, as we have come to learn, Bill Clinton's Arkansas was a very strange place."

In retrospect, Morrison hasn't *really* given Clinton much breathing room. After all, the author has already clearly established the president's irrevocable connection with the "Mysterious Mena" mess. So that leaves nothing uncertain about the Clinton involvement with this scandal, as dwelled on by Morrison in his closing paragraph—except for the final sentence:

"After all, as we have come to learn, Bill Clinton's Arkansas was a very strange place."

37

IT'S BUSH AND CLINTON

Bill's Getting Edgy over George

On May 26, Clinton and Bush roared toward their respective parties' certain nominations when they captured the primaries in Kentucky, Arkansas, and Idaho.

Clinton won 56 percent of the Democratic vote to 28 percent uncommitted in Kentucky's final returns. A fading Jerry Brown pulled a humbling 8 percent.

In his home state, Clinton grabbed 71 percent of Arkansas's precincts, uncommitted pulled 18 percent, and Brown straggled past the finish line with 11.

Idaho's Democrats gave Clinton a 50-plus percent of their delegates to 18 percent for Brown, with the balance in the uncommitted category.

Bush won so many delegates in this three-state romp that his nomination was drained of all suspense.

By June 2, it was all over in the primary races. Bush, who had sewn up his nomination weeks earlier, was joined by his rival in that euphoric plateau by taking the primaries in just three of the six states that held contests on that Tuesday. Needing less than 100 of the 700 delegates at stake in the half-dozen state derby, Clinton got the votes he needed in New Jersey, Ohio, and Alabama even before the polls closed in the West. He climbed above the 2,145 total needed to win nomination.

Victories in New Mexico, Montana, and the big California grab bag for delegates weren't needed by Clinton. He had won the 105-day primary campaign that began in New Hampshire the previous winter. Bill Clinton had defied those who had written his political obituary so many times before and emerged the certain Democratic nominee.

Yet the curtain came down on the primary processional with voters even more angry and dissatisfied. The real winner of the five-month voting marathon seemed to be the as-yet unannounced candidate who wasn't even on the ballot.

Ross Perot would have won both the Republican and Democratic primaries in California, according to TV network exit polls. Even Ohio voters who helped put Clinton over the top said they'd sooner vote for Perot than Clinton.

After the primaries, the good news for Clinton was that, despite nagging doubts about his "electability," public opinion polls showed him running about even with President Bush.

The bad news was that both Clinton and Bush appeared to be running behind

Perot.

Former Democratic National Chairman John C. White offered a perceptive view about Perot as both major candidates scrambled to energize their dispirited loyalists.

"There's more shock than anything else, that (Clinton and Bush) might be edged out by a billion-dollar Bubba from Texas. They're going to have to find some way to deal with Perot, because you can't let this thing just sit there and solidify. The theory that he's going to go away is not a strategy—it's a prayer."

On his way to Madison Square Garden, Bill Clinton seemed to be trying desperately to alienate more voters. Clinton chose Jesse Jackson's National Rainbow Coalition's leadership summit in Washington, D.C., to once more anger his critic—now his reluctant host—once more. Given the dais to speak, Clinton attacked black rap star Sister Souljah for denigrating the character of whites and declaring that blacks couldn't be racist. She intimated, moreover, that blacks should kill whites. Sister Souljah had spoken at the conference the day before, June 12.

"If you took the words 'white' and 'black' and reversed them, you might think David Duke was giving that speech," declared Clinton to an audience that seemed almost as shocked as Jackson, who sat stone-faced at the banquet table on stage and rolled his eyes.

"We have an obligation, all of us, to call attention to prejudice wherever we see it," Clinton continued.

The governor cited his own "mistake" of playing golf at all-white country clubs and called criticism of him "justified." But that did not lessen the effect of a statement that went beyond any rational political calculation.

Jackson was asked to comment about the question of racism raised by Clinton.

Clinton Steps on Jackson's Toes

"It was unnecessary," Jackson stated. "It was a diversion. It was not at all helpful."

Saying that Sister Souljah told him that Clinton had misquoted her, Jackson called the criticism "an unfair attack on her—her character, her reputation." He added, "I do not know the cause of this diversion...Bill Clinton has agreed to speak to Sister Souljah himself...the rippling effect through the conference has been traumatizing."

Asked whether Clinton's comments were an attempt to placate conservative voters while still trying to round up black votes, Jackson responded, "I don't know that. I hope not."

Clinton had stirred further dismay among listeners when he almost totally ignored the coalition's new "Rebuilding America" program and, instead, reiterated the planks of his own plan.

"You will soon be seeing my version of your program," he said grandly, further straining his relationship with Jackson.

Barely a week went by before Jackson and Clinton exchanged broadsides again. Jackson refueled the controversy over the Arkansan's remarks about Sister Souljah by telling the *New York Times* that Clinton's speech was part of a calculated, two-year effort on Clinton's part to distance himself from the traditional "multiracial" wing of the Democratic Party.

Jackson accused Clinton of engineering a showdown with the Democratic National Committee headed by Ron Brown, a black, and the minister's close political associate.

"This was not just aimed at me in a personal sense," Jackson said. "This was a move by the right wing of the party to pull away from the DNC because the DNC was too multiracial for them and too democratic. And of course they did not agree fundamentally with the election of Ron Brown [as chairman]...the further attempt to isolate the Rainbow is just another dimension of their strategy."

Jackson characterized Clinton's comments about Sister Souljah as "a political calculation of the lowest order" comparable to "a sneak attack designed to embarrass us at our own convention."

Clinton himself didn't reply directly to this attack but let it hang while press secretary Dee Dee Myers tried once again to do damage control.

"Bill Clinton...has been very up front about the need to change the direction of the party even before he decided to run for president. And it's working. A year ago people in the Democratic Party weren't talking about such ideas as welfare-to-work, streamlining and reinventing government or bringing the budget under control. Now they are being talked about all the time."

But the Clinton-Jackson flap showed no sign of abating. A plea from New York Governor Cuomo, urging Clinton to make peace with Jackson, fell on deaf ears.

"For the sake of the country and certainly for the sake of the Democrats, "Cuomo appealed, "someone should get the three together." He suggested Ron Brown as the mediator.

The principals weren't receptive. Especially after Clinton refused to apologize to Sister Souljah and declared, "I don't know why all of this rewriting of history is going on—basically depriving me of the right of expressing my opinion on racial division and divisiveness." Repeating his refusal to apologize, he said, "I've got to stand for what I believe and say what I believe."

As the feud boiled, Clinton was scalded from yet another steamy front: The Republican National Committee. It accused Democrats of illegally helping finance Clinton's primary campaign and demanded the government cut off federal campaign matching funds for his candidacy.

The complaint filed with the Federal Election Commission alleged Clinton wrongly used $395,000 of his party's general-election money to help raise funds for his cash-strapped primary campaign, which finished April more than $2 million in debt. How the Clinton brain trust could owe that amount of money after the big Arkansas businesses (Tyson Foods, International Paper, etc.) had kicked into Bill's campaign coffers is one of the most perplexing mysteries of Campaign '92.

That questioned $395,000 was used for Clinton's half-hour TV appearance on NBC-TV the previous week when, during the airing, the candidate's toll-free, fund-raising number was trailered across the screen several times, the complaint charged.

More Campaign Funding Hanky-Panky

Clinton replied that his campaign strategists had sought legal advice before they dipped into the Democratic National Committee's funds.

"We feel good about it and we certainly asked before we did it," Clinton blustered. He left it to Dee Dee Myers to explain what he himself wasn't anxious to tackle.

"This is all a political ploy"—but, yes, "flashing the fund-raising number was a mistake...there was a technical error," she tried to explain.

If this admission of the "truth" is to be believed, then what can be made of this further effort to exonerate Bill Clinton of using federal campaign matching funds illegally?:

"The campaign corrected the mistake by refusing to accept any contributions from people who called the fund-raising number to pledge money as a result of the show."

Dee Dee didn't say that callers who dialed that toll-free number to offer contributions for Bill Clinton's campaign *were referred to another toll-free number to call.*

Bill-bashing didn't end with Jackson or the GOP National Committee.

A gang of gay activists stormed into Broadway's Saint James Theater and disrupted a celebrity-studded fund-raiser for Clinton. They demanded he explain why his state had outlawed fellatio, cunnilingus, and all forms of buggery when he was attorney general from 1976 to 1978.

As supporters Alec Baldwin, Richard Dreyfuss, and Blair Brown waited for a reply, Clinton grabbed the microphone at center stage in the venerable Times Square playhouse and took his out:

"That's right. I was attorney general. I wasn't governor. I didn't sign the law. I did my best to defeat the law. Those are the facts."

What a relief!

But a big question remained because it wasn't asked.

Did Bill Clinton consider himself as a violator of the Sodomy Act enacted by the legislature when he engaged in oral sex with Gennifer Flowers?

After the hecklers were evicted from the mezzanine, Clinton told his audience that when he was growing up in Arkansas, he never anticipated he'd one day stand on a Broadway stage "with the cultural elite."

The bash raised $300,000—pretty close to covering the $395,000 the GOP said Clinton spent illegally on his TV appearance. Did the Clinton campaign return that money to the Federal Election Commission?

No, it did not.

38

THE DEMOCRATIC CONVENTION

Jimmy Breslin Bashes Bill

As July dawned, the Democrats prepared to rally in New York for their four-day exercise in the obvious. At the same time, they were reminded by Jimmy Breslin that even if Clinton could waltz into Madison Square Garden with a lock on all 4,287 delegates, they weren't bound to fulfill their pledges.

The acerbic columnist's theme, *Clinton? Throw The Bum Out*, was prefaced by a reminder that Ross Perot wasn't to blame for threatening the two-party system. It was, as Breslin viewed it, past Democratic debacles:

"The ones who did this are the tiny number of Democratic Party primary voters who in 1984 gave you Walter Mondale, who bored so many people to death that he might as well have used a machine gun. Then in 1988 they gagged the country with this fellow Dukakis, who in the end was detested by people and was the one most disastrous candidate in all of memory.

"And now this time we have the guy who could absolutely end one of the two parties forever, the Democratic Party. That is Bill Clinton, who is nothing more than a cheap waitress chaser."

Breslin cast a cold eye on candidate Clinton.

"If there is any spirit, any verve, any sense of adventure left in the Democratic Party," urged the Runyanesque journalist "it will walk into Madison Square Garden next month and revolt against the candidate.

"Throw the bum out."

Breslin said New York was the place to start the "movement to get rid of the nominee" since "everything good in this country comes from this city."

Citing the 1967 Coalition For a Democratic Alternative, which started on Manhattan's West Side and which led to the "Dump Johnson" movement, Breslin suggested the United States of America would have been a different country if Robert F. Kennedy, who was racing headlong to the presidency, hadn't been assassinated.

"Clinton is an even easier case" than the effort that sent LBJ back to his Texas ranch in retirement. "Just throw him out," urged Breslin, "and forget he ever was around. How pleasant!"

Dispatching Bill Clinton back to Little Rock could be accomplished "in a matter of moments on a convention floor," offered Breslin (a colleague and commuting companion of the author's on Hearst's *New York Journal-American* in the early 1960s and on the *New York Post* in the 1970s).

"Let many members of one delegation—New York—scream that they don't want Clinton and the convention falls apart in front of you," Breslin lectured.

"Start a riot in the seats. For the first time in so many years, let people be thrilled by politics. You could even start people talking about being better."

Breslin offered absolution to Clinton delegates turning their coats as he urged, saying they "were not elected as robots who, upon hearing the name Clinton, must raise their hands."

Clinton, Breslin wrote, "deserved to come into this city and have the nomination taken right out of his hands. For we are real and he is false."

Breslin then cited Clinton's record that showed him to be

- from a Right to Work state (meaning organized labor be damned.)
- in favor of Desert Storm, "even though his own background as a cheap draft dodger gave him no right to ask anybody else to get shot at."
- a governor who conducts executions in Arkansas "that are nothing more than torture."
- a candidate who has "no conviction except that he should have this job."
- a saxophone player on the "Arsenio Hall Show" "who gives only the feeling of a smoky room and waitresses running around—'Damn! Will you ever look at that one!'—and the hour going late and everybody going home with somebody they shouldn't be with."
- a guy who had his chance in Los Angeles and "lost it" when he failed to excite the world "to a higher dignity than fire and looting." But "instead, he was so afraid of offending all his people in low IQ states, Arkansas and Louisiana and Mississippi and Virginia, that he mumbled how he sure could be 'an agent of change,'" a phrase whose meaning Breslin said eluded him.

Calling for Clinton to be "summarily dismissed" by the delegates and to get "a real Democrat or lose a party," Breslin asked—and answered—his own question:

"How can you take it away from him after all that hard work" he put in after going through the long, arduous ordeal of the primaries?

"Easily. By a few people giving an exciting, healthy scream in Madison Square Garden:

"'Clinton! Take a walk!'"

It's Gore the Bore for Veep

Four days before the Democratic convention was to convene, Bill Clinton put the ticket and the party's future into the custody of two centrist baby boomers with southern accents.

He picked Al Gore, Jr., to be his running mate.

"Gore The Bore," as many pundits labeled the candidate long before he was chosen by Bill Clinton, fulfilled a childhood dream.

Gore, who learned politics at the feet of his father, a U.S. senator, was born in the tiny town of Carthage, Tennessee, March 31, 1948—19 months after Clinton. He had a mostly big-city upbringing as he lived in Washington during the years Al Sr. served in the House of Representatives, then the Senate.

Al Jr. graduated from Harvard in 1969, served in Vietnam as an army journalist, later worked as a reporter, and dabbled in home building in Nashville while studying law and religion, part-time, at Vanderbilt University.

When 28, he wrote "30" to his journalist's career and entered politics. He won a seat in the House of Representatives. Detractors claimed he was stiff, arrogant, overly ambitious and opportunistic. But they never accused him of being shallow.

In 15 years in the House and Senate, Gore came to be regarded as a deep—at times ponderous—thinker.

He followed his ambition to run for national office in 1988, and received a luke-warm reception. The kibosh was put on his developing campaign for the presidency when he came into New York City. There Mayor Edward I. Koch indirectly helped bury it when he took the opportunity to bash Jesse ("New York is hymietown") Jackson by saying, "Jews and others who care about Israel would be crazy to vote for Jackson."

The statement, intended to enlist support for Gore among Jews, turned that year's New York Democratic primary into a black-Jewish confrontation that triggered shifts to Massachusetts Governor Michael Dukakis—and effectively buried Gore.

Once Clinton had selected Gore as his running mate, *Newsday* sent Jack Sirica to Carthage to see what his hometown folks thought of Al Jr. While most praised him, a 54-year-old waitress named Lois Dixon cut him down to size.

"In my opinion, I'd just as soon vote for my dog," she said. "Because neither Gore nor his father had done a thing for Smith County, as far as I can see."

One more reaction—from Jesse Jackson:

"It takes two wings to fly, and here you have two of the same wing."

In picking Gore for the ticket, Bill Clinton didn't have to worry that embarrassing questions would hound the Tennessean as they had him all through the primaries.

Gore had answered questions about his youthful experimentation with marijuana and his "pampered" Vietnam-era military service during his unsuccessful bid in 1988. He responded straightforwardly—not hesitantly, untruthfully, or with double-talk as Clinton had done in '92.

Gore, father of four young children and married to Mary Elizabeth Aitcheson Gore, 43, brought pluses to the ticket that neither Clinton nor Hillary possessed. Mrs. Gore, nicknamed "Tipper" since childhood, projected a very different image than Hillary who had said, "You know, I suppose I could have stayed home and baked cookies and had teas, but what I decided to do was to fulfill my profession."

Tipper Gore's father, Jack Aitcheson, who ran a family-owned, wholesale plumb-ing supply business in northern Virginia at the time, contrasted his daughter-in-law and the wife of the presidential candidate:

"My daughter has been a housewife primarily. She is primarily very interested in her family and her home, as opposed to Mrs. Clinton's vocation as a lawyer."

But Mrs. Gore didn't always sit at home. Not after Tipper—a one-time rock drummer in her single years—bought her eight-year-old daughter a copy of Prince's "Purple Rain" album and discovered it contained offensive lyrics referring to masturbation.

She promptly called friends like Susan Baker, wife of then-Treasury Secretary James Baker in Ronald Reagan's administration, and later secretary of state and director of George Bush's reelection campaign. The two wives formed the Parents Music Recording Center (PMRC) with the goal of informing parents what their children were hearing.

Soon, Senator Gore was orating in senate hearings on the morals of popular music. In four years, the effort exerted enough influence to move two dozen states to legislate mandatory labeling of offensive lyrics.

The Recording Industry Association of America agreed, finally, in 1990 to have record companies sticker singles and albums with labels warning "Explicit Lyrics."

This gave Tipper Gore a "'family values' credential that even Dan Quayle will not be able to top," commented David Hinckley in the *New York Daily News*. "She has not only talked about cultural rot [as when the veep rapped TV's Murphy Brown for being an unmarried mother raising a child as a single parent], but she can say she has helped do something about it—without government intervention."

Breaking with tradition by not picking a running mate who offered a balance in ideology, region, and politics, Clinton went to the convention waving this century's first "unbalanced ticket."

Now to Madison Square Garden.

The Comeback Kid's Big Night

"America needs Bill Clinton," said the booming voice of Mario Cuomo as he gave a stirring nomination speech reminiscent of his mesmerizing keynote address at the 1984 Democratic National Convention.

"...Because he will remind us that we are too good to make war our most successful enterprise, because he does not believe that the way to win political support is to pit people against one another...instead he will work to make the whole nation stronger, by bringing people together."

The governor worked on his speech for 10 days, confining himself mostly to the executive mansion in Albany, poring over nominating speeches dating back to the 1920s and composing several drafts.

He rehearsed his delivery the day before in the Garden before he made final revisions in a midtown hotel. Then in sweltering summer heat, he walked a mile back to the Garden for a final run-through.

Praising Clinton highly, Cuomo also delivered a scathing attack on the GOP, reminding the nation that the communal "city of despair" he described in his address had suffered even more from GOP neglect.

Cuomo lashed out at the GOP as the party of the rich who "detect a callus on their palms and concluded it's time to put down their polo mallet."

Charging that Republicans had sacrificed the middle class to the rich, he chided President Bush for being able to find billions of dollars for war and disasters but not a penny to rescue the nation's most vulnerable.

"Bill Clinton asks...why can't we find the wealth to respond to the quiet catastrophes that every day oppress the lives of thousands, that destroy our children with drugs, that kill thousands with terrible new diseases like AIDS?"

Recalling the post-Gulf War victory parades, Cuomo called for one more parade:

"...to march with you behind President Bill Clinton through cities and rural villages where all the people have safe streets, affordable housing, and health care when they need it."

Nowhere in his speech did Mario Cuomo suggest that Clinton join a parade of the American Legion, the Veterans of Foreign Wars, the Vietnam Veterans, or the Disabled Veterans of America.

The New York governor closed his nominating speech by demanding, "Step aside, Mr. Bush. You've had your parade. It's time for a change. It's time for someone smart enough to know, strong enough to do, sure enough to lead.

"The Comeback Kid. A new voice for a new America...the man from Hope, Arkansas."

So, the "Comeback Kid," who had survived and yet would still be dogged by bruising questions about his character, honesty, and integrity, was nominated. Clinton received 3,367 delegate votes; Jerry Brown, 594; Paul Tsongas, 209; and others, 77.

Although Alabama, Alaska, and Arizona are listed ahead of Arkansas in their alphabetical order, the honor of casting her state's 43 ballots first went to Virginia Kelley, the candidate's mother.

Now all Bill Clinton had to do was to convince the voters.

39

A DIRTY CAMPAIGN GETS DIRTIER

More Military Muckraking

No sooner was the Democratic nomination his than Bill Clinton went off to barn-storm the country with blarney about what a great commander in chief he'd make.

But the *unthinkable* seemed always to happen to Clinton. Trouble loomed just when he set out to woo the American Legion. Despite his record as a draft evader, Clinton asked his audience to overlook that and focus on the future.

"If any of you choose to vote against me because of what happened twenty-three years ago," Clinton told the convention of legionnaires in Chicago on August 25, "that's your right as an American citizen and I respect that.

"But it is my hope you will cast your vote while looking toward the future with hope rather than remaining fixed to the problems of the past."

By long-standing policy and tradition, the American Legion doesn't endorse can-didates for political office. So when Clinton addressed the legion, he didn't ask for that. Instead he tried to win favor with the veterans by beseeching them not to hold it against him for being a slacker.

The other speaker at the same convention acknowledged the nonpartisan nature of the veteran's meeting. He didn't directly compare his military record to Clinton's. Nevertheless, President George Bush appeared happy to dwell briefly on his past military experience:

"At the age of eighteen, I went off to fight. Like many of you, I was scared—but I was willing."

Bush didn't have to remind the veterans about his heroic and highly decorated service in World War II. They knew all about it:

Bush volunteered to serve in the Navy at age 18—the same age Clinton was when he first schemed on ways to beat the draft.

After his enlistment, Bush was commissioned the youngest pilot in naval aviation history and flew combat missions in the Pacific. He was shot down twice by Japanese Zeros during some of the war's bloodiest engagements in the battle for Iwo Jima.

No sooner had Bill Clinton left the podium than he was confronted with another charge that contradicted his oft-repeated claim:

"I never received any unusual or favorable treatment to avoid military service."

The new disclosure established that shortly before Clinton graduated from Georgetown University in 1968, his Hot Springs draft board reclassified him 1-A (ready for induction). The date was March 20.

Yet the records reflect that Clinton was the only draftee whose pre-induction physical was put off for more than 10 months—more than five times longer than virtually all area men of comparable eligibility.

And then he didn't get the call at all.

"I never received any unusual or special treatment to avoid military service."

That's what Bill Clinton told the American Legion. How else to describe the events of March 1968 in Little Rock, than to say bluntly that *the fix was in to keep Bill Clinton out of serving in the military*?

We don't know how many young men in the Hot Springs area were called up for Clinton and put their lives on the line in Vietnam. The war memorial in Washington, D.C., could certainly supply some of those names.

But the controversy that developed over Clinton's draft record had less to do with his efforts to avoid the "unpopular war," as it was put by *Los Angeles Times* reporter William Rempel, and more to do with questions of whether his public statements during the campaign were candid or complete.

Significantly, Clinton has never volunteered any information about his draft dodging efforts. Even after they were made public.

When contacted by the *Los Angeles Times'* reporter while on a campaign swing, asking him to comment about just-published revelations of his uncle pulling strings to keep him out of uniform, Clinton replied testily, "I have two things to say: Everyone involved in the story is now dead. Number two, I said everything I have to say at the American Legion, I have nothing else to say about that. I have no comment."

Then, perhaps on second thought, Clinton put in, "I've told you the truth about my draft status, I have told you the only military option I have ever considered or that I was ever offered was the one that was reported to you [the University of Arkansas ROTC]...the only records we could get are the ones you have. Now you want me to respond to every rumor and every innuendo."

As just cited, the records (from the U of A ROTC) didn't tell the full story.

Nor was Clinton telling the truth when he said, "Everyone involved in the story is now dead."

Very much alive was Robert Corrado, another surviving member, besides Opal Ellis, of the Hot Springs draft board from that time. His story can now be told.

"Bill Clinton's treatment was unusual," according to Corrado. "The only explanation for the long delay would be some form of preferential treatment. But I wasn't privy to the details..."

Uncle Raymond Clinton's longtime friend and personal attorney at the time, James Britt, who later became an Arkansas circuit court judge (now retired), was also very much alive. He spoke just before Labor Day, 1992, to Bill Rempel for his *Los Angeles Times* exposé.

The draft board was "handled successfully," said Britt.

He Got Preferential Treatment

Britt admitted he *"assisted in the lobbying efforts."*

Moreover, Britt "recounted details of a calculated campaign to *'get what Bill wanted'*—the opportunity to attend Oxford University.

"'We started working as soon as [Raymond] got word Billy was going to be drafted,' after graduating from Georgetown, he said.

"Britt discounts the possibility that Clinton was unaware of his uncle's lobbying efforts. *'Of course Billy knew about it* [author's emphasis in all cases],' Britt said."

A Republican who lost a bid to be his party's candidate in Arkansas's 1960 gubernatorial election, Britt recalled that Bill Clinton's uncle Raymond had "one goal in my judgment—to delay, delay, delay" so his nephew could attend Oxford.

The law made no allowances for deferments to graduate students, except those in medical school.

"According to Britt," the *Los Angeles Times* story went on, "Raymond Clinton also personally lobbied Will 'Bill' Armstrong, the head of Hot Springs Draft Board No. 26, and Lieutenant Commander Trice Ellice, Jr., commanding officer of the local Naval Reserve unit.

"Raymond Clinton, Britt, Armstrong, and Ellice all were founding members of the Hot Springs chapter of the U.S. Navy League, a national service organization.

"Britt said the pursuit of the navy reserve billet was intended to stall the draft process."

Again, the words "Everyone involved in the story is now dead." came back to haunt Bill Clinton.

Several others besides Robert Corrado, Mrs. Opal Ellis, and James Britt were also alive. One important figure in documenting that Clinton lied was Trice Ellice, who served in the Hot Springs Naval Reserve Unit in 1992.

That's the same unit Bill Clinton would have entered had he taken the Naval Reserve assignment created especially for him in 1968—but which he turned down. He could afford to, for Uncle Ray by then had worked a fix with the draft board that stalled Bill's call-up for more than 10 months.

"Ellice confirmed that he persuaded officials of the Eighth Naval District in New Orleans to create a billet, or enlistment slot, especially for Bill Clinton," *Newsday*'s Timothy Clifford reported.

Clinton's double-talk and outright lies began early in the presidential campaign when he was asked whether he served in the military. He responded by claiming he *"had a four-year deferment, had made myself available for the draft, got a high lottery number, and never was called."*

None of that was even remotely true.

After the *Los Angeles Times* story broke, Clinton was confronted for comment by *Newsday*'s Washington Bureau Chief Gaylord Shaw.

"I don't know anything about it…it's all news to me," Clinton insisted.

Refusing to respond in detail, Clinton persisted in an interview in Baltimore:

"I have spoken the truth about my draft status."

Later, in Rockville, Maryland, a Washington suburb, he addressed a community college campus. He bashed President Bush for not caring about the middle class and said that rising costs had priced college "out of range for so many Americans."

The Bush campaign then distributed a statement by Education Secretary Lamar Alexander that accused Clinton of playing "fast and loose with the facts." Alexander said Clinton won't be able to improve schools (not anymore so than he had in Arkansas during his more than dozen years as governor) with "teacher union leaders [who dislike Clinton intensely] and the Democrats in Congress draped around his neck."

During this stop, Clinton was again asked to comment on the *Times* draft evasion story.

"I have nothing more to say," he thundered.

By now the Bush campaign was on top of him about the new reports which "raise serious questions about Clinton's already dubious credibility."

Torrie Clark, Bush's campaign press secretary, said, "Clinton stands in front of the American Legion and says he's going to bare his soul. Well, not quite.

"He owes the American people, he owes the veterans, some explanations.

"...How many times is he going to lie and say, 'I've told you everything there is?'"

The Bush campaign also distributed a statement from Dominic DeFrancesco, past national commander of the American Legion. He said the new story of Clinton's draft dodging scheme raised questions about his pledge to "set the record straight."

"Regardless of one's views about the war or the draft, don't the American people deserve the truth on these important issues?" DeFrancesco asked.

Fix Is Handled "Successfully"

Two days later, New York's *Daily News* had a screaming headline:

Bill flip-flops on draft record

"I didn't mean to suggest that the latest questions about my Vietnam draft record were all news to me now," Clinton said at a press conference called in an attempt to rehabilitate him yet again.

"I think it was just a misunderstanding. I don't know anything about it...it's all news to me."

That was his statement on Wednesday.

"I don't know where all this stuff comes from...the reports are all absolutely untrue...they're nothing but rumor and innuendo concocted by Republicans who are opposed to me."

That was his statement on Thursday.

On Friday, Clinton, at long last, acknowledged that as recently as five months ago, in March, Commander Ellice told him of how his uncle, Raymond Clinton, had tried to get him into the Naval Reserve in 1968.

That was the first he knew of any effort to help him avoid the Vietnam draft, Clinton said.

"I did not know about any efforts to secure a Naval Reserve assignment before Mr. Ellice mentioned it to me in Hot Springs," Clinton insisted, sticking to the script.

"There was no way to document or confirm what he told me. The only military option I was offered and considered was the ROTC."

Which ROTC option was Clinton referring to? The two-year run he had at Georgetown University between 1964 and 1966, then quit to avoid active military service?

Or the one at the University of Arkansas, which he obtained fraudulently by concealing his draft call-up notice and hiding his Georgetown University ROTC service?

Clinton didn't say, because the country was told only about his ROTC experience at the University of Arkansas.

Now, after he revealed what sounded like the truth—that he had created a spot in the Naval Reserve "especially for Bill Clinton"—Commander Trice Ellice was confronted by reporters for more details.

Ellice stated that he talked to Clinton about his uncle's efforts to get him into the Naval Reserve at a March 20, 1992, party in Hot Springs.

"I said, 'I thought you were going navy. I was surprised you didn't show up for your navy exams,'" Ellice said he told Clinton.

"He looked at me and said, 'What do you mean?' and I told him the story.

"I told him, 'Your uncle Raymond called me and told me you wanted in the navy. I called up to see if there was a billet. Bill said, 'That was the first time I have heard that story.' He told me it was 'news to me.'"

Although Ellice had earlier told *Los Angeles Times* reporter William Rempel that he persuaded officials at the Eighth Naval District to give preferential treatment to Bill Clinton, in a later interview with reporters the commander denied Clinton received preferential treatment in the reserve assignment his uncle sought.

The Republicans, assembling in Houston for the GOP Convention, were emboldened by this latest dirt, hoping it would help George Bush make mincemeat of Bill Clinton at the November election.

Clinton had yet to level with the American people about his shameless, indeed fraudulent, manipulations of his country's draft laws.

Had it not been for the statute of limitations, these disclosures could have subjected Clinton to arrest, indictment, prosecution, conviction, and sentencing to a federal penitentiary for falsifying a public instrument (his draft notice), perjury (lying about his standing with the draft board to the ROTC) and conspiracy (importuning the various persons who put in the fix for him with the draft board and Naval Reserve).

Note: See Appendix: How Clinton Escaped Prison as a Draft Dodger.

The statute of limitations had no bearing on the phone call Clinton's campaign strategist, Betsey Wright, received on August 10. She wasted no time getting the word to her chief.

"Bill, Don Bankston just phoned. He wants you to know that Dianne Welch has just been sprung."

Clinton's bank-robbing, drug-trafficking stepsister had won her appeal after losing the first round with the Texas Court of Appeals in 1987. Thus she was now free as the driven wind.

Dianne had served six years and 40 days of hard time in Texas's tough Mountain

View Maximum Security Prison in Gatesville, and finally she had been turned loose on grounds that her 45-year incarceration had been improperly imposed.

"Good for her," was Clinton's retort upon hearing the news. But his flip disposal of this information was to take on a much more somber note in a few short weeks.

40

THE REPUBLICAN CONVENTION

A Lilting Aria for the Gipper

By the time the new scandals about Bill Clinton's draft evasions had fully surfaced, the Republican National Convention was under way in Houston's colossal Astrodome.

New York Daily News correspondent Lars-Erik Nelson's analysis was perhaps the best of all accounts that came out of the indoor arena. It sang a lilting aria for the Gipper. The *News'* Washington bureau chief wrote, "It took Ronald Reagan to provide the magic and the music that has been missing from this campaign—the sunny vision, the lighthearted put-downs of Democrats and liberals, the sense of historic sweep and the pride in the virtuous victories of Americans.

"It may seem like blarney when you compare Reagan's rhetoric to reality. But with his stirring recollection of the Reagan Revolution, 81-year-old Ronald Reagan managed to upstage his designated successor, George Bush.

"And when you add the fire of the last true Reaganaut, Pat Buchanan—calling Republicans in a fiery holy war against homosexuality, abortion, environmentalists and big-spending leftist draft-dodgers like Bill Clinton—well, at the end of the night, genteel President Bush seemed like tame goods."

Reagan's performance, said Nelson, was one "to cap a storybook lifetime, and he made the most of it. The Republicans who rode to victory on his coattails in 1980 must have listened with a bittersweet sense of nostalgia and regret. Bush cannot match the Old Master when it comes to inspiring people."

The president's acceptance speech was alternately defiant and apologetic. He defended his accomplishments and sarcastically likened Bill Clinton, whom he didn't mention by name, to "Elvis." At the same time, he likened himself to Harry S. Truman. (He hadn't voted for Truman in 1948, but for Thomas E. Dewey. Reagan, by contrast, a Democrat at the time, cast his ballot for the scrappy HST.)

Although his speech "lacked the poetry of his widely admired 1988 convention address," as *Newsday*'s Susan Page put it, he nevertheless "took a slashing tone toward Clinton and a defensive one about his own accomplishments. It had the air of a speech written by committee—which it was—and it lasted just short of an hour."

It was received with explosive cheering and roars of "Four more years!"

When he finished his speech, Bush was surrounded by First Lady Barbara, their children, and a raft of grandchildren as more than 150,000 red, white, and blue balloons cascaded from the rafters and fireworks exploded in the huge, 50,000-plus seat indoor, all-weather arena.

By morning, the polls showed Bush narrowing Clinton's lead dramatically. An ABC News survey put Clinton nine points ahead among likely voters, 50–41 percent, with a margin of error of five percentage points. A CBS News survey had Bush cutting Clinton's lead to 11 points, compared with 18 points only a week earlier. Clinton led Bush 51–40 percent in that poll.

It had become a real horse race.

"George Bush is a lot more interested in beating me than helping you," Clinton shouted at a Detroit rally as he fell back on Bush's vow to do "whatever it takes" to win.

Bush shot back that Clinton favored hiking taxes. "Elvis economics" that would have America "checking into the Heartbreak Hotel," he called them. And the president ripped into Clinton's character with acid ridicule.

"What about the leader of the Arkansas National Guard—the man who hopes to be commander in chief?" Bush demanded at a campaign stop in Gulfport, Mississippi. It was an unmistakable reference to Clinton's draft dodging.

Reading Clinton's own words when he waffled his support of the Gulf War—even after the Democratic-controlled Senate approved it—Bush demanded, "What kind of a message would that send to a man like Saddam Hussein?"

"At least on the first day after the Republican National Convention," noted the *New York Post*'s Washington Bureau Chief Deborah Orin, "the Clinton camp seemed to be on the defensive."

It remained on the defensive as Bush barreled into Springfield, Illinois, and invaded a steamy livestock arena at the annual state fair. Keeping the promise he made in his Houston nomination speech not to let up, Bush blasted incumbent Congressman Richard Durbin in an updated version of President Truman's 1948 campaign against the "do-nothing 80th Congress."

He beat the drums for Republican candidate John Shimkus, who was battling Durbin for his House seat. Bush declared, "The congressman from this district voted against us on Desert Storm."

More than 4,000 loyalists, many clanging cow bells, were fired up by the president's words and cheered their approval.

George Is Giving 'Em Hell

When a spectator yelled, "Give 'em hell!" Bush responded, "No, it's not give 'em hell, but they're going to think it's hell when I get through with 'em."

He later led the crowd in chants of, "Clean the House!"

Newsday's Martin Kasindorf noted from Springfield that Bush's emphasis on Congress "is part of a Republican strategy to tie the Democratic ticket of Arkansas Governor Bill Clinton and Tennessee Senator Al Gore to a Washington lawmaker set that is thought to be in ill favor with the public."

He quoted the president, "'We've got to change the Clinton-Gore gridlocked Congress!'"

The campaign was on. And it promised to get more brutal, more ugly, and bloodier as it got nearer to the November 3 showdown.

****

One question mark loomed: the matter of presidential debates. That they'd be held, there was little doubt. President Bush had vowed as September went into its third week, "I'll show up."

And a spokesman for Bill Clinton chimed in, "We'll be there."

But when, where, and how many times Bush and Clinton would face each other before a nationwide TV audience remained in question. The answers were closely guarded by the Bush-Quayle campaign brain trust, headed by White House Chief of Staff James A. Baker, who had resigned as secretary of state to help reelect the president.

Clinton said he'd abide by the rules proposed by the bipartisan Commission on Presidential Debates. He gave his word to show up in East Lansing, Michigan, for the first face-off on September 22, whether the president came or not.

Bush wasn't saying what he'd do. But he sought changes in the commission's plans. He appeared to want to follow Baker's advice. Baker wanted his own set of rules for the three presidential debates and the single vice-presidential debate—each of 90 minutes duration.

But the debate issue wasn't the prime factor in the campaign with six weeks remaining to election day.

While it didn't seem to matter much to some voters—particularly baby boomers— that Clinton spent six years of his life maneuvering to stay out of Vietnam, what did matter to Republicans, especially to Bush's political director, Mary Matalin, was that they had found an incendiary issue, minus the extramarital sleaze, that made the challenger uncomfortable.

"Whenever there is a new component to the [draft] story, we are going to raise it until he answers the question," promised Miss Matalin.

Since the *Los Angeles Times*' account of his uncle's efforts to keep Clinton out of the war, the press and the Republicans had relentlessly kept the issue alive.

Both Senate Republican Leader Bob Dole and Vice President Quayle used the issue—and there were strong hints from the president's campaign that Bush himself would bring it up.

So, after being the beneficiary of two months of the most favorable coverage since he was nominated, Clinton all at once began ducking a press he complained was being unfair to him.

Then his staffers, appearing in disarray, began doing what political campaign people never should do—they got into physical altercations with reporters to keep them from grilling the candidate.

Betsey Wright, using another of her innumerable job titles, "research director," charged that the press was being used "as a Republic pawn" by writing that Clinton had not been candid in his explanations of his draft history, which she called "absolutely a lie."

"The people most concerned and acutely tuned in [to the issues] are the press, and the Republican strategy is to keep the press on it until it does have a spillover effect," Miss Wright offered. "They may succeed in instilling a lie."

Newsday's David Firestone, Susan Page, and Martin Kasindorf combined to produce a story about a Clinton staffer who discussed the draft issue. The staffer requested anonymity. This made it appear the informant was one of those members of the Clinton campaign who had a falling out with Hillary Clinton's interference and had almost resigned.

"The campaign isn't worried about the impact of the [draft] issue on voters, because polls do not show that it has caused Clinton any damage," *Newsday* reported.

"But the staffer said the campaign is very concerned about the way the draft issue has hobbled Clinton's generally successful ability to get out his preferred message."

"It acts as a noise," the staffer was quoted. "It interrupts an economic dialogue, a health-care dialogue...our goal is to not let our campaign be driven by others."

While Bush himself had not yet alluded to Clinton's draft history, he nevertheless made an implied contrast when he referred again and again to his own valorous service in World War II.

Draft Issue Is Getting to Bill

Bush senior adviser Charlie Black suggested that the point wasn't Clinton's patriotism or military fitness, but the favorite issue of character.

"The question is not the draft," Black said, suddenly becoming animated as he cheerily skewered Clinton on NBC-TV's "Today" show. "It's not the Vietnam War...the issue is the truth. It's Bill Clinton's credibility."

"Political experts agree that the Republicans may be able to turn what is essentially a tired issue to their advantage if they can continue to make Clinton look shifty and evasive in his evolving explanations of the past," reported the *Newsday* team of Firestone, Page, and Kasindorf. "Such offensives work best they say, when they play into preconceptions about a candidate's veracity, as this one does."

Ed Goeas, a GOP pollster with the Tarrance Group, a public opinion research firm, said the draft issue had become effective for Bush. It was pushing up the president's polling numbers on days when Clinton was bogged down defending himself against the draft issue.

"I think the press is reacting this way because they sense this is how the American public feels," said Goeas, who conducted a daily opinion poll for *Hotline*, an independent political digest. "Even those people who like Clinton, who tend to lean his way, are questioning the way he has handled this."

Clinton's own people acknowledged that he had to come up with a forthright explanation of his draft-related activities if he hoped to stay on the offensive in the closing weeks of the campaign.

"In the debates, Clinton is going to have to construct an answer that sounds really candid," said Terry Michael, a former Democratic Party official who now was running the nonpartisan Washington Center for Politics and Journalism.

"He needs to give the answer he should have given in the first place—which is that like millions of other Americans, he opposed the Vietnam War and used all legal means not to be inducted.

"That should have been his original answer, and I hope he has learned the lessons about the problems he has cost himself by not giving it..."

As election day approached, there was no concern that the "Yellow Ross of Texas" would figure in the balloting for president. Eccentric billionaire Perot faded away as quickly as he had appeared on the political scene.

Fading with him was the talk that the Texan had only to win one or two states in a close election to block either major party's candidate from gaining the 270 electoral college votes needed to win the presidency. After Perot declined to enter the race as an announced candidate it was a standard election again.

Bill Clinton was in a showdown with the president of the United States. He had overcome so many seemingly insurmountable odds to fulfill his dream. And to think, just a few months back his name was mud.

****

Only recently, Mike McAlary, the investigative reporter/columnist of the *New York Post* had written, "What can you really say about Bill Clinton, even in victory? That he made a run at his dream? There is a responsibility in dreams. You don't just grab something because you can reach it. Bill Clinton, the flawed candidate, can't beat George Bush, the vulnerable president."

McAlary had written that in April—three months before the Democratic National Convention.

"...maybe some other Democrat can [defeat Bush]. At some point, you would hope, even Bill Clinton will be responsible enough to step aside in favor of a greater dream. With each day that Clinton remains in the race, the window of opportunity on George Bush closes.

"In the end—win or lose—Bill Clinton is just another New York story. The sidewalks are crowded with them: would-be singers working as waitresses, would-be artists selling insurance, would-be authors writing traffic tickets."

Would-be saxophone player running for president.

"The Arkansas governor shares an ordinariness with an awful lot of New Yorkers," McAlary went on. "Clinton is the Broadway showgirl who couldn't kick high enough. He is the Felt Forum boxer who couldn't hit hard enough. He is the Carnegie Hall trumpet player who never quite hit the high note.

"Bill Clinton is the guy who wasn't quite big enough."

Saying that Bill Clinton came to New York to win the state's primary as Slick Willie and was leaving as "Billy Liar," the writer noted the excuses Clinton made to apologize for his Mafioso remarks about the state's governor, the Colombian pot he smoked, and his lies about the draft:

"That isn't me on the tape. Sorry, Governor Cuomo, that is me on the tape. I didn't inhale. I did inhale. I didn't dodge. I did dodge. I did play golf. I didn't play golf."

McAlary unleashed both barrels:

"...there is the whole tabloid thing. Frankly, I don't know why Bill Clinton thinks he has been garroted by the press. You answer this slight with the work of Hillary Clinton, intrepid smut reporter. What supermarket tabloid in the country, having seen Mrs. Clinton's machinations in getting a rumor about George Bush into print, doesn't want to hire her? And don't give New Yorkers that stuff about an 'off-the-record' comment. Mrs. Clinton's quotes were read back to her a week before they were finalized in the copy that went to *Vanity Fair*. And Hillary Clinton signed off on them.

"One of the reasons people don't want Bill and Hillary Clinton in the White House has to do with the vision thing," continued McAlary.

"People have an innate ability to know just how much of a couple they can bear. They know how much of a physical presence they can withstand. And who out there really wants to live with four years of Bubba and Mrs. Fields?"

McAlary wrote that column on April 7, the day New Yorkers went to the polls to vote in the state primary. He conceded that "no one is voting their dreams in this election. Most people, it seems, are voting their fears."

The writer's suggestion that "New Yorkers...do a grand and noble thing [by not voting for Clinton]," did not pan out. Clinton carried the Empire State and won all the marbles at the convention.

New York did not go out "and save the whole country" that day, as McAlary wished.

Nor had the Democratic National Convention taken Jimmy Breslin's advice to tell their pretender to the throne, "Take a walk!"

41

THE LAST ONE HUNDRED YARDS

Eight Weeks to the Election

Four months of primaries.

Two national conventions.

A slew of slashing election television commercials.

Much character assassination—most of it the character of Bill Clinton.

That was the story of the 1992 presidential campaign until Monday, September 7.

With the arrival of Labor Day, the quadrennial election madness turned from marathon to sprint.

Just eight weeks remained in this volatile election campaign. And the president of the United States and governor of Arkansas were engaged in a combat that would resort to a multitude of weird political gymnastics. Between Labor Day and election day the candidates would do all of the following:

- Hopscotch the national landscape to win votes.
- Attend ethnic and religious rallies and eat food they pretended to like but deep down hated with a passion.
- Shake hands they would never deign to touch at another time and kiss babies they didn't care a whit about.
- Wear funny jackets and funnier hats and pretend they didn't feel foolish in those getups.
- Give speeches and make promises about programs they knew had no chance to ever get past Congress.
- Spend some $70 million on their respective newspaper and TV campaign advertising with money that didn't belong to them.
- Engage in three presidential debates and suddenly find themselves facing jug-eared Ross Perot after he weaseled his way back into the race.

The bottom line on Labor Day was that Clinton was leading in the polls conducted since the Democratic convention in July. His margins over Bush had grown hearteningly—ranging from 45 percent to 63 percent—in the two months since the Democratic convention.

While Bush had been close to Clinton in some polls, the disheartening fact for Republicans was that the president lagged consistently in the nations' six most respected polls. His support never rose above 42 percent, separating him from his opponent by margins of as little as 3 percent and as much as 21 percent.

Analysts judged the disparity to mean that about six of every ten voters were deciding they wanted to vote *against* Bush.

But at the same time, they were not indicating they were *for* Clinton.

One of the top poll-takers, Cable News Network-*USA Today*, on Labor Day weekend showed Clinton ahead of Bush by a solid 43-to-29 percent margin. That 14-point differential was almost the same as the popularity deficit President Harry S. Truman faced on Labor Day 1948 before he launched his historic "give 'em hell" drive.

Truman had squeaked to victory on November 2, the only president in this century to win election after trailing his opponent on the first Monday of September.

As election day '92 loomed, Bush began comparing himself to Truman. He promised to carry out the most intensive politicking campaign ever. He exuded confidence that his tactics would prevail. However, Truman had three pluses in his favor that Bush lacked:

• The polls didn't consistently project Truman as an underdog as they did Bush.

• Dewey refused to roll up his sleeves and come out fighting the way Clinton had done against the incumbent.

• Truman could claim credit for a booming, post-World War II economy. Bush couldn't do the same after Desert Storm, a period when he dropped from an unprecedented 82 percent approval rating to a dismal 29 percent—an unheard-of 53 percent plunge.

Bush's task was made more formidable by the size of the uncommitted electorate, fully 28 percent of the people polled. To make his comeback—the president would have to win 75 percent of that number. Many political sages were inclined to believe that was impossible.

How, then, could George Bush avoid early retirement?

A possible answer came from top Democratic pollster Geoffrey Garin:

"The best and the only hope for the Bush campaign is to make people feel that Bill Clinton is too great a risk to elect. They just might be able to pull it off."

However, Garin cautioned, "Keep in mind that Clinton's conversion this summer from just another politician to the candidate-of-change is far from a firm or settled conclusion..."

In short, the Arkansas governor had made considerable progress since his early disastrous debuts in the New England primaries. He had established himself as a candidate to be reckoned with only after he walked away with the nomination in Madison Square Garden. Now if he only could hold on to that image, he just might pull it off.

Aware of Clinton's potential as the *candidate-of-change*, the GOP knew what it had to do to defuse this image with the electorate. They had to raise their candidate's "comfort level" while at the same time lowering Clinton's.

Thus began what was to be one of the most relentless attacks ever in a presidential race—hammering attacks on Clinton's character and candor, most especially on the ways he avoided the draft.

As they hit the campaign trail on Labor Day, Bush and Clinton both broke into full gallop.

Bush flew to Wisconsin and addressed 7,000 friendly listeners in Waukesha. Again, he compared himself to Truman by pointing to their similarities: both had "do-nothing" Congresses, both served their country honorably in wartime (a dig at Clinton's non-service), and both he and Truman were decisive on issues (while Clinton was wishy-washy, always "waffling and wavering.")

To ridicule this comparison, Clinton broke a Democratic tradition of rallying with national labor leaders in Detroit's Cadillac Square. He stood before a statue of Harry S. Truman in his hometown of Independence, Missouri, and proclaimed, "George Bush cast his first vote against Harry Truman...George Bush's legacy is the destruction of that very middle class. Harry Truman did not wake up every morning worrying about how to lower taxes one more time on millionaires."

Nicaragua: Bush's Achilles' Heel

More questions on his Vietnam War draft record threw Clinton into a lather at a fire station just before his tribute to Truman. He called on the news media to investigate—as zealously as they were his military record—recent reports contradicting Bush's claim that he knew nothing about the mid-1980s' arms sale to Iran in exchange for the release of hostages. Clinton did not mention his own role in the two-way traffic of Colombia cocaine in exchange for arms to the Contras, which he countenanced for years as governor.

"There is a memorandum between two [Reagan] cabinet members...that, if true, would call into question not only the president's [Bush's] veracity but his support for illegal conduct, which you [reporters] all don't ask him about."

The memo Clinton referred to was written in 1987. It surfaced in a court case against former Secretary of Defense Caspar Weinberger. In it, a damning charge was made against Bush by an aide to former Secretary of State George Schultz. He claimed Reagan's vice president was aware of the differing views among cabinet members over the arms sales—and that Bush favored the deal despite objections by both Weinberger and Schultz.

The issue would stay at the top of Clinton's Bush-bashing agenda throughout the campaign. And just before election eve, it would explode with a force that would leave no doubt the illegal sale of arms to Iran and diversion of the profits to Nicaraguan contras was Bush's Achilles' heel.

Yet, why didn't George Bush ever mention Clinton's dark role in the very similar—and just as illegal—role in the Bobby Seal/Mena airport scheme?

A week after Labor Day Clinton zoomed into comfortable leads in 17 big states, enough to give him the 270 electoral votes needed to win the White House, a Field Institute survey showed. That poll came on the heels of a *New York Daily News* poll giving Clinton a nearly 70 percent knockout margin in New York City and a 57-to-30 percent overall lead in the Empire State.

Meanwhile, at a time when family values and child care were hot issues, it was disclosed that Clinton once used Arkansas state funds to pay for a nanny for daughter Chelsea.

According to the story, the nurse was hired in 1980, initially to watch the child at night. Later, she tended Chelsea during the day. She was paid $9,785 that was supposed to have been the salary for a security guard at the governor's mansion.

A state senator described the gimmickry employed to engage the nanny as "pretty blatant." Clinton defended it by claiming it had been approved by his finance department—whose members served at his pleasure.

"It appears that the only baby Bill Clinton has ever required the people of Arkansas to care for is his own," criticized Bush strategist David Tell, linking the revelation to the campaign debate over family leave for newborn baby care and medical emergencies.

Ironically, while Clinton's campaign pledge had him backing a federal family-leave law, as 32 states provided on their own at the time, his own Arkansas wasn't among them.

"Once again, Clinton is proposing to require that American businesses do something that he hasn't required Arkansas businesses to do," David Tell complained.

The Clinton flacks simply turned their backs on an avalanche of questions on that issue.

Into late September, Clinton became increasingly inaccessible to reporters.

Nine months earlier, when he was an unknown candidate in New Hampshire, Clinton was eager to speak to reporters.

Now, Clinton talked to the press via satellite: he dispatched comments via faxes or on pre-recorded videotapes. In short, he was freezing out the media.

"You ask questions about stories that are not accurate, it's our legitimate right not to answer them," Clinton spokeswoman Dee Dee Myers protested, referring to the draft issue.

Miss Myers claimed her boss was now paying for having had a honeymoon with the press early on.

"You guys are all trying to make up for this sense that you've been too easy on Clinton," she fumed. "It's ridiculous!"

Meanwhile, in Yorba Linda, California, seat of Orange County, one of the nation's most Republican enclaves, Representative Robert K. Dornan, the California Republican who had attacked Clinton's draft shenanigans on the House floor, led several thousand at a rally in counting to 58 to mark the number of missions Bush flew in World War II as a Naval aviator.

Dornan said flatly that a President Clinton "will not have the moral authority to send troops into battle" because he is "Chicken Little from Little Rock—a big zero."

Former President Reagan joined the rally: "Bill Clinton cannot venture forth and campaign in Orange County because of its Santa Ana winds. He prefers to steer clear of drafts."

Meanwhile, Clinton returned to his Little Rock TV interviews to let the country know he was gearing up for a debate on the Michigan State University campus.

"Billy, Baby, Go Debate Yourself!"

"There's a debate scheduled for September twenty-second in East Lansing," Clinton trumpeted. "We're going to be there. We hope the president will."

The answer from the Bush camp was, "Billy, baby, you go and debate by yourself. Our George isn't gonna be anywhere near that stage."

The Bush campaign dispatched an ultimatum to the Clinton campaign, giving them until September 17 to agree to its terms on presidential debates—or else there wouldn't be any.

The GOP terms were at odds with the debate format proposed by the bipartisan commission and already accepted by the Democrats. Clinton/Gore national campaign chairman Mickey Kantor, replying to Bush/Quayle campaign chairman Robert Teeter, was just as tough:

"There is no counteroffer...quit running and hiding, because it's time the American people see these two candidates on the same stage."

Teeter proposed the debate rules used in the 1988 presidential face-offs: three presidential debates and one vice-presidential debate, with opponents to be questioned by a panel of journalists.

That was the formula created by White House chief of staff James Baker. The recently resigned secretary of state had led the Republican side in debate negotiations since Reagan's first presidential campaign in 1980.

But Kantor wouldn't negotiate with the Bush people. He stood fast on the rules enacted by the bipartisan Commission on Presidential Debates: three presidential debates and one vice-presidential debate, with opponents to be questioned by a single moderator rather than a panel of journalists.

The GOP's response was, "No negotiations, no debates."

The draft issue was still making headlines into the late days of September. Clinton became so concerned about the thrashing Bush was giving him that he had a change-of-heart about addressing the Utah National Guard Association in Salt Lake City. He had turned down an invitation earlier in the month. Now, after hearing that Bush was to speak at the gathering, Clinton decided to show up.

In his speech Bush didn't directly attack Clinton. Instead he said that the issue wasn't whether or not a candidate served in the military, but the more basic question of honor.

"Does that mean that if you've never seen the awful horror of combat that you can never be commander in chief?" Bush asked before answering his own question. "Of course not. But it does mean that we must hold our presidents to the highest standard, because they might have to decide if our sons and daughters should knock early on death's door."

Climbing the rostrum, Clinton praised the National Guard and said he was ready to be commander in chief and to order combat.

"I do not relish this prospect," he offered, "but neither do I shrink from it."

Clinton's effusive praise for the National Guard created an ironic wrinkle in the Democratic Party's strategy of criticizing Vice President Dan Quayle for joining the guard to avoid service in Vietnam. No longer could Quayle's action be likened to Clinton's avoidance of military service.

The draft did not remain a high priority issue much longer. Distant thunder was heard from the Lone Star State.

****

Sixty-four days had passed since Ross Perot had walked away from his shot at the White House. Since then he had spent the time teasing, cajoling, threatening, and generally being a royal pain to the two major candidates. He had been trying all along to have the rivals court him, to exert an extraordinary power over the election.

On September 18, Perot's supporters filed petitions that put his name on the ballot in Arizona, the 50th state to do so. He used the occasion to issue an ultimatum to Bush and Clinton.

Newsday's David Firestone said it first and best about Perot's ploy to have one or the other candidate adopt "his flinty plan to cut the budget deficit." The political correspondent offered, "To the candidate who agrees to do so, according to associates, he may offer the glittering prize of his endorsement, which could be worth millions of votes. But if neither candidate adopts his plan, Perot may well make good on his threat to enter the race as a formal candidate, a decision that could cripple Bush's chances but also posed pitfalls for Clinton."

Clinton got a boost the next day when Admiral William Crowe, retired chairman of the Joint Chiefs of Staff, endorsed the governor.

"There has been an inordinate amount of attention in this campaign paid to Governor Clinton's lack of military service," Crowe announced at the governor's mansion in Little Rock.

"I served in uniform for forty-seven years. I know and have worked with many others who didn't serve in uniform, including a number of key national security figures in the Bush administration. That fact never affected my ability to work with them or my high regard for them."

The endorsement by Crowe, appointed by President Reagan to the nation's top military post in 1985 and who served until President Bush named General Colin Powell, was a coup for the Democrats. But it was shortly countered by the general who had directed the Persian Gulf War.

Norman "Stormin' Norman" Schwarzkopf went on record proclaiming that avoidance of the draft raised serious questions.

"How does a person who admits that he deliberately did not agree with the war, and therefore did not want to go to that war, how does he handle it when he has to send other people to war?"

Perot Holds the High Card

Now in October, the last full month before Tuesday, November 3—just 34 days to the election—all at once it was again a three-man race for the presidency.

For weeks Ross Perot had been asked what he wanted when he intruded into the presidential campaign.

The blunt, eccentric Texas billionaire had "invited" President Bush and Governor Clinton to send delegates to Dallas to brief *him* on how their campaigns were addressing the issue he held dearest: reduction of the federal budget.

Both camps caved in and slavishly sent high-ranking delegates to Perot's Dallas headquarters to massage his Texas-sized ego.

Perot had engineered these pilgrimages in a classic demonstration of his manipulative nature. Perot claimed this was not the case—that the goal of his movement was to "take back the grass roots of America" and that it was "driven from the bottom up."

At a raucous press conference in Dallas on the morning of October 1, the man who was never really in the race but was never fully out of it, announced that he was running for the presidency.

"I promise you I will give it everything I have," said Perot. Claiming that an American public had made him its candidate, Perot vowed, "I look forward to squarely presenting these issues day after day to the American people."

Clearly cognizant that his about-face had not strengthened his credibility, Perot told voters, "My decision in July hurt you. I apologize. I thought I was doing the right thing. I made a mistake. I take full responsibility for it."

Perot tried to give the impression that he left the race in July because he believed the two major political parties would address the issue. But he now judged they had failed to do that. Thus he was becoming a third-party candidate.

For a running mate, Perot reached out for 68-year-old former Admiral James Stockdale, who was captured in Vietnam and held prisoner of war for more than seven years. Stockdale's most significant contribution in the campaign was to offer his view of the Democratic candidate for president:

"The demonstrations by Bill Clinton and other protesters hurt the U.S. war effort in Vietnam. They cost American lives and prolonged the captivity of prisoners such as myself.

"Those comrades of mine that died...the extra ten, fifteen, twenty-thousand—that blood is on your hands, you war protesters!

"You strung it out. You didn't stop it a minute.

"Every time in prison, we would hear that they had one of these big galas of the sort that Clinton was arranging here and there in the world.

"'Huh!' we would say. 'Another year in this place. We're not going to get out of here until we bomb Hanoi.'

"And they couldn't do that until they beat that opposition down."

Bush did not hesitate to fire anti-patriot missiles at Clinton either.

"Maybe I'm old-fashioned, but I can't understand why anyone would demonstrate against our country in a foreign land," Bush declared on the October 7 "Larry King Live" talk show on CNN.

"Bill Clinton should level with the American people on whether he participated in Vietnam anti-war demonstrations abroad and about a trip he made as a student to Moscow in 1970."

High Stakes Debates

Barely a week into October, with the election now a three-horse race, negotiators for Bush and Clinton had hammered out a compromise for a schedule of debates that appeared to satisfy both sides.

The game plan was four debates to be held October 11, 13, 15, and 19.

The first, third, and fourth debates were for the presidential candidates, the second for their running mates. The GOP and Democratic camps also agreed to let Perot take part.

The first presidential debate was held the night of October 11 in St. Louis. Bush, Clinton, and Perot wrangled with a controlled civility for 90 minutes and batted questions posed to them by four panelists on subjects ranging from Medicare to AIDS, taxes to foreign affairs, the demand for change vs the need for experience.

The most dramatic moment came when Clinton charged that Bush had "questioned my patriotism" in criticizing his anti-war activities. Clinton accused the president of employing the very tactics his father, the late Senator Prescott Bush (R-Connecticut) had once battled.

"Your father was right to stand up to Joe McCarthy; you were wrong to attack my patriotism," Clinton said, turning to address Bush directly on his left. "I was opposed to the war, but I loved my country."

Avoiding Clinton's angry glare, Bush retorted, "I find it impossible to understand how anyone could have demonstrated in a foreign country, England, during the war, and I question whether he can serve as commander in chief and order American troops into battle."

The debate was viewed as a draw on most of the nation's media scorecards. *Newsday*'s Washington correspondent Susan Page concluded, "It was a high stakes, high tension confrontation that broke little ground, had no knockout punches, no gaffes—but nonetheless offered a television audience estimated at 70 million an opportunity to see the three candidates answer questions side-by-side for the first time

Two nights later, October 13, the spotlight was beamed on Atlanta and on Vice President Dan Quayle and challengers Al Gore and James Stockdale. Quayle turned the debate into the most combative and free-wheeling exchange of the political year.

Quayle called Bill Clinton the "man who can't be trusted." Gore fired back that the Republican administration created and then ignored America's economic ills.

The man in the middle of the stage, white-haired Admiral Stockdale, commanded all the laughs. Avoiding confrontations with either rival, he seemed content to let Quayle and Gore fire shots at each other—and to swivel his head from one to the other as though watching a Ping-Pong game.

In the middle of the debate, Stockdale brought the house down by asking, "Who am I? Why am I here?"

Near the end of the debate, Stockdale huffed like the scholar in philosophy that he is at Stanford University's Hoover Institution:

"I think America is seeing right now the reason this nation is in gridlock."

New York Daily News Washington Bureau chief Lars-Erik Nelson summed up the veep jab-fest by suggesting that Quayle, by repeatedly assaulting Clinton as a liar, had set "the tone for what is likely to be the Bush campaign's strategy from now until election day." Then Nelson concluded, "...Quayle all but drowned out [Gore] and his cool mastery of issues in their lone vice-presidential debate.

"In terms of getting his message out and doing the job he was programmed to do, Quayle won...he stuck to his guns—even at the expense of tiresome repetitions."

A converted field house at the University of Richmond in Virginia was the scene for the second presidential debate. It brought out an audience that turned the program into an unprecedented town-hall-type give-and-take.

Rising with polite persistence all night long, the audience made it clear they were less than interested in Clinton's Vietnam draft status and Bush's role in the Iran-Contra scandal—a theme that Clinton had been hammering at with the same intensity that Bush had in hitting his challenger's war record.

Clinton seemed most comfortable in the town-hall format. He took advantage of the intimacy with the audience and ticked off his record in Arkansas and the provisions of his economic proposals for the country.

Bush seemed defensive, detached and tentative, glancing at his watch and, at times, not seeming to understand the questions or to connect with the 209 questioners in the field house. He wasn't as aggressive as his aides wanted him to be. Afterward, Republican Party chairman Rich Bond conceded that "the format did not lend itself to the kind of bitter free-for-all that characterized the vice-presidential debate."

While Perot continued to amuse everyone with his homespun humor, he seemed better equipped at outlining the nation's problems than in offering the specific solutions the audience was seeking.

An instant post-debate nationwide poll by CBS taken with people who used touch-tone phones to call in their selections, gave Clinton a resounding 54 percent of the 1,394 respondents' votes, more than double the 25 percent for Bush and 20 percent for Perot.

The final face-off was held the night of October 19 at the Michigan State University campus in East Lansing.

Clearly, it was the liveliest of the three presidential face-offs. It was highlighted by much finger-pointing, considerable arm-waving, and clashes on a broad range of issues. The candidates also mounted harsh attacks on one another's past performances on issues ranging from the nation's troubled economy to the handling of Iraq's Saddam Hussein.

Perot ended the debate as he had started the first one: "claiming what appeared to be mystical kinship with the American people," as Lars-Erik Nelson put it, "...as though he and the public would govern without the need for messy things like governments, lobbyists, congressional representatives, and the like."

Bush was more aggressive than in the previous two debates. He vigorously challenged Clinton's economic proposals, saying, "Mr. and Mrs. America...watch your wallets!"

While he also came across strongly with his assertion that Clinton would be forced to raise taxes on middle-income families, Bush had to defend himself against Clinton and Perot's attacks about his record in foreign policy and his agenda for solving the nation's economic ills.

100 Million View Final Face-Off

The final face-off, viewed by nearly 100 million Americans—an all-time record TV audience—was narrowly given to Bush by an Associated Press panel of judges. The president was awarded 126 points of a possible 150, Clinton received 125 points, and Perot, 122.

The campaign gained intensity as President Bush continued to sharply contrast the differences between himself and Clinton.

Meanwhile, Clinton refused to be complacent, although he was ahead in some polls by double-digit figures.

"I've got to keep on fighting," he said. "Two weeks from now is still two weeks from now."

A week before the election, when he was beginning to make slight gains in the polls, Perot pulled a grandstand play that backfired. He was left holding the bag of a dirty-tricks story that not only queered what slight chance he had of winning a few votes in the electoral college, but also cast strong doubts that he'd ever again rise as a factor in politics.

"He's a Perot-noid!" screamed the headlines.

On October 25, campaigning in Pennsylvania and New Jersey, Perot addressed crowds in Pittsburgh and Flemington with a "revised version" of why he dropped out of the race in July. It wasn't, as he had originally claimed, for the sake of his country and because he didn't want his candidacy to create the turmoil of throwing the election into the House of Representatives.

Perot stunned the crowd into silence with the "real reason" he quit:

"I found myself in a situation where I had three reports that the Republican Party intended to publish a false photograph of my daughter, who was getting married on August twenty-third, and smear her before her wedding and actually disrupt the wedding ceremony. That was a risk I couldn't take. I love her too much to have her hurt."

After he dropped out, he said, his daughter Caroline was married, went on her honeymoon, and returned to plead with her father to reenter the race, which he then did.

Perot's allegations of GOP dirty tricks brought instant reaction from White House spokesman Marlin Fitzwater, traveling with President Bush on a campaign trip to Denver.

"He seems to have latched onto this theory much like other people latch onto UFO theories, and he seems to believe it."

Other comments from Bush spokespeople:

"Perot is paranoid...he's crazy...he's a person who has delusions."

Perot went public with his dirty-tricks story because he was burned the night before in the Sunday prime-time "60 Minutes" broadcast. The entire program was based on Perot's "hair-brained claim" that the Republicans planned to do a smear on his daughter.

The program concluded that Perot's sources were unbelievable, that the attack on his daughter was a fiction of his imagination—just as when, on prior occasions, Perot discerned conspiracy theories that others could not.

For years, Perot claimed the North Vietnamese marked him for death after his efforts to free America POWs in the early 1970s. He claimed (skeptics said he *fantasized*) a squad of rifle-toting Black Panthers had stormed his estate but were chased off by a pack of guard dogs that "took a big bite on the backside" of one of the intruders as he fled.

Real or imagined conspiracies against him aside, Perot seemed also to have a *thing* about "compromising photographs."

In one instance, after he failed to persuade the Defense Department's Richard Armitage to go along with his plan on POW matters, Perot alerted the *Washington Post* that he had a "compromising photo" of Armitage with an Asian woman.

Another time, incensed over a negative story about his son Ross Jr., Perot confronted the publisher of the *Fort Worth Star-Telegram* with a claim that he had an "embarrassing picture" of a staffer on the newspaper.

Blatant blackmail tactics by Perot?

Not quite.

It's blackmail when the threat is made before the protested act or action can be taken. When it becomes a *fait accompli*, the threat to blacken the image of the person who committed that act or action is *sour grapes*, a harmless practice and not prosecutable as a crime.

Syndicated gossipist Liz Smith, who cited Perot paranoias at great length in one of her columns, concluded that he was "a flake...adorable, charismatic, smart, and extremely dangerous."

"60 Minutes" executive producer Don Hewitt concluded that Ross Perot is just a plain *unmitigated liar*. He spoke up after Perot tried to explain at a press conference why he aired his allegation that the Republicans planned to embarrass his daughter:

"I brought it up to my volunteers yesterday because '60 Minutes' was going to run it last night. I didn't want '60 Minutes' to run it. I didn't give them the story. I told '60 Minutes' when they first called me, I said approach this with great skepticism. They decided to run the story."

Hewitt revealed that Perot had brought the story to "60 Minutes" after his July 16 withdrawal from the presidential race.

"He told me personally that he dropped out because Republicans 'were going after my kids,'" Hewitt revealed.

"He can say all he wants that he didn't want the story to come out and that I dragged it out of him. But the fact is that he was the one who urged me to pursue it."

Taking Perot's tips, CBS investigative journalists had followed trails that lead them to dead ends. They were given two unidentified sources whom Perot called "good friends" but declined to name. He did offer one name, that of Scott Barnes, who allegedly informed Perot, as he said the other two had, that the Republicans planned to distribute a doctored photo of his daughter, depicting her as a lesbian.

An ex-policeman in Inglewood, California, and subsequently a bridal shop owner in Prescott, Arizona, was one side of Scott Barnes. His other side showed his history included the following:

- He gave accounts of exploits as an undercover agent and special forces commando on Rambo-type missions involving American POWs. Army Colonel Joseph Schlatter, former head of the Defense Intelligence Agency's special office for POW/MIA affairs, said Barnes "is not now, nor has he ever been employed by the DIA, the CIA, Drug Enforcement Administration, FBI, or any other federal intelligence or law enforcement agency."

• He was convicted in 1988 of illegally recording telephone calls in California and got off with a reduced charge after the judge concluded Barnes suffered from "an undercurrent" of delusions.

In 1983, *Soldier of Fortune* magazine accorded Barnes the ultimate salute by calling him "My Favorite Flake."

POW/MIA activists were astounded that Perot had given credence to Barnes.

"It's the funniest damn thing I ever heard of," said a laughing Ann Mills Griffin, director of the National League of Families of the Missing.

"That a reportedly serious candidate for president could take this guy seriously—it just blows my mind," said Ms. Griffin.

Less than 24 hours after voicing his story about GOP dirty tricks, Perot called a press conference in Dallas and lashed out bitterly at skeptics.

"I am sick and tired of you all questioning my integrity without a basis for it," he flailed at reporters who kept asking for his sources—other than the discredited Scott Barnes.

"Would you give us one credible person that actually saw it happen, other than a person that says you told them it happened?" Perot was asked by a reporter.

"Hey, look I don't have to prove anything to you people, to start with," Perot exploded. "Number two, I have given you proof that would satisfy any reasonable group in the country on an issue that's not related to the president's race.

"Was I making up stories or not?

"No, I wasn't.

"That's all you need to know."

42

THE ELECTION: A NEW PRESIDENT

A Torch Passes

Dog-tired and with a raspy voice he was unable to raise above a whisper, Bill Clinton returned to Little Rock and stretched out on a couch in the governor's mansion. He was a man fulfilled.

How far away it all now seemed, those voices that had shouted at him last February in the New England winter, voices that shouted questions:

"Did you sleep with Gennifer Flowers?"

"Are you afraid you're going to lose your lead in the polls?"

"Will you drop out of the race if you don't win the New Hampshire primary tomorrow?"

"Are you angry at the media?"

Questions that had brought him to his knees and made him cringe and despise journalists. That was his first all-out encounter with a dogged, abrasively unrelenting national press corps. How different from the friendly, look-the-other-way Arkansas reporters he'd become accustomed to in more than a dozen years in public life!

The turning point in Clinton's relations with the press was reached at an eatery called Blakes' Coffee Shop, nestled in the New Hampshire Mountains in the once-bustling community of Manchester. It was now a relic of a rich industrial past, suffering the same precipitate economic decline that other New England communities had experienced for too many years.

That state of affairs had brought Bill Clinton into the race for the presidency in the first place—he wanted to do something about the nation's economy. He had come to New Hampshire to offer one man's solution to the country's shaky domestic crisis, a predicament that the incumbent president had not fully grasped. George Bush had scorned his brain trust's advice to "get back in touch with the voters" and "give the people an aggressive economic stimulus package."

That advice came from the likes of top GOP campaign advisers such as Fred Malek and Bob Teeter. How did George Bush handle such counsel at a time shortly after the end of the Gulf War, when his approval rating soared briefly to a stratospheric 82 percent?

"If you're so damn smart," he sniffed, "how come I'm president and you're not?"

Bill Clinton saw the monumental odds he faced. The Gennifer Flowers revelations were demonstrably injurious. *Womanizing* disclosures had destroyed Gary Hart's bid for the presidency four years earlier. Now they rose to haunt Bill Clinton.

What could he do to salvage the little, the *very* little hope that seemed left for his survival as a viable candidate?

After breakfast at Blakes' Clinton left for the campaign trail with thoroughly embarrassed Hillary at his side. She was devastated by one of her husband's responses

"If I did [sleep with Gennifer], I wouldn't tell you."

Hillary is reported to have snapped something that sounded like, "You bastard!" If she smiled when she said it that's because she had tolerated his behavior for so long. She had learned to put him in his place with a smile.

(Soon after Bill and Hillary's residency in the White House began, a secret serviceman reported that during a somewhat high-strung family dispute, the first lady hurled a lamp at the president. And *she had a smile on her face when she let go.* Soon after that incident was reported in *Newsweek*, Clinton proposed replacing the White House Secret Service with a "private guard." That idea was shot down as swiftly as Clinton's later effort to fire the White House Travel Office staff and substitute its services with an Arkansas travel office operated by a Clinton cousin.)

Booting Sam Donaldson et al.

Bill Clinton's itinerary that February morning after breakfast at Blakes' took him and Hillary to a picturesque clapboard dwelling at 83 Boynton Street. He had an appointment to speak with local residents in a homey encounter on the front porch.

He found, instead, a regiment of reporters, photographers, and electronic media people with microphones, booms, cameras, and miles of wire snaking over the by-now thoroughly trampled New England snow.

"What the hell is this?" Clinton asked in bewilderment. "Where are the voters?"

This was Bill Clinton's moment of truth. No more wise-guyish, embarrassing queries from Sam Donaldson or his churlish media colleagues, the candidate told himself.

"If they want me to talk," the new Bill Clinton informed Hillary and his campaign aides, "I'll talk to Larry King instead. I'll talk with Ted Koppel. Those guys from the news side are too hard-nosed for me. And the same goes for the reporters from the print media. They can go screw..."

That was a seemingly unorthodox transformation. For a candidate to snub such an important and influencing factor as the press during a primary campaign, didn't augur well.

Nevertheless, he bucked the odds. The greatly diminished role Bill Clinton consigned to journalists during his campaign had begun—in earnest.

"That can't last long," one member of the fourth estate after another protested. "He'll drown in his ignorance of the press's real importance in any candidate's campaign."

Not so. Bill Clinton largely turned his back on the press from that day forward. He limited his responses to a few words—always words of denial—whenever the sensation-seeking tabloids and even the most distinguished broadsheets screamed about the various scandals attributed to him.

Stormy as it was at times, Clinton weathered the squalls and came out a survivor. He had set his agenda to shaft the press—and it succeeded. He invented a new dynamism in politics for relations with the fourth estate. And he won.

The election results proved that...thanks to the beneficence of a press that took Clinton's punches lying down.

The Final Hours Before

Bill Clinton had every reason to be weary and hoarse in the early hours of election day, November 7, 1992.

Minutes before arriving at the governor's mansion, he stepped off his campaign plane with Hillary and daughter Chelsea. They were returning from a torturous, 29-hour, 4,106-mile tour across the country. Clinton spoke at every stop until, literally, he lost his voice.

Now back in the friendliest of surroundings, Little Rock, he accepted the ebullient greetings of his supporters.

"I'm glad its over...we're gonna win."

It was morning and the polling places had opened. Clinton relaxed on the sofa for a few minutes. Then he rose, showered, ate breakfast, and took a seat before the TV, where he promptly fell asleep. When he awakened, he was off with Hillary and Chelsea for the polls.

"I'm pooped," Clinton remarked before entering the voting booth. "I fell asleep in a chair after getting back. We were watching a John Wayne movie on TV. I guess I had about three-and-a-half hours of sleep. That's enough for me."

Then the Clintons returned to the governor's mansion. In late afternoon, despite a steady rainfall, Clinton donned shorts and T-shirt, slipped into running shoes, and went for a jog. Chelsea accompanied her dad for a way, then hopped into the limousine that trailed behind.

Soon the entourage (mostly secret servicemen) arrived at a McDonald's. This pit stop gave Clinton one of his last opportunities to speak to the public as governor. For at midnight, when he addressed the people again, he would do so as president-elect.

"This place keeps me alive," he quipped as he swallowed thirstily from a glass of water.

He then jogged back to the mansion and found another huge gathering of well-wishers.

"My voice is coming back a bit," he said. "I'm going to go up there," he went on, pointing to an upper floor of the governor's residence, "and sit with Chelsea and my family and have dinner and wait to see what happens."

Bill Clinton was a man at peace with himself, at long last. He had weathered the arduous, often impossible roller-coaster ride of a 10-month political campaign.

He had refused to take for granted polls that showed him comfortably ahead of both President Bush and Ross Perot. He wanted to fight to the end—and he did.

But Ross Perot wasn't the only distant thunder Bill Clinton had to countenance from Texas. Dianne Dwire Welch all at once became an ominous *fourth party candi-*

date in the election, now just hours away.

"What the fuck do you mean she's going to the *National Enquirer* with her story!" Clinton shouted into the phone to the caller, once again said to be Don Bankston, the Lone Star State's Democratic Party's chief fund-raiser

The author was not privy to the exchange, but sources of unimpeachable integrity inside the Clinton campaign committee agreed that Clinton barked a command on this order:

"Kidnap the dirty bitch! Take her out of circulation. We can't have that cunt screwing me in the final hours of this fucking race."

No sooner said than done. And for the upshot of the caper, let's go to Dianne Dwire Welch herself:

"It all started with a phone call from Don Bankston. He said to me, 'What the hell are you trying to do? Don't you realize Bill Clinton's got to be elected president? Do you want to upset the apple cart?'

"My response was, 'Look, Don, you tossed me overboard when my ass was in a jam and I had to do six years and more of hard time. I don't have any means to get by on anymore, and the *Enquirer* is giving me a chance to make some money that I need desperately'

"His answer was, 'Bullshit! After your brother's elected president you won't ever have to worry a thing about your future or from where the next buck's gonna come from.'

"So I said to him, 'What the hell am I supposed to do, just sit tight and choke to death?'

"Bankston had the answer at his fingertips. 'Just stay on an even keel. I'm gonna make certain you don't lose out.'"

Dianne stayed cool and waited. But not for long.

"A man named Arthur came over to the house. I never heard him give me his last name. He talked to my boyfriend, John Rodriguez, who was back living with me after I got out of prison. Arthur told John that the Clinton people were saying I had medical problems and that I should be put away in a sanitarium or hospital.

"John told the guy to go screw himself. He said there was nothing wrong with me. But John didn't disagree with Arthur that I shouldn't talk to the *Enquirer*. So…"

Rodriguez told Arthur that he could handle the *problem*. "I'll keep her out of Clinton's hair until after the election," he is said to have promised Clinton's emissary.

But the very next day—Sunday, November 1, 1992, two days before the election—Rodriguez had to leave town and Dianne was left alone and helpless in coping with the visitor who appeared at her door.

"Don Bankston came to tell me that he was going to salt me away until after the election. He said that there were very powerful people who wouldn't hesitate to dispose of me in a very unceremonious way if I put up any resistance.

"'Get your things together,' he ordered me. 'I'm taking you to a hideout for a couple of days, until after the election.'"

Dianne told the author that she was compelled to go to the Holiday Inn on Route 6 in Houston, just a stone's throw from her $400-a-month apartment that she shared with John Rodriguez.

"Bankston told me an eighty-dollar-a-night room was reserved for me at the motel for two nights. He told me I was to stay there until Wednesday—after the election.

"And he also put a hundred and fifty dollars in my hand.

"'If you want more money, just ask for it,' he said to me. 'But be sure and stay there for the next two nights. Your room is paid for in full.'"

Dianne said that her son, Jeff, who was also living with her, drove his mother to the Holiday Inn.

"But after I was there for about four or five hours, I panicked. I was scared and confused. I called Jeff to come take me home."

According to Dianne, her incarceration was over.

"Bankston phoned the next morning and demanded to know why I hadn't stayed at the motel. I told him that I didn't need to be put away like that—that I wasn't going to blow it for my brother Bill by blabbing to the *Enquirer* or to any other tabloid.

"Bankston put in the last word. 'You just better not!' he said sternly, 'because it won't be good for you.'"

Of course, by this late date—just 24 hours before the election, there was no chance that the supermarket tabloid that had waved the big bucks at Dianne could ever publish her story in time to change the outcome of the election. But the concern in the Clinton camp at this late stage wasn't the *Enquirer*, but the possibility a wide circulation daily, such as the *Los Angeles Times*, might break the story about Clinton's relationship with his ex-convict stepsister.

That never happened. Dianne Dwire Welch, her lips sealed, sat before the TV in her apartment on election night and cheered her stepbrother as he steamrollered to victory.

Bill in an Electoral Landslide

The suspense was over before it even began. The first results trickling in from the precincts where Bill Clinton found the roughest early going, New Hampshire, put him ahead of President Bush and Ross Perot as they broke out of the starting gate.

He would retain the lead for the next 10 hours as the tabulation of the election returns continued until a candidate was officially proclaimed the winner.

No sooner did the polls in the East close, and before votes in the country's other two time zones were counted, than Clinton was seen as the clear-cut winner.

Less than an hour after the voting in New York ended, at 9:00 p.m., all three networks and CNN projected Clinton as the victor.

The Arkansan had won victory by taking New England, the Northeast, and the Midwest swing states. He overcame the GOP's domination of the South and Mountain States, then claimed the voter-rich far West.

Clinton won more than a 2 million vote plurality, an amazing outcome when viewed in the light of a three-way race. The Clinton/Gore ticket won 43 percent of the popular vote, compared with 38 percent for Bush/Quayle, and 19 percent for Perot/Stockdale.

The results were even more profound in the electoral college which tallied a 357–

168 showing, a brutal arithmetical rejection for the incumbent. As political scientist Everett Barll Ladd put it, "It was a contest between the personal doubts about Clinton and the desire for economic change. Change won."

Bush suffered one of the most decisive rejections of an incumbent president in history. He received the lowest popular-vote percentage since William Howard Taft lost his bid for a second term in 1912 in a similar three-way racc.

Bush was hurt more than he was helped by Perot, whose $60 million bullhorn on-again, off-again campaign won him the largest electorate backing since the renegade Bull Moose candidate, former President Theodore Roosevelt. He grabbed 88 electoral votes to Taft's 8, leaving Democrat Woodrow Wilson to sweep the election with 435 of the prized electoral college ballots.

Some Last Words from the Boys

Newsweek noted that by amassing 19 percent, the eccentric Texan "seemed guaranteed to [win] a seat at the national talk-show table."

He was not seated in such a setting on election night. Perot played hide-and-seek with his supporters all day in Dallas. When he emerged finally, via a telephone hookup, he chided, "Is this the end?" Then with an ear-to-jughead-ear grin, he commanded the band to strike up his theme song, "Crazy."

Not since FDR defeated Hoover in 1932, while the band played "Happy Days Are Here Again," had a song fit the candidate better than in 1992 when the odd man out accepted the inevitable.

"The American people have spoken," Perot said in another peek-a-boo appearance before supporters. Some booed the outcome and almost drowned out their hero's last words:

"[The people] have chosen Governor Clinton. Congratulations."

George Bush went out "clannish," as the headline in the *New York Daily News* put it.

"Looking good," Bush said half-heartedly when informed early on that he won the midnight vote in tiny Dixville Notch, New Hampshire. "Great day!"

Bush watched election returns in Houston, his permanent residence, while a small crowd of supporters gathered a mile or so away, in a hotel ballroom booked for a victory celebration.

Barely two hours after the polls in Texas closed, the president told campaign director James Baker to prepare a concession statement.

"Keep it short," Bush said. "I don't want it to be a speech."

After a telephone call to Little Rock congratulating Clinton on his victory, Bush spoke to the America that had given him one of the most resplendent victories of any presidential election four years ago—and now had denied him a second term.

"Here's the way I see it...and the country should see it," Bush said somberly. "The people have spoken and we respect the majesty of the democratic system."

His voice choked as he turned and thanked wife Barbara for her work and support.

"He [Clinton] did run a strong campaign," said Bush, who let it be known he phoned his victorious rival in Little Rock. "I wish him well in the White House. I want the country to know my entire administration will work closely with his team to assure the smooth transition of power...America must come first."

In Little Rock, where the Christmas decorations had been hung early and lights were strung over the city, huge crowds descended on the governor's mansion where Clinton remained out of view until just after midnight. At that hour, he was beamed around the world as he spoke with his wife, daughter, in-laws, and other family members and friends gathered around him in a celebrative mood:

"My fellow Americans, on this day, with high hopes and brave hearts, in massive numbers, the American people have voted to make a new beginning.

"This election is a clarion call for our country to face the challenges of the end of the Cold War and the beginning of the next century."

In the end, the voters had the last word. They had spoken and sent the message across the land loud and clear: they wanted change.

Change in the way the economy was handled.

Change in the way senators carry on—three were sent into involuntary retirements.

Change in the way Native Americans had been ignored; the first such tribal member was elected to the Senate.

And change in the length of congressional terms; all 14 states that carried the term-limit proposition on their ballots passed the measure.

Newsweek's Howard Fineman summed it up:

"Clinton has survived one of the great character ordeals of political history, a gauntlet of innuendo and attack that had seemed to doom his candidacy before the first primary.

"His relentless cheerfulness, his stoicism and his shrewdness will all stand him in good stead in the hard years ahead. And they will be hard. For unlike his idol [John F. Kennedy], Clinton takes the helm on an ebb tide. His moment in history is in some ways the mirror opposite of Kennedy's.

"While JFK could volunteer his countrymen to pay any price, bear any burden, lift the world toward a New Frontier, Clinton must now ask their children to save themselves from an age of slow but ominous decline.

"It is a challenge that is perhaps even greater than the one Kennedy so confidently faced three decades ago."

Now, for good or ill, the burden of America's leadership had been shifted upon William Jefferson Blythe Clinton's broad shoulders to carry.

He had made 1992 the Year of the Voter, and the voter had spoken.

America had changed the guard.

43

THE BANKERS' ECONOMIC DEMOLITION AGENT

The Acceptance Speech Giveaway

When Bill Clinton delivered his July 16 nomination acceptance speech in Madison Square Garden, he said he admired two people the most: President John F. Kennedy and Professor Carroll Quigley.

Just the mention of Quigley's name sent a clear message to the American—indeed the world's—banking community.

He was telling bankers everywhere that, if elected, he'd carry out the economic theories of the renowned economist and professor of history at the Foreign Service School of Georgetown University, who was Clinton's teacher when he was an undergraduate—and had since written a massive, 1,348-page tome titled *Tragedy and Hope: A History of the World in Our Time*.

The book was originally published by the MacMillan Company in 1966. Although the publisher reportedly was pressured by "powerful forces" to take the book off the market, thousands of copies became collectors' items for a West Coast publisher, who has now made them available through GSG Associates, P.O. Box 6448, Rancho Palos Verdes, California 90734.

In the book, Quigley, now dead, gives one of the most telling accounts about the "world's secret power structure," a mysterious super leadership alluded to at times for the past 150 years by such authorities as Britain's nineteenth-century prime minister Benjamin Disraeli and that same country's twentieth-century learned publication, the *British Intelligence Digest*.

Disraeli said, "The world is governed by very different personages from what is imagined by those who are NOT behind the scenes."

A century and a half later, the *Intelligence Digest* noted, "There is a small but powerful control group behind the scenes which is extremely influential in manipulating world events."

Because the *Digest* seemed to have inside contacts with the group, it did not identify any powers by name. It simply referred to the control group as "Force X."

However, Dr. Quigley pulled no punches. He not only identified individuals in the power structure by name, he also clearly and forcefully defined the diverse roles they played in the secret power structure's day-to-day activities.

The most incisive analysis of Professor Quigley's motivation in exposing "one of the best kept secrets in the world" was advanced by one of America's foremost scholars of political conspiracies, W. Cleon Skousen, a 16-year veteran of the FBI, one-time chief of police of Salt Lake City, longtime editorial director of the nation's leading police magazine, *Law and Order*, and later a law professor at Brigham Young University.

In a 143-page review and commentary on Dr. Quigley's *Tragedy and Hope,* published under the title *The Naked Capitalist*, Skousen described Bill Clinton's idol as one of the elite "insiders" of the secret world power complex. (Skousen has updated his book with additional commentary and analysis, and the revised edition, retitled *Tragedy and Hope: Understanding the New World Order*, is also available through GSG Associates.

"...[Quigley] knew the scope of this power complex and he knew that its leaders hope to eventually attain total global control. Furthermore, Dr. Quigley makes it clear throughout his book that by and large he warmly supports the goals and purposes of the 'network.'"

At the podium in Madison Square Garden, Bill Clinton didn't allude to any of this. He merely let himself pass as a name-dropper. He didn't inform the convention who Quigley really was and what he stood for.

Since Quigley himself admitted that he supported the "network," why did he expose it and disclose many of its most secret operations?

Why did he alert the millions of people who are the conspiracy's intended victims and possibly arouse them to resistance?

Professor Skousen: "[Quigley's] answer appears in a number of places but is especially forceful and clear on pages 979–980. He says, in effect, that it is now too late for the little people to turn back the tide. In a spirit of kindness he is therefore urging them not to fight the noose which is already around their necks. He feels certain that those who do will only choke themselves to death.

"On the other hand, those who go along with the immense pressure which is beginning to be felt by all humanity will eventually find themselves in a man-made millennium of peace and prosperity."

Throughout the book, Dr. Quigley tosses assurances out to his readers that those "benevolent, well-meaning men who are secretly operating behind the scenes, can be trusted."

"They are the *HOPE* of the world," Skousen declares. "All who resist them represent *TRAGEDY*. Hence, the title for Quigley's book."

What is to be drawn by Bill Clinton's salute to Professor Quigley?

Was he giving a message to the bankers that, if elected, he'd carry out Quigley's—and the world's secret power structure's—economic "takeover" theories?

If not, why had the banking community rallied to him as soon as he was a candidate and sweetened his campaign kitty with a cascade of contributions?

Why, too, had the media—also run predominantly by the big-buck people—

hitched themselves to Clinton's caravan?

Did they see parallels between Quigley's writings that stress a *new world order* and Clinton's economic agenda, a process that began taking shape more than five weeks before he took the oath of office?

Clinton's Rx for the Economy

Clinton's "prescription for fixing the economy" was established at a two-day "economic summit" in downtown Little Rock's Robinson Center. The summit was attended by 326 invited participants, mostly high-powered business people, academics, and corporate economists from all over the United States.

Thirty-one of the crème de la crème participants sat with Clinton and his economic advisers in red leather chairs behind tables arranged in a horseshoe. The remaining 295 invited guests were on the outside perimeter. Cameras were trained on those who spoke so their images could be viewed by the elite group on three TV sets inside the oval. C-span broadcast the two-day session live, carrying it for its full 11 hours on opening day and a nine-hour stretch during the second round.

Clinton's avowed purpose in calling the summit was to get input on ways to jump-start the nation's economy. But the experts seemed divided on how to accomplish that. Not surprisingly, most proposals closely paralleled the line Clinton espoused during the campaign:

To compete globally, the United States needed a plan of new investment in education and infrastructure, combined with deficit reduction and cuts in health care costs.

Clinton made an impassioned pitch for health-care reform. He argued that the economy would not improve unless medical costs were brought under control.

"We are kidding each other," Clinton said as he fumbled with his glasses, "we are all just sitting here making this up, if we think we can fiddle around...and get control of this budget if we don't do something about health care.

"It is not a joke. It is going to bankrupt the country."

While the president-elect was attentive, appeared knowledgeable about even obscure topics, and gently cross-examined many speakers, he was not without wife Hillary's strong influence.

She sat in the audience section next to conference organizer Mickey Kantor and took copious notes. She frequently consulted a three-inch-thick briefing book prepared for Clinton's top staff. At the private receptions and meals, she joined prospective cabinet nominees to solicit the views of conference participants.

Most noticeable was Hillary's silence. Yet, although she didn't utter a word while the TV cameras were on her, her clout was clearly in evidence. She passed Kantor note upon note. Each time he scurried to the conference table and whispered in Clinton's ear.

The message was clear: Hillary Clinton was going to be a hands-on first lady, no less so than she was the iron lady behind the throne in Little Rock.

That Bill was not going to run the presidency without his wife's input became obvious during the final hour of the opening session when the need for lifetime education, a topic on which Hillary was presumed to have some expertise, was being discussed.

Clinton, who was leading that talk, finally decided to close the session. But not before turning to look at Hillary. Clinton's newly appointed chief of staff, Mack McLarty, spoke with Hillary, then approached Clinton.

"She doesn't want to speak," he was overheard to say.

Clinton gaveled the meeting to a close.

When Clinton opened the two-day conference, he refused to recognize the recent signs of a resurging economy. He stressed that urgency remained to implement a long-term economic strategy, as he'd advocated during the campaign.

"We must never let a blizzard of statistics blind us to the real people and the real lives behind them," Clinton declared. Too many skilled people were out of work and one hundred thousand people a month were losing their health insurance.

"Clintonomics," as his program for the country's economic revitalization came to be called, met a few resistors. Marion Sandler, president and chief executive officer of World Savings Bank in Oakland, California, was one.

Sandler complained that some of the people at the session were "nibbling around the edges" of the real problem: Social Security and Medicare entitlements were too high.

Vice President elect Al Gore also took criticism from Robert Allen, AT&T's chairman and chief executive officer. He opposed the veep's proposal for a government-funded technology network.

"I may disagree," Allen protested politely after Gore held forth for several minutes on the idea.

Most of the speakers advocated massive investments of government funds to rebuild the nation's infrastructure (an "investment" of up to $90 billion) to rehabilitate cities and at the same time create jobs.

"Without growth, there can be no deficit reduction," said Felix Rohatyn of Lazard-Freres. He was the former chairman of New York City's Municipal Assistance Corporation who almost single-handedly saved the Big Apple from bankruptcy.

Rohatyn noted that New York pulled itself out of the 1975 fiscal crisis by spending more than $4 billion a year on its infrastructure, a debt it amortized over a longer period.

No Decision on Budget Deficit

After the summit ended, Clinton conceded that there was a consensus on the need for early investment to rebuild the nation's inner cities. He was undecided on whether to plunge the nation further into debt by spending those huge amounts of cash up front.

"Am I going to deliberately increase the deficit in this budget year?" he asked. "The answer is, I have not made up my mind."

Of the 326 participants, the largest state contingent—50—was from New York, with 45 from corporations, institutions, public agencies, or other concerns centered in the city proper.

"That's no surprise because New York is the financial and big business capital of the country," said Dee Dee Myers, newly appointed as Clinton's "transition press secretary."

The assemblage included representatives from every conceivable arena of commerce and industry: investment banking and institutions, hospitals and unions, state and city agencies, cable television, real estate concerns, manufacturers and public research groups, charitable foundations, retail businesses, minority communications, and more.

For all their differences, the delegates left with a single view of the meeting and of the president-elect. Dennis Rovera, president of Local 1199 of the Hospital and Health Workers Union in New York, summed it up:

"It was unfolding in front of our eyes. We were watching President-elect Clinton taking over the leadership of the country."

With Bill Clinton's seeming devotion to the teachings of Dr. Carroll Quigley, we must ask how committed is he to the proposition advanced by his former mentor, that the stage for the coming conflict between traditional Americans and the powerful secret combination of the global establishment is set?

Dr. Quigley had no doubt about the final outcome—he equated hope and press with the establishment, tragedy and horse-and-buggy backwardness with traditional Americanism.

If one looks at Washington, New York, the United Nations Headquarters, or the capitals of any major nation in the world, massive evidence is to be found to support Dr. Quigley's bias.

His people are everywhere. They *are* running things.

Who are these people or groups?

Unmistakably, one is the Bilderberg Society—a classic example of Quigley's global establishment in action.

Don't forget that Bill Clinton was an honored, invited guest at the June 1991 Bilderberg Conference held in Baden-Baden. Clinton never told anyone what transpired at this secret conclave other than that he tried to drum up investments for Arkansas.

"Every once in a while, the network lets down its guard long enough for us to get a slight but alarming peek into the inward parts of the mammoth machine which Dr. Quigley believes is now too big to stop," Cleon Skousen offers in his analysis of Quigley's writings.

"When one contemplates the interlocking global ramifications which this power structure had developed, it is little wonder that Dr. Quigley feels so tremendously confident about its ultimate and irrevocable victory."

Skousen looks at the "conferences" called by this global establishment and concludes, "These are held each year as an international master planning conclave.

"They are secret and attendance is restricted to invited 'guests.' These turn out to be about 100 men from the top inner circle representing their four major dimensions of power: the international banking dynasties, their corporations involved in vast, international enterprises, the American tax-exempt foundations, and the *establishment representatives who have gained high offices in government, especially the United States government* [author's emphasis].

"These conferences always have the same chairman—his royal highness Prince Bernhard of the Netherlands who, with his family, owns a massive fortune in the Royal Dutch Shell Oil Corporation.

"Then close at hand will always be David Rockefeller [former chairman of the Chase Manhattan Bank] representing his family and especially Standard Oil of New Jersey which is one of the largest corporate structures in existence.

"It is interesting that [during the 1950s and 1960s] when political revolutions...occurred in various parts of the world, these two companies usually end up with all the oil and natural gas concessions. This had been largely true in Africa, the Middle East, South America, and the Middle East.

"These are also the companies whose installations seem to be virtually off limits to the bombers in both sides of any recent war. We mention this simply to demonstrate the fact that Dr. Quigley does seem to be correct in alleging that the political and economic forces of the earth are being woven into a gigantic monolith of total global power.

"As Raymond B. Fisdick, one of those who nearly always attends these Bilderberg Conferences, has said, the Bilderberg partners are spinning 'the infinity of threads (economically and politically) which bind peace together.'

"And of course the 'peace' they have in mind is compulsive cooperation, which a socialized world government could enforce upon humanity to the exclusion of any significant resistance—hence there would be peace as THEY envision it."

Strange Secrecy at Bilderberg

"Most significant about the Bilderberg get-togethers," Skousen writes, "is that no secretary takes notes, no reporters sit in on the debates, and when Prince Bernhard brings down the gavel to close the conference, no handouts, policy statements, or copies of their adopted resolutions are given to the press.

"The conferees depart to the four corners of the earth to carry out their adopted goals that the world is never given the slightest hint as to what has been decided.

"This is particularly frustrating to Congress which has tried several times to ferret out the activities of these Bilderberg Conferences. Even when top government officials such as Navy Secretary Paul Nitze were placed under oath and interrogated, it became virtually impossible to learn anything of significance."

In the light of this great amount of information about a secret order taking over the world, shouldn't Congress ask the new president, who has a personal experience with the Bilderberg Conference, to discuss what goes on behind the locked doors of their meeting?

Aren't the voters entitled to know whether Clinton was programmed to guide America's destiny in a manner ordained by the secret society?

Shouldn't the nation be told whether Clinton will lead America into "the new world order" in which bankers take over the globe and middle-class Americans, who think they will retain their property and constitutional rights, are dreamers?

Shouldn't Clinton tell his views about Dr. Quigley's blunt—if not scary—pronouncement that the international bankers who've set out to remake the world are perfectly confident they can use their money to eventually control the Commu-nist-Socialist conspiratorial groups—as they are now doing in Russia and its former satellites?

In fact, to further buttress the belief that Bilderbergers "programmed" Bill Clinton for the presidency, one has only to examine the history of John Ruskin, who took the first seat as professor of fine arts at Oxford in 1870 and advocated the emancipation of England's poverty-stricken masses by the wealthy aristocracy. Ruskin inspired Cecil Rhodes' dream to establish a strip of British territory across Africa from the Cape of Good Hope to Egypt and ultimately link them with a Cape-to-Cairo Railway.

In addition to establishing the scholarships in his name for deserving students in the English-speaking world and allied friendly nations, Rhodes joined forces with one of Ruskin's most devoted disciples, Alfred (later Lord) Milner. Together they estab-lished the Rhodes-Milner Round Table Groups which advocated a world federation along socialist lines.

Their credo was to put all property, industry, agriculture, communications, trans-portation, education, and political affairs in the hands of a small cadre of financially controlled political leaders. They would organize the world in a way that would com-pel everyone to do what was good for the new world society.

Skousen interprets the significance of this view professed by Clinton's "hero," Quigley:

"It may seem somewhat contradictory that the very people whom Marx identified as the epitome of 'Capitalism' should be conspiring with the followers of Marx to overthrow traditional Capitalism and replace it with Socialism. Studies further show that in many countries where the conspirators have taken over, the people would have risen up and overthrown them years ago if it had not been for the most sinister kind of depraved maneuvering behind the scenes by the agents of these wealthy master plan-ners."

Despite this sinister *modus operandi*, Quigley pleads that these London-Wall Street manipulators have the best of intentions and are really angels in disguise:

"The chief aims of this elaborate, semi-secret organization were largely com-mendable: to coordinate the international activities and outlooks of all the English-speaking world into one…to work to maintain the peace; to help backward, colonial, and underdeveloped areas to advance toward stability, law and order, and prosperity *along lines somewhat similar to those taught at Oxford and the* University of Lon-don."

The author emphasizes this quote from Quigley's book to highlight Bill Clinton's teacher's admission that the remaking of the world by the super-rich was to be along socialist lines taught at the two key British institutions that view global socialism as the hope of the world.

"Human beings are treated *en masse* as helpless puppets on an international chess board," writes Skousen. On that chess board, that the "giants of economic and politi-cal power subject them to wars, revolution, civil strife, supports the Quigley conten-tion that this is precisely what has been happening. The reason is rather simple.

"Power from any source tends to create an appetite for additional power. Power coming from wealth tends to create an appetite for political power and vice versa. It was almost inevitable that the super-rich would one day aspire to control not only their own wealth, but the wealth of the whole world. To achieve this, they were perfectly willing to feed the ambitions of the power-hungry political conspirators who were committed to the overthrow of all existing governments and the establishment of a central world-wide dictatorship along socialist lines."

The London-Wall Street Axis

Perhaps the most frightening section of the 1,348 pages of Quigley's tome is his discussion of "the secret society of the London-Wall Street axis" that he describes as "the master planners."

As summarized in *The Naked Capitalist*, Clinton's hero stresses that the secret society has "attempted to control the global conspiratorial groups by feeding them vast quantities of money for their revolutionary work and then financing their opposition if they seemed to be getting out of control. This policy has required the leaders of London and Wall Street to deliberately align themselves with dictatorial forces which have committed crimes against humanity in volume and severity unprecedented in history.

"It has required them to finance and support international intrigue by the most ruthless kind of political psychopaths [who practice] confiscation, subversion, indoctrination, manipulation, and outright deception as it suits their fancy and their concocted schemes for world domination."

Having been exposed to Rhodes scholar's teachings—and to Quigley's pronouncements—will Bill Clinton, now in the Oval Office, make the United States subservient to the Bilderberg/Rhodes-Milner Round Table?

Will he follow the principles of "the new world order" in which bankers take over the world?

Will middle-class Americans who think they're going to hold onto their property be allowed to keep it?

Or will banker-power snatch their hard-earned possessions from them, as President Clinton's teacher suggests?

Lastly, will their constitutional rights be taken from them, as Dr. Quigley asserts they will be?

Another one-time Rhodes scholar—and Clinton *hero*—Senator J. William Fulbright, advocated, "Let's scrap the Constitution!"

44

THE CO-PRESIDENTS PICK A CABINET

A Well-Earned Yuletide Respite

Bill and Hillary had every good reason to welcome the Christmas holidays after their extended struggle with interest-group politics and its influence on the tedious selection of the president's cabinet.

Clinton had kept one of the deadlines he set for his presidency: to have his new administration in place before Christmas. His goal was accomplished with great fanfare in the Arkansas capital.

When morning broke, attired in a jogging outfit and sneakers, the ebullient president-elect ate a hearty, country-style breakfast with his family. Overnight guests included Hillary's two brothers, her parents, and the governor's mother and stepfather. Half-brother Roger Clinton also flew in from Los Angeles to help arrange the musical selections for the various orchestral groups that would play at the pre-inaugural "ringing bells" celebrations, leading up to the grand finale the night of January 20 after the swearing-in ceremony.

Following breakfast, the mountain of presents piled around the Christmas tree were opened. Clinton's gifts to Hillary and Chelsea were birthstone rings. He received a set of golf clubs from Hillary. The rest of the day was spent in relative quiet until dinnertime. The gathering then was seated around the huge dining room table for a sumptuous spread similar to the Clintons' Thanksgiving dinner of Virginia ham; Tyson home-grown Arkansas turkey; heaping servings of potatoes, the sweet and Irish variety; topped with a choice of several pies.

After dinner, Clinton huddled with top aides in his office at the mansion and reflected on the tasks ahead, as he had the day before when he introduced the last of his 33 appointments. The final four filled the last of 16 critical cabinet posts.

"I'm not finished," Clinton said. "I've still got a lot of [lesser] appointments to make. At least we got the cabinet done."

Indeed he had. And to many keen political observers it seemed that his main objective was to keep himself out of trouble. One of Clinton's earliest media endorsers, the *New York Daily News*, observed in a lead editorial that his choices were made with an eye to keeping himself from the bad side of "women's groups, Congress, with anyone who might possibly object that a constituency was being neglected or a political base left uncovered. As a result," editorial page editor Ellis Cose noted, "the group is not distinguished by fresh faces, or by appointees known for bold, unconventional views, but neither is it a collection of mediocrities."

Overall, Clinton was given favorable grades for honoring his campaign pledges on most of his first appointments. One of the nation's foremost scholars, Stephen Hess, of the Brookings Institute, a former official in Nixon's White House, offered what was judged to be a consensus view about the cabinet:

"It shows that he keeps his promises, or tries to. He's given us a fair amount of diversity.

"He knows where the votes are. He knows the coalition he wants to keep together to get himself reelected and to build a new Democratic era."

Clinton was pleased with the results of the hectic selection process that brought more women and blacks into the inner circle than any previous chief executive had, and straddled the Democratic Party's ideological fault lines.

"They come from all across America," Clinton offered about his nominees. They included four African Americans, three women, and two Hispanic men to cabinet jobs, as well as two other women to positions that Clinton pledged to elevate to cabinet level.

"From the state capitals and the U.S. capital, from the city halls and the board rooms, and the classrooms," Clinton continued.

"They come from diverse backgrounds and we will all be better and stronger for that diversity. I can say with pride that I believe the cabinet and these other appointees represent the best in America."

The delicate juggling he performed to finesse competing interests was evident. He assembled a team that gave him confidence he could fulfill the full menu of promises made during the campaign.

He did it with what *Newsday* viewed as a "style that blends activism with caution and consensus-building along with an understanding of political symbolism and perception."

Let the Selections Begin

He had started the ball rolling on the morning of Thursday, December 10, after repeating his top campaign theme:

"Economic prosperity is the top priority of our administration."

Clinton was addressing a news conference in Little Rock's statehouse.

"These people are seasoned, skilled, incredibly able and ready to work for the American people," Clinton told the gathering. "I am going to work my heart out with these people to construct a strong, long-term plan for economic growth, for jobs, for incomes, and to reduce our national debt."

The first two appointments came as no surprise—only because the names had been bandied about in newspapers and over airwaves for days.

He named 71-year-old Democratic Senator Lloyd Bentsen of Texas as secretary of the treasury. A member of the upper house since 1970, Bentsen was the best known of the cabinet appointees because he had been Michael Dukakis's running mate in

1988. Chairman of the Senate Finance Committee, Bentsen was regarded highly for his skill at forging compromises.

Bentsen was seen as an odd choice for Clinton to have made. Yet it was assessed to be his way of currying favor not only with Congress, where the senator was highly respected, but also *with Wall Street*, which considered Bentsen their fair-haired boy *because of his big-business advocacy.*

Bentsen was viewed by some as the wrong choice for a teammate who'd be expected to conform to the president's promised aim of bringing about a "wrenching transformation of society" and changing "the very foundation of our civilization."

But the *New Republic* suggested Bentsen's selection was predicated by an ulterior motive:

"If, as treasury secretary, Bentsen insists on larding up the president's tax program with special-interest loopholes...Clinton can order him to stop or fire him. With Bentsen in the Senate, Clinton can only cajole or persuade."

(The author earlier, in chapter 43, focused on what is possibly Clinton's *real* reason for picking this Wall Street darling to be secretary of the treasury.)

Panetta's Picked after Bentsen

Clinton's second selection, a sub-cabinet post, but an all-important one in the executive agencies category, that of director of management and budget, went to 54-year-old Congressman Leon E. Panetta. The California Democrat had served in Congress 16 years and was chairman of the House Budget Committee. A distinguished student of the federal budget, Panetta was known as an advocate for fiscal responsibility.

Odd that Panetta was picked for that post after he had criticized Clinton's economic proposals during the campaign?

"Not at all," Clinton said with a broad smile when a reporter raised that issue. "I'm going to give him a chance to teach me some math."

The second of Clinton's picks for sub-cabinet posts was New Yorker Robert Rubin, 54, a co-chairman of the Wall Street banking investment firm Goldman, Sachs & Company. He was named chairman of the newly created National Economic Council. Rubin had credentials to spare, for he also was a member of a Securities and Exchange Commission committee and a director of the New York Stock Exchange.

New York investment banker Roger C. Altman, 46, was chosen as Bentsen's deputy, and Alice Rivlin, 61, the first director of the Congressional Budget Office, as Panetta's deputy.

Panetta and Rivlin came aboard with reputations as "deficit hawks" who advocated higher taxes, entitlement reforms, and other spending curbs to infuse new life in a sagging economy.

With his first-day appointments, Clinton sent some important signals. He was obviously determined to keep his promise to straighten out America's economy. To do so, he seemed to have turned a deaf ear to his campaign advisers' stresses for an economic stimulus that favored federal "investment"—or spending—over an immediate reduction of the nation's trillion-plus dollar budget deficit.

While Clinton promised an administration that "looks like America and will bring a healthy economic turnaround to the country," his first appointments were familiar power brokers—just the cast of characters to conform to the ideologies of Prince Bernhard's Bilderbergers and Professor Quigley.

His earliest critics faulted Clinton for having picked an all-Caucasian team with only one woman aboard.

Assessing those initial appointments, Brookings Institute's Stephen Hess noted, "They could have been made by almost any president, except Ronald Reagan, since the end of World War II."

Two devil's advocates commented on Clinton's initial appointments.

David Blitzer, chief economist at Standard & Poor's Corporation, warned, "There are lots of things that Clinton is talking about that overlap with Bush's proposed programs, but Clinton knows that he'd better get them passed if he doesn't want to be like Bush four years from now."

Newsday's acerbic columnist Robert Reno, who hadn't the foggiest notion that his sister Janet Reno would soon join the cabinet as attorney general, was most critical:

"And so now we know the people who will form the core of Bill Clinton's economic team: a 71-year-old conservative Texas Senator, a couple of Wall Street tycoons and a congressman who cut his teeth serving the Nixon administration and bounced only 12 checks at the House bank.

"They're all male, white and have not been convicted of pig stealing.

"Still, on paper, it's a curious first step in administration building for a candidate who drew his most lopsided majorities among liberals, blacks, the distressed inner cities, the poor, the feminists. I guess you can safely say of Lloyd Bentsen, Robert Rubin, Roger Altman and Leon Panetta, that *they won't spook the bond market, if that's what Clinton was elected not to do* [author's emphasis]. But neither did Nicholas Brady, the incumbent treasury secretary or Richard Darman, the present budget director. And they helped get us in the mess we're now in."

Reno concluded that Clinton "feels not the slightest need to appoint anywhere high on his economic team somebody to reassure the liberals, the disadvantaged, the unemployed, the minorities, the urban masses, the people who have nothing to invest and who voted for him by such huge margins."

Most of the above appears to be a sound analysis. However, Reno's view that "*the investment community didn't vote*" for Clinton is contradicted as previously cited in chapter 43.

Clinton had signaled America's investment community from the rostrum of the Democratic National Convention that, should he be elected president, he'd serve as *The Bankers' Economic Demolition Agent.*

He virtually said so in his acceptance speech.

"Tonight I want to talk with you about my hope for the future, my faith in the American people, and my vision of the kind of country we can build together.

"As a teenager, I heard John Kennedy's summons to citizenship. And then, as a student at Georgetown, I heard that call clarified by a professor...Carroll Quigley, who said America was the greatest country in the history of the world because our people have always believed in two great ideas: first, that tomorrow can be better than today, and second, that each of us has a personal, moral responsibility to make it so."

By his own words, Bill Clinton raised a question that he could truly champion the little people. How can he, after embracing the teachings of Quigley, an admitted intimate associate of the dynastic families of the super-rich?

More Cabinet Appointments

Friday, December 11, another overflow crowd came to the statehouse and heard the president-elect proclaim, "During the campaign I pledged that I would bring people to Washington who offered new perspectives and new creativity to the challenges we face."

Addressing an afternoon press conference, Clinton explained that his choice of cabinet officers announced earlier in the day differed vastly from the previous day's selections (which had a decidedly establishment tint) to fashion economic policy.

"My appointees today are people who promise to bring energy, dynamism, and fresh thinking to the task of carrying out our mandate for change," he declared.

He named two more members of his cabinet: University of Wisconsin Chancellor Donna Shalala as secretary of health and human services and Harvard lecturer Robert B. Reich as secretary of labor.

Two other non-cabinet posts were filled with the appointment of California economist Laura D'Andrea Tyson as chairperson of the Council of Economic Advisers, and Florida environmental official Carol Browner to head the Environmental Protection Agency.

After the press conference, Clinton returned to the governor's mansion to continue long hours of interviewing cabinet prospects who arrived from the airport in limousines with smoked-glass windows, which had been pressed into service from the governor's motor pool.

Reaction to the second round of appointments was generally positive. There were some expressions of concern, indeed apprehension about one or another of the selections.

The 51-year-old Donna Shalala, a former president of New York's Hunter College and an assistant secretary of the Department of Housing and Urban Development in the Carter administration, was given high marks for her "dynamic leadership capabilities." Those who knew her described her as a tough, but fair master administrator and creative thinker—qualities that could serve her well in administering the government's biggest bureaucracy.

Ms. Shalala made a point of thanking Hillary Clinton, a key ally whom she had succeeded as chairperson of the Children's Defense Fund. Hillary reportedly was the "chief driving force" in promoting Ms. Shalala's candidacy. It was her first chief act of influence as a cabinet maker—the co-presidency had begun!

While Ms. Shalala didn't come to her office with a health-policy background, in Wisconsin she had been responsible for a 488-bed teaching hospital funded by a $260-million annual budget.

Despite that lone connection to a health facility, advocates of health-care reform privately expressed concerns about Ms. Shalala's lack of hands-on expertise in the field. They noted that the bulk of her experience was in education, with a brief time out to tackle housing and urban affairs in her previous service in government.

She swiftly jumped to her own defense.

"I'm a quick study," she said as she prepared to leave academia again and wrestle with national health-care reform, one of Clinton's—and the first lady's—foremost priorities. The appointee let it be known that combating AIDS and reforming health care would be her two most pressing priorities at the Department of Health and Human Services.

From Shalala to Pal Bob Reich

At the age of 46 and with the lilliputian stature of 4 feet 11 inches, Robert Reich was given a much warmer welcome to his appointment as secretary of labor. While he hadn't been closely associated with labor issues, he was nevertheless hailed by two of the country's foremost labor leaders as someone who would make workers' issues central to economic decision-making in the new administration.

AFL-CIO president Lane Kirkland said, "The president-elect has chosen someone who recognizes the primary role of the labor of human beings in economic progress."

Victor Gottbaum, former militant leader of New York's Municipal Employees Union and the current director of Labor-Management Policy Studies at the City University of New York, said Reich's lack of close experience with labor issues were of no concern.

"He is sensitive to labor needs and his writings show it," Gottbaum said. Among Reich's public works was *The Work Of Nations*, which was riding the nation's bestseller list on the day of his appointment.

Economist Greg Tarpinian, executive director of the Labor Research Association, noted approvingly that Reich had argued for "the best economic policy for America" by calling for "a human capital strategy, which means upgrading the skills and educational level of the American working force."

Reich was introduced in chapter 4 as the Oxford-bound, seasick classmate of Bill Clinton aboard the liner United States. For the six days of the Atlantic crossing, Clinton had tended to the stricken Reich in his cabin. That kindness made Reich a lifelong friend of Clinton's. Long before he became a candidate for the presidency, Clinton leaned on Reich for advice and support in shaping some of Arkansas's most innovative economic ideas, including the need to promote competitiveness through worker retraining.

When Clinton launched his presidential campaign, Reich was Johnny-on-the-spot again, molding the economic platform for the candidate.

Clinton's choice to head the Environmental Protection Agency, Carol Browner, was also almost universally well received.

A 36-year-old lawyer and a Washington insider, Mrs. Browner became Senator Al Gore's chief legislative aide in 1988, after serving in a similar capacity for then-Senator Lawton Chiles (D-Florida).

Before Clinton picked her to head EPA, Mrs. Browner headed Florida's giant 1,700-employee Department of Environmental Regulation. She had been installed in that position in 1990 after her former boss, Chiles, was elected governor.

A Miami native, Mrs. Browner lent a touch of informality to the second day's ceremonies conducted by Clinton by bringing her 5-year-old son, Zachary, to stand beside her during the announcement.

She engaged in some light-hearted repartee with Reich after he joked about his 4-foot-11 stature by saying he always knew he was on Clinton's "short list" for secretary of labor.

When Mrs. Shalala, a mere three inches taller than Reich, offered to form a new caucus with him and Alice Rivlin, another shortie, named budget director the previous day, Mrs. Browner said she was afraid she couldn't join the group. As she stood laughing next to the 6-foot-2 Clinton, the new EPA head seemed almost as tall as the president-elect.

Mrs. Browner's appointment was a clear indication of Vice President Gore's unmistakable stamp on the administration's environmental policy making. Gore had not forgotten the key role the new EPA head had played in the complex negotiations that led to the sweeping 1990 amendments to the Federal Clean Air Act, which Gore had shepherded through the Senate.

"She's got a great relationship with the vice president, and that's going to be very important," said Fred Drupp, executive director of the Environmental Defense Fund.

Praise for Mrs. Browner was heard in a chorus of bipartisan voices after Republican Florida State Senator Malcolm Beard, chairman of the appropriations subcommittee that sets the budget for the FDER, recognized the appointee's fearless management of that agency.

Mrs. Browner settled a lawsuit that accused the state of inadequately protecting the Everglades from fertilizer pollution by negotiating a deal in which Florida agreed to spend $350 million over a 20-year period, building artificial marshes to trap and filter runoff from sugar cane farms.

"I would say she's a liberal, but she's also extremely capable," Senator Beard said. "She was one of a bunch of people Chiles brought back with him from Washington, and she did a better job than just about all of them."

In the authoritarian world of economics, 45-year-old Laura D'Andrea Tyson had a reputation as a lively consensus builder: one who was always ready to entertain opposing points of view, according to colleagues at the University of California at Berkeley.

Undoubtedly Clinton was aware of that favorable estimation when he picked her to ride herd over his Council of Economic Advisers. A baby-boomer, as was Robert Reich, Miss Tyson and her husband, Eric Tarloff, were, like Bill and Hillary, a high-powered couple.

Tarloff is a screenwriter best known for scripts that made "M*A*S*H" and "All In The Family" two of the most outstanding and successful long-running series in television history.

Raised in New Jersey, with a summa cum laude graduate degree from Smith College and a doctorate in economics from Massachusetts Institute of Technology, Miss Tyson began teaching at Berkeley in 1978. By 1993 she was a tenured professor of economics and business administration. She brought to the cabinet the prestige of having won 1982's Distinguished Teaching Award and the experience of having served as a member of the Washington-based Economic Policy Institute. She had also been on Governor Mario Cuomo's Commission on Trade and Competitiveness.

Miss Tyson came to her new job firmly believing that "national security depends on the United States' ability to compete in industries that demand high skills and involve new technologies."

Her immediate superior at Berkeley, John Quigly, chairman of the economics department, lauded her:

"One distinguishing characteristic of Laura is her high level of energy and enthusiasm and her openness to others."

His Picks Getting High Marks

President-elect Clinton's second round of appointments received all-around praise. Harriet Woods, president of the National Women's Political Caucus lauded the first two women chosen for the cabinet.

"We are continuing to press for diversity in terms of color, which is not yet there, and for breakthrough positions like attorney general, which have never been held before by women."

Bill Clinton must have been listening.

Some 20 hours after he had named the second round of cabinet and cabinet-level appointees, Clinton took some historic steps before returning to the statehouse to name another two key appointments.

During a morning jog, he confided in reporters who accompanied him on his run that he felt somewhat sentimental about moving to Washington after spending the last 12 years as governor of Arkansas.

Pausing outside Rally's Hamburgers, he resisted the temptation to order a burger and fries and instead talked about his "unemployed status."

Clinton had just resigned as governor and would not begin receiving paychecks again until after he was sworn in on January 20 as president of the United States.

The reins of government were turned over to Lieutenant Governor Jim Guy Tucker, but the Clintons had no concern about being evicted from the governor's mansion just yet. Tucker and the Arkansas Legislature had agreed to extend the Clintons' occupancy, rent-free, until they moved to the White House some five weeks hence.

After the jog, Clinton showered, ate breakfast, then left the mansion for the statehouse. If the Secret Service seemed to give the president-elect extra-careful protection that morning, it was because of an incident the day before at Little Rock's AmeriSuites Inn, where the agents assigned to protect Clinton were involved in a shoot-out.

Clinton was not nearby when the agents, who were staying at the inn, came under fire from four bandits fleeing the lobby after an abortive attempt to rob the hotel.

The agents, who had just been relieved by other secret servicemen in their assignment to guard Clinton, ducked the bullets fired at them, drew their guns, jumped into their cars, and pursued the suspects as they fled on foot.

As more shots were fired at them, the agents returned the fire and felled two of the fugitive bandits, who were taken to a hospital. A third robber was captured unharmed. The remaining bandit escaped but was arrested later by Little Rock police.

At the statehouse, Clinton went to the stage and put his arms around one of his dearest friends, 46-year-old Thomas F. (Mack) McLarty, the affable 5-foot-10, 175-pound Arkansas utility company VIP, and Clinton's boyhood friend in Hope.

McLarty was chairman and chief executive officer of Arkansas Louisiana Gas Company, the state's largest utility. He was touted by his new boss as a collegial loyalist who could be expected to act as "an honest broker rather than a forbidding doorkeeper" in the critical White House chief-of-staff role.

His arms still embracing his childhood chum, Clinton told reporters, "My friend Mack McLarty...will make sure everyone's voice is heard before I make an important decision. Action and results are what the American people demanded, and that's what we're going to give them."

In picking McLarty, Clinton shunned advice that he should take on an "inside-the-Beltway" strongman to head the White House staff. He decided instead on McLarty because of his "even temperament and unquestioned devotion."

A onetime Arkansas state legislator and former state Democratic chairman, McLarty didn't go to Washington without some controversy following him. He had been the target of criticism among some of Clinton's own people after his company, ARKLA, was hit with a $545 million lawsuit in October.

That action was brought by the Resolution Trust Corporation. It involved a failed Houston savings and loan that had once been owned by a company that unloaded it in a sale just before ARKLA acquired it in 1988.

Because of that lawsuit, McLarty agreed not to take part in discussions about thrifts that Clinton's transition team engaged in during the campaign.

But McLarty's selection as chief of staff raised another question that hadn't surfaced when Clinton was governor. While his appointees served on the Arkansas Public Service Commission, which regulates ARKLA, the relationship between the governor and the utility's boss hadn't raised serious conflict-of-interest questions in Arkansas. Although at times the Clinton-appointed PSC was the object of harsh criticism for granting rate raises to ARKLA that many felt were too generous.

McLarty let it be known that being chief of staff wouldn't be a problem for someone with a natural gas background such as his.

The question was raised because Clinton himself has advocated increased use of natural gas as a way of coping with the nation's energy needs.

"I wouldn't see that as a conflict for anyone in natural gas," said McLarty, who was said to have holdings of ARKLA bonds estimated to be worth several hundred thousand dollars—gains made while Clinton PSC appointees were granting frequent generous rate increases to the governor's old chum's utility.

Clinton made one other appointment on the third round held that Saturday of December 12. It was a reward for a job well done during the sometimes bumpy road to the White House.

Rewarding a Party Loyalist

Democratic National Chairman Ronald H. Brown, 51, had been reared among the Harlem elite. He was Clinton's choice as secretary of commerce, the first African American named to the president-elect's cabinet.

Brown's selection surprised some, who expected Clinton to reward a Republican who supported his campaign such as Apple Computer chief John Scully. Scully would have been an ideal choice, but he was put on the back burner when Brown lobbied for the job after hearing that he was being considered for a lower-profile position, such as ambassador to the United Nations.

Brown, a corporate lawyer with a reputation as a partisan politician and a "Mr. Fixit" for clients that included blue-chip corporations and foreign countries, blustered that he had higher expectations—such as secretary of state, attorney general, or U.S. trade representative.

When he learned that Clinton had others in mind for those cabinet posts, Brown settled for a shot at becoming secretary of commerce.

In several private meetings with Clinton, Brown "sold himself for the job in commerce" by insisting he was "ready for the challenge to revamp commerce and restore its effectiveness, which has been hampered because of its hodgepodge of responsibilities."

Clinton was impressed with Brown's sale pitch.

"I am an eternal optimist by nature," Brown told the man he helped through the thick and thin of scandal during the campaign and played perhaps the most significant role of anyone in bringing about Clinton's nomination. "I know institutions can change if leadership and commitment are brought to bear."

Brown's father had managed the Theresa Hotel in Harlem, a gathering place for black athletes and artists—and the hotel where Cuban dictator Fidel Castro mocked the United States by roasting chickens in his suite when he was attending United Nation's sessions.

In those days Ron Brown was acquiring an education at some of the country's finest schools. He was a scholarship student at the exclusive Hunter College Elementary School in New York and graduated in 1962 from Middlebury College in Vermont. Then it was back to his native New York to receive a law degree from St. John's University.

After he was admitted to the bar, he served with the Urban League for 11 years and became chief counsel to the Senate Judiciary Committee. Then, while associated with the Democrats' liberal wing, he joined Massachusetts Senator Edward M. Kennedy's Washington office as general counsel and staff director. Later he conducted Kennedy's successful 1980 presidential primary campaign in California, although Teddy was defeated by incumbent President Jimmy Carter, who won most of the other state primaries and renomination.

Brown eventually severed his ties with Kennedy and joined the powerhouse law firm of Patton, Boggs & Blow, as their first black partner, at a six-figure salary. With what is believed to be the capital's best-connected lobbying force, his clients ranged from Japanese companies to the former regime of infamous Haitian dictator Jean-Claude "Baby Doc" Duvalier.

While still a partner at Patton, Brown served as convention manager for the Rev. Jesse Jackson during his unsuccessful 1988 bid for the Democratic presidential nomination. He was tapped to head the Democratic National Committee in 1989.

Brown's appointment to commerce was met with some skepticism.

"Why Ron Brown?" asked Ken Goldstein, an economist at the Conference Board, a business research group. "Having said that four years ago people could have asked, 'Why Robert Mosbacher?'"

Mosbacher had made it as secretary of commerce in much the same way as Brown had, by showing loyalty to Vice President George Bush in his 1988 race against Michael Dukakis. Mosbacher was chief fund-raiser for the Republican candidate.

As a wheeler-dealer in affairs of blue-chip corporations and foreign countries as Brown had been, did Clinton again choose a capable ally, conceivably to work in tandem with him should he decide to follow the urgings of Prince Bernhard and Professor Quigley in shaping a *world secret power structure*?

In any event, Clinton's two cabinet selections on that Saturday, Mack McLarty and Ron Brown, were clearly studies in contrasts:

A Washington *outsider* for the most *inside* of jobs at the White House, chief of staff, and a quintessential Washington *insider* for the most *outside* of jobs, secretary of commerce.

After taking time out to hold his much-anticipated two-day conference designed to aim his "laser beam on the economy," Clinton summoned reporters to the statehouse on Thursday, December 17, and announced he had appointed two more minorities to his cabinet.

Former San Antonio Mayor Henry G. Cisneros was his pick for secretary of housing and urban development and Vietnam veteran Jesse Brown was to be secretary of veterans' affairs.

Clinton named Hershel Gober, 56, also a Vietnam veteran, who headed Arkansas's Department of Veterans' Affairs, to be Brown's deputy secretary. These concurrent appointments—like those of Roger Altman as deputy to Secretary of the Treasury-designate Lloyd Bentsen—suggested a pattern of pairing Clinton loyalists with outsiders.

Bill Pats Himself on His Back

"These individuals have one thing in common—they have lived the issues they will now address in the government," Clinton told the news conference after he introduced his latest appointees. "Devoting their lives to public service and to finding creative solutions to the problems of others, they represent the best in a new generation of policy leaders."

The 45-year-old Cisneros, who rose to national prominence in the 1980s as the first Hispanic mayor of a large American city (San Antonio), served four terms, from

1981 to 1989.

His promising political career was besmirched in 1988 after he acknowledged an extramarital affair with political fund-raiser Linda Medlar. Although he reconciled with his wife, Mary Alice, he felt there was no future for him in public office and turned to the private sector.

He became chairman of an investment firm bearing his name which today manages $525 million in pension funds and other assets. He also established Cisneros Communications, which furnishes his commentaries to news outlets, and Cisneros MetroAir Service, Inc., a small charter air service.

Cisneros holds a doctorate in public administration from George Washington University and taught college before entering politics and winning election to San Antonio's City Council.

As mayor, he fused government and private-sector efforts to improve downtown tourism and convention business, and pushed for construction of a down-river mall and a $180-million domed stadium.

Cisneros attempted to make a political comeback after serving Clinton as a senior campaign adviser and transition team member. He had asked recently elected Texas Governor Ann Richards to appoint him to the Senate seat Bentsen was vacating to take the treasury appointment, but she declined.

It was then that Clinton chose Cisneros to head HUD.

"I sense that we have limited time for America," Cisneros said after his appointment. "That we cannot talk about the economy and not talk about our cities and towns, our poor of all races, and that we must use the best of technology and the best of our talents to pull it all together to create quality of life...all across America."

The 48-year-old Jesse Brown came into his cabinet post with a record as an advocate for disabled veterans for more than a quarter century, since an ambush in a Vietnam rice paddy left him with a paralyzed right arm.

The former Marine first went to work for the Disabled American Veterans in 1967. When he was appointed to head the new administration's veterans' affairs business, he was executive director of the DAV's Washington office, from which he was lobbying Congress on behalf of disabled vets.

"He's a pretty gracious kind of guy, and he's obviously an insider in veterans' affairs," observed Paul Egan. "We're excited he isn't going to have a long learning curve here."

Brown said he looked eagerly toward his confirmation by Congress, so "I can attend to the need to reform veterans' health care [the largest public health care system in the nation].

"I will be a secretary *for* veterans' affairs, not a secretary *of* veterans' affairs."

One of his early tasks was to build ties with veterans' groups that had a low visibility during the Bush administration.

Jesse Brown joined his namesake Ron Brown as one of two African Americans named to Clinton's cabinet. That brought to three the number of minorities among the seven named to the cabinet to date.

Four days later, Clinton introduced two more cabinet appointees: Hazel O'Leary, a Minnesota energy executive, as secretary of energy, and former South Carolina Governor Richard Riley as secretary of education.

Although the 55-year-old Mrs. O'Leary was the second woman—and third African American—named to his cabinet, Clinton found himself lobbied by leaders of major women's organizations for still more nominations of women to high-level positions.

Standing firm against suggestions that his selections were being influenced in large part by activists' demands, Clinton flatly asserted that Mrs. O'Leary's name was not suggested by anyone calling for more minority or female appointments. He also criticized women's groups for "diminishing" his sub-cabinet selections of Carol Browner for Environmental Protection Agency administrator and Laura D'Andrea Tyson to chair the president's Council of Economic Advisers.

"They're playing quota games and math games," Clinton fumed. "And they would have been counting those positions against our administration, those bean counters who are doing that, if I had appointed white men to those positions."

His remarks quickly drew the ire of at least one women's group.

"We should never be denigrated by being called a bean counter," protested Eleanor Smeal, president of the Fund for the Feminist Majority. "If people call us a little overactive, better that than sitting on the sidelines."

Patricia Ireland, head of the National Organization of Women, put in, "He sounds a little defensive." This followed her dispatch of a letter just before the weekend that urged Clinton to appoint no fewer than six women to cabinet posts to break what she called the "glass ceiling" precedent of three female cabinet members in the Reagan and Bush administrations.

Clinton chose his words carefully:

"This counting-of-the-cabinet issue has been amazing to me, the way they do it. People who are doing this talking by and large, are talking about quotas. I don't believe in quotas."

But he said the appointment of more Hispanics was possible and promised that his cabinet would be the most "diverse" as well as giving real "clout" to its women and minority members.

He cited his latest minority cabinet designee as an example: Hazel O'Leary, the 55-year-old executive vice president of Northern States Power Company of Minneapolis and a former Energy Department official.

In her role with a major nuclear and coal-fired utility, she had crossed swords occasionally with environmentalists. But those who worked with her said she was likely to seek a reasonable balance.

"The industry is trying to make changes and be environmentally responsible, and it doesn't happen overnight," asserted Don Storm, chairman of the Minnesota Public Utilities Commission.

Mrs. O'Leary, who joined Northern States in 1989, participated in the field as an independent energy consultant with her husband, John, until 1987, when he died. O'Leary had been a former Carter administration energy official.

At the Minneapolis-based utility, which served 1.6 million customers in the upper

Midwest, Mrs. O'Leary was executive vice-president of corporate affairs. Under her aegis in 1991, Northern States launched a two-year, $35 million plan to promote electricity conservation.

After receiving a law degree from Rutgers University in 1966, Mrs. O'Leary became an Essex County prosecutor and an assistant attorney general for New Jersey. President Carter named her head of the Economic Regulatory Administration, which managed conservation programs and handled overcharge cases against oil companies.

The new secretary of energy came to her post with environmentalists' praises for her commitment to energy conservation. But they felt she still had to prove her concern for the environment.

"She's an intelligent woman," said George Crocker, a Minnesota environmental leader. "My concern is whether she really will wear a *different hat* now."

Environmentalist's Car's a Gas

She did come with a *different car*. To show her concern for the environment, Mrs. O'Leary brought to Washington a car that runs either on gasoline or cleaner-burning natural gas. And she vowed to do all in her power to convert as many of the government's motorized fleets to the fuel powering her car.

Her appointment was suggested by Chief of Staff Mack McLarty after Clinton learned some truths about his top candidate for the post, retiring Colorado U.S. Senator Timothy E. Wirth.

One unmistakable quality Clinton exhibited in making cabinet selections was that he could be ruthlessly unsentimental. He felt no compunction in making decisions that treaded on feelings of old friends or supporters.

Senator Wirth had been considered as a candidate for both energy and EPA as his reward for stumping incessantly for Clinton in the late months of the campaign and acting as one of his most loyal surrogate speakers.

Many of Clinton's aides and Wirth were confident that he would receive one of those top posts.

Later, Clinton discussed this possibility with Wirth, who then spent anxious days waiting for a decision. When none was forthcoming, he continued to assume the job would be his.

But members of the Senate, who regarded Wirth as abrasive and too outspoken, sent word to Clinton that they didn't want to see the retiring senator given any place in the administration.

This initially had little effect on Clinton. He was choosing his cabinet in a slow, deliberate process, a sharp contrast to the pell-mell way he assembled his campaign team. An aide—a close friend of many years—addressed that issue:

"I've seen a new side of Bill Clinton in picking the cabinet. During the campaign, we threw together a staff, hiring people sometimes on the fly. But on this [the cabinet selections] he's spent hour after hour."

In every instance, Clinton insisted that no matter who his transition team recommended for cabinet or other posts, his decision would at all times be the final one.

Yet he couldn't ignore McLarty's advice. He raised warning signals against

Wirth. Besides the animosity of his Senate colleagues, he also was tainted by allegations of ethical problems in his ties to cable television and savings and loan interests.

After Clinton closed the door to an appointment, he defended Wirth publicly by saying that he wanted to name him to an administration post but found the charges of the Coloradan's "political enemies" too much to ignore.

No such problems involved the appointment of fellow Southerner Richard Riley, the South Carolina governor who served as the transition team's personnel director with responsibility for sub-cabinet appointments.

Riley, nearly 60, earned a law degree from the University of South Carolina in 1959, three years after being discharged from the navy with a painful spinal inflammation.

After a brief spell in private law practice, Riley turned to politics and was elected to the state senate. Then, as a near-unknown, he was elected governor in 1978. Four years later, he was reelected with 70 percent of the vote.

In his second term Riley joined a half-dozen Southern governors, including Clinton, in trying to reshape their region with dramatic changes in public school class sizes, for better-paid teachers, higher graduation standards, and—most important, but difficult of all—extra taxes to pay for those improvements.

Education experts applauded Riley's school-reform plan as the broadest and most effective among those implemented in the region.

"In his own quiet way, he made South Carolina number one in education reform," praised Ernest Boyer, president of the Carnegie Foundation for the Advancement of Teaching.

Thus when President-elect Clinton tapped Riley as his secretary of education, he was commanded to lead a similarly broad-based campaign to energize American schools and colleges.

"The education secretary can be a spur for creativity and for change," Clinton proclaimed. "And he can do it in a way that makes education everywhere in America the exciting venture it should be."

Mark Musick, president of the Southern Regional Education Board, offered the last word on Riley:

"If you were casting a movie for a successful politician, you would not pick him. Once you meet him, you know you're dealing with an earnest man of reliability, a special kind of person."

Huddlin' and Decidin' Some More

Clinton spent the following day and most of the next, Sunday and Monday, December 20 and 21, with his circle of advisers who'd been with him in the sitting room of the governor's mansion nearly every day since Thanksgiving.

The objective now was to name a national security and foreign policy team. Some 20 hours were spent in deliberations on eight appointments.

A top aide described how the prospects were reviewed.

"It was a nonstop round of juggling, juggling, and more juggling...Bill had the last say in each selection. There were times when we put nominees' names on the table somewhat forcefully. And that was not the way to go. Bill always resisted being boxed into a decision. Whenever he sensed that we were bowing to outside pressures and he didn't feel comfortable with the candidate, he abruptly changed course and began considering someone else."

Still bristling and displaying calculated independence from interest groups, Clinton announced his national security and foreign policy team on December 22. His voice was a hoarse croak, not only from the late nights, but also from shouting at pressure groups. At one point, he became so incensed with them that National Public Radio broadcast his reaction:

"President-elect Bill Clinton is so rankled by pressure from women's groups to have more top level representation in his administration that he came right out and said, 'I will not be Mau-Maued by a bunch of crazy feminists."

Clinton created no surprises when he tapped the experienced Warren M. Christopher as secretary of state and Wisconsin's Democratic Congressman Les Aspin, the House expert on military affairs, as secretary of defense.

Sensing he would be criticized for choosing a team heavy with Carter administration veterans that included Madeleine Albright as ambassador to the United Nations and R. James Woolsey, Jr., as director of Central Intelligence, Clinton rasped, "I have picked a creative and an illustrious group of Americans...to call them retreads from the Carter administration would be totally unfair.

"That's the only Democratic administration we've had in twenty-five years, so I did not think I should appoint people who had not lived interesting, full, productive lives in which they had garnered the experience and judgment necessary to fill these positions."

Clinton named his remaining choices: Samuel Berger as deputy national security adviser, Clifton Wharton as deputy secretary of state, and retired Admiral William Crowe, Jr., to head the Foreign Intelligence Advisory Board.

The team Clinton chose was widely hailed as "experienced, centrist, and basically cautious" in national security affairs. It was seen as a viable force in emphasizing *continuity* in foreign policy rather than *change*.

However, *Newsday* editorialized, "That is a wise course for him to have chosen, but it does not raise the issue of where a vision of a *new world order* [author's emphasis] will come from and whether his team will be able to do any more than react— even if sagely—to rapidly changing foreign developments."

Newsday, which had supported General Colin Powell, chairman of the Joint Chiefs of Staff, for secretary of state, conceded "there can be no criticizing the choice of Christopher." The newspaper cited the 67-year-old Los Angeles lawyer's role as Carter's deputy secretary of state and the patience and good judgment he exhibited as a negotiator "that led to the safe return of the 52 American hostages held in Iran."

Christopher, known among his friends as "Mr. Neat" and "Mr. Cool," is slight, gray-haired, and almost always somber-faced. He was born in Scranton, North Dakota. After graduation from Stanford Law School, he went to Washington as law clerk for Supreme Court Justice William O. Douglas, one of the most liberal justices ever to sit on the high court. Christopher later became a top assistant to another liberal, Attorney General Ramsey Clark.

Since leaving government at the end of the Carter administration, Christopher ran O'Melveny & Myers in Los Angeles, one of the nation's largest and most prestigious law firms. He also headed commissions that investigated the Rodney King beating in Los Angeles and the city's police department.

A staff member of the Senate Foreign Relations Committee said that Christopher is "no James Baker [who served in the Bush administration]. Christopher does not have his presence. Clinton picked someone who will not outshine the president. But he got a secretary in which he has complete trust and who has experience with issues that are not familiar to Clinton."

High grades were also given to the 54-year-old Congressman Aspin. A Yale graduate, Aspin, like Clinton, had studied at Oxford. He came to Washington in 1971 as a liberal and an opponent of the Vietnam War.

For seven years before he was named to Clinton's cabinet, Aspin had been the shadow secretary of defense. He helped to establish Pentagon policy to the delight of the military brass, but to the dismay of some fellow Democrats.

Described by a national security consultant as "one of the few people who understands the whole military budget and appropriations process," Aspin was seen playing a central role in Clinton's promise to tailor the American military for new missions: peacekeeping, humanitarian operations, and possibly for limited warfare in a world no longer threatened by a Cold War or nuclear holocaust. But he blundered during the Somalia food relief efforts by refusing to send tanks to protect America's GI's, causing unnecessary deaths during a Somali uprising.

Aspin would be the first Clinton cabinet member to throw in the towel, on December 15, 1993, a month short of his first year in the office.

A Nixon Loyalist Wins Favor

Clinton's choice for national security adviser was Anthony Lake, who developed a rich background as a foreign service officer in Vietnam before joining President Nixon's National Security Adviser Henry Kissinger's staff.

Lake was viewed by many as having a more personal relationship with his new boss than other appointees.

For when Anthony Lake was a youngish 33 back in 1972, he was as active as anyone could have been for Senator George McGovern's candidacy for president. Thus it wasn't surprising that the Clintons' relationship with Lake went back to that time, when Bill and Hillary took time off from Yale Law to run McGovern's campaign in Texas. Here they met Lake, who was on the senator's national campaign committee.

Lake got his initial experience in government in 1962 when he served in John Kennedy's State Department. He became a foreign service officer in Vietnam before joining Kissinger's staff after briefly serving as national security adviser to President Nixon. In 1970, Lake quit his post in protest of the invasion of Cambodia.

In 1976, Lake was President Carter's international affairs adviser during the transition from the Ford administration. The following year he was named director of policy planning at the State Department. After Carter's defeat, Lake joined the faculty of Amhurst College as a professor of international relations before going into another professorship at Mount Holyoke College.

When Clinton summoned him to the national security adviser's post, Lake brought not only hands-on government experience, but also a university professor's perspective.

He is of a mind that on balance, political appointees have too much sway over professionals. At least he found that so during the Carter administration when he witnessed the 1979 fall of Nicaragua's Anastasio Samoza. The ouster was forced by the United States and led to the mushrooming problems and scandals in the Reagan and Bush administrations.

In his other security and foreign selections, Clinton again picked veterans of foreign affairs.

R. James Woolsey, Jr., never served in the intelligence bureaucracy but was a National Security Council aide to Nixon. He gained further experience by holding positions in arms control and Defense Department operations for several administrations.

The 51-year-old Woolsey had been a captain in the army and served as undersecretary of the navy in the Carter administration. In the private sector, he sat on the boards of several defense companies, including Martin Marietta Corporation.

That prompted questions by at least one critic, a former Pentagon analyst, who pointed out that Woolsey, as the navy's number two official, was committed to reforming Pentagon spending practices. Nevertheless, he was "one-hundred percent behind the contractors and always maximized the procurement budget."

This alumnus of Stanford University, who, like Clinton, is a Rhodes scholar and a Yale Law School graduate, took over a multi-tiered intelligence organization that had been forced to swallow a significantly reduced budget due to new intelligence priorities created by the Soviet Union's disintegration.

Woolsey was praised by two predecessors, Richard Helms, Nixon's CIA director ("He's an excellent choice") and William Colby, Helms' successor, who said the new spy chief was "a very well contained, solid...very sophisticated fellow" about intelligence matters.

In tapping Madeleine Albright for the ambassador's seat in the United Nations, Clinton was giving a loyal Democrat her reward for working diligently.

The 53-year-old Georgetown University professor of international affairs and president of a Democratic-oriented think tank, the Center for National Policy, is the daughter of a Czech diplomat. She was to be the only member of the Clinton administration born outside the country.

Like a predecessor, Jean Kirkpatrick, Mrs. Albright, a divorcée and mother of three daughters, came to her UN seat after teaching at the president's alma mater. She also shared a strong interest in women's issue.

Unlike Mrs. Kirkpatrick, a Democrat who complained that the party strayed too far left and became a dropout, Mrs. Albright has been steadfastly loyal to the party. She participated in the national campaign of such Democrats as former Senator Edmund Muskie and former Governor Michael Dukakis's unsuccessful efforts for the presidency, and in ex-Congresswoman Geraldine Ferraro's vice presidential race.

Despite these defeats, Mrs. Albright never complained.

"I have had this fantastic life," she told the *Washington Post*. "For someone like me, who came to this country when I was eleven years old, to end up working in the White House and having all these amazing opportunities—I mean, I am kind of this American story. This is an amazing country."

Her prior experience with the White House was during a brief tenure with the National Security Council in the last days of the Carter administration.

Clinton named three others to round out his foreign policy and national security team.

Sam Berger, a lawyer who headed the transition staff's search for a national security chief, was awarded the deputy's role under the man he helped pick, Anthony Lake.

Two other transition aides, Leon Furth and Nancy Soderberg, were appointed to lesser National Security Council jobs.

To serve as Warren Christopher's deputy, Clinton tapped Clifton Wharton, Jr., an African American and chairman of the Manhattan-based $112 billion Teachers Insurance and Annuity Association and the College Retirement Equities Fund. Some observers said Wharton's credentials were more impressive than the secretary of state he was to serve. Wharton was also chairman of the Rockefeller Foundation, president of Michigan State University, and chancellor of the 380,000-student State University of New York system.

Clinton made a point of recognizing Wharton's achievements and skills.

"He is truly legendary," the president-elect said about the appointee who would run the State Department's day-to-day operations.

There may have been something of a "thank you" in Clinton's appointment of retired Admiral William Crowe, Jr., to head the Foreign Intelligence Advisory Board.

Chairman of the Joint Chiefs of Staff in the Reagan and Bush regimes, Crowe undoubtedly merited the appointment not only because of his vast military experience, but also for forcefully defending Clinton in the campaign against attacks that he was a draft dodger during the Vietnam War.

****

'Twas the day before Christmas and all through the Old Statehouse, reporters had gathered there, in hopes that Bill Clinton had finished choosing his cabinet—with great care.

Indeed he had. When the president-elect went to the lectern and announced his choice for attorney general, 40-year-old Connecticut corporate lawyer Zoe Baird, clues to Clinton's thinking were never more apparent. He had run a mine field to reach his decision. Most of the hindrances were on his staff, riding Clinton's back to appoint women and minorities to the remaining domestic posts.

A Fine Ethnic and Minority Mix

It was generally agreed that Clinton had fulfilled his commitment of diversity in his final choices of four blacks, three women, and two Hispanic men to cabinet jobs, as well as two other women to high posts that the president pledged to soon elevate to cabinet level.

The delicate juggling of competing interests was evident in the appointees he introduced the afternoon of December 24.

His secretary of agriculture nominee was former Congressman Mike Espy of Mississippi, a 39-year-old African American.

Former Arizona Governor Bruce Babbitt, 54, picked to be secretary of the interior, addressed the environmental activists who championed a man of his caliber and mindset for ecology reforms.

Another minority goal was met when Clinton tapped former Denver Mayor Federico F. Peña, 45, an American born of Mexican parents, to be secretary of transportation.

His choice for surgeon general pleased activists calling for more minority representation in the White House hierarchy. Clinton reached into his own Arkansas to fill the position. Not to the discredited Dr. Fahmi Malak, the former chief medical examiner of the state. The choice was Malak's boss, Dr. M. Joycelyn Elders, the Arkansas Health Director, a 56-year-old African American, whose contributions to the Clinton Arkansas administration have been described at length in earlier chapters.

Rounding out the last-day selections were Mickey Kantor, 52, a Los Angeles lawyer and the Clinton campaign's chairman, to be United States trade representative; and John H. Gibbons as executive director of the Office of Technology, a role that called upon him to be the president's science adviser.

The *New York Times* concluded that Clinton's nominees "rounded out a selection of advisers who generally prefer a larger role for government than the country has seen under Republican rule, but who are also less enamored of federal spending programs than Democrats have favored in the past."

Clinton's resistance to outside pressures, and even to the urgings of his own advisers, was never more in evidence than in his choice of attorney general.

The process by which Clinton chose Brooklyn-born Zoe (pronounced ZOH-ee) Baird, a graduate of the University of California at Berkeley and its law school, was one of the most circuitous he had taken.

Initially, Clinton turned to Federal Appeals Court Judge Patricia Wald. She had several qualities he wanted: government experience, a strong reputation within the national legal community, and a commitment to public-interest legal work.

Mrs. Wald turned down the offer because her husband was beset with serious health problems. Other candidates were interviewed. As each potential appointee fell out of contention, Clinton seemed to move toward Washington attorney Brooksley Born, a favored candidate of women's groups.

As Mrs. Born seemed to be the likely choice, FBI agents checking the backgrounds of potential nominees, turned their investigative spotlight on her. But before they could illuminate her background, she was gone. Clinton and some advisers had reservations about Mrs. Born, principally her lack of government service and experience in managing large organizations.

Clinton turned to Zoe Baird, whom he knew, along with her husband, Yale Law School constitutional scholar Paul M. Gerwitz. Miss Baird had cut her teeth as a newly admitted member of the bar in the Office of Legal Counsel in the Carter Justice Department.

"I've never forgotten how proud I felt each day as I went to work, knowing that my only mission was to do my best for my country," said Miss Baird. She was prepared to reshape and redirect Justice away from what it had become over a dozen years of Republican administrations: headquarters for the aggressive promotion of conservative legal and social agendas.

"She is tough, tenacious, and gifted," Clinton said when announcing her appointment. "She's a very, very able manager and has proven that she can resolve difficult cases and bring order to complex organizations."

The president-elect came down hard on the Bush Justice Department. He cited infighting and lifted an eyebrow at its reputation as one of the government's "fat cat" agencies. The department employees 80,000 people and its annual budget approaches $11 billion. When Ronald Reagan took office in 1981 and appointed William French Smith attorney general, justice had half that many employees and about a fifth the budget.

In what has been described as "small-scale rehearsal for the job she was to face," Miss Baird had managed a major restructuring of the Aetna Life and Casualty Company shortly after she arrived at the insurer's corporate headquarters in Hartford. When she departed the company to take up her new duties in government, she left behind 120 lawyers with a budget of $90 million a year for legal fees.

Ronald E. Compton, Aetna's chairman and chief executive officer, predicted Miss Baird would encounter no problems as the first woman attorney general.

"She's used to being in a very high-pressured, high-velocity environment," he observed. "She was the first woman vice president of Aetna, and she has handled that extremely well. It would be very, very hard to intimidate this woman. Let's put it this way: I haven't seen it happen yet."

In 1981, Miss Baird and another Carter administration lawyer, Terrence Adamson, were asked to give pointers on how to run the Justice Department to President Reagan's newly appointed Attorney General Smith.

Pulling no punches, Miss Baird and Adamson advised that "personal integrity and well-meaning intentions are not enough, noting that Smith's principal qualification for the job "can fairly be said to be as the president's friend and personal lawyer." Their last word to Smith was to remember that his "ultimate client must be the people of the U.S."

Miss Baird wouldn't have left Washington in the first place had her husband, one of the nation's leading constitutional scholars, not been named to his distinguished chair as Potter M. Stewart professor of law at Yale. The Gerwitzes, parents of a three-year-old son, were seen likely reversing the roles of tailoring career to fit the spouse's. In 1990, Miss Baird pulled up stakes in Washington and ended her commuter marriage. However, there was talk now that she was returning to the nation's capital and that her husband might follow her there.

Moreover, the speculation in the early days of the new administration was that Gerwitz might also become a Clinton appointee—to the U.S. Supreme Court.

****

Bill Clinton met the Christmas deadline. He picked his cabinet and the other top people in his administration. He had jockeyed hard to please many groups, although he criticized them for playing a "quota game." He did appoint women and minorities to several important positions, who are now to be judged not by what they represent in ethnicity and race, but by what they do.

That can be said of President Bill Clinton, too. He surrounded himself with Washington insiders in his attempt to meet his "diversity" goals and come up with a low-wattage cabinet. It seemed he wanted to do the "heavy lifting." To that end he stepped into the White House with sleeves rolled up and, with a Democratic Congress, he came prepared to turn Washington upside down.

Having campaigned on a platform of change, not just change from the Reagan-Bush formula, but even from the Democratic practices of the past, Clinton claimed that government was handcuffed in its ability to effect good, that individual responsibility had to be a priority over entitlement.

Above all, he maintained that he was realistic and unwilling to settle for easy answers.

Only time would tell whether or not he'd usher in the dramatic changes he maintained were essential to bring about the *new world order* he envisioned for America.

****

His presidency was in the 523rd day of its 1,460-day term—less than a year and a half old—when the words Bill Clinton had once spoken about his boyhood pal, Mack McLarty, no longer applied. McLarty obviously had not lived up to the promise the president foresaw for his chum, that he'd "make sure everyone's voice is heard before I make an important decision."

For on that Monday, June 27, 1994, President Clinton, his arms no longer embracing McLarty as they had the day he announced the appointment, McLarty was shorn of his duties as chief of staff and shunted off to be *counselor to the president*. The *counselor's* title was vacated by David Gergen, the communications expert from the Nixon and Reagan White Houses, who had come aboard only months ago to "improve President Clinton's deteriorating image."

Gergen, who did not appear to have met much success in that endeavor, remained a *senior White House adviser*. He was then dispatched to the State Department to try his hand in reclamation work on Secretary Warren Christopher, whose handling of U.S. foreign policy had reached "a deplorable state" and left him with an image so tarnished that his own future seemed to be in dire straits.

But Gergen wasn't long for that job either. Early in 1994, he privately expressed disgust at "all these know-nothing Razorbacks" in the administration, and let it be known he would abandon ship and head for smoother sailing by accepting a significant appointment on the Duke University campus later in the year.

McCarty's place was taken by budget director Leon Panetta, the former congressman from California and reputedly a tough-minded administrator who "can be nice to your face, but be tough and merciless when he wants to be." His deputy, Alice Rivlin, was to be his replacement—but needed congressional approval first.

It took almost a year and a half for Clinton to follow the advice offered him when picking his cabinet—that he had to have an "inside-the-Beltway" strongman to head the White House staff. As that White House staff—mostly home-grown Arkansans—looked on glumly during the mid-afternoon televised Oval Office shocker (no advance warning was given to anyone but the principals about what was coming), Clinton finally saw the errors of his ways:

"No one in Washington has a better understanding of both ends of Pennsylvania Avenue than Leon Panetta, and no one has earned greater respect at both ends."

If the gloom on the faces of the staffers seemed to deepen before the ceremony was over, that was because Panetta was given the floor to let it be known, "I'll be making further staff changes in consultation with the president."

Dee Dee Myers and George Stephanopoulos appeared to be the most depressed after that proclamation.

45

LET THE INAUGURAL BAWLS BEGIN

Everyone's Ticketed—but Why?

President-elect Bill Clinton and First Lady Hillary Rodham Clinton ["That's the way I want to be addressed from here on," she again emphatically declared] ordained three days of inauguration events before the oath of office was administered on the fourth day.

People who planned on attending the presidential inauguration, along with the various dinners, balls, and other festivities, had to have tickets to attend.

Those not among the 250,000 of the Clintons' friends and supporters had as much chance of getting their hands on those tickets as they had of picking up front-row orchestra tickets for a performance of *Les Miserables* on Broadway, or 50-yard-line seats for the Super Bowl in Miami.

Printed "invitations" totaled a mere 65,000, or a fourth the number of admissions needed for all who hoped to attend one of the 10 inaugural balls. The main inaugural ball entrance fee commanded $125 a pop.

Basically those not already an F.O.B. (Friend of Bill)—or well connected—had to forget it. Many of the parents, wives, and families of those serving on the inaugural staff couldn't be accommodated. Many had obtained airline tickets and booked inflated-priced hotel accommodations in Washington they couldn't use.

For those willing to settle just to be at the same overcrowded events as the first family during the five-day celebration (it carried over to the day after the inauguration with tours through the White House as the Clintons' guests), eight free public events were offered, from January 17 to 21.

Those pre-inaugural festivities included an extensive menu of events:

Sunday, January 17 - "America's Reunion on the Mall," a 10 a.m. outdoor festival featuring regional foods, music, and crafts highlighting America's cultural diversity, and at 3 p.m. "A Call for Reunion," concert and fireworks at the Lincoln Memorial. Uncounted thousands attended.

Monday, January 18 - "The American Gala," a festive entertainment given at the Capital Centre in suburban Largo, Maryland, at 7:30 p.m. Free tickets were required because of limited seating, and only a handful of the thousands who wanted to attend were able to do so.

Tuesday, January 19 - "Salute to Children" at the John F. Kennedy Center, from 1:30 p.m. to 2:30 p.m. While admission tickets were free, limited facilities excluded most who wanted to be there. At night, the same story: free tickets, but comparatively few who wished to be there were able to get in for the "Presidential Gala" at the Capital Centre.

Included among the 10 inaugural balls around the city were two very special ones.

Arkansans, who suffered through attacks on their "last-place" state during the campaign, had their revenge at one of the balls exclusively open to them.

Tennesseeans likewise had their official state ball, with B. B. King and Dolly Parton among the most honored guests. The president played his sax at this do. Vice President elect Gore and wife Tipper were in their element at their home state gala, but the second lady elect did not play her drums.

Hillary's Gowning Glory

At each of the 10 inaugural balls, Bill Clinton looked most presidential in his tailor-crafted tuxedo and bow tie, while Hillary looked ravishing in her fitted, floor-length, violet lace ball gown designed by the young and relatively unknown New York designer, Sarah Phillips.

The dress was given the ultimate salute by Patrick McCarthy, publisher of the international style bible, *Women's Wear Daily*.

"I think the dress is really beautiful," he cheered. "It's flamboyant, and looks as though [it suits] her style very nicely."

More encomiums for the dress from Liz Tilberis, editor of glossy *Harper's Bazaar*:

"It's terribly pretty and really glamorous, and it [photographed] very well."

Ms. Tilberis added that it was "a fantastic time for Sarah Phillips. She just started her own company and this...really [gives] her the limelight."

Sarah Phillips's business boomed even before Hillary slipped into the dress. The *New York Daily News'* Orla Healy broke the story about the gown and its designer on Friday, January 15, and turned her into the fashion world's most envied premier seamstress.

But not for very long. For, the story goes, Ms. Phillips neglected some of her clients to cater most attentively to the first lady's wardrobe needs—so much so that some of her steady customers were compelled to turn elsewhere.

Still, Sarah Phillips realized her 15 minutes of fame. Her needle and thread turned Hillary Rodham Clinton into the belle of the inaugural ball.

Next day, it was on to the sober business of installing America's 42nd president.

- 46 -

A FLAWED PRESIDENCY STARTS

Bill's Inaugural Address Plagiarizes the Preacher

William Jefferson Blythe Clinton IV became the 42nd president of the United States on Wednesday, January 20, 1993. Under a cloudless, cerulean sky, he took the oath of office from Chief Justice William H. Rehnquist.

George Herbert Walker Bush, who only months before seemed certain to be reelected to his second term, watched somber-faced from his seat on the flag-draped platform erected on the western facade of the Capitol steps.

A sea of 250,000 people stretched out from the nearest vantage point, below the gathering of VIPs, for a mile over the huge mall to the marble and granite monuments of Presidents Washington, Jefferson, and Lincoln.

Among the many millions of listeners and viewers tuned into their radio and television stations, one lonely but enthralled watcher sat before the tube in her Houston apartment and wiped tears of joy from her eyes.

"I just kept thinking back to how differently Bill's path took from mine," Dianne Dwire Welch reflected. "This was a far cry from those early days we shared in Hot Springs, however brief they were.

"But there's no getting away from it. Bill is my brother and he had just been sworn in as president of the United States. I would have loved to have been in Washington for his inauguration, but I hadn't been invited.

"It hurts to be left out—what sister wouldn't want to be there in the flesh when her brother's sworn into the highest office in the land? But I'm not surprised that I didn't get an invitation. Yet I remain with fond hopes that a day will come that I'll be able to kiss my brother's cheek and wish him luck in the world's most important job."

In a 14-minute address, Clinton told Americans that they would be asked to assume greater responsibility for their country's future and "must do what America does best: offer opportunity to all and demand more responsibility from all." The oratory sounded like an echo of John F. Kennedy's inaugural address.

That is, the vast majority of journalists reached that conclusion. But one among them, syndicated columnist Jimmy Breslin, did not. He assessed Clinton's speech as flawed—an address torn from the handbook of someone like Delaware Democratic Senator Joe Biden, one of the political world's most notorious plagiarists.

In critiquing Clinton's address, Breslin broke from custom by introducing two news photos in his column.

One shot shows the Rev. Gardner Taylor, pastor emeritus of the Concord Baptist Church in Brooklyn, preaching on the morning of inauguration day at an interfaith service in Washington's Metropolitan AME Church.

The other picture shows Clinton seated in the first row of the church, flanked by Hillary on his right, and Al and Tipper Gore on his left. Clinton is writing on note paper with a pen held in his left hand.

Explaining the first picture that shows Pastor Taylor at the pulpit, Breslin wrote, "He is saying at this very moment: 'On this fateful day when we enter a springtime we believe of a new beginning, there may be spring rains and storms, but it's spring-time in America. As we enter this new era.'"

Then the columnist referred to the second photo:

"Here, Clinton is brazenly copying Gardner Taylor's words. Clinton has just whispered to Hillary and both smiled, and he turned to Al Gore and both nodded emphatically."

After putting the words "This is ours" in Clinton's mouth, Breslin noted that "Clinton then went into his inside jacket pocket and came out with his pen."

Breslin speculated that Clinton already "had a phrase in the speech that came from the late Rev. Timothy Healy." He was referring to the Jesuit priest who ran the New York Public Library for many years. Just before he died, Healy had faxed the phrase to Clinton for his inaugural address, "Force the spring."

"Somebody had announced that he had finished his inaugural address at four in the morning. Which appears incorrect," Breslin went on. "Bill Clinton is finishing that speech right here in these pictures that I am smart enough to show you when nobody else does. They are taken from a tape of the sermon personally rushed to me by Brian Lamb of C-Span.

"His press people said that Clinton made 'small editing changes' after hearing the sermon. The pictures suggest that he might have put what you call 'a new top' on his address."

Echoes of JFK in Inaugural Address? No Way!

Breslin picked up on that address and quoted directly from the inaugural speech the president gave a few hours later:

"My fellow citizens, today we celebrate the mystery of American renewal...this ceremony is held in the depth of winter, but by the words we speak and the faces we show the world, we force the spring. A spring reborn in the world's oldest democracy."

"In his long religious life," Breslin wrote, "Reverend Taylor has counseled sinners on avarice and adultery, on lying and lousiness, on slander...greed [and] stealing. But never had he been told of the horrible pain that shoots through the body at the moment your best thoughts are stolen during hours of bright daylight."

Breslin's column was splashed in newspapers across the country under the head-line **The Preacher and the Plagiarist**.

The scandalous road to the White House had been traveled. A flawed presidency had started.

MYSTERY MURDERS ON THE WHITEWATER

Deaths: The Key to Riches for the Clinton-McDougal Axis

Bill and Hillary Clinton and Jim and Susan McDougal rubbed their hands in glee while their Whitewater Development Corporation flourished during its 12-year heyday between 1978 and 1990, before they pulled up stakes singing a lachrymose, but patently phony tune about their *losses.*

The Clintons and McDougals profited enormously in the dozen years of their partnership. They did it by hook and by crook—mostly by crook—and they managed to hide their huge profits in a manner that would have made Al Capone ashamed to call himself a gangster.

These powerhouse schemers raked in hundreds of thousands of dollars in what now appears to have been under-the-table profits.

The evidence examined by the author leaves no doubt that the Clintons and McDougals funneled their ill-gotten funds into secret stashes, in a manner so clever that it totally eluded detection by the Internal Revenue Service!

The world would not have known about their tactics had it not been for Jim McDougal's inadvertent release of Whitewater's records in late April 1994. He was hoping to make another fast buck by selling several thousand documents, at 50 cents a page, on the firm's land dealings.

That blew the lid off Whitewater's underhanded operations and imprudently set up not only McDougal as a target for criminal investigation, but his ex-wife and the Clintons as well.

The case of Clyde Soapes, Jr., a Texas grain elevator operator, is a classic example of the Whitewater Development Corporation's style of rip-off—a practice begun just as Bill Clinton, in the earliest days of his gubernatorial reign, was calling himself a *consumer advocate* while at the same time beginning to turn the screws on Whitewater's clientele.

It is an axiom of real estate practice in the *civilized* states of America for a mortgagee to receive a deed to the property on which the mortgage agreement is drawn.

Not in Arkansas. It is no *Land of Opportunity* for a purchaser when it comes to granting a developer the wherewithal—loophole is a far better word for it—to deal with purchasers of limited financial means, such as Soapes evidently was.

In 1984, Soapes closed on his commitment to buy a plot of Ozark Mountains vacation land along the White River, where he planned to put up a fishing cottage one day.

He signed a contract that obligated him to pay $14,000 for the land.

Soapes put up $3,000 as down payment and agreed to pay the balance with $244.69 monthly installments for the next four years.

Nothing like the deal Susan McDougal trumpeted in the commercial: "Reckon a feller could live off the land here if he was of a mind to...just ten percent down and seven years to pay it off."

Soapes had to put up more than 20 percent down and was allowed only four years to "pay it off." With amortized interest, Soape's place in the summer sun would cost him $14,745.

The trap that Soapes—and hundreds of other Whitewater Development buyers—fell into was signing the *Purchase Agreement*. That's the document *people of limited financial means* sign, as the laws of Arkansas allow, to buy real estate. Ostensibly, the buyer is emancipated from a credit check, but is hopelessly committed to ante up a sizable, *non-refundable* down payment and to meet the monthly installments *on time*—with no ifs, ands, or buts.

The Purchase Agreement included no bona fide warning to the buyer about what would happen to the deal if that payment wasn't made when it was due!

Soapes learned the hard way—on the third anniversary of his mortgage. Until that time he had been scrupulously prompt with payments. He had met 35 of the 48 installments under the mortgage contract totaling $8,564.15. With the $3,000 down payment, Soapes had advanced the Clinton-McDougal partnership $11,564.15.

He was less than $2,500 away from the prideful ownership of his little slice of paradise.

Did he write to Whitewater Development Corporation and explain his situation—that he was desperately ill with diabetes and was unable to make that 36th payment?

Yes, he did.

Did he ask for understanding and an extension on the due date of that payment?

Yes, he did.

The partners' response?

A notification to Soapes that he had defaulted on his note and that he was out in the cold. No grace period was allowed, nor were there any foreclosure proceedings.

He simply no longer had the land—and if he wanted to restore his stake in it in the future, the Clinton-McDougal firm would be pleased to do business with him.

And they would be willing to advance him the same terms as before: $3,000 down and 48 equal monthly payments of $244.69, for the grand total of $14,745.12.

But what about the $11,564.15 that he paid to the Clinton-McDougal firm?

Forget about it!

The Clintons and McDougals weren't through making money on the land bought by Soapes, whose diabetes led to his death at age 59 in 1990, three years after he lost his $11,564.15. Their own Whitewater Development records show that the Clintons and McDougals resold Soapes's land to another buyer, a Nevada couple, who signed a Purchase Agreement on even tougher terms than the previous purchaser.

They agreed to ante up $18,000 for that land and made a total of $16,500 in payments before they missed a month in early 1990. They lost the land just as Soapes had—getting not a dime out of all the money they paid the Clintons and McDougals.

Then it happened a third time, after another buyer went through those same exercises and was left holding an empty bag after failing to make payments beyond $6,400.

Finally, a fourth buyer came along, completed some $20,000 in payments to Whitewater for that thrice-sold land, and received the deed.

On just this one parcel of land, the Clintons and McDougals raked in approximately $63,000 by recycling it four times!

Is that the whole story about how Whitewater operated?

No way.

The 2,300 pages of records McDougal sold at 50 cents each are only a partial picture of the entire operation. Remember, McDougal had delivered more than 10,000 pages to the Clintons at the gubernatorial mansion back in 1986—and the author has already reported the widespread suspicion that many of those records were incinerated in the fireplace.

The documents McDougal put up for sale in 1994 were sent to him by the Clinton White House—undoubtedly, as many suspect, after they were sanitized. Yet even that wasn't enough to conceal the trickery and cheating that went on at Whitewater Development, as the Clyde Soapes case demonstrates.

Soapes and the others cited as losers on that one piece of property on the White River were hardly the only victims. There were hundreds who lost their life's savings to Whitewater's four operators, Bill and Hillary Clinton and Jim and Susan McDougal.

It is believed that, all told, more than $5 million dollars—not hundreds of thousands of dollars, as available records show—was grabbed off by this quartet of land manipulators from their gullible victims.

Need proof that the Clintons and McDougals were dealing in *under-the-table* moneys and funneling them into a *secret stash*?

The land records of Marion County (where the Ozarks vacation property is located) have no entry of Soapes's transaction.

Why?

Because under the rules that applied in Bill Clinton's Arkansas, if a buyer defaulted on a land purchase, it was as if the transaction never occurred!

No record of it was kept!

Uncle Sam never got a smell of it—so the money went into the operators' deep pockets, a tax-free benefit!

Multiply this *omission* by the hundreds of parcels the Clintons and McDougals sold, recovered, and resold—and it's easy to see how they made out like bandits.

What view do experts in real estate transactions hold about Whitewater's dealings?

"That is clearly not a very consumer-oriented method of selling [land] at all," said Bruce May, an Arizona real estate lawyer and chairman of an American Bar Association committee on land sale regulation.

May politely concedes, "You couldn't get away with that in Arizona or, I believe, in most other states. It's common for states to protect purchasers from these kind of agreements."

Yet when one listens to Arkansas real estate lawyer Hal Kemp critiquing such contracts drawn up in his state, he equivocates:

"This is a poor man's real estate financing. In return for loose approval terms—no credit checks or appraisals and low down payments—such contracts often deal severely with anyone who defaults.

"Typically, the contract says that if a person skips a payment, all previous payments are considered 'rent,' and any equity in the land is lost."

A spokesman for the Arkansas Real Estate Commission told one of the author's researchers, "Quite frankly, we received very few, if any, complaints about Purchase Agreements—and we have absolutely no record of a single complaint against Whitewater Development."

Left unsaid by this spokesman was that members of the Real Estate Commission served at the pleasure of Governor Bill Clinton, all of them his appointees.

A Bludgeoning for a Deep-Digging Reporter

It's a long road from New York's Brooklyn to Arkansas's Russellville, Mena, and Little Rock. But that's the road L. J. Davis traveled to dig up dirt on the Clinton, McDougals, Whitewater, Madison Guaranty, and the Rose Law Firm.

The fruits of his powerful investigation appeared in the April 4, 1994, edition of *The New Republic* under the headline "An Arkansas Thriller: The Name of Rose."

That this reporter, who is also a contributing editor to *Harper*'s magazine, lived to write his expository story is a miracle.

After spending an entire week poring over financial documents in government depositories and interviewing scores of people at the three aforementioned locales, Davis returned to the Legacy Hotel in Little Rock, which he had made his headquarters while in Arkansas.

This was February 14, St. Valentine's Day.

It was early evening—no later than 6:30 p.m.—when the lights suddenly went out as Davis entered his room to shower and dress for dinner after a rugged day on the road.

A power failure hadn't caused the blackout—a whack to the head blacked out Davis.

"The last thing I remember is unlocking the door of room five-oh-two to go in," Davis recalled with a shudder. "The next thing I remember, four hours later, at ten-thirty at night, was waking up on the floor of the foyer of my hotel room partially paralyzed with a lump the size of a darning egg over my left ear."

In pain when he came to, Davis looked around for a clue to what had happened.

"There was nothing to hit my head on," he professed. "I was not drunk. There was no furniture in the foyer.

"I knew I couldn't have been the victim of a robbery because my watch was still on my wrist and my wallet still contained a couple of hundred bucks...but I did find that about four pages of my notebook in a very significant portion were torn out."

At that moment, thoughts of the recent past raced through his mind.

"I should have heeded warnings I received from the office of a high government official in Washington. The exact phrase...used was, 'You've gotten into a red zone.'

"And my contact urged me, 'Work your ass off and get out of there as fast as possible.'"

That's precisely what Davis did after he was coldcocked so unceremoniously.

Next day in Brooklyn after leaving Little Rock terrified, Davis went to his doctor, who examined the lump behind his left ear.

"You were struck by a powerful blow," the doctor told Davis. "You have a concussion."

Davis now knew why "it felt like I was on a trampoline for the last twenty-four hours."

The feeling persisted over the next 48 hours while he took medication "to dissolve a blood clot on my brain," which he said his doctor diagnosed.

By March 8, Davis was his old self again and busily fashioning his story in Brooklyn for *The New Republic*. Late that afternoon, he tapped the *send* key on his word processor and dispatched a partial draft of the story to the magazine's Manhattan offices.

Three hours later, Davis's phone rang.

"What you're doing makes Lawrence Walsh [the Iran-Contra special counsel] look like a rank amateur."

The voice was a rich baritone, but not otherwise even remotely identifiable.

"Who is this?" Davis demanded.

"Seems to me you've gotten your bell rung too many times," replied the male voice. "...But did you hear what I just said?"

"...Yes...I did...," he stammered. "Is this..."

Before he could complete the sentence, the man on the other end hung up.

All of this caused L. J. Davis to conclude, "Somebody seems to be reading my computer transmissions. Whoever called me knew what I'd just sent to *The New Republic*.

"There are only three of us who know what was in that [transmission]."

Was he including the mystery caller?

"That makes four." Davis added about the events that could have cost him his life, "I used to laugh at things like this—until I ended up on the goddamn floor."

Burglaries and Burnings

Reporter David Brock, it will be recalled, interviewed the Arkansas state troopers who served as "pimps in uniform" for then-Governor Bill Clinton. He had completed his investigation in Little Rock in late August 1993 and returned to Washington.

Brock filed a preliminary report on his findings to *The American Spectator* magazine and managing editor Wladyslaw Pleszczynski gave him thumbs up to write the story.

On September 3, even as Brock was caught up at home writing the story, Pleszczynski walked into his magazine's office in Arlington, Virginia, and discovered a break-in.

"All the desk drawers were ajar; it appeared that someone had gone through them," he explained. "The only things that seemed to have been taken were a boom box and a Sony Walkman."

Entry was gained through an unoccupied section of the top floor, which enabled the burglar to "cut a hole in a thin wall into the mailroom."

Seven days later, another middle-of-the-night break-in—through the same wall, after it had been repaired.

On September 22, the magazine's studio apartment on Manhattan's Upper East Side was burglarized.

"These are the first break-ins in our twenty-seven-year history," Pleszczynski said. "We didn't necessarily connect them with David Brock's research, but it makes you wonder."

Deroy Murdock, a New York writer and president of Loud & Clear Communications, a marketing and media consultancy, conducted his own investigation of the L. J. Davis attack and *American Spectator* break-ins and wrote about them in *Human Events*, a widely read conservative weekly.

Murdock conducted an extensive examination of other violent happenings that appeared to revolve around Whitewater matters and people connected with them, and he concluded that there may be more to the violence than coincidence.

He was intrigued particularly by a fire that broke out shortly before midnight of January 24, 1994, on the 14th floor of Little Rock's Worthen Tower, headquarters of the Worthen Bank, "which loaned $3.5 million to the Clinton presidential campaign and held on deposit $55 million in federal matching funds for the fall 1992 race against George Bush."

The grabber in the fire was its target—the offices of the Pete Marwick accounting firm, which had been used by the White House to audit the travel office when the Clintons decided to give the seven-member staff the ill-fated heave-ho and give Bill's cousin in the travel business the opportunity to rake in the big bucks.

Murdock, whose findings also were published in the *New York Post*, was especially intrigued by the Marwick firm's rehabilitative audit on Madison Guaranty Savings & Loan's books that was commissioned by Jim McDougal in 1986.

Although he quotes a Marwick spokeswoman, Barbara Kraft, as pouring cold water on the idea that skullduggery was involved in the fire, Murdock nevertheless sounds this suspicion:

"...The timing of the blaze seems significant coming just four days after the appointment of Whitewater special prosecutor Robert Fiske and within three days of the Rose Law Firm's reported shredding of documents that belonged to...Vincent Foster."

It remained for the *Arkansas Democrat-Gazette* and London's *Sunday Telegraph* to tie up the loose ends on one of the more baffling acts of violence that bears a direct link not only to Whitewater—but to President Clinton personally.

10 Bullets for Clinton's Security Chief

Until September 26, 1993, Luther "Jerry" Parks ran a lucrative private security guard agency, American Contract Services, Incorporated, one of Arkansas most prestigious.

He was destined to cross paths with Governor Bill Clinton in a most incomprehensible way in late 1991 after he declared for the presidency. Clinton retained Parks's American Contract Services to provide security guards for him—despite the fact that as a viable and visible candidate he automatically received cost-free Secret Service protection.

"Bill felt more comfortable having homegrown guards around him than the intrusive protection the overly watchful Secret Service provides," a Clinton insider confided to the author on condition of anonymity.

"He wanted Parks's guards to be his buffers when he did his screwing on the campaign trail."

And they did just that—until the campaign ended and Clinton was elected president. Parks supplied guards for just a while longer to hold forth at Clinton's transition headquarters in Little Rock. Their tour was over when Bill's team went to Washington to carry out the changeover in administrations with President Bush's people.

Campaign funds had paid Jerry Parks and his American Contract Services—but evidently that wasn't enough to buy the security chief's silence on what he learned about his client. Not any more so than those Arkansas state troopers, who had rounded up trollops by the carload for their governor, could be silenced with bribes of cushy jobs on the federal payroll after Clinton began to run the country.

Parks decided to write an exposé on aspects of Clinton's licentious life that was hidden from the public. Parks knew, just as the state police did, that Clinton's righteous pose before the public as a man with "strong family values and morals" stands as just so much hogwash.

Parks became so obsessed with his project that he expanded his efforts to chase down all the reports that had surfaced about Clinton's infidelities since the beginning of his political career in 1974.

By mid-September 1993, the investigator had sniffed out considerable data, working backward in time. He felt comfortable with the information he had gathered, which by then reached back to Clinton's 1983 gubernatorial campaign.

But he still had a long way to go before attaining his goal.

The fruits of Parks's investigation—files of paramours' names, accounts of their ententes with Clinton, and photos—were kept in the bedroom of his home in Little Rock, where he lived with his wife, Jane, and their son, Gary, now 23.

Then "on or about September 15," as Mrs. Parks recalled, "our home was broken into. The phone lines were cut, knocking out our security system. When we checked around to see what might have been taken we found Jerry's files on Clinton were missing. I suppose they must have been stolen."

Because of the secret nature of Parks's work, no complaint of the break-in was filed with the Little Rock Police Department.

But that department did open a file on Luther "Jerry" Parks on the night of September 26—a *murder* file!

Parks had gone to a Mexican restaurant for dinner with a client. On his way home, Parks was shot dead on the street. This was no mugging, but an out-and-out assassination, deliberate and determinedly thorough. For the target of the killer's .9 millimeter, semi-automatic pistol was drilled by ten bullets.

The assassin fled into the night and has not been apprehended—and there's little likelihood he ever will be.

In an interview with the *Arkansas Democrat-Gazette*, Mrs. Parks was quoted:

"I believe it was premeditated. I believe someone has been watching us."

In a recent interview with London's *Sunday Telegraph*, her son, Gary, who recently ended a tour with the navy as a submarine navigator, called his father's rub-out a "premeditated, cold-blooded killing committed to silence him."

Bitter because authorities have gotten nowhere with their investigation, young Parks said, "I believe they had my father killed to save Bill Clinton's political career."

Sergeant Clyde Steelman of Little Rock's detective division, who is in charge of the murder investigation, does not dispute what Gary and his mother said about the events leading up to Parks's murder.

"If they say that some files were missing, then I can tell you those files were missing. The Parks family aren't lying to you."

Sudden Death for the Whistle-Blowing Dentist

Because of the intriguing aspects in Jerry Parks's mysterious murder and its ties to President Clinton, the *Sunday Telegraph* dispatched its Washington, D.C., correspondent Ambrose Evans-Pritchard to Arkansas to do some further digging.

One of his earliest scores was making contact with Dr. Ronald Rogers, a dentist in the tiny hamlet of Royal, just a stone's throw from Clinton's mother's cabin on Lake Hamilton outside Hot Springs.

What was Dr. Rogers offering to the London newsman?

"He was going to share some knowledge of a sensitive nature about personalities and transactions there," Evans-Pritchard said cryptically.

Evans-Pritchard's trip to meet Dr. Rogers never materialized. The intermediary who arranged the meeting with the dentist phoned the Englishman in Washington and told him to skip the trip to Arkansas.

"They got him last night," the contact said. "He went down in a plane crash that killed him and the others aboard."

Rogers had driven his car to Dallas and caught a flight to Denver on a commuter plane, a twin-engine Cessna. At 10:30 p.m. on March 3, shortly after the pilot reported electrical trouble, according to the Federal Aviation Administration, the plane vanished from the radar screen near Lawton, Oklahoma.

According to David Keating, a reporter with KFDX-TV in Wichita Falls, Texas, the FAA reported that the pilot, who radioed the tower in Lawton that he planned to land there, transmitted a curious second message.

"I'd like clearance to land at Lawton so I can refuel."

The plane had left Dallas with a full tank of gas and couldn't possibly have used up much of its fuel in the half hour it was airborne.

The reason the radar tracker lost sight of the northbound plane was that it crashed 45 miles south of Lawton, just three miles east of Shepard Air Force Base in Wichita Falls.

KFDX-TV's David Keating arrived at the crash scene at about 3 a.m. and reported what he saw:

"The plane took a complete nose dive. The front of the plane was totally demolished and the back was intact. The whole thing is weird.

"Bad weather was not a factor that evening. It was clear as could be. I saw the stars myself at three o'clock in the morning. Yet it appears the plane may have been lost. I don't know why they'd be this far off course."

Keating said that a map and magnifying glass were found in the wreckage of the forward part of the plane.

Had the *electrical problem* the pilot reported knocked the plane's gyro out of whack and also played havoc with the fuel gauge, leading the pilot to fly "by the seat of his pants" with the map and magnifying glass and report he was coming down to refuel?

No answers because the pilot and his three passengers, including Dr. Rogers, were killed in the crash.

Evans-Pritchard, who is also a contributor to the *Wall Street Journal* and to William F. Buckley's conservative *National Review*, offers the next-to-last word on this experience and several other hair-raising encounters he's had in Arkansas:

"It's a bit difficult for people to understand that this is going on in the borders of the U.S. There's a serious shutting-up operation under way."

Why Did Bill's Three Secret Service Agents Die at Waco?

As these final words were being written on the life and times of Bill and Hillary Clinton, one of the author's researchers obtained a videotape produced by Linda D. Thompson, an enterprising free-lance investigative journalist, lawyer, and founder of the Indianapolis-based American Justice Foundation. It was a documentary of the February 1993 raid on the Branch Davidians in Waco, Texas, by the Federal Alcohol, Tobacco, and Firearms Bureau.

The account narrates and depicts the botched raid upon the followers of religious zealot David Koresh. Yet it doesn't jibe with the so-called "official" version that appeared in print and on television—after reporters and photographers were *exiled* to a location three miles from the sprawling, multi-story farmhouse in the Texas countryside outside Waco so they couldn't directly eyeball the action at the compound under siege.

Never reported or depicted in the edited film and videotaped footage release by the ATF are scenes of the way the foray was actually conducted. Linda Thompson's documentary was filmed by a camera, secretly emplaced in a nearby observation post, trained on the first steps of the raid.

The scene opens with two teams of four agents leading the assault. They are seen climbing a ladder to a wide, second-floor roof overhang.

No one can be seen shooting at the agents, who are carrying fully automatic rifles and .9 millimeter pistols in their hip holsters. The guns have no safeties on them, as it soon becomes apparent.

One of the agents climbing the ladder pulls out his handgun from its holster and, before it can be positioned for use in the assault, he discharges it accidentally—shooting himself in the foot.

It appears to be only a glancing blow that causes him to slip a few rungs down the ladder before he arrests his fall. Then he continues his climb to the roof.

A moment later, the camera panning on this agent and his two ATF confederates captures a telltale scene as they reach the roof and gingerly enter the second-story window.

According to information supplied the author by sources at the raid, the agents were said to be Steve Willis, 32, of Houston; Todd McKeehan, 28 of New Orleans; and Conway LeBleau, 30, also of New Orleans.

In the irony of ironies, these three—fated to die minutes later—had served as Bill Clinton's Secret Service bodyguards during the presidential campaign. It isn't known why they were detached from that duty, but the Treasury Department has a policy of relieving its agents from strenuous and hazardous assignments periodically for mandatory rest and rehabilitation.

Serving as a personal bodyguard for a public figure, who at any moment of the day or night could be a target of an assassin, is considered *strenuous* and *hazardous* duty.

As this trio disappear after going through the window, a fourth agent, having climbed to the roof setback, reaches for one of two grenades dangling from his belt.

Taking it in hand, he pulls the pin and, inexplicably, tosses the grenade through the window.

Then, without aiming, he sprays an indiscriminate burst from his machine gun into the room. The fire is returned from the inside and bullets pierce the wall and exit the exterior siding above the roof setback.

The agent who unlimbered the first round triggers another into the room. Then, all at once, he's hit by returning fire from within. Bullets strike the back of his helmet and he falls to the roof grabbing his head. He's unhurt, but momentarily dazed.

Recovering quickly, he rises to his feet and lobs the second grenade into the room. Even before the missile explodes, he triggers another burst from his machine gun that sprays bullets into the room where his three fellow ATF agents have gone.

Agents Steve Willis, Todd McKeehan, and Conway LeBleau, who had served as Clinton's Secret Service bodyguards during his presidential campaign, were all killed in this incredible videotaped episode.

The fourth agent to die in the raid was Robert J. Williams, 26, who was shot by a burst of gunfire as he tried to come out of a "cattle car" (an enclosed truck that conveys military personnel in a much cruder fashion than a bus). There was no clue on the tape to ascertain who drilled the bullets into Williams.

But proof that the three agents who went through the window were slain (by the fourth, unidentified treasury man) is to be found in the March 3, 1993, *Dallas Morning News*: according to the ATF itself, all three secret servicemen "were killed inside the Branch Davidian farmhouse at Waco."

The big question that remains in light of this bewildering recorded revelation: were agents Willis, McKeehan, and LeBleau *exiled* to Waco and marked for death in the raid—to be gunned down by one of their own confederates in the Treasury Department?

Why, if that is the case, were they so targeted?

Was it something they learned about Bill Clinton during their tour in the campaign that made them expendable?

Just as private eye Luther "Jerry" Parks, who served jointly with the three T-men as a Clinton guard, had been taken out of circulation?

No answers to these questions and the scores of others that are invited by this puzzling episode which has all the frightening characteristics of cold-blooded murder.

From the Ozarks to the Potomac: A Blood-Splattered Trail

Ambrose Evans-Pritchard had the next-to-last word about the miasmic findings he came across in Arkansas.

Now for the last word, which comes from Deroy Murdock, who first recalls yet another baffling plane crash that occurred three days before the Wichita Falls tragedy.

A plane crash with an even closer connection to the Clinton White House.

On March 1, Herschel Friday, head of Friday, Eldridge & Clark, Arkansas's largest law firm (actually somewhat bigger in staff than the Rose Law Firm), was returning to Little Rock from a trip in his private plane.

Friday, an experienced pilot, was wealthy enough to have his own airfield alongside his home. It was nearly dusk, and Friday's son was guiding his father's plane by radio for the landing.

It was drizzling, so the lights on the landing strip were turned on. But the plane didn't make it. It crashed just short of the field and Friday was killed.

"Something happened that got him disoriented and he dropped out of sight," his widow, Beth, said afterward. "The landing lights in the rain might have caused him to lose perspective."

Yet Mrs. Friday and her son are thoroughly at a loss to accept the circumstances on face value.

"He had landed here so many times," Mrs. Friday pointed out. "He was a very excellent pilot."

Herschel Friday, the author learned, was to be questioned by special prosecutor Kenneth Starr about Bill Clinton's 1992 presidential campaign finances.

Friday was a key member of the president's Campaign Finance Committee, whose contributions and payments are currently a highly significant issue in the tangled maze of the Whitewater-Madison Guaranty mess that Fiske is probing.

Here now is New York writer Deroy Murdock's last word, first expressed in *Hu-*

man Events when he wrote about the "mysterious coincidences" cited earlier that appear to tightly connect with "the many violences" growing out of Whitewater:

"Can any of this be tied to the White House? Who knows? Journalists as well as investigators working for special prosecutor Kenneth Starr should move quickly to kick over the Whitewater-related rocks from the Potomac to the Ozarks and see if anything under them tries to burrow away from the sunlight.

"Also, properly handled congressional hearings would help drag all of this into the open where it can be explained as either a brutal cover-up or an interesting but irrelevant series of coincidences.

"Until then, all America can do is take President Bill Clinton at his word. As he insists, 'I haven't done anything wrong.'"

A Postscript to "Mystery Murders on the Whitewater"

Is there a larger body count around Bill and Hillary Clinton than what all of the above facts and figures depict from the *official* record?

As chronicled in chapter 36, Barry Seal, the nation's most notorious drug smuggler, became a target for death when he was turned loose to a Salvation Army halfway house instead of being imprisoned for life for his many sins against society.

Certainly Seal's murder must stand as more than a coincidence in the roll call of deaths that lay so ominously at Bill and Hillary Clinton's doorstep.

Just as certainly, yet another closely configured Clintonite's sudden departure raises unanswered questions—that of C. Victor Raiser II, 52, the co-chairman of the Clinton for President National Finance Committee.

Raiser and his son, R. Montgomery, 22, were killed with three others in the crash of a private plane outside Dillingham, Alaska, on July 30, 1992. No cause for the crash was ever advanced by the Federal Aviation Administration.

Raiser, whose experience as a political fund-raiser was gained as national finance chairman of the Democratic National Committee, was killed at a critical time in Clinton's campaign—when finances for his presidential race were hitting rock bottom and the campaign was $395,000 in the hole.

Immediately after Raiser's death, the Clinton campaign received an infusion of fresh contributions that fueled the Democratic front-runner's locomotive with a full head of steam to his destination as the party's nominee.

The count of dead bodies with connections to Bill and Hillary Clinton during their Arkansas years and their year and a half as America's first couple doesn't end after Raiser became a statistic. Although there is no doubt that the next series of deaths was entirely coincidental, the increasing number of deaths of those with links to the Clintons seems to suggest that even the slightest association could be the *kiss of death*.

On March 25, 1993, 22 days after secret servicemen Willis, McKeehan, and LeBleau were slain at Waco, five navy pilots from the aircraft carrier *USS Roosevelt*, which had just been deployed to the Mediterranean from its home port in Norfolk, Virginia, lost their lives in a mystery crash.

The pilots, all aboard an early warning E-2C Hawkeye, had just completed their first operational mission: night combat patrol off the Yugoslav coast, clearing the airways for German-based cargo planes flying food drops to starving Muslims in the besieged former province of Bosnia.

The five fliers were returning to their carrier in the Ionian Sea when their Hawkeye crashed, killing the entire crew.

Those five men had been Clinton's escorts aboard the *Roosevelt* earlier in the month when he went aboard the carrier off the Virginia coast—his initial visit to a military installation and first official function as commander in chief. The president, according to the *Washington Post*, received a relatively warm welcome—but was roundly ridiculed behind his back by the crew because of his draft-dodging history.

Fourteen months later—May 19, 1994—a VH-60N Blackhawk helicopter crashed in a thickly forested area alongside the Potomac River some 40 miles southwest of Washington, D.C. All four Marine Corps crew members lost their lives: Major William S. Barkley, Jr., 27, of Hickory, North Carolina; Captain Scott J. Reynolds, 33, of Wausau, Wisconsin; Staff Sergeant Brian D. Haney, 32, of North Ridgeville, Ohio; and Sergeant Timothy D. Sabel, 27, of Ripon, Wisconsin.

Barkley was one of eight pilots assigned to the presidential squadron in January 1990. He had flown George Bush on a number of occasions from the White House lawn to Camp David—and had performed flight duty on just one occasion for Bill Clinton after he was inaugurated in January of '93.

Barkley piloted the Hawkeye that flew Clinton to the *Roosevelt* off the Virginia Coast and returned him to the White House grounds.

Haney flew that same mission with Clinton, for he was the quality assurance representative on every presidential flight made on Hawkeyes, regardless of which craft in the fleet of nine VH-60Ns was designated to make the trip.

Likewise, Sabel had also accompanied Clinton on the single flight just after he took office. Sabel was responsible for maintenance on all aircraft assigned to ferry presidents.

Unlike his tribute at a Treasury Department memorial service for the three Secret Service agents who guarded him during the campaign and were murdered in Waco, Clinton spoke no eulogy for the eight navy fliers who played vital roles in his historic debut at sea as commander in chief on the March 25, 1993.

The last in this long-running catalog of deaths is the mid-May 1994 suicide of Trooper Danny Ferguson's ex-wife, who died of a shotgun blast in the mouth.

Ferguson's former wife's life ended just as his involvement in the Paula Jones controversy became increasingly significant to the Clinton White House. The question loomed large at the time: would the trooper side with Clinton (deny any sexual approach occurred at the hotel) or team with the former Arkansas state employee (to confirm her claim that Clinton made such an attempt)?

Early reports suggested Ferguson would deny Paula's tale. But then his ex-wife died—and just as swiftly reports filtered out of Arkansas hinting that the trooper's ex-wife may have been silenced because she "knew too much" about her former husband's experiences as Bill Clinton's *pimp in uniform* and was "ready to tell all."

As of early June, Ferguson was reported "stunned beyond belief" over his ex-wife's "suicide" and was said by his lawyer Bill Bristow to have reached a decision on whose side he would take.

Bristow came on the scene after Ferguson was named in Paula Jones' suit because of his role in escorting her to Clinton's hotel room in Little Rock—and blabbing about it to *The American Spectator* and the *Los Angeles Times*.

"My job is to do what is best for my client," Bristow said cryptically, stopping just short of stating that Ferguson would side with Paula in the controversy.

"If it were the decision that we should be as specific as possible, that would be what we would do," Bristow declared.

How minds change!

In chapter 39, the reader will find Lieutenant Commander Trice Ellice, Jr., commanding officer of the local Naval Reserve unit in Hot Springs, telling the *Los Angeles Times*' William Rempel shortly before Labor Day, September 7, 1992, that he had "persuaded officials of the Eighth Naval District in New Orleans to create a billet, or enlistment slot, especially for Bill Clinton" that would keep him immune from the draft.

Soon after that story shook up Clinton on the campaign trail, Ellice backed off that version and denied the Democratic nominee for president had received preferential treatment in the reserve assignment that Bill's uncle Raymond Clinton had desperately sought for him.

How minds change!

On June 10, 1994, trooper Danny Ferguson, who provided all the succulent details about the way Paula Corbin Jones' encounter with Bill Clinton came about, had a refreshing change of recollection. Suddenly Ferguson remembered he had done virtually nothing in arranging the governor's meeting with the Arkansas Industrial Development Commission employee.

Ferguson denied he told Paula, "The governor would like to meet you," but instead claimed Paula was the one who was interested in meeting Clinton. Yet his involvement in the case appeared to be deep enough to compel Ferguson to level that he at least "rode the elevator" with Paula up to the governor's floor and pointed her to "a particular room of the hotel."

Clinton's $400-an-hour attorney, Robert Bennett, put on a face that was configured to demonstrate complete satisfaction that his defense of the president had taken a distinct turn for the better. But Paula's attorney, Joseph Cammarata, saw it far differently.

"On the critical question, he puts her in a hotel room with him," Cammarata hammered with an ear-to-ear grin at the *admission* in Ferguson's *recantation*.

"As to Paula approaching Ferguson first (the trooper said it was Paula, not he, who made the first approach to meet Clinton), there will be witnesses who contradict that."

****

There were no witnesses on lonely Louisiana Highway 159 shortly after midnight on Saturday, September 6, 1986, when Benjamin Paul Talbot, Sr., lost his life while driving his car on that interstate.

Markings on the pavement appear to have satisfied the state police as to what happened at the accident scene, two miles south of the Louisiana-Arkansas state line.

The car the 58-year-old, wealthy Arkansas businessman was driving through a slight mist, but on a dry road, "ran off the highway and traveled a long distance before rolling end-over-end and hitting a tree," the police report said.

"The victim, who was not wearing a seat belt, was thrown from the vehicle and apparently died instantly."

Talbot, who operated the family-owned Talbot's Department Store in Magnolia, Arkansas, was also a real estate developer, a member of the Chamber of Commerce, president of the Rotary Club, and involved in a host of other civic activities in that community in the southernmost section of the state.

However, his most significant role on the Arkansas landscape was that of chairman of the Governor's Task Force on Small Business. As such, Talbot headed the 60-member commission that was studying ways the state could help small businesses.

Talbot's appointment was made in early July 1982—in the second year of Governor Frank White's term (while Bill Clinton was putting his campaign in high gear for the November election to unseat the incumbent, who defeated him in 1980).

In fact, Talbot's son, Benjamin P. Talbot, Jr., then 31, had entered the 1982 race for lieutenant governor on the Republican line, but withdrew from contention for the No. 2 job, saying "There's only twenty-four hours in a day...my commitments to the family businesses are so extensive that I feel I could not serve in the office of lieutenant governor in the way I intended to."

As already cited, Clinton deposed Frank White in the election and began serving his second two-year term in January 1983. One of Clinton's first acts upon his return to office, the record reflects, was to dismantle the Governor's Task Force on Small Business.

Because, as the record establishes with indisputable clarity, Clinton was not a caring governor of *small businessmen*, but a hard-nosed protagonist of *big businessmen* (Tyson Foods, International Paper, the Ford Motor Company, etc.)

The last thing he wanted was a "small businessman," as Talbot Sr. called himself, to mess in the governor's agenda that called for huge tax breaks and incomprehensible special concessions for the *big boys*.

Talbot's reputation in the realm was impeccable. He had served as chairman of the Arkansas delegation to the White House Conference on Small Business, whose aim was to "map a plan for implementing 60 recommendations for legislation and affirmative action" for his state.

Virtually no progress was made—because Clinton was then serving in his first term. His successor, White, made a stab at it but because he was not a two-fisted governor, nothing meshed in that effort. Then, with Clinton's return to power, Ben Talbot's efforts to lobby legislation to aid the "survival of small business in the state" went down the drain.

Although Talbot grew and prospered and eventually became a *big businessman*, he never fancied himself to be anything but a *small businessman*. Thus he continued to champion the causes of the little guy in business—much to Governor Clinton's distress.

On April 1, 1986, former Governor White threw his hat into the Republican primary for another crack at the incumbent Clinton. Almost at once, Ben Talbot, Sr., got behind White and promised to "campaign for Frank as vigorously as I humanly know how."

Clinton was vulnerable. He knew he was. So he turned the '86 campaign into what concededly was one of the dirtiest in Arkansas's political history (see chapter 22 for details).

But when November 4 passed into history, Bill Clinton had soundly trounced his challenger by a whopping 64–36 percent margin.

One highly significant occurrence came about as the campaign went into the homestretch of the seven-week dash to the wire. Ben Talbot, Sr., was speaking his mind on the campaign trail and telling the voters just how neglected the *small businessmen* were and that a new governor, who had their interest at heart, should be elected, when—wham!

Talbot was dead.

On that road there were no witnesses and only some sketchy, inconclusive evidence of the way the accident happened to a man who, according to his son, Ben Jr., "never sat behind the wheel of his car without fastening his seat belt."

Ben Jr., who had told the author in an earlier conversation that he had once been friends with Bill Clinton and "smoked pot and snorted coke with him," had one final, solemn word about Ben Sr.'s death:

"Ya know, they say that Lyndon B. Johnson left a lot of bodies lying on the Texas countryside in his march to the presidency. But I ask you to look at the road Bill Clinton traveled to the White House.

"Clinton's journey makes Johnson's look like that of a piker."

Ben Jr. stopped just short of suggesting Clinton himself had anything to do with his father's death. But he did say, "Somebody up there in that ol' statehouse sure as hell didn't want my ol' man buzzing about a subject [the best interests of the *small businessman*] that Clinton and his Mafia wanted kept at arms-length from his administration."

In all good conscience, the author cannot speculate whether Bill Clinton ever did—or even had the capacity to—order a death. The closest *evidence* of what, in all fairness, seems a most remote possibility, is to be found in a quote attributed to Clinton by the *Washington Post*'s Bob Woodward, who together with Carl Bernstein won a Pulitzer Prize for early findings on Watergate.

Woodward claims to have spent 18 months studying what goes on behind the locked doors of 1600 Pennsylvania Avenue, and his recent book, *The Agenda: Inside the Clinton White House* (Simon and Schuster), details his findings.

Woodward's book, which was roundly panned by the White House staff as "old hat" and "he had nothing in it that's new," described the first year of the Clinton administration as chaotic and the president as indecisive and prone to temper tantrums.

One example is cited now so as to close out this chapter on what may or may not be a significant note.

During the presidential campaign, Woodward claims Clinton was infuriated over a flunky's actions at a Little Rock function and flew off the handle by supposedly screaming, "*I want him dead! I want him killed! Get him horsewhipped!*"

That's the closest anyone's ever come to putting words of such threatening consistency in Clinton's mouth.

All the deaths cited here—18 in toto, beginning with the Clintons' Whitewater land deals and ranging across the landscape throughout their years as Arkansas's first couple and into the first 18 months of the co-presidency—what is to be made of them?

The question need not be answered until a late report about Kathy Ferguson, trooper Danny Ferguson's wife, is chronicled.

Kathy Ferguson worked at Quachita Hospital in Little Rock—where Bill Clinton's mother had been employed throughout her entire career as a nurse-anesthetist.

Kathy went to work at the hospital some years after Virginia Kelley was ousted as a staffer. But in death, Kathy Ferguson left a shuddering reminder that the bullet that took her life—fired into her mouth—may not be all it seems as a messenger of suicide.

In this author's experience with more than 2,000 murder cases he has covered in his career, the one thing he learned from any number of medical examiners in his rounds is this:

Women bent on suicide never forsake the one thing that has held them together in life—vanity.

The words of one pathologist, Dr. Sydney B. Weinberg, chief medical examiner for more than a quarter of a century in Suffolk County on Long Island, stand out:

"Women are vain. When they decide to kill themselves, they leave this planet looking as well as they can appear. They don't take their lives in the nude. They don't end it all by destroying their good looks, like blowing out their brains.

"This is what I found in my long experience as a medical examiner. I believe this is what you'll find if you talk to any number of pathologists around the country."

The author did and found universal agreement among the forensic specialists he interviewed—that Dr. Weinberg was talking horse sense.

Ironic that Kathy Ferguson, who knew so much about Bill Clinton's affair with Paula Jones should die?

Consider this: Kathy Ferguson told co-workers at the hospital, "Danny [her husband, the trooper] told me he solicited women by the dozens for Bill Clinton...and Paula Jones was among those women my husband told me he recruited for the governor's sexual gratification. Paula Jones has spoken the truth."

Special prosecutor Kenneth Starr should certainly be able to track down the validity of these and all other allegations and see whether or not they fly, and whether Kathy Ferguson's death, most especially, is a suicide—or murder. Or if he can't, certainly those legislators on the Hill could give it a crack to answer this question:

Can all of the above-enumerated deaths be mere coincidence—or are they more correctly attributable to a *kiss of death*?

While it remains for special prosecutor Starr and/or Congress to provide answers, it could be a wait well worth the time it takes to decide. For the findings may also resolve the ultimate issue:

Whether William Jefferson Blythe Clinton IV—and Hillary Rodham Clinton, as well—can be believed when they say they did nothing wrong.

HOW MUCH LONGER CAN SLICK WILLIE AND SLIPPERY HILLARY GET AWAY WITH IT?

Last Words on the Co-Presidents

A time comes when the writing must stop.

It's been a long time in coming.

This book, begun as a manuscript, was seeded with a first word; it has grown to some 225,000 words.

The preceding pages have told the story about two ambitious, politically astute people who used every known ploy—and invented numerous devices of their own—to steamroller their way through a labyrinth of dark shadows while governing the nation's bottom-rung state of Arkansas. They emerged from those dank depths and found a bright horizon promising new conquests on a scale so huge as to defy description.

Nicknamed The Land of Opportunity, their state truly was all of that for this ambitiously ravenous couple with insatiable appetites, whose "integrity" could never remotely qualify even as one of their lesser strengths.

Their wiles and weaseling enabled them to claw their way out of the morass they left behind to reach the highest office of the land—where they continued performing in a manner no better, and at times a great deal worse, than the lock-tight control they exercised over every piece of unethical or illegal business they could put their hands on back home.

What stands as the bottom line is that the real story about these two people has been told here to its fullest—to the best of this author's ability.

There's little to add to the chronicles of the scandalous road to the White House that led to *America's first co-presidency*, except to update the reader on the more momentous matters hanging fire as the Clintons teeter along on the shakiest legs through the second year of the presidency.

Virtually all are issues that Bill and Hillary would just as soon see swept under the rug. But the record is indelibly inscribed with these blemishes and, despite their power as America's first couple, they can do nothing to alter what the future holds.

The Clintons live in a fishbowl, the presidential mansion at 1600 Pennsylvania Avenue in Washington, D.C.: so different from Little Rock, and so fortunate for America, where their every move subjects them to microscopic scrutiny by a national press and an ever-watchful public.

A far cry from Center Street's gubernatorial mansion where they lived for years with imperious oblivion to the needs and wants of the people they had made their patsies.

Whitewater: A Billary Downfall?

"When will it cease?" Americans are asking. "This Bill and Hillary Clinton festering chicanery, evasiveness, slickness, deception, double-dealing, double-talking, and unethical and most probably criminal behavior that gets more abhorrent and egregious with almost every passing day?"

Increasing numbers of political columnists and editorial writers are demanding to know whether the president and first lady "have no vestiges of self-esteem or decency left to call halt to the putrefaction they have spread over the White House after a residency barely a year old."

Many members of Congress are voicing the thoughts of their constituents and asking, "Do the Clintons believe they can still get away performing with the utterly corrupt and unspeakable unseemly ways they supervised the state of Arkansas, leaving it torn, tattered, and teetering after their dozen years of wreck and ruin rule?

"Will they be permitted to survive their past sins and to continue committing new ones without being brought to the bar of justice?"

Those questions were asked for some time. And it seemed no answers were forthcoming. But the situation's changed—for the better.

A special prosecutor, Robert B. Fiske, Jr., began trawling for those answers.

Then a new special counsel, Kenneth Starr, stepped in.

And congressional committees suddenly began their own inquiries.

The questions crying for those answers involved their curious and apparently illegal loans from the bankrupt Madison Guaranty Savings and Loan, their diversion of depositor funds from Madison to their Whitewater Development Corporation, which engaged in the Ozark Mountains vacation-land settlements, and the mystifying shredding of documents after the death of Hillary's former Rose Law Firm partner, *close friend*, and White House counsel, Vincent Foster.

All of the above issues—and so many others that were begging to be explained—were brought to a head on February 24, 1994, by what many view as the Clintons' "unpardonable sin"—the "insider information" that the White House received on a criminal investigation being conducted by the Resolution Trust Corporation, the

Treasury Department branch that was probing whether laws were broken when the Clintons obtained those loans from the failed thrift.

This intelligence might never have come into the open had it not been for the Senate Banking Committee and its alertness in questioning Deputy Treasury Secretary Roger C. Altman, to learn that he'd gone to the White House to see his old pal, the president, and wife Hillary. The committee learned of Altman's "heads up" meeting with them and with White House counsel Bernard Nussbaum; Hillary's chief of staff, Margaret Williams; and Harold Ickes, the administration's *new kid on the block* and former counsel and *shepherd* of the corrupt, mob-dominated Hotel and Restaurant Workers' Union in New York.

Of all assignments to receive, Ickes—whom the FBI declined to clear as an uninvolved member of the union's waywardness into mob control—is now characterized as the president's "political troubleshooter on Whitewater"!

Altman acknowledged under questioning by Republicans of the banking committee that he went to the White House to discuss the problem that Madison Guaranty was posing for the RTC.

Altman said he wanted to inform the White House that the statute of limitations applying to any civil lawsuit against Rose or its partners was less than a month away.

Altman committed one of the worst offenses by doing this, since he headed an independent regulatory agency that's supposed to function without political considerations.

More scandalously, the briefing was attended by senior advisers to the Clintons, who themselves were subject to the agency's investigations.

Even worse still, the shocked Senate Banking Committee was to learn Altman had two prior *briefing* sessions with the White House going back as long ago as September 1993!

Republicans immediately pointed to the briefings as evidence that the White House had been *controlling* the inquiries into Madison and Whitewater.

Without any question it was unethical and—judging from the depth of involvement the president and first lady had in the case—probably highly illegal.

A flabbergasted Congressman Jim Leach, an Iowa Republican and the ranking GOP member on the House Banking Committee, labeled the meetings "thoroughly unseemly" and declared that the Clinton White House had undermined "the credibility of the regulatory process."

Leach fumed, "Nothing could be more inappropriate. The Resolution Trust Corporation should be arms length from both the executive branch and from Congress. These are process issues that should be handled in appropriate ways." The Resolution Trust's primary commitment, as it concerns the Clintons, was configured around being able to reach a decision on whether or not the agency should bring fraud charges against executives or borrowers connected with Madison—or whether there were conflicts of interest involving Hillary Clinton and the Rose Law Firm.

The heart of the issue is that Hillary represented Madison before an Arkansas regulator who was appointed by her husband. After Madison went belly-up in 1989, federal regulators hired Rose to sue the savings institution's accountants—the case cited earlier that was handled by Webster Hubbell.

"I'd describe it as a heads-up [meeting]," Altman weaseled about his get-togethers with the White House honchos. "...They should be aware of the internal processes and the types of criteria which the RTC was going to be following in order to reach a decision by February 28, 1994."

Why February 28?

That was the last day when any civil lawsuit against Rose or its partners had to be filed before the statute of limitations ran out.

Altman doesn't spell this out too clearly for the committee, nor does he go into details on what other aspects of the investigation he discussed with the president's people—nor what the RTC proposed to do about the fast-approaching deadline.

The author learned that Altman actually *personally informed* Bill and Hillary Clinton—and their counselors—in separate meetings, that among the RTC's options were filing a civil suit before the February 28 deadline or asking those involved to waive the statute of limitations. Either would produce renewed embarrassment for the White House.

The belief is that the RTC had no intention of asking for an extension of the deadline—that it wanted to let the statute of limitations run out so the president, first lady, and the rest of the cabal who took Madison Guaranty to the cleaners would be completely off the hook from further civil and/or criminal proceedings.

Hanging 'Em out to Dry

But Senator Al D'Amato made certain the president, his wife, and all others involved in the Madison Guaranty scam would be duly hung out to dry, if they so deserved.

The wily New York legislator saw to it that they didn't escape without what he deemed was a deserved turn they had coming—to be thoroughly investigated. He demanded—and received from Congress—an extension to the statute of limitations into 1995.

Time enough for the RTC and Bob Fiske to carry on their back-to-back inquiries without concern about time running out on them before they could lodge charges, if warranted.

Altman claimed he saw nothing inappropriate about having asked for meetings with the White House bigwigs. He explained that they were no different from the briefings he provided earlier to members of Congress concerned about whether the inquiry into Madison would be hampered by the statute of limitations.

However, Altman didn't address the difference between discussing the case with the congressional body that commissioned the RTC's investigation and talking such matters over with the targets of that inquiry—clearly, the "enemy."

"We explained the process which the RTC would follow in reaching a decision before that February twenty-eighth, that it would be exactly identical to procedures used in any other cases," Altman offered weakly.

But the Republicans on the banking committee attacked the meeting as a sign of how the Clinton administration had purposefully failed to conduct a proper examination of Madison and Whitewater.

And, moreover, of the way the White House had been trying not only to downplay the importance of the case—but also doing all it could to deep-six it.

D'Amato commented, "Can you imagine if I or another senator brought someone to the RTC to ask for an update of a lawsuit?

"What would they think of us?

"It is totally inappropriate and presents the worst of appearances.

"And these were Clinton's personal lawyers. They were Nussbaum and Ickes and Williams."

Harold Ickes was beside himself to learn such a fuss followed Altman's briefing on which way the RTC investigation was headed.

"It was a very short meeting. He came in, advised us of the status of the statute of limitation, and left."

Spoken like a true-blue White House loyalist—in language no different from the tongue-twisting gibberish he offered in his defense against charges that in his eight years as counsel and organizer for New York's Local 100 of the Restaurant and Hotel Workers Union, he was aware it was mob-operated.

Special counsel Robert Fiske, who on June 30, 1994, ruled that Foster's death was a suicide, issued a companion ruling that absolved the Treasury Department officials called before his grand jury of committing *crimes* when they discussed Whitewater-related matters with federal regulators.

However, Fiske offered no voice or view on the *ethical* questions that were raised and brought a sharp rejoinder from Senator D'Amato, the ranking minority member of the Banking Committee in the upper house, where the hearings on Whitewater were to be held in late July.

"If the purpose of these contacts between administration officials was not to obstruct justice or influence an ongoing investigation," D'Amato asked, "what was their purpose? We have a right to know."

Whitewater to Outdo Watergate?

On the very day the assistant treasury secretary caused the banking committee to wonder what kind of administration it was dealing with, Bob Fiske dispatched a message to the White House that read, "Hold tight, guys, I'm a-gonna let you see what kind of ruck you're dealin' with."

Those were Fiske's moves that held the promise to many of making the 1970s' *Spiro Agnew contretemps* and attendant *Dick Nixon Watergate follies* seem like mere preliminary acts to a 1990s' spectacle that holds all the ingredients for the biggest political scandal of the twentieth century:

• The special prosecutor's office in Washington, D.C., was put in the hands of Roderick C. Lankler, whose primary assignment was to get the lowdown on Vincent Foster's strange death. Lankler, 56, had a long career investigating public corruption. He spent more than eight years in the 60s as a prosecutor of the most difficult homicide cases in New York County. He was seen as one of the nation's most qualified probers, with the supreme capability of being able to sort out whether Foster's case was a suicide—as officially labeled—or a murder, which seemed more likely when weighed against the evidence found at the death scene, the quick and indiscriminate destruction of his personal papers on Whitewater (both in the White House and the Rose Law Firm), and the shameless stonewalling of an FBI investigation. These three factors, all taken together, went to the heart of the case—**M-O-T-I-V-E**. Yet the findings rendered on June 30, 1994—that Foster was downtrodden over his poor management of his White House duties and took his own life—appeared to put that questioned death to rest.

- Besides Washington, D.C., Fiske opened offices in Little Rock and in Manhattan, the latter being a place where his staff can meet and store documents, and have lawyer Susan Thomases close at hand to experience the kind of muscle the *New York Times*' Jeff Gerth lacked when he tried to press the heavy-duty barbells the Clintons threw in his path after he sought to penetrate their Ozark Mountains gymnastics.

- Fiske also hand-picked Russell Hardin, Jr., a former Texas prosecutor, to look into the case against former Municipal Court Judge David Hale, who lifted the lid on the Whitewater scandal by declaring that Clinton and Madison Guaranty's Jim McDougal pressured him to advance funds from his Small Business Administration treasury to bail the troubled S&L out of its hopeless financial dilemma.

Hale, who cut a deal with Fiske, became the first person to testify under oath before the grand jury who had the shots to link Bill and Hillary Clinton to the criminal conspiracy Bob Fiske was trying to unearth.

It could well be all the thrust the new special prosecutor, Kenneth Starr, may need to decide what the Clintons' fate will be.

But Hale wasn't alone in his ground-breaking role as a sworn testifier before a duly convened legal body. Bob Fiske sent his operatives—without any advance alert sounded to the White House—to knock on the front doors of the executive mansion with a batch of subpoenas, the ink on them barely dry.

They were delivered to Clintons' *Gang of Six*, the ones who put their heads together with Roger Altman when he allegedly "did nothing more than alert them to the statute of limitations."

In alphabetical order, the billy-do's commanding the deponents' presence before the grand jury went to the following:

Lisa Caputo, Hillary Clinton's press secretary; Mark D. Gearan, the White House communications director; Harold Ickes, the deputy chief of staff; Bruce Lindsey, a senior adviser to the president; Bernard Nussbaum, the White House counsel; and Maggie Williams, the chief of staff to the first lady.

Another batch of subpoenas descended on the Treasury Department and were slapped on Roger Altman, the deputy treasury secretary; Jack DeVore, Treasury Secretary Lloyd Bentsen's chief spokesman; Jean Hanson, the Treasury Department's chief counsel; and Josh Steiner, chief of staff to Secretary Lloyd Bentsen.

Ten subpoenas! For openers!

All of them directed at key persons who appeared to have been involved in furnishing the Clinton White House the kind of *inside information* that even the Nixon White House, in its most trying times, was unable to obtain from government probers.

And while the initial phase of Fiske's inquiry gave the White House people a bit of room to breathe by his finding that they *committed no crime*, they were not home free by any means.

They were facing far greater caloric confrontations in the Senate, where the questioning not only was to be under oath, but also before a vast nationwide audience of television viewers, who could come to their own conclusions as to the kind of label to post on the information they gleaned about the RTC inquiry from Treasury Department officials.

The Co-Presidents Are Shanghaied from Shangri-La

2:30 p.m. Sunday, June 12, 1994.

The euphoria has ended. The thrill of an eight-day hegira to Italy, France, and England is over.

President William Jefferson Blythe Clinton IV and First Lady Hillary Rodham Clinton have returned from a continent that gave them a temporary tenancy in *Shangri-La*—3,000 miles from the cares and concerns of the White House and of Whitewater.

Together the *co-presidents* honored American GI's who gave their lives in the Anzio and D-Day landings, paid homage to the surviving military men for their valorous deeds on the beaches and in the hedgerows and trenches during World War II, and basked with puffed chests in the goodwill their mission commanded.

They even had their cake iced with the doctorate that the Oxford University faculty of 2,500 refused in 1985 to grant to their then-British Prime Minister Margaret Thatcher (the vote was 1,738 nays and only 319 yeas).

Yet the dons chose to confer Oxford's highest award, an honorary Doctorate of Civil Law by Diploma, to their most notorious *dropout*!

Yet what could one expect from the "cosseted bulwarks of socialism, reactionary in defense of the welfare state and medieval in rejection of demands for accountability," as it was put in *Human Events* by Washington, D.C., attorney Andrew J. Morris, himself an Oxford graduate?

With the ceremony of majestic medieval pomp over, the Clintons were conveyed to Air Force One, where their journey to that mythical kingdom ended abruptly and most unceremoniously with a jarring call on the *hot line*.

No, North Korea hadn't invaded South Korea.

Nor had Saddam Hussein unleashed nuclear warhead missiles on Israel.

The news that couldn't wait for the Clintons' return to the White House was that special counsel Robert Fiske wanted to question the president and first lady as soon as they got back!

As the hatch of the presidential jet was shut and the pilot synchronized the engines for takeoff, one couldn't blame the Clintons if suddenly they were disposed to feel their trip home was to another *Lost Horizon*—but far different than James Hilton's imaginary setting where life approaches perfection.

Life was anything but perfect on the Sunday afternoon of June 12 when Bob Fiske and his top deputy, Roderick Lankler, accompanied by a court stenographer, strode into the White House and were ushered into the Treaty Room, on the opposite end of the mansion from where the Clintons have their official offices.

Clinton, accompanied by White House counsel Lloyd N. Cutler and the first family's personal lawyer, David E. Kendall, entered the Treaty Room that's used as a study by the president and for formal signings of legislation and decrees.

When the president raised his right hand and swore to tell the truth as the court stenographer administered the oath, history was made.

For after Clinton answered questions about his and the White House staff's actions bearing on Vince Foster's death in the summer of 1993 and about the give-and-take that went on between the first family's aides and the Treasury Department's Roger Altman, it marked the first time that a sitting president had given a deposition about his official conduct. His questioning lasted 90 minutes.

History was made a second time when Hillary followed her husband to the dock and testified under oath for a full 60 minutes. That was also the first time a sitting first lady had ever been interviewed by law-enforcement officials about her actions while in the White House.

After their back-to-back encounter with the special prosecutor, the Clintons could only look for more of the same. For Fiske indicated clearly that he planned a return engagement.

Next time he was going to quiz the president and first lady about matters more directly related to the scandalous Whitewater Development Ozark Mountains venture and the Madison Guaranty Savings and Loan mess.

Meanwhile, the cry of "When will it cease?" was heard once again when Americans across the country expressed outrage after the Clinton White House confirmed a widely circulated rumor that had been put out by the Oval Office as a trial balloon: the formation of a "defense fund" for the president and first lady!

That occurred on June 28, 1994, when Clinton "became the first commander in chief ever to pass the hat to help pay his legal bills." That's the way the *New York Post*'s Deborah Orin and Marilyn Raubert reported the news from their newspaper's Washington bureau. "The White House said Clinton and wife Hillary decided to make history by soliciting $1,000-a-year contributions because they face bills of up to $2 million for Whitewater and Paula Jones' charges of sexual harassment."

Dee Dee Myers quickly went into her *damage control* configuration. "It's in the best interest of the country and the president to have those bills paid," the press secretary said about having the nation shell out shekels to defend the first couple against the innumerable crimes they committed in Arkansas.

Political analyst Bill Schnider protested: "This attempt to fund the Clintons' kitty for their legal defense will hurt their image totally, because that's unseemly for a president [and first lady] to be begging, particularly when he's paid $200,000."

Another source added, "It's particularly outlandish to ask the people to pay their lawyers' bills after they cleaned up with all those hundreds of thousands—if not millions—of dollars through their Whitewater rip-offs and other schemes they pulled in Arkansas."

The headline on the *New York Post* story summed it up: **It's official: Bill and Hill become a charity case**.

It certainly seemed that this was going to be a *long, hot summer* for Bill and Hillary Clinton—perhaps their longest.

If not, then why had the president installed a staff in basement offices in the West Wing to monitor Whitewater developments at what the White House press corps refers to as damage-control meetings?

Indeed, what a vastly different ball game is played in Washington than the pastime the Clintons were so accustomed to in Little Rock.

The nation's capital isn't Little Rock, these two erstwhile *untouchable* big shots are finding out at long last.

They built their road to the White House with huge paving blocks of scandal.

Those weighty slabs now threaten to become their political gravestones.

APPENDIX

THE DRAFT-DODGING LAWS CLINTON BROKE

The author and his researchers conducted an exhaustive investigation and study of Clinton's experiences with his Vietnam protests and many efforts to evade military service. It takes a finite measure of the man who would be commander in chief of America's armed forces that has never been attempted before.

Bill Clinton would not be president of the United States today had he not pulled strings and broken laws to manipulate and subvert authorities into a conspiracy to aid and abet his cause: to keep him out of the military, as well as out of a penitentiary!

As an ex-con, or a dishonorably-discharged military yardbird, which he would have been had he not slithered out of the law's clutches time and again, he couldn't have run for Congress, for Arkansas attorney general, or five times for the governorship of that state—and most certainly not for the presidency!

He wouldn't even have been eligible to *vote* in an election!

****

Clinton began breaking the statutes enunciated in the "American military bible" known as the *United States Code of Federal Regulations*, a voluminous book that spells out all the laws governing each aspect of military service as applied to those who serve, as well as to those who do not through deceit, chicanery, forgery, perjury, and fraud.

That book, coupled with another government legal binder, the similar, but briefer, *Code of Federal Regulations*—along with considerable guidance and advice generously advanced by many sources (please see Author's Credits)—aided the author and his researchers in preparing this study on the legal ramifications of the president's avoidance of military service.

Bill Clinton committed an accountable 26 criminal acts against his country over a period of seven months when he compressed every wile and manipulation he could enlist into an all-out effort to evade military service.

His violations of the laws began on or about May 13, 1969, when his induction notice arrived at his mother's Hot Springs home—while he was at Oxford—and he was ordered to report for active military duty on July 28, 1969.

To beat the gun against induction, the already-drafted Clinton returned home and dashed to the Fayetteville campus of the University of Arkansas—after U.S. Senator J. William Fulbright and nearly a dozen others of equal political clout—set the stage for Colonels Eugene Holmes and Clinton Jones to grease the 23-year-old Georgetown University graduate's way into the U of A Law School Reserve Officers Training Corps.

That ROTC unit was already filled to capacity and brimming with prospective candidates on a long waiting list that was closed to additional applicants.

That fact evidently didn't make a difference to the Colonels Holmes and Jones, since they were obviously willing to go along with the "fix" and unlawfully slip Clinton into their roster—an act that in itself subjected both career army officers to a court-martial and the prospect of being drummed out of the service for these reasons under:

USCS = 891, Article 92. Failure to obey order or regulation:

(1) violates or fails to obey any lawful general order or regulation

(2) having knowledge of any other lawful order issued by a member of the armed forces, which it is his duty to obey, fails to obey the order; or

(3) is derelict in the performance of his duties;
shall be punished as a court-martial may direct.

As the architect of the scheme to have the officers violate their trust, Clinton was subjected to the same penalties that Holmes and Jones faced—as a conspirator.

Clinton himself committed any number of serious breaches of the law in applying for the U of A ROTC. Three of the most glaring were as follows:

1.   He did not reveal that he had received a notice to report for active military duty. As stipulated in **Section 50 USCS Appx = 465** of the *United States Code of Federal Regulations*, bearing on **War and National Defense:**

"…no person shall be accepted for [ROTC] enlistment after he has been issued an order to report for induction, unless authorized by the Director and the Secretary of Defense…"

No such authorization was ever received—or granted.

2.   His acceptance into the ROTC was fraudulently negotiated. Therefore, the telephone call that Colonel Jones told us he made to the draft board in Hot Springs to remove Clinton's name from its selective service 1-A listing, because of his enrollment in the ROTC, did not exonerate the candidate from his primary legal obligation to report for duty, as ordered by the draft notice he received on May 13. Clinton's enrollment was illegal to begin with. By failing to report for induction on July 28, Clinton broke the second law; he was in violation of **10 USCS = 801, N 543**, which provides:

"Where person had registered for draft, was delinquent, and was mailed notice to report before certain date or he would be in military service of United States, he was subject to trial by court-martial after that date, and it was not necessary to show his receipt of notice…"

3.   When Clinton signed up for the ROTC at the Arkansas school, he was not officially enrolled there as a student. Consequently, he couldn't be legally accepted into that school's ROTC because he abrogated the *Code of Federal Regulation*'s **Section 32 CFR Ch V**, which specifies:

(c) Students desiring enrollment in a unit must: (1) be enrolled in and attend-

ing full time a regular course of instruction at a school participating in the program.

When Clinton obtained deferment from the draft after his illegal enrollment in the ROTC, he opened a Pandora's Box that overflowed with other criminal activities he had engaged in, and which subjected him to further charges under existing laws—since he got his release under false pretenses and by committing perjury.

His enlistment in the U of A ROTC was accomplished not only by withholding the fact that he had received a draft induction notice, but also by unlawfully failing to reveal his prior two years of ROTC experience at Georgetown University.

In rejoining the ROTC, he automatically committed himself to serve a mandatory two years of active duty in the army. This was a step he declined to take on the Hoya campus in his junior year, because by signing up for third-year ROTC he would then have committed himself to that dreaded two-year hitch in the military.

He chose instead to take his chances with the draft—and with the help he could enlist from people with political clout to keep him out of uniform.

The *Code of Federal Regulations* cites several applicable laws that spell out the consequences for not complying with that obligatory term of service in the third or fourth year of ROTC membership.

Section 10 USCS = 2105 most clearly enunciates the action that is to be taken against a student for "failure to complete" the ROTC "advanced training" course:

A member of the program who is selected for advanced training...and who does not complete the course of instruction...may be ordered to active duty by the Secretary of the military department concerned to serve in his enlisted grade or rating for such period of time as the Secretary prescribes but not for more than two years.

Clinton did not adhere to this provision of the law. He opened himself to prosecution in a federal court or at a possible court-martial when he withdrew from the U of A ROTC program by submitting his nonbinding resignation in the letter he sent to Colonel Holmes in late December 1969—the day after the new Nixon-enacted U.S. draft lottery went into effect, a method of picking recruits, that by "the luck of the draw" freed Clinton from the draft forever.

But that happy day for Clinton did not dawn for several more months. During the early summer, Bill was caught between the proverbial rock and a hard place. He either had to resign himself to being drafted or seek the alternative of a place in the ROTC that would effectively postpone the day he had to slip into khaki and serve his country as a soldier.

However illegal were the methods by which he slipped into the ROTC, the fact is that he was very much a member of the reserve army unit anyway. Thus it's in order to dwell on that ROTC experience by examining the key regulations defining such service:

Section 50 USCS = 562.28 Enrollment explicitly specifies the college student's obligation once he signs up for advanced ROTC training, such as Clinton committed himself to perform at the Arkansas university. He must **...complete that course as a requirement for his graduation, unless relieved of this requirement by regula-**

tions prescribed by the Secretary of the Army.

Clinton didn't obtain such permission; he merely took it upon himself to quit cold, which was an illegality that Colonel Holmes—but not Colonel Jones, so far as the latter has indicated to the author—committed for reasons that the senior ROTC commander has never divulged.

To suppose Holmes was deluged by the "fixers" to accept the informal resignation—just as he was inundated by pressures from Senator Fulbright and others to enroll Clinton in the ROTC—may not be far-fetched.

According to the many sources the author and his researchers consulted, there is no doubt that laws were broken by Clinton. They carried varying penalties ranging from a *simple reprimand* to the *death sentence*.

According to the various interpretive notes, decisions, and possible legal ramifications culled from the sources researched, the additional laws Bill Clinton allegedly flouted are listed here, along with the applicable punishment for those crimes:

10 USCS = 883. Fraudulent enlistment, appointment, or separation

Any person who...procures his own separation from the armed forces by knowingly false representation or deliberate concealment as to eligibility for that separation, shall be punished as a court-martial may direct.

10 USCS = 891, Art. 92. Failure to obey order or regulation

Clinton (1) failed to obey the "lawful general order" to report for active duty, (2)) knew the order was lawful but was derelict in his duty to obey it, and (3) was, therefore, derelict in the performance of his duties as a soldier—and subject to punishment that a court-martial may direct.

32 CFR = 1632.14. Duty of registrant to report for and submit to induction

Clinton did not respond to the Order to Report for Induction (SSS Form No. 253) mailed to him by his Hot Springs Selective Service Board. It was his duty to respond to the board and apprise it of his whereabouts in the event there was a change in plans to induct him for active military duty on July 28.

32 CFR = 1621.16. Permit to depart from the United States

Before leaving for Oxford, Clinton failed to submit SSS Form No. 300, Permit for Registrant (of Selective Service) to Depart from the United States. Thus his draft board was not officially aware of his whereabouts out of the country, as they should have been, rather than hearing of it by word of mouth.

32 CFR = 1641.3. Communications by mail

Clinton was unable to receive mail directly from the selective service board in Hot Springs because he hadn't officially informed them of his change of address to England.

10 USCS = Art. 86. Absence without leave

Clinton faced a court-martial for the two, above-cited failures to keep his selective service board informed of his whereabouts as well as for this one: absenting himself from his place of duty in the United States, where he was required to be instead of in England.

10 USCS = Art. 104. Aiding the enemy

Acknowledging that he led anti-Vietnam rallies in England at a time when his country was at war in that Southeast Asian nation, Clinton **without proper authority, knowingly harbors or protects or gives intelligence to, or communicates or corresponds with or holds any intercourse with the enemy, either directly or indirectly.**

The law governing this covenant specifies that the offender **shall suffer death or such other punishment as a court-martial or military commission may direct.**

The same law applied to Clinton's trip in 1969-70 to take part in a peace rally in Moscow and have a layover in Prague with a founder of Czechoslovakia's Communist Party, which could be regarded as an **attempt to aid the enemy with arms, ammunition, supplies, or other things.**

10 USCS = 894. Art. 94. Mutiny or sedition

Again, as a member of the armed forces either by dint of being a "soldier" who failed to report for duty, or an ROTC cadet who was an army reservist, Clinton was subject to this chapter's conditions, which hold that any member of the armed forces who **refuses...to obey orders or otherwise do his duty...is guilty of mutiny, which shall be punished by death or such other punishment as a court-martial may direct.**

18 USCS = 2383. Rebellion or insurrection

When he led the two anti-Vietnam peace rallies in England, and took part in Senator Eugene McCarthy's anti-war rally in Moscow, Clinton was subject to the weight this law carries for anyone who **incites, sets on foot, assists, or engages in any rebellion or insurrection against the authority of the United States or the laws thereof,** or **gives aid or comfort thereto [and] shall be fined not more than $10,000 or imprisoned not more than ten years, or both and shall be incapable of holding any office under the United States.**

32 CFR = 562.29a. Discharge or disenrollment

To enlist in the ROTC at the U of A Law School, Clinton executed and signed form DA Fpr. 597, Advanced Course Students' Contract, which requires straight answers about the applicant's background. Had he honestly filled out the application, he would have cited his prior ROTC experience. This could have made a world of difference when he renounced his obligation to the ROTC. His commitment to serve in the U of A ROTC would have been irrevocable.

10 USCS = 932. Art. 132. Frauds against the United States

In its simplest terms, this law challenges the honesty of those who submit vouchers for reimbursement of out-of-pocket payments they've incurred on military business. Clinton is known to have received reimbursement for travel on at least two occasions between Hot Springs and Fayetteville in connection with his enrollment in the U of A ROTC. The penalty, which is punishable by whatever term is imposed by court-martial, can be lodged in Clinton's case because he assertedly knew that statements he made in form DA Fpr. 597 were false.

10 USCS = 885. Art. 85. Desertion

This article provides that **any member of the armed forces who (1) without authority goes or remains absent from his unit, organization, or place of duty with intent to remain away therefrom permanently; (2) quits his unit, organiza-**

tion, or place of duty with intent to avoid hazardous duty or to shirk important service...is guilty of desertion...or attempt to desert [and this crime] shall be punished, if the offense is committed in time of war, by death or such other punishment as court-martial may direct."

18 USCS = 2388, Activities affecting armed forces during war (Treason, Sedition)

Whoever, when the United States is at war, willfully makes or conveys false reports or false statements with intent to interfere with the operation or success of the military or naval forces of the United States or to promote the success of its enemies [as Clinton had when he attended a peace rally in the Soviet Union and visited the chairman of the Communist Party in Czechoslovakia] **shall be fined not more than $10,000 or imprisoned not more than twenty years, or both.**

18 USCS = 2381. Treason

Whoever, owing allegiance to the United States, levies war against them or adheres to their enemies, giving them aid and comfort within the United States or elsewhere [as Clinton indisputably had at the Moscow rally staged by Senator McCarthy] **is guilty of treason and shall suffer death, or shall be imprisoned not less than five years and fined not less than $10,000; and shall be incapable of holding any office under the United States.**

18 USCS = 2387. Treason, Sedition

Whoever, with intent to interfere with, impair, or influence the loyalty, morale, or discipline of the military or naval forces of the United States: (1) advises, counsels, urges, or in any manner causes or attempts to cause insubordination, disloyalty, mutiny, or refusal of duty by any member of the military [Clinton admitted in his lengthy, cathartic missive to Colonel Holmes that he wrote a letter to the draft board for a fellow American student at Oxford, who was a fugitive because he refused to be inducted into service] **shall be fined not more than $10,000 or imprisoned not more than ten years, or both, and shall be ineligible for employment by the United States or any department or agency thereof, for the five years next following his conviction.**

Had Clinton been prosecuted and punished for the above-cited act of treason and/or sedition and been hit with the maximum 15-year ineligibility to hold government employment, he could not have run for any of his public offices.

10 USCS = 884. Art. 84. Unlawful enlistment, appointment, or separation

Any person subject to this chapter [it applies to both Colonels Holmes and Jones] **who effects an enlistment or appointment in or a separation from the armed forces of any person who is known to him to be ineligible for that enlistment, appointment, or separation because it is prohibited by law, regulation, or order shall be punished as a court-martial may direct.**

Colonels Holmes and Jones both joined the conspiracy to recruit Clinton into the ROTC's ranks when he was ineligible to be taken on because the roster was closed to additional applicants.

Holmes also allowed Clinton to slip out of the ROTC by accepting his resignation, forwarded to him in a letter that wasn't even formalized by a notarized witness.

As cited earlier, Clinton faced the same penalties as the colonels because of his role in the conspiracy. What punishment has Clinton eluded after committing the aforementioned illegalities against the United States?

In one scenario—assuming "the book was thrown at him" for crimes that fell short of treason—Clinton could conceivably have been subjected to the severest punishment prescribed by **Section 128** of the **Military Selective Service Act of 1967: ...if a registrant or a person required to present himself for and submit to registration fails to perform any duty prescribed by the selective service law, or directions given pursuant thereto, within the required time, he shall...upon conviction in any district court of the United States of competent jurisdiction, be punished by imprisonment for not more than five years or a fine of not more than $10,000, or by both such fine and imprisonment, or if subject to military or naval law may be tried by court-martial, and, on conviction, shall suffer such punishment as a court-martial may direct.**

Yet, if one were to carry the theoretical possible punishment to its furthest extreme, attention is directed to **10 USCS = 843. Art. 43. Statute of limitations**

(a) A person charged with desertion or absence without leave in time of war, or with aiding the enemy, mutiny, or murder, may be tried and punished at any time without limitation.

At the very least, again in theory at best, time has not run out on the statutes that, arguably, prescribe the severest form of punishment for Bill Clinton. For, in the view of some authorities, his railings as a "drafted soldier" at the rallies in England against America's participation in the Vietnam War, and his support, as he admitted giving, to a fugitive draft dodger in wartime, constituted treason—the unforgivable crime.

Realistically, however, the likelihood of a trial for Bill Clinton for any of the 26 crimes he committed against his country, is moot, if not far-fetched.

Returning a last time to Clinton's shameless gymnastics with the ROTC, it can be said that Bill spat in the face of two opportunities this military experience had to offer him—to better serve as a president of the United States and as commander in chief of its military institutions.

The citation in **CFR = 562.4** lists the noble benefits the ROTC had in store for him:

...motivate and prepare [the candidate] with potential to serve as commissioned officer...understand the concept and principles of military art and science...develop potential to lead and manage...understand other professions...develop honor, and responsibility...appreciate the need for national security..."

Bill Clinton never completed that course.

AUTHOR'S NOTES AND ACKNOWLEDGMENTS

No book dwelling on facts can be written without the generous assistance of others. Biographies are the most difficult to research because they require meticulous, painstaking investigation about the subject. Biographies of two people, as this book is, are extremely rare, and understandably are doubly difficult to shape because they require twice the research effort.

This book was made more of a challenge because the subjects, William Jefferson Blythe Clinton IV and Hillary Diane Rodham Clinton, declined to be interviewed. Moreover, they closed access to aides and spokesmen in the governor's office in Little Rock and at the White House—yet that attempt did not succeed, as the considerable *inside* information on the Clintons demonstrates throughout this volume.

The fact that the Clintons themselves declined to cooperate in the preparation of this book turned into a plus for the project. For the author was enabled then to proceed with total immunity from the taint of possible prejudice toward his subjects on one side of the scale or the other. He assumed the role of *an unbiased juror*, much as in the practice of a venireman seated in judgment at a criminal court proceeding. Such a *decider of the facts* is admonished by the trial judge "not to speak with the *defendant[s]* nor form an opinion until you have heard all of the evidence."

Thus my work was cut out for me. I was compelled to draw upon my more than 50 years of investigative reporting experience to sniff out the *who*, *what*, *when*, *where*, *how*, and *why* on each of the Clintons, totally independent of their *assistance* in landing sources who undoubtedly could do little less than lean to the side of prejudice in discussing the first couple.

****

I began by reading much of everything that had been written about the couple. The library at the *Arkansas Democrat-Gazette* was a wondrous font of information about Bill and Hillary Clinton, as well as the members of their immediate families, from their earliest days in the Land of Opportunity to the very present time. Special thanks must go to head librarian Alfred Thomas for the extensive research and culling of stories about my subjects that he and his staff conducted for me. I am deeply indebted to three of his librarians for the lengths they went to in gathering material on the Clintons; my sincerest thanks to Doris Hale, Rosie Dixon, and Betty Seegar.

I am also indebted greatly to the *Arkansas Democrat-Gazette*'s photo department, which supplied the lion's share of the photos appearing in this book. Appreciation goes to Barry Auther, the picture editor, John Sykes, chief photographer, and Mark

Wilson, the staff photographer who worked exhaustively in this newspaper's files to assemble the photos that appear in chronological order in the picture section of this book.

I was assisted greatly in my research and fact-finding missions by publishers, editors, writers, and reporters from many areas of the United States, but especially in Arkansas. I am most indebted to them for their advice, guidance, and help in supplying indispensable information—given directly or through intermediaries or assistants and, as in some instances, through their own published works.

I will list the names and identities of all these fine people in the order in which the material obtained from them appears in the book (rather than presenting them in alphabetical order).

****

Nigel Hamilton, author of *JFK: Reckless Youth*; Henry Leon Ritzenthaler, Bill Clinton's half brother; Adele Cofelt, Ritzenthaler's mother and second wife of Clinton's natural father, William Jefferson Blythe III; Wanetta Ellen Alexander Blythe, the third wife of Clinton's father; Sharon Blythe Pettijohn, Clinton's half sister, born in their father's third marriage; feature writer Martha Sherrill of the *Washington Post*; the staff of Quachita Hospital in Little Rock, where Clinton's mother, Virginia Kelley, served as a nurse-anesthetist; Jeannie Snodgrass Almo, Hillary Rodham Clinton's friend; the staff of Johnny Carson's "The Tonight Show"; the staff of the Oak Park racetrack in Hot Springs; Carolyn Staley, Clinton's friend since childhood; columnist-commentator Gary Wills, whose works about the subjects of this book appeared in a number of national publications; Carolyn Wilson, a classmate of Clinton's at Hot Springs High School; Patty Criner, a childhood friend; correspondent Todd S. Purdom of the *New York Times*; writer Joe Klein of *New York* magazine; the clerks and record keepers at the Garland County Chancery Court in Hot Springs; Thomas Caplan, a classmate of Clinton's at Georgetown University; the press-public relations officials at Georgetown University; Stefanie Weldon, a classmate at Georgetown; Phillip Plascencia, who was Clinton's student company commander in the ROTC at Georgetown; Lee Williams and other staffers who served with Senator J. William Fulbright; Jan Piercy, Hillary Rodham's roommate at Wellesley College; Betsy Johnson Ebeling, Hillary's friend in Park Ridge, Illinois; Opal Ellis, secretary for the Selective Service System's Draft Board 26 in Hot Springs; Neil Grimaldi, a classmate at Georgetown; Michael Kinsley, senior editor of *The New Republic* and co-anchor on TV's "Crossfire"; Robert Reich, his Oxford classmate and now the secretary of labor in Clinton's administration; Robert Corrado, a member of the Hot Springs draft board; retired Arkansas Circuit Court Judge James Britt; reporter Bill Rempel of the *Los Angeles Times*; Lieutenant Commander Trice Ellice, Jr., of the Hot Springs Naval Reserve unit; reporter Charles Allen of the *Arkansas Gazette*; Strobe Talbott, Clinton's classmate at Oxford University and now ambassador-at-large in the Clinton administration; Tamara Eckles-Williams Kennerly, Clinton's girlfriend at Oxford; reporter David Gardner of the *London Daily Mail*; Professor Leslie Campbell, associate dean of history at Auburn University in Alabama; Ron Hathaway, a high school principal in New Braunfels, Texas; reporter Ralph Frammolino of the *Washington Times*; reporter Jeffrey H. Birnbaum of the *Wall Street Journal*; Army Colonel Eugene J. Homes, commander of the ROTC at the University of Arkansas; Lt. Colonel Clinton D. Jones, administrator of the ROTC program at the U of A; reporters Richard E. Lauter and Doug Jehl of the *Washington Times*; the press and public relations staffs at Wellesley College; likewise the people in similar capacities at Yale University Law School; writer David Wattenberg of *The American Spectator*; Judith Warner, author of *Hillary Clinton: The Inside Story* (Signet Books); the Rev. Richard McSorley, a Jesuit priest who directed the Center for Peace Studies at Georgetown University; Betsey Wright, longtime Clinton aide, campaign spokeswoman, and White House aide to the president; reporter David Rosenbaum of the *New York Times*; the Czechoslovakian Consulate in New York City; reporter Maureen Dowd of the *New York Times*; Anne Wexler-Duffey of the Connecticut Democratic State Committee; David Matthews, Lou Hardin, and Morril Harriman, students in Clinton's law class at the U of A who were influenced to enter politics by their teacher; Dianne Dwire Welch, Clinton's stepsister when his mother married her father, Jeff Dwire; Sarah Ehrman, friend and co-worker when the Clintons' campaigned for Senator George McGovern; Representative John Paul Hammerschmidt (R-Arkansas); the press and public relations staffs at the University of Arkansas Law School in Fayetteville; Floyd G. Brown, of the Citizens United organization and author of *Slick Willie: Why America Cannot Trust Bill Clinton* (Annapolis Publishing Company); author-journalist Gail Sheehy in *Vanity Fair* and other publications; Senators Dale Bumpers and David H. Pryor, both Arkansas Democrats; attorney William R. Wilson, Jr., of Little Rock; Gennifer Flowers, Clinton's girlfriend for 12 years; editor John Robert Starr of the *Arkansas Democrat*; Cal Ledbetter, Jr., professor of political science at the U of A; reporters Howard Fineman and Mark Miller of *Newsweek*; former Arkansas Governor Frank White; press relations staffers at International Paper Corporation and Tyson Foods in Arkansas; real estate broker-banker James B. McDougal; his former wife, Susan McDougal; attorney James B. Blair of Tyson Foods; reporters James Gerth, Dean Baquet, and Stephen Lebaton of the *New York Times*; investigative reporter-columnist Ray Kerrison of the *New York Post*; writer Lisa Schiffren in *The American Spectator*; former Internal Revenue Service Commissioner Donald Alexander; Bill Goodman, chairman of the Arkansas Legislative Joint Budget Committee; White House Chief Counsel Bernard Nussbaum; staffers at the Rose Law Firm in Little Rock, who spoke on condition of anonymity; Larry Nichols, official of the Arkansas Development Finance Authority; John Rupp of the Tiger Employment Agency in New York City; Arkansas State Representative John E. Miller; attorney David Kendall, the Clintons' personal lawyer; Diane Brown Cox of Dierks, Arkansas; Billy Ray Washington of Hot Springs; Drs. William Schuelte, James Griffin, and William Johnson of Quachita Memorial Hospital; Dr. Fahmi Malak, chief medical examiner of Arkansas; the record room staff at Arkansas State Supreme Court in Hot Springs; J. Sky Tapp of Hot Springs; Dr. M. Joycelyn Elders, former Arkansas Health Director and currently surgeon general of the United States; reporter Brian Ross and the staff of the television magazine "Dateline NBC"; reporter Joe Nabbefeld of the *Arkansas Gazette*; syndicated gossip columnist Cindy Adams of the *New York Post*; the staff of the

ABC-TV Sally Jessy Raphael Show for interview material on Sally Perdue; Colonel Thomas (Tommy) Goodwin, commander of the Arkansas State Police; the Federal Bureau of Investigation in Little Rock; the Federal Drug Enforcement Administration; the Little Rock Police Department; the North Little Rock Police Department; U. S. Attorney Asa Hutchinson of the Western District of Arkansas; U.S. Attorney George W. Proctor of the Eastern District; the Arkansas Chamber of Commerce in Little Rock; columnist Ernie Dumas of the *Arkansas Gazette*; reporter George Church of *Time* magazine; Thomas McRae, president of the Winthrop Rockefeller Foundation; reporters Michael Weisskopf and David Maraniss of the *Washington Post*; black activist Robert "Say" McIntosh of Little Rock; Bobbie Ann Williams, who claims she bore "Bill Clinton's mulatto child"; corroborative material of Clinton's profligacies with black women was culled from the *Washington Post, Chicago Tribune, Newsday, Los Angeles Times, Times of London,* and *London Telegraph*; the Rev. Tommy Knots, aide to Hillary Clinton at Rose Law; Phil Bunton, editorial director of the *Globe* weekly magazine and his staff, including editor Dan Dolan and reporters Ken Harrel, Bob Boyd, Stan Wulff, Bob Temmey, and George Hunter; Virginia Kelley's autobiography *Leading With My Heart: My Life* (Simon & Schuster) for details about the cabin in Lake Hamilton; journalist Neal Travis, author of the gossip column "New York" in the *New York Post*; Mrs. Kelley's Lake Hamilton neighbors Darlene Lewis and Effie Kirby; Arkansas State Police Captain Raymond (Buddy) Young; Lucille Bolton, Bobbie Ann Williams' sister; Dan Williams, Bobbie Ann's husband; Susan Whiteacre, press secretary for Bill Clinton when governor; Arkansas State Police Troopers Larry G. Patterson, Roger L. Perry, Danny Ferguson, and Ronnie Anderson; investigative reporter David Brock, author of *The Real Anita Hill* (Free Press), for his article "His Cheatin' Heart" in *The American Spectator*; David Hale, businessman and operator of a Small Business Administration Loan branch in Little Rock; U.S. Attorney Paula Casey in Little Rock; former U.S. Attorney Jay Stephens, currently chief investigator for the Resolution Trust Company that is probing Whitewater-Madison Guaranty Savings and Loan matters; investigative reporter Mike McAlary in the *New York Post* (and now plugging for the *New York Daily News*); reporter Charles Allen of the *Arkansas Gazette*; Sheffield Nelson, chairman of the Arkansas Industrial Development Commission; Bob Lamb, chairman of the Arkansas State Chamber of Commerce; Don Bankston, an attorney and leader in the Fort Bend County (Texas) Democratic Party; teller Jessie McClure of the Gold Coast Savings and Loan in Sugarloaf, Texas; Ronald H. Brown, as chairman of the National Democratic Committee; Senator Alfonse D'Amato (R-New York) and his staff in New York and Washington; Lisa Caputo, press secretary for Hillary Rodham Clinton; Representative Jim Leach (R-Iowa) and his staff in Washington; reporter Bob Wells of the *Arkansas Gazette*; attorney Scott Trotter of Little Rock; former Governor Edmund G. Brown, Jr., of California; former Governor Michael Dukakis of Massachusetts; the Reverend Jesse Jackson; political consultant Jerry Russell of Little Rock; former Arkansas State Assemblyman Rudy Moore; Arkansas State Representative David Matthews; former Arkansas Attorney General Steve Clark; former U.S. Representative Sonny Robinson of Arkansas; columnist Murray Kempton of *Newsday*; Arkansas Supreme Court Justice Jack Holt,

Jr.; editor Phyllis D. Brandon of the *Arkansas Democrat*; Paula Corbin Jones, former employee of the AIDFA; Steve Jones, her husband; Pamela Blackard, another employee of the AIDFA; the manager's office staff at the Excelsior Hotel in Little Rock; attorney Robert Bennett, special counsel to president Clinton; Paula Jones' lawyers Daniel Traylor, Joseph Cammarata, and Gil Davis; employees of B. J.'s Star-Studded Honky Tonk in Little Rock, who did not wish to be identified; the *Time* magazine team reporting on the Paula Jones case that comprised David Ellis, Jane Sims Podesta, Kate Klise, Jane Sanderson, Joseph Harmes, Tom Cunneff, Johnny Dodd, Lyndon Stambler, and Clare Mead Rosen; White House communications director Mark Gearan; investigative reporters Michael Isikoff, Charles Shephard, and Sharon LaFraniere of the *Washington Post*; former State Department spokeswoman Margaret D. Tutwiler; Clay Farrow, the late Virginia Kelley's son-in-law by marriage; Dr. William R. Mashburn, Garland County (Hot Springs) coroner; Senator J. Robert (Bob) Kerrey (D-Nebraska); former Senator Paul Tsongas (D-Massachusetts); Senator Tom Harkin (D-Iowa); Patrick Buchanan (as a candidate in the GOP primaries of 1992); Roger Wood, president and publication director of the *Star* magazine; Gennifer Flowers' mother, Mrs. Mary Hirst; Miss Flowers' friend, Dallas real estate agent/interior designer Lauren Kirk; Bill Clinton press aide Mike Gauldin; Bill Gaddy, director of the Arkansas Employment Security Division; Judy Gaddy, special assistant to Governor Clinton; Don K. Barnes, chairman of the Arkansas Board of Review; Charlette Perry, administrative assistant in the Arkansas Board of Review; correspondents Timothy Clifford and Shirley Perlman of *Newsday*; reporter Jonathan Alter of *Newsweek*; reporter Eleanor Clift of *Newsweek*; Georgia Secretary of State Max Cleland, the Vietnam triple amputee; the late Lewis Puller, the Vietnam double amputee and author of *Fortunate Son*, his autobiography; Senator Kerrey's senior adviser Bob Shrum; political correspondent Susan Milligan of the *New York Daily News*; Washington bureau chief Deborah Orin of the *New York Post*; Professor Charles Wolfram of Cornell University; staffers who didn't want their names used at the National Association for the Advancement of Colored People; anchorman David Stanton of WIS-TV in Columbia, South Carolina; David Willhelm, Bill Clinton's national campaign director; Dave Howell, news director of KTSP-TV in Phoenix; Larry Klein, station manager of KTSP-TV; assistants in the office of Christy Hefner, editor of *Playboy*; columnists William Safire in the Sunday *New York Times* magazine; Richard Bond, chairman of the Republican National Committee; editorial page editor Eric Breindel of the *New York Post*; private investigator Jack Palladino of San Francisco; country singer Tammy Wynette; Miss Wynette's husband and manager, George Richey; talk show hostess Devon O'Day of WSIX-FM radio in Nashville; staff correspondent David Firestone of *Newsday*; staffers at the campaign offices of Ross Perot in Dallas; reporter Steve Dunleavy of the Fox Television Network's "A Current Affair" program; Jack Aitcheson, father of Tipper Gore; Torrie Clark, Bush's campaign press secretary; correspondent Martin Kasindorf of *Newsday*; Senator Bob Dole (R-Kansas) and his staff in Washington; former Vice President Dan Quayle and staff; Vice President Al Gore, Jr., and staff; GOP pollster Ed Goeas with the Tarrance Group; Terry Michael of the nonpartisan Washington Center for Politics and Journalism; the pollsters of the

Cable News Network-*USA Today*; Clinton/Gore national campaign chairman Mickey Kantor; Bush/Quayle campaign chairman Robert Teeter; retired Admiral James Stockdale; Washington bureau chief Lars-Erik Nelson of the *New York Daily News* (and now pitching for *Newsday*); columnist Robert Reno of *Newsday*; David Blitzer, chief economist at Standard & Poor's Corporation; Patrick McCarthy, publisher of *Women's Wear Daily*; Liz Tilberis, editor of *Harper's Bazaar*; L. J. Davis, contributing editor to *Harper* and *The New Republic*; writer Deroy Murdock, president of Loud & Clear Communications; Mrs. Jane Parks and her son Gary; Sergeant Clyde Steelman of the Little Rock Police Department Homicide Division; correspondent Ambrose Evans-Pritchard of London's *Sunday Telegraph*; reporter David Keating of KFDX-TV in Wichita Falls; Mrs. Herschel Friday, widow of the head of the Arkansas law firm of Friday, Eldridge & Clark; Dr. Sidney B. Weinberg, former chief medical examiner of Suffolk County on Long Island.

****

I further want to thank and express appreciation to my *primary* sources who contributed information that has made it possible—without the cooperation of the subjects—to wrap up *Clinton Confidential: The Climb to Power—The Unauthorized Biography of Bill and Hillary Clinton* with a profusion of details and facts that fulfill my promise as biographer to produce the most complete work on Bill and Hillary Clinton ever written.

I interviewed most of these sources either in person or on the telephone; my researchers also spoke with the sources listed here when I was unable to conduct the interviews or investigations myself.

My heartfelt thanks to the following:

Cliff Jackson, Bill Clinton's classmate at Oxford and today an attorney-at-law in Little Rock, for his many insights on the president and his efforts to avoid the draft when a college student.

British journalist Paul Donnelley, who headed my team of researchers in England and facilitated the investigation into Clinton's Oxford years.

The Federal Election Commission in Washington, D.C., for counseling me about Bill Clinton's Presidential Election Committee's misuse of $395,000 of its general-election funds.

Reporter Rodney Bowers of the *Arkansas Democrat* (now the *Arkansas Democrat-Gazette*) for his incisive, four-part series about the Iran-Contra drug/arms smuggling conspiracy operating out of Intermountain Regional Airport at Mena, Arkansas.

Max Brantley, editor and publisher of the *Arkansas Times*, for background information and expository data on the Mena Airport scandal and insights on Bill Clinton as governor.

Colonel Thomas "Tommy" Goodwin, commander of the Arkansas State Police who, in a series of interviews with my researchers, explained points of the investigation conducted into Roger Clinton and Dan R. Lasater's drug trafficking activities, and also threw light on some areas of the probe into the Mena Airport smuggling activities.

David Lee Miller, reporter for the Fox Television Network's "A Current Affair," for invaluable discoveries about the airport scandal.

Lawrence T. Patterson, founder and publisher of *Criminal Politics*, for extensive information and analysis bearing not only on the surreptitious Mena Airport activities, but also for his critique of the '92 presidential election and his eye-opening article on "The Clinton Cocaine Connection" that was combined with an intensely thorough study of Roger Clinton's involvement in the drug scene.

Arkansas's Polk County Sheriff's Department, whose sources asked for anonymity in providing invaluable insight into the Mena Airport drug smuggling/money launder-ing schemes that involved both Bill Clinton and George Bush over a 10-year period.

Frank Sneps, a writer whose story on the Mena Airport doings was published in New York's avant-garde weekly, *The Village Voice*, during the presidential primaries and provided excellent leads for the author.

John C. White, former Democratic national chairman, for his penetrating views about Ross Perot, who gave birth to the slogan the jug-eared Texan is a "billion dollar Bubba."

The FBI office in New York City and the U.S. Attorney's Office in the Southern District of New York for information about Secretary of Commerce Ronald H. Brown and Local 100 of the Restaurant and Hotel workers Union headed by Harold Ickes.

Linda D. Thompson, freelance investigative journalist, lawyer, and founder of the Indianapolis-based American Justice Foundation, who produced a documentary on the Federal Alcohol, Tobacco, and Firearms Bureau raid on the Branch Davidians in Waco, Texas.

Benjamin P. Talbot, Jr., former GOP candidate for lieutenant governor in Arkan-sas, for information about his father's mysterious death while campaigning for Gov-ernor Clinton's reelection rival and other information that helped shape this book.

George S. Gabric, who provided the author with the most penetrating commentar-ies about President Clinton's Georgetown professor Carroll Quigley, author of *Trag-edy and Hope: History of the World in Our Time* (MacMillan Company). Gabric also introduced the author to the works of former FBI agent and ex-Salt Lake City Chief of Police W. Leon Skousen, one of America's foremost scholars of political conspira-cies. His book, *The Naked Capitalist*, was a gold mine of information in understand-ing the conspiracy of taking over the world that Clinton's *hero*, Professor Quigley, espoused.

I further wish to acknowledge the counseling and assistance I received in the preparation of the appendix: "How Clinton Escaped Prison as a Draft Dodger." Counselors and librarians of Touro College Jacob D. Fuchsberg Law Center in Hunt-ington, N.Y., pointed me in the many directions I took to gather the information in this most significant section of the book. The staff also furnished advice, guidance, and interpretations/applications of the laws governing the violations Clinton commit-ted.

Others who must be saluted for the help they contributed: the office of the Joint Chiefs of Staff in the Pentagon and the library at that facility; the Library of Congress; the Half Hollow Hills Library on Long Island; the Department of the Army in Wash-ington; the Selective Service Bureau in Washington; the Department of the ROTC,

Washington; the Clinton White House (for directing my researchers to some of the agencies cited here); the former members of the Selective Service System's Draft Board 26 in Hot Springs, Arkansas, whose names are listed throughout the pages of this book along with the information they provided.

I also want to state that in the course of conducting my vast research for *Clinton Confidential*, I obtained material on the daily accountings and happenings of Bill and Hillary Clinton from the following newspapers: *The New York Times*, *New York Post*, *New York Daily News*, *Newsday*, *Washington Post*, *Washington Times*, and *Los Angeles Times*. In every instance, the by-liners who were credited for the stories on the pages of their newspapers have been acknowledged as the sources throughout the text of this book.

I owe special thanks to Christopher Bowen, the chief librarian at *Star*, who was also my colleague for many years at the *New York Post*. Working as my chief researcher in the Metropolitan New York area, Chris trudged to libraries far and wide to come up with any and all fragments of information on Bill and Hillary Clinton. He was ably assisted in those endeavors by his deputy, Mary-Beth Buckout.

And I want to salute Stephen P. Lehmann for his invaluable assistance with the Paula Jones case.

Before my final tribute, I want to acknowledge the help provided by the late Stan Mays, the London-based Express Newspapers bureau chief in the United States. His help was invaluable and without it this book could not have been what it is.

Lastly, my heartfelt thanks to Mark Weaver of radio station WMAL in Washington, D.C., and columnist Jack Wheeler for steering me to my most fortuitous association with the wondrous and supremely helpful people at Emery Dalton Communications. First, there was David Ross, who made some of what I wrote more readable and understandable. Then there was Jacquelyn Dapper, who put the final touches to my manuscript and made it lilt like an aria at the Metropolitan. I must also salute Mark Fleming, who gave me guidance and advice on pursuing leads and sources with the thoroughness and accuracy that only the most disciplined of editors and/or lawyers would demand. Lastly, I take my hat off to Michael Dalton Johnson, who had the courage and determination to publish this book whereas others chickened out.

– GEORGE CARPOZI, JR.

INDEX

—A—

—H—

—T—